MOON HANDBOOKS

D0311520

OAXACA

BRUCE WHIPPERMAN

PUEBLA

Tehuacán

Lagunas
de Temascal
National
Park

Río
Coyolapa

Temescal
Reservoir

Chazumba

Cerro Rabón
2,350m

Río
Capalapa

Huautla
de Jiménez

Teotitlán del
Camino

Cerro de Oro
Reservoir

Río Santo Domingo

Tequixtepec

Río
Xiquila

Río
Salada

Cerro Cheve
3,255m

Cuicatlán

Valle
Nacional

Río
Mixteco

CERRO DE
LAS MINAS

**THE
MIXTECA**

NORTHER
OAXACA

Huajuapan
de León

Coixtlahuaca

Tamazulapan

Cerro
el Pelón
3,270m

Río
Grande

Llano de las
Flores

Yosocuta
Reservoir

YUCUITA

Cerro Yucuiña
3,250m

Nochixtlán

Ixtlán de Juárez

Villa

Tonalá

Teposcolula

Cerro San Felipe
3,250m

Guelatao

Yalala

HUAMELULPAN

Cerro Negro
3,250m

Benito Juárez
National Park

Juxtlahuaca

Etla

Tlaxiaco

**MONTE
NEGRO**

MONTE ALBÁN

**OAXACA
CITY**

Benito Juárez

Cerro de los Sortenejos
2,850m

Putla de Guerrero

Cuajimolo

**Cerro Piedra de Olla
3,350m**

Río
Hinas

Zaachila

Tlacolula

Mitla

GUERRERO

Río
Atoyac

Zimatlán

**THE VALLEY
OF OAXACA**

Huixtepec

Cerromandingas
3,050m

San Sebastián de
las Grutas

Cerro El Labrador
2,840m

San Pedro
Amusgos

Cerro La Neblina
2,300m

Ejutla

Cacahuatepec

Río Atoyac

Cerr
Quixe
3,750

Miahuatlán

San Pedro
Juchatengo

Pinotepa
Nacional

Jamiltepec

Río
Verde

Juquila

Cerro Iguana
2,760m

San José del
Pacífico

Río

Nopala

San Gabriel
Mixtepec

**PACIFIC RESORTS
AND SOUTHERN
SIERRA**

Río Cope

Laguna
Corralero

Río Grande

*Lagunas de Chacahua
National Park*

Laguna
Manialtepec

Candelaria

Pluma H

PACIFIC

Río Colotepec

Pochutla

Santa María
Huatulco

OCEAN

Puerto
Escondido

Santa
de Hu

Puerto Ángel

Bo

© AVALON TRAVEL

Contents

Discover Oaxaca

Experience the best of Mexico, both old and new, in Oaxaca. Once isolated and little visited, this Mexican state is now fulfilling its promise. New superhighways and airline routes have increased access to its capital city, a gateway to an abundance of both colonial history and rich cultural heritage, which includes 16 separate living languages, spoken in dozens of distinct dialects and spread among hundreds of ethnically separate indigenous groups.

A generation ago, the United Nations recognized Oaxaca City's unique gifts by naming it a UNESCO World Heritage Site. The city acknowledged the compliment, rebuilding and refurbishing its graceful colonial-era buildings, churches, and monuments, including the venerable Iglesia de Santo Domingo. But the city is as much about the present as the past. By day, people linger at plaza-front sidewalk cafés beneath shady arches; by night, the same central plaza comes alive with entertainment, from arts and crafts stalls to folkloric dance.

The cultural wealth is even more evident as you move outside the city. The surrounding Valley of Oaxaca is ringed by ancient ruins, including magnificent Mitla and Yagul. On the south side, explore mysterious and revered Zaachila. To the southwest, Monte Albán, Mesoamerica's first true city, still reigns from its mountaintop throne.

These ghosts of the ancients exist side by side with vibrant native markets, one for practically each day of the week, decorated with stalls offering everything from colorful carpets and pottery to embroidered dresses and *alebrijes,* Oaxaca's celebrated wooden animals. The less-traveled Mixteca region offers its share of magnificent Dominican churches, barely explored ancient kingdoms, and natural wonders such as emerald waterfalls, limestone caves, and crystal springs. And southeast on the Isthmus, you can join the celebration at near-continuous festivals. More contemporary pleasures can be found on the golden strands of Pacific coastal resorts like Puerto Ángel, the Bahías de Huatulco, and Puerto Escondido.

Wherever you wander in this rich land, you'll find excitement, lots of friendly folks, relatively low prices, and a host of traditional Mexican delights.

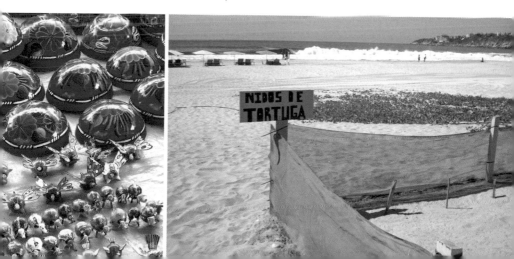

Planning Your Trip

▶ WHERE TO GO

Oaxaca City

The capital city occupies the strategic intersection of the three great arms of the Valley of Oaxaca. From the city, the three subvalleys diverge south, northwest, and east, like the thumb, index finger, and middle finger of a single hand. Aztec conquerors called that crucial hub Huaxyacac (oo-AHSH-yah-kahk) for a forest of flowery, pod-bearing trees that still carpets the hillside. The Spanish shifted that name to the more-pronounceable Oaxaca (wah-HAH-kah).

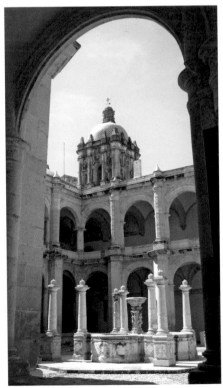

The Valley of Oaxaca

A feast of old-Mexico sights and experiences awaits outside the city: colorful markets, crafts villages, archaeological sites, venerable churches, and natural wonders. Notable handicrafts villages include Teotitlán del Valle and Santa Ana del Valle, on the east side; San Bartolo Coyotepec and Ocotlán to the south; Arrazola toward the southwest; and Atzompa and Etla on the west. Among the archaeological sites are Mitla and Yagul, on the east side; Zaachila on the southwest side; Monte Albán to the west; and San José El Mogote and Suchilquitongo to the northwest.

Pacific Resorts and Southern Sierra

The Pacific coast is a long, lazy land of eternal summer, embellished by its resort trio: Puerto Ángel and Huatulco, on the east side, and Puerto Escondido on the west. Enjoy beachcombing, horseback riding, sportfishing, swimming, snorkeling, and scuba diving. On the Puerto Ángel–Huatulco side, add plenty of golf and tennis, river rafting, and jungle coffee farms. On the Puerto Escondido side, add abundant wildlife-viewing opportunities at pristine Laguna Manialtepec and Parque Nacional Lagunas de Chacahua.

The Mixteca

This homeland of the Mixtecs, Oaxaca's "People of the Clouds," is a grand, virtually untouristed domain, stretching over the whole of northwestern Oaxaca, across both fertile valleys and tragically eroded wastelands. The Mixteca is an adventurer's paradise, offering natural springs, the towering cliffs of El Boquerón, the great gorge of the Río Mixteco, and groves of ancient *sabino* trees at the charming farm village of Tonalá. The Mixteca's markets are also among Oaxaca's most captivating.

Northern Oaxaca

An exploration of northern Oaxaca begins in the towns and villages of the Sierra Juárez, scarcely an hour north from Oaxaca City. Farther west, from Ixcatlán, the highway climbs past the gigantic whale-back massif of the Cerro Rabón, the holy mountain of the Mazatec people, to the summit, at Huautla de Jiménez, their spiritual home. Stroll the lively *tianguis* lanes and shop for prized Mazatec ribbon-decorated *huipiles*. On another day, head out for half an hour by road to enjoy the cool spray at the twin waterfalls of Las Regaderas, or explore the monumental limestone cave near Eloxochitlán village.

The Isthmus

Nothing embodies the independent Isthmus spirit more than its near-continuous menu of fiestas, locally called *velas*. Women dress up in their spectacularly floral *huipiles* and sway with their sombreroed partners to the lovely, lilting melody of "La Sandunga," the song of the Isthmus. Tehuántepec and Juchitán are the towns where *istmeño* hearts beat fastest. Exciting excursions include the legendary crystal-blue springs at Tlacotepec, fishing hamlets of Playa Copalito and Rincón Juárez, and the grand canyon of the Río Zanatepec.

► WHEN TO GO

The most popular times to visit the city of Oaxaca are Christmas–New Year's, the Guelaguetza (gay-lah-GET-zah) dance festival in July, and Día de los Muertos (Day of the Dead) week, around November 1. Although the crowds are biggest and hotel prices are highest, these are the times when Oaxaca City is at its merriest and most colorful.

By contrast, beaches are at their most popular twice yearly: during the Christmas–New Year's holiday and Semana Santa, the pre-Easter week. Droves of folks, both foreign and local, crowd restaurants and lodgings and push up hotel rates.

Weather-wise, it's important to know that Oaxaca (and most of Mexico) has two sharply defined seasons: wet summer–fall and dry winter–spring.

People often say Oaxaca is too hot in the summer. This, however, isn't necessarily the case. In fact, increased summer cloud cover and showers can actually create average daily temperatures in July, August, and September that are cooler than clear and very warm late April, May, and early June temperatures.

The other summer advantage is the vegetation. If you like lush, green landscapes, summer–fall may be your season. This is

THE DAY OF THE DEAD

Instead of mourning the dead, Mexicans celebrate the memory of their deceased relatives with a festive holiday, **El Día de los Muertos** (Day of the Dead). The roots of this celebration go back for countless generations, long before the Spanish Conquest, to the ancient holiday of Mictecacihuatl, the guardian-goddess of the dead, whom many of the original Mexicans celebrated around the month of August.

The Spanish shifted the date to November 1 to coincide with the Catholic religion's observation of All Saint's Day. Eventually a second day, November 2, was added. Today, folks celebrate November 2 all over Mexico, and most intensely in the indigenous southeast regions of Michoacán, Guerrero, Chiapas, and the entire state of Oaxaca. While it's best known as El Día de los Muertos, it's also sometimes called El Día de los Angelitos, or Day of the Little Angels.

El Día de los Muertos amounts to a joyous reunion of all family members – both living and dead. At the end of October, people gather in their hometowns and villages to reunite with their loved ones. By the afternoon of November 1, preparations are well under way. People converge on the cemeteries, clean up the gravesites, and polish the tombstones. They scatter flower petals and burn candles to mark the path. By early evening on November 2, everything is ready. The graves are festooned with a collection of fruit and glowing candles, and decorated with flowers and dishes loaded with the favorite foods of the deceased. Most important, every-

one has arrived. As the evening wears on, people curl up beneath blankets and spend the night in a happy vigil to welcome their departed loved ones back into the family fold once again.

true especially in the highlands around Oaxaca City, northern Oaxaca, and the Mixteca, where myriads of multicolored wildflowers decorate the roadsides and the clouds seem to billow into a 1,000-mile-high blue sky.

If you don't mind crowds and want to experience lots of local color, go during one of Oaxaca's festivals. If, however, you shun crowds but like the sunny, temperate winter,

January, a low-occupancy season, is a good bet, especially on the beach.

October, November and the first half of December are also good times to go (except possibly for the crowded, expensive high-holiday El Día de los Muertos week, around November 1 and 2). Hotel prices are cheapest, the landscape is lush and green, beaches are beautifully uncrowded, and it's cooler and not so rainy as July, August, and September.

▶ BEFORE YOU GO

Passports, Tourist Cards, and Visas

Your passport (or birth or naturalization certificate) is your positive proof of national identity. Don't leave home without one. U.S. Immigration rules require that all U.S. citizens must have a valid passport in order to re-enter the United States.

For U.S. and Canadian citizens, entry by air into Mexico for a few weeks could hardly be easier. Airline attendants hand out tourist cards *(tarjetas turísticas)* and officers make them official by stamping them at the immigration gate. Business travel permits for 30 days or fewer are handled by the same simple procedures.

Immunizations and Precautions

A good physician can recommend the proper preventatives for your Oaxaca trip. If you are going to stay pretty much in town, your doctor will probably suggest little more than updating your basic typhoid, diphtheria-tetanus, hepatitis, and polio shots.

For remote tropical areas—below 4,000 feet (1,200 meters)—doctors often recommend a gamma-globulin shot against hepatitis A and a schedule of chloroquine pills against malaria. Use other measures to discourage mosquitoes and other tropical pests. Common precautions include mosquito netting and rubbing

on plenty of pure DEET (N,N dimethyl metatoluamide) "jungle juice," mixed in equal parts with rubbing (70 percent isopropyl) alcohol.

Getting There and Around

The majority of visitors reach Oaxaca by air and a large fraction of those through Mexico City. There, travelers transfer to flights bound for either Oaxaca City, Puerto Escondido, or Bahías de Huatulco-Puerto Ángel.

But bus travel rules in Mexico. Hundreds of sleek luxury- and first-class bus lines roar out daily from the border, headed south. The route to Oaxaca along the Pacific shore, although the longest, requiring one or two transfers and at least three full 24-hour days, is the most scenic. Within Oaxaca, a host of lines connect virtually every town and most villages. Three distinct levels of service—luxury or super-first class, first class, and second class—are generally available.

If you're adventurous, but still want to have all the comforts of home, you may enjoy driving your car or RV to Oaxaca. On the other hand, consideration of cost, risk, wear on both you and your vehicle, and the congestion hassles in towns may change your mind. Oaxaca car rentals are not cheap. With a 15 percent or more "value added" tax tacked on and mandatory Mexican car insurance, they run more than in the United States.

What to Take

Everyone should bring a hat for sun protection and a light jacket or sweater for the occasional cool evening. Loose-fitting, handwashable, easy to-dry clothes make for trouble-free tropical vacationing. In all cases, leave showy, expensive clothes and jewelry at home. Stow valuables in your hotel safe or carry them with you in a sturdy zipped purse or a waist pouch on your front side.

Explore Oaxaca

▶ THE BEST OF OAXACA

This two-week adventure explores Oaxaca's most fascinating, charming, and simply beautiful places. First-time visitors will want to spend their time in and around Oaxaca City and valley and enjoy a few days relaxing on the coast. Returning visitors might choose to wander off the beaten path into other regions, such as the Mixteca or the Isthmus.

Although you could successfully begin this itinerary most any day of the week, the ideal would be to plan your Thursday, Friday, and Sunday for visiting the Valley of Oaxaca towns of Zaachila, Ocotlán, and Tlacolula, when their *tianguis* (native markets) are at their biggest and best. The itinerary below consequently starts in Oaxaca City on Monday, Tuesday, and Wednesday, and then switches to the valley towns, beginning with Zaachila, on Thursday.

Day 1

Monday: Arrive in Oaxaca. Stroll the *zócalo* (central plaza), visiting the cathedral and mysterious Santa Cruz de Huatulco. Take a table and enjoy the scene and dinner at a plaza-front café, or at Casa de la Abuela upstairs.

Days 2-3

Tuesday: After breakfast, stroll through the Mercado Juárez and continue to the adjacent San Juan de Dios church and market. Return uphill along Andador Macedonio Alcalá, sampling the handicrafts shops and the sights (Museo de Arte Contemporaneo, Ex-Convento de Santa

sweet shop in downtown Oaxaca City

embroidery (bordado) at Tlacolula

masks for sale in Oaxaca City

fresh candied apples at the zócalo

Catalina). Enjoy lunch at the Hostería de Alcalá restaurant.

Spend the full afternoon at the Iglesia y Ex-Convento de Santo Domingo and the Museo de las Culturas de Oaxaca. Eat dinner at either Los Pacos restaurant or Manantial Vegetariana. In the evening, take in a Guelaguetza folkloric dance performance.

Wednesday: Follow your individual interests. For arts and handicrafts, check out the shops and galleries you missed on Day 2, or visit the Museo de Rufino Tamayo or the ethno-botanical garden by the Iglesia de Santo Domingo. For churches, visit the beloved San Agustín and the Basilica de Nuestra Señora de la Soledad and its museum. During the evening, enjoy a music concert (Oaxaca State Band, Marimba Ensemble, or Oaxaca Orchestra) in the zócalo.

Alternatively, you might travel northwest of town, first to San José El Mogote archaeological zone and its community museum, continuing to the market at Etla, and then northwest to Suchilquitongo Community Museum and the Cerro de la Campana archaeological zone.

Days 4-5

Thursday: By 8 A.M. head southwest to Zaachila to explore the archaeological site and the market. Have lunch at a Zaachila market food stall or La Capilla restaurant.

Return via the Cuilapan de Guerrero church and Arrazola woodcarver's village.

Friday: Head out early to the Ocotlán market. In town, visit the Casa de Cultura Rudolfo Morales and the Templo de Santo Domingo and do lunch at La Celebración restaurant.

On your return, visit handicrafts villages San Antonino Castillo Velasco, Santo Tomás Jalieza, San Martín Tilcajete, and San Bartolo Coyotepec.

Days 6-7

Saturday: Enjoy a midmorning visit to Monte Albán. Allow around three hours, including the bookstore and museum. Eat lunch in the cafeteria or bring a picnic. Return downhill via Santa María Atzompa pottery village and handicrafts market.

Sunday: Head east early, first to the great El Tule tree. Continue to the wool textile store-workshops and community museum at Teotitlán del Valle. Have a noon lunch at Restaurant El Patio on the highway.

Continue to Tlacolula for an hour and a half at the market and the Capilla del Señor de Tlacolula. By 2:30 P.M. head east for at least an hour's visit to the Mitla archaeological zone.

Day 8

Since the Oaxaca coast stretches about 200 miles (320 km) from east to west, it's best to

Puerto Ángel

divide your overnights between Puerto Ángel, on the east side, and Puerto Escondido, on the west side. Arrive in Puerto Ángel. Stroll the beachfront and follow the *andador* (walkway) to Playa Panteón for sunning, swimming, or snorkeling. Have dinner at Beto's or Restaurant Alquimista.

Days 9-10

Spend Day 9 enjoying the nearby beaches. Drive or bus west to Playa Zipolite and its diminutive Roca Blanca district. Breakfast at Restaurant San Cristóbal; swim, surf, and sun for an hour or two, and then continue via Playa San Agustinillo village for a visit to the Centro Mexicano de la Tortuga at Mazunte. Stroll Mazunte village and beach; visit the Fábrica Ecología de Cosméticos Naturales de Mazunte, a cosmetics and soap factory. Have lunch or an early dinner at either Tanya's or Armadillo restaurant.

On Day 10, drive, tour, or ride a *colectivo* to Crucecita for a day in Huatulco; transfer to a taxi to Santa Cruz de Huatulco early enough to catch one of the excursion boats to tour Bahías de Huatulco. Return midafternoon and go to Crucecita for a walk around the plaza-front handicrafts shops and market. Dine at Restaurant La Crucecita, or splurge at the Italian Restaurant Giardino del Papa.

Days 11-12

Travel west an hour to Puerto Escondido. Stroll the *adoquín* (pedestrian walkway) and soak in the scene from a shady beachfront restaurant. Catch a boat ride (or a taxi) for either or both Bahía Puerto Ángelito and Bahía Carrizalillo for more beach fun, and lunch at a beachfront *palapa* restaurant. Head back east over to Playa Zicatela for a sunset dinner at the Hotel Santa Fe restaurant. Cap the evening with a balmy stroll, shopping, and nightclubbing along the *adoquín*.

On Day 12, head out for a wildlife-viewing excursion at Laguna Manialtepec by private tour, car, or bus (independent travelers get off and hire a boat at lagoon-front Isla El Gallo).

Days 13-14

Depending on your own inclination, Day 13 might be a good time for simple poolside or beachfront relaxing, watching the daredevil surfers at Playa Zicatela or perusing the *adoquín* shops. If you're up for adventure, enjoy a day (or overnight) excursion west to Lagunas de Chacagua or an upland overnight in either Nopala or Juquila, to visit Oaxaca's adored Virgen de Juquila.

Wind down on Day 14 by taking a morning walk along Playa Zicatela or the seafront *andador* from the main Puerto Escondido beach. Alternatively, go on a fishing excursion, do some snorkeling at Playa Carrizalillo, get a scuba lesson, or ride horseback along Playa Zicatela.

▶ TREASURES OF OLD MEXICO

Oaxaca preserves a wealth of tradition in its museums, galleries, festivals, historic churches, pilgrimage shrines, and archaeological sites. You can also find Oaxacan culture alive today in its shops and native markets.

Oaxaca City

Along your city route, be sure to include the Museo de las Culturas de Oaxaca and its neighboring Iglesia de Santo Domingo. Of the churches, don't miss the Basilica

the ruins of Monte Negro

TIANGUIS: NATIVE MARKETS

Most important Oaxaca towns have a public outdoor market every day but a *tianguis* (tee-AHN-gees) only once a week. The word *tianguis* is an ancient native expression, synonymous with "awning," the colorful tarpaulins that shade the mini-mountains of fruits, vegetables, crafts, and merchandise. Native people flock to *tianguis* everywhere in Oaxaca to buy and sell.

Although trade appears to be the prime mover, people really come to *tianguis* for human contact, not only in the buying and selling itself, but for gossip, entertainment, flirtation – all of the other diversions that make life worth living.

Oaxaca City

Abastos .... Saturday

The Valley of Oaxaca

Tlacolula	Sunday
Miahuatlán	Monday
Atzompa	Tuesday
Etla	Wednesday
Zimatlán	Wednesday
Zaachila	Thursday
Ejutla	Thursday
Ocotlán	Friday

Pacific Resorts and Southern Sierra

Nopala	Saturday and Sunday
Juquila	Saturday and Sunday
Santa María Huatulco	Saturday and Sunday
Cacahuatepec	Sunday
Sola de Vega	Sunday
Pinotepa Nacional	Monday
Pochutla	Monday
Huamelula	Thursday
Jamiltepec	Thursday
Astata	Saturday

Mixteca

Nochixtlán	Sunday
Putla	Sunday
Tamazulapan	Wednesday
Juxtlahuaca	Thursday, Friday biggest
Chalcatongo	Thursday
Tonalá	Friday
Huajuapan	Saturday
Tlaxiaco	Saturday

Northern Oaxaca

Yalalag	Sunday
Huautla	Sunday
Ixtlán de Juárez	Sunday
Valle Nacional	Sunday
Tuxtepec	Sunday
Cuicatlán	Sunday
Villa Alta	Monday
Teotitlán del Camino	Wednesday and Sunday
Jalapa de Díaz	Thursday and Sunday
Ojitlán	Wednesday

The Isthmus

Juchitán	every day
Tehuántepec	Wednesday and Sunday

Tlaxiaco Saturday market

fine wool weavings of Oaxaca Valley

de Nuestra Señora de la Soledad and the Catedral de Oaxaca, with its legendary Santa Cruz de Huatulco (Holy Cross of Huatulco).

Oaxaca City overflows with handicrafts. Stroll along the Andador Macedonio Alcalá to visit the finest source shops, such as La Mano Mágico (masks and textiles), Oro de Monte Albán (gold jewelry), and the first-rate, female-operated MARO (Mujeres Artesanías de las Regiones de Oaxaca) on Calle Cinco de Mayo, a block south of Alcalá.

The Valley of Oaxaca

Three very worthwhile community museums welcome visitors in Teotitlán del Valle, Santa Ana del Valle, and San José El Mogote. Along the way, don't miss the beautifully restored, lovely 16th-century churches in Tlacolula and Ocotlán.

Make certain to visit the monumental ruins, unmissable at Mitla and Monte Albán. The sites at Yagul and Lambityeco on the east side, and San José El Mogote and Suchilquitongo on the west side are also worthwhile if you have the time.

Go to the source in the celebrated handicrafts villages of Teotitlán del Valle (for wool weavings), San Bartolo Coyotepec (for black pottery), San Martin Tilcajete and Arrazola (for carved wooden animals), San Antonino Castillo Velasco (for embroidered blouses and dresses), and Atzompa (for pottery).

Pacific Resorts and Southern Sierra

The Oaxaca Pacific's unmissable museum is the Centro Mexicano de la Tortuga (Turtle Museum) in Mazunte. The most interesting

Atzompa pottery

embroidered Mazatec-style *huipiles* for sale

churches to visit are (moving east to west) at Santa María de Huatulco (with its mysterious Santa Cruz de Huatulco) and the pair of beloved pilgrimage shrines, the Santuario de Nuestra Señora de Juquila and the Capilla del Pedimento, at Santa Catarina Juquila.

Most of the Oaxaca Pacific's handicrafts are made on the west-side Mixtec coast. Primary are masks (in Huazololotitlán and Pinotepa Don Luis), *pozahuancos* (indigenous Mixtec wraparound skirts) in Pinotepa Nacional and vicinity, and the embroidered *huipiles* sold at San Pedro Amuzgos.

The Mixteca

Some professionally prepared community museums in the Mixteca welcome visitors: Memorias de Yucundaayee at San Pedro y San Pablo Tequixtepec, Bee Nu'u at Yucunama, and Ihitalulu at San Martin Huamelulpan are all well worth a visit. Furthermore, the Mixteca boasts some of Mexico's most celebrated Dominican church gems, notably at Teposcolula, Yanhuitlán, and Coixtlahuaca.

Also along your Mixteca route, you can visit a number of archaeological sites, the most accessible being the Cerro de las Minas, at Huajuapan, and the site at Huamelulpan. For pure wonder, however, visit the haunting and fascinating mountaintop ruined city at Monte Negro (near Tilantongo). Finally, for the rarest of archaeological treats, hike to the Puente Colosal, near Tepelmeme, to view the big red glyph of the yet-undeciphered Mesoamerican Ñuiñe written language.

The entire Mixteca Baja is a source of soft, pliable palm sombreros, baskets, and mats. One shop, Artesanías de Palma in Huajuapan, sells all these and more. At the

Juxtlahuaca market, indigenous Trique women offer embroidery and their richly decorated red and black wool *huipiles,* while also in town, master Alejandro Jesús Vera Guzmán offers expertly carved masks. At the big Tlaxiaco Saturday market, in addition to the above-mentioned woven goods, there are also carved *calabazas* (gourds) and embroidered *huipiles,* and leather belts, purses, and billfolds are plentiful.

Northern Oaxaca

Head north out of Oaxaca City to visit petite Guelatao and its shrine and museum in honor of Benito Juárez. Farther north in Tuxtepec, find the remarkable, unreconstructed Castillo de Moctezuma pyramid. Up the mountain, at the Huautla de Jiménez market, shop for bright, ribbon-decorated Mazatec *huipiles,* and don't miss visiting the wondrously mysterious María Sabina mural.

The Isthmus

Circle southeast to the Isthmus for a visit to Tehuántepec and its early-16th-century Templo y Ex-Convento de Santo Domingo. While in both Tehuántepec and neighboring Juchitán, shop for the famous, spectacularly flower-embroidered *huipiles.*

► ECOTOURISM LODGES

Cabañas ecoturísticas offer a unique opportunity for visitors weary of the city tourist rush who desire more contact with the local people and the local cultures. Many of the participating communities produce uniquely fine handicrafts and enjoy scenic, wildlife-rich locations. For modest fees, these local communities also furnish guides who lead visitors along scenic trails, past springs, caves, meadows, and mountain vistas, while identifying useful plants and birds and animals along the way. Some communities rent mountain bikes and offer instruction in rappelling and rock climbing and other outdoor diversions.

The Oaxaca Federal-State Department of Tourism (SEDETUR) first built these tourist cabin complexes in communities on the east side of the Valley of Oaxaca during the 1990s. Although five of the original nine are not now being used, several more *cabañas ecoturísticas* have been built, mostly in Northern Oaxaca and the Mixteca, raising the total to about 14 complexes that are now operating. About two dozen Oaxaca communities now invite visitors to stay in their community tourist lodging.

The *cabañas* are government constructed but locally managed, modern-standard but usually rustic. Each bungalow typically sleeps four, with private hot-water shower/bath and toilet and perhaps a kitchenette.

The Valley of Oaxaca

Santa Ana del Valle: Master weavers' shops, museum, lake, scenic views, hikes.

Hierve El Agua: Hikes, scenic vistas, mineral springs, frozen stone cascades.

The Mixteca

Apoala: Idyllic village, wild canyon, cave, cascade, springs, camping.

San Francisco Yosocuta: Reservoir, boating, fishing, RV and tent camping.

San Martín Huamelulpan: Ruined city, museum, hikes to other archaeological sites.

San Miguel Tequixtepec: Museum, hike to hieroglyphic rock paintings, palm weaving, restored 17th-century church.

Tepelmeme de Morelos: Museum, canyon hike to Puente Colosal natural bridge and rare Ñuiñe glyph.

Northern Oaxaca

Ixtlán de Juárez: Cloud forest, wildlife-viewing, Benito Juárez's birthplace and museum, limestone cave.

Santa Catarina Ixtepeji: Hiking trails, campground, colonial-era church.

Benito Juárez: Cool pine-scented air, camping, panoramic views.

Cuajimoloyas: Mountain-top village, hiking, rock climbing.

Llano Grande: Woodland hikes, wildflowers.

Butterflies are one of the delights seen in summer and fall strolls in Oaxaca's tropical evergreen and deciduous forest paths.

great white heron

Iñè Lola del Serpiente waterfall in Apoala

Reservations

Two agencies handle reservations for most of the *cabañas*. The Oaxaca state ecotourism (Murguia 206, Oaxaca, tel. 951/516-0123, info@aoaxaca.com, www.oaxaca.travel) reserves Santa Ana del Valle, San Miguel del Valle, Hierve El Agua, Ixtlán de Juárez, Santa Catarina Ixtepeji, Apoala, and Yosundua. They've also published a class-act photo- and information-filled Guía Ecoturística (Ecotourism Guidebook)—in Spanish, but very informative nevertheless.

The other reservations agency, Expediciones Sierra Norte (M. Bravo 210, tel 951/514-8271, fax 951/514-3631, sierranorte@oaxaca.com, www.sierranorte.org.mx) handles *cabaña* reservations for the six communities collectively organized as the Pueblos Mancomunicados: Benito Juárez, Cuajimoloyas, and Llano Grande, and three neighboring communities, Santa Catarina Lachatao, La Guacamaya, and San Miguel Amatlan.

Cactus-like *maguey* grows nearly everywhere in the state of Oaxaca.

► ON LAND AND SEA

Oaxaca abounds with natural wonders and outdoor adventures: hills and mountains for hiking and climbing; rivers for kayaking and rafting; caves for exploring; and coasts, offshore islands, and mangrove lagoons for kayaking, boating, bird-watching, and much more. Moreover, Oaxaca is a veritable wildlife treasury, home to myriad species, from iguanas and crocodiles to dolphins, whales, and white herons.

Hiking, Biking, and Horseback Riding

In Oaxaca City, walk uphill to the top of breezy Cerro del Fortín, or, at Hierve El Agua, follow the *sendero peatonal* (footpath) that circuits the entire fascinating site.

In Huatulco, follow the forest paths to Bahía El Organo and Bahía Cacaluta, hike or ride horseback along the Río Copalita, or hike to the coffee farm in Pluma Hidalgo.

The Mixteca abounds with unforgettable walks. For example, in Apoala, follow the spectacular trail into the gorge of Las Dos Peñas Colosales to the hidden valley of the La Peña Donde Murió El Aguila con Dos Cabezas. In Tepelmeme, hike to the spectacular natural bridge, Puente Colosal.

Oaxaca's northern mountains are full of outdoor opportunities, especially plenty of hiking and mountain biking, beginning not far from Oaxaca City, around the pine-scented Benito Juárez, Cuajimoloyas, and Ixtlán de Juárez villages.

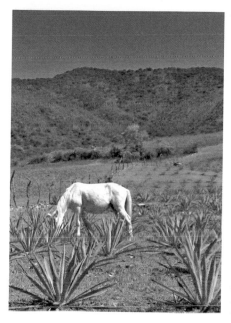

lancha (launch) in Huatulco, Puerto Ángel, or Puerto Escondido. You can also rent a fully equipped fishing boat at either Huatulco or Puerto Escondido.

If you prefer to go after freshwater fish, such as *mojarra* (bass) or tilapia, launch your own boat or rent a *lancha* at either Yosocuta reservoir in the Mixteca or Temascal reservoir in northern Oaxaca.

Caverns, Waterfalls, and Natural Springs

In the Valley of Oaxaca, start your exploring at the monumental limestone cavern complex near San Sebastián de las Grutas down Highway 131, south of Zimatlán.

Moving counterclockwise around the Mixteca, start at Apoala to explore the limestone cavern, natural spring, and waterfall. Farther northwest, continue to Juxtlahuaca to the emerald-green Laguna Encantada, a crystal-clear, spring-fed lake. Nearby, explore the triple wonder of limestone cavern, natural spring river, and lake at San Miguel de la Cueva.

In northern Oaxaca and on the Isthmus, most spectacular are the crystalline springs Monte Flor and Zuzul and the limestone cavern at Eloxochitlán, near Huautla de Jiménez.

River Rafting and Kayaking

When the water conditions are right (usually in the fall), outfitters take parties for rafting on the Río Copalita near Huatulco. Moreover, a number of other coastal rivers, notably (moving from east to west) the Ríos Zimatán, Colotepec, Verde, and Arena, appear negotiable during the fall and early winter seasons for skilled rafters and kayakers with their own equipment.

Fishing

Fish thrive all along the Oaxaca Pacific coast. From the beach or shoreline rocks, pluck them out of the surf with a net or rod and tackle at Huatulco's Bahía Chahue, at the Bahía Puerto Ángel, and at Playa Carrizalillo near Puerto Escondido. For deep-sea fishing, either launch your own boat or rent a

Kayaking

At Huatulco, for easy bay boating or kayaking, start out from the sheltered Marina Chahue with your own boat or by kayak from Playa Entrega in the Bahía Santa Cruz or the beach at Bahía Maguey. More challenging kayaking opportunities abound in the less sheltered Huatulco Bahías El Organo, Cacaluta, and San Agustín. Near Puerto Escondido, easy boating or kayaking is doable from the landings at Las Hamacas, La Alejandria, or Isla El Gallo in Laguna Manialtepec.

BEST BEACHES

BEST OVERALL
Playa San Agustinillo (Puerto Ángel and vicinity, page 126)
Playa Entrega (Huatulco, page 149)
Playa Manzanillo (Puerto Escondido, page 173)

BEST SURF-FISHING
Bahía Chahue (Huatulco, page 149)
Playa Bachoco (Puerto Escondido, page 173)

BEST SNORKELING
Playa Estacahuite (Puerto Ángel and vicinity, page 125)
Playa Manzanillo (Puerto Escondido, page 173)

BEST SURFING
Playa Zipolite (Puerto Ángel, page 125)
Playa Zicatela (Puerto Escondido, page 173)

BEST SUNSETS
Playa Zipolite (Puerto Ángel and vicinity, page 125)
Playa La Ventanilla (Puerto Ángel and vicinity, page 127)
Bahía Tangolunda (Huatulco, page 149)
Playa Zicatela (Escondido, page 173)

BEST FOR KIDS
Playa Panteón (Puerto Ángel and vicinity, page 123)
Bahía el Maguey (Huatulco, page 150)
Playa Principal (Puerto Escondido, page 172)

BEST FOR CAMPING
Playa Zipolite (Puerto Ángel and vicinity, page 125)
El Playon at Bahía San Agustín (Huatulco, page 151)

MOST PRISTINE
Playa La Ventanilla (Puerto Ángel and vicinity, page 127)
Bahía Chachacual (Huatulco, page 150)
Playa Carrizalillo (Puerto Escondido, page 173)

MOST INTIMATE
Bahía El Organo (Huatulco, page 150)
Playa Carrizalillo (Puerto Escondido, page 173)

MOST SPECTACULAR
Bahía Cacaluta (Huatulco, page 150)

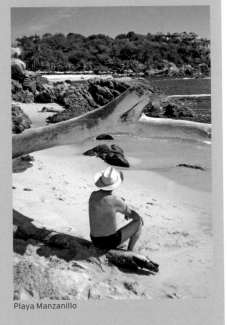

Playa Manzanillo

OAXACA CITY

The fortunate city of Oaxaca (pop. 375,000, elev. 5,110 feet/1,778 meters) is both the governmental capital of Mexico's fifth-largest state by area (about tenth largest by population) and the de facto capital of Mexico's southern indigenous heartland. And Oaxaca is southern indeed. It lies farther south than all of Mexico's state capitals save one, Tuxtla Gutiérrez, the capital of the state of Chiapas, and consequently enjoys abundant sunshine—fortunately without suffering from tropical heat. Oaxaca nestles in a temperate highland valley, blessed with a year-round balmy, springlike climate, prized by both residents and visitors alike.

Every year, for two weeks starting in mid-July, Oaxaca (wah-HAH-kah) City becomes the focus of the extraordinary diversity of its entire state. In the celebrated Guelaguetza (The Giving) festival, indigenous Oaxaca people, speaking 16 unique languages and representing hundreds of Oaxaca's separate ethnic groups, converge in the city for a grand two-week party of food, dancing, music, and general merrymaking.

The Guelaguetza, like virtually all of Oaxaca's civic revelries, starts at the *zócalo* (central plaza), sprinkled all around by relaxing sidewalk cafés and bordered by the porticoed Palacio de Gobierno on its south side and the distinguished baroque bulk of the **Catedral de Oaxaca** on its north side.

From there, the city's street grid, originally laid out by city founders in 1529, spreads south past the town's vibrant pair of central markets, the **Mercado Juárez** and the Mercado

HIGHLIGHTS

◖ Mercado Juárez: A regiment of stalls offers the best traditional Oaxaca merchandise, from *huaraches* and *huipiles* to mountain-gathered remedies and spit-roasted chickens (page 34).

◖ Catedral de Oaxaca: The recently restored facade and the inner chapel, which enshrines one of the four replicas of the Holy Cross of Huatulco, highlight a visit to this plaza-front gem (page 35).

◖ Basilica de Nuestra Señora de la Soledad: Five pounds of gold and 600 diamonds crown Oaxaca's adored patron, and a fascinating adjacent museum preserves her beloved legacy (page 38).

◖ Ex-Convento de Santa Catalina: Wander the tranquil inner courtyards of this richly restored ex-convent, now a distinguished hotel (page 39).

◖ Centro Cultural de Santo Domingo: Explore the celebrated duo – the art-swathed Iglesia de Santo Domingo, and the adjacent Museo de las Culturas de Oaxaca, with its golden treasure of Monte Albán's Tomb 7 (page 39).

◖ Los Arquitos: The original 18th-century aqueduct still stands, in Oaxaca City's uptown northwest corner, in a quaint string of arches called Los Arquitos. The surrounding neighborhood is ripe for strolling winding village lanes and lingering at a sprinkling of shops, small cafés, and an all-natural Saturday food market (page 41).

◖ MARO: Do a major part of your Oaxaca handicrafts shopping at this store, run by a remarkable group of native Oaxacan women artisans (page 64).

LOOK FOR ◖ TO FIND RECOMMENDED SIGHTS, ACTIVITIES, DINING, AND LODGING.

San Juan de Dios, and north, uphill, along the very strollable pedestrian walkway, the Andador Macedonio Alacalá. The walkway connects the *zócalo* with Oaxaca's uptown monuments, most notably Oaxaca's jewel, the **Centro Cultural de Santo Domingo,** made up of the Iglesia y Ex-Convento de Santo Domingo and the adjacent magnificent Museo de las Culturas de Oaxaca.

Finally, the city streets climb even more steeply, and as the Guelaguetza throng does in July, the westbound streets reach the grand outdoor dance stage and amphitheater atop Oaxaca's storied hillside of Cerro del Fortín. This hill, originally known as the hill of Huayxacac, was named for the forest of pod-bearing trees that still cover its slope. In fact, Huaxyacac was the city's original name, and the Spanish transliterated it to the more pronounceable Oaxaca.

HISTORY
Before Columbus

As early as perhaps 20,000 years ago, small bands of people, whose ancestors had migrated from Asia, were gathering wild grains, vegetables, and fruits and hunting wild game in the present Valley of Oaxaca. They foraged from the bounty of forest and meadow while following the great herds—bison, camels, deer, horses, and mammoths—that roamed Ice Age America.

Later, around 8000 B.C., the climate had warmed, and the animal herds were gone. The people, no longer following the vast game migrations, settled into a more sedentary life. They began to sow and cultivate the fruits, vegetables, and grains they had originally gathered. A few thousand years later, many of those original humble fields and gardens had become productive fields supporting permanent settlements of thatched houses, not unlike many remote Oaxacan hamlets today.

Finally, around 600 B.C., people speaking a Zapotec mother tongue founded Monte Albán on a mountaintop above the present city of Oaxaca. Monte Albán ruled the Valley of Oaxaca for more than a millennium, climaxing as a sophisticated metropolis of as many as 40,000, controlling a large and populous area of southern Mexico and enjoying diplomatic and trade relations with distant kingdoms. But for reasons unknown, Monte Albán declined to a shadow of its former glory by around A.D. 800.

Zapotec-speaking city-states such as Zaachila, Dainzu, Mitla, and Lambityeco in the surrounding valleys filled the power vacuum left by the decline of Monte Albán. They ruled small valley-floor kingdoms, each controlling a small flock of satellite towns. Later, Mixtec-speaking people from the northwest invaded the Valley of Oaxaca and took over Monte Albán, using it mostly as a burial ground. Their chiefs subjugated many of the Zapotec city-states and ruled as an upper-crust nobility over much of the Valley of Oaxaca, until the Aztecs invaded during the 1440s.

In 1488, after a generation of struggle against combined Mixtec and Zapotec forces, the victorious Aztecs established a garrison on the hill of Huaxyacac (now called El Fortín), overlooking the present city of Oaxaca. Although Aztec settlers had established a model colony by 1500 (including districts with well-known Valley of Mexico names that still exist, such as Xochimilco), their rule was brief. On December 25, 1521, after a token skirmish, conquistador Francisco de Orozco and his soldiers replaced the Aztecs on the hill of Huaxyacac scarcely five months after the Spanish tide had flooded the Aztecs' Valley of Mexico homeland.

Conquest and Colonization

Spanish settlers began arriving soon after the conquistadors. Hernán Cortés, hearing of the beauty and bounty of the Valley of Oaxaca from both his lieutenants and emissaries from the Zapotec king, decided early on to stake out the Valley of Oaxaca as his personal domain. Time and again during the 1520s he ordered the settlers evacuated from Huaxyacac, only to find a year or two later that they had returned. During Cortés's absence on an expedition to Honduras, the settlers petitioned for and received a charter from King Carlos V for their town, which they christened Antequera after the old Roman city in Spain. Determined not to be outmaneuvered, Cortés personally went to Spain to plead his case and returned triumphant with the royal title of Marqués del Valle de Oaxaca. This included a grant of hundreds of thousands of acres and rights to the labor of thousands of indigenous subjects in a grand checkerboard domain stretching from the Valley of Mexico to the Isthmus of Tehuántepec. Cortés's lands surrounded the settlers' entire town of Antequera. In desperation, the townspeople petitioned the queen of Spain for land on which to grow vegetables: They were granted a one-league square in 1532, now the core of the modern city of Oaxaca.

For hundreds of years, Cortés's descendants reigned; the townspeople prospered, the church grew fat, and the natives toiled—in corn, cattle, cane, and cochineal.

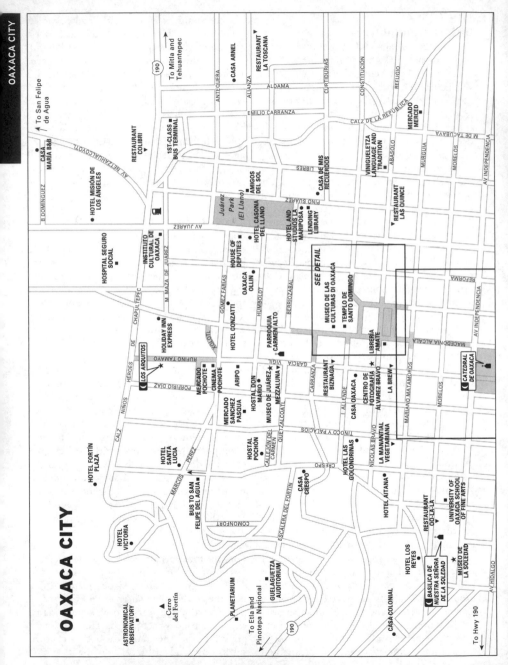

OAXACA CITY

ASTRONOMICAL OBSERVATORY

Cerro del Fortín

PLANETARIUM

GUELAGUETZA AUDITORIUM

To Etla and Pinotepa Nacional

190

CASA COLONIAL

HOTEL VICTORIA

HOTEL FORTÍN PLAZA

BUS TO SAN FELIPE DEL AGUA

HOTEL SANTA LUCÍA

CASA CRESPO

HOTEL LAS GOLONDRINAS

HOTEL AITANA

HOSTAL POCHÓN

CALLEJÓN DEL CARMEN

MERCADO SÁNCHEZ PASQUA

HOSTAL DON MARIO

MERCADO POCHOTE

CINEMA POCHOTE

ARIPO

MUSEO DE JUÁREZ

MEZZALUNA

RUFINO TAMAYO

HOLIDAY INN EXPRESS

HOTEL CONZATTI

HOSPITAL SEGURO SOCIAL

INSTITUTO CULTURAL DE OAXACA

HOUSE OF DEPUTIES

OAXACA OLLIN

PARROQUIA CARMEN ALTO

LOS ARQUITOS

LA MANANTIAL VEGETARIANA

CASA OAXACA

RESTAURANT BIZNAGA

CENTRO DE FOTOGRAFÍA ÁLVAREZ BRAVO

LA BREW

LIBRERÍA AMATE

MUSEO DE LAS CULTURAS DI OAXACA

TEMPLO DE SANTO DOMINGO

SEE DETAIL

HOTEL AND STUDIOS LA MARIPOSA

LENDING LIBRARY

HOTEL CASONA DEL LLANO

AMIGOS DEL SOL

Juárez Park (El Llano)

AV JUÁREZ

CASA DE MIS RECUERDOS

VINIGULETZA LANGUAGE AND TRADITION

RESTAURANT LAS QUINCE

CATEDRAL DE OAXACA

MACEDONIA ALCALÁ

AV INDEPENDENCIA

REFORMA

UNIVERSITY OF OAXACA SCHOOL OF FINE ARTS

RESTAURANT OO-LA-LA

HOTEL LOS REYES

MUSEO DE LA SOLEDAD

BASÍLICA DE NUESTRA SEÑORA DE LA SOLEDAD

AV HIDALGO

To Hwy 190

HOTEL MISIÓN DE LOS ÁNGELES

CASA MARÍA B&B

RESTAURANT COLIBRÍ

AV NETZAHUALCOYOTL

To San Felipe de Agua

B DOMÍNGUEZ

190

To Mitla and Tehuantepec

CASA ARNEL

RESTAURANT LA TOSCANA

1ST-CLASS BUS TERMINAL

ANTEQUERA

ALDAMA

EMILIO CARRANZA

ALIANZA

CURTIDURÍAS

CALZ DE LA REPÚBLICA

CONSTITUCIÓN

REFUGIO

MERCADO MERCED

M DE TACUBAYA

AV INDEPENDENCIA

MORELOS

MURGUÍA

ABASOLO

PINO SUÁREZ

BERRIOZABAL

HUMBOLDT

GÓMEZ FARÍAS

M MAZA DE JUÁREZ

CHAPULTEPEC

DE

HÉROES

NIÑOS

CALZ

PÉREZ

MARCOS

ESCALERA DEL FORTÍN

COMONFORT

TINOCO Y PALACIOS

CRESPO

QUETZALCOATL

NICOLÁS BRAVO

J ALLENDE

CARRANZA

GARCÍA VIGIL

MARIANO MATAMOROS

MORELOS

PORFIRIO DÍAZ

REFORMA

AV INDEPENDENCIA

To Hwy 190

SEE "DOWNTOWN OAXACA CITY" MAP

MUSEO PHILATELICA ★ DE OAXACA

HOTEL MAELA ●

HOTEL CASA VERTIZ ●

CLINICA HOSPITAL CARMEN ■

HOTEL VILLA DE LEÓN ■

ETHNOBOTANICAL LIBRARY ■

APTS CASA DE LOS ABUELOS ■

CASA BUGAMBILIAS ■

ETHNOBOTANICAL GARDEN ■

GALERIA QUETZALLI ■

CAFE LA ANTIGUA ▶

RESTAURANT LOS PACOS ■

MUSEO DE LAS ★ CULTURAS DE OAXACA

RESTAURANT CASA OAXACA ■

COFFEE BEANS ●

MONEDAS Y ANTIGUIDADES ■

EX-CONVENTO DE SANTA CATALINA ★

CENTRO CULTURAL DE SANTO DOMINGO ◀

TEMPLO DE SANTO DOMINGO ■

RESTAURANT EL CHE ▶

TEOTITLAN RUGS ■

CASA OLIVO ▶

Plazuela Labasti'da

MUNICIPAL TOURIST INFORMATION ★

GALERIA INDIGO ■

SHOPPING PLAZA SANTA DOMINGO ■

ORO DE MONTE ALBAN ■

BAR LA PASION/ RESTAURANT ▶ MAYORDOMO

INSTITUTO DE ARTES GRAFICOS ★

LOS DANZANTES ▶

LIBRERIA AMATE ■

HOSTERIA ▶ A.CALA

US CONSUL ▶

LA CANTINITA ▶

POSADA DE CHENCHO ■

VILLA MARIA ●

HOSTAL CHACAHUA ■

To Pochutla (Puerto Angel)

ATLANTIDA VANS ■

ECLIPSE 70 VANS ■

UNO LANGUAGE CENTER ■

Plaza de Armas (Zócalo)

MERCADO JUAREZ ◀

Mercado 20 de Noviembre

EL ARTE OAXAQUEÑO ■

MERCADO DE ARTESANIAS ■

PAULINA YOUTH HOSTEL ●

EXCELENCIA COLLECTIVE VANS ■

HOTEL RIVIERA DEL ANGEL/ VIAJES TURISTICOS MITLA ■

To 2nd-Class Bus Terminal

Mercado Abastos

Rio Atoyac

PROL DE VICTORIA

To Monte Albán

To Airport, Ocotlan, Puerto Angel, and Puerto Escondido)

To Zaachila

To Arrazola, Cuilapan, and Zaachila

CARRETERA MONTE ALBAN

0   100 yds
0   100 m

© AVALON TRAVEL

Independence, Reform, and Revolution

In contrast to its neighbors in the state of Guerrero, conservative Oaxaca was a grudging player in the 1810–1821 War of Independence. But as the subsequent republican tide swept the country, local fervor produced a new state constitution, including a state legislature and governmental departments, such as public instruction and the Institute of Arts and Sciences.

By the 1850s, times had changed. Oaxacans were leading a new national struggle. Benito Juárez, a pure Zapotec native Mexican, was rallying liberal forces in the War of the Reforms against the oligarchy that had replaced colonial rule. Born in Guelatao, a mountain village north of the Valley of Oaxaca, Juárez at age 12 was an orphan sheepherder. A Catholic priest, struck by the boy's intelligence, brought him to the city as a servant and taught him Spanish in preparation for the priesthood.

Instead, Benito became a lawyer. He hung out his shingle in Oaxaca, as a defender of the poor. He then became state legislator, governor, chief justice, and finally the president of Mexico. In his honor, the city's official name was again changed—to Oaxaca de Juárez—in 1872.

In 1861, after winning the three-year civil war, Juárez's Reformista forces had their victory snatched away. France, taking advantage of the preoccupation of the United States with its own civil war, invaded Mexico and installed an Austrian Hapsburg prince as Emperor Maximilian of Mexico.

It took Juárez five years to prevail against Maximilian and his conservative Mexican backers. Although Maximilian and Juárez paradoxically shared many of the same liberal ideas, Juárez had Maximilian executed after his defeat and capture in 1867. Juárez bathed Mexico in enlightenment as he promulgated his Laws of the Reform (which remain essentially in force). Although the country rewarded him with re-election, he died of exhaustion in 1871.

Another Oaxacan of native Mexican descent, General Porfirio Díaz, vowed to carry Juárez's banner. Díaz, the hero who defeated the French in the battle of Puebla on Cinco de Mayo (May 5) of 1862, was elected president in 1876. "No Reelección" was his campaign cry. He subsequently ruled Mexico for 34 years.

Under Díaz's "Order and Progress" programs, Mexico, and to a lesser degree Oaxaca, was modernized at great human cost. As railroads, factories, and mines mushroomed, property ownership increasingly became concentrated among rich Mexicans and their foreign friends. Smashed protest marches, murdered opposition leaders, and rigged elections returned Díaz to office time and again.

But not forever. The revolt that ousted Díaz in 1910 has, in theory, never ceased. For the last three generations of the 20th century, the PRI (Partido Revolucionario Institucional, or the Institutional Revolutionary Party) presided over a uniquely imperfect Mexican form of democracy. During that time, the lives of native Oaxacans improved gradually. Although indigenous families now go to government health centers and more of their children attend government rural schools, the price for doing so is to become less indigenous and more Mexican.

In the late 1980s, UNESCO recognized Oaxaca as one of several world sites belonging to the "cultural patrimony of mankind." The government took notice and began preparing Oaxaca for an influx of visitors. Museums were built, monuments refurbished, and the venerable buildings restored. Burgeoning tourism during the 1990s has visibly improved the economic well-being of many Oaxaca families. In 1995, moderate PRI governor Diodoro Carrasco Altamirano pushed through an unprecedented law that legalized Oaxacan native rights to their indigenous language and their traditional, town-meeting form of government.

Nevertheless, by developed-world standards, most Oaxaca City families remain poor. The political system, moreover, remains far from perfect. In 2000, the victory of opposition presidential candidate Vicente Fox promised a new day for democracy in Oaxaca. Although

Fox couldn't work miracles during his six-year term, one of his major achievements was to add transparency to the workings of the Mexican government.

Unfortunately, despite President Fox's efforts at the national level, serious political trouble surfaced in Oaxaca in mid-2006. It started mildly enough. In May 2006, Oaxaca's statewide teachers union went on their perennial strike for much-needed higher wages. They accused PRI governor Ulises Ruiz of diverting millions of dollars in education funds to his controversial pet public works projects. Soon, hundreds of teachers were camping out in the *zócalo* and staging daily political rallies. Their rhetoric increasingly focused on the credibility of Governor Ruiz, who consistently refused to negotiate with them.

By mid June, when teachers began barricading streets around the *zócalo*, Ruiz sent in his police, who brutally manhandled the nonviolent middle-class demonstrators. The protest escalated quickly. The teachers allied themselves with their left-leaning supporters, forming an umbrella protest organization, the APPO (Popular Assembly of the People of Oaxaca), and added the demand that Governor Ruiz must step down.

During the summer months of July, August, and September, the protests turned violent. Highways were blocked, buses were burned, a radio station was occupied, and a handful of people were shot to death. By the end of September, downtown Oaxaca City resembled a ghost town. Tourism had evaporated and, consequently, all businesses, including hotels and restaurants, had shut their doors.

The focus then shifted to Mexico City, where teachers, negotiating with federal authorities, got their requested wage increase. Furthermore, the federal Chamber of Deputies voted overwhelmingly that Governor Ruiz must vacate his office.

In late October, President Vicente Fox, spurred by the killing of an American news reporter, acted. He sent a brigade of federal troops and police to Oaxaca, where they removed the street barricades and dispersed the protestors while inflicting only minimal injuries.

The local townspeople, breathing a sigh of relief, turned out, and in two days they swept up the mess, painted over the accumulated graffiti, and opened their businesses. Townspeople filled the streets, buying flowers to celebrate their subsequently peaceful November 1–2 Day of the Dead holiday, and equally tranquil and joyful Christmas celebrations.

During 2007, aside from a few minor APPO ("AH-poh") demonstrations, relegated to the city outskirts, Oaxaca continued returning to normal. Local and national visitors responded, frequenting downtown hotels, restaurants, and shops in increasing numbers. By November 2007, a growing trickle of foreign visitors was joining the influx, fueling predictions by some experts that in 2008 international visitors would come back, big-time.

Oaxaca is certainly ready for them. Virtually all of the favorite restaurants and shops are open for business; the same is true of hotels, several of which have remodeled and are welcoming visitors with bargain rates, making the prospect of a long Oaxaca stay more tempting than ever. And best of all, despite past political tensions, the people of Oaxaca remain appreciative of visitors and look forward with renewed enthusiasm to sharing their lovely city's celebrated handicrafts, delicious cuisine, and beloved fiestas with them.

PLANNING YOUR TIME

You could spend a month of Sundays exploring the city of Oaxaca and still have plenty left over. However, in about four fairly relaxed days, you can take in most of the downtown highlights. Start out with a leisurely day of people-watching and café-lounging around the invitingly tranquil old *zócalo*. For activity, explore the nearby Palacio de Gobierno, the colorful **Mercado Juárez**, the exquisitely baroque **Iglesia y Ex-Convento de San Agustín,** and the **Catedral de Oaxaca** with its mysteriously intriguing Santa Cruz de Huatulco.

Spend your second day relaxing along the **Andador de Macedonio Alacalá pedestrian**

© BRUCE WHIPPERMAN

Ex-convento de Santo Domingo

mall, checking out the many fine handicrafts shops, **the Museo de Arte Contemporaneo,** and the **Ex-Convento de Santa Catalina,** now restored as the Hotel Camino Real. Be sure to enjoy lunch on the relaxingly cool patios of the Danzantes or Hostería Alcalá restaurants.

Highlight your downtown exploration with at least a day around the **Centro Cultural de Santo Domingo,** which includes a pair of unmissable stops: the world-class **Museo de las Culturas de Oaxaca,** and Oaxaca's pride, the radiantly lovely **Iglesia y Ex-Convento de Santo Domingo.**

Spend your fourth day following your own interests, such as investigating more handicrafts stores, especially **MARO** (Mujeres Artesanís de los Regiones de Oaxaca); visiting small museums, notably, the **Casa de Juárez** and the **Museo Prehispanico de Rufino Tamayo;** or more sights, such as the intimate Arquitos and San Felipe del Agua village neighborhoods or the gemlike **Basílica de Nuestra Señora de la Soledad** and adjacent museum, **Museo de la Soledad.**

Sights

GETTING ORIENTED

The streets of Oaxaca still run along the same simple north–south grid the city fathers laid out in 1529. If you stand at the center of the old *zócalo* and look out toward the *catedral* across Avenida Hidalgo, you will be looking north. Diagonally left, to the northwest, you'll see the smaller plaza, **Alameda de León,** and directly beyond that, in the distance, the historic hill of Huaxyacac, now called **Cerro del Fortín.**

Along the base of that hill, the Pan American Highway (National Highway 190) runs generally east–west through the northern suburbs. Turn around and you'll see the porticoed facade of the former **Palacio de Gobierno,** now a museum, where Oaxaca's governor used to tend to the state's business. Half a mile (0.8 km) behind that (although you can't see it from the *zócalo*), the **periférico** (peripheral boulevard)

loops around the town's south end. There it passes the yawning but often dry wash of the **Río Atoyac** and the sprawling **Mercado Abastos,** a market and second-class bus terminal on the southwest. Finally, if you find a clear vantage point, you'll see the hill of **Monte Albán** looming 1,000 feet (300 meters) above the southwest horizon.

AROUND THE *ZÓCALO*

The venerable restored downtown buildings and streets, some converted to traffic-free malls, make a delightful strolling ground for discovering traditional Mexico at its best. The shady old *zócalo* basks at the heart of it all, a perfect place for taking a seat at one of many sidewalk cafés and watching the world glide by. Officially called Jardín Juárez, the *zócalo* was laid out in 1529. Its portals, clockwise from the

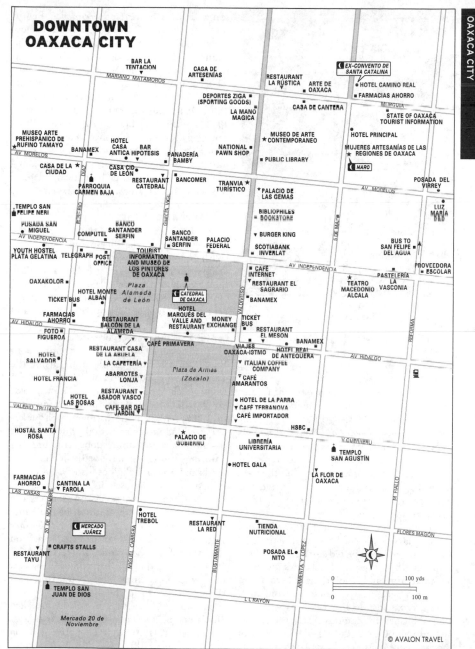

DOWNTOWN OAXACA CITY

BAR LA TENTACION
MARIANO MATAMOROS
CASA DE ARTESENÍAS
RESTAURANT LA RÚSTICA
ARTE DE OAXACA
EX-CONVENTO DE SANTA CATALINA
HOTEL CAMINO REAL
FARMACIAS AHORRO
DEPORTES ZIGA (SPORTING GOODS)
LA MANO MAGICA
CASA DE CANTERA
MURGUIA
STATE OF OAXACA TOURIST INFORMATION
MUSEO ARTE PREHISPÁNICO DE RUFINO TAMAYO
BANAMEX
HOTEL CASA ANTICA HIPOTESIS
BAR
PANADERÍA BAMBY
AV MORELOS
NATIONAL PAWN SHOP
MUSEO DE ARTE CONTEMPORANEO
HOTEL PRINCIPAL
MUJERES ARTESANÍAS DE LAS REGIONES DE OAXACA
CASA DE LA CIUDAD
DIAZ
CASA CID DE LEÓN
RESTAURANT CATEDRAL
BANCOMER
PUBLIC LIBRARY
MARO
PARROQUIA CARMEN BAJA
TRANVIA TURÍSTICO
PALACIO DE LAS GEMAS
AV MORELOS
POSADA DEL VIRREY
TEMPLO SAN FELIPE NERI
ES RIO
GRECIA VIGIL
BIBLIOPHILES BOOKSTORE
LUZ MARIA
POSADA SAN MIGUEL
AV INDEPENDENCIA
COMPUTEL
BANCO SANTANDER SERFIN
BANCO SANTANDER SERFIN
PALACIO FEDERAL
BURGER KING
5 DE MAYO
YOUTH HOSTEL PLATA GELATINA
TELEGRAPH POST OFFICE
TOURIST INFORMATION AND MUSEO DE LOS PINTORES DE OAXACA
SCOTIABANK INVERLAT
BUS TO SAN FELIPE DEL AGUA
OAXAKOLOR
HOTEL MONTE ALBÁN
Plaza Alameda de León
CATEDRAL DE OAXACA
VALDIVIESO
CAFÉ INTERNET
AV INDEPENDENCIA
RESTAURANT EL SAGRARIO
BANAMEX
TEATRO MACEDONIO ALCALA
PASTELERÍA LA VASCONIA
PROVEEDORA ESCOLAR
TICKET BUS
FARMACIAS AHORRO
AV HIDALGO
RESTAURANT BALCÓN DE LA ALAMEDA
HOTEL MARQUÉS DEL VALLE AND RESTAURANT
MONEY EXCHANGE
TICKET BUS
RESTAURANT EL MESON
BANAMEX
FOTO FIGUEROA
RESTAURANT CASA DE LA ABUELA
CAFÉ PRIMAVERA
VIAJES OAXACA-ISTMO
HOTEL REAL DE ANTEQUERA
AV HIDALGO
HOTEL SALVADOR
LA CAFETERÍA
ITALIAN COFFEE COMPANY
HOTEL FRANCIA
ABARROTES LONJA
Plaza de Armas (Zócalo)
CAFÉ AMARANTOS
HOTEL LAS ROSAS
RESTAURANT ASADOR VASCO
HOTEL DE LA PARRA
CAFÉ TERRANOVA
VALERIO TRUJANO
CAFÉ-BAR DEL JARDIN
CAFÉ IMPORTADOR
HOSTAL SANTA ROSA
PALACIO DE GOBIERNO
LIBRERÍA UNIVERSITARIA
HSBC
V GUERRERO
TEMPLO SAN AGUSTÍN
HOTEL GALA
FARMACIAS AHORRO
LAS CASAS
CANTINA LA FAROLA
LA FLOR DE OAXACA
M FIALLO
20 DE NOVIEMBRE
MERCADO JUÁREZ
HOTEL TREBOL
RESTAURANT LA RED
TIENDA NUTRICIONAL
FLORES MAGÓN
RESTAURANT TAYU
CRAFTS STALLS
MIGUEL CABRERA
BUSTAMANTE
POSADA EL NITO
ARMENTA Y LÓPEZ
TEMPLO SAN JUAN DE DIOS

Mercado 20 de Noviembre

LL RAYON
REFORMA

0 _____ 100 yds

0 _____ 100 m

© AVALON TRAVEL

OAXACA CITY

In Oaxaca, it's fun to take a *zócalo* seat and watch the world pass slowly by.

© BRUCE WHIPPERMAN

west side, are named Flores, Clavería, Juárez, and Mercaderes.

Palacio de Gobierno

Give the guards at the front door of the former statehouse—now museum (south side of the zócalo, no phone, 9:30 A.M.–5 P.M. daily except Mon.) a cheery *"buenos días"* or *"buenas tardes"* and step inside. City fathers first built a city hall on the same site in 1576. Repeated earthquakes led to reconstructions, until 1948, when the present building, a modernized and strengthened version of the previous 1884 structure, was finished.

Straight ahead, across the central patio and up the stairs, you'll find the main mural, by Arturo Bustos, completed during the 1980s. It depicts the struggles of Oaxaca's independence, reform, and revolutionary heroes. On the upper right, in his trademark bandanna, is *insurgente* José María Morelos y Pavón, who published the famous *El Correo del Sur* newspaper in Oaxaca during Mexico's War of Independence. In the center is Oaxaca's favorite

son and Mexico's revered *presidente,* Benito Juárez, and his wife, Margarita Maza. Below them is Juárez's *reformista* cabinet (notice the young, restive General Porfirio Díaz third to the right of Juárez, with the sword on the right), which struggled through two bloody wars, finally emerging, with Juárez, triumphant in 1867. On the mural's far left, you see Oaxaca's 1910 revolutionary hero in turn-of-the-20th-century Marxian-style spectacles, Ricardo Flores Magón. Also take a look at Bustos's other mural, above the right (east) side staircase, upstairs, before you exit. It dramatically depicts Mexico's pre-Hispanic and conquest eras.

ⓒ Mercado Juárez

The traditional Juárez market occupies the one-block square that begins just one block south and one block west of the *zócalo*. Stroll around for fun and perhaps a bargain in the honeycomb of traditional leather, textile, and clothing stalls. Although there are many exceptions, most shops are open by 8 A.M. and close by 6 P.M.

While at the market, be sure to step to the southwest corner of 20 de Noviembre and Rayón for a history lesson in art inside the **Templo y Ex-Convento de San Juan de Dios,** which stands on the site of Oaxaca's oldest church. The present structure, completed in 1703, replaced the former earthquake-damaged 1535 town cathedral, which itself replaced the original 1521 adobe structure. Big paintings lining the nave walls depict landmarks in Oaxaca's religious history. Inside the front door, to the left, see Bishop las Casas protecting his native charges against soldiers and settlers. Farther inside is an oil of the Santa Cruz de Huatulco (see the *Catedral de Oaxaca* section); next comes Oaxaca's first mass, on the banks of the Río Atoyac, on November 25, 1521, and after that, the baptism of Cosijoeza, the last Zapotec king. Also, you'll find a series of oils showing the discovery, persecution, revolt, and reacceptance of the so-called "Idolators of Los Cajonos," whom Spaniards discovered worshipping their native gods on September 14, 1700.

Templo y Ex-Convento de San Agustín

Off-*zócalo* side streets are studded with Oaxaca's old church gems. One of the most precious and most accessible is the San Agustín church and ex-convent one block due east from the Palacio de Gobierno along Calle Guerrero. One of the few Oaxacan works of the Augustinian order, the original adobe church on this site was finished in 1596, but it was seriously damaged by subsequent earthquakes. The present church, finished in 1722, replaced the original. A generation after the Augustinians were expelled in the 1860s, Bishop Gillow of Oaxaca acquired and reactivated the church in 1893 and started the Casa de Cuna, a children's home and school, which still exists next door.

San Agustín's baroque facade blooms with a pious pastoral sculpture of a bearded San Agustín, fifth-century Bishop of Hipona, North Africa, above the entrance arch. Below, flanking the entrance portal, stand sculptures of Augustinian Saints Alipio, on the left, and Thomas of Valencia, on the right.

Inside, the same saints grace the grand, gilded main altarpiece, with the addition of Augustinian founding fathers San Juan Sahagún and San Fulgencio. The gilded south (right) transept altarpiece displays a heavenly image of Santa Monica, mother of San Agustín. Finally, look below the pulpit for the glass capsule that contains a bone-fragment relic of San Agustín, gift from the Roman Augustinians.

Catedral de Oaxaca

Return to the *zócalo*'s opposite, north side, for a look at the present cathedral. It replaced the 1550 original, demolished by an earthquake in 1696. Finished in 1733, with appropriately burly twin bell towers, the present cathedral is distinguished by its Greek-marble main altar, where a polished Italian bronze Virgin of the Ascension is being drawn upward to the cloud-tipped heavenly domain of the Holy Spirit (the dove) and God (the sunburst). Notice the glass images of noble, bearded St. Peter and St. Paul flanking opposite sides of the altar.

Of considerable historical interest is the

© BRUCE WHIPPERMAN

Oaxaca City's sturdy, earthquake-resistant cathedral rises from the broad plaza that marks the city center.

MARGARITA MAZA:
A LIFE OF COURAGE AND CONVICTION

Calle M. Maza, a modest two-block lane on Oaxaca City's northern downtown edge, memorializes Margarita Maza, wife of Mexico's revered president Benito Juárez and heroine who gave her all for love and country. Her greatness and that of her husband were inextricably intertwined by their own strong liberal ideals and their collective fate. Years before Margarita was born, Benito, of pure Zapotec blood, came to Oaxaca City seeking both his sister and his fortune. He found his sister working as a cook in the household of Italian immigrant and merchant Antonio Maza and his wife, Petra Parada.

Benito also found refuge and warmth in the Maza household; through the Mazas, Benito found work and social connections that led to education and introduction into Oaxacan society. Benito was 20 years old when Margarita, the Mazas' youngest child, was born. He bounced the baby on his knee and played with her like an older brother as she matured and while Benito's career as a lawyer, then Oaxaca state legislator, blossomed.

By the time Margarita was 17, their mutual affection had bloomed into love, and Benito, a successful attorney at 37, proposed marriage.

They were married in the church of San Felipe de Neri, in Oaxaca City, on July 31, 1843. Even today such a match would be unusual; in the Oaxaca of 1843 it was unheard-of. That he, a poor, dark brown Zapotec, and she, a lily-white daughter of a prominent merchant, were even able to associate, much less to marry, is testament to the Mazas' liberal views.

The same liberal views and their iron determination to do something about them scarred the last half of Benito and Margarita's 26 years of married life. From around 1854, when Benito was driven into exile in New Orleans, civil war, foreign invasion, and assassination attempts forced the family to be nearly always on the move, living in unfamiliar and trying circumstances, hounded and threatened by enemies, and continually lacking money.

One of the most dangerous episodes came in 1858, when Margarita, at the age of 32, had to move her brood of five children and entire household from Oaxaca to Veracruz, where Benito was running the liberal Mexican government-in-exile. Fearing spies and assassins, Margarita took the tortuous, roundabout route over the heart of the Sierra Madre, traveling at night, on foot beside their burro-train,

---

Santa Cruz de Huatulco (Holy Cross of Huatulco), enshrined in a chapel at the middle, south (right) side of the nave. The cross, about two feet high, in the glass case atop the chapel altar, is one of four made in 1612 by Oaxaca bishop Juan Cervantes from the original mysterious cross worshipped by the natives on the southern Oaxaca coast long before the conquest. An explanation, in Spanish, gives three versions of the story of the cross, which, the natives reported to the conqueror Pedro Alvarado in 1522, was erected long before by a strange, white-robed holy man who soon departed and never returned. Bishop Cervantes sent the three other copies of the cross, respectively, to authorities at Santa María Huatulco town, Mexico City, and Rome. (For more information, see the sidebar *The Holy Cross of Huatulco* in the *Pacific Resorts and Southern Sierra* chapter.)

NORTHWEST OF THE *ZÓCALO*
Templo de San Felipe Neri

Just two blocks west of the cathedral, along Independencia, at the corner of Tinoco and Palacios, rises the distinguished facade of the Templo de San Felipe Neri (open for worship 8 A.M.–11 P.M.). The building is immediately notable, for it faces south, unlike the great majority of Oaxaca's churches, which follow tradition and face west.

Its builders finished the structure, once a convent of the order of San Felipe Neri, and dedicated it to the Virgin of Patrocinio in disguising herself in native *huipil* and sleeping by day in farmhouses of friendly Zapotec campesinos.

Later, Benito and Margarita enjoyed two years of peace together, beginning in 1861, after the liberal triumph in the civil War of the Reforms. Their marriage, although severely tried by hardship and separation, was a supremely happy one. Twelve children resulted; seven – six girls and a boy – outlived their parents. Two boys and three girls died when still young. Their love, although profoundly deep, had few pretensions. Benito called her his "old lady." She called him "Juárez" and, when asked, replied that "he is very homely but good."

Their peace together was short lived. The French invasion forced Benito to travel the country, managing the government in a black carriage, one jump ahead of the French army. Margarita took the family on a hopscotch path into northern Mexico and finally to New York and Washington, D.C. There, she reached the depths of despair when two of her three sons died. She wrote to Benito: "The loss of my sons is killing me . . . I prefer death a thousand times more than life . . . I do not blame persons who

kill themselves . . . If I had been braver I should have done it a year ago."

Eventually Margarita recovered her equilibrium, buoyed by the birth of her first grandchild, a baby girl, and the admiring attention of American society, including General Ulysses S. Grant and President Andrew Johnson.

On June 19, 1867, Juárez had the French-installed Emperor Maximilian executed. This was Margarita's signal to return home. A month later, with her party of 14, she arrived in Veracruz, showered by bouquets as she walked down the gangplank.

Reunited for three happy years with Margarita in Mexico City, Benito worked like a demon to turn his dreams for Mexico into reality. But overwork took its toll, and Benito suffered a stroke in October 1870. He recovered partially to discover that Margarita was fatally ill. She died on January 2, 1871, of cancer. Although weak, Benito strained with all of his strength and with tears in his eyes to lift her body into the coffin. All of Mexico, both friends and former enemies, joined in grief with their president for their beloved Margarita Maza, who had given as much as any heroine could for both love and country.

1773. The subsequent 1795 earthquake caused extensive damage, which was not completely repaired until the 20th century. Unfortunately, more earthquakes, in 1928 and 1931, inflicted additional destruction. The present restoration was completed in 1985.

The result appears well worth the effort. Original builders crafted the facade in the 17th-century "plateresque" tradition, so-named for the designs, similar to those of fine silverware, using muted green volcanic *cantera* stone. The sole exception is the noble statue of San Felipe Neri, carved of contrasting yellow *cantera,* in clerical hat and bishop's cape, that presides above the front door.

Walk inside to admire the temple's glorious golden *retablo* (altarpiece). It towers three stories, inhabited by a host of apostles, saints, angels, and cherubs, all reigned over by the Virgin and finally San Felipe de Neri at the very top.

Museo Arte Prehispánico de Rufino Tamayo

Just one block farther north, this museum (503 Morelos, tel. 951/516-4750, 10 A.M.–2 P.M. and 4–7 P.M. Mon. and Wed.–Sat., 10 A.M.–3 P.M. Sun.) exhibits the brilliant pre-Columbian artifact collection of celebrated artist Rufino Tamayo (1899–1991). Displays include hosts of animal motifs—Colima dogs, parrots, ducks, snakes—whimsically crafted into polychrome vases, bowls, and urns.

the basilica of Oaxaca's patron, La Señora de la Soledad

🄲 Basilica de Nuestra Señora de la Soledad

Continue three blocks west, past the University of Oaxaca School of Fine Arts and the airy Plaza of Dances, to the baroque Basilica de Nuestra Señora de la Soledad. Inside, the Virgen de la Soledad (Virgin of Solitude), the patron of Oaxaca, stands atop the altar with her five-pound solid golden crown, encrusted with 600 diamonds.

Step into the **Museo de la Soledad** (tel. 951/516-5076, 8 A.M.–2 P.M. and 4–7 P.M. daily) at the downhill side of the church, on the rear end. A multitude of objects of adornment—shells, paintings, jewelry—crowd cabinets, shelves, and aisles of musty rooms. Large stained-glass panels tell of the images of Jesus and the Virgin that arrived miraculously in 1620, eventually becoming Oaxaca's patron symbols.

ANDADOR DE MACEDONIO ALCALÁ

The tranquil Andador de Macedonio Alcalá pedestrian mall, named after the composer of the Oaxacan hymn "Dios Nunca Muere" ("God Never Dies"), leads north from the *zócalo*. Paved with Oaxaca green stone in 1985 and freed of auto traffic, the mall connects the *zócalo* with a number of unmissable Oaxaca sights.

Teatro Alcalá

Among them is the Alcalá theater (900 Independencia, tel. 951/516-8312 or 951/516-8344, 10 A.M.–4 P.M. daily, admission free except during events). From the back of the cathedral head right one block along Independencia to the corner of Independencia and Cinco de Mayo. Christened by a 1909 opening performance of *Aida*, the Teatro Alcalá houses a treasury of Romantic-era art. Above the foyer, a sumptuous marble staircase rises to a bas-relief medallion allegorizing the triumph of art. Inside, soaring above the orchestra, a heavenly choir of muses, representing the arts, decorates the ceiling. Check at the theater box office for a list of performances, which customarily include classical ballet, folkloric dance, opera, and orchestral music.

Museo de Arte Contemporaneo de Oaxaca

Continuing north along the Alcalá pedestrian mall, you soon pass the so-called **Casa de Cortés,** now the Museo de Arte Contemporaneo de Oaxaca (Macedonio Alcalá 202, tel. 951/514-1055, 10:30 A.M.–8 P.M. daily except Tues). Past the bookstore (mostly Spanish but some English-language history, art, and guidebooks), exhibitions feature works of local and nationally known modern artists. Although named popularly for Hernán Cortés, the building is at least a hundred years too new for Cortés to have lived there. The coat of arms on the facade above the door reveals it to have been the 17th-century home of a different Oaxaca family.

(For a change of pace, enjoy an airy 45-minute ride around town on the motorized trolley **Tranvia Turístico,** which takes off hourly, half a block downhill from the Museo de Arte Contemporaneo, at the corner of Alcalá and Morelos, $3 per person.)

◖ Ex-Convento de Santa Catalina

Continue uphill and, at Murguia, detour right again, to the Ex-Convento de Santa Catalina (Cinco de Mayo 600, tel. 951/516-0611, free public tours 5 P.M. Wed., Thurs., and Fri.), the second-oldest women's convent in New Spain, founded in 1576. Although the quarters of the first novitiates were spare, the convent grew into a sprawling chapel and cloister complex decorated by fountains and flower-strewn gardens. Juárez's reforms drove the sisters out in 1862; the building has since served as city hall, school, and movie theater. Now it stands beautifully restored as the Hotel Camino Real. Note the native-motif original murals that the renovation revealed on interior walls.

◖ Centro Cultural de Santo Domingo

Return to the Alcalá pedestrian mall and continue another block uphill to Oaxaca's pride, the Centro Cultural de Santo Domingo (corner of M. Alcalá and I. Allende, 951/516-2991 or 951/516-3721), which contains two main parts, side by side: the Museo de las Culturas de Oaxaca and the Iglesia y Ex-Convento de Santo Domingo, both behind the broad Plaza Santo Domingo maguey garden and pedestrian square.

Inside, the **Iglesia de Santo Domingo** (7 A.M.–1 P.M. and 5–8 P.M. daily) glows with a wealth of art. Above the antechamber spreads the entire genealogical tree of Santo Domingo de Guzmán, starting with Mother Mary and weaving through a score of noblemen and women to the saint himself over the front door.

Continuing inside, the soaring, Sistine Chapel–like nave glitters with saints, cherubs, and Bible-story paintings. The altar climaxes in a host of cherished symbols—the Last Supper, sheaves of grain, loaves and fishes, Jesus and Peter on the Sea of Galilee—in a riot of gold leaf.

Continue next door to the **Museo de las Culturas de Oaxaca** (tel. 951/516-2991 or 951/516-3721, 10 A.M.–6 P.M. Tues.–Sun.), which occupies the completely restored convent section of the Santo Domingo church. A very informative audio tour headset and player

Museo de las Culturas de Oaxaca is housed in the cloister of the Santo Domingo church.

is available for rent, for $5, just past the entrance security gate.

Exhibitions begin on the bottom floor in rooms adjacent to the massive convent cloister, restored in 1998 to all of its original austere beauty. A downstairs highlight is the long-neglected but now safely preserved Biblioteca (Library) de Francisco Burgoa, which you can walk right through and examine some of the more important works on display. The collection, 23,000 titles in all, includes its earliest work, a 1484 commentary on the works of Aristotle by Juan Versor. Although not part of the original library collection, a set of four fascinating glyphs, in the largely yet-to-be-decoded classical Mixtec Ñuiñe written language, were on display at the time of this writing.

A Museo sign points you upstairs via a glitteringly restored, towering domed chamber, adorned overhead with the Dominican founding fathers, presided over by Santo Domingo de Guzmán himself.

It's hard not to be impressed by the seeming miles of meticulously prepared displays divided into about two dozen long rooms covering various historical periods. One room exhibits priceless Monte Albán–era artifacts, including one of the most important of the original so-called *danzantes*, with the typically mutilated sex organs. The climax comes in the Tesoros de Tumba 7 (Treasures of Tomb 7) room, where the entire gilded treasure discovered at Monte Albán Tomb 7 is on display. Beside a small mountain of gold and turquoise ornaments, notice the small but masterfully executed golden head of Ecéchatl, god of the wind, made eerie by the omission of facial skin over the jaw, to produce a nightmarishly skeletal piece of jewelry.

The museum also includes a big **jardín etno-botánico** (ethno-botanical garden) in its big backyard. The staff customarily conduct tours, but the schedule seems to change often. The announced schedule for the two-hour tour in Spanish is 10 A.M., noon, and 2 P.M. daily except Sunday, $5 per person; tours in English are at 11 A.M. Tuesday and Thursday, $10 per person. Inquire (check for the tour schedule on the door) at the ethno-botanical library (tel./fax 951/516-5325, 951/516-7915) at the garden entrance, at the northwest corner of Reforma and Constitución, two blocks behind the Santo Domingo churchfront.

Small Museums

Back outside, step across Alcalá, a few doors uphill, into the rust-colored old building now tastefully restored as the museum of the **Instituto de Artes Gráficas de Oaxaca** (tel. 951/516-6980, 10 A.M.–8 P.M. daily except Tues.). Inside, displays exhibit mostly contemporary etchings, wood-block prints, and paintings by artists of both national and international renown. Exhibits change approximately monthly.

Head west one block (along the Plazuela del Carmen, off Alcalá across from the museum) to the **Casa de Juárez** museum (609 Garcia Vigil, tel. 951/516-1860, 10 A.M.–7 P.M., closed Mon.). The modest but beautifully restored house was the home of Juárez's benefactor, priest, and bookbinder Father Antonio Salanueva. Rooms decorated with homey mid-19th-century furnishings realistically illustrate the life and times of a man as revered in Mexico as his contemporary, Abraham Lincoln, north of the border.

Later, if you have time, return to the Santo Domingo church plaza and continue east past the church along Constitución to the new **Museo Philatelica de Oaxaca** (Reforma 504, just uphill from the corner of Constitución, tel. 951/514-2366, 10 A.M.–8 P.M. daily except Mon.). Inside, showcases display the noted collection of José Cosino y Cosio—a library of international postal paraphernalia. Planners project that the museum's collection, of mostly Mexican and Oaxacan postage stamps, will grow steadily during succeeding decades.

Return a block and a half down Reforma and turn right at Abasolo, which, past Alcalá, becomes M. Bravo. Continue a block to the **Centro de Fotografía Manuel Alvarez Bravo** (M. Bravo 116, corner of Garcia Vigil, tel. 951/516-9800, 9 A.M.–3 P.M., 5–8 P.M. daily except Tues.). Here, galleries display the work of both locally prominent and internationally acclaimed photographers, while instructors in classrooms conduct photography classes for children, adult beginners, and professionals.

Back downhill, at the north edge of the *zócalo,* at the corner of Independencia and Garcia Vigil, stands a regally restored colonial-era house, formerly the Oaxaca state tourism headquarters, now home to the **Museo de los Pintores Oaxaqueños** (Museum of Oaxacan Painters, tel. 951/516-5645, 10 A.M.–8 P.M. daily except Mon.). It houses an eclectic, revolving collection of modern art, sometimes primitive, sometimes erotic, and mostly abstract, on two floors around a central patio. The house itself, built in 1695, has gone through several transformations: first a girl's school, then, in succession, the Manuel Fiallo family home, a regional museum, city hall, and finally the Oaxaca *Turismo* (Tourism Secretariat) for several years before its 2004–2005 restoration to its austerely noble present incarnation. Presently *Turismo* maintains a tourist information desk, to the left as you enter the museum.

◖ LOS ARQUITOS

Long ago, Oaxaca's city fathers provided for a permanent town water supply. They tapped the bountiful natural springs flowing from the mountains rising directly north of the city, topped by the towering Cerro San Felipe (elev. 10,200 feet/3,100 meters). The aqueduct they built gave rise to the name San Felipe del Agua, the foothill village where the aqueduct begins. Although now replaced by underground steel pipes, the original 18th-century aqueduct still stands, paralleling the downhill road from San Felipe and ending in a quaint string of arches, called Los Arquitos, in the city neighborhood several blocks northwest of Iglesia de Santo Domingo.

Walking Tour

The following walking tour consists of two separate parts. First, a one- or two-hour stroll through the relatively close-in Los Arquitos neighborhood, and next, an out-of-downtown two- or three-hour (or more) exploration of the cooler, leafy heights of picturesque San Felipe de Agua village.

Starting from the Santo Domingo church-front, at the corner of Alcalá and Allende, walk a block west along Allende to Garcia Vigil, turn right and continue uphill three blocks to Calle Cosojopi. If it's Friday or Saturday between 9 A.M. and 3 P.M. you're in for a special treat. Step into the garden-courtyard (half a block beyond Calle Cosojopi, on the left as you're heading uphill), of the Cinema Pochote (G. Vigil 817). Inside, find the **Pochote Market,** a collection of stalls offering all-organic home-grown selections of fruit, vegetables, drinks, and food. Don't miss sampling some *porchaca* (por-CHA-kah), genuine indigenous Oaxacan pizza, washed down with delicious *tejate,* "the drink of the gods," made of pressed sweet corn juice and natural floral flavors.

Continue uphill along Vigil; pass Calle Xolotl (show-LOH-tuhl) immediately on the right, where Calle Garcia Vigil changes its name to Calle Rufino Tamayo, which continues, paralleling the arches for three blocks,

to thoroughfare Calzada Niños Héroes. The most entertaining thing about the Los Arquitos neighborhood is the way the residents have adapted to the aqueduct, ingeniously tucking their individual home and store doorways beneath the arches. Don't miss the little shrine built beneath one arch, at Tamayo 802, and also the tiny café, El Pavito (The Little Peacock), beneath another. Also notice the colorfully picturesque contrast between the arches' red brick and light green volcanic *cantera* stone construction. Finally, be sure to explore some of the side lanes, such as the one opposite Tamayo 818 that heads beneath an arch and opens into a tiny plaza presided over by Archangel Gabriel.

During your walk, you might also stop by the diminutive **Café Pochotita** (Rufino Tamayo 814, no phone, 9 A.M.–8 P.M. Mon.–Sat.) for some savory coffee and maybe a snack (*tortas,* banana bread, baguettes, light meals $3–6). If you'd like to linger overnight in Los Arquitos, ring the doorbell at **Casa Los Arquitos** bed-and-breakfast (818 Rufino

arquitos (little arches)

The Los Arquitos neighborhood is ripe for back-lane strolling.

Tamayo) and take a look inside. (For details, see *Bed-and-Breakfasts North and East of the Zócalo,* under *Accommodations,* later in this chapter.)

For the second part of the North-End tour, especially for those in the mood for more active adventures, it's easiest to first hire a taxi ($5) to San Felipe del Agua village. Alternatively, you can get there via a city **bus** marked Hospital San Felipe (on Niños Héroes, uphill six blocks from Santo Domingo church). Or, near the *zócalo,* catch a bus labeled San Felipe, heading north, either from the corner of Independencia and Reforma, or uphill along Pino Suárez.

Alternatively, you can drive the five miles uphill to **San Felipe del Agua** village. The jumping-off point is Avenida Netzahualcoyotl (nay-tzah-oo-wahl-coh-YOH-tuhl), which heads uphill at its intersection with the Highway 190 thoroughfare (Calz. Niños Héroes), at the big green San Felipe sign, one block east of the Pemex station.

Continue about two-thirds of a mile (one km) uphill; at Calle Naranjos, at the hotel sign, bear left around the curve, then take the first right. After one more uphill block, go left; a long block later, you'll see the aqueduct. Turn right at the aqueduct, and you'll be on your way uphill, heading along Calzada San Felipe, which parallels the old stone aqueduct on your left. In a few miles the road becomes San Felipe's Calle Hidalgo, which leads you to San Felipe Apostol Church behind the pocket-sized village plaza on the right.

If at this point you simply want a leisurely stroll, take a turn around the plaza and church and a couple side streets. For a real treat walk a block or two uphill from the plaza, along the main street to the lovely, relaxing **Hacienda Los Laureles** (driveway on the right, at Hidalgo 21, tel. 951/520-0890; see *North-Side Suburban Luxury Hotels,* under *Accommodations*) for lunch or early dinner (about $15 per person) and a walk around the luscious grounds.

If, on the other hand, you hanker for more adventure, continue by taxi, bus, or car another half mile to the road's-end bus turnaround at the foot of Cerro San Felipe. Here the air is fresh and cool, and the view, both uphill and down, is inspiring. Below spreads the city and valley both left and right, while uphill rises the green, pine-tufted massif of Cerro San Felipe.

Continue (on foot if necessary) along the road that runs north below the bus turnaround. After about a quarter mile (0.4 km) arrive at the **Parque Comunal de San Felipe** trailhead and guard station. See the map at the guard station that traces tracks that lead (with an experienced guide only) steeply uphill through pine-shadowed glens and past a waterfall all the way to the top of the mountain. It's a stiff, all-day 4,000-foot (1,200-meter) uphill hike. Your guide knows the way, and you start hiking early enough (preferably before 9 A.M.); if clouds don't gather, the stupendous mountaintop view will be your reward. Under any conditions, be prepared with a hat, water, lunch, and sturdy shoes.

Accommodations

Oaxaca offers a wide range of good lodgings. Air-conditioning is not particularly necessary in temperate Oaxaca, although hot-water showers (furnished by all lodgings listed below) feel especially comfy during cool winter mornings and evenings. Many of the less expensive hotels, which generally do not accept credit cards, are within easy walking distance of the colorful, traffic-free *zócalo*. With but a few exceptions, Oaxaca's plush, resort-style hostelries dot the northern foothill edge of town. During holidays and festivals (Easter week, July, August, late October–early November, December 15–January 6), many Oaxaca hotels raise their prices 20–50 percent above the numbers listed below. (*Note:* Many of the following lodgings and many more are advertised on websites, notably **www.mexonline.com** and others listed under *Internet Resources* in the *Resources* chapter.)

All hotels below are positive recommendations, grouped by location in relation to the *zócalo*, and listed, within each location group, in ascending order of double-room price. For other lodging options, see the *Bed-and-Breakfasts, Homestays, and Apartments; Hostels;* and *Trailer Parks and Camping* sections immediately following *Accommodations*.

HOTELS
Near the *Zócalo*
UNDER $50

For economy, consider the nine-room **Hotel Salvador** (20 de Noviembre 204, tel. 951/516-4008, $25 s, $30 d, $40 t), a block west of the zócalo, next door to the north of the Hotel Francia. Here, you can get a plain but decent upstairs room with bath, with the bonus of a good restaurant downstairs, but with no parking or credit cards accepted.

Another good, close-in budget option is the modest, gay-friendly **Posada Nito** (Armenta y López 416, tel. 951/514-6668, hotelnito@ yahoo.com, $25 s, $33 d, $43 t), a block east

and two blocks south of the *zócalo*'s southeast corner. Guests at this simple, 10-room hotel enjoy clean, light rooms, thoughtfully decorated with hand-hewn bedspreads, rustically attractive tile floors, reading lamps, and shiny hot-water bathrooms. There's no parking, telephones, or credit cards accepted. Downstairs, guests enjoy a tranquil, intimate inner patio, with chairs, table, and a shade umbrella for relaxing and socializing. Reserve one of the upstairs rooms for maximum privacy and light.

Head northeast a few blocks east of the *zócalo*'s northeast corner to the busy, traveler-favorite, 39-room **Posada del Virrey** (1001 Morelos, tel. 951/516-5555 or 951/516-5141, fax 951/516-2193, www.hotelesdeoaxaca.com/ hotelposadadelvirrey.html, $35 s or d in one bed, $45 d in two beds, $50 t). Only four blocks (five minutes) east of the zócalo, the authentically colonial Posada del Virrey offers two floors of rooms surrounding a spacious inner restaurant patio, which in the mornings and evenings is often half-filled with mostly foreign travelers, reading, conversing, and relaxing. The rooms are clean and comfortably furnished, including one, two, or three double beds, with attractive brown and bright-orange bedspreads and handsome rustic handmade wooden furniture. Rooms come with cable TV, phone, fan, parking (9 P.M.–9 A.M.), and MasterCard accepted. Get your reservations in early, especially during holidays.

(For quieter, more intimate ambience, consider the bed-and-breakfast Casa Luz María, across the street. See the *Bed-and-Breakfasts, Homestays, and Apartments* section for more details.)

Even closer in, just half a block west of the zócalo's southwest corner, is the petite and popular **Hotel Las Rosas** (Trujano 112, tel./ fax 951/514-2217, $34 s, $38 d, $55 t). Climb a flight of stairs to the small lobby, relatively tranquil by virtue of its second-floor location. Beyond that, a double tier of rooms surrounds a homey inner patio. Adjacent to the lobby is a cheery sitting room with a big, beautiful tropical aquarium and a TV, usually kept at subdued volume. In the rear, guests enjoy an airy terrace for reading and relaxing. The rooms themselves, although plainly furnished, are clean and tiled (except some bathrooms, which could use an extra scrubbing). Prices are very reasonable for such a well-located hotel. Discounts are negotiable for a one-week stay. No credit cards, parking, or wheelchair access, however.

Walk a block north to the northwest side of the zócalo to the leafy Alameda de León square in front of the cathedral and the **Hotel Monte Albán** (Alameda de León 1, tel. 951/516-2777 or 951/516-2330, fax 951/516-3265, hotelmontealban@prodigy.net.mx, $30 s, $45 d, $55 t). This popular old standby hostelry encloses a big patio/restaurant that hosts folk-dance shows 8:30–10 P.M. nightly. During your first evening this could be understandably exciting, but after a few days you might feel as if you were living in a three-ring circus. The 20 rooms, which surround the patio in two floors, are genuinely colonial, with high-beamed ceilings and big bedsteads. Rates are modest for such a well-located hotel; no parking, but credit cards are accepted.

Ideally situated just east of the zócalo's northeast corner, the best-buy colonial-era **Hotel Real de Antequera** (Hidalgo 807, tel. 951/516-4635, fax 951/516-4020, www.oaxaca-mio.com/real.htm, hra5109@prodigy.net.mx, $40 s, $45 d, $58 t) offers plenty for reasonable rates. The 29 comfortable rooms, in two stories around an inviting old world–style restaurant-patio include breakfast, bath, fans, cable TV, phones, parking, and credit cards accepted.

Just a block south of the zócalo's southwest corner, the (**Hotel Trebol** (at Flores Magón 201, tel./fax 951/516-1256, reservacioneshotrebol@prodigy.net.mx, www.oaxaca-mio.com/trebol.htm, $47 s or d in one bed, $58 d in two beds, $80 t) remains an enduring jewel among Oaxaca's close-in moderately priced hotels. Guests can choose from about 40 rooms,

artfully sprinkled in three stories around an airy, plant-decorated inner patio. The recently renovated rooms are comfortably furnished with rustic tile, hand-hewn wooden furniture, table lamps, color-coordinated bedspreads, and shiny, modern-standard shower-baths. Rooms include fans, telephone, cable TV, parking, travel agent, and good restaurant.

A block west of the zócalo's southwest corner, find the **Hóstal Santa Rosa** (Trujano 201, tel. 951/514-6714, 951/514-6715, fax 951/514-6715, $40 s, $48 d). The streetside lobby leads past an airy restaurant to the rooms, recessed along a meandering inner passageway and courtyard. Inside, the rooms are very clean, comfortably furnished, and decorated in pastels. Rates continue to be reasonable except during festivals and holidays, when they might rise as much as 40 percent. It offers TV, phones, parking, limited wheelchair access, and an in-house travel-tour agency, but no credit cards are accepted.

$50-100

Just a block west of the zócalo, find the long-time **Hotel Francia** (20 de Noviembre 212, tel. 951/516-4811 or 951/516-4120, fax 951/516-4251, reservaciones@hotelfrancia.com.mx, www.hotelfrancia.com.mx, $50 s or d, $60 t). Savvy new managers have brightened up the Francia with fresh white paint, a bright chandelier, potted palms, shiny lobby tile, and a new restaurant. They have also added a renovated colonial-era section (once a separate hotel next door) built around an invitingly traditional interior patio. Rooms are clean and spacious, with high ceilings and old-world dark wood furniture. The 62 rooms feature baths, hot water, fans, TV, phones, and credit cards accepted; parking $5/day.

Although somewhat removed (three blocks south, three blocks west, ten easy minutes) from the zócalo, the **Hotel Rivera del Ángel** (Mina 518, tel. 951/516-6666, fax 951/514-5405, hotelriveradelangel@prodigy.net.mx, www.hotelriveradelangel.com, $48 s, $55 d, $60 t) offers a number of advantages. Downstairs, an airy, shiny, but busy lobby and restaurant area offers nothing special, but through the lobby windows, feast your eyes on the inviting big blue pool and sunny central patio. Upstairs, you'll find the rooms semi-deluxe, clean, spacious, and comfortable, several with private terraces overlooking the pool patio. The hotel's main drawback, besides the questionable neighborhood (streetwalkers, low-life bars, and drunks at night), is street noise from buses along Mina. Avoid this by reserving a *tranquilo* off-street room, next to or above the inner pool-patio. Amenities include cable TV, fans, phones, passable restaurant, secure parking, travel agency, and tour buses to Mitla and Monte Albán. Credit cards accepted but discounts are available for cash.

Just a few doors south of the *zócalo*'s southeast corner, consider the popular 1980s-mod **Hotel Gala** (Bustamante 103, tel. 951/514-2251 or 951/514-1305, fax 951/516-3660, Mex. toll-free 800/712-7316, galaoax@prodigy.net.mx, www.gala.com.mx, $60 s, $68 d, $76 t, $86 junior suite). Here, guests enjoy comfortable, modern, deluxe accommodations at relatively moderate prices right in the middle of the *zócalo* action. Rooms, although tastefully decorated and carpeted, are smallish. Get one of the quieter ones away from the street. The 36 rooms rent have offers phones, TV, fans, and a restaurant, and parking 9 P.M.–9 A.M.; credit cards are accepted.

Return just two blocks west of the *zócalo*'s northwest corner to the class-act **⊂ Parador San Miguel** (Av. Independencia 503, tel./fax 951/514-9331, sanmigueloaxaca@hotmail.com, www.paradorsanmigueloaxaca.com, $74 s or d, $100 t). Here, little seems to have been spared in transforming a colonial-era mansion into a lovely hotel. Inside, a plethora of old-world details—leafy, tranquil inner patio, sunny upstairs corridors, brilliant stained glass-decorated staircase, scrolled wrought-iron railings, handsome hand-carved wooden doors—are bound to please lovers of traditional refinement. A correspondingly elegant restaurant, the Andariega, completes the gorgeous picture. The 19 rooms and four suites are no less than you'd expect, attractively furnished with custom-woven bedspreads and curtains,

handcrafted bamboo and leather furniture, elegantly tiled shower-baths, and a choice of king, single, or double beds. If the Parador San Miguel has a drawback, it's the traffic noise from busy Calle Independencia just outside the front door; ask for a room away from the street. But never mind, the place is simply exquisite and prices are not unreasonable; add about 50 percent during festivals and holidays. All with air-conditioning, cable TV, and credit cards accepted.

OVER $100

Alternatively, check out the queen of *zócalo*-front hotels, the long-time **Hotel Marques del Valle** (on the north flank of the *zócalo*, Portal Clavería, tel. 951/514-0688 or 951/516-3474, fax 951/516-9961, reservaciones@hotelmarquesdelvalle.com.mx, www.hotelmarquesdelvalle.com.mx, $119 s or d, $145 t). Guests enter through a restored lobby, bright with gleaming chandelier, mirrors, and shiny dark-wood paneling. Upstairs, however, massive wrought-iron fixtures cast gloomy nighttime shadows through the soaring, balconied central atrium. The 96 rooms, nevertheless, retain their original 1940s polish, with hand-crafted cedar furniture and marble-finished baths. Deluxe rooms have TV, carpets, and some balconies looking out onto the *zócalo*. With a good restaurant/bar, limited wheelchair access, credit cards accepted, and parking 8:30 P.M.–8:30 A.M.

North of the *Zócalo*
UNDER $50

One of the most popular budget options, **Casa Arnel** (Aldama 404, Colonia Jalatlaco, tel./fax 951/515-2856, casa.arnel@spersaoaxaca.com.mx, www.casaarnel.com.mx, standard rooms $35 s, $40 d, $50 t, shared bath $15 s, $25 d) is also farthest north (actually, less than a mile) from the *zócalo*. Casa Arnel stands at the edge of downtown, so removed from the urban bustle that it feels as if it's embedded in another era. As one local resident explained, Jalatlaco, the formerly separate village, is "old, with stone streets . . . It's *so* Oaxaca." In front of

Casa Arnel, the streets are indeed cobbled with stone, and across from it stands the ancient village church, San Matias Jalatlaco, beside its shady neighborhood plaza. Casa Arnel is a family home that grew into a hotel, with about 20 rooms around a jungly garden blooming with birdcalls, flowers, and big, leafy plants, with a monument of a library in the middle of it all. Additional amenities include a broad roof deck with umbrellas, tables, and chairs for sunning and relaxing. The standard rooms, all renovated, are attractively furnished with new bedspreads, curtains, and shiny furniture and fixtures. There's a travel agency, a decent restaurant, and it's just three blocks from big, shady El Llano Park with its good restaurants and services. Bargain for a cheaper long-term rate.

Much closer in, halfway between the *zócalo* and Iglesia de Santo Domingo, right in the middle of the tranquil Calle Cinco de Mayo restaurant and shopping district, find the old-fashioned **(** **Hotel Principal** (Cinco de Mayo 208, tel./fax 951/516-2535, hotelprincipal@gmail.com, $29 s, $33 d, larger, superior rooms $53 d), like a slice out of the 1940s. Past the entry, the two stories of 14 rooms surround a quiet, geranium-decorated interior patio. A few sofas line the patio and upstairs corridor. The rooms are clean, with high ceilings, tiled floors, and shaded bed lamps. No TV or phones, but with hot-water baths all day. All rooms have private shower-baths and fans, but no parking nor credit cards accepted.

A few blocks farther north stands another well-located budget choice, the **Hotel Villa de León** (Reforma 405, tel. 951/516-1958, fax 951/516-1977, $30 s, $40 d, $45 t), adjoining the back side of the Iglesia de Santa Domingo grounds. Past the reception and inner-courtyard restaurant, most of the approximately 20 rooms encircle an upstairs balcony. In the past, accommodations were cheap and often in need of repair, but renovations are under way. All rooms have hot-shower-baths, and credit cards are accepted. Reserve a room away from the heavily trafficked street.

Nearby, budget-minded travelers should also consider the inviting **Hotel Maela** (Constitución 206, tel./fax 951/516-6022, maela@prodigy.net.mx, www.mexonline.com/maela.htm, $41 s, $46 d, $60 t, suites for four $70), one block east of the Iglesia de Santo Domingo compound. Inside, just past the small reception, the hall tiles shine, the ceilings are gracefully high, and the 24 rooms and two suites, in two stories, are spacious, with private shower-baths and attractive handmade wood dressers, beds, and end tables. Ceiling lights are bare-bulb, but nighttime reading lamps are shaded. Rooms come with fans, TV, wireless Internet, and parking.

On the northwest side, about three blocks west of the Iglesia de Santo Domingo, is the very inviting and super-popular **(** **Hotel Las Golondrinas** (Tinoco y Palacios 411, tel. 951/514-3298 or tel./fax 951/514-2126, lasgolon@prodigy.net.mx, lasgolonoax@yahoo.com, $42 s, $46 d, and $55 t). Rooms enfold an intimate garden, lovingly decorated with festoons of hothouse verdure. Leafy bananas, bright bougainvillea, and platoons of potted plants line pathways that meander past an intimate fountain patio in one corner and lead to an upstairs panoramic vista sundeck on the other. The care also shows in the rooms, which are immaculate and adorned with spartan-chic, pastel earth-toned curtains and bedspreads and natural wood furniture. Guests additionally enjoy use of laundry facilities, a TV sitting room, a shelf of paperback books, and a break-fast restaurant open 8–10 A.M. In addition to the 27 regular rooms, two honeymoon suites rent for about $55 each.

For yet another economical and highly recommended north-side lodging option, see the Hotel and Studios Las Mariposas in the *Bed-and-Breakfasts, Homestays, and Apartments* section.

$50-100
Start several blocks north of Iglesia de Santo Domingo at the **Hotel Casona de Llano** (Av. Juárez A701, tel. 951/514-7719 or 951/514-7703, fax 951/516-2219, $50 s, $63 d, and $79 t). This hotel is a favorite of visitors

who enjoy the shady, untouristed ambience of Oaxaca's big Sunday park, officially called Parque Paseo Juárez, but popularly referred to as **El Llano** (YAH-noh, Plain or Flat Place). The memorable time to arrive is in the evening, when the hotel puts on its most impressive face: You enter the lobby, crowned with high ceilings hung with gleaming chandeliers, continue past polished mahogany Doric columns, and enter a graceful Porfirian dining room, where guests often linger after dinner. You hear music, investigate, and find someone playing a tune on a handsomely preserved and polished upright piano in a side parlor. Your room, by contrast, is modern, comfortably furnished, and very clean. In the morning, you open your door and look out upon a tranquil, grassy, inner tropical garden. The 28 rooms include fans, TV, phones, parking, and credit cards accepted. Reserve ahead.

On the other side and south of El Llano, step into **(Hotel Casa Vertíz** (Reforma 404, tel. 951/516-1700 or tel./fax 951/516-2525, reservaciones@hotelvertiz.com.mx, www.hotelvertiz.com.mx, $90 s, $95 d, $110 t), arguably the most inviting small hotel in Oaxaca. Here you find a masterfully rebuilt former colonial house with air, light, and space that invites lingering. Past the reception, guests enjoy a refined, airy patio restaurant and an exquisitely naturalistic tropical rear garden. Upstairs, rooms open onto a spreading top-floor terrace shaded on one side by a grand old tree. The 14 rooms, both upstairs and down, open directly to all these graceful amenities. Accommodations are luxuriously appointed with designer-rustic tile floors, earth-toned bedspreads and curtains, deluxe tiled baths (four rooms have tubs), and queen-size beds. Rentals include cable TV, phone, in-room Internet connection, air-conditioning, parking, and credit cards accepted.

OVER $100

Oaxaca's classiest downtown hotel, the **(Camino Real** (Calle Cinco de Mayo 300, tel. 951/516-0611, toll-free U.S./Can. tel. 800/722-6466, fax 951/516-0732, reservascro@prodigy.net.mx, oaxaca@caminoreal.com,

www.caminoreal.com/Oaxaca, $350 d) occupies the lovingly restored former convent of Santa Catalina, four blocks north and one block east of the *zócalo*. Flowery secluded courtyards, massive arched portals, soaring beamed ceilings, a big blue pool, and impeccable bar and restaurant service combine to create a refined but relaxed old-world atmosphere. Rooms are large, luxurious, and invitingly decorated with antiques and folk crafts and furnished with a plethora of modern conveniences. If street noise is likely to bother you, request a room away from bustling Calles Abasolo and Cinco de Mayo; if not, bring earplugs. The hotel entertains guests and the paying public (about $35 per person) with a weekly class-act in-house buffet and folkloric dance performance. Rooms have phones and cable TV, but parking is not included; credit cards are accepted. Sometimes they offer promotional packages that run about $260 d including breakfast.

North-Side Suburban Luxury Hotels
$50-100

Just above north-side Avenida Niños Héroes (Highway 190), the **Hotel Fortín Plaza** (Av. Venus 118, Colonia Estrella, tel. 951/515-7777, fax 951/515-1328, reservaciones@hotelfortinplaza.com.mx, www.hotelfortinplaza.com.mx, $80 s, $95 d) is hard to miss, especially at night. Its yellow-lit six-story profile tops everything else in town. The hotel offers the usual resort facilities—restaurant/bar, pool, live music Tuesday–Saturday, disco, and parking—in a compact, attractively designed layout. Upstairs, guests enjoy deluxe, clean, and comfortable rooms with private city-view balconies (whose tranquility is reduced, however, on the highway side, by considerable traffic noise—best reserve for a more *tranquilo* mountain-view room on the opposite side). Rooms come with phones, TV, wireless Internet, wheelchair access, and parking; credit cards accepted. Ask for a discount or a *paquete* (package), especially during weekdays and the low-occupancy months of January, May, June, and September.

OVER $100

Hotel Misión de Los Angeles (Calz. Porfirio Díaz 102, tel. 951/502-0100, fax 951/502-0111, info@misiondelosangeles.com, www.misiondelosangeles.com, rooms $110 d, junior suites $134 d) rambles like a hacienda through a spreading oak- and acacia-decorated garden-park two blocks uphill from Avenida Niños Héroes (Highway 190), about a mile uphill, north, of the city center. After a rough few days on the sightseeing circuit, this is an ideal place to kick back beside the big pool or enjoy a set or two of tennis. The 162 rooms and suites are spacious and comfortable, decorated in earth tones and pastels and have big garden-view windows or balconies. Upper rooms are quieter and more private. (Some rooms, however, may not be as favorably located; look at more than one before deciding.) Amenities include phones, parking, and restaurant; credit cards accepted.

Several blocks west, a couple of blocks past the Hotel Fortín Plaza, the **Hotel Victoria** (Km 545, Blvd. Adolfo Ruiz Cortínez 1306, Carretera Panamericana, tel. 951/515-2633, fax 951/515-2411, reservaciones@hotelvictoriaoax.com.mx, www.hotelvictoriaoax.com.mx, rooms $100, villas $115, junior suites $130) spreads over a lush hillside garden of panoramic vistas and luxurious resort ambience. The 1960s-modern lobby extends from an upstairs bar, downhill past a terrace restaurant to a flame tree and jacaranda-decorated pool patio. Rooms come in three grades, all comfortably deluxe, that vary by size and location. The smallest are the rooms in the original hotel building; somewhat larger are the villas downstairs around the pool, and most spacious are the junior suites, in the newer wing detached from the lobby building, with double-size bathrooms and private-view balconies. The 150 rooms come with cable TV, phones, air-conditioning, tennis court, live music Friday and Saturday evenings, handicrafts shop, parking, and wheelchair access; credit cards accepted.

Cooler, breezier **San Felipe village,** in the foothills north of Oaxaca town, has recently become home to a number of restful luxury lodgings. Choicest among them, (**Hacienda Los Laureles** (Hidalgo 21, San Felipe del Agua, tel. 951/501-5300, 951/520-0890, Mex. toll-free tel. 800/508-7923, fax 951/501-5301, bookings@hotelhaciendaloslaureles.com, www.hotelhaciendaloslaureles.com, or reserve through booking agent Mexico Boutique Hotels toll-free U.S./Can. tel. 800/728-9098, www.mexicoboutiquehotels.com, deluxe rooms $195 s or d, superior deluxe $250 s or d) is the labor of love of personable German expatriate owner-managers Ligia and Peter Kaiser. After a career of managing hotels in Europe, Africa, and the United States, Peter and Ligia decided to create their version of heaven in Oaxaca. During the late 1990s they rebuilt a venerable hacienda, tenaciously preserving its rustic old-world essence while installing the best of the new. Now, Hacienda Los Laureles's centerpiece is its lush interior garden of grand tropical trees and climbing vines that, at night, is transformed by shadowed lighting and the serenades of crickets and tree frogs into an enchanted forest. The Hacienda's 25 rooms, which all open onto this precious scene, are decorated in elegant simplicity, with high ceilings, handsome tile floors, and hand-hewn mahogany furniture. Bathrooms are likewise luxurious and comfortable. Suites for 3–6 or more are also available. All come with air-conditioning, cable TV, pool with whirlpool tub, and an excellent terrace restaurant. *Temazcal* and a menu of spa services are also available at an extra cost.

BED-AND-BREAKFASTS, HOMESTAYS, AND APARTMENTS

Many Oaxacans offer either lodging in their homes or apartment and house rentals. If you're interested in such options in Oaxaca now (or are going to be in Oaxaca looking), be sure to see the classified sections of the English-language newspapers *Oaxaca Times* and *Go-Oaxaca,* which customarily list a number of bed-and-breakfast, room, and apartment rentals both in their print and online (www.oaxacatimes.com and www.go-oaxaca.com) versions.

Lacking an Internet connection, you can either get copies at their respective editorial offices (see the *Information and Services* section), or find both newspapers' print editions at hotels, shops, and at the Oaxaca state tourism information office (Murgia 206, tel. 951/516-0123, 951/502-1200) three blocks northeast of the *zócalo,* between Cinco de Mayo and Constitución.

Moreover, many websites, such as www.mexonline.com, customarily advertise a number of Oaxaca lodgings. For more options, see the *Internet Resources* section at the back of this book. Finally, the Oaxaca state tourism information office lists a number of economical home-style lodgings. Also, language schools (see *Language Instruction and Courses* later in this chapter) arrange homestays with families.

Meanwhile, read on to find out about a number of promising lodging options sprinkled around town. Unless otherwise stated, prices given below are daily rates, often subject to healthy discounts for long-term stays.

North and East of the *Zócalo*

Oaxaca bed-and-breakfast lodgings as a group are not particularly economical, since they are a North American transplant that appeal to foreign visitors who are accustomed to paying somewhat elevated prices.

UNDER $50

One of the more attractive, economical, and centrally located Oaxaca bed-and-breakfasts is homey but exclusive **Casa Luz María** (1002 Morelos, tel. 951/516-2378, f_fagoaga@hotmail.com, luzmago30@hotmail.com). Since it's her home, the owner chooses her clients carefully. If you qualify, your reward will be one of her several comfortable, immaculate (albeit a bit worn around the edges) modern rooms and apartments, all built around a pair of flowery, sunny interior patios. Some of the accommodations have private baths, others are shared; with hot water and fans, but no phone, TV, or

parking and no credit cards accepted. Rentals include a hearty breakfast with coffee, tea, fruit, bread, eggs, and sweet rolls. The owner assured me that her prices, which she declined to state, are both flexible and moderate.

For another worthy budget option check out the **Casa los Arquitos** (Rufino Tamayo 818, tel. 951/132-4975, ventas@casalosarquitos.com, www.casalosarquitos.com, $40–65), where a welcoming Mexican couple have converted their modest home into an inviting small hotel tucked into the heart of the charming north-end Los Arquitos neighborhood. Their five immaculate rooms with bath, simply but attractively decorated, offer a choice of either one single bed, two single beds, or one king-sized bed with full kitchenette, including refrigerator, stove, microwave oven, dishes and utensils, and a private patio to boot. Amenities include in-house Internet and a generous continental breakfast with choice of savory organic coffee, hot chocolate, or tea, and breads, yogurt, granola, and fresh seasonal fruit.

(For a very economical, hostel-style but with private rooms bed-and-breakfast option, see **Paulina Youth Hostel** in the *Hostels* section.)

Go a mile north of the *zócalo,* two blocks uphill past Avenida Niños Héroes (Highway 190) and your reward will be **◖ Casa María** (Belisario Domínguez 208, Colonia Reforma, tel./fax 951/515-1202, maria@oaxacalive.com, www.oaxacalive.com/maria.htm, rooms $36 s, $46 d, suites $80), project of welcoming owner María Luz Díaz. Her 18-room abode basks behind a flowery, spacious green garden, perfect for reading and relaxing. Past the inviting terrace and dining/living area, the rooms, several upstairs, are clean, modern, and comfortably furnished. A separate kitchen is available for guest use. Breakfast is hearty American-style, but served only between 8 and 9 A.M. María usually has many guests, who often head out in the morning but linger on the terrace and in the living room during the evenings, comparing their experiences of the day over coffee and tea. Bungalows (kitchenette apartments) run about $70 d, $500/month, breakfast not included. A large family apartment for five costs about $115. Prices rise about 25 percent during festivals and holidays. All with private shower-baths and fans; some parking in her four-car garage. Massage and traditional *temazcal* treatments are available at an extra cost.

$50-100

Much closer in, just two blocks behind Ex-Convento Santo Domingo, you'll find **Casa de las Bugambilias** (Reforma 402, tel./fax 951/516-1165, bugambilias@lasbugambilias. com, www.lasbugambilias.com, $42–85 s, $60–100 d), with eight seven rooms and one suite, artfully tucked behind its good street-front restaurant. (*Note:* Casa de las Bugambilias has an unusually convenient U.S-direct telephone connection that allows you to contact an English-speaking person at Casa de las Bugambilias from your U.S. telephone simply by dialing 321/249-9422.) The rooms, immaculate and thoughtfully appointed with art and handicrafts, are all different. Some open onto a lovely rear garden. Take a look at as many as possible before choosing. Rules include minimum three-night stay, children over 12 only, no pets, and no smoking. Amenities include private bath, breakfast, Internet access, a *temazcal* (at extra cost); credit cards accepted, but no parking included.

On the far northwest edge of downtown, about ten blocks from the *zócalo* (but only four blocks west of Santo Domingo), consider the petite, gay-friendly **Casa Crespo** bed-and-breakfast (Crespo 415, tel. 951/514-1102, casa-crespo@go-oaxaca.com, www.casacrespo.com, $90 s or d) Personable owner-artist-publisher Oscar Carrizosa offers two large, elegantly appointed rooms that open to a tranquil inner fountain patio and are traditionally decorated with polished hand-hewn furniture, antiques, paintings, and reading lamps. Amenities include full breakfast, wireless Internet connection, shiny, tile-decorated bathrooms, big beds, fans, and cooking classes at a 20 percent discount for guests.

Another promising bed-and-breakfast in the same north-side neighborhood (but a few blocks west of El Llano park) is ◖ **Bed-and-**

Breakfast Oaxaca Ollin (oh-YEEN) (Quintana Roo 213, tel. 951/514-9126, U.S./Can. tel. 619/787-5141, reservations@oaxacaollin.com, www.oaxacaollin.com, $65–75 d, honeymoon suite $100), life project of guide Judith Reyes López and her husband Jon McKinley. Judith and Jon offer 11 comfortable double rooms in their large house, located on a quiet side street a block north and a block east of the Centro Cultural de Santo Domingo. Rooms are immaculate and comfortably appointed with natural wood furniture, reading lamps, and lovely Talavera-tile bathrooms. Extras abound, such as a lovely blue swimming pool and patio, living room, library, reading room, gratis Internet access and local phone calls, and much more. Prices include a hearty breakfast.

Back on the northeast side, from Casa de las Bugambilias (above), go east two blocks and turn north a block to the bed-and-breakfast gem **Casa de Mis Recuerdos** (House of My Memories, Pino Suárez 508, tel. 951/515-8483, tel./fax 951/515-5645, misrecue@prodigy.net. mx, www.misrecuerdos.net, $40–45 per person). Enter the front gate and continue through a blooming, bougainvillea-festooned garden to the private home of the Valenciana family, which has been accommodating students and foreign visitors for years. The rented rooms occupy rear and front sections. The four front rooms, immaculate, spacious, and lovingly decorated with folk art and furnished with handmade wooden furniture, have two bathrooms between them. They are closer to the busy streetfront than the five similarly furnished rear rooms, which, although they have private baths, are smaller. Guests also have the use of an airy, shaded rooftop gazebo for reading and relaxing. Breakfast, included with rentals, is served in the inviting downstairs family dining room. Rates approximately double during festivals and holidays; all linens and cleaning service included.

OVER $100

Elegant **Casa Oaxaca** (Garcia Vigil 407, tel. 951/514-4173, fax 951/516-4412, casaoax@ prodigy.net.mx, www.casa-oaxaca.com, $190 s or d for the four smallest, yet spacious units,

$300 s or d for a larger suite, and $390 for a two-story apartment above the rear courtyard) is straight uphill four blocks and a world apart from the *zócalo*. Its sky-blue colonial facade reveals nothing of its singularly unique interior. The lobby, which appears more like an art museum foyer than a lodging entrance, provides the first clue. Past that, you enter a spacious, plant-decorated courtyard, with the wall plaster artfully removed here and there to reveal the brick underlay. Continue to a rear courtyard, which centers on a blue designer pool and a *temazcal*. All six rooms, which border the courtyards, are luxuriously austere and uniquely appointed with antiques, crafts, and contemporary wall art. Rates include gourmet continental breakfast in the exclusive Casa Oaxaca restaurant; credit cards are accepted. *Temazcal* treatments, complete with native healer, run about $50 per person.

South and West of the *Zócalo*
$50-100
Only a few bed-and-breakfast lodgings dot the south and west sides of town. Here are two gems, however.

Start several blocks southeast of the *zócalo* with **Posada de Chencho** (4ta Privada de la Noria 115, tel./fax 951/514-0043, pchencho@prodigy.net.mx, www.mexonline.com/chencho.htm, $37 s, $58 d). Part of the attraction here is the spark-plug owner, Inocencio "Chencho" Velasco, a friendly Mixtec version of Santa Claus. Such a stream of visitors from all over the world stay at his place that he seems to know someone everywhere. Moreover, very well-informed, English-speaking Chencho is a treasury of information about Oaxaca, both local and statewide. His compound, 22 immaculate rooms in two stories, surrounds an inviting, green garden patio. The rooms themselves are comfortably and thoughtfully decorated, with Western-standard baths. Downstairs, guests enjoy a dining room and a big sitting room/library, besides patio nooks for reading and relaxing. Some rooms in the sun might get hot during the summer. If heat bothers you, be sure to select one in the shade, with a ceiling

fan. If your room has no fan, ask Chencho to supply one. Rates include breakfast. Add $24 per person for all meals. Ask for a cheaper long-term rate. Get to Chencho's by walking east, along Guerrero, from the southeast corner of the *zócalo*. After four blocks, at Xicotencatl (shee-koh-tayn-KAH-tuhl), turn right and continue another four blocks south to Calle La Noria; 4ta Privada de la Noria is one of the one-block streets to your left that run south from La Noria.

On the west edge of downtown, about 10 blocks due west of the *zócalo*, stands **Casa Colonial** (Calle Miguel Negrete 105, tel./fax 951/516-5280, toll-free U.S./Can. tel. 800/758 1697, oaxaca@casa-colonial, reservations@casa-colonial.com, www.casa-colonial.com, $40–95). Personable owners Jane and Thornton Robison, who seem to know everyone in town, call their domain the "posada with no sign," because they don't advertise and only accept guests with reservations. Upon arrival, you immediately see why Casa Colonial is such a favorite among savvy visitors. Low-rise rooms and apartments enfold a spacious, gracefully lovely inner garden. Rooms vary from high-ceilinged, antique-decorated Victorians to smaller, one-person garden-side units. Besides the leisurely tropical ambience, guests enjoy the use of a spacious, refined but homey living room with a fine library and Internet connection. Room prices vary according to size and elegance; ten percent discount for cash. For information on their Casa Colonial Tours, visit their website.

Apartments
An increasing number of visitors are opting for longer Oaxaca stays, and a number of recommendable small apartment complexes are ready to accommodate them.

UNDER $50
In the southeast quarter, an easy five-block walking distance to the *zócalo*, you'll find the attractive (**Villa María** (Arteaga 410 A, tel. 951/516-5056, fax 951/514-2562, villamaria22@hotmail.com, $45–65 d per night,

$400–600 per month). Villa María is the labor of love of trilingual (English, French, Spanish) owner-manager María Garcia and her sister Mari Carmen. Step inside their domain and you'll see the other reason for Villa María's popularity: about 15 apartments surrounding an inviting, plant-adorned inner patio, where stairways rise to rooftop sundecks furnished with comfortable chairs and shady umbrellas. The immaculate, thoughtfully decorated one-bedroom housekeeping apartments, with themes such as "Mixteco," are completely furnished, including dishes, silverware, in-house Internet, optional phones, and maid service. The one- and two-bedroom apartments vary in cost depending on location, size, and amenities

About five blocks north of the *zócalo,* right in front of Iglesia de Santo Domingo and its plaza, is **Departmentos del Fraile** (Macedonio Alcalá 501, tel./fax 951/516-4310, cell in town 044-951/5070, goodwood@prodigy.net.mx, $600/month). Family owner-managers offer four compact, modern, rustic-chic apartments, hidden behind a street-front wall, and tucked within a quiet leafy inner courtyard. The renovated units have one bedroom, bathroom, and kitchenette. Rentals are monthly only.

Behind (east of) the Iglesia de Santo Domingo block, find **La Casa de Rosita** (formerly La Casa de los Abuelos, House of the Grandparents) (Reforma 410, tel. 951/516-1982, lacasadelosabuelos@hotmail.com, www.lacasa-de-rosita.com, $50/day, $350/week). This charmingly quirky colonial-era complex is the life project of personable owner-builder Luis Arroyo Nuñez, who inherited it from his *abuelos* (grandparents). This former priests' residence for Iglesia de Santo Domingo was confiscated by the government after the *cristero* revolt of the late 1920s. Luis's six completely renovated apartments, built around two quiet inner patios, are replete with unique details, such as exposed original brick walls, old family photos, bric-a-brac, and sturdy wooden staircases leading up to bedroom lofts. Rentals include invitingly furnished living-dining rooms, kitchenettes, queen-size beds, and shower-baths. Asking rates are negotiable by the month; with

fans, TV, purified bottled water, and wireless Internet connection.

Nearby, a block east and a block north, just south of El Llano park, **Hotel and Studios Las Mariposas** (Pino Suárez 517, tel. 951/515-5854, ventas@lasmariposas.com.mx, www.lasmariposas.com.mx, $45 s, $50 d) is strongly recommended by previous customers for either short- or long-term stays. Welcoming and knowledgeable owner Teresa Dávila offers six comfortable studio kitchenette suites with private baths in her restored 19th-century family house. In addition, seven rooms (with baths but without kitchenettes) rent for about $40 s, $45 d. Ask for a discount for a long-term stay. Besides the happy customers, pluses include use of fax machine, Internet connection, wireless Internet access, coffee, TV, credit cards accepted, optional breakfast at extra cost, but no kids under 12.

(You might also consider the good long-term rental possibilities at Casa Luz María, Casa María, Posada de Chencho, and Casa Colonial, described earlier in this section.)

HOSTELS

Oaxaca offers several recommendable hostel-style lodgings: Cheapest of all, and also closest in, is artsy-scruffy **Plata Gelatina** (501 Independencia, tel. 951/514-9391, platagelatina@hotmail.com, leviatano@hotmail.com, dorms $7 per person, rooms $18 d), just a block west of the *zócalo.* The location, right in the middle of the downtown action, is the major advantage of Plata Gelatina (Gelatin Plate), so named by the photographer-owner, whose black-and-white gelatin silver plate prints decorate the reception. Upstairs, two dorms—one mixed 10-bed and one female seven-bed—and four stuffy rooms with shared baths provide the lodging options. A pizza oven at street level downstairs also cooks at least one of the rooms upstairs. The bathroom-shower room is decently clean, but is small and probably crowded during times of high occupancy.

Another cheap but decent and relatively close-in choice, two blocks east and five blocks south of the *zócalo's* southeast corner, is **Hostal Chacahua** (Fiallo 803, tel. 951/516-9057, www.advantagemexico.com/oaxaca/hostels .html, dorms $8 per person, rooms $20 d). This small, clean but bare-bones lodging house in a solid working-class neighborhood offers dorm beds and private rooms.

For more amenities, check out a pair of hostels in the picturesque Los Arquitos neighborhood on the far northwest side of downtown, two blocks west and nine blocks north (15 minutes) from the zócalo's northwest corner. There you'll find **Hostal Pochón** (Calle del Carmen 102, tel. 951/516-1322, hostalpochon@yahoo. com, www.hostalpochon.com, dorms $9 per person, rooms $23 d). Owners offer lodging for about 28 guests in six separate four-person dorms and one double room with shared bath.

In the same northwest neighborhood is the very worthy **Hostal Don Mario** (Cosijopi 219, tel./fax 951/514-2012, hostaldonmario@hotmail.com, www.posadadonmario.com, dorms $10 per person, rooms with shared bath $15 s, $20 d, $30 t, rooms with private bath $25 s or d), on a quiet side street. Hardworking owner Norma Moran offers ten rooms and a dormitory, tucked around an intimate downstairs patio and an airy upstairs porch, furnished with comfy chairs and couches for reading and relaxing. Breakfast runs $2–4.

The first choice hostel by far is the beautifully restored ◖ **Paulina Youth Hostel** (V. Trujano 321, tel. 951/516-2005, reservations@paulinahostel.com, www.paulinahostel.com, dorms $14 per person, rooms $28 s, $30 d, $45 t, $60 q), just three blocks west of the zócalo. Here, owners have created the best of all possible hosteling worlds, with a good cafeteria and inviting, spacious common areas, all within attractive garden grounds. The comfortable, squeaky-clean rooming options include separate male and female dorms and private rooms with shower-baths, all with comfortable orthopedic mattresses, roof terrace, hot water, and hearty breakfast thrown in for free. Get your reservations in early.

TRAILER PARKS AND CAMPING

Oaxaca has two trailer-camping parks. Most accessible, but less inviting, is the **Oaxaca**

Trailer Park (900 Av. Violetas, owner's tel. 951/515-0376, or dial cell 044/569-5528 in town, hookups $15, tents $10), at the far northeast side of town. Once a very popular facility, the Oaxaca Trailer Park has been partly converted to offices and apartments as of this writing. Nevertheless, it lives on, still with dozens of all-hookup spaces and tent spaces remaining. Amenities include big shade trees and diagonal parking space for the largest rigs, clean hot-water showers and toilets, a manager-watchman, and the original sturdy security fence. Get there by turning left at Violetas, marked by the big green Colonia Reforma sign over the highway, at the baseball stadium, several blocks east of the first-class bus terminal on Highway 190. Continue uphill six long blocks to the trailer park on the left.

Although more remote, the second choice trailer park has its advantages. For those who prefer a bit of adventure and wide-open spaces, the **San Felipe del Agua Trailer Park** (Camino de la Chigolera 10, San Felipe del Agua, tel. 951/516-0654 or 951/520-0947, info@oaxacanstuff.com, www.oaxacanstuff.com, tents $7, RVs $15) will probably be the best choice for tenters and for rigs 25 feet (7.5 meters) or smaller. It perches atop a valley-view knoll in foothill San Felipe del Agua village, about four miles (six km) north of downtown. The San Francisco, California, expatriate owner (and former Oaxaca consular agent) Roberta French and her son Doug French offer all hookups for about 10 rigs in a large country lot with scant shade but plenty of mezcal plants and room for tents. A small clubhouse with kitchenette, shower, and toilet is also available for resident use. Prices include water, electricity, and drainage. Reservations are possible but probably not necessary.

Their hilltop location, at the jumping-off point for rough hiking trails, past waterfalls and meadows, en route to the summit of towering, pine-tufted Cerro San Felipe (elev. 10,300 feet/3,140 meters), appears ideal for experienced, prepared hikers and backpackers. Look at the map at the community park guard station a quarter mile (0.4 km) uphill from the San

Felipe bus turnaround for hiking route information. The trailer-park manager might serve as your guide; figure on paying him about $30 for a day's outing.

Get there by bus, taxi, or car to San Felipe del Agua village. By bus, ride San Felipe–marked Choferes del Sur bus from the corner of Independencia and Reforma, two blocks east of the *zócalo,* thence following Pino Suárez uphill, past El Llano park. Get off at the San Felipe del Agua village plaza (see the old church on the right) and follow the driving directions below. (*Note:* The end-of-the-line bus turnaround is a half-mile farther uphill from the village plaza. From there, you can hike a quarter mile (0.4 km) via the road that continues beneath the turnaround, to the Parque Comunal San Felipe guard station and trailhead.)

For drivers, the jumping-off point to the trailer park is Avenida Netzahualcoyotl (nay-tzah-oo-wahl-coh-YOH-tuhl), which heads uphill at the big green San Felipe sign from its intersection with the Highway 190 thoroughfare (Calz. Niños Héroes), one block east of the Pemex station. Drivers, continue about two-thirds of a mile (one km); at Calle Naranjos (see the hotel sign), bear left around the curve, follow the first right one block, then left after one long block; a long block later, at the big traffic intersection, you'll see the aqueduct. Turn right, uphill, at the aqueduct, and you'll be on your way heading along Calzada San Felipe, which parallels the old stone aqueduct on your left. In a few miles the road becomes San Felipe's Calle Hidalgo, which leads you to San Felipe Apostol Church behind the pocket-sized village plaza on the right.

To get to the trailer park, turn left (west) just before the church and village plaza, on to Calle Iturbide, then right again at the first street, Morelos, then another quick left onto the "Prologation of Iturbide." After another long block or two downhill, at the arroyo bottom, turn right onto Chigolera; continue, climbing steeply uphill 0.4 mile (0.6 km) to the trailer-park sign and gate on the left.

Food

SNACKS, FOOD STALLS, AND COFFEEHOUSES

During fiestas, snack stalls along Hidalgo at the cathedral-front Alameda de León square abound in local delicacies. Choices include *tlayudas,* giant crisp tortillas loaded with avocado, tomato, onions, and cheese; and *empanadas de amarillo,* huge tacos stuffed with cheese and red salsa. For dessert, have a *buñuelo,* a crunchy, honey-soaked wheat tortilla.

At non-fiesta times, you can still fill up on the sizzling fare of taco, *torta,* hamburger, and hot dogs (eat 'em only when they are served hot) at stands that set up in the same vicinity.

For relatively economical local fare, go to the acre of food stalls inside the **Mercado 20 de Noviembre,** two blocks south of the *zócalo's* southwest corner. Adventurous eaters will be in heaven among a wealth of succulent *chiles rellenos;* piquant *moles* (moh-LAYS); fat, banana leaf–wrapped *tamales Oaxaqueños;* and savory *sopas* (soups) and *guisados* (stews). Insist, however, that your selection be served hot.

Alternatively, take a look around the completely untouristed Sánchez Pasqua market (8 A.M.–2 P.M. daily except Sun.) for some pleasant surprises. (From the *zócalo* Cathedral, walk uphill along Garcia Vigil seven blocks to Humboldt and turn left a block to Porfirio Díaz. The market is past the gigantic laurel tree.) Enjoy the town's tastiest *comal* (charcoal-fired griddle) cooking. Ask for Carmen Hernández Ramírez and order her *memelas* (big, thick, open-face tortillas smothered in beans, $1.50) and/or the luscious, plump tamales ($1.50) of Catalina Minerva Paz.

Much farther up the economic scale, sample the delicious offerings of ◖ **Hostería Alcalá** (Alcalá 307, 8:30 A.M.–11 P.M. daily, $5–15), four blocks north of the *zócalo.* The airy, tranquil patio ambience is ideal for a relaxing refreshment or lunch break from sightseeing along the Alcalá pedestrian mall.

For coffee and dessert, you have a number of additional downtown choices, notably **Coffee Beans** (Cinco de Mayo 400, cell tel. 951/162-7171, 8 A.M.–11 P.M. daily), five blocks north of the zócalo; or nearby **Restaurant La Antigua** (a block east at Reforma 401, tel. 951/516-5761, noon-11 P.M. daily, $3–8), just uphill from Abasolo.

For baked goods, a quartet of good carryout bakeries stand within a stone's throw of the zócalo. First, try the sweet offerings of **Tartamiel Pastelería Frances** (on Trujano, half a block west from the southwest corner of the zócalo, tel. 951/516-7350, 7 A.M.–8 P.M. Mon.–Sat., 8:30 A.M.–7 P.M. Sun.). Continue clockwise, north of the zócalo a block, to **Panadería Bamby** (at the northwest corner of G. Vigil and Morelos, 6 A.M.–9 P.M. Mon.–Sat.). A block east of the zócalo, stop by either the 🅒 **Pastelería and Café La Vasconia** (Independencia 907 between Cinco de Mayo and Reforma, tel. 951/516-2677, 8 A.M.–9 P.M. daily, $2–6), with an inviting arched interior patio and a luscious selection of pastries, cakes, salads, and sandwiches. Another option is **Pastelería Quemen** (8 A.M.–9 P.M. daily), across the street.

CAFÉS AND RESTAURANTS
Around the Zócalo

Oaxaca visitors enjoy many good eateries right on or near the zócalo. In fact, you could spend your entire Oaxaca time enjoying the fare of the several zócalo-front sidewalk cafés. Of the eight cafés, seven offer recommendable food and service. Moving counterclockwise from the northwest corner, they are **Primavera, La Cafetería, Del Jardín, Importador, Terranova, Amarantos,** and the zócalo-front café of the **Hotel Marques del Valle.**

First place overall goes to the pricier, upper-class **Terranova** at the southeast corner, and the **Hotel Marques del Valle** on the north side, for their professionally prepared and served lunch and dinner entrées. For good, economical breakfasts, however, go to **Primavera,** at the northeast (Hidalgo) corner. The adjacent westside **La Cafetería** and **Del Jardín** (with loud marimba music most nights) rate generally good for food (notably Del Jardín's tummy-warming apple strudel), but their service can be spotty. While service at **Amarantos** is usually good, its food is only fair. Newcomer **El Importador** is trying harder with entertaining, not-too-loud live music and passably good food, at lower prices than neighboring Terranova. They all are open long hours, about 8 A.M.–midnight, and serve from very recognizable menus, with morning breakfasts ($2–5), soups, salads ($3–6), and pasta, meat, poultry, and fish ($5–$12).

Note: The zócalo's west side is generally shadier, cooler, and more pleasant during the warm March, April, and May dry season. On the other hand, the east side, which gets the afternoon sun, is the warmer and often more pleasant side during the cooler months of November, December, and January. As for zócalo-front seating, nonsmokers can escape to the open-air tables, thus avoiding the cigarette and cigar smoke beneath the portal.

The one drawback of zócalo-level eating is the persistent flow of vendors, which can be unnerving. If, however, you refuse (or bargain for) their offerings gently and with humor, you might begin to accept and enjoy them as part of the entire colorful scene. (If they really get to you, best take an inside table or retreat to the two restaurants that shoo them away: the Terranova and the Marques del Valle.)

Note: Also, for the time being, it is best not to eat any of the French-fried *chapulines* (grasshoppers) that some vendors offer. Both the grasshoppers and certain kinds of locally made candy have been found to contain large amounts of lead, which is harmful, especially to children, even in amounts as small as a hundred-thousandth of a gram. Mexican health authorities are very aware of this problem, and are working to correct it quickly.

As for zócalo-front restaurants, serious-eating longtimers return to **El Asador Vasco** (Portal Flores 10A on the second-floor balcony above the Restaurant Jardín, tel. 951/514-4755, 1 P.M.–midnight daily, $25–35). The menu specializes in hearty Basque-style country cooking: salty, spicy, and served in the decor of a medieval Iberian manor house. Favorites include fondues (bean, sausage, and mushroom), garlic soup, salads, veal tongue, oysters in hot sauce, and the carnes asadas (roast meats) house specialties.

Longtimers also swear by the Oaxacan specialties at ◖ **Casa de la Abuela** (Grandmother's House) (above the Primavera café, tel. 951/516-3544, 11 A.M.–10 P.M. daily, $7–17) at the *zócalo*'s northwest corner. Here you can enjoy tasty, professionally prepared regional dishes and airy *zócalo* vistas from the

A OAXACAN MENU

Oaxacan food adds another layer to the already rich Mexican food tradition. Oaxacan meals must start off with appetizers, such as *quesillo a la plancha*, Oaxaca's famous white cheese, served melted with guacamole and black beans. An appetizer list wouldn't be truly Oaxacan without *chapulines*, small grasshoppers grilled with minced onion in oil until crunchy.

Next come the Oaxacan *sopas* (soups), such as *sopa de guías*, a delicious stewed medley of squash flowers, tender baby squash, small corn dumplings, fresh whole corn kernels (*elote*), and tender vine shoots. Other typically served soups include *caldillo de nopales*, a broth of fleshy cactus leaves, often cooked with bits of pork, chicken, or small shrimps, and *sopa de frijoles*, black bean soup with cheese chunks and tortilla chips.

Main courses must include *moles* (MOH-lays), the most Oaxacan of all dishes. Very typical is *mole negro* (black *mole*), a spicy-sweet mixture of chocolate, chilies, garlic, peanuts, and a score of spices and other flavorings, cooked to a sauce, then baked with chicken or turkey. The turkey variation, called *mole de pavo*, is so *típica* that it's widely regarded as the national dish.

The *mole* list goes on, through *mole amarillo* (yellow *mole*) to *mole colorado* (red *mole*), a sauce of chilies, sesame seeds, almonds, raisins, bananas, tomatoes, and spices, served over chicken with rice seasoned with *chepil*, a wild local herb.

Oaxacan main-dish sauces are not necessarily chili based. Some menus feature fruit- and nut-based sauces, such as *almendrado*, an almond sauce spiced with tomatoes, green olives, and herbs and served over chicken. Oaxacans also enjoy local variations on

the usual Mexican *antojitos*, such as *chiles rellenos de picadillo*. Here the cook replaces the usual chiles rellenos cheese stuffing with minced spiced pork, beef, or chicken and serves them with guacamole, grilled onion, and refried black beans.

Menu meat selections often include *cecina* (say-SEE-nah), thin slices of spicy cured pork, frequently served with bean sauce and cheese, or *tasajo*, thinly sliced grilled beef, often dished up with *chilaquiles* (tortillas cooked in chili-tomato sauce).

Finally, top off your meal with a local dessert, such as flan (egg custard), and a drink, such as *té de poleo*, a tea brewed from *poleo*, a local, mintlike herb, or *café de la olla*, a rich regional coffee sweetened with *panela*, the dark brown sugar that market vendors sell by the chunk.

© BRUCE WHIPPERMAN

Dried chilies are a basic ingredient for flavoring Mexican dishes.

balcony. Call for reservations and a table with a view.

For fine Oaxacan specialties in a graceful, old-world setting, try **Andariega Restaurant** (Independencia 503, tel./fax 951/514-9331, 7:30 A.M.–9 P.M. daily, $8–12) in the Parador San Miguel, two blocks west of the cathedral. Here's one of your best chances to try some of Oaxaca's *moles*, such as *almendrado* (almond), *verde* (green), *amarillo* (yellow), or *negro* (black), over chicken, beef, or pork. Other favorites are *chiles rellenos*, stuffed with cheese and *picadillo* (spiced meat), and red snapper in orange sauce. An excellent daily four-course *comida* (set lunch) runs about $8.

For many loyal local upper-class patrons, **Restaurant Catedral** (Garcia Vigil 105, tel. 951/516-3285, 8 A.M.–midnight Mon.–Fri., 8 A.M.–2 A.M. Sat. and Sun, $8–16), two blocks north of the *zócalo*, at the corner of Morelos, serves as a tranquil daytime refuge from the street hubbub. The refined ambience—music playing softly in the background, tables set around an airy, intimate fountain patio crowned by the blue Oaxaca sky above—is half the show. The finale is the very correct service and quality food for breakfast, lunch, or supper. The Aguilar family owners are especially proud of their *moles* that flavor their house specialties. These include fillets, both meat and fish ($9–16), and regional dishes, such as banana leaf–wrapped *tamales Oaxaqueños* ($8).

Back on Hidalgo, just past the *zócalo's* northeast corner, the spotless little *fonda* **El Mesón** (Hidalgo 805, tel. 951/516-2729, 8 A.M.–11:30 P.M. daily) specializes in buffet food. For about $5, you can select your fill of fresh fruit, salads, *frijoles charros* (chili beans), and several entrées, including roast beef and pork, chicken, *moles*, tacos, tamales, and enchiladas.

More good eating, in a genteel, relaxed atmosphere, awaits you at the very popular **Restaurant El Sagrario** (120 Valdivieso, tel. 951/514-0303 or 951/514-3319, 8 A.M.–midnight daily, $7–12), around the corner behind the church. Mostly local, youngish upper-class customers enjoy a club/bar atmosphere

(lower level), pizza parlor booths (middle level), or restaurant tables (upper level). At the restaurant level during the evening, you can best take in the whole scene around you—chattering, upbeat crowd; live guitar, flute, jazz, or salsa melodies; and elegantly restored colonial details. Then, finally, comes the food, beginning, perhaps, with an appetizer, continuing with a soup or salad ($4), then an international or regional specialty ($7–12), which you top off with a light dessert and a savory espresso. Music volume goes up later in the evening. Credit cards accepted.

North of the *Zócalo*

Devotees of light, vegetarian-style cuisine get what they're hungering for at **La Manantial Vegetariana**, with two locations. The original branch is just above Matamoros (at west-side Calle Tinoco y Palacios 303, tel. 951/514-5602, 8 A.M.–11 P.M. daily except Sun.), two blocks west and three blocks north of the *zócalo;* the new branch occupies the center of the busy Santo Domingo shopping plaza (diagonally across Alcalá from the Iglesia de Santo Domingo, 8 A.M.–9 p.m. daily, $2–5) and is consequently not very relaxing. At the east-side branch, tranquil patio ambience sets the tone for the house specialty, a set lunch *comida*. Typically they might offer soup (onion or cream of zucchini), salad (mixed greens or tomato cucumber), stew (mushroom or soya steak), bread, fruit drink, dessert, and coffee or tea for about $6 until 7 P.M., $8 after that.

If you're in the mood for a little bit of Italy in Oaxaca, go to **Restaurant la Rústica** (upstairs, above the northeast corner of Alcalá and Murguia, tel. 951/501-1318 or 951/516-7696, 11 A.M.–10:30 P.M. daily, $5–12), a few blocks uphill from the *zócalo*. This is a place that has customers when everywhere else is empty. It's like a picture out of old Sicily, with arched ceilings, old-world religious wall paintings, Pavarotti in the background, and a tasty menu of most everything Italian: *antipasti,* ($3–6), 185 spaghetti options ($5–9), lasagna, and delicious pizza in a dozen variations ($7–12).

If you're unfamiliar with (or unconvinced about) Oaxaca's *mole* sauces, walk two blocks east of the front of Iglesia de Santo Domingo to ((**Restaurant los Pacos** (Abasolo 121, tel. 951/516-1704, noon–about 10 P.M. Mon.–Sat.). Your meal automatically comes with a *mole* appetizer sampler, which treats you to six—*coloradito, verde, negro, estofado, Amarillo,* and *chichilo*—of Oaxaca's *moles* right off the bat. It only gets better after that, especially if you continue with one of the good salads, from Caesar to tomato ($4–7), then follow up with a traditional Oaxaca specialty, such as *enchiladas coloradito con picadillo* ($9), *espinazazo de puerco con mole verde* ($10), or *entomatadas* either *solas* or with beef ($9).

Also behind Santo Domingo, half a block north of Abasolo, **Café La Olla** (Reforma 402, in front of Casa de las Bugambilias bed-and-breakfast, tel. 951/516-6668, 8 A.M.–10 P.M. Mon.–Sat.) enjoys a loyal following of long-time North American expatriates. Here, the dark-beamed ceiling, subdued spotlighting of the art-decorated walls, quiet music, and candlelight set the refined, romantic tone. Select from a long but light menu of skillfully prepared and presented soups (Aztec soup is nearly a meal in itself, $5), salads, Oaxacan specialties, and meats ($6–14). La Olla's main drawback is street noise, which you can minimize by taking an upstairs table.

Right across the street is **Café La Antigua** (Reforma 401, tel. 951/516-5761, 9 A.M.–11 P.M. Mon.–Sat.), enjoyed by a long list of loyal patrons for entirely different reasons. Here, the main course is conversation and fine on-site roasted "Pluma" (from the mountains above Puerto Escondido) Oaxaca coffee. Along with their savory lattes, cold cappuccinos, and mocha frappés, patrons can enjoy fresh baked goods, crepes, sandwiches, eggs, and juices ($2–7). The prime mover behind all this is friendly coffee grower and owner Diego Woolrich Ramírez.

Continue east two blocks and north two more to the relaxing garden of **Mariscos Jorge** (on Pino Suárez, across from El Llano park, tel. 951/513-4308, 8 A.M.–6:30 P.M. Wed.–Mon.,

$8–14), standout standby of local middle- and upper-class patrons. Choose from a long menu of seafood (14 cocktail selections, including, shrimp, squid, and clams, $4–6), salads and soups ($4), and entrées, including fish fillets, from breaded and baked to *a la diabla,* octopus, and much more ($8–14). Also pleasant for breakfast.

South of the *Zócalo*

Only a few good sit-down restaurants sprinkle the neighborhoods south of the *zócalo.* A quartet of them, three well known for Oaxacan cuisine, and one for seafoood, stand out.

Local folks strongly recommend the nononsense, country-style (but refined) **La Flor de Oaxaca** (Armenta y López 311, tel. 951/516-5522, 7:30 A.M.–10 P.M. Mon.–Sat., 9 A.M.–3 P.M. Sun.), a block east and half a block south from the *zócalo*'s southeast corner. Along with spotless linen and very correct service, you'll get the customary bottomless plate of warm corn tortillas to go with your entrée. The *mole*-smothered regional specialties come mostly in four styles: *con tasajo* (thin broiled steak), *con pollo* (chicken), *con cecina* (roast pork), all about $8, or *sola* (without meat, $6). Besides those, you can choose from an extensive menu of equally flavorful items, such as *tamales Oaxaqueños* (wrapped in banana leaves, $5), pork chops ($8), several soups, spaghetti, and much more. Vegetable lovers get started off right with their crisp *ensalada mixta* (sliced tomato, cucumber, onion, avocado, and lettuce with vinegar and oil dressing, $4). Credit cards accepted.

A block west and two blocks south of the *zócalo*'s southwest corner, ((**Restaurant Tayu** (20 de Noviembre 416, tel. 951/516-5363, 8 A.M.–6 P.M. daily except Sun.) allows you to step back to Oaxaca "as it used to be." Take a table and relax in the refined, old-world, TV-free ambience. Mornings, select from a host of tasty breakfasts ($3–5); afternoons, choose one of their four-course $5 *comidas* that include a choice between several hearty entrées, such as short ribs, chicken, chiles rellenos, with soup, rice and dessert included. Arrive 2:30–4:30 P.M. and enjoy their live instrumental music.

Lovers of fresh seafood can join the loyal brigade of local folks who frequent the airy and unpretentious **Restaurant La Red** (The Net), one of five Oaxaca branches (corner of Bustamante and Colón, tel. 951/514-8840, 11 A.M.–9 P.M. daily), one block south of the *zócalo*'s southeast corner. Customers get their heart's delight of generous seafood cocktails ($5), heaping bowls of shrimp ($16), fish fillets ($10), octopus ($12), and much more.

Splurge Restaurants

The Oaxaca visitor influx during the 1990s has nurtured a crop of fine restaurants. If at all possible, visit the uniquely elegant **Los Danzantes** (Alcalá 402, tel. 951/501-1184, 951/501-1187, 1:30–11:30 P.M. daily), where everything seems designed for perfection. We enjoyed their surprisingly economical ($10 until 6 P.M.) set lunch, which changes every day. In the luxuriously airy dining atrium, beneath blue sky and sunlight filtering through curtains artfully draped overhead, waiters scurried, starting us off with yummy chilled artichoke soup, continuing with savory spinach lasagna with Oaxaca *requesón* cheese, accompanied by mildly delicious pressed guava-apple juice. They topped it all off with delectable dark-Oaxaca chocolate mousse and espresso coffee. Bravo! After such an introduction, you'll be tempted to return on another day.

For dinner, expect to pay at least $35 per person, if you include a glass of wine. Reservations strongly recommended.

Hotel manager and chef Alejandro Ruiz of **Casa Oaxaca** (Garcia Vigil 407, tel. 951/514-4173, 951/516-8889, 1–11 P.M. daily except Sun.) puts his all into blending the best of old and new cuisine. For example, start off with duck pâté ($8) and continue with *flor de calabaza*, stuffed with cheese and accompanied by *tostaditas* (toasted corn) and guacamole ($6). Follow through with broiled shrimp in their juice, with lentils ($18), or baked *robalo* (snook) with lemon ($22), all accompanied with a bottle of Concha y Toro Sauvignon Blanc from Chile. Finish off with either baby coconut custard, mango pie, or *guanabana* mousse, or a sampling of all three ($10). Reservations required.

In the far northeast corner of downtown, showplace **Restaurant La Toscana** (at the corner of Cinco de Mayo and Alianza, in the old Jalatlaco neigborhood, tel. 951/513-8742, 2–11 P.M. daily) offers a long, elegant Mediterranean menu, spiced with a dash of traditional Oaxaca. Although it would be hard to go wrong with most anything here, I enjoyed the lettuce and tomato salad with goat cheese ($7), shrimp fettuccine ($9), leg of *jabalí* (wild pig, $14), and, for dessert, croquettes of coconut and banana ($8). Reservations recommended.

Entertainment, Events, and Recreation

AROUND THE *ZÓCALO*

The Oaxaca *zócalo*, years ago relieved of traffic, is ideal ground for spontaneous diversions. Regular concerts serenade from the *zócalo* band kiosk at 7 P.M. virtually every evening: the Oaxaca state band, Tuesday and Thursday; Marimba band, Monday, Wednesday, and Friday; and the Oaxaca orchestra, Sunday. At other times, divert yourself by running like a kid over the plaza, bouncing a 10-foot-long *aeroglobo* into the air. (Get them from vendors in front of the cathedral.) If you're in a sitting mood, watch the world go by from a *zócalo* sidewalk café. Later, take in the folk dance performance at the Hotel Monte Albán on the adjacent Plaza Alameda de León, 8:30–10 P.M. nightly, for about $9. After that, return to a *zócalo* café and enjoy the musicians who entertain most every evening until midnight.

FESTIVALS

There seems to be a festival somewhere in the Valley of Oaxaca every week of the year.

Oaxaca's wide ethnic diversity explains much of the celebrating. Each of the groups celebrates its own traditions. Sixteen languages, in dozens of dialects, are spoken within the state. Authorities recognize around 500 distinct regional costumes.

All of this ethnic ferment focuses in the city during the July **Lunes del Cerro** festival. Known in pre-Hispanic times as the **Guelaguetza** (gay-lah-GAY-tzah, or Offering), tribes reunited for rituals and dancing in honor of Centeotl, the god of corn. The ceremonies, which climaxed with the sacrifice of a virgin who had been fed hallucinogenic mushrooms, were changed to tamer, mixed Christian–native rites by the Catholic Church. Lilies replaced marigolds—the flower of death—and saints sat in for the indigenous gods.

For the weeks around the two Mondays following July 16, the **Día de la Virgen de Carmen** (Virgin of Carmen day), Oaxaca is awash with native Mexicans in costume from all seven traditional regions of Oaxaca. The festivities, which include a crafts and agricultural fair, climax with dances and ceremonies at the Guelaguetza amphitheater on the Cerro del Fortín hill northwest of the city. Entrance to the Guelaguetza dances runs about $30; bring a hat and sunglasses. Make hotel reservations months ahead of time. For more Guelaguetza tickets ($40 per person), contact the state tourist information office (Murguia 206, between Cinco de Mayo and Reforma, tel. 951/516-0123, 951/502-1200, 8 A.M.–8 P.M. daily, info@aoaxaca.com, www.oaxaca.travel), two blocks north and a block and a half east of the rear of the cathedral.

Note: If the first Monday after July 16 happens to fall on July 18, the anniversary of Benito Juárez's death, the first Lunes del Cerro shifts to the succeeding Monday, July 25.

On the Sunday before the first Lunes del Cerro, Oaxacans celebrate their history and culture at the Plaza de Danzas adjacent to the Iglesia de la Virgen de la Soledad. Events include a big sound, light, and dance show and

Dancers from Tehuántepec entertain at the grand Guelaguetza festival in July.

© BRUCE WHIPPERMAN

depictions in tableaux of the four periods of Oaxaca history.

Besides the usual national holidays, a number of other locally important fiestas liven up the Oaxacan calendar. The first day of spring, March 21, kicks off the **Juegos Florales** (Flower Games). Festivities go on for 10 days, including the crowning of a festival queen at the Teatro de Alcalá, poetry contests, and performances by renowned artists and the National Symphony.

On the second Monday in October, residents of Santa María del Tule venerate their ancient tree in the **Lunes del Tule** festival. Locals in costume celebrate with rites, folk dances, and feats of horsemanship beneath the boughs of their beloved great cypress.

As in many southern-Mexico locales, Oaxaca folks celebrate a robust **Día de los Muertos** (Day of the Dead) November 1 and 2. Families gather at cemeteries, where they decorate the graves of their departed with the favorite foods of the deceased and lights to guide their beloved ancestors to reunite (albeit temporarily) with the family once again.

Oaxacans venerate their patron, the Virgen de la Soledad, December 16–18. Festivities, which center on the Virgin's basilica (on Independencia six blocks west of the *zócalo*), include fireworks, dancing, food, and street processions of the faithful bearing the Virgin's gold-crowned image decked out in her fine silks and satins.

For the **Fiesta de los Rábanos** (Festival of the Radishes) on December 23, celebrants fill the Oaxaca *zócalo*, admiring displays of plants, flowers, and figures crafted of giant radishes. Ceremonies and prizes honor the most innovative designs. Food stalls nearby serve traditional delicacies, including *buñuelos* (honey-soaked fried tortillas), plates of which are traditionally thrown into the air before the evening is over.

Oaxaca people culminate their *posada* week on **Nochebuena** (Christmas Eve) with candle-lit processions from their parishes, accompanied by music, fireworks, and floats. They converge on the *zócalo* in time for a midnight cathedral mass.

FOLKLORIC DANCE SHOWS

If you miss the Lunes del Cerro festival, some towns and villages stage smaller Guelaguetza celebrations year-round. So do a number of hotels, the most reliable of which occurs nightly at 8:30 P.M. at the Hotel Monte Albán (on Plaza Alameda de León, adjacent to the *zócalo*, tel. 951/516-2777, $9). At other hotels, days may change, so call ahead to confirm: Hotel Camino Real (tel. 951/516-0611, 7 P.M. Fri., $30 show with dinner, not including drinks); Restaurant Casa de Cantera (Murguia 102, tel. 951/514-7585, 8:30 P.M., $10 per person).

PERFORMING ARTS AND FINE ARTS

Many Oaxaca institutions, such as the **Museo de Arte Contemporaneo de Oaxaca**, the **Teatro Macedonio Alcalá**, the **Instituto de Artes Graficos de Oaxaca**, (see the *Sights* section) and the art-film **Cinema El Pochote** (Garcia Vigil 817, tel. 951/514-1194, films at 6 and 8 P.M. Tues.–Sat.), sponsor first-rate cultural events. Local sources of events information include the weekly **El Grito** events newsletter of the Oaxaca State Secretary of Culture (www.cultura.oaxaca .gob.mx), the Oaxaca state tourist information office (Murguia 206, between Cinco de Mayo and Reforma, tel. 951/516-0123, 951/502-1200), and possibly the English-language newspapers *Oaxaca Times* and *Go-Oaxaca*.

NIGHTLIFE

When lacking an official fiesta, you can create your own at a number of nightspots around town.

Some sidewalk cafés around the *zócalo* regularly have live music. Just follow the sound to café **El Importador** (southeast *zócalo* corner), the marimba band in front of the El Jardón (southwest corner), and seasonally at the **Hotel Marques del Valle** restaurant (north side of *zócalo*). Music typically continues until about 11 P.M. daily.

Nearby, behind the cathedral, the restaurant **El Sagrario** (120 Valdivieso, tel. 951/514-0303 or 951/514-3319, 8 A.M.–midnight daily, $7–12) has live music nightly beginning about 9 P.M.

OAXACA CITY

Bar La Farola (20 de Noviembre 314, corner of Las Casas, 951/516-5352, 11 A.M.–2 A.M. daily), a block west and a block south of the *zócalo*, founded 1916, claims to be Oaxaca's longest-running cantina. The Farola's dignified old-style pub ambience attracts a middle-to-upper-class local clientele, some young, some old, who come to relax over food, drinks, and the rhythms of a live latin-jazz-salsa trio.

Moving uphill, north, from the *zócalo*, the action is often livelier and louder (recorded hip-hop, reggae, and salsa) at restaurant-bar **Tentación** (Matamoros 101, open 8 A.M. until sometimes as late as 2 A.M. Tues.–Sat.).

One of the most intense in-town nightspots is **Candela** (Murguia 413, corner of Pino Suárez, tel. 951/514-2010, from about 10 P.M. Thurs.–Sat.), which jumps with hot salsa and African-Latin rhythms. Arrive at 10 P.M. for dance lessons; call to confirm. (Women, be aware that a well-known cadre of local Romeos regularly frequents this and other such downtown spots.)

The hottest new nightspot in town among 20-somethings is the class-act **Bar La Pasion** (hidden beyond the rear of Restaurant Mayordomo, Alcalá 303, noon–3 A.M. daily) with giant flat TV screens, studio lighting, and loud, live music. On Friday, Saturday, and Sunday, you can recognize it easily after about 8 P.M. by the large crowd out in front.

The success of Bar La Pasion has spawned a number of newer nightspots. One of the liveliest is **La Cantinita** restaurant-bar across the street (Alcalá 302, tel. 951/516-8169, 1 P.M.–2 A.M. daily). Above the front door, a sign announces "entrance prohibited to all persons who like to fight, are in a bad mood, or are angry." The attraction is loud, live salsa and hip-hop and lots of folks in their 20s and 30s dancing, drinking, and eating.

For a more subdued atmosphere, try the luxury hotels, which host live dance music in their lobby bars especially on weekends and holidays. Call to confirm programs at Camino Real (tel. 951/516-0611), the Victoria (tel. 951/515-2633), and the Fortín Plaza (tel. 951/515-7777).

SPORTS AND RECREATION
Swimming, Tennis, and Golf

Swimmers can do their laps and laze the afternoon away by the big pool (unheated but usually swimmable) at in-town **Hotel Rivera del Ángel** (Mina 518, tel. 951/516-6666, $10 adults, $5 kids 5 and under).

For both tennis (about seven courts) and a nine-hole golf course, go to the relaxed country club–style **Club Brenamiel** (at the intersection of Hwy. 190 and Calle San Jacinto, tel. 951/512-6822, clubbrenamiel@hotmail.com), on the left just past the Hotel Villas del Sol, about three miles north of the town center. Alternatively, on the other side of town, try the well-equipped (half a dozen tennis courts, two pools, gymnasium) YMCA-like **Oaxaca Deportivo** (Km 6.5, Carretera a El Tule, tel. 951/517-5271, 951/517-5974, 951/517-7312), off Highway 190 on the way to El Tule, about four miles east of town. *Note:* Although both Club Brenamiel and Oaxaca Deportivo are membership organizations, they do accept day guests for a fee.

For both swimming and tennis, you can also stay at either the **Hotel Victoria** or the **Hotel Misión de los Angeles** (see *Accommodations*), which have a pool and courts.

A modest sporting goods and clothing selection is available at **Deportes Ziga** (on the southwest corner of Alcalá and Matamoros, next to La Mano Mágico handicrafts shop, 9 A.M.–3 P.M. and 4–9 P.M. Mon.–Sat., 11 A.M.–2 P.M. Sun.).

Jogging and Walking

For jogging, try the public **Ciudad Deportiva** (Sports City) fields on the west side of Highway 190 about two miles (three km) north of the town center. Closer in, you might also jog around the big **Parque Paseo Juárez** (El Llano), on Avenida Juárez, three blocks east and about 10 blocks north of the *zócalo*.

For an invigorating in-town walk, climb the **Cerro del Fortín.** Your reward will be a panoramic city, valley, and mountain view. The key to getting there through the maze of city streets is to head to the **Escalera del Fortín** (staircase), which will lead you conveniently to the instep of the hill. For example, from the northeast *zócalo* corner, walk north along the Alcalá mall. After five blocks, in front of the Iglesia de Santo Domingo, turn left onto Allende, continue four blocks to Crespo, and turn right. After three blocks, you'll see the staircase on the left. Continue uphill, past the sprawling Guelaguetza open-air auditorium, to the road (Av. Nicolas Copernicus) heading north to the **Planetarium** (tel. 951/514-7500, 7–9 P.M. Nov.–May, check the events schedule) to enjoy the panoramic city and valley view. (Besides daytime movies and star shows, the planetarium is customarily open for evening telescopic viewing of the moon, planets, and stars.)

Past the planetarium, you can keep walking along the hilltop for at least another mile. Take a hat and water. The round-trip from the *zócalo* is a minimum of two miles (three km); the hilltop rises only a few hundred feet. Allow at least a couple of hours.

Shopping

The city of Oaxaca is renowned as a handicraft shopper's paradise. Prices are moderate, quality is high, and sources—in both large traditional markets and many dozens of private stores and galleries—are manifold. In the city, however, vendors do not ordinarily make the merchandise they sell. They buy wholesale from family shops in town, the surrounding valley, and remote localities all over the state of Oaxaca and Mexico in general. If your time is severely limited, best buy from the good in town sources, many of which are recommended below.

If, on the other hand, you have the time to benefit (both because of lower prices and person-to-person contact with the artisans) by going to the villages, consult *The Valley of Oaxaca* chapter for sources of local village handicrafts.

TRADITIONAL MARKETS

The original town market, **Mercado Juárez**, covers the entire square block just one block south and one block west of the *zócalo*. Many dozens of stalls offer everything; cotton and wool items—such as dresses, *huipiles*, woven blankets, and serapes—are among the best buys. Despite the overwhelming festoons of merchandise, bargains are there for those willing to search them out.

Before diving into the Juárez market's cavernous interior, first orient yourself by looking over the lineup of stalls on the market's west side, along the block of 20 de Noviembre between Las Casas and Trujano. Here, you'll be able to select from a reasonably priced representative assortment—*alebrijes* (fanciful wooden animals), black and green pottery, cutlery, filigree jewelry, *huipiles*, leather goods, pewter, tinware—of much that Oaxaca offers.

After your Juárez market tour, walk a block west, to J. P. Garcia, and three and a half blocks south, between Mina and Zaragoza, for a look inside the **Mercado de Artesanías** (handicrafts market). Here, you'll find more of the same—a ton of textiles—*huipiles, camisas* (shirts), *blusas* (blouses), and *tapetes* (carpets), plus *alfarería* (pottery), *alebrijes*, and some for-tourist masks.

While you're south of the *zócalo*, head back up J. P. Garcia half a block and visit the unique private store El Arte Oaxaqueño (at Mina 317, corner of J. P. Garcia, tel. 951/516-1581, 10 A.M.–8 P.M. Mon.–Sat.). Their diverse, carefully selected offerings run from lovely wool weavings and bright one-of-a-kind pottery to fetching wooden toys and precious metalware Christmas ornaments. Each piece comes with a detailed explanation of its history and the craftsperson who made it.

PRIVATE HANDICRAFTS SHOPS

Although pricier, the private shops generally offer the choicest merchandise. Here you can select from the very best: *huipiles* from San Pedro de Amusgos and Yalalag, richly

© BRUCE WHIPPERMAN

the hand-embroidered "Oaxaca Wedding Dress" from San Antonino Castillo Velasco

embroidered "wedding" dresses from San Antonino Castillo Velasco, rugs and hangings from Teotitlán del Valle and Santa Ana del Valle, pottery (black from San Bartolo Coyotepec and green from Atzompa), carved *alebrijes* from Arrazola, whimsical figurines by the Aguilar sisters of Ocotlán, mescal from Tlacolula, and masks from Huazolotitlán.

Most of the best individual shops lie scattered along three streets—Cinco de Mayo, Macedonio Alcalá, and Garcia Vigil, which run uphill, north of the *zócalo*.

MARO

Somewhere along your handicrafts route, you must take a serious look around MARO, **Mujeres Artesanías de las Regiones de Oaxaca** (Craftswomen of the Regions of Oaxaca) (204 Cinco de Mayo, tel./fax 951/516-0670, 9 A.M.–8 P.M. daily). From behind the Cathedral, walk uphill, first passing Independencia; one block farther, at Morelos, turn right, continue a block and turn left and walk half a block uphill to MARO, on the right.

Here a remarkable all-Oaxaca grassroots movement of women artisans has gotten the government to pay the rent for a building, where they sell their goods and demonstrate their manufacturing techniques. The artisans are virtually pure native Mexicans from all parts of Oaxaca, and their offerings reflect their unique effort. Hosts of gorgeous handicrafts—wooden masks, toys, carvings; cotton *traje* (native clothing) such as *huipiles, pozahuancos, quechquémitles;* wool serapes, rugs, and hangings; woven palm hats, mats, and baskets; fine steel knives, swords, and machetes; tinplate mirrors, candlesticks, and ornaments; leather saddles, briefcases, wallets, and belts—fill the shelves of several rooms. Don't miss it; better still, do a major part of your Oaxaca shopping at this store.

Other Private Shops

From the *zócalo*, head north along the Alcalá pedestrian mall; just a block north of the Cathedral, you'll arrive at a Oaxaca favorite, the **Palacio de las Gemas** (corner of Morelos and Alcalá, tel. 951/514-4603, 10 A.M.–8 P.M. Mon.–Sat.). Although specializing in semiprecious stones and jewelry, it has much more, including a host of charming hand-painted tinware Christmas decorations, Guerrero masks, and pre-Columbian reproductions in onyx and turquoise.

Continue north on Alcalá a block and step into **La Mano Mágico** (on the west side, just below the corner of Murguia, at Alcalá 203, tel./fax 951/516-4275, 10:30 A.M.–3:00 P.M. and 4–8 P.M. Mon.–Sat.). The shop offers both a colorful exposition of crafts from all over Mexico and a patio workshop where artisans work, dyeing wool and weaving examples of the lovely, museum-quality rugs and serapes that adorn the walls.

Across the street, step into **Cuchillos Alcalá** (Alcalá 206, tel. 951/514-7943, 10 A.M.–8 P.M. Mon.–Sat.) for an interesting selection of cutlery—knives, swords, scissors—and much more from a longtime Oaxacan tradition.

Take a one-block detour west along Matamoros to **Casa de Artesanías** (Matamoros 105, corner of Vigil, tel. 951/516-5062,

9 A.M.–8 P.M. Mon.–Sat.). Here, a cooperative of about six dozen Oaxaca artisan families offers a wide handicrafts selection, including rainbows of fantastic *alebrijes,* from Tilcajete and Arrazola, a treasury of glistening black pottery from Coyotepec, and preciously embroidered dresses from San Antonio Castillo Velasco.

Return and continue uphill on Alcalá, a block farther north, to the **Plaza Alcalá** complex, southwest corner of M. Bravo, which has both an outstanding courtyard restaurant and some good shops. Best among them is an exceptional bookstore, **Librería Amate** (307 Alcal, tel. 951/516-6960, 951/516-7181, amatebooks@prodigy.net.mx, 10 A.M.–8 P.M.). Personable owner Henry Wangeman stocks an expertly selected library of English-language books about Mexico, including archaeology, cookbooks, ethnography, guides, history, literature, maps, postcards, and much more.

If you're interested in fine weavings, step directly across Alcalá to the **Tapetes de Teotitlán** shop (11 A.M.–7:30 P.M. Mon.–Sat., 1–7 P.M. Sun.) of the Martínez family of the famous Teotitlán del Valle weaving village (see *The Valley of Oaxaca* chapter). Here, you're looking at the real thing: fine, mostly traditional designs, made of all-natural dyes.

Half a block farther uphill, be sure to look inside **Oro de Monte Albán** jewelry store (Alcalá 403, tel. 951/514-3813, 10 A.M.–8 P.M. Mon.–Sat., noon–8 P.M. Sun.), across from the Iglesia de Santo Domingo. This extraordinary family-run enterprise carries on Oaxaca's venerable goldsmithing tradition as the sole licensed manufacturer of replicas from the renowned treasure of Monte Albán Tomb 7. Besides the luscious, museum-quality reproductions, Oro de Monte Albán offers a fine assortment of in-house silver and gold earrings, charm bracelets, necklaces, brooches, and much more.

While you're at Alcalá be sure to peruse the colorful outdoor displays of for-sale local paintings and native-style women's blouses, skirts, dresses *(blusas, enredos, vestidos)* and *huipiles* that decorate *Plaza Labastida* just south, across Abasolo, from the Santo Domingo church.

Rewards await shoppers who are willing to walk a few long blocks farther uphill to the state-run **IAO** (Instituto Oaxaqueño de las Artesanías) (Garcia Vigil 809, tel. 951/514-4030 or 951/514-0861, 9 A.M.–8 P.M. Mon.–Sat., 9 A.M.–5 P.M. Sun.). You can pick from a broad, authentic, and very traditional selection of carved animals, ceramics, *huipiles,* masks, tinware, wedding dresses, and much more. Prices vary: cheap on some items and high on others.

FINE ARTS GALLERIES

The tourist boom has stimulated a Oaxaca fine-arts revival. Several downtown galleries bloom with the sculpture and paintings of masters, such as Rufino Tamayo, Rudolfo Morales, Francisco Toledo, and a host of up-and-coming local artists. Besides La Mano Mágico, listed in the *Private Handicrafts Shops* section, a number of galleries stand out. Foremost among them is **Arte de Oaxaca** (Murguia 105, between Alcalá and Cinco de Mayo, tel. 951/514-0910, www.artedeoaxaca.com, 11 A.M.–3 P.M. and 5–8 P.M. Mon.–Fri., 11 A.M.–6 P.M. Sat.), the gallery of the Rudolfo Morales Foundation.

Also outstanding is **Galería Quetzalli** (Constitución 104, between Reforma and Cinco de Mayo, tel. 951/514-2606, fax 951/514-0735, www.quetzalli.com, 10 A.M.–2 P.M. and 5–8 P.M. Mon.–Sat.), local outlet for celebrated artist Francisco Toledo, opposite the south wall-flank of Iglesia de Santo Domingo.

Also well worth visiting is **Galería Arte Mexicano** (southwest corner of Alcalá and Allende, tel. 951/514-3815, 10 A.M.–8 P.M. Mon.–Sat., 11 A.M.–5 P.M. Sun.), in the Santo Domingo shopping complex, diagonally across Alcalá from the Iglesia de Santo Domingo.

For something unusual, go to **Galería Indigo** (Allende 104, corner of Alcalá, tel./fax 951/514-3889, galeriaindigoart@prodigy.net.mx, www.indigoarts.com, 11 A.M.–3 P.M. and 4:30–8 P.M. Mon.–Sat.), across from Iglesia de Santo Domingo. Inside, several spacious rooms contain dramatic displays of modern paintings and exquisite one-of-a-kind handicrafts, both traditional and innovative, from Mexico, Central America, and Asia.

Completely different but just as fascinating is the longtime coin, antique bric-a-brac, and art store **Monedas y Antiguidades** (Coins and Antiques, Abasolo 107, between the upper end of Cinco de Mayo and Reforma, tel. 951/516-3935, 11 A.M.–3 P.M. and 6–9 P.M. Mon.–Sat., noon–3 P.M. Sun.). Browsers enjoy a potpourri of art, from kitsch to fine, plus a for-sale museum of dusty curios, from old silver coins and pioneer clothes irons to revolutionary photos and Porfirian-era tubas.

CUTLERY AND METALWORK SHOPS

Oaxaca is well known for its fine metal crafts. A few families produce nearly everything, which at least three of them sell from their own shops. While in Mercado Juárez, stop by stall number 5 to see the fine swords, knives, and scissors of **Miguel Martínez** and family (tel. 951/514-4868, 9 A.M.–9 P.M. daily). Walk a few blocks west and south to see an even wider selection, plus artisans at work, at **Guillermo** Aragon's street-front shop (J. P. Garcia 503, tel. 951/516-2658, 9 A.M.–3 P.M. and 4–8 P.M. Mon.–Sat.).

GROCERIES, WINE, AND NATURAL FOOD

For fruits and vegetables, the cheapest and freshest are in the Juárez market, which takes up the square block immediately southwest of the *zócalo*.

For simpler, straightforward grocery shopping, plus the English *News* and a small selection of good wines, go to handily located **Abarrotes Lonja** (8 A.M.–9:30 P.M. daily), on the *zócalo*'s west side, next to La Cafetería café.

Local natural-food devotees get their heart's content of teas—arnica, anise, manzanilla—and ginseng, organic grains, granola, and soy burgers, two blocks west of the *zócalo* at **Tienda Naturista Trigo Verde** (J. P. Garcia 207, tel. 951/516-2369, 9 A.M.–9 P.M. Mon.–Sat., 9 A.M.–6 P.M. Sun.).

Information and Services

TOURIST INFORMATION

The state government maintains a good information office (Murguia 206, tel./fax 951/516-0123, 951/502-1200, info@aoaxaca.com, www.oaxaca.travel, 8 A.M.–8 P.M. daily) between Cinco de Mayo and Reforma, two blocks north and a block and a half east of the rear northerly corner of the cathedral.

Secretaría de Turismode Oaxaca (tel./fax 951/516-0123 or 951/502-1200) also maintains an information desk at their former location (now the Museum of Oaxacan Painters), at the north edge of the *zócalo*, half a block north of the cathedral-front, on Independencia, corner of Garcia Vigil.

PUBLICATIONS

One of the absolute best sources of English-language books about Mexico is the **Librería** **Amate** (on the ground floor of Plaza Alcalá, Alcalá 307, tel. 951/516-6960, fax 951/516-7181, amatebooks@prodigy.net.mx, www.amatebooks.com, 10 A.M.–8:30 P.M. Mon.–Sat., 2–7 P.M. Sun.), four blocks north of the *zócalo*.

Another good source is bookstore **Librería Universitaria** (Guerrero 104, tel. 951/516-4243, 9:30 A.M.–2 P.M. and 4–8 P.M. Mon.–Sat.), half a block east of the *zócalo*. It has English paperbacks, both used and new; a number of indigenous language dictionaries; and guides, cookbooks, art, and history books.

The interesting **Librería de Bibliofiles de Oaxaca** (Bibliophiles' Bookstore of Oaxaca, M. Alacalá 104, just downhill from Iglesia de Santo Domingo, tel. 951/516-9901, 10 A.M.–9 P.M. daily) offers a big collection of

© BRUCE WHIPPERMAN

A motorized tourist streetcar leaves for downtown tours.

new, mostly Spanish, books, but with a good number of art, crafts, archaeology, and cultural books in English.

Oaxaca's largest general book source (nearly completely in Spanish, however) is **Proveedora Escolar** (Scholar's Supplier, Independencia 1001, tel. 951/516-0489, fax 951/514-5655, 9 A.M.–8 P.M. Mon.–Sat.), which, as its name implies, is especially useful for those seeking a wealth of detailed historical, geographical, touristic, cultural, and archaeological information about Oaxaca. It's a cultural experience in itself to visit the place. The materials you'll probably most want to peruse are on the upper floors.

Pick up a copy of the daily English-language **News,** usually available late mornings, at the stand beneath the portal at the southwest corner of the *zócalo.*

Also, copies of the useful tourist newspapers, **Go-Oaxaca** and **Oaxaca Times** are available free at hotels, shops, travel agents, and the Oaxaca state tourist information office. If you can't locate a copy, contact the publishers:

Go-Oaxaca (Crespo 415, tel. 951/514-1102, www.go-oaxaca.com) and *Oaxaca Times* (Alcalá 307, upstairs, tel./fax 951/516-3443, www.oaxaca times). At their best, in season, the newspapers list local events, feature cultural and historical articles, have tourist hints, and advertise room and apartment rentals and bed-and-breakfast accommodations.

LIBRARIES

The city **biblioteca** (public library, corner of Morelos and Alcalá, tel. 951/516-5681, 9 A.M.–8:30 P.M. Mon.–Fri.), two blocks north of the *zócalo* in a lovingly restored former convent, is worth a visit, if only for its graceful, cloistered Renaissance interiors and patios.

Visitors starving for a good read will find satisfaction by borrowing at least one of the thousands of volumes at the **Oaxaca Lending Library** (Pino Suárez 519, tel. 951/518-7077, library@oaxlibrary.com, www.oaxlibrary.com, 10 A.M.–2 P.M. and 4–7 P.M. Mon.–Fri., 10 A.M.–7 P.M. Sat.), about five blocks north of the *zócalo* on the east side of El Llano park.

VOLUNTEER WORK AND DONATIONS

Local residents and visitors have bonded together to provide help for Oaxaca's street children and poor single-parent families. Their **Centro de Esperanza Infantile** (formerly Grassroots) organization (Crespo 308, tel. 951/501-1069, streetchildren@spersa oaxaca.com.mx, www.oaxacastreetchildren grassroots.org or www.shinealight.org/CEI .html, 9 A.M.–1 P.M. and 4–7 P.M. Mon.–Fri., 10 A.M.–3 P.M. Sat.) operates cooperatively out of its center about four blocks north, three blocks west of the zócalo.

The all-volunteer organization raises money for food, schoolbooks and uniforms, housing, foster care, and much more for homeless children and destitute single mothers and their children. They welcome donations and volunteers, and visitors are always welcome.

Outside of Oaxaca, you can send contributions: Mail checks, addressed and written to the order of Oaxaca Street Children Grassroots, to Donations, P.O. Box 29226, Brooklyn Center, MN 55429.

MONEY EXCHANGE

Several banks, all with ATMs, sprinkle the downtown area. (*Note:* Remove your ATM card promptly; some local machines are known to "eat" them if left in more than about 15 seconds after the transaction is finished.) The most convenient is **Banamex** (on Valdivieso directly behind the cathedral, 9 A.M.–4 P.M. Mon.–Fri.).

The best-bet, full-service bank is long-hours **HSBC** (one block north, one block east of the zócalo, corner of Guerrero and Armenta y López, tel. 951/516-9754, 8 A.M.–7 P.M. Mon.–Sat.).

A full-service **Banamex** branch (Hidalgo at Cinco de Mayo, tel. 951/516-5900, 9 A.M.–4 P.M. Mon.–Fri., 10 A.M.–2 P.M. Sat.), nearby, receives customers just one block due east of the zócalo. If Banamex is too crowded, go to HSBC or **Banco Serfin** (on the Independencia corner, north of the Cathedral, tel. 951/516-1100, 9 A.M.–4 P.M. Mon.–Fri., 10 A.M.–2 P.M. Sat.), U.S., Canadian, Japanese, and many European currencies and travelers checks changed; or Serfin's neighboring brother branch (three doors west, across Garcia Vigil, at Independencia 605, tel. 951/516-2526, 9 A.M.–4 P.M. Mon.–Fri., 10 A.M.–2 P.M. Sat.).

After bank hours, go to **Casa de Cambio Internacional de Divisas** (on the Alcalá pedestrian mall just north of the zócalo, behind the cathedral, tel. 951/516-3399, 9 A.M.–6 P.M. Mon.–Fri., 9 A.M.–5 P.M. Sat.). Although it may pay about a percent less than banks, it changes many major currencies and travelers checks.

TRAVEL AND TOUR AGENCIES AND GUIDES

Viajes Mexico Istmo and Caribe (one block northeast of the zócalo behind the cathedral at the corner of Valdivieso and Independencia, tel. 951/516-2700 or 951/516-2919, fax 951/516-7475, 9 A.M.–8 P.M. Mon.–Sat.) is a good source for most travel services, especially air tickets.

Other agencies are more experienced at tours. Among these are **Viajes Xochitlán** (M. Bravo 210A, tel. 951/514-3271 or 951/514-3628, fax 951/514-2556, oaxaca@xochitlan-tours.com.mx, www.xochitlan-tours.com.mx, 9 A.M.–2 P.M. and 4–7 P.M. Mon.–Sat.). Go in comfort to all and any Oaxaca City and Valley sites and villages, such as Monte Albán, Mitla, Teotitlán del Valle, Tlacolula, and much more. They specialize in individuals and groups, tourist and business services, and travel agent services, such as air and bus tickets and hotel bookings.

Another reliable, long-time travel and tour agent is **Viajes Turísticos Mitla** (at Hóstal Santa Rosa, Trujano 201, tel./fax 951/514-7800 or 951/514-7806, fax 951/514-3152), a block west of the zócalo's southwest corner. They offer many tours, including guide and transportation, for small- or medium-sized groups. Their main office is at the Hotel Rivera del Ángel (F. J. Mina 518, tel. 951/514-3152), three blocks west, three blocks south of the zócalo's southwest corner. They also provide very economical bus-only tourist transportation to a plethora of Valley of Oaxaca sites, with multiple daily departures to Monte Albán. For more information and reservations, contact the bus departure ticket desk at the Hotel Rivera del Ángel (tel. 951/516-6175).

A Oaxaca regiment of **private individual guides** also offer tours. Among the most highly recommended is English-fluent **Juan Montes Lara** (Prol. de Eucaliptos 303, Colonia Reforma, tel./fax 951/513-0126, jmonteslara@ yahoo.com, $25/hour), backed up by his wife Karin Schutte. Besides cultural sensitivity and extensive local knowledge, Juan and Karin also provide comfortable transportation in a GMC Suburban wagon.

Moreover, satisfied customers give guide **Sebastian Chino Peña** rave reviews for his guided tours ($20/hour) anywhere you would like in the city or Valley of Oaxaca. Contact him in town (cell 044-951/508-1220) or email him (sebastian_oaxaca@hotmail.com).

More athletic travelers might enjoy the services of **Zona Bici** (Garcia Vigil 409C, tel. 951/516-0953, boccaletti@prodigy.net.mx), five blocks due north of the *zócalo*, which rents bikes and also conducts bike tours into the countryside.

For even more extensive backcountry adventure bicycling, hiking, and camping in the mountains on the pine-scented crest just north of the Valley of Oaxaca (see the *Northern Oaxaca* chapter), contact **Expediciones Sierra Norte** (M. Bravo 210, tel./fax 951/514-8271, sierran-orte@oaxaca.com, www.sierranorte.org.mx).

For other more diversified and farther-ranging guide and tour recommendations, see *Getting Around* in *The Valley of Oaxaca* chapter. Also, you might inquire for a guide recommendation at the state tourist information office (Murguia 206, tel./fax 951/516-0123, 951/502-1200, info@aoaxaca.com, www.oaxaca.travel, 8 A.M.–8 P.M. daily).

CAR RENTALS

Car rentals offer another convenient means of exploring Oaxaca City and environs. Although town and valley roads present no unusual hazards, drive defensively, anticipate danger, and keep a light foot on the accelerator. Also be aware that road hazards—animals, people,

potholes, barricades, rocks—are much more formidable at night.

To rent a car, all you need is a current driver's license and a credit card. However, car rentals, which by law must include adequate Mexican liability insurance, are expensive, running upward of $40 per day. Save *mucho dinero* by splitting the tariff with others.

Get your rental through either a travel agent or, before departure, through U.S. and Canadian toll-free car rental numbers, or in Oaxaca locally: **Hertz** (at Labastida 115, tel. 951/516-2434, 951/516-8268, hertz_oax@ hotmail.com), **Alamo** (at Cinco de Mayo 203, tel./fax 951/514-8534, fax 951/514-8686, oax-alamo@hotmail.com), and **Europcar** (at airport, tel./fax 951/143-8340, and at Labastida 104, tel. 951/516-9305, or toll-free Mex. tel. 800/201-3333, www.europcar.com.mx).

COMMUNICATIONS

The Oaxaca *correo* (post office, tel. 951/516-1291, 8 A.M.–7 P.M. Mon.–Fri., 10 A.M.–5 P.M. Sat.) is across from the cathedral at the corner of the Alameda de León square and Independencia. The **telecomunicaciones** offers money orders, telephone, and public fax (a block west, at the corner of Independencia and 20 Noviembre, tel. 951/516-4902, 8 A.M.–7:30 P.M. Mon.–Fri., 9 A.M.–4 P.M. Sat., 9 A.M.–noon Sun.).

For long-distance and local telephone service, buy a Ladatel phone card (widely available in stores; look for the yellow Ladatel sign) and use it in public street telephones.

Answer your email and access the Internet at any one of a number of spots around the *zócalo*. For example, try the small shop behind the cathedral (Valdevieso 120, tel. 951/514-9227, 9 A.M.–11 P.M. daily).

HEALTH AND EMERGENCIES

If you get sick, ask your hotel desk to recommend a doctor. Otherwise, go to the 24-hour **Clinica Hospital Carmen** (Abasolo 215, tel./ fax 951/516-0027), staffed by English-speaking IAMAT Doctors Horacio Tenorio S. and Germán Tenorio V.

For routine medicines and drugs, go to one of many pharmacies, such as the **Farmacias Ahorro** (on Cinco de Mayo, near the northeast corner of Murguia, one block east, two blocks north of the cathedral, 7 A.M.–11 P.M. daily). After hours, call Farmacia Ahorros's free 24-hour delivery service (951/515-5000).

For fire or police emergencies, call the emergency number 060, or get a taxi to the municipal police station *policia municipal* (tel. 951/516-0455), or call the firefighters *(bomberos)* (tel. 951/506-0248).

CONSULATES AND IMMIGRATION

The **U.S. consular agent** (Alcalá 407, tel. 951/514-3054 or 951/518-2853, fax 951/516-2701, 10 A.M.–3 P.M. Mon.–Fri.) is upstairs at Plaza Santo Domingo, across from the Santo Domingo church. The **Canadian Consul** (700 Pino Suárez, local 11B, tel. 951/513-3777, fax 951/515-2147, 11 A.M.–2 P.M. Mon.–Fri.) does the same for Canadian citizens. In an emergency, call the Canadian Embassy in Mexico City (toll-free Mex. tel. 800/706-2900).

Other consuls that may be available in Oaxaca are the **Italian** (Alcalá 400, tel. 951/516-5058) and the **Spanish** (Porfirio Díaz 340, tel. 951/515-3525 or 951/518-0031). For more information, look for consulate contact numbers in the *Oaxaca Times* or the telephone directory Yellow Pages, under *Embajadas, Legaciones, y Consulados,* or call the U.S. or Canadian Consuls above for information.

If you lose your tourist permit, make arrangements with **Migración** at least several hours before your scheduled departure from Mexico. Take proof of arrival date in Mexico—stamped passport, airline ticket, or copy of the lost permit—to the airport Migración (tel. 951/511-5733).

LANGUAGE INSTRUCTION AND COURSES

A long list of satisfied clients attests to the competence of the language instruction of the **Instituto Cultural de Oaxaca** (at the north-side corner of Niños Héroes/Hwy. 190 and Juárez, tel. 951/515-3404, fax 951/515-3728, info@icomexico.com, www.icomexico.com), in a lovely garden campus.

Also very highly recommended is the **Becari Language School** (N. Bravo 210, tel./fax 951/514-6076, becarioax@prodigy.net.mx, becari@becari.com.mx, www.becari.com.mx). Offerings include small-group Spanish instruction, as well as cooking and dancing classes. If you desire, the school can arrange homestays with local families.

Similarly experienced is the **Vinigulaza Language and Tradition** (Vinigulaza Idioma y Tradición) school (Abasolo 503, corner of Los Libres, about six blocks east, four blocks north of the plaza, tel. 951/513-2763, info@vinigulaza.com, www.vinigulaza.com), associated with the local English-language Cambridge Academy. Offerings include informative (and even fun) small-group Spanish instruction. Schedules are flexible, and prices are reasonable.

Alternatively, for more lightweight instruction, try **Español Interactivo** (Interactive Spanish, Armenta y López 311B, tel./fax 951/514-6062, spanishmaestra@yahoo.com, www.studyspanishinoaxaca.com), one block east and half a block south of the *zócalo,* by Iglesia de San Agustín. The school offers several levels that provide, respectively, 15–40 instructional hours per week. Classes have a maximum of five students.

All the language schools also arrange **homestays** with Oaxaca families and often offer classes in folkloric and salsa dancing, weaving, and painting on clay and wood.

Inexpensive Spanish instruction is customarily available from volunteers at the **Oaxaca Lending Library** (Pino Suárez 519, tel. 951/518-7077, library@oaxlibrary.com, www.oaxlibrary.com), about five blocks north of the *zócalo* on the east side of El Llano park.

OAXACAN COOKING AND CULTURE

Susana Trilling, Oaxaca resident and author of *My Search for the Seventh Mole* (as in MOH-lay), offers an unusual mix of Oaxacan culture, cooking, and eating, with a lodging option, at her **Seasons of My Heart** cooking school (Rancho Aurora, tel./fax 951/518-7726, local cell 044-951/508-0469 or 044-951/508-0044, long-distance 951/504-0469 or 951/508-0044, info@seasonsofmyheart.com, www.seasonsof myheart.com) in the Etla Valley, north of the city. Susana's simplest offering is a one-day cooking adventure, including a morning trip to a local native market to buy food, then preparing and eating later at Susana's ranch. Other options are a long Thursday–Tuesday cooking and cultural adventure, or an extended one-week version of the same thing. Farther-ranging cooking excursions regularly include outlying parts of Oaxaca, such as the Isthmus of Tehuántepec or northern Oaxaca, around Tuxtepec.

PHOTOGRAPHY

Downtown has some good photo shops, most on 20 de Noviembre, a block west of the *zócalo*. Best of all is **Oaxakolor** (20 de Noviembre 108, tel. 951/516-3487, 9 A.M.–9 P.M. Mon.–Sat.), perhaps the best-stocked photo store in Oaxaca. It carries dozens of cameras—digital

point-and-shoot, SLRs, professional medium format—as well as an abundance of film, a host of digital accessories and professional color, slides, sheet, black and white film.

More ordinary, but still well stocked, is **Foto Figueroa** (Hidalgo 516, corner 20 de Noviembre, tel. 951/516-3766, 9 A.M.–8 P.M. Mon.–Sat.). With plenty of Kodak digital and film accessories, it offers quick digital and develop-and-print service.

Half a block farther down, **Express Kolor** (20 de Noviembre 225, tel. 951/516-1492, 9 A.M.–8 P.M. Mon.–Sat.) is better stocked, with scores of point-and-shoot digital and film cameras and many Minolta, Vivitar, and Olympus accessories. It also stocks Konica, Fuji, Kodak, and Agfa films in color and black and white, both roll and sheet.

LAUNDRY

Get your laundry done at conveniently located **Super Lavandería** (at the corner of Hidalgo and J. P. Garcia, tel. 951/514-1181, 8 A.M.–8 P.M. daily), two blocks west of the *zócalo*'s northwest corner.

Getting There and Away

BY AIR

The Oaxaca airport (code-designated OAX) has several daily flights that connect with Mexico City and other Mexican and international destinations. Many of the Mexico City flights allow same-day connections between Oaxaca and many U.S. gateways.

Continental Airlines (toll-free Mex. tel. 800/900-5000) fortunately has eliminated the oft-difficult stop in Mexico City en route to Oaxaca and now flies nonstop to and from Houston daily (flight time only 2.5 hours).

Mexicana Airlines (toll-free Mex. reservations and flight information tel. 800/502-2000 and 800/801-2010, local reservations and information tel. 951/516-8414 and 951/516-7352) flights connect a number of times daily with Mexico City.

Aeroméxico (reservations tel. 951/516-1066, 951/516-7101, 951/516-3765, flight information tel. 951/511-5055, 951/511-5044) flights also connect daily with Mexico City.

Mexicana Airlines affiliate **Click** (reservations tel. 800/125-5425, in addition to the Mexicana numbers above) flights connect with Mexico City and eastern destinations of Tuxtla Gutiérrez, Villahermosa, Mérida, Cancún, and Puerto Escondido.

Aviacsa Airlines (information and reservations tel. 951/518-4555 or 951/518-4556, toll-free Mex. tel. 800/006-2200, toll-free in Oaxaca tel. 800/284-2272, flight information tel. 951/511-5039) connects with Mexico City and Tijuana via Mexico City, and also with Acapulco, continuing to Hermosillo and Tijuana.

Azteca Airlines (reservations tel. 951/501-0190, 951/501-0192) flights connect directly with Tijuana via Mexico City and Guadalajara.

Alma Airlines (reservations toll-free Mex. tel. 800/800-2562, local tel. 951/143-8601, www.alma.com.mx) connect with Guadalajara, Tuxtla Gutiérrez, and Mérida.

Avolar Airlines (reservations toll-free Mex. tel. 800/212-8052, www.avolar.com.mx) flights connect with Guadalajara, Tijuana, and Cuernavaca.

Alternatively, light charter airlines (in the general aviation terminal, the building to the right as you face the main terminal) connect Oaxaca City with various points within Oaxaca. **Aerotucan** (Alcalá 201, upper floor, suite 204, tel. 951/501-0530, toll-free outside Oaxaca Mex. tel. 800/640-4148, infor@aerotucan.com.mx, www.aerotucan.com.mx) regularly connects Oaxaca City with Puerto Escondido, Huatulco, Tuxtla Gutiérrez, and Puebla.

From the same general aviation terminal, **Aerovega** (tel. 951/516-2777), the dependable local air-taxi service, routinely connects Oaxaca City with Puerto Escondido and Huatulco.

The Oaxaca airport provides a modicum of services, such as a good upstairs restaurant with a view; several shops; an international newsstand with magazines and paperback novels; car rentals; a mailbox *buzó* (downstairs by the staircase to the restaurant); and ATMs downstairs.

Arrival transportation for the six-mile (10-km) trip into town is easy. Buy tickets at the booth at the far right end of the terminal as you exit. Fixed-fare *colectivo* (shared taxi) tickets run about $3.50 per person for downtown ($7 to north-side Hotels Misión de los Angeles, Fortín Plaza, and Victoria). For the same trip, a *taxi especial* (private taxi) ticket runs about $15 for four persons; larger GMC Suburbans cost $28 for up to 8 persons. No public buses run between the airport and town.

Car rental agents stationed regularly at the Oaxaca airport are: Hertz (tel. 951/516-8268, hertz_oax@hotmail.com), Alamo (tel./fax 951/514-8534, fax 951/514-8686, oax-alamo@hotmail.com), and Europcar (tel. 951/516-8258, www.europcar.com.mx).

For **departure,** save taxi money by getting your *colectivo* airport transportation ticket ahead of time, at **Transportacion Terrestres** (on the west side of Plaza Alameda de León, across from the cathedral, tel. 951/514-4350, 9 A.M.–2 P.M. and 5–8 P.M. Mon.–Sat.).

Furthermore, keep enough dollars or pesos for your $12 international departure tax (which may be collected in Mexico City) if your air ticket doesn't already cover it. If you lose your tourist permit, take proof of arrival date in Mexico, such as a stamped passport, airline ticket, or copy of lost permit, to airport **Migración** (tel. 951/511-5733, 9 A.M.–1 P.M. Mon.–Fri.) a minimum of several hours prior to departure from Mexico.

BY CAR OR RV

Paved (but long, winding, and sometimes potholed) roads connect Oaxaca City with all regions of Oaxaca and neighboring states.

Four alternative routes connect Oaxaca City south with the Pacific coast: Two of them, via Highways 175 and 131, connect directly south over the super-scenic but rugged Sierra Madre del Sur. Especially during the June–October rainy season, travelers are subject to landslides and bridge washout delays. The longer but less rugged (and more dependable in rainy weather) route connects via Highway 190 southeast with Tehuántepec, thence Pacific coast Highway 200 west. The fourth route, also less direct, but still rugged and winding, connects west via Highway 190, thence south with the Pacific coast, via Highway 125.

Narrow national **Highway 175** connects along 148 winding, sometimes potholed miles (238 km) with its junction with coast Highway 200 at Pochutla (thence six miles/10 km to Puerto Ángel). The road climbs to more than 9,000 feet (2,700 meters) through winter-chilly pine forests and indigenous Chatino and Zapotec villages. Fill up with gas at the last-chance Pemex in Mihuatlán heading south and at Pochutla (north edge of town) heading north; carry water and blankets and be prepared for emergencies. Under dry, daylight conditions, count on about seven hours at the wheel if heading south from Oaxaca to Puerto Ángel, or about eight hours in the opposite direction.

About the same is true for the paved **National Highway 131** route south from Oaxaca, which splits off of Highway 175 two miles (three km) south of San Bartolo Coyotepec. On your way out of town, fill up with gasoline at the Oaxaca airport Pemex. Continue, via Zimatlán and Sola de Vega (fill up with gas again), over the pine-clad Pacific crest, a total of 158 miles (254 km) to Puerto Escondido. Under dry, daylight conditions, allow about seven hours southbound, or about eight hours in the opposite direction. Unleaded gasoline is regularly available mid-route at the Sola de Vega Pemex only.

Highway 190 connects Oaxaca City southeast with Tehuántepec, along 155 miles (250 km) of well-maintained but winding highway. Allow about 4.5 hours to Tehuántepec (downhill), or five hours in the opposite direction.

At Tehuántepec, connect west with Highway 200, via Salina Cruz, to the Oaxaca Pacific coast, and Bahías de Huatulco (100 miles/161 km, three hours), Pochutla–Puerto Ángel (124 miles/200 km, four hours), and Puerto Escondido (170 miles/274 km, five hours) via a paved, lightly traveled but secure highway.

The very long 229-mile (368-km) **Highway 190-Highway 125** route connects Oaxaca southwest with coastal Pinotepa Nacional, via the Mixtec country destinations of Yanhuitlán, Teposcolula, and Tlaxiaco. Although winding most of the way, the generally uncongested road is safely drivable (subject to some potholes, however) from Oaxaca in about nine driving hours if you use the *cuota autopista* northwest of Oaxaca City (exit to old Highway 190 at Nochixtlán). Add an hour for the 7,000-foot (2,100-meter) climb in the opposite direction.

The 350-mile (564-km) winding

Highway 190-Highway 160 from Oaxaca to Cuernavaca, Morelos, and Mexico City via Huajuapan de León requires a very long day, or better two days for safety. Under the best of conditions, the Mexico City–Oaxaca driving time runs 11 hours either way. Take it easy and stop overnight en route. (Make sure you arrive in Mexico City on a day when your car is permitted to enter. See the sidebar *Mexico City Driving Restrictions* in the *Essentials* chapter.)

Alternatively, you can cut your Mexico City–Oaxaca driving time significantly via the Mexico City–Puebla–Oaxaca *autopista*, combined 150D-131D, which, southbound, takes off from the southeast end of Mexico City's Calzada General Ignacio Zaragoza. Northbound, follow the signs on Highway 190 a few miles north of Oaxaca. Allow about six hours driving time at a steady 60 mph (about 100 kph). Tolls, which are worth it for the increased speed and safety, run about $30 for a car, much more for a big RV.

BY VAN

Eight-to-sixteen-passenger vans, although less comfortable than first-class buses, provide faster service (at about the same price). They are becoming increasingly popular for medium-distance connections, especially for Pacific coast destinations of Pochutla–Puerto Ángel and northwest destinations in the Mixteca.

At least two operators provide Oaxaca–Pochutla connections, from stations about one block east, three blocks south of the *zócalo*'s southeast corner. The first option is **Eclipse 70,** which departs about every half hour during the day from Armenta y López 540 (tel. 951/516-1068, Pochutla $12). Alternatively, around the second left downhill corner, you can ride **Atlántida** (Noria 101, tel. 951/514-7077) every two hours for the same price.

The northwest (Nochixtlan, Teposcolula, Tlaxiaco, Putla) van connection is **Excelencia** (Díaz Ordaz 305, tel. 951/516-3578), three blocks west, one block south, from the *zócalo*'s southwest corner.

BY BUS
Luxury and First Class

In contrast to vans, buses are much more comfortable and remain a popular option, especially for longer trips. Omnibus Cristóbal Colón and Autobuses del Oriente, Oaxaca's major luxury- and first-class carriers and their associated minor carriers, operate out of their shiny new terminal on Highway 190 (Calz. Héroes de Chapultepec 1036, at Carranza, on the north side of town). All bus lines accept credit cards and are bookable via the information and reservation line (toll-free Mex. tel. 800/702-8000). At the terminal, passengers enjoy a squad of public telephones out front, snack stands, luggage lockers, and cool, refined Restaurant Colibri across the street.

Moreover, all of the carriers that use the Héroes de Chapultepec terminal cooperate through the joint agency **Ticket Bus,** which sells tickets at two town-center offices: one a block west of the *zócalo* (20 de Noviembre 103D, tel. 951/514-6655, toll-free Mex. tel. 800/702-8000, www.ticketbus.com.mx), and the other behind the Cathedral (corner of Independencia, tel. 951/502-0560, www.ticketbus.com.mx). Both are open 8 A.M.–10 P.M. Monday–Saturday and 8 A.M.–9 P.M. Sunday.

Omnibuses Cristóbal Colón (OCC) offers service to most major Oaxaca destinations. Buses connect northwest with Mixteca destinations of Nochixtlán, Tamazulapan, and Huajuapan de León, continuing to Puebla and Mexico City. Westerly, they connect with the Mixteca Alta, via Teposcolula, Tlaxiaco, Juxtlahuaca, and Putla de Guerrero. Southerly they connect (via the surer, but long, Isthmus route) via Salina Cruz, with Huatulco, Pochutla–Puerto Ángel, and Puerto Escondido; southeasterly with Tehuántepec, Tuxtla Gutiérrez, and Tapachula; and northerly with Villahermosa.

Autobuses del Oriente (ADO) offers limited Oaxaca connections, mostly along the Highway 190 corridor, connecting northwest with Mexico City (Tapo Tasqueña and Norte stations), via Nochixtlán and Huajuapan de León, and southeast with Tehuántepec and Salina Cruz. Other departures connect northwest with Veracruz, Coatzacoalcos, Villahermosa, Palenque, and Mérida.

Regional **Cuenca** buses connect with northern Oaxaca points along Highway 175, including Ixtlán de Juárez, Valle Nacional, Tuxtepec, and Tierra Blanca, continuing all the way to Veracruz.

Sur departures connect with Mexico City Tapo station, along old Highways 190 and 160, via Huajuapan de León, Izucar de Matamoros, Puebla, and Cuatla, Morelos.

Autobuses Unidos (AU) departures connect with Mexico City along the fast *autopista* expressway via Nochixtlán, Coixtlahuaca, and Puebla; or along the old Highway 131 via Cuicatlán, Teotitlán del Camino, Tehuacán, and Puebla.

Second Class

A swarm of long-distance second-class buses runs from the **camionera central segunda clase** southwest of downtown, just north of the Abastos market. Get there by taxi or by walking due west about eight blocks from the *zócalo* to the west end of Calle Las Casas. Take care crossing the busy *periférico* straight across the railroad tracks. Keep walking the same direction, along the four-lane street for two more blocks, to the terminal gate on the right. Inside, you'll find an orderly array of snack stalls, a cafeteria, luggage lockers, a long-distance telephone and fax, and a lineup of *taquillas* (ticket booths).

With one exception (see the last paragraph of this section) all ticket booths line up along the terminal to your left as you enter. **Fletes y Pasajes** (tel. 951/516-2270) dominates the terminal, with three separate ticket booths. All three Fletes y Pasajes booths sell tickets to most of their destinations. They offer very broad second-class service, connecting with nearly everywhere in Oaxaca except north: westerly, with Mixteca destinations of Nochixtlán, Tamazulapan, Huajuapan, and Tlaxiaco, connecting all the way via Highway 125 to Pinotepa Nacional on the coast; easterly, with Mitla and Mixe destinations of Ayutla, Zacatepec, and

Juquila Mixes; and southeasterly, with Isthmus destinations of Tehuántepec, Juchitán, and Salina Cruz. Besides all of the above, Fletes y Pasajes offers luxury-class "super" expressway connections with Mexico City.

In approximate consecutive order, moving left from the entrance, first find **Transportes Oaxaca Istmo** (tel. 951/516-3664). Departures connect with dozens of destinations east and south. These include the east Valley of Oaxaca destinations of Tlacolula and Mitla, continuing to the Isthmus destinations of Tehuántepec, Juchitán, and Salina Cruz. From Tehuántepec and Salina Cruz, they connect west, with Pacific coast destinations of Huatulco, Pochutla–Puerto Ángel, and Puerto Escondido.

Cooperating **Auto Transportes Oaxaca-Pacífico** (tel. 951/516-2908) and **Autobuses Estrella del Valle** travel the Highway 175 north–south route between Oaxaca and Pochutla–Puerto Ángel. Both lines continue, connecting along east–west coastal Highway 200 with Bahías de Huatulco, Puerto Escondido, and Pinotepa Nacional.

Estrella Roja del Sureste and **Trans Sol** (with some first-class) buses, tel. 951/516-0694,

connect directly with Puerto Escondido along Highway 131 north-south via Sola de Vega (with side trip to Juquila pilgrimage shrine). From Puerto Escondido, you can make coastal connections with Pochutla–Puerto Ángel, Bahías de Huatulco, Jamiltepec, and Pinotepa Nacional.

Several other semi-local lines connect mostly with Valley of Oaxaca points: **Choferes del Sur,** with the northwest Valley of Oaxaca, ranging from San Felipe del Agua north of the city to Etla northwest; **Autobuses de Oaxaca** connects south with Cuilapan and Zaachila; and **Sociedad Cooperativa Valle del Norte** connects west with Teotitlán del Valle and Tlacolula. Finally, if you hanker for a long, sometimes rough but scenic back-roads adventure, ride **Flecha de Zempoaltépetl** northeast to the remote Zapotec mountain native market towns of Villa Alta and Yalalag, via Tlacolula and Cuajimoloyas.

Finally, to the right of the entrance as you enter, **Pasajeros Benito Juárez** buses climb the mountains edging the Valley of Oaxaca's north side to the cool, pine-shadowed mountain-top communities of Benito Juárez and Cuajimoloyas (koo-ah-hee-moh-LO-yahs).

THE VALLEY OF OAXACA

The riches, both cultural and economic, of the city of Oaxaca flow largely from its surrounding hinterland, the Valley of Oaxaca, a mountain-rimmed patchwork expanse of fertile summer-green (and winter dry) fields, pastures, villages, and reed-lined rivers and streams. By far Oaxaca's largest valley, both in size and population, with an aggregate population of about half that of the central city, the Valley of Oaxaca consists of three subvalleys—the Valley of Tlacolula, the Valley of Ocotlán, and the Valley of Etla—that each extend, respectively, about 30 miles east, south, and northeast of Oaxaca City.

The Valley of Oaxaca is unique in a number of ways. Most importantly, the inhabitants are nearly all indigenous Zapotec-speaking people. You will often brush shoulders with them, especially in the big markets in Tlacolula,

Ocotlán, Zaachila, and Etla. The women traditionally dress in attractive bright skirts and blouses, with their hair done up in colorful ribbon-decorated braids. Although only a fraction of them speak fluent Spanish, they will nearly always understand and appreciate a smile and friendly *"buenos dias"* or *"buenas tardes."*

The Valley of Oaxaca's vibrant and prosperous native presence flows from a fortunate turn of history. During the mid-1800s, Mexico's Laws of the Reform forced the sale of nearly all church lands throughout the country. In most parts of Mexico, rich Mexicans and foreigners bought up much of these holdings, but in Oaxaca, isolated in Mexico's far southern region, there were few rich buyers, so the land was bought at very low prices by the local people, most of them indigenous farmers. Moreover, after the Revolution

HIGHLIGHTS

◖ **Santa María del Tule:** Townsfolk have literally built their town around their gigantic beloved El Tule tree, a cousin of the giant red wood trees of California (page 82).

◖ **Teotitlán del Valle:** Fine wool carpets and hangings, known locally as *tapetes*, are the prized product of dozens of local family work-shop-stores (page 84).

◖ **Mitla:** Explore the monumental plazas and columned buildings, handsomely adorned by a treasury of painstakingly placed *greca* (Grecian-like) stone fretwork (page 90).

◖ **San Bartolo Coyotepec:** A small city of roadside home-workshops and an unmissable museum display the famously pearly-black pottery pioneered by celebrated potter Doña Rosa a generation ago (page 95).

◖ **Zaachila:** Its monumental archaeological zone and riotously colorful *tianguis* make Zaachila a Thursday destination of choice in Oaxaca (page 105).

◖ **Monte Albán:** Any day is a good day to visit this, Mesoamerica's earliest true metrop-olis, which to some still seems to rule from its majestic mountain-top throne (page 107).

◖ **San José El Mogote:** Its regal recon-structed pyramids and plazas and the unfor-gettably red *diablo enchilado* displayed in its community museum, plus the neighboring Etla market, make San José El Mogote a worthwhile Wednesday out-of-town excursion (page 114).

LOOK FOR ◖ TO FIND RECOMMENDED SIGHTS, ACTIVITIES, DINING, AND LODGING.

of 1910–1917, progressive federal-government land-reform policies awarded many millions of acres of land to *campesino* communities, notably to Oaxaca Valley towns Teotitlán del Valle and Santa Ana del Valle, whose residents now hus-band many thousand acres of rich valley fields and foothill forests.

Although the grand monuments, fascinat-ing museums, good restaurants, and invit-ing handicrafts shops of Oaxaca City alone would be sufficient, a visit to Oaxaca is dou-bly rich because of the manifold wonders of the surrounding Valley of Oaxaca. The must-see highlights of the valley are the timeless Mitla and Monte Albán archaeological sites and the fetching crafts—wool weavings, pearly black pottery, floral-embroidered blouses and dresses, and *alebrijes* (wood-carved animals). You could spend a week or more of your time touring the Valley of Oaxaca, and all the sights are easily accessible from your base in Oaxaca City.

You can even let the valley's *tianguis* (lit-erally, "shade awnings" and synonymous with "native markets") guide you along your

THE VALLEY OF OAXACA

To Yalalag and Villa Alta

To Hierve el Agua and Ayutla

To Tehuantepec and Bahías de Huatulco

To Ixtlán de Juárez and Tuxtepec

Yavesia

Las Vigas

El Llano

San Miguel del Valle

Díaz Ordaz

MITLA

Mitla

190

Amatlán

Lachatao

Cuajimoloyas

Benito Juárez

Santa Ana del Valle

Lambityeco

Yagul

San Lucas Quiaviní

TEOTITLÁN DEL VALLE

EL PATIO

Tlacolula

San Bartolomé Quialana

Cerro Piedra del Sol 2,850m

Latuvi

Maculxóchitl

Dainzu

Guelavia

San Marcos Tlapazola

Santa Catarina Ixtepeji

La Cumbre

175

Lachigolo

Tlacochahuaya

San Sebastián Abasolo

Santa Cruz Papalutla

Guelaxe

San Juan Teitipac

Santo Tomás Jalieza

To Ejutla and Puerto Ángel

Cerro San Felipe 3,250m

San Andrés Huayapan

SANTA MARÍA DEL TULE

Rojas de Cuauhtémoc

OAXACA SPORTS (TENNIS, GYM, POOL)

SAN BARTOLO COYOTEPEC

San Sebastián Teitipac

Ocotlán

Ánimas Trujano

175

San Martín Tilcajete

San Antonino Castillo Velasco

OAXACA

CLUB BRENAMIEL (GOLF, TENNIS)

Cacaotepec

(TOLL)

COCHINEAL FARM

ZAACHILA

Huixtepec

131

To Nochixtlán, Huajuapan, and Mexico City

Suchilquitongo

Etla

San Antonio

Santa María Atzompa

MONTE ALBÁN

Monte Albán

Arrazola

Cuilapan de Guerrero

Zimatlán

135 190

Río Atoyac

SAN JOSÉ EL MOGOTE

Soledad Etla

Tejalapan

Jalapa del Valle

Santa Ines del Monte

Río San Bernardo

San Pablo Huitzo

135 D

To Nochixtlán, Coixtlahuaca, Puebla, and Mexico City

To Sola de Vega, Juquila, and Puerto Escondido

0   5 mi
0   5 km

© AVALON TRAVEL

excursion path. Along the way, beneath the shadowed market canopies and the shops of Oaxaca's welcoming local people, you can look, choose, and perhaps bargain for the wonderful handicrafts that travelers from all over the world come to the Valley of Oaxaca to buy.

PLANNING YOUR TIME

If your time is limited, your enviable task is to pick, according to your own interests, the best of the best from the Valley of Oaxaca's treasury of colorful markets, bucolic handicrafts villages, mysterious archaeological sights, and community museums. In a whirlwind four or five days, you can soak in the valley's celebrated highlights, scheduling your time according to the weekly market days.

Given the limited hotel choices in the Valley of Oaxaca and the relatively short distances (10–30 miles/16–48 km) to valley sights from Oaxaca City, you could use your lodging in the city as a home base and take excursions from there to explore the valley.

For transportation, you could hire a guide for about $150–300 per day, which includes a car for 4–5 people; rent a car for around $50 per day ($250 per week); or use the tourist bus transportation for $10–15 per person. Each option can get you to most of the valley's high lights over three or four days. Although touring by local buses from the second-class bus station (Camionera Central Segunda Clase) is much cheaper, it requires twice the time.

Some sights you won't want to miss are the archaeological sites **Mitla,** on the east side, and **Monte Albán,** on the southwest side of the valley. Of the markets, the biggest are the **Tlacolula** Sunday market, the **Ocotlán** Friday market, and the **Zaachila** Thursday market. Fascinating crafts villages along the way are **Teotitlán del Valle** (on the way to Tlacolula and Mitla); Santo Tomás Jalieza, San Martín Tilcajete, and **San Bartolo Coyotepec** (on the way back to Oaxaca City from Ocotlán); and the Santa María Atzompa pottery village on the way to or from Monte Albán.

If your time is very limited, you could skip the Tlacolula market, but make sure to visit the Thursday market in **Zaachila,** unbeatable for its intensely colorful ambience and exotic fruits and foods. Nearby, be sure to include the Zaachila archaeological site in your visit.

On the other hand, if you have an extra day, it would be worthwhile to visit the **San José El Mogote** archaeological site and the adjacent community museum. Continue to the **Etla** market, especially good on Wednesdays.

GETTING AROUND
Buses and Rental Cars

Droves of buses from the west-side Abastos *camionera central segunda clase* (second-class bus terminal) run everywhere in the Valley of Oaxaca and beyond. Arrive early any day and you could cover most major valley destinations in about a week that way: two days east (Teotitlán, Tlacolula, Mitla), two days south (crafts villages, Ocotlán market), two days southwest and west (Zaachila market and archaeological site, Cuilapan, Arrazola, Monte Albán, and Atzompa), and one day northwest (Etla market and San José El Mogote). For second-class bus destination details, see *By Bus* in the *Getting There and Away* section of the *Oaxaca City* chapter.

Get to the second-class bus terminal by walking one block south from the *zócalo*'s southwest corner, turn right at Las Casas, and keep walking about seven blocks. With caution, cross the *periférico*. The big terminal is two blocks farther, on the right.

More leisurely options would be to rent a car or take a tourist bus, or both. Get your car rental through either a travel agent or U.S. and Canadian toll-free car rental number before you leave home, or in Oaxaca locally: **Hertz** (tel. 951/516-2434, fax 951/516-0009, hertz_oax@hotmail.com), **Alamo** (tel. 951/514-8534, fax 951/514-8686, oaxalamo@hotmail.com), and **Europcar** (tel./fax 951/143-8340, tel. 951/516-9305, toll-free Mex. tel. 800/201-3333, www.europcar.com.mx).

For tourist buses, a good bet is to go with **Viajes Turísticos Mitla,** which offers economical tourist bus transportation to a number of

Valley of Oaxaca sites, with multiple daily departures to Monte Albán. For more information and reservations, contact the bus departure ticket desk at the Hotel Rivera del Ángel (F. J. Mina 518, tel. 951/516-6175)—from the *zócalo*'s southwest corner, walk three blocks west, then three blocks south. For private tour options, contact their main office (tel. 951/514-3152), also at the Hotel Rivera del Ángel.

Alternatively, other agencies offer similar arrangements. For example, try **Agencia de Viajes Caracol** (tel. 951/514-1574), at the Hotel Trebol (corner of Flores Magon and Miguel Cabrera, a block south of the *zócalo*'s southwest corner). Their regular departures include Monte Alban, El Tule–Mitla, and Cuilapan–Zaachila–Arrazola. Many hotels also have economical tourist bus arrangements. See your desk clerk or lobby travel agency.

Guided Tours

Many private individual guides offer tours. Among the most highly recommended is English-fluent **Juan Montes Lara** (Prol. de Eucaliptos 303, Colonia Reforma, tel./fax 951/513-0126, jmonteslara@yahoo.com), backed up by his wife Karin Schutte. Besides cultural sensitivity and extensive local knowledge, they can also provide comfortable transportation in a GMC Suburban wagon for $25/hour.

Moreover, satisfied customers give guide **Sebastiañn Chino Peñ** (tel. 044-951/508-1220, fax 951/562-1405, sebastian_oaxaca@hotmail.com) rave reviews for his guided tours ($20/hour) anywhere you would like in the city or Valley of Oaxaca.

Another promising guide option is to go with **Judith Reyes López** (tel./fax 951/514-9126, judithreyes37@hotmail.com or reservations@oaxacaollin.com, www.oaxacaollin.com), who operates through her **Art and Tradition** tours. Judith offers alternatives ranging from half-day city tours and whole-day Valley of Oaxaca archaeological and crafts-village outings to farther-reaching explorations of the art and architecture of venerable Dominican churches in the Mixteca. Contact her at her bed-and-breakfast, Oaxaca Ollin (Quintana Roo 213),

a block north and a block east of the Centro Cultural de Santo Domingo.

On the other hand, folks interested in the exceedingly diverse natural world of Oaxaca might appreciate a tour led by biologist **Fredy Carrizal Rosales** (tel. 951/515-3305, in-town cell 045-951/164-1897, long-distance out-of-town cell 951/164-1897, ecologiaoaxaca@yahoo.com.mx), owner-operator of **Tourism Service in Ecosystems.** Fredy offers customized explorations of many Oaxaca locations—pine-oak woodlands, coastal mangrove wetlands, semi-desert highlands, lush coastal foothill forest coffee plantations—viewing and identifying plants and animals and enjoying nature in general.

Customized explorations of Oaxaca's indigenous communities, traditions, and natural treasures are the specialty of native Zapotec guide **Florencio Moreno,** who operates **Academic Tours in Oaxaca** (Nieve 208A, Colonia Reforma, home tel./fax 951/518-4728, in-town cell 044-951/510-2244, long-distance out-of-town tel. 951/134-4189, info@academictoursoaxaca.com, www.academictoursoaxaca.com). Florencio's tours reflect his broad qualifications: fluency in native dialects, historical knowledge, cultural sensitivity, personal connections with indigenous crafts communities, and expertise in wildlife-viewing and identification. His excursions can be designed to last a day or a week and include any region of Oaxaca, exploring anything from folk art and hidden archaeological sites to the colorful indigenous markets and festivals of the Mixteca or the Isthmus.

For more guide recommendations, ask at the state **tourist information office** (Murguia 206, tel. 951/516-0123, info@aoaxaca.com, www.oaxaca.travel, 8 A.M.–8 P.M. daily), between Cinco de Mayo and Reforma, two blocks north and a block and a half east of the rear of the cathedral.

Higher up the economic scale, **commercial guided tours** also provide a hassle-free means of exploring the Valley of Oaxaca. Travel agencies, such as **Viajes Turisticos Mitla, Viajes Xochitlán,** and others offer such tours. See *Information and Services* in the *Oaxaca City* chapter.

COMMUNITY MUSEUMS

Oaxaca's many community museums *(museos comunitario)* provide visitors with a potentially rewarding alternative for getting to know local people. The museums, which now number about 20, sprinkle the Valley of Oaxaca, the Mixteca, and the Pacific coast. The first community museums began as a result of archaeological digs. Later museums arose from the local need to house historic community documents and the myriad artifacts that folks have been digging up on their own all over the state for centuries.

During the 1980s and 1990s, the government funded the construction of museums and and installation of exhibits in a number of indigenous communities, in both the Valley of Oaxaca and the Mixteca. Now, excellent small museums in the communities of **Teotitlán del Valle** and **Santa Ana del Valle**, in the east Valley of Oaxaca, and **San José El Mogote** and **Suchilquitongo**, in the northwest valley, welcome visitors during regularly maintained hours. See the individual community sections in this chapter for more information.

The same is more or less true for the well-organized Mixteca museums in **Huajuapan de León, San Pedro y San Pablo Tequixtepec, Yucunama Huamelulpan,** and **Tututepec** on the Mixtec Coast. See the individual community sections in the *Mixteca and Pacific Resorts and Southern Sierra* chapters for details.

A number of other small communities also have established museums but do not yet maintain regular hours. Nevertheless, local contact persons are available to open their museums for visitors. In the Valley of Oaxaca, such museums exist at San Pablo Huixtepec (on Hwy. 131, south of Zimatlán) and San Pablo Huitzo (northeast, off of Hwy. 190); see the *Valley of Oaxaca* map. The same is true, in the Mixteca, for the communities of Yucuita, San Miguel Tequixtepec, Tepelmeme de Morelos, San José Progeso, San Juan Mixtepec, Santa María Cuquila, and Santa María Yucuhiti. See the *Mixteca* chapter for map locations and museum details for most of these communities.

REACHING OUT

By establishing museums for public viewing, the communities are reaching out as never before. Your interest in visiting them will most likely be seen as a compliment by the local people. If you're interested in seeing more than just the museum, ask the museum attendant to suggest a guide who can show you around. Most of these museums have regular guides who are available to lead visitors to notable local sites, such as ruins, sacred caves, lakes, springs, mountain summits, and artisans' shops.

Always volunteer to pay *(donar al museo:* "donate to the museum") for such services. If necessary, be sure to bring along your own English-speaking guide or a Spanish-speaking friend to interpret.

For more information and possible reservations, contact the Oaxaca state tourism office in Oaxaca City (Murguia 206, tel. 951/516-0123, info@aoaxaca.com).

A local community museum guide pauses at a valley-view overlook above Santa Ana del Valle.

© BRUCE WHIPPERMAN

THE VALLEY OF OAXACA

East Side: The Textile Route

The host of colorful enticements along this path could tempt you into many days of delightful exploring. For example, on Saturday you could head out, visiting the great El Tule tree and the weavers' shops in Teotitlán del Valle and continuing east for an overnight at Mitla. Next morning, explore the Mitla ruins, then return, stopping at the hilltop Yagul archaeological site and the Sunday market at Tlacolula. In either direction, going or coming from the city, you could pause for a brief exploration at the Dainzu and Lambityeco roadside archaeological sites.

One more day would allow time to venture past Mitla to the remarkable mountainside springs and limestone mineral deposits at Hierve El Agua. Stay longer and have it all: a two- or three-day stay in a colorful market town, such as Tlacolula, with a side trip to visit the textile market and community museum at **Santa Ana del Valle** and also perhaps

to a quiet backcountry village, such as San Bartolomé Quialana or San Marcos Tlapazola, south of Tlacolula.

EL TULE AND TLACOCHAHUAYA
🚉 Santa María del Tule

El Tule is a gargantuan Mexican *ahuehuete* (cypress), probably the most massive tree in Latin America. Its gnarled, house-size trunk divides into a forest of elephantine limbs that rise to bushy branches reaching 15 stories overhead. The small town of Santa María del Tule, nine miles (14 km) east of Oaxaca City on Highway 190, seems built around the tree. A crafts market, a church, and the town plaza, where residents celebrate their El Tule with a fiesta on October 7, all surround the beloved 2,000-year-old living giant.

Note: Eastbound Highway 190 to El Tule divides inbound traffic, either to the left along a town bypass, beneath a viaduct, or to the right, passing over the viaduct to the town and the El Tule tree.

Tlacochahuaya

At San Jerónimo Tlacochahuaya (tlah-koh-chah-WYE-yah), about four miles (seven km) east of El Tule, stands the village's pride and joy, the venerable 16th-century **Templo y Ex-Convento de San Jerónimo.** Dominican padres and their native acolytes, under the guidance of Father Jordán de Santa Catalina, began its construction in 1586 and completed it a few decades later.

Tlacochahuaya is usually a quiet little town except during holidays, notably the eight days of processions, dances, fireworks, and food that climax on September 30, the feast day of San Jerónimo.

The church's relatively recent 1991 restoration glows so brilliantly, especially from the white baroque facade, that, standing beneath the spreading wild fig tree in the courtyard (or more precisely, atrium), you can feel the

El Tule, one of Latin America's largest trees

facade reflecting the warmth of the late afternoon sun. The atrium appears big enough to assemble a crowd of about 5,000 folks, probably the number of local *indígenas* the padres hoped to convert during the 16th century. At the atrium's corners stand the three open-air but arch-roofed chapels, or *pozas,* where the conversions took place.

Above the entrance portal, see San Jerónimo standing piously, his left hand on a skull, listening for the voice of God. Inside, glance upward at the lovely nave ceiling and appreciate the still-vital spirit of those long-dead artists who created its flowery, multicolored swirls. Look for the group of oil paintings depicting the legend of the **Virgin of Guadalupe**, with the last showing the roses miraculously tumbling from Juan Diego's cape, emblazoned with her image.

Once when I visited, near the entrance was the pledge of the Sacerdote de Cristo (Priest of Christ), which, translated, reads:

The priest of Christ offers
THIS MASS
As if it were your
FIRST MASS
As if it were your
ONLY MASS
As if it were your
LAST MASS

Get there by car, guide, or the Sociedad Cooperativa Valle del Norte or Fletes y Pasajes local bus from the *camionera central segunda clase* in Oaxaca City.

DAINZU AND LAMBITYECO ARCHAEOLOGICAL SITES

Among the several Valley of Oaxaca buried cities, Dainzu and Lambityeco, both beside the highway, are the most accessible. Dainzu comes first, on the right about six miles (nine km) east of El Tule.

Dainzu

Dainzu (in Zapotec, "Hill of the Organ Cactus," 10 A.M.–5 P.M. daily) spreads over an approximate half mile square, consisting of a partly restored ceremonial center surrounded by clusters of unexcavated mounds. Beyond that, on the west side, a stream runs through fields, which at Dainzu's apex (around A.D. 300) supported a town of about 1,000 inhabitants.

The major excavation, at the foot of the hill about a hundred yards south of the parking lot, reveals more than 30 bas-reliefs of ball players draped with leather head, arm, and torso protectors. Downhill, to the west, lies the partly reconstructed complex of courtyards, platforms, and stairways. The northernmost of these was excavated to reveal a tomb, with a carved door supporting a jaguar head on the lintel and arms—note the claws extending down along the stone doorjambs. The jaguar's face, with a pair of curious vampire teeth and curly nostrils, appears so batlike that some investigators have speculated that it may represent a composite jaguar-bat god.

A couple of hundred yards diagonally southwest you'll find the ball court running east-west in the characteristic I-shaped layout, with a pair of "scoring" niches at each end and flanked by a pair of stone-block grandstand-like seats. Actually, archaeologists know that these were not seats, because the blocks were once stuccoed over, forming a pair of smooth inclined planes (probably used for glancing shots) flanking the central playing area.

Lambityeco

Six miles (10 km) farther, Lambityeco (10 A.M.–5 P.M. daily) is on the right, a few miles past the Teotitlán del Valle side road. The excavated portion, only about 100 yards square, is a small but significant part of Yegui (Small Hill in Zapotec), a large buried town dotted with hundreds of unexcavated mounds covering about half a square mile. Salt-making appears to have been the main occupation of Yegui people during the town's heyday, around A.D. 700. The name "Lambityeco" may derive from the Arabic-Spanish *alambique,* the equivalent of the English "alembic," or distillation or evaporation apparatus. This would explain the intriguing presence of more than 200 local

TOWN NAMES

Town names in Oaxaca (and in Mexico) generally come in two pieces: an original native name, accompanied by the name of the town's patron saint. Very typical is the case of San Jerónimo Tlacochahuaya, a sleepy but famous little place covered in this chapter. Combining both the saint's name (here, San Jerónimo) and the native name often makes for very unwieldy handles, so many towns are known only by one name, usually the native name. Thus, in the west side of the Valley of Oaxaca, San Jerónimo Tlacochahuaya, Santa María del Tule, Tlacolula de Matamoros, and San Pablo Villa de Mitla, for example, are commonly called Tlacochahuaya, El Tule, Tlacolula, and Mitla, respectively.

Nevertheless, sometimes a town's full name is customarily used. This is especially true when a single name – such as Etla, northwest of Oaxaca City – identifies an entire district, and thus many towns, such as San Agustín Etla, San Sebastián Etla, and San José Etla, must necessarily be identified with their full names. In this book, although we may mention the formal name once on a map or in the text, we generally conform to local, customary usage for town names.

mounds. It's tempting to speculate that they are the remains of *cujetes,* raised leaching beds still used in Mexico for concentrating brine, which workers subsequently evaporate into salt.

In the present small restored zone archaeologists have uncovered, besides the remains of the Valley of Oaxaca's earliest known *temazcal,* a number of fascinating ceramic sculptures. Next to the parking lot, a platform, mound 195, rises above ground level. If, after entering through the gate, you climb up its partially restored slope and look down into the excavated hollow in the adjacent east courtyard, you'll see stucco friezes of a pair of regal, lifelike faces, one male and one female, presumably of the personages who were found buried in the royal grave (Tomb 6) below. Experts believe this to be the case, because the man was depicted with the symbol of his right to rule—a human femur bone, probably taken, as was the custom, from the grave of his chieftain father.

Mound 190, sheltered beneath the adjacent large corrugated roof about 50 yards to the south, contains a restored platform decorated by a pair of remarkably lifelike, nearly identical divine stucco masks. These are believed to be of Zapotec rain god Cocijo (see the water flowing from the mouths). Notice also the rays, perhaps lightning, representing power, in one hand, and flowers, for fertility, in the other.

◖ TEOTITLÁN DEL VALLE

Teotitlán del Valle (pop. 5,000), nine miles (14 km) east of El Tule, at the foot of the northern Sierra, means "Place of the Gods" in Nahuatl; before that it was known, appropriately, as Xa Quire (shah KEE-ray), or "Foot of the Mountain," by the Zapotecs who settled it, archaeologists estimate, at least 2,000 years ago. From the age of artifacts uncovered beneath both the present town and at nearby sites, experts estimate that approximately 1,000 people were living in Teotitlán by A.D. 400.

Present-day Teotitlán people are relatively well off, not only from sales of their renowned *tapetes,* but from their rich communal landholdings. Besides a sizable swath of valley-bottom farmland and pasture, which every Teotitlán family is entitled to use, the community owns a dam and reservoir and a small kingdom of approximately 100,000 acres of sylvan mountain forest and meadow, spreading for about 20 miles (32 km) along the Valley of Oaxaca's lush northeastern foothills.

Getting Oriented

Teotitlán del Valle has two principal streets: Juárez, the entrance road, which runs northerly about 2.5 miles (four km) from the highway, and Hidalgo, which intersects it at the center of town. Turn right at Hidalgo (where the pavement becomes cobbled) and you'll be looking east, toward the town plaza and, behind it, the 17th-century town church.

Textile Shops

Nearly every Teotitlán house is a mini-factory where people card, spin, and color wool, often using hand-gathered natural dyes. Each step of wool preparation is laborious; obtaining pure water is even a chore—families typically spend two days a week collecting it from mountain springs. The weaving, on traditional hand looms, is the final, satisfying part of the process.

Visiting the workshop-stores should be first on your itinerary. The home workshops, once confined to the town center, now sprinkle nearly the entire entrance road. Be sure not to miss the shop of renowned master **Isaac ("Bug in the Rug") Vasquez** (tel. 951/514-4122, 10 A.M.–6 P.M. daily), on the right a few blocks before the town center at Juárez 244, or on main cross-street Hidalgo, number 30 (turn left at the town center). Also, be certain to look inside the store of the cooperative shop **Mujeres Que Tejan** (Women Who Weave, tel. 951/166-6174, joker213@brownpride.com). The shop is managed by Josefina Jiménez and displays the fine for-sale woven products of 28 women weavers. Find it on the road into town, on the right side, at Juárez (old address number 86, new number 162) about a quarter-mile (0.5 km) from Highway 190.

The best weaving is generally the densest, typically packing in about 45 strands per inch (18 strands per centimeter); ordinary weaving incorporates about half that. Please don't bargain too hard. Even the highest prices typically bring the weavers less than a dollar an hour for their labor.

Another good place to see weavers at work is the workshop-store-restaurant-hotel **El Descanso** (Juárez 51), at the town-center corner of Juárez and Hidalgo (see the *Food and Accommodations* section).

Community Museum

Reserve enough time to visit the community museum **Balaa Xtee Guech Gulal** (tel. 951/524-4463, 10 A.M.–6 P.M. Tues.–Sun.) whose name translates from the local Zapotec as "Shadow of the Old Town." It's on the north side of Hidalgo, about a block east of Juárez. Step inside and enjoy the excellent exhibits that illustrate local history, industry, and customs. One display shows the wool-weaving tradition, introduced by the Dominican padres, including sources of some natural dyes—*cochinilla* (red cochineal), *musgo* (yellow moss and lichens), *anil* (dark blue indigo), and *quizache* bean (black). Another exhibit shows the local practice of service to the bride's parents by a prospective groom, with a house mock-up showing the prospective bride making tortillas for him. Be sure to get a copy of the good English-language explanatory pamphlet.

A Walk Around Town

If you ask, a community museum volunteer may be available to lead you on a walking tour of the town and environs. They especially recommend English-speaking Zeferino Mendoza. Highlights often include visits to weavers' homes, the church, a traditional *temazcal*, the recently reconstructed foundation stones of the ancient town, the dam and lake, and the hike to Picacho, the peak above the town's west side.

Lacking a guide, simply stroll out on your own self-guided tour. After seeing the museum, head east on Hidalgo. If you haven't already, take a look around the plaza-front textile stalls, then continue to the **Templo de la Preciosa Sangre de Cristo** (Church of the Precious Blood of Christ). Here, community adoration focuses during both the July 1–15 patronal festival and the September 7–9 Fiesta del Señor de La Natividad (Festival of the Lord of the Nativity), which include processions, fireworks, and the spectacular Danza de las Plumas (Dance of the Feathers).

The Teotitlá Church

The church itself, built over an earlier Zapotec temple, contains many interesting pre-Columbian stones, which the Dominican friars allowed to be incorporated into its walls. Notice the corn motif carved into the front doorway arch, similar in style to the monolith built into the outside wall at the right of the church entrance steps. Inside, admire the nave's flowery overhead decorations and the colorful Bible-story paintings. Continue from the nave into the intimate *claustro* (cloister) and see the Zapotec god of the wind, with stone curls carved to represent the wind (in the southwest corner, to the right as you enter from the nave).

Outside, behind the church, continue to the reconstructed foundation corner of the original **Zapotec temple.** Notice the uniquely Zapotec stone fretwork, similar to the famous *greca* remains at Mitla, 20 miles (32 km) farther east.

More Options

If you have time, you can venture even farther afield. One option is to walk or drive along the bumpy but passable uphill gravel continuation of main street Calle Juárez about a mile (1.6 km) to the **town dam.** After the summer rains, the reservoir fills and forms a scenic lake, good for swimming, picnicking, and even possibly camping, along its pastoral mountain-view shoreline. If you plan to camp at the Teotitlán reservoir, first ask for permission at the museum or the *presidencia municipal.*

Travelers can extend their Teotitlán adventure all the way into the neighboring mountains. From the Teotitlán reservoir, hike (be prepared with water, good shoes, and a hat), hitchhike, taxi, or drive about 12 more miles (19 km) uphill (with an elevation gain of 5,000 feet/1,500 meters) along the good gravel road to pine-shadowed **Benito Juárez** and **Cuajimoloyas** mountain hamlets. (See the *Northern Oaxaca* chapter for details.)

Back at the Teotitlán reservoir, you can also venture up the slope of **Picacho,** the steep, peaked hill a mile (1.6 km) west of town. The usual route from town is along Calle 2 de Abril, which heads west, bridging the west-side arroyo. Continue uphill, bearing right at the fork at the base of the hill. First you'll pass some houses, then continue, curving left around the hillside. Eventually, before the summit, you'll pass some *cuevitas* (small caves), a holy site where local folks have been gathering for sacred ceremonies

each New Year's Day since before anyone can remember.

Food and Accommodations

Sample Teotitlán's best at the traditional **Tlamanalli** restaurant (on Juárez, about a block south of Hidalgo, no phone, 1–4 P.M. daily except possibly Mon. and Thurs., longer hours when more people stop by). Their menu of made-to-order Zapotec specialties, such as *sopa de calabaza* (squash soup, $5) and *guisado de pollo* (chicken stew, $10) is limited, but highly recommended by Oaxaca City chefs.

If Tlamanalli is closed, go to the inviting **Restaurant El Descanso** (Juárez 51, tel. 951/524-4152, weaving shop and restaurant open 8 A.M.–6 P.M. daily). Your hosts will be the welcoming family of Edmundo and Alicia Montaño, who, besides crafting and selling lovely wool weavings, also serve tasty country fare and offer a number of rooms ($40 d) that open on to their leafy and lovely inner garden-patio. Choices include king-sized, regular double bed, and single beds.

Alternatively, for a lunch or early dinner treat, stop at showplace **C Restaurant El Patio** (out on the highway, 0.8 mile/1.2 km east of the Teotitlán entrance road, tel. 951/514-4889, 10 A.M.–6 P.M. Tues.–Sun.). The restaurant centers around an airy patio, decorated by antique country furniture and a fetching gallery of scenes from the 1940s-era films of the Mexican Golden Age of cinema. The finale is the food, of tasty traditional Oaxacan dishes such as *ensalada Oaxaqueña* ($4), Zapotec soup ($3), and the house specialty *botana* Don Pepe ($7).

Getting There

You can go to Teotitlán by car, tour, taxi, or bus. Drivers, simply turn left from Highway 190 at the signed Teotitlán del Valle side road, nine miles (14 km) east of El Tule. By bus, ride a **Fletes y Pasajes** Tlacolula- or Mitla-bound bus from the *camionera central segunda clase* (in Oaxaca City by the Abastos market at the end of Las Casas, past the *periférico* west of downtown). Alternatively, ride the hourly **Valle del**

Norte bus from the *camionera central segunda clase* parking lot. Get off at the signed bus stop and walk, taxi, or hitchhike the 2.5 miles (four km) into town.

SANTA ANA DEL VALLE

This is a sleepier version of Teotitlán, where virtually every family speaks the Zapotec tongue at home and earns at least part of its living through weaving. Many older folks understand Spanish only with difficulty. Santa Ana del Valle, like Teotitlán, has thousands of acres of communal lands in the valley bottom and mountains north of the town. Nearly all households tend plots of corn, beans, and vegetables. Most also graze cattle, sheep, and goats in specified communal areas. These lands have been traditionally held by the town since before the conquest. Families may buy or sell shares of their allotted land, but only within the Santa Ana del Valle community.

Community Museum

Your first stop should be the excellent community museum **Shan Dany** (tel. 951/562-1705, 10 A.M.–2 P.M. and 3–6 P.M. Mon.–Sat.), on the town plaza opposite the *presidencia municipal*. The exhibits include an archaeological section with pre-conquest remains found during a recent plaza-front construction project. Also notice the ponderous monolith, brought from the mountain above town, carved with the visage of Cocijo, the god of lightning and rain. Another museum section details 1910–1917 revolutionary history, when townsfolk had to flee to the hills and wage a guerrilla war against rampaging forces of "Primer Jefe" General Venustiano Carranza.

Toward the rear of the museum, a pair of excellent displays illustrate more community lore: One shows many of the naturally occurring dyes, including avocado seeds, *guaje* bark, and *copal* bark, that local weavers gather and use; the other explains the Danza de la Pluma (Dance of the Feathers), in which a dozen young men dance and brighten the town plaza with their huge, round feathered hats. This dance takes place during the July 26

and August 14–16 split-date festival in honor of Santa Ana.

A Walk Around Town

Ask and a museum volunteer may be able to find a guide (offer to pay) to lead you on a two- or three-hour *recorrido* (tour) around town, including the *presa* (dam and small reservoir), a creek (where you can cool off during the summer rainy season—bring your bathing suit), a breezy *mirador* (viewpoint) for a spectacular valley vista, and an old gold, silver, and copper mine. During the walk, your guide might identify and explain the uses of the many medicinal plants along the path. Be sure to ask them to point out the poison oak–like *mala mujer* (bad woman) bush to you. Finally, ask them to take you to shops of outstanding local weavers for demonstrations and possible purchases of their work.

If you can't get a guide, you can still do most of the walk on your own. The path to the dam takes off from Calle Plan de Ayala, on the east, uphill side of town. After about half a mile (0.8 km), bear left, around the hill. If you get confused, ask a younger person (most likely to understand Spanish) "*¿Donde está la presa*" (PRAY-sah), "*por favor?*" The viewpoint, the big moss-mottled rock about halfway up the steep, left-hand slope, sticks out of the hillside above the path to the dam.

Accommodations

The comfortable Santa Ana tourist **cabaña ecoturística** is on the entrance road to town. It is well situated for exploring, being just a few blocks from the center of town. Reserve a spot here through the state tourist information office, alternative tourism section (Murguia 206, up the driveway in the back, tel. 951/516-0123, 951/502-1200, info@aoaxaca.com, www.oaxaca.travel).

Shopping

Although Santa Ana weavers sell much of their work through shops in Teotitlán del Valle and Oaxaca, they also sell directly in town, from both the **Mercado de Artesanías** on the town plaza and their home workshops. For suggestions of whom to visit, ask at the museum, or go directly to **Casa Martínez** (Matamoros 3, corner of V. Carranza, tel. 951/562-0366), the house of personable master weaver Ernesto Martínez, around the corner a few doors downhill from the town plaza. You'll also be welcome at the home shop of the friendly weaving family of **Alberto Sánchez García** (Sor Juanes Inés de la Cruz 1, no phone), a few blocks from the town plaza.

For some good Santa Ana and Teotitlán del Valle tips, visit Ron Mader's super websites (www.planeta.com/ecotravel/mexico/oaxaca/santana.html and www.planeta.com/ecotravel/mexico/oaxaca/teotitlan.html).

Getting There

You can go to Santa Ana del Valle by car, tour, taxi, or bus. Drivers, turn left at the fork across Highway 190 from the Tlacolula Pemex *gasolinera* 24 miles (38 km) east of Oaxaca City. After half a mile (0.8 km), turn left again at the signed Santa Ana del Valle side road. Continue another few minutes; pass the tourist *cabaña ecoturística* on the right, and arrive at the town plaza a few blocks farther. By bus, you can ride a Tlacolula- or Mitla-bound bus from the *camionera central segunda clase* in Oaxaca City by the Abastos market, end of Las Casas, west of downtown. Get off at the Tlacolula stop on Highway 190 by the Pemex station. Cross to the side road on the north side of the highway and take a taxi, ride the Transportes Municipal del Santa Ana del Valle local bus, or hike the four miles (6.4 km) from the highway—walk the side road half a mile (0.8 km) to a signed Santa Ana fork; go left and continue for two more miles (3.2 km), passing the *cabaña ecoturística* on the right, and then on to the town plaza a few blocks farther.

TLACOLULA

The Zapotec people who founded Tlacolula (pop. 15,000, 24 miles/38 km east from Oaxaca) around A.D. 1250 called it Guichiibaa (Place Between Heaven and Earth). Besides its beloved church and chapel and famous Sunday

fine wool weavings for sale at the Tlacolula market

© BRUCE WHIPPERMAN

market, Tlacolula is also renowned for *mescal,* an alcoholic beverage distilled from the fermented hearts of maguey. Get a good free sample at the friendly **Pensamiento shop** (Juárez 9, 9 A.M.–7 P.M. daily), as you head from the highway gasoline station (along Juárez) toward the market. Besides many hand-embroidered Amusgo *huipiles* and Teotitlán weavings, Pensamiento offers *mescal* in more than 20 flavors, with many more for women than men.

Just before the market, take a look inside the main town church, the 1531 **Parroquia de la Virgen de la Asunción.** Although its interior is distinguished enough, the real gem is its attached chapel, **Capilla del Señor de Tlacolula,** which you enter from the nave of the church. Every inch of the chapel's interior gleams with sculptures of angels and saints, paintings, and gold scrollwork. Notice the pair of floating angels, each holding a great pendulous solid silver censer, on opposite sides of the altar; also, admire the solid silver fence in front of the altar. Saints seem to live in every corner of the chapel. Especially graphic are the

© BRUCE WHIPPERMAN

The Pensamiento shop in Tlacolula offers dozens of mescal flavors.

martyrs, who reveal the way they died, such as a sorrowful San Sebastián, his body shot full of arrows, and a decapitated San Pablo, above the right transept, his head on the ground.

Ordinarily tranquil, the church grounds seem to nearly burst with the faithful during the five-day **Fiesta del Santa Cristo de Tlacolula,** climaxing on the second Sunday of October, when the plaza is awash with mer rymakers. It is then that folks enjoy their favorites, the **Danza de los Jardineros** (Dance of the Gardeners) and the spectacular **Danza de las Plumas** (Dance of the Feathers), along with a *pelota mixteca* (traditional Mixtec ball game) tournament.

The big gate bordering the church grounds leads you to the Tlacolula market. One of Oaxaca's biggest and oldest, the Tlacolula market draws tens of thousands from all over the Valley of Oaxaca every Sunday. Wander around and soak it all in—the diverse crowd of buyers and sellers, and the equally manifold galaxy of merchandise. How about a hand-hewn yoke for your oxen, or a new stone *mano* and *metate*

for your kitchen? If not, perhaps some live (or ground) *chapulines* (grasshoppers), maybe a live turkey for dinner tomorrow, or a hunk of sugarcane to chew on while you stroll?

For **food and accommodations,** try the basic but clean downtown Tlacolula lodging, the **Hotel and Restaurant Calenda** (Juárez 40, tel. 951/562-0660, $21 s or d, and $28 t). They offer about 30 rooms with hot-water shower-baths and fans in three floors around an interior restaurant courtyard. Their restaurant ($3–7) serves a wholesome country menu that, although specializing in *barbacoa* (barbecue) *pollo, chivo,* or *borrego* (chicken, goat, or lamb), offers many more hearty choices, such as pork chops, spaghetti, eggs, fish, and chiles rellenos.

YAGUL ARCHAEOLOGICAL ZONE

The regal remains of Yagul (Zapotec for "old tree," 10 A.M.–5 P.M. daily) preside atop their volcanic hilltop, 28 miles (45 km) east of Oaxaca City. Although only six miles (10 km) from Mitla and sharing architectural details, such as Mitla's famous *greca* fretwork, the size and complexity of its buildings suggest that Yagul was an independent city-state in its own right. Local folks call the present ruin the Pueblo Viejo (Old Town) and remember it as the forerunner of the present town of Tlacolula. Archaeological evidence, which indicates that Yagul was occupied for about a thousand years, at least until around A.D. 1100 or 1200, bears them out.

One of Yagul's major claims to fame is its **Palace of Six Patios,** actually three nearly identical but separate complexes of two patios each. In each patio, rooms surround a central courtyard. The northerly patio of each complex is more private and probably was the residence, while the other, more open patio served administrative functions.

South of the palace sprawls Yagul's huge **ball court,** the second largest in Mesoamerica, shaped in the characteristic Oaxaca I configuration. Southeast of the ball court is Patio 4, consisting of four mounds surrounding a

THE VALLEY OF OAXACA

courtyard. A boulder sculpted in the form of a frog lies at the base of the east mound. At the courtyard's center, a tomb was excavated; descend and explore its three *greca*-style, fretwork-decorated chambers.

If it's not too hot, gather your energy and climb to the hilltop above the parking lot for a fine view of the ruin and the entire Valley of Oaxaca. The name for this prominence, the Citadel, probably was accurately descriptive, for Yagul's defenders long ago added rock walls to enhance the hilltop's security.

◖ MITLA

The ruins at Mitla (about 31 miles/50 km from Oaxaca city, 8 a.m.–5 p.m. daily) are a "must" for Valley of Oaxaca sightseers. Mitla (Liobaa in Zapotec, the Place of the Dead) flowered late, reaching a population of perhaps 10,000 during its apex around A.D. 1350. It remained occupied and in use for generations after the conquest.

During Mitla's heyday, several feudalistic, fortified city-states vied for power in the Valley

of Oaxaca. Concurrently, Mixtec-speaking people arrived from the north, perhaps under pressure from Aztecs and others in central Mexico. Evidence suggests that these Mixtec groups, in interacting with the resident Zapotecs, created the unique architectural styles of late cities such as Yagul and Mitla. Archaeologists believe, for example, that the striking *greca* (Grecian-style) frets that honeycomb Mitla facades are the result of Mixtec influence.

Exploring the Site

In a real sense, Mitla lives on. The ruins coincide with the present town of San Pablo Villa de Mitla, whose main church actually occupies the northernmost of five main groups of monumental ruins. Virtually anywhere archaeologists dig within the town they hit remains of the myriad ancient dwellings, plazas, and tombs that connected the still-visible landmarks.

Get there by forking left from main Oaxaca Highway 190 onto Highway 176. Continue about two miles to the Mitla town entrance, on the left. Head straight through town, cross

stone fretwork at Mitla archaeological site

MITLA

CHURCH GROUP

MITLA CHURCH

P

■ HANDICRAFTS STALLS

GATE

PALACE OF COLUMNS

ADOBE GROUP

SHRINE

COLUMN OF LIFE

COLUMNS GROUP

TOMBS

ARROYO GROUP

Arroyo

Mitla River

SOUTH GROUP

● HOTEL AND RESTAURANT LA ZAPOTECA

■ ARTESENIAS ACACIA

THE FRISSELL MUSEUM ★

Mitla Town Plaza

● HOTEL AND RESTAURANT MITLA

● HOTEL DON CENOBIO

To Hwy 190, Oaxaca, and Tehuantepec

0   100 yds
0   100 m

© AVALON TRAVEL

THE VALLEY OF OAXACA

a bridge, and, after about a mile, arrive at the site. Of the five ruins clusters, the best preserved is the fenced-in Columns Group. Its exploration requires about an hour. The others—the Arroyo and Adobe groups beyond an arroyo, and the South Group across the Mitla River—are rubbly, unreconstructed mounds. Evidence indicates the Adobe and South groups were ceremonial compounds, while the Arroyo, Church, and Columns groups were palaces.

Although the Church Group (marked by the monumental columns that you pass first on your right after the parking lot) has suffered from past use by the local parish, it deserves a few minutes' look around inside. It consists of a pair of regal courtyards, labeled A and B, adjacent to the triple red-domed 16th century church. You first enter courtyard B, enclosed by monumental stone-framed doorways. A passageway leads to smaller courtyard A, where you can see the fascinating remnants of the red hieroglyphic paintings of personages, namedates, and glyphs that once covered its walls.

Back outside, on the main entrance path, continue past the tourist market and through the gate to the **Columns Group.** Inside, two large patios, joined at one corner, are each surrounded on three sides by elaborate apartments. A shrine occupies the center of the first patio. Just north of this stands the **Palace of Columns,** the most important of Mitla's buildings. It sits atop a staircase, inaccurately reconstructed in 1901.

Inside, a file of six massive monolithic columns supported the roof. A narrow "escape" passage exits out the right rear side to a large patio enclosed by a continuous narrow room. The purely decorative *greca* facades, which required around 100,000 cut stones for the Columns Group complex, decorate the walls. Remnants of the original red and white stucco that lustrously embellished the entire complex hide in niches and corners.

Walk south to the second patio, which has a similar layout. Here the main palace occupies the east side, where a passage descends to a tomb beneath the front staircase. Both this and

another tomb, beneath the building at the north side of the patio, are intact, preserving their original crucifix shapes. (The guard, although he is not supposed to, may try to collect a tip for letting you descend.) No one knows who and what were buried in these tombs, which were open and empty at the time of the conquest.

The second tomb is similar, except that it contains a stone pillar called the **Column of Life;** by embracing it, legend says, you will learn how many years you have left.

The interesting **Church Group** (notice the church domes) is on the far north side of the Palace of Columns. Builders used the original temple stones to erect the church here. On its north side is a patio leading to another interior patio surrounded by another *greca*-decorated palace.

The Frissell Museum

The Frissell Museum (a block west of the town entrance road, by the Mitla town plaza) has been closed for several years due to earthquake damage. Thankfully, it is slated to be repaired and reopened in the near future, displaying its exceptionally fine artifact collection, including a host of finely preserved ceramic figurines, yet-to-be-deciphered Zapotec glyphs, and a Zapotec marriage certificate in stone.

Besides its collection, the museum's historic venerable hacienda-style home is notable in its own right. From the mid-19th century, as the **Posada La Sorpresa,** it served as a lodging, owned and operated by the longtime local Quero family. In 1950, they sold it to American artifact collector Ervin R. Frissell, who turned the hotel into both his home and a repository for his growing collection and that of his friend, Howard Leigh, noted scholar of Mixtec language and culture. Upon their deaths, the entire building and artifact collection passed to the University of the Americas.

Fiesta del Apóstol de San Pablo

Mitla (pop. 15,000), although famous, is a quiet town where tranquility is disturbed only by occasional tourist buses along its dusty, sun-drenched main street. A major exception occurs during Mitla's key fiesta, which centers on the town's venerable 16th-century church, dedicated to San Pablo Apóstol (St. Paul the Apostle). If you plan your visit during the eight days climaxing around January 25 (or also around June 29, the day of San Pablo and San Pedro), you can join with the townsfolk as they celebrate their *patrón* with masses, processions, a feast, fireworks, *jaripeo* (bull roping and riding), and dancing.

Accommodations and Food
Directly across the street from the Frissell Museum, stop for a refreshment at the homey **Hotel and Restaurant Mitla** (Benito Juárez 6, tel. 951/568-0112, 8 A.M.–7 P.M. daily), domain of the sparkplug mother-daughter team of Teresa and Gloria González de Quero. Here you can enjoy Mexico as old-timers remember it, in a charmingly ramshackle hacienda-style farmhouse, where roosters crow, dogs snooze, and guests can have their seasonal fill of bananas, avocados, mandarins, and papayas from a shady backyard *huerta* (orchard). Their 16 rooms ($15 s, $22 d) vary. Most rooms in the upstairs tier—plain but clean, with the essentials, including hot water—are acceptably rustic. Parking is included.

Across the plaza from the museum is the new four-star neo-colonial-style **Don Cenobio Banquet Salon and Hotel** (3 Calle Juarez, tel. 951/568 0330, fax 951/568-0050, info mas@ hoteldoncenobio.com, www.hoteldoncenobio .com, $70 d), with about 20 beautifully decorated rooms built around a large, inviting grassy green pool patio. It has a wealth of facilities, including a restaurant and banquet hall for 500 people. Rooms come with air conditioning, cable TV, queen and king-sized beds, and much more. The only drawback to all of this is that they rent the place out to hundreds for conferences and parties quite often. Best to check by telephone before reserving an overnight.

Alternatively, about five blocks north, closer to the archaeological zone, try the family-run ⌑ **Hotel and Restaurant La Zapoteca** (5 de Febrero 12, tel. 951/568-0026), on the right just before the Río Mitla bridge. The spic-and-span restaurant (7:30 A.M.–7 P.M. daily), praised by locals for "the best chiles rellenos in Oaxaca," is excellent for meals, and the 20 clean, reasonably priced rooms ($15 s, $20 d, $27 t), with hot water and parking, are fine for an overnight.

Shopping
Instead of making handicrafts, Mitla people concentrate on selling them, mostly at the big **handicrafts market** adjacent to the archaeological zone parking lot. Here you can sample from a concentrated all-Oaxaca assortment, especially textiles including *huipiles*, wool hangings and rugs, onyx animals and chess sets, fanciful *alebrijes*, and leather huaraches, purses, belts, and wallets.

For a fine private for-sale collection, stop by **Artesanias Acacia** (Morelos 32, 9 A.M.–8 P.M. daily, tel. 951/568-0539), on the main street to the ruins, on the right, a fraction of a block past the Frissel Museum. The main attraction is hundreds of lovely hand-embroidered dresses, blouses, tie-dye, and innovatively attractive *pescaderos* (embroidered blouses, sold as a set with embroidered, pedal-pusher-length pants).

Getting There
Bus travelers can get to Mitla from Oaxaca City by Fletes y Pasajes bus from the *camionera central segunda clase*. Drivers get there by forking left from main Oaxaca Highway 190, at the big Mitla sign, onto Highway 176. Continue about two miles (3.2 km) to the Mitla town entrance, on the left. Head straight through town, pass the town plaza, continue across the bridge over the (usually dry) Río Mitla, and after about a mile (1.6 km), arrive at the site.

HIERVE EL AGUA MINERAL SPRINGS
Although the name of this place translates as boiling water, the springs that seep from the side of the limestone mountain less than an

hour's drive east of Mitla aren't hot. Instead, they are loaded with minerals. These minerals over time have built up into rock-hard deposits, forming great algae-painted slabs in level spots and, on steep slopes, accumulating into what appear to be grand frozen waterfalls. *Note:* A local community dispute has unfortunately led to the closure of Hierve El Agua *cabañas* and sometimes even the whole park. Before planning a visit, check with the state tourist information office in Oaxaca City (Murguia 206, tel. 951/516-0123, 951/502-1200, info@aoaxaca.com, www.oaxaca.travel).

The Springs

Although the springs may be crowded on weekends and holidays, you'll probably have Hierve El Agua nearly to yourself on weekdays. The first thing you'll see after passing the entrance gate is a lineup of snack and curio stalls at the cliff-side parking lot. A trail leads downhill to the main spring, which bubbles from the mountainside and trickles into a huge basin that the operators have dammed as a swimming pool. Bring your bathing suit.

Part of Hierve El Agua's appeal is the panoramic view of mountain and valley. On a clear day, you can see the tremendous massif of **Zempoatepetl** (saym-poh-ah-TAY-pehtl), the grand holy mountain range of the Mixe people, rising above the eastern horizon.

From the ridge-top park, agile walkers can hike farther down the hill, following deposits curiously accumulated in the shape of miniature limestone dikes that trace the mineral water's downhill path. Soon you'll glimpse a towering limestone formation, like a giant petrified waterfall, appearing to ooze from the cliff downhill straight ahead, on the right.

Back uphill by the parking lot, operators have augmented the natural springs with a resort-style swimming pool where, along with everyone else, you can frolic to your heart's content.

Hikers can also enjoy following a *sendero peatonal* (footpath) that encircles the entire zone. Start your walk from the trailhead beyond the bungalows past the pool, or at the other end, at the cliff edge between the parking

lot and the entrance gate. Your reward will be an approximately one-hour, self-guided tour, looping downhill past the springs and the great frozen rock cascades and featuring grand vistas of the gorgeous mountain and canyon scenery along the way.

The Hierve El Agua zone and surrounding country is habitat for a hardy dry-country palm you'll probably see plenty of while strolling around. Lack of winter–spring moisture usually keeps the palms small, sometimes clustering in great gardens, appearing like regiments of desert dwarfs. Local people gather and weave their fronds into *tenates* (baskets), *petates* (mats), *escobas* (brooms), and more, which they sometimes sell in the stalls by the parking lot.

Accommodations and Food

The Hierve El Agua tourist **C cabañas ecoturísticas** have in the past provided the key for a restful one- or two-night stay. The several clean and well-maintained housekeeping bungalows, with shower-baths and hot water, rent for about $7 per person, or around $40 for up to six in a bungalow, with refrigerator, stove, and utensils.

For food, you can bring and cook your own in your bungalow or rely upon the strictly local-style beans, carne asada (roast meat), tacos, tamales, and tortillas offered by the parking-lot food stalls. In any case, fruit and vegetable lovers should bring their own from Oaxaca. Produce selection in local San Lorenzo village stores will most likely be minimal.

Getting There

Get there by riding an Ayutla-bound Fletes y Pasajes bus east out of either Oaxaca City *(camionera central segunda clase)* or Mitla on Highway 179 just east of town. Get off at the Hierve El Agua side road, about 11 miles (18 km) past Mitla. Continue the additional five miles (eight km) by the local bus marked San Lorenzo–Hierve El Agua.

Drivers, head east from Mitla along Highway 179. After approximately 11 miles (18 km), follow the signed gravel side road that forks right another five miles (8 km), through San Lorenzo village to Hierve El Agua. (*Warning:* Until they get around to paving it, the clay roadbed through San Lorenzo village and beyond is *extremely slippery* when wet with rain.

Under such conditions, unless you're driving a good-traction four-wheel-drive vehicle, park your car in the village and walk the final quarter mile (0.4 km), which steeply descends to the Hierve El Agua entrance.)

South Side: The Crafts Route

Travelers who venture into the Valley of Oaxaca's long, south-pointing fingers, sometimes known as the Valleys of Zimatlán and Ocotlán, can discover a wealth of crafts, history, and architectural and scenic wonders. These are all accessible by day trips from Oaxaca City by car or combinations of bus and taxi. Most reachable are the renowned crafts villages of Coyotepec, Tilcajete, Jalieza, and others along Highway 175, between the city and the colorful market town of Ocotlán (best to plan a visit to all on Friday, Ocotlán's market day; start at Ocotlán early and work your way north back to Oaxaca City). Another day, you can either continue farther south, off the tourist track, to soak in the feast of sights at the big market in Ejutla, or fork southwest, via Highway 131 through Zimatlán, to the idyllic groves, crystal springs, and limestone caves hidden around San Sebastián de las Grutas.

◖ SAN BARTOLO COYOTEPEC

San Bartolo Coyotepec (Hill of the Coyote), on Highway 175 14 miles (23 km) south of Oaxaca City, is famous for its pottery and its August 24–27 festival, Fiesta de San Bartolomé. During the fiesta, masked villagers costumed as half-man half-woman figures in tiaras, blond wigs, tin crowns, and velvet cloaks dance in honor of their patron.

The town's black pottery, the renowned *barro negro* sold all over Mexico, is available at the signed **pottery Mercado** on the right and at a number of cottage factory shops (watch for signs) off the highway, scattered along left (east side) Calle Juárez, marked by a big Doña Rosa sign. Doña Rosa, who passed away in 1980, pioneered the technique of crafting

lovely, big, round jars without a potter's wheel. With their local clay, Doña Rosa's descendants and neighbor families regularly turn out acres of glistening black plates, pots, bowls, trees of life, and fetching animals for very reasonable prices (figure on about $20 for a pearly black three-gallon vase, and perhaps $2 for a cute little rabbit).

San Bartolo Museum

Across the highway from the town church, on the town plaza's southern flank, stands the elaborate, new **Museo Estatal de Arte** (Plaza

The celebrated black pottery of San Bartolo Coyotepec is prized for its pearly sheen.

BUILDING CHURCHES

Although European architects designed nearly all of Mexico's colonial-era churches, embellishing them with old-world Gothic, Renaissance, baroque, and Moorish decorations, native artists blended their own geometric, floral, and animal motifs. The result was a hybrid that manifested in intriguing variations all over Mexico. This was especially true in Oaxaca, where droves of faithful worship before gilded altars and flowery ceilings built and decorated by their long-gone ancestors. Local materials further distinguish Oaxacan churches from others in Mexico. The spectrum of soft pastels of local *cantera* volcanic stone, from yellow through gray, including green in Oaxaca City, marks Oaxacan walls and facades.

Sometimes the native influence led to poor ("provincial") versions of European designs; other times (notably, the Templo y Ex-Convento de Santo Domingo in Oaxaca City), artists merged brilliant native decorations with the best of European-style vaults, arches, and columns.

THE LAYOUT

Mexican church design followed the Egypto-Greco-Roman tradition of its European models. Basically, architects designed their churches beginning with the main space of the nave, in the shape of a box, lined with high lateral windows. Depending on their origin and function, the churches fit into three basic groups – the monk's **convento** (monastery or convent), the bishop's **catedral** (cathedral), and the priest's **templo** or **parroquia** (parish church). Most Oaxacan monastic churches (nearly all now ex-convents) were begun during the 16th and 17th centuries by the missionary orders – a handful by the Franciscans, Jesuits, and Augustinians, and the overwhelming remainder by the Dominicans.

In Oaxaca, faced with the constant threat of earthquake, the Dominican padres built massively thick walls supported on the exterior with ponderous buttresses. Key elements were naves, with or without **cruceros** (transepts), cross spaces separating the nave from the altar, making the church layout resemble a Christian cross. They placed the **coro** (choir) above and just inside the entrance arch.

At the opposite, usually east (or sunrise) end of the church, builders sometimes extended the nave beyond the transept to include a **presbiterio** (presbytery), which was often lined with seats where church officials presided. The building ended past that at the **ábside** (apse), the space behind the altar, frequently in semi-circular or half-octagonal form. Within the apse rose the gilded **retablo** (retable or altar-piece) adorned with sacred images, attended by choirs of angels and cherubs.

Larger churches usually incorporated side altars presided over by images of locally popular saints, nearly always including the Virgin of Guadalupe.

THE FACADE

Outside, in front, rises the **fachada** (facade), sometimes in a uniform style, but just as often a mixture of Renaissance, Gothic, and baroque, with some *mujedar* (Moorish) worked into the mix. A proliferation of columns nearly always decorates Oaxacan church facades, from the classic *Toscano, Dórico, Jónico,* and *Corintio* (Etruscan, Doric, Ionic, and Corinthian) pillars to spiraled *Salomónico* (Solomonic) barber's poles and bizarre *estipites*. *Estipite* columns, a baroque feature of Plateresque facades (so-named for their resemblance to elaborate silverware designs), usually begin with a classical capital (base) but rise, curiously, like an inverted obelisk, widening to a pair or trio of elaborately carved prismatic blocks and narrowing quickly again to an identical capital at the top.

CONVENTS

The monastery- (or convent-) style churches included, in addition to all of the above, living and working quarters for the members of the order, typically built around a columned patio called the **claustro** (cloister). A corridor through an arched **portería** (porch) adjacent to the nave usually leads to the cloister, from which monks and nuns could quickly reach the dining hall, or **refectorio** (refectory), and their private rooms, or **celdas** (cells).

The Oaxacan missionary fathers always designed their churches with an eye to handling the masses of natives whom they hoped to convert. For them, padres included an **atrio** (atrium), a large exterior courtyard in front of the facade. For the partly initiated natives, they often built a **capilla abierta** (open chapel) on one side of the atrium. Conversions also occurred at smaller open chapels called **pozas,** built at the corners of the atrium.

OAXACA STANDOUTS
(an asterisk "*" denotes especially recommended churches)
Outstanding examples (nearly all Dominican) of Oaxacan church architecture are scattered throughout the state, notably in the following locations:

Oaxaca City
Basilica y Ex-Convento de Nuestra
    Señora de la Soledad*
Catedral de Oaxaca*
Iglesia y Ex-Convento de San Agustín
Iglesia y Ex-Convento de Santo Domingo*
Templo de San Felipe Neri

Valley of Oaxaca
Cuilapan*
Ocotlán
Tlacochahuaya
Tlacolula*

Mixteca
Coixtlahuaca*
San Juan Teposcolula
San Miguel Achiutla*
Santo Domingo Tonalá
Tamazulapan
Tejupan
Teotongo
Teposcolula*
Tlaxiaco*
Yanhuitlán*

Northern Oaxaca
Calpulalpan*
Ixtlán de Juárez*
Santa Catarina Ixtepeji

The Isthmus
Juchitán
Tehuántepec*

Iglesia y Ex-convento de Santo Domingo

Principal, no phone, 9 A.M.–5 P.M. Tues.–Sun.). Although the main event is a fine exposition of San Bartolo's famed black pottery, the museum also exhibits a surprisingly innovative range of some of the best crafts that the Valley of Oaxaca offers. Besides Doña Rosa's classic pearly-black examples, a host of other pieces— divine angels, scowling bandidos, buxom señas, fierce devils—that reveal the remarkable talent of Doña Rosa's generation of students and followers.

Cochineal Farm

On your way either to or from Coyotepec and Ocotlán, you're in for an unusual treat if you stop at the small demonstration cochineal farm and museum **Rancho la Nopalera** (Km 10.5 Carretera Oaxaca–Puerto Ángel, Calle Matamoros 100, tel./fax 951/551-0030, info@ aztecacolor.com, www.aztecacolor.com), just off the highway at Santa María Coyotepec just north (Oaxaca side) of San Bartolo Coyotepec, a few miles south of the Oaxaca airport. The farm, officially called the **Centro de Difusión del Conocimiento de la Grana Cochinilla y Colorantes Naturales,** is the labor of love of retired chemical engineer Ignacio J. del Río Dueñas and his son-in-law, engineer Manuel Loera Fernández. They graciously welcome all visitors—schoolchildren, visiting scholars, neighbors, tourists—to their ranch for the purpose of breathing life into the ancient Oaxaca tradition of cochineal dye, the source of the bright reds in many of the Oaxaca weavings. (See the sidebar *Cochineal—Nature's Richest Red Dye* in the *Background* chapter.)

Others besides Señores Dueñas and Fernández believe in cochineal and support its use as a natural dye. Its color, so intensely scarlet that it is sometimes known as the "blood of the nopal," is produced from the bodies of the scale insect, *Dactylopius coccus,* that thrives on the thick leaves of the nopal (prickly pear) cactus, found all over Mexico and much of the western United States. Precisely *because* cochineal is a natural, non-synthetic, product, it's gaining favor as a food and cosmetic (lipstick) coloring. The small amount of cochineal that the farm produces sells

for about $200 per kilogram (compared with silver, at about $100), and requires the processing of about 600 nopal leaves.

They will be happy to show you around their cactus cultivation house and demonstrate how the insects are harvested, and explain their several interesting museum exhibits, which illustrate the history and uses of cochineal.

Get there by bus from the *camionera central segunda clase* in Oaxaca City, via regional buses Estrella del Valle, Oaxaca Pacifico, or Estrella Roja del Sureste, or more local Choferes del Sur buses.

By car, turn right, southbound, at the small roadside sign Grana Cochineal Tlapanochestli at the southern edge of Santa María Coyotepec village, on Highway 175, 4.7 miles (7.5 km) south of the Oaxaca airport. After a few hundred yards westbound on a dirt road, another sign directs you left to the ranch.

CRAFTS VILLAGES ON THE ROAD TO OCOTLÁN

Each of the three little crafts villages not far north of Ocotlán has something unique to offer. In order to visit all of them, plus Coyotepec and Ocotlán, on Friday, you'll need to get an early start. If you're inclined to linger, it's best to allow two days for your visit, with an overnight in Ocotlán. Under any circumstances, visit **San Antonino Castillo Velasco** on the same Friday that you visit Ocotlán, because it also has its *tianguis* on Friday. Two things to look for are the wonderful breads, fresh and yummy (in the morning, sold out by afternoon) as you come into town, and the famous *vestidos de San Antonino,* sometimes known as "Oaxaca wedding dresses," marked by their elaborately fancy and colorful animal and floral embroidery.

First stop for the *vestidos de San Antonino* should be the small **Artesanías de Castillo Velasco** (on the San Antonino entrance road, Av. Castillo Velalsco, on the right, two blocks from the highway, tel. 951/571-0623). Your hosts will be friendly Enrique Lucas G. and his wife Maria Luisa Amador H., who manufacture and offer lovely embroidered *vestidos,* *blusas,* and *servilletas* (dresses, blouses, and napkins), and much more. Their finest *vestidos,* elaborately adorned with fetchingly colorful floral and animal designs, sell for $100 and up. Besides the goods they display up front, they also can show you much more, including men's wedding shirts, from their rear storeroom.

For more embroidery options, a few women sell dresses and blouses in the regular market on Friday (turn left at the first block after the bread stalls). If you arrive and no one seems to be selling any dresses, mention *vestidos de San Antonino,* and someone will lead you to a woman who makes them. Alternatively, ask for friendly **Rosa Canseco Godines** (go DEE-nays, Calle Guerrero 33), one of the local *maestras* of the craft. If she's home, she'll gladly show you examples of her beautiful work.

Bus passengers, take a taxi or walk the mile (1.6 km) from Ocotlán. Drivers, turn west at the San Antonino sign just at the northern (Oaxaca) edge of Ocotlán.

San Martín Tilcajete and Santo Tomás Jalieza

San Martín Tilcajete (teel-kah-HAY-tay), about 21 miles (37 km) south of Oaxaca City (not far north of the Hwy. 131 fork), is a prime source of the *alebrijes,* fanciful wooden creatures occupying the shelves of crafts stores the world over. Both it and Santo Tomás Jalieza (south of the Hwy. 131 fork), a mile or two farther south, can be visited as a pair on any day.

The label *alebrije,* a word of Arabic origin, implies something of indefinite form, and that certainly characterizes the fanciful animal figurines that a generation of Oaxaca woodcarvers has been crafting from soft copal wood. Dozens of factory-stores sprinkle Tilcajete town. Start on the front main street, but also be sure to wander the back lanes and step into several cottage workshops, whose occupants will be happy to show you what they have and demonstrate how they make them. You'll find lots more than funny animals. Artisans have branched out to plants such as purple palm trees and yellow cactus. Some items, such as imaginatively painted jewel boxes and picture frames, are practical, while others, such as miniature sets of tables and chairs, are for kids 3–90. Find some of the most original examples at the back-street shop of **Delfino Gutiérrez** (Calle Reforma, tel. 951/524-9074), who specializes in free-form elephants, frogs, turtles, armadillos and much more.

Jalieza (Centro de Artesanías, Plaza Principal, 9 A.M.–5 P.M. daily), on the other hand, is known as the town of embroidered *cinturones* (belts). Townsfolk, virtually all of whom practice the craft, concentrate all of their selling in a single many-stalled market in the middle of town. Step inside and you'll be tempted not only by hundreds of hand-embroidered leather belts, but also by a wealth of lovely hand-loomed and embroidered purses, shawls, dresses, blouses, small backpacks, and much more. Furthermore, asking prices are very reasonable.

OCOTLÁN

Your first stop in district capital Ocotlán (pop. 20,000, 26 miles/42 km south of Oaxaca) should probably be the interesting trio of family workshops run by the Aguilar sisters, Irene, Guillermina, and Josefina. Watch for signs reading "Aguilar," on the right, on the outskirts, about a quarter mile (0.4 km) on the Oaxaca side from the town plaza. Their creations include a host of fanciful figures in clay: vendors with big ripe strawberries, green and red cactus, goats in skirts, and bikini-clad blondes. The workshops are open 9 A.M.–6 P.M. daily.

The main Ocotlán attraction (unless you're lucky enough to arrive for the big fiesta on the third Sunday of May) is the huge Friday market. Beneath a riot of colored awnings, hordes of merchandise—much modern stuff, but also plenty of old-fashioned goodies—load a host of tables and street-laid mats. How about a saddle for your donkey? If not that, why not four or five turkeys, a goat, or perhaps half a dozen bags of hard-to-get wild medicinal plants? And be sure to pick up a kilo or two of *cal* (lime or quicklime) for soaking your corn. If you're looking for lots of native costumes, you'll have

THE VALLEY OF OAXACA

to head for the mountains, because few women (except for their ribbon-decorated braids) and virtually no men wear *traje.* You'll hear plenty of Zapotec, however. At least half of the local people are native speakers.

Since markets are best in the morning, you should make Ocotlán your first Friday stop. Drivers could get there by heading straight south out of the city, arriving in Ocotlán by mid-morning. Spend a few hours, then begin your return in the early afternoon, stopping at the sprinkling of crafts villages along the road back to Oaxaca. Gasoline is available at the Pemex *gasolinera,* on the highway, on the north edge of Ocotlán.

Bus travelers could hold to a similar schedule by riding an early Autobuses Estrella del Valle or Autotransportes Oaxaca–Pacífico from the *camionera central segunda clase,* then returning, in steps, by bus, or more quickly by taxi, stopping at the crafts villages along the way.

Casa de Cultura Rudolfo Morales

During the 1980s and 1990s, Ocotlán came upon good times, largely due to the late Rudolfo Morales, the internationally celebrated but locally born artist who dedicated his fortune to improving his hometown. The Rudolfo Morales Foundation has been restoring churches and other public buildings, reforesting mountainsides, and funding self-help and educational projects all over Ocotlán and its surrounding district. The bright colors of the plaza-front *presidencia municipal* and the big church nearby result from the good works of Rudolfo Morales.

The Morales Foundation's local efforts radiate from the Casa de Cultura Rudolfo Morales (Morelos 108, tel. 951/571-0198, 10 A.M.–2 P.M. and 4–8 P.M. Mon.–Fri.), in the yellow-painted mansion three doors north from the Ocotlán plaza's northwest corner. In the Casa Cultura's graceful, patrician interior, the Morales family and staff manage the foundation's affairs, teach art and computer classes, and sponsor community events.

The foundation staff welcomes visitors. For advance information, contact the foundation's headquarters in Oaxaca City (Murguia 105, between Alcalá and 5 de Mayo, tel. 951/514-2324 or 951/514-0910, galeria@artedeoaxaca.com, www.artedeoaxaca.com, 11 A.M.–3 P.M. and 5–8 P.M. Mon.–Sat.).

Templo de Santo Domingo

Local people celebrate Rudolfo Morales's brilliant restoration of their beloved 16th-century Templo de Santo Domingo. Gold and silver from the infamous Santa Catarina Minas (mines), in the mountains east of Ocotlán, financed the church's initial construction. When overwork and disease had tragically decimated the local native population by around 1600, the mines had to be abandoned, and work on the church stopped. Although eventually completed over the succeeding three centuries, it had slipped into serious disrepair by the 1980s.

Fortunately, the Templo de Santo Domingo is now completely rebuilt, from its bright blue, yellow, and white facade to the

Ocotlán's beautifully restored Templo de Santo Domingo

© BRUCE WHIPPERMAN

© BRUCE WHIPPERMAN

restored doors, Templo de Santo Domingo

baroque gold glitter of its nave ceiling. Inside on the right side, you'll pass a pious Saint John the Baptist, with Mary Magdalene at his feet. Up front, above the main altar, a white-haired, bearded Creator reigns, resembling an indigenous Father Sun, with a halo of golden rays bursting from behind his head. Below him, Jesus hangs limply on the cross, flanked below by Mother Mary with a knife in her breast and St. John the Baptist lamenting at Jesus's feet.

Walk to the nave's south (right) side, to a gilded chapel dedicated to the Señor de la Sacristía (Lord of the Sacristy), the image above the altar. Also notice the adjacent oil painting of the Virgin of the Rosary, singular for her mestizo facial features. The Señor de la Sacristía is the object of community adoration in a festival of food, fireworks, processions, high masses, and dances climaxing on the third Sunday in May.

Practicalities

Ocotlán has at least two good restaurants. For relaxation, take a seat at the airy plaza-view veranda of the ℂ **Restaurant Celebración** (cell 044-951/544-4254, 7 A.M.–10 P.M. daily, $3–10), on the upstairs floor of the Plaza las Portales, on the east side of the central plaza. Although welcoming owner Jorge Guzman serves from a very recognizable à la carte menu of Mexican country breakfast, lunch, and supper choices, his afternoon four-course *comida* (soup, rice, entrée, and dessert, $4–6) is what keeps most of their local customers returning day after day.

Alternatively, you can usually free yourself of the Friday downtown crowd at the rustic-chic **La Cabaña** (tel. 951/571-0201, 8 A.M.–7 P.M. daily, $3–8), an open-air *palapa* restaurant by the *gasolinera* on the highway, at the north, Oaxaca, edge of town.

If you decide to linger overnight in

Ocotlán, the newish, clean, and modern **Hotel Rey David** (16 de Septiembre 248, tel. 951/571-1248, $20 s or d in one bed, $30 d or t in two beds) can accommodate you. The hotel offers about 20 comfortable, attractively decorated rooms. Find it on the south-side Highway 175 ingress-egress avenue, Avenida 16 de Septiembre, where it runs east–west, about three blocks east of the market and central plaza.

Do your money business at the Ocotlán **Banamex** (9 A.M.–4 P.M. Mon.–Fri.), with ATM, on the north side of the town plaza.

EJUTLA

Tour buses usually skip Ejutla de Crespo (pop. 20,000) because of its distance, about 36 miles (59 km, one hour) from Oaxaca City. This is a pity, because Ejutla (ay-HOOT-lah) hides some surprises, not the least of which is its huge, colorful **Thursday market.** Folks troop in from country villages all over the huge Ejutla governmental district and farther, to haggle over everything from *hamacas* and huaraches to radios and refrigerators. Moreover, Ejutla also offers accommodations, at Hotel 6, the graceful hacienda-turned-hotel at the south edge of town.

Sights

Take a walk around Ejutla's shady plaza to get your bearings. The portico-fronted *presidencia municipal* stands on the plaza's south side, the market is on the north, and the big, proud **Templo de la Natividad** towers above the southeast corner. Sometime around 1750, the present church replaced the 16th-century original (which itself replaced a big pre-conquest Zapotec pyramid). Over the years, earthquakes took their toll; it was extensively restored around 1900.

Several large hieroglyph-decorated stone blocks built into the church's walls attest to the fact that the entire town remains an unexplored archaeological zone. You can find more evidence of this about two blocks north and two blocks east of the church, near the corner of Calles Altimirano and 16 de Septiembre. A big house compound encloses what appears to be a small hill, which is actually a buried temple-topped pyramid. Look for the several hieroglyph-decorated pre-conquest monoliths that have been incorporated into modern walls.

Since the church is usually open, you might as well step into the cool interior and contemplate the town's patron, the **Virgin of the Nativity,** presiding above the altar in what at first glance appears to be a bridal gown. In the lovely transept chapel on the right of the nave, you'll see another image of the same patron. Local people celebrate both, with a big fiesta centering around December 8.

For something else interesting, step over to the *presidencia* and look on the wall for Ejutla's official *escudo* (coat of arms), which incorporates no arms at all. It's a portrait in tile of a bean vine, encircling a view of the sun rising from behind a likeness of Cerro El Labrador, the town's sacred mountain, towering in the east. A poem in praise of the "SUN, which rises here earlier than other lands . . . the source of life . . . without which there would be nothing" is included at the base of the *escudo*.

Practicalities

Another of Ejutla's surprises is the ❰ **Hotel 6** (Km 61.5 Carretera Oaxaca–Puerto Ángel, tel. 951/573-0350, $20 s or d in one bed, $40 d or t in two beds), "probably the best in North America," claims the owner-operator, friendly former Olympic wrestler and civil engineer Mario E. Corres. A sign, which strikingly resembles Motel 6 signs all over the United States and Canada, draws you into the parking lot. You know you're in for something unique when you pull up to a portaled, old hacienda as big as a baseball field, with a jungle on one side, complete with tree house and a swinging rope walkway.

Inside, you'll find everything completely in order, from three spreading courtyards, a pool, and two big function rooms to a huge living room, dining room, and spotless, shining, old-fashioned kitchen. The climax to all this is Señor Corres's museum, which includes his family tree and which he gladly explains to visitors (in Spanish, of course).

The 14 rooms, which after everything else seem an afterthought, are plain but clean. Some are more inviting than others. Take a look at two or three, small and large, before choosing. If the weather's warm, you'll need a fan, which some rooms have. All this plus parking, hot-water shower-baths, and an elegantly homey dining room.

You'll encounter most of Ejutla's services during your stroll around town—most of the available stores and institutions are right on or near the plaza. Starting at the *presidencia municipal,* on the south and moving clockwise, first, at the southwest plaza corner is the town's best place to eat, **Comedor Mary** (8 A.M.–7 P.M., $2–6), where a squad of hardworking teenage girls serve hearty country food.

From there, head down the street south, away from the plaza. At the first corner stands the bus station where (some first-, but) mostly second-class Autotransportes Oaxaca–Pacífico, Autobuses Estrella del Valle, and Fletes y Pasajes buses will take you anywhere along Highway 175 between Puerto Ángel and Oaxaca City.

Switch back to the Comedor Mary and walk west away from the plaza; near the first street corner, find the **Telecomunicaciones** (for money orders, public fax, and telephone). A few steps south of the same corner, find **Farmacia San Antonio and Clinica Urgencias** (tel. 951/573-0304, 8 A.M.–2 P.M. and 5–8 P.M. Mon.–Sat.), with Dr. Lorenzo Antonio Elorza.

To mail a letter or buy stamps, reverse direction, continue a full block north, then turn left (west) and continue two blocks and a fraction to the *correo* (post office). Return east, to the northwest plaza corner, where you'll see **Casa Altamirano** (8 A.M.–9 P.M. daily), the *abarrotes* (grocery), and half a block east of that the open-air market (8 A.M.–6 P.M. daily) where you can get the fresh items that the grocery store doesn't have.

Continuing north, at the street corner past the market, is the *huarachería* **La Principal** (9 A.M.–7 P.M. Mon.–Sat.) with a huge assortment of down-home footwear, nearly all made

on-site by the owner's daughter. One short block behind that (north) is the **Clínica San Gabriel** (tel. 951/573-0244), with a gynecologist and a general practitioner–surgeon on call 24 hours. If you need another *farmacia,* you have your choice of either the **Santa Fe** (9 A.M.–9 P.M. daily), on the plaza's northeast corner, or the **Farmacia Liliana** (9 A.M.–9 P.M. daily), a block east of the plaza, next to the church. Gasoline is available at the highway **Pemex** *gasolinera* at the north edge of town.

DOWN HIGHWAY 131
Zimatlán

Travelers who head far enough along Highway 131, which branches west about 22 miles (35 km) south of Oaxaca City through the Valley of Oaxaca's southwest side, are in for more than just one treat. They pass some of Oaxaca's most productive farmland: lush fields and pastures that in summer and fall appear like a verdant carpet reaching to the foot of pine- and oak-studded mountains.

Zimatlán (pop. 25,000), the capital of all this, appears simply as a workaday farming town, with a modicum of strictly local-style services. Zimatlán's pace quickens, however, on Wednesdays, when the town market overflows with a flood of Zapotec buyers and sellers from the surrounding mountains. Excitement peaks during the eight days around January 15, when folks celebrate the unique **Fiesta del Dulce Nombre de Jesús.** Keeping by their traditional ways, townspeople enjoy old-fashioned events including processions, a big everyone-invited barbecue, *jaripeo,* and the Danza de las Plumas (Feathers) and Danza de los Jardineros (Gardeners), plus a *pelota mixteca* (pre-conquest ball game) tournament.

San Sebastián de las Grutas

It's hard not to fall in love with this idyllic hidden corner of the Valley of Oaxaca. Don't be put off by the scruffy, tourist-*comedor-*cluttered Highway 131 right turnoff intersection, 45 miles (73 km) south of Oaxaca City. After a quarter mile (0.4 km) toward the *grutas* (caves), the road becomes a gently winding, sylvan creekside drive. The jade-green brook (sometimes muddy in wet season) gurgles downhill over little rocks and giant boulders, pausing here and there in picture-perfect swimming holes. Meanwhile, from overhead, a regal host of towering, gnarled *sabinos* (*tules* or *ahuehuetes*) shades the creek, appearing every bit as ancient and grand as their northern cousins, the California redwoods. Now and then, you pass by the rustic wooden homes and the cornfields of the local farm families. Or you might glimpse the big cylindrical fermentation vats of a rough-and-ready roadside *mescal* factory.

About eight miles (13 km) past San Sebastián de las Grutas town (pop. 2,000) you reach the caves. The creek emerges clear and pristine, as if by magic, from beneath a big rock at the foot of a mountain.

A hundred yards uphill are the caves, which you can tour for a fee of about $2. A guide with a pair of strong flashlights will lead you on an easy, mostly level walk through the cave's several chambers, which vary from about 20 feet (six meters) to more than 200 feet (60 meters) in height. He's used to getting a tip of about $2 per person.

The cave you will see is only one of the several partly explored caves honeycombing the mountain, Cerro Cruz del Lado. Its five or six main chambers stretch about 500 yards (about 0.5 km) into the mountain. Inside, the formations, which include many towering stalagmites and plenty of bulging stalactites, initially appear, in the semi-darkness of the flickering flashlights, to be gargantuan mounds and columns of half-melted vanilla-chocolate-swirl ice cream. However, when your eyes get accustomed to the darkness, most of the formations, more than any cave I've ever seen, take on fanciful shapes. Bring your own flashlight and have fun dreaming up your own interpretations instead of merely seeing the guide's camel, turtle, shark, alligator (which looked like a seal to me), or tiger.

PRACTICALITIES

One could spend several enjoyable days hiking, bird-watching, swimming in the creek, sitting in the town plaza, and getting to know the local people. They're generally friendly, having seen enough visitors that they're not afraid and don't think you're too strange. The shady streamside, moreover, appears ripe for camping, either in your tent or (self-contained) RV. Get permission first from the municipal authorities at the *presidencia* in San Sebastián de las Grutas, a mile (1.6 km) downstream from the cave parking lot.

A number of downscale eating stands near the caves sell basic local meals, which, if hot, should be wholesome. Water, drinkable directly from the pristine spring source by the caves, is not a problem here.

Get there by bus via the Solteca or Estrella Rojo del Sureste bus from the *camionera central segunda clase* next to the Abastos market on the southwest side of Oaxaca City. The Solteca buses, some of which go right to the caves, leave several times a day, beginning around 6 A.M. The Estrella Rojo del Sureste may only drop you at the intersection, eight miles (13 km) from the caves. Take a taxi or *colectivo* van or truck from there. Drivers, follow Highway 131, a total of 53 miles (76 km) south of Oaxaca City. Allow about two hours' driving time. In the reverse, north direction, the *grutas* are 119 miles (190 km) north of Puerto Escondido. For safety, under the best of conditions, allow about four hours of daylight driving time.

Sola de Vega

San Miguel Sola de Vega (pop. 13,000), diminutive capital of the remote, sprawling governmental district of the same name, is the main service stop on Oaxaca–Puerto Escondido Highway 131. The town, 59 miles (95 km) south of Oaxaca City (99 miles/159 km north of Puerto Escondido), presides over a lush mountain-valley checkerboard of corn, cane, and cattle. The lovely *sabino*-shaded Río Sola de Vega ripples right past the town, crossed by quaint but practical suspension footbridges. It looks as if the people have plenty of fun, spending about half their time in the water. Camping by tent or RV appears promising in shady spots by the river. Get permission from authorities at the *presidencia municipal* at the town plaza, about three blocks north from the highway.

If you arrive on Sunday, Sola de Vega's traditional market day, be sure to visit the local *tianguis* around the town plaza.

PRACTICALITIES

A few stores near the plaza can supply basic groceries. For cooked food, try one of the many country *comedores* by the highway or, if you prefer, the dining room of the plain but clean **Hotel Aguirre** (tel. 951/574-0046 or 951/574-0047, $15 s, $20 d, $30 t; dining room 7 A.M.–10 P.M. daily, $2–6), on the highway. Its 15 rooms come with hot-water showers. You will not generally need a reservation, unless you're arriving late (perhaps after 9 P.M.).

Drivers, fill up with gasoline at the **Pemex** station on the north side of town, since gasoline is scarce in most of the country along Highway 131. For other essential services, you have the *correo* and *telégrafo* by the plaza, a *centro de salud* on Independencia, off the plaza, and a private physician, Dr. Vicente Mendoza Martinez, also on Independencia. For nonprescription medicines and phone calls, go to the *farmacia-caseta larga distancia* San Miguel, right on the highway at the south (Puerto Escondido) end of town. Also on the highway you'll find the Solteca and Estrella Roja del Sureste bus stations.

SOUTHWEST SIDE
◖ Zaachila

About 10 miles (16 km) south of Oaxaca City, Zaachila (pop. 30,000), like Mitla, overlies the ruins of its ancient namesake city, which rose to prominence after the decline of Monte Albán. Although excavations have uncovered many Mixtec-style remains, historical records nevertheless list a number of Zapotec kings (including the greatest, Zaachila Yoo, for whom the town is named) who ruled Zaachila as a virtual Zapotec capital during the 14th and 15th centuries. Nevertheless, by the eve of the conquest, in the early 16th century, a noble Mixtec minority dominated the

Zapotec-speaking inhabitants, whose leaders the Mixtec warriors had sent fleeing for their lives to Tehuántepec.

The big forested hill that rises north of the market plaza is topped by a large, mostly unexplored pyramid. Several unexcavated mounds and courtyards dot the hill's north and south flanks. The site parking lot and entrance gate are adjacent to the colonial church just north of the plaza.

In 1962, archaeologist Roberto Gallegos (guarded from hostile residents by armed soldiers) uncovered a pair of unopened tombs beneath the summit of the Zaachila pyramid. They yielded a trove of polychrome pottery, gold jewelry (including a ring still on a left hand), and jade fan handles. Tomb 1 descends via a steep staircase to an entrance decorated with a pair of cat-motif heads. On the antechamber walls a few steps farther are depictions of owls and a pair of personages (perhaps former occupants) inscribed respectively with the name-dates 5-Flower and 9-Flower. Do not miss the bas-reliefs on the tomb's back wall that depict a man whose torso is covered with a turtle shell. (Tomb 2, although open for inspection, contains no remaining sculptures or inscriptions.)

Hint: The narrow tomb staircase is negotiable by only a few persons at a time and often requires an hour for a tour-bus crowd to inspect it. Rather than waste your market time standing in line, go downhill, stroll around the market, and return when the line is smaller. If driving, arrive early, around 9 A.M. on Thursday, to avoid tour-bus crowds. Return in early afternoon, allowing time to visit Cuilapan and Arrazola.

After visiting the archaeological site, you might take a look inside the smallish but robustly buttressed colonial-era Zaachila church, which appears to have been erected atop one of the town's original pre-conquest ceremonial platforms. Inside, atop the altar, an unusual black Jesus presides above the glass-encased town patron, the Virgin of the Nativity. In her honor, townsfolk stage a big fiesta during the eight days around September 8, which, besides the exhilarating carnival rides, challenging games of chance, tasty food, and flashing fireworks, also features the spectacularly colorful Danza de las Plumas (Dance of the Feathers). The Thursday **tianguis** is Zaachila's weekly main event. It spreads for blocks below the archaeological site and church. Thousands of Zapotec-speaking country people stream into town to buy, sell, gossip, flirt, and fill up with their favorite delicacies. A few highlights are the luscious, scarlet-red *pitacaya* (pee-tah-KAHY-yah) fruits, and the foamy-tan *tecate* (tay-KAH-tay) drink, corn-based and deliciously flavored with chocolate, *rosita* flower petals, and ground seeds of *mamey*, all sweetened with brown sugar juice and honey. For a breezy change of pace, hop into one of the buzzing *moto-taxis* (motorized rickshaws) for a 10-minute jaunt (for about $1.50) around town.

If you're in the mood for food, wholesome (make sure you get it served hot) country fare is available at the regiment of *fondas* in the permanent, roofed section of the market. Alternatively, enjoy lunch at the showplace C **Restaurant La Capilla** (tel. 951/528-6115, 7 A.M.–7 P.M. daily, $5–10). Get there on foot or by asking your *moto-taxi* driver to let you off at La Capilla (kah-PEE-yah), on the main east–west Oaxaca ingress street, a few blocks west of the market.

By bus, get to Zaachila via **Autobuses de Oaxaca,** from the *camionera central segunda clase* in Oaxaca City, or by private tourist bus.

By car from Oaxaca City, head south from downtown to the *periférico*. Do not continue south via the airport Highway 131–175. Instead, from the *periférico* a block west of the airport-highway intersection (watch for the Monte Albán sign), follow the four-lane boulevard that angles southwest, away from the *periférico*, across the Río Atoyac bridge. Just after crossing the bridge, do not continue straight ahead toward Monte Albán, but take the second left (south) onto the old (scenic route) Zaachila road, which also passes Cuilapan and Arrazola. (*Note:* The first left fork heads along the no-nonsense new highway, in a straight four-lane bee-line toward Zaachila, bypassing Cuilapan and Arrazola.)

Cuilapan de Guerrero and Arrazola

Southwest of Oaxaca City, on the old road between Zaachila and Arrazola, Cuilapan de Guerrero is famous for its elaborate but unfinished **Ex-Convento de Santiago,** or Saint James (visible from the highway, 9 A.M.–5 P.M. daily), where Vicente Guerrero, father of the Mexican republic, was infamously executed in 1831. Although construction began in 1535, the cost of the basilica and associated monastery began to balloon. In 1550, King Philip demanded humility and moderation of the builders, whose work was finally ended by a 1570 court ruling. The extravagances—the soaring, roofless basilica, magnificent baptismal font, splendid Gothic cloister, and elaborate frescoes—remain as national treasures.

Arrazola, a few miles farther north, toward Oaxaca City, is one of the sources (along with Tilcajete) of the intricately painted *alebrijes* (ah-lay-BREE-hays)—fanciful wooden creatures that decorate the shelves of handicrafts shops all over Mexico and foreign countries. Bus travelers, get there either by second-class bus or by tourist bus from Oaxaca City. Drivers, turn west (left) onto signed Highway 145 a few miles north of Cuilapan or, traveling south, 3.2 miles (5.1 km) south of the Río Atoyac bridge in Oaxaca City. Pass through San Javier village and continue from the turnoff a total of three miles (five km) to the Arrazola town plaza. Turn right immediately before the plaza onto Calle E. Zapata and turn left after one block, at Independencia. After one more block you will be at Calle Obregón, where everyone seems to be making *alebrijes*. Although you should visit a number of family workshops along the street, be sure to visit **Pepe Santiago** and his Santa's workshop of craftspersons (10 A.M.–6 P.M. daily). Inside the Santiago compound (on the right, just below the hilltop), men and boys saw and carve away while a cadre of young women and girls painstakingly add riots of painted brocade to everything from whimsical dragons and gargoyles to armadillos, giraffes, and rabbits.

West Side: The Archaeological Route

Although all of these interesting destinations are readily reachable from Oaxaca City, they are far too rich to be visited in a single day. As a minimum, be sure to visit Monte Albán, which can be conveniently combined with a side trip to Atzompa. On another day, preferably a Wednesday, visit the Etla market, with stops at the community museums and key archaeological sites at El Mogote and Suchilquitongo nearby.

◖ MONTE ALBÁN

Monte Albán ranks among Mesoamerica's most regally spectacular ruined cities. Known in ancient times by its Zapotec name, Danni Dipaa, the site's present "Monte Albán" label was probably coined by a local Spaniard because of its resemblance to a similarly named Italian hilltop town.

Monte Albán's original inhabitants cultivated beans, chilies, corn, fruits, and squash on the hillsides and in adjacent valleys, occasionally feasting on meat from deer, small game, and perhaps (as did other native Mexicans) domesticated dogs. Tribute from surrounding communities directly enriched Monte Albán's ruling classes and, by extension, its artisans and farmers.

The great city atop the hill reigned for at least 1,200 years, between 500 B.C. and A.D. 750, as the capital of the Zapotecs and the dominant force between Teotihuacán in the Valley of Mexico and the Maya kingdoms of the southeast. Archaeologists have organized the Valley of Oaxaca's history from 500 B.C. to the conquest into five periods, known as Monte Albán I–V. Over those centuries, the hilltop city was repeatedly reconstructed with new

Monte Albán's enigmatic Building J, foreground

© BRUCE WHIPPERMAN

THE VALLEY OF OAXACA

THE VALLEY OF OAXACA

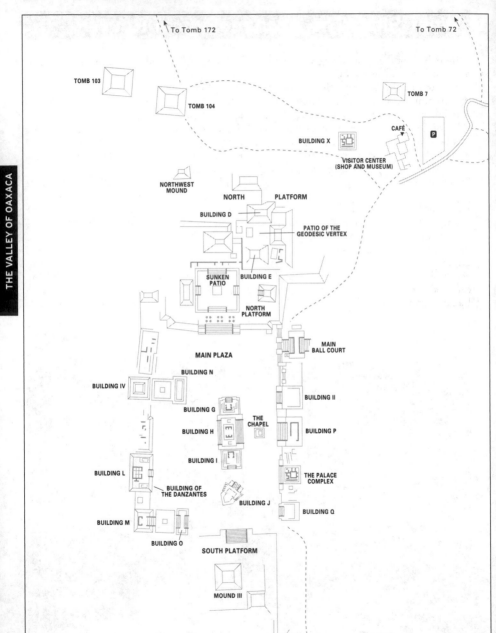

To Tomb 172

To Tomb 72

TOMB 103

TOMB 104

TOMB 7

CAFÉ

P

BUILDING X

VISITOR CENTER
(SHOP AND MUSEUM)

NORTHWEST
MOUND

NORTH   PLATFORM

BUILDING D

PATIO OF THE
GEODESIC VERTEX

SUNKEN
PATIO

BUILDING E

NORTH
PLATFORM

MAIN
BALL COURT

MAIN PLAZA

BUILDING N

BUILDING IV

BUILDING II

BUILDING G

THE
CHAPEL

BUILDING H

BUILDING P

BUILDING I

BUILDING L

THE PALACE
COMPLEX

BUILDING OF
THE DANZANTES

BUILDING J

BUILDING Q

BUILDING M

BUILDING O

SOUTH PLATFORM

MOUND III

© AVALON TRAVEL

To 7-Deer Complex (250m)

To Oaxaca

SMALL BALL
COURT

TOMB 105

MONTE ALBÁN

0   100 yds

0   100 m

walls, plazas, and staircases, which, like layers of an onion, now overlie earlier construction.

Remains from Monte Albán Period I (500 B.C.– A.D. 1) reveal an already advanced culture, with gods, permanent temples, a priesthood, a written language, numerals, and a calendar. Sharply contrasting house styles indicate a differentiated, multilayered society. Monte Albán I ruins abound in graceful polychrome ceramics of uniquely Zapotec style.

Concurrent Olmec influences have also been found, notably in the buildings known as the **Danzantes** (Dancers), decorated with unique bas-reliefs similar to those unearthed along the Veracruz and Tabasco coasts.

Monte Albán-II people (A.D. 1–300), by contrast, came under heavy influence from Chiapas and Guatemala in the south. They built strange, ship-shaped buildings, such as Monte Albán's mysterious **Building J,** and left unique remains of their religion, such as the striking jade bat-god now on display in the Anthropology Museum in Mexico City.

Monte Albán reached its apex during the classical Period III (A.D. 300–800), attaining a population of perhaps 40,000 in an urban zone of about three square miles (eight sq. km), which spread along hilltops (including the El Gallo and Atzompa archaeological sites) west of the present city of Oaxaca.

Vigorous Period III leaders rebuilt the main hilltop complex as we see it today. Heavily influenced by the grand style of the Teotihuacán structures in the Valley of Mexico, the buildings were finished with handsome sloping staircases, corniced walls, monumental carvings, ball courts, and hieroglyph-inscribed stelae depicting gods, kings, and heroic scenes of battle.

By A.D. 750, few foreign influences were continuing to enrich Monte Albán's uniquely Zapotec pottery styles. Quality declined until they seemed like mere factory copies. Concurrently, the Zapotec pantheon expanded to a horde of gods, as if mere numbers could protect the increasingly isolated Valley of Oaxaca from the outside world.

In A.D. 800, Monte Albán, mysteriously cut

off from the rest of Mesoamerica, was declining in population and power. By A.D. 1000, the city was virtually abandoned. The reasons—whether drought, disease, or revolt—and the consequent loss of the necessarily imported water, wood, salt, and food supplies remain an enigma.

During Periods IV and V, Mixtec peoples from the north invaded the Valley of Oaxaca. They warred with valley Zapotecs and, despite their relatively small numbers, became a ruling class in a number of valley city-states. The blend of Mixtec and Zapotec art and architecture sometimes led to new forms, especially visible at the west valley sites of Yagul and Mitla.

Monte Albán, meanwhile, although abandoned, was not forgotten. It became both a refuge and a venerated burial place. In times of siege, local people retreated within the walls of a fortress built around Monte Albán's South Platform. At other times, Mixtec nobles opened tombs and reused them as burial vaults right up until the eve of the conquest.

Exploring the Site

Visitors to Monte Albán (8 A.M.–5 P.M.) enjoy a panoramic view of green mountains rising above the checkerboard of the Valley of Oaxaca. Monte Albán is fun for a picnic; alternatively, it is an auspicious place to perch atop a pyramid above the grand Main Plaza, etched by lengthening afternoon shadows, and contemplate the ages. Allow at least two hours for your visit.

As you enter past the visitors center, north is on your right, marked by the grand **North Platform,** topped by clusters of temples. The **Ball Court** will soon appear below on your left. Twenty-foot-high walkways circumscribe the sunken I-shaped playing field. To ensure true bounces, builders spread smooth stucco over all surfaces, including the slopes on opposite sides (which, contrary to appearances, did not seat spectators). This, like all Oaxacan ball courts, had no stone ring (for supposed goals), but rather four mysterious niches at the court's I-end corners.

The **Main Plaza,** 1,000 feet long and exactly two-thirds that wide, is aligned along a precise north–south axis. Probably serving as a market and civic/ceremonial ground, the monumentally harmonious Main Plaza was the Zapotec "navel" of the world.

Monte Albán's oldest monumental construction, the **Danzantes** building (surmounted by newer Building L, on the west side of the plaza between Buildings M and IV), dates from Period I. Its walls are graced with a host of personages, known commonly as the *danzantes* (dancers) from their oft-contorted postures—probably chiefs vanquished by Monte Albán's armies. Their headdresses, earplugs, bracelets, and necklaces mark them among the nobility, while glyphs around their heads identify each individual.

Building J (circa A.D. 1), one of the most remarkable in Mesoamerica, stands nearby in mid-plaza at the foot of the South Platform. Speculation has raged since excavators unearthed its arrow-shaped base generations ago. It is not surprising that Alfonso Caso, Monte Albán's original principal excavator, theorized it was an astronomical observatory. In the mind's eye, it seems like some fantastic ocean (or space?) vessel, being navigated to some mysteriously singular southwest destination by a ghostly crew oblivious to its worldly, earthbound brother monuments.

The **South Platform** affords Monte Albán's best vantage point, especially during the late afternoon. Starting on the right-hand, Palace-complex side, **Building II** has a peculiar tunnel on its near side, covertly used by priests for privacy or perhaps some kind of magical effect. To the south stands Building P, an undistinguished, albeit multiroom palace.

The South Platform itself is only marginally explored. Looters have riddled the mounds on its top side. Its bottom four corners were embellished by fine bas-reliefs, two of which had their engravings intentionally buried from view. You can admire the fine sculpture and yet-undeciphered Zapotec hieroglyphs on one of them, along with others, at the South Platform's plaza-edge west side.

Still atop the South Platform, turn

THE VALLEY OF OAXACA

© BRUCE WHIPPERMAN

North Platform, Monte Albán archaeological site

southward, where you can see the Seven-Deer complex, a few hundred yards away, labeled for the name-date inscribed on its great lintel.

Turning northward again, look just beyond Building J to Buildings G, H, and I at plaza center, erected mostly to cover a rocky mound impossible to remove without then-unavailable dynamite. Between these buildings and the palace complex on the right stands the small chapel where the remarkable bat-god jade sculpture was found.

On Monte Albán's northern periphery stand a number of tombs that, when excavated, yielded a trove of artifacts, now mostly housed in museums. Walking west from the Northern Platform's northeast base corner, you will pass Mound X on the right. A few hundred yards farther comes the **Tomb 104** mound, presided over by an elaborate ceramic urn representing Cocijo, the Zapotec god of rain. Just north of this is **Tomb 172,** with the skeletons and offerings left intact.

Heading back along the northernmost of the two paths from Tomb 104, you will arrive at **Tomb 7** a few hundred feet behind the visitors center. Here, around 1450, Mixtec nobles removed the original eighth-century contents and reused the tomb, burying a deceased dignitary and two servants for the netherworld. Along with the bodies, they left a fabulous treasure in gold, silver, jade, alabaster, and turquoise, now visible at the museum at the Centro Cultural de Santo Domingo in Oaxaca City.

A few hundred feet toward town on the opposite side of the road from the parking lot is a trail leading past a small ball court to the Cerro de Plumaje (Hill of Plumage), site of **Tomb 105.** A magnificent entrance door lintel, reminiscent of those at Mitla, welcomes you inside. Past the patio, descend to the mural-decorated tomb antechamber. Inside the cruciform tomb itself, four figures walk in pairs toward a great glyph, flanked by a god and goddess, identified by their name-dates.

Visitors Center

The Monte Albán Visitors Center (tel. 951/516-1215, 8 A.M.–5 P.M.) has an excellent museum, good café with airy terrace, and information counter. Also, a well-stocked store offers many books—guides, histories, art, folklore—on Mesoamerica. First, take a look inside the museum, which displays a number of Monte Albán's famous finds. Most notable are several of the original *danzantes* monolith reliefs, recognizable by their mutilated genitals.

In the bookstore (tel. 951/516-9180), you might purchase a copy of the very useful *Guide to Monte Albán,* by Monte Albán's director, Neli Robles. You might also pick up a copy of the very authoritative, in-depth *Oaxaca, the Archaeological Record,* by archaeologist Marcus Winter, that covers many Oaxaca archaeological sites, including the valley sites of Dainzu, Lambityeco, Mitla,

THE TRAGIC STORY OF PRINCESS DONAJI

The fabled marriage of King Cosijoeza (koh-see-hoh-AY-zah) of the Zapotecs to Coyollicatzin (koh-yoh-yee-KAH-tseen), daughter of Emperor Moctezuma II of the Aztecs, around 1490, was a happy one. It resulted in five children, the youngest of whom was a charming little girl.

The king asked his soothsayers what their divinations told of his little daughter's future. They replied that her life would be filled with tragic events and that she would finally sacrifice herself for her people. The king, saddened by the news but happy that she would turn out to be so selfless, named her Donaji (Great Soul).

Earlier, Cosijoeza, who ruled the Zapotec Isthmus domains from his capital at present-day Tehuántepec, had been an uneasy ally of his old enemy, King Dzahuindanda (zah-ween-DAHN-dah) of the Mixtecs. In 1520, with the Aztec threat diminished by the Spanish invasion, Cosijoeza recklessly attacked the fierce Mixtecs, losing the initial battle and then nearly his life as the Mixtecs pressed their advantage.

However, the Spanish, in the person of Hernán Cortés's lieutenant, Francisco Orozco, soon imposed a Mixtec-Zapotec treaty in which Dzahuindanda received Princess Donaji as a hostage to guarantee the peace.

Having Donaji as a prisoner at Monte Albán (known as Danni Dipaa in those days) was not exactly an advantage to Dzahuindanda, for he suspected that she was as much a spy as a hostage. His guess was right. Donaji gleaned intelligence vital to the Zapotec counterattack her father

Cosijoeza was planning. At the moment Dzahuindanda's forces were most vulnerable, she sent her father a secret message to attack, which he did, with complete success, except for one thing.

With the treaty broken, the outraged Mixtecs decided to do away with Donaji. They decapitated her and buried her body before her father could rescue her. Later, some Zapotecs found Donaji's remains on the bank of the Atoyac river. They were surprised to see a lovely violet wild iris blossoming from her blood. Even more surprising, they found the flower's roots growing around her head, which was without any sign of decomposition.

Three hundred years later, the Oaxaca government decided to honor the heroine who sacrificed herself for her people by adding an image of Donaji's head to the Oaxacan coat of arms, where it remains to the present day.

Princess Donaji sacrificed her life in order to protect the safety of her Zapotec kinfolk.

© BRUCE WHIPPERMAN

San José El Mogote, and Suchilquitongo, and several other important sites in the Mixteca.

Getting There

Get to Monte Albán economically and very conveniently by one of the **tourist buses,** run by Viajes Turísticos Mitla, that departs many times daily from downtown Hotel Rivera del Ángel (Mina 518), five blocks west of the *zócalo* in Oaxaca City. (See the *Getting There and Away* section in the *Oaxaca City* chapter.)

By car, get to Monte Albán via the most scenic route. Starting from Oaxaca City's south side, at the *periférico*, about a mile due south from the *zócalo* past the end of southbound Calle M. Cabrera. At the *periférico*, watch for a Monte Albán sign. Cross the *periférico*, then bear right (southwest) and immediately cross over the Río Atoyac bridge. Continue ahead, following other Monte Alban signs, about five miles (eight km), uphill, to Monte Albán.

Alternatively, get to Monte Albán by following Highway 190 northwest from downtown Oaxaca City. After just about two miles (three km) from the city center (look for a Monte Albán sign), curve left, around the big monument and traffic circle, reversing your direction, then immediately turn right (west) and continue across the Río Atoyac bridge. Follow the signs about six more miles (10 km) uphill to Monte Albán.

SANTA MARÍA ATZOMPA

The present-day town of Santa María Atzompa (pop. 5,000) spreads over the western end of the greater Monte Albán archaeological complex, overlying hundreds of acres of unexplored ancient remains. The majority of modern Atzompans, however, have little time for the past. They are busy producing their distinctive pottery creations—fetching emerald green–glazed cooking pots, bowls, baking dishes, plates, and more—famous all over Mexico and the world.

Now, however, they make much more than these, having developed a host of new styles such as multicolored vases, some with artfully cut holes for placing dried or fresh flowers, as well as lily-adorned crosses, vases, plates, and red pottery, inscribed with fetching floral motifs.

pottery selection, Atzompa Mercado de Artesanías

Atzompa's artists, moreover, make it very easy to select from their wares, with an inviting **Mercado de Artesanías** (Handicrafts Market, tel. 951/558-9232, 9 A.M.–7 P.M. daily), on the entrance road (right side) after a long initial lineup of private stores. Each of the *mercado* displays contains the name and address of the artist, whom you can contact nearby in town. (*Note:* Recently, some artists have been trying harder, building individual stores on the road before the official Mercado de Artesanías. For the best selection, however, pass these and go straight to the official market.)

For lunch at the handicrafts market, try the adjacent, airy **(Restaurant Patio** (11 A.M.–6 P.M. daily). They offer an inviting menu of many Mexican country specialties, including a number of *moles* (with chicken, $4) and the reliable favorite, chiles rellenos ($4).

Get to Atzompa by bus, from the Abastos *camionera central segunda clase* in Oaxaca City, or by car, heading northwest out of town, along the Highway 190 exit boulevard in the direction of Mexico City. After about two miles (three km) from the city center, follow the Monte Albán sign, bearing left around the traffic circle, which heads you momentarily back toward town. Immediately turn right, cross the Río Atoyac bridge, and continue for about half a mile (0.8 km), turning right (north) at an Atzompa-signed intersection. Continue another 2.5 miles (four km) to the Mercado de Artesanías and the restaurant on the right.

SAN JOSÉ EL MOGOTE

Finds uncovered at San José El Mogote have shed considerable light on Valley of Oaxaca prehistory, especially during the thousand-year period preceding the founding of Monte Albán, around 500 B.C. Remains reveal that El Mogote was founded around 1500 B.C. and developed into a sophisticated center, with factory workshops supervised by elite merchants, which manufactured mica mirrors and jewelry for local and regional trade.

Old San José El Mogote lives on, literally, in the backyards of its present Zapotec residents. The people had forgotten what was buried in the seven or eight *mogotes* (mounds) dotting their village. From the pottery shards littering their fields, however, they suspected something was buried beneath the mounds. Archaeologists came and dug up the treasures now displayed in the community museum, the restored **Hacienda del Cacique.**

Museum

El Mogote people take justifiable pride in their museum, housed in a gorgeously restored old hacienda, the former ranch home of a local founding *cacique* (political boss) family. Its intriguing displays include shell jewelry, ceramic and stone burial offerings, a reconstructed tomb, a pre-Columbian adobe wall, a photo of a *danzante* monolith (still situated in the ruins) like those found at Monte Albán, and exquisite ceramic sculptures. Outstanding among these is the amazing *diablo enchilado,* with a half-scowling, devilish grin, exactly like a scary red Halloween demon.

Note: If you arrive unannounced, you may find the museum closed. However, someone is usually in charge, and, if available, he or she will open it for you. To inquire, say (or point to) this phrase *"Donde está el encargado del museo?"* ("Where is the person in charge of the museum?") The Presidencia Municipal (town hall) is usually the best place to make your inquiry.

Exploring the Site

The archaeological zone consists of eight mounds in all, which extend over a local half-mile square. Only one of them, the biggest, immediately behind the museum, has been extensively explored. Climb its reconstructed stone staircase to a broad courtyard. On the courtyard's north side is an excavated shaft, customarily locked, with the *danzante* monolith at its bottom. Climb the regal, stair-stepped pyramid adjoining the courtyard. At the summit, you can glimpse the other mounds, scattered near and far. Most notable among these is a partly excavated ball court, a five-minute walk to the northwest, once used for the *pelota mixteca* ball game, still played locally.

Farther afield, a 10-minute walk to the southwest side of the zone past a modern but now unused stone *era* (threshing circle), local people can lead you to a corrugated iron roof that shelters the stone foundation of what archaeologists believe to be an elite family house.

While exploring the site, you may see a scattering of tiny yellow daisies. Local folks call this *yerba de conejo* (herb of the rabbit). They take it as a tea, or mixed with beans, for *comida,* especially before siestas. Some say that its aphrodisiac effect is potent indeed.

Festival of San José

Arrive during the third week in March and join in the fun of the patronal festival of San José, which climaxes on the weekend closest to March 19. Festivities include processions, fireworks, dances of giant figures (called *monos* or *marmotas*), and a *pelota mixteca* tournament. While at the museum, ask the volunteers to show you the *hule* (natural rubber) ball and the leather mitts currently used to play the game.

Getting There

You can reach El Mogote in a number of ways. Easiest is to go by tour or taxi from downtown Oaxaca City. You can also go solo by second-class bus from the *camionera central segunda clase,* just north of Abastos market. Catch the Choferes del Sur bus to Nazareno town. Alternatively, you can catch a *colectivo* on the prolongation of V. Trujano, which runs along the north side of the second-class bus station.

Drivers, head north along Highway 190 out of Oaxaca City. About 7.5 miles (12 km) from downtown, at the fork to the new *cuota autopista,* stay on the *libre* (free) old route. After about two miles (three km), turn left (west) at the San José El Mogote (also Nazareno) side road (marked by the pyramid archaeological symbol sign). Pass over the railroad tracks, continue about half a mile (0.8 km), and at the bus stop shelter, turn left. Continue to the museum just past the water towers on the left.

ETLA

The name Etla strictly refers to a county-size district northwest of Oaxaca City that contains a number of small towns (such as Soledad Etla, San Miguel Etla, and San Gabriel Etla) that cluster around the central hub town of San Pedro y San Pablo Etla, site of the famous Etla Wednesday market. Consequently, this is the place that most folks refer to simply as Etla (or sometimes Villa de Etla). Although the Etla Wednesday market invariably has stalls overflowing with its celebrated "Oaxaca" (but more correctly "Etla") cheese, vendors offer plenty of other old-fashioned merchandise. How would you like, for example, some fresh sheepskins, burro pack frames, green Atzompa pottery, or banana-leaf-wrapped red Oaxaca tamales?

The market's main attraction, however, is the battalion of native country women offering mounds of carrots, forest-gathered herbs, nopal cactus leaves, onions, and much more.

For food, head to country-style *comedor* **La Fonda** (no phone, 8 A.M.–7 P.M. daily, $2–5), adjacent to the market's east side. Elderly Señora Julia both cooks and directs a bustling cadre of helpers in serving up a wholesome menu of home-made breakfasts, *sopas* (soups), and *guisados* (stews), all served up with generous portions of rice and beans and steaming stacks of hand-made tortillas. Alternatively,

The food is excellent at La Fonda.

try **Restaurant Chefy**(8 A.M.–8 P.M. daily, $3–8)for a wholesome, home-style breakfast or lunch, on the left side of the main street as you enter town from the highway.

Get to Etla much as you would get to El Mogote. Preferably arrive at the market by about 10 A.M. to allow time for visits to El Mogote and/or Suchilquitongo later. By bus from Oaxaca City, ride a Choferes del Sur Etla–marked bus from the *camionera central segunda clase,* or a *colectivo* from the north side of the *camionera central segunda clase.*

By car, head north along old *libre* Highway 190 about nine miles (15 km) from the center of Oaxaca City and turn left at the big green Etla highway sign. The market is the prominent light-yellow stone building, uphill from the rail station, about a quarter mile (0.4 km) from the highway.

SUCHILQUITONGO AND CERRO DE LA CAMPANA ARCHAEOLOGICAL ZONE
Suchilquitongo

Before heading uphill to investigate the important Cerro de la Campana archaeological zone, look around the nearby Suchilquitongo town plaza. Suchilquitongo (Place of Flowers in the Mixtec language; pop. 5,000) is the seat of the surrounding Suchilquitongo *municipio,* a rich domain of hills and mountains enclosing the emerald vale of the upper Río Atoyac. Using irrigation, bottomland farmers routinely bring in three crops per year, achieving some of Mexico's highest yields per acre in corn, beans, alfalfa, and squash. If only the rest of Oaxaca were so productive. Although virtually all of the bottomland is privately owned, much of the surrounding hills and mountains is undeveloped town communal pastureland.

The Suchilquitongo **Museo Comunitario** (no phone, 10 A.M.–3 P.M. and 5–7 P.M. daily), on the town plaza, is one of best of the network of community museums sprinkled around the state. It displays artifacts, reproductions, and an actual-size mock-up model of the famous Tomb 5, discovered in the Cerro de la Campana (formerly Huijazoo) archaeological zone in 1985. A glance at the archaeological displays reveals why it's considered the most important Zapotec city-state tomb uncovered to date. It was literally a house of the dead, with the remains of at least 20 noble personages of at least three generations, with calendrical birth names, such as 5-Earth, 5-Serpent, and 12-Monkey. Before the excavation, they lay at rest in a massive three-room, 15-foot-deep crypt complex among piles of jewelry, supplied with elaborate goods for the afterlife and surrounded by bright murals of ceremonial scenes, including a grand procession of feathered and helmeted ball players. Before you leave the Tomb 5 mock-up, be sure to see the **sphere of day and night,** and the richly engraved columns and tomb entrance door, both embossed with as-yet-untranslated Zapotec glyphs.

Another museum room illustrates the Spanish-Mexican custom of *mayordomía,* as acted out by Suchilquitongo people for their major fiesta, the July 22–27 fiesta of Santiago (St. James). Everyone participates—cooking food, making costumes, rehearsing for the dancing, setting up *ramadas* for shade, spiffing up the church, donating money—especially the *mayordomo,* the man or woman nominated by the *presidente municipal* and approved by a grand church meeting of the entire community to head all this up. The *mayordomo,* nearly always a person of means, usually ends up his or her term of office poorer, but rich with community affection and prestige.

Before you leave Suchilquitongo, you might want to visit one of the town's **basket weavers** at work. For a small fee, maybe the equivalent of a couple of dollars, the person at the museum desk may be able to guide you (or find someone who can) to one of their workshops.

Suchilquitongo's other significant craft is **stonemasonry.** Local quarries mine three types—*morada* (pink), *blanco* (meaning white, but actually a pale green), and *amarillo* (pale yellow)—of the soft *cantera* (volcanic tufa) for which Oaxaca is famous. As you exit at the highway, go left a few hundred yards, and on the right you'll see the covered workshop of

© BRUCE WHIPPERMAN

A few elderly craftspersons still weave baskets in Suchilquitongo.

master stonemason **Cenobio Ausencio Pinelo Martínez** (tel. 952/528-4569), who's teaching his sons his disappearing craft.

Exploring Cerro de la Campana

From the town plaza, you can see the Cerro de la Campana cluster of hilltops above the northern horizon. The site is about a two-mile (three-km), 500-foot (150-meter) climb. If it's hot, hire a taxi. If not, be sure to wear a hat, sturdy shoes, and take water. Atop the hill, you'll find Tomb 5 (hopefully open to the public after years of restoration), a ball court, three courtyards, and three partly restored pyramids.

After you arrive atop the hill, look closely at the knolls in the immediate vicinity and you'll see that they too are topped by pyramids, approximately 20 in all. Also, as you walk next to a road-cut section of hillside, look carefully and you'll be able to spot and examine 1,500-year-old pottery shards.

Climb to the highest—the cross-topped—pyramid, and your reward will be a breezy view of the entire Etla Valley and mountain panorama. Notice the dark Monte Albán ridge, far

to the southeast, to the right of distant Oaxaca City (below the Cerro San Felipe massif on the left). You can immediately see Cerro de la Campana's advantages: direct signal-fire communication with its contemporary, Monte Albán; a strong defensive position; and fertile riverbank fields. Why it was abandoned, like Monte Albán, around A.D. 800, remains a puzzle for future generations of archaeologists to decipher from the bones, stones, and mute, mysterious glyphs Cerro de la Campana's builders have left behind.

Getting There

Get to Suchilquitongo by bus via one of the *Cooperativa de Autobuses* Suchilquitongo buses, which leave from the *camionera central segunda clase* just north of the Abastos market in Oaxaca City, west of the *periférico*. Alternatively, you can go by a Suchilquitongo-bound *colectivo* on the prolongation of V. Trujano, which runs along the bus station's north side.

Drivers, head out of Oaxaca City along Highway 190 in the direction of Mexico City, northwest. Bear right onto *libre* (toll-free) Highway 190 where the *cuota autopista* (toll expressway) splits off to the left, about 7.5 miles (12 km) from the city center. Continue another several miles along *libre* Highway 190, pass an industrial park entrance on the left and, within a few minutes, turn left 17 miles (27 km) from the city center at the big Suchilquitongo entrance arch on the left. Pass over the railroad tracks and continue straight ahead to the Community Museum, another half mile (0.8 km) to the town plaza. Climb the plaza stairway on the right to the museum.

(For the Cerro de la Campana archaeological zone, return to the railroad tracks, where Calle Victoria forks left, uphill north, passing a church, continuing a total of about 1.5 miles, or 2.5 km, to the hilltop archaeological zone.)

THE VALLEY OF OAXACA

PACIFIC RESORTS AND SOUTHERN SIERRA

Historically, Oaxaca's southern coastal residents have both earned their livelihoods and sought their connections with the outside world by the Mar del Sur, the Southern Sea, the traditional Mexican name for the Pacific Ocean. Before roads were built, the Oaxaca coast slumbered, every bit like an isolated South Seas island, dependent upon occasional ships for trade and news from the exterior world.

The major cause of the isolation was the towering, cloud-capped wall of the Sierra Madre del Sur (Mother Range of the South). Oaxaca's high southern Sierra, always remote and mysterious, was finally unveiled in its majesty only in the 1980s, when satellite photo measurements revealed that Cerro Quiexobra (kee-ay-SHOW-brah), at 12,300 feet (3,750 meters), was by far Oaxaca's tallest mountain massif, a scarce 50 miles (80 km) due north of the Bahías de Huatulco.

From such high, cool, pine-crested summits along its entire 200-mile (320-km) rampart, the Sierra Madre del Sur plunges precipitously downward more than two miles (three km) through lush vine-hung canyon and foothill forest to the Pacific shore, an acacia-tufted expanse of endless summer.

There, as if forced southward by the weight of the high mountains, the coastline bulges to Oaxaca's (and nearly the entire country's) most southerly point, near the petite bay and resort of Puerto Ángel. From there, the Oaxaca coastline bends northerly—on its east side toward the Isthmus, and on its west side toward the Mixtec Coast, often called the Costa Chica (Little Coast) in southern Mexico.

© BRUCE WHIPPERMAN

HIGHLIGHTS

◖ Playa Estacahuite: This intimate cove, sheltered by friendly offshore rocks, enfolded by breeze-swept headlands, and teeming with colorful fish, ranks among Oaxaca's loveliest beaches (page 125).

◖ Playa Zipolite: A little bit for everyone – surf, sun, and plenty of clean golden sand – makes Zipolite a choice spot for a relaxing day, week, or a season (page 125).

◖ Centro Mexicano de la Tortuga: Far-seeing government action and community cooperation has converted a former turtle processing factory into a center for the recovery of Oaxaca's Pacific sea turtles (page 127).

◖ Playa Zicatela: The two types of Zicatela waves, simply mountainous and super-mountainous, make for lots of excitement, for both the intrepid surfers and the spectators on the beachfront (page 173).

◖ West-Side Beaches: Rewarding off-beach snorkeling, golden sand, and *palapa* restaurants make Playas **Manzanillo, Carrizalillo,** and **Bachoco** local favorites for Sunday family outings (page 173).

◖ Laguna Manialtepec: Easy access, mirror-smooth oft-fresh water, and dozens of bird species identifiable in an afternoon make this a prime adventure ground for kayakers, boaters, and campers (page 188).

◖ Santuario de Nuestra Señora de Juquila: Several duplicate images of the beloved patron are accessible to accommodate the hundreds of thousands of adoring pilgrims who arrive in Juquila yearly (page 195).

◖ La Capilla del Pedimento: This small hilltop chapel is a necessary second devotional stop for Juquila pilgrims, who adorn a life-size replica image of the Virgin of Juquila with daily dozens of *milagros* (metal wish tokens) (page 196).

◖ Huaxpáltepec Pre-Easter Fair: If you can, plan your Oaxaca trip to coincide with this exceptionally colorful Mixtec country fair on the fourth Friday of Lent (page 204).

◖ Pinotepa Market: Among the picked-from-the-garden vegetables, mountain-gathered herbal remedies, and piñatas, you may see an heirloom *pozahuanco* (Mixtec wraparound skirt) for sale at this market (page 206).

PACIFIC RESORTS

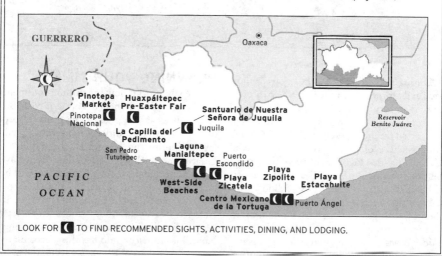

LOOK FOR ◖ TO FIND RECOMMENDED SIGHTS, ACTIVITIES, DINING, AND LODGING.

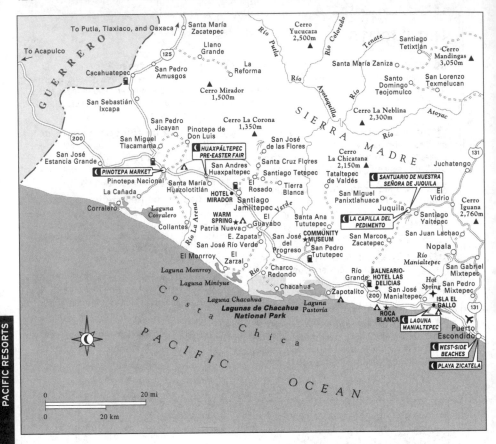

During the 1970s and 1980s, paved highways and airlines ended the Oaxaca coast's isolation and brought a trickle of Mexican and foreign visitors to the region. The government recognized the area's potential and began developing a new, ecologically correct vacationland at the Bahías de Huatulco. Meanwhile, visitors were discovering the South Seas village resorts of Puerto Ángel and Puerto Escondido.

Now the steady stream of vacationers can choose from a growing menu of outdoor diversions, from strolling the sand and snorkeling in hidden coves to rescuing sea turtle eggs, splashing in upland waterfalls, and lodging comfortably overnight at rustic jungle coffee farms.

PLANNING YOUR TIME

Where you go and how much time you spend on Oaxaca's sun-drenched southern coast depends on what you prefer. The prime resorts of Puerto Ángel (and its neighboring villages Zipolite and Mazunte), the Bahías de Huatulco, and Puerto Escondido each have their distinct charms. In all three, you will be able to enjoy beautiful beaches and good restaurants; but there the similarity ends. Puerto Ángel is heaven for those who prefer sleepy Mexico beach-village ambience. On the other hand, Puerto Escondido has the spectacularly awesome breakers of **Playa Zicatela,** the most famous (and most challenging) surfing beach

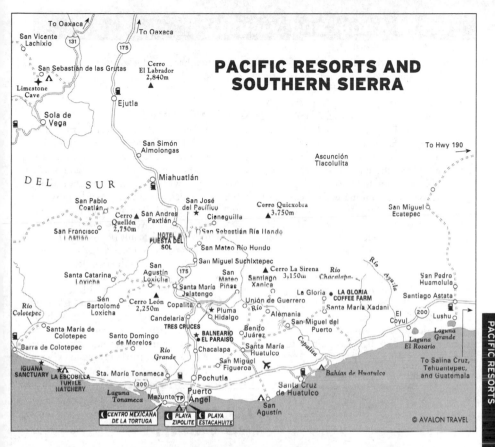

PACIFIC RESORTS AND SOUTHERN SIERRA

© AVALON TRAVEL

in Mexico; plenty of handicrafts shopping; and a pair of lovely hidden coves, while the up-to-date Bahías de Huatulco resort has the widest range of hotels, from modest to luxurious; several very good restaurants; and a small kingdom of sylvan forests that enfold its nine, coral-strewn blue bays.

If you have a week, you could spend it all at one place, spending half of your time on the beach, in the water, and by the pool. For more activity, in Puerto Ángel, spend two or three days on excursions, to the **Centro Mexicano de la Tortuga** in Mazunte, La Ventanilla for bird- and crocodile-watching, maybe continuing for a day upcountry in

Chacalapa for a stroll to the waterfall, and continuing to the pine-scented sierra summit at San José del Pacifico. In Huatulco, you can easily spend a day on a catamaran tour exploring the Bahías, another day rafting or kayaking the Río Copalita, and a third day visiting La Gloria Coffee Farm in the tropical foothill forest. In Puerto Escondido be sure to spend a day wildlife-viewing at sylvan **Laguna Manialtepec,** maybe continuing farther afield to explore Parque Nacional Lagunas de Chacahua, and finally heading uphill into the Chatino indigenous heartland to visit the **Santuario de Nuestra Señora de Juquila** pilgrimage shrine.

Puerto Ángel and Vicinity

During his three presidencies, Oaxaca-born Benito Juárez shaped many dreams into reality. One such dream was to better the lot of his native brethren in the isolated south of Oaxaca by developing a port for shipping the lumber and coffee they could harvest in the lush Pacific-slope jungles of the Sierra Madre del Sur. The small bay of Puerto Ángel, directly south of the state capital, was chosen, and by 1870 it had become Oaxaca's busiest port.

Unfortunately, Benito Juárez died two years later. New priorities and Puerto Ángel's isolation soon wilted Juárez's plan, and Puerto Ángel lapsed into a generations-long slumber.

In the 1960s, Puerto Ángel was still a sleepy little spot connected by a single frail link—a tortuous cross-Sierra dirt road—to the rest of the country. Adventure travelers saw it at the far south of the map and dreamed of a south-seas paradise. They came and were not disappointed. Although that first tourist trickle has grown steadily, it's still only enough to support the sprinkling of modest lodgings and restaurants that now dot the beaches and hillsides around Puerto Ángel's tranquil little blue bay.

Getting Oriented

Puerto Ángel is at the southern terminus of Highway 175 from Oaxaca City, about six miles (nine km) downhill from its intersection with Highway 200. It's a small place, where nearly everything is within walking distance along the beach, which a rocky bayfront hill divides into two parts: Playa Principal, the main town beach, and sheltered west-side Playa Panteón, the tourist favorite. A scenic boulder-decorated shoreline *andador* (watch out for gaps and holes in the concrete) connects the two beaches.

A paved road winds west from Puerto Ángel along the coastline a couple of miles to Playa Zipolite, lined by a colony of hammock-and-bamboo beachfront *cabañas,* popular with an international cadre of budget-minded seekers of heaven on earth. Continuing west, the road passes the former turtle-processing village

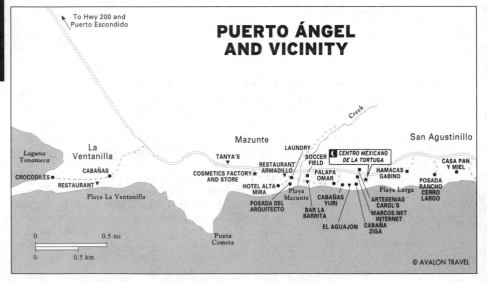

beaches of Playa San Agustinillo and Playa Mazunte. From there it goes on another four miles, joining with Highway 200 (and thence Puerto Escondido) at San Antonio village at Kilometer 198.

The major local service and transportation center is **Pochutla** (pop. 35,000), a mile north along Highway 175 from its Highway 200 junction.

Getting Around

Local *colectivo* taxis ferry passengers frequently between Pochutla and Puerto Ángel (fare around $0.50) from about 7 A.M. until 8 P.M., stopping at the Highway 200 intersection. Some taxis continue to Zipolite after stopping on Bulevar Virgilio Uribe, Puerto Ángel's main bayfront street. To continue to Playa San Agustinillo and Playa Mazunte, you must transfer to another *colectivo* (arriving from the opposite direction) in Zipolite. Private taxis also routinely make runs between Puerto Ángel and either Zipolite or Pochutla for about $5.

You can also get around (much more expensively) by boat. Captains routinely take parties of up to eight for sightseeing, snorkeling,

and picnicking to a number of nearby beaches. Bargain at Playa Panteón (the rate should run about $20/hour).

Tours and **Rental Cars** are other options for getting around. See *Tours* and *Travel Agent and Car Rental* in the *Puerto Escondido and Vicinity* section.

SIGHTS AND BEACHES
Playas Principal and Panteón

Playa Principal's 400 yards of wide golden sand decorate most of Puerto Ángel's bayfront. Waves can be strong near the pier, where they often surge vigorously onto the beach and recede with a sometimes strong undertow. Swimming is always more tranquil at the sheltered west end toward Playa Panteón. The clear waters are good for casual snorkeling around the rocks, on both sides of the bay.

Sheltered Playa Panteón (Cemetery Beach) is Puerto Ángel's sunning beach, lined with squadrons of beach chairs and umbrellas in front of beachside restaurants. **Playa Oso** (Bear Beach) is a little dab of sand beside a rugged seastack of rock beyond Playa Panteón, fun to swim to from Playa Panteón.

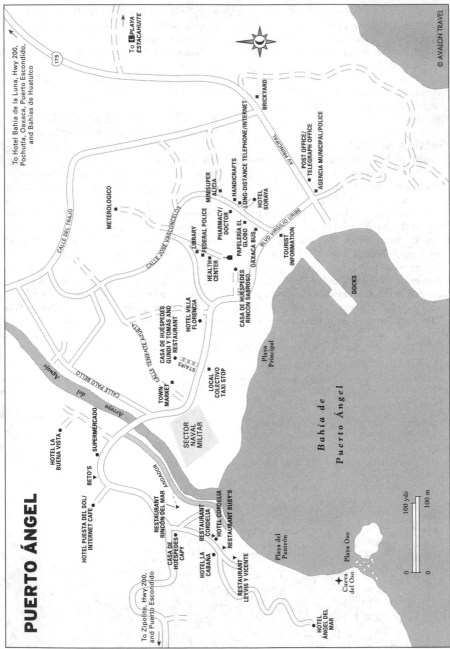

PACIFIC RESORTS

PUERTO ÁNGEL

To Hotel Bahía de la Luna, Hwy 200,
Pochutla, Oaxaca, Puerto Escondido,
and Bahías de Huatulco

To Zipolite, Hwy 200,
and Puerto Escondido

175

To ◗ PLAYA
ESTACAHUITE

© AVALON TRAVEL

BRICKYARD

POST OFFICE/
TELEGRAPH OFFICE
AGENCIA MUNICIPAL/POLICE

AV. PRINCIPAL

HANDICRAFTS
LONG-DISTANCE TELEPHONE/INTERNET
MINISUPER
ALICIA
HOTEL
SORAYA

METEROLOGICO

PHARMACY/
DOCTOR
PAPELERÍA EL
GLOBO
OAXACA BUS

BLVD VIRGILIO URIBE

LIBRARY
FEDERAL POLICE

TOURIST
INFORMATION

CALLE DEL TRAJO

CALLE JOSÉ VASCONCELOS

HEALTH
CENTER

CASA DE HUÉSPEDES
RINCÓN SABROSO

DOCKS

CALLE TENIENTE AZUETA

CASA DE HUÉSPEDES
GUNDI Y TOMÁS AND
RESTAURANT

HOTEL VILLA
FLORENCIA

Playa
Principal

STAIRS

CALLE PALO BELLO

Arroyo del Aguaje

TOWN
MARKET

LOCAL
COLECTIVO
TAXI STOP

*Bahía de
Puerto Ángel*

HOTEL LA
BUENA VISTA

SUPERMERCADO

SECTOR
NAVAL
MILITAR

BETO'S

HOTEL PUESTA DEL SOL/
INTERNET CAFE

RESTAURANT
RINCÓN DEL MAR

ANDADOR

RESTAURANT
CORDELIA
HOTEL CORDELIA
RESTAURANT SUSY'S

CASA DE
HUÉSPEDES
CAPY

HOTEL LA
CABAÑA

RESTAURANT
LEVIS Y VICENTE

Playa del
Panteón

Playa Oso

Cueva
del Oso

HOTEL
ÁNGEL DEL
MAR

100 yds

100 m

0

0

© B3 JCE WHIPPERMAN

view across Bahía de Puerto Ángel, toward Playa Panteón

❰ Playa Estacahuite

Decorating the rocky shoreline, about half a mile outside the opposite (east) side of Puerto Ángel bay, Playa Estacahuite (ay-stah-kah-WEE-tay) is actually two beaches in one: a pair of luscious coral-sand nooks teeming with fish grazing the living reef just offshore. (Don't put your hands in crevices; a moray eel may mistake your finger for a fish and bite.) A pair of *palapa* restaurants perched picturesquely above the beaches provide food and drinks. Get there in less than a mile by taxi or on foot via the dirt road that forks right off the highway, about 400 yards uphill from beachfront Bulevar Uribe.

❰ Playa Zipolite

Playa Zipolite (see-poh-LEE-tay), a wide, mile-long strand of brilliant golden sand enfolded by headlands and backed by palm groves, is simply stunning. It stretches from the intimate little cove and beach of **Playa del Amor,** tucked on its east side, to towering cactus-festooned sea cliffs rising behind the new-age Shambala retreat on the west end.

Playa Zipolite, although often good for

wading and for casual swimming (with care), its surf, usually tranquil in the mornings (but always with significant undertow), can turn thunderous by the afternoon, especially when offshore storms magnify both the swells and the undertow. Experienced surfers love these times, when everyone but experts should stay out.

Zipolite has evolved from a lineup of stick and thatch beachfront *cabañas* to sturdy concrete (cheap, and mostly scruffy) hotels, most with oceanfront *palapa* restaurants. Many of these share a new, paved two-block main street-front known locally as the **Adoquín** (ah-doh-KEEN), along with a procession of home-grown restaurants and small businesses, from grocery and pharmacy to surf shop, laundry, and money exchange. All of this, a neighborhood known as **Colonia Roca Blanca,** is now Playa Zipolite's new town center. Get there, heading west from Puerto Ángel, by turning left after the children's school.

Good surfing notwithstanding, Zipolite's renown stems from its status as one of the very few nude beaches in Mexico. Bathing au naturel, practiced nearly entirely by visitors and a few local young men, is tolerated only grudgingly by local people, many of whose livelihoods depend on the nudists. If you're discreet and take off your clothes at the more isolated west end (behind the big rock), no one will appear to mind (and women will largely avoid voyeuristic attentions of Mexican boys and men).

Playas San Agustinillo and Mazunte

About a mile west of Zipolite, a wide, mile-long, yellow-sand beach curves past the village of San Agustinillo. On the open ocean but partly sheltered by offshore rocks, its surf is much like that of Zipolite, varying from gentle in the morning to rough in the afternoon, depending mostly upon wind and offshore swells. Small village groceries and beachside *palapa* restaurants supply food and drinks to the occasional Zipolite overflow and local families on weekends and holidays. Fishing is excellent, either in the surf from nearby rocks, by rented *panga,* or your own boat launched from the beach. Beach camping is customary,

especially in front of beachfront restaurants, and at a few rustic, hammock-hung roadside *ramadas,* such as **El Paraiso,** at the east (Zipolite) end of the beach.

Remnants of the local turtle industry can be found at the rusting former processing factories on Playa San Agustinillo (west end) and Playa Mazunte two miles farther west.

The half-mile-long, yellow-sand Mazunte Beach, like San Agustinillo, is semisheltered and varies from tranquil to rough. Fishing is likewise good, beach camping is customary (as a courtesy, ask nearby business owners if it's okay), and local stores and seafood *palapa* restaurants sell basic supplies and food.

San Agustinillo and Mazunte people, including a group of European (mostly Italian) resident-entrepreneurs, have been renovating their houses and building *cabañas* to accommodate an increasing number of visitors. Signs along the road and at the beach advertise their lodgings and restaurants. (For details, see *San Agustinillo* and *Mazunte* in *Accommodations,* later in this section.)

a sandy, sheltered nook, at Playa San Agustinillo

© BRUCE WHIPPERMAN

cuddly turtle trinkets for sale across the road from the Mazunte Turtle Museum

◄ Centro Mexicano de la Tortuga

The former turtle-processing plant at Mazunte lives on as the Mazunte Turtle Museum (on the main road, east end of the village, tel./fax 958/584-3376, 10 A.M.–4:30 P.M. Wed.–Sat., 10 A.M.–2:30 P.M. Sun.). At the museum, which includes an aquarium, study center, and turtle hatchery, you can peruse displays illustrating the ongoing turtle research and conservation program and see members of most of Mexico's turtle species paddling in tanks overlooking the beach where their ancestors once swarmed. Guided tours are offered in a number of foreign languages, including English, German, and Italian. For lots of good information, visit www.tomzap.com/turtle.html.

Fábrica Ecología de Cosméticos Naturales de Mazunte

About half a mile farther west along the main road through Mazunte village is a cosmetics factory and store. Initially funded partly by the Body Shop Foundation and spearheaded by the local community, local workers manufacture and sell all-natural shampoo, skin cream, hair conditioner, and more. The staff is working hard to assure that the effort catches on, so that locally grown products such as coconut, corn, and avocado oils and natural aromatics will form the basis for a thriving cottage cosmetics industry.

Playa La Ventanilla

Continue about 1.5 miles (2.4 km) west along the main road over the low hill west of Mazunte and turn left at the signed dirt road to pristine wildlife haven Playa and Laguna La Ventanilla. Now protected by local residents, swarms of birds, including pelicans, cormorants, and herons, nest there, and a population of wild *cocodrilos* and *lagartos* is making a comeback in a bushy mangrove wetland.

Boatmen headquartered at the sturdy **visitors center** *palapa,* past the beach village road's end parking lot, guide visitors on a two-hour ecotour ($4 per adult, kids half price), which includes a stop for refreshment at a little mid-lagoon island. The boatmen are known for their wildlife sensitivity and allow no motor vehicles within 100 yards of their communally owned lagoon-sanctuary.

(*Note:* A second latecomer cooperative, that merely conducts lagoon tours while doing little for conservation, may try to intercept you in the parking lot. Simply avoid them and continue to the original conservation cooperative's beachfront visitors center, to get your lagoon-tour ticket.)

The Playa La Ventanilla community (lervenanillamx@yahoo.com.mx) has taken responsibility for protecting the turtles that arrive on their beach against poachers. During both February and June through October, hundreds of sea turtles come ashore to lay eggs. If necessary, community volunteers help the exhausted turtles up the steep beach, where they lay their eggs. Volunteers then gather the eggs and rebury them in a secure spot. After the hatchlings emerge about a month and a half later, volunteers nurture them for about three months and release them safely back into the ocean. For more information and photos, visit www.tomzap.com/ventanil.html.

A TURTLE ARRIVES AT PLAYA LA VENTANILLA

It was raining, and the wind, although not cold, was driving the surf high on Playa La Ventanilla. On the rocky headland above the beach, a small hole, like a round window, appeared to have been carved in the rock. Our guide, Pedro, who had just rowed us through the community wetland ecological preserve, explained.

"That's why we call this La Ventanilla. Because of that hole that the sea and wind have carved out."

"It's like a little window, a *ventanilla*."

"Yes, that's right."

He then went on to tell us something we didn't expect.

"We are waiting for the turtles to arrive. They come this time of year, especially when the wind blows toward shore like this. Yesterday afternoon and night nearly 80 turtles came and laid about 8,000 eggs."

It seemed too many.

"Eight thousand? Are you sure?"

"Yes . . . and they're buried right here."

He pointed to a fenced-off area in the sand, laid out in a grid of several dozen stakes.

"Each turtle lays about 100 eggs, and we buried each one's eggs separately under each of these stakes."

Before I could answer, a lookout atop the headland yelled something.

"A turtle has come ashore."

We scanned the beach. A black, pointed silhouette showed at the edge of the sand.

"There it is."

Two or three young male villagers raced toward the beach. They stopped several steps short of the turtle, however.

"We don't want to interfere with its egg-laying."

For several minutes, we watched the turtle, not large, perhaps 50 pounds and two feet long, struggle to climb one last small sand ridge before reaching the flat part of the beach. We asked what kind of turtle it was.

"It's a *golfina* turtle," Pedro explained. "Two other kinds arrive here. The *laut*, and the *sacasillo*. The *laut* can be big, maybe as much as a ton. They arrive in February."

After watching the turtle struggle for a few minutes longer, Pedro decided to help. He picked it up by the shell and placed it on level sand a dozen feet farther inland. He sympathized with the turtle's plight.

"The turtle seems very tired. It's small and weak."

The boost seemed to encourage the turtle.

Besides lagoon tours and saving turtles, La Ventanilla cooperative maintains the excellent beach-view **Restaurant Maiz Azul** (8 A.M.–7 P.M. daily, $2–6), run by half a dozen dedicated women. They specialize in local recipes, such as savory banana-leafed-wrapped tamales, baked turkey smothered in mole sauce, and yummy chiles rellenos. They also sell their own home-ground fresh peanut butter.

Furthermore, the Ventanilla community invites visitors to stay in their comfortable rustic accommodations. They offer two options: either four clean and cozy cabañas (on the left as you enter), with choice of one king-size bed, two double beds, or one double bed, all with mosquito nets and private hot-water shower-bath, for $35 s or d; or a four room dormitory-style *cabaña,* each room with two bunk beds for a total of four persons per room, with shared toilets and showers, for $15 per person.

ACCOMMODATIONS

The Puerto Ángel area offers dozens of accommodations, most of which are modest, home-grown guesthouse-style lodgings. The successful ones have given their legion of savvy repeat customers what they want: clean, basic, tepid-water accommodations in tranquil, television-free settings where Puerto Ángel's natural isolation and tropical charm set the tone for long, restful holidays.

Visitors have their choice of several

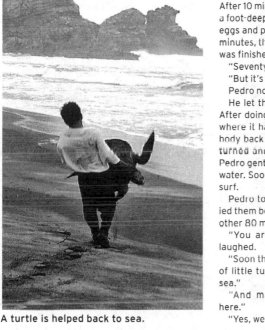

It immediately began digging with its flippers. After 10 minutes it began depositing its eggs in a foot-deep hole. Pedro promptly removed the eggs and placed them in a bucket. After a few minutes, the seemingly near-exhausted turtle was finished. Pedro had kept count.

"Seventy-five eggs. Not many."

"But it's better than nothing."

Pedro nodded his head in agreement.

He let the turtle cover up the empty hole. After doing so, it packed down the sand over where it had deposited the eggs, rocking its body back and forth with its flippers. Then it turned and headed back toward the waves. Pedro gently lifted it up and placed it near the water. Soon the turtle was gone, beneath the surf.

Pedro took the bucket of 75 eggs and buried them beneath a new marker alongside the other 80 markers.

"You are the turtle papa," we said. He laughed.

"Soon these eggs will hatch into thousands of little turtles, which we will return to the sea."

"And maybe many of them will return here."

"Yes, we hope so."

A turtle is helped back to sea.

© BRUCE WHIPPERMAN

neighborhoods. In Puerto Ángel itself, hotels and guesthouses dot the hillside above the main town beach, the pier, and the single main business street. The Playa Panteón lodgings, by contrast, are on the sleepier west side of the bay, above the lineup of rustic *palapa* restaurants along petite Playa Panteón.

Outside of Puerto Ángel visitors also have many choices, mostly right on the beach, but some atop breezy view hillsides, above the plumy, west-side country beachfront hamlets of Zipolite, San Agustinillo, and Mazunte.

Unless otherwise specified, prices listed below are year-round rates, excepting Christmas–New Year's and Easter holiday seasons, when rates customarily rise 25–50 percent, depending on demand.

Puerto Ángel: Main Town
UNDER $25

The splendidly isolated **Casa de Huéspedes Rincón Sabroso** (tel. 958/584-3095, $18 s or d, $20 t room-temperature water, $27 s or d, $30 t hot water) is accessible by stairway from beachfront main street Uribe, about a block west of the town pier. Atop a bay-vista hill, guests enjoy lodgings that open onto a hammock-hung view breezeway adorned by luscious tropical greenery. Inside, rooms are very clean (but dark), with white walls, tile floors, shiny bathrooms, and natural wood furnishings. Guests have the additional option of good food and each other's company in an airy café, perched above a heavenly bay and sunset panorama.

PACIFIC RESORTS

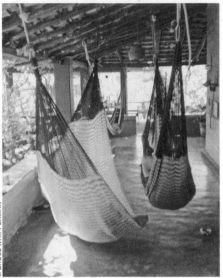

© BRUCE WHIPPERMAN

afternoon siesta time in the lazy hammocks at Casa de Huéspedes Gundi y Tomás

PACIFIC RESORTS

$25-50

Puerto Ángel's most welcoming lodging is the exceptional **Casa de Huéspedes Gundi y Tomás** (tel. 958/584-3068, gundtoma@ hotmail.com, www.puertoangel-hotel.com, $25–50 depending on room), the life project of personable German-born Gundi Ley and her sons, Bastian and Fabian López. Their homey, rustic-aesthetic complex rambles up a leafy hillside to a breezy bay-view *palapa* where patrons relax, socialize, and enjoy food and drink from their kitchen. Just above that, guests enjoy a double row of several clean, simply furnished rooms, shaded by a shared hammock-strewn view porch. Besides all this, they change U.S.-dollar travelers checks, volunteer information about local sights, do laundry, and pick up and drop off guests at the Huatulco airport. In addition, Bastán and Fabián, both accomplished surfers, offer surfing lessons in English, German, or Spanish.

Their accommodations, which include the **Almendro** tropical-garden *posada* near the beach downhill, consist of 14 rooms—some shared shower and toilets, some private—and

one bungalow (50 percent discount for one week rental), all with fans and a good restaurant. Get there via the lane (see the sign, uphill side) that stair-steps uphill near the west end of Puerto Ángel's main beachfront street.

Travelers who enjoy being right in the middle of the Puerto Ángel beachfront street scene choose the petite **Hotel Villa Florencia** (Blv. Virgilio Uribe s/n, tel./fax 958/584-3044, villaserenaoax@hotmail.com, $20 s, $30 d, $35 t, add $3 for a/c). Here, in the shady interior lobby-patio, past the good porch-front café, tranquility reigns as soft classic songs and instrumental music play in the background, while guests read and relax on comfortable chairs and couches. Upstairs, the approximately 15 rooms with bath are immaculate and thoughtfully decorated with local art and handicrafts.

Another very worthy Puerto Ángel accommodation is **Hotel La Buena Vista** (P.O. Box 48, tel./fax 958/584-3104, reservations@ labuenavista.com, www.labuenavista.com, $50–70), tucked on the hillside that rises just west of the mid-town Arroyo de Aguaje bridge. The hotel's five accommodations levels stair-step artfully (but steeply) up the forested slope. First- and second-level rooms look out onto verdure-framed bay views. On the third level are more rooms and a luxuriously airy restaurant *palapa* that opens to a picture-perfect bay vista. The hotel climaxes with several large onyx-tile-floored fourth- and fifth-floor rooms that share an entire private view patio with hammocks. There, owners have provided a luxurious **view pool-patio** for their guests. All rooms are immaculate, light, and simply but tastefully furnished, with spotless bathrooms. Several of the approximately 20 rooms have private hammock-hung view balconies; all come with fans, mosquito curtains, and good breakfast and supper restaurant, but with room-temperature water only.

Back on the east side of town, find the 1960s motel-style **Hotel Soraya** (Priv. José Vasconcelos 2A, tel./fax 958/584-3009, hotelsorayadepuertoangel@hotmail.com, $30 s or d, $45 t fan only, $50 s, $65 d, $80 with a/c), perched on the bluff above the pier. The well-managed hotel includes a restaurant with an airy bay view, fine for bright morning breakfasts and sunset-glow dinners. Outside, two tiers of spartan but light and comfortable rooms enclose a parking patio. Although some rooms have air conditioning, the fan-only ones may be preferable, since they avoid the air-conditioner noise and oft-associated mildew. Check before moving in. Rent on the upper story for maximum privacy, air, and light.

Playa Panteón

UNDER $25

Heading around the curve of the bay to the Playa Panteón neighborhood, you'll find one of Puerto Ángel's old standby budget lodgings, **Casa de Huéspedes Capy** (tel./fax 958/584-3240, $10 s, $15 d in one bed, $18 d, $22 t in two beds), perched on the bay-view hillside by the road fork to Zipolite. Rooms, stacked in two stories, with views toward Playa Panteón, are basic but clean with fans and cool-water private baths. Good family management is the Capy's strong suit. This shows in the shady view restaurant, **Arcely,** where good food

Playa Panteón offers shade, fresh seafood, and vistas of Puerto Ángel's petite blue bay.

in a friendly atmosphere encourages guests to linger, reading or talking, for hours. The family also watches the community TV at night; if it bothers you, ask them to turn it down.

$25-50

Downhill stands Puerto Ángel's only truly beach-front lodging, **Hotel Cordelia** (right on Playa Panteón, tel. 958/584-3109, fax 958/582-3231, azul_profundomx@hotmail.com, $35 s or d, $65 t or q). The Cordelia's seven rooms, most with bay views, are sparely but pleasingly decorated with rustic whitewashed walls, attractive native floor tiles, natural wood furniture, and artful tile touches in the modern-standard baths. No phones, no TV, just the murmur of the gentle Playa Panteón surf to lull you to sleep. With fans and good restaurant downstairs.

Bahía de la Luna

OVER $50

Visitors who long for the delights of a hidden south seas hideaway can have it, at Bahía de la Luna (on the coast about two miles east of Puerto Ángel, tel. 958/589-5020, info@bahia-delaluna.com, www.bahiadelaluna.com, $55 s, $65 d, $110 suite, $185 villa). New owners have revitalized this mini-paradise, set on a petite, palm-shaded half-moon strand, lapped by gentle waves and enfolded by rocky headlands. They offer about a dozen comfortable rustic-chic thatched, adobe *cabañas,* some with panoramic views, on the forested hillside above the beach, and others, tucked in the leafy shade, right on the beach below. Rentals feature one room with big bed, reading lamps, and private tepid-water shower-bath, and include hearty breakfast in their restaurant, hammocks for snoozing, shady beach *palapas* and recliners, and snorkeling equipment for guest use. A pair of larger similarly comfortable units—a suite accommodating four, and a villa accommodating eight—are also available. Get there via the signed but rough side road, east off of Highway 175, about five miles (eight km) downhill from the Highway 200 Pochutla junction, or two miles (three km) uphill from Puerto Ángel. After about two bumpy miles from the turnoff, the road steepens and becomes impassable for all but sturdy four-four-wheel drive vehicles. Best to go by taxi.

Zipolite
UNDER $25
The *cabañas* of **Lo Cósmico** (Playa Zipolite, fax 958/584-3151, 958/584-3152, 958/584-3153, admin@locosmico.com, www.locosmico.com, $15–30 d) nestle on a cactus-decorated rocky knoll at Playa Zipolite's sheltered west end. White spheres perched on their thatched-roof peaks lend a mystical Hindu-Buddhist accent to the *cabañas'* already picturesque appearance. In the restaurant atop the knoll, you're likely to find Antonio Nadurille, Lo Cósmico's Mexican owner-manager. He watches after both the *cabañas* and restaurant, specializing in a dozen varieties of tasty crêpes. His hillside and beach-level *cabañas* are clean, candle-lit, and equipped with hammocks and concrete floors; rates depend upon location and amenities. Recently, Antonio has built a number of sturdy, rock-walled, hurricane-proof designer rooms on his view hilltop. *Note:* All of Lo Cósmico's very clean toilet and shower facilities are separate from the accommodations, a short walk downhill.

$25-50
Shambhala (shambhala_vision@excite.com, www.advantagemexico.com/shambhala, $25 s or d), which shares the same forested, west-side headland as Lo Cósmico, is as it sounds—a tranquil Buddhist-style retreat. Shambhala's driving force is the articulate owner–community leader Gloria Esperanza Johnson, who arrived in Zipolite by accident in 1970 and decided to stay, eventually adopting Mexican citizenship.

Shambhala is a quiet, alcohol-free haven for lovers of reading, sunbathing, hiking, yoga, and meditation. It perches atop an enviable few acres at the edge of a sylvan hinterland. Adjacent cactus-studded cliffs plummet spectacularly to surf-splashed rocks below, while paths fan out through lush green (July–Dec.) tropical deciduous forest. An excellent macrobiotic panoramic-view restaurant completes the attractive picture.

Gloria has built Shambhala from the ground up; she now offers four rustic view *cabañas* (on a no-reservation, first-come-first-served basis only), two on the beach and two in the leafy (green summer–early winter) forest overlooking lovely Zipolite beach. Choices include a beachfront *cabaña* accommodating two to four, with shared toilet and shower; two smaller view *cabañas*, tucked in the uphill forest, each with private toilet and shower-bath; and a larger view *cabaña*, also in the uphill forest, accommodating three, with shared toilet and shower. All *cabañas* come with fans and mosquito nets.

Get to both Shambhala and Lo Cósmico by turning toward the beach from the main Puerto Ángel–Zipolite road onto the signed dirt driveway at Zipolite's west end. Bear right at the first fork, then left at the next for Lo Cósmico, right for Shambhala.

Smack at the center of the Zipolite beachfront action stands **Posada Mexico** (tel. 958/584-3194, info@posadamexico.com, www.posadamexico.com, $20 s, $30 d private bath, $25 d shared bath), with its dozen south-seas rustic *cabañas* basking in a flowery beachfront garden. The *cabañas* are attractively and individually decorated, each with upstairs bamboo and thatch sleeping *palapa*, with a private toilet and room-temperature shower and a hammock-hung porch below at beach level.

The scene at Posada Mexico is all relaxation, by private hammock or at the hotel's popular Italian-Mexican beachfront restaurant, where the mostly youthful guests enjoy late breakfasts, stroll out for swims, read thick novels, and kick back and enjoy convivial conversation with mostly North American and European fellow vacationers. Rentals include with mosquito nets.

Alternatively, consider **◖ Solstice Yoga and Vacations** (info@solstice-mexico.com, www.solstice-mexico.com, $33–49), at the tranquil east, Puerto Ángel end, of Playa Zipolite. Welcoming European-born yoga instructor/owner Brigette Longueville manages an inviting, authentically rustic minicolony of two-story *cabañas* on the gorgeous Zipolite beachfront. Accommodations are in Robinson Crusoe, south-sea islands, open style in all-natural wood, with ladders leading to upstairs sleeping-lounging areas, furnished with serape-draped beds, hung with gauzy mosquito nets. Guests are about evenly divided between beach vacationers and yoga devotees, who attend sessions in the in-house studio.

Accommodations go for about $33 d low season (June–Nov.), $42 high (Dec.–May), for the smaller unit, and about $39 low, $49 high for the three larger units; $6 per extra person, with private bath with toilet and tepid-water shower-baths. Breakfast is available at extra cost. Dormitory accommodations are also available, for $11 per person low season, $14 high. Brigette offers Hatha yoga classes, for $7 per 1.5 hours, and weeklong workshops.

Bungalows ◖ **Las Casitas** (local cell tel. 044-958/587-8464, info@las-casitas.net, www.las-casitas.net, $20–65), back on Zipolite's far west end, occupy the same leafy hilltop as, but west of, Shambhala. Las Casitas is the labor of love of friendly Italian builders-owners Daniela and Bruno Canibus, who have created their vision of paradise in Zipolite's summer-green tropical forest. They offer four rustically picturesque housekeeping bungalows, meticulously hand-built of all-natural materials, in a lovingly tended naturalistic garden of meandering stone pathways, sea views, refreshing breezes, and a thatched *palapa* restaurant (breakfast $3–5, supper $9–12), fine for enjoying leisurely meals and conversation with fellow guests. A path leads downhill to Zipolite beach.

The four bungalows, each unique, come with kitchenettes equipped with gas stove, utensils, and purified water. Two of the bungalows, El Organo and La Tortuga, the most private options, are spacious studios, furnished with one double bed and private toilet and shower-bath, and renting for about $50 and $45 d, respectively. The other two bungalows, Los Platanos and La Ceiba, accommodate six and nine people respectively in three separate bedrooms with shared kitchen and bathroom facilities. The Los Platanos bungalow rooms, for one, two, and three people each, rent for $20, $28, $36, and respectively. The rooms in the larger La Ceiba bungalow, for two, three and four people each, rent for about $45, $55, and $65, respectively. Get to Las Casitas via the dirt road to Lo Cósmico and Shambhala, which you will pass along the way. Continue uphill about two hundred yards more to the Las Casitas gate.

San Agustinillo
$25-50

A number of lodgings sprinkle the San Agustinillo beachfront and view hillside above the road. Here, you can enjoy it all: Mexican beach village ambience, stores and small restaurants nearby, and hammock-hung verandas with gorgeous views of the foaming San Agustinillo surf and hundreds of yards of golden sand to wander upon.

One of the most popular options, where you can walk out your door right onto the sand, is **Mexico Lindo** (fafinyleila@latinmail.com, no phone, $50 d) hotel and restaurant. Italian-born owner-manager Fausto offers five spacious individually decorated *cabañas* in two stories, with soft beds and private shower-baths. Amenities include fans and Fausto's good (but sometimes noisy) restaurant next door.

Nearby, removed two long blocks along a signed uphill driveway, find **Casazul** (tel. 958/587-4627, casazulplus@hotmail.com, www.casazulposada.com, $35–55), the lovely life-project of friendly owner Yolanda Quintana. Her hillside-perched stucco-and-tile, art-decorated complex offers four guest lodgings. They include two deluxe kitchenette studio apartments ("casitas"), each with two double beds and private baths, sharing a hammock-hung gorgeous-view-veranda, for $55 d; one rustic palm-thatched bungalow-in-the-round casita with a queen-sized bed, small refrigerator, and private bath for $35 d; and one "relaxation-room" casita, with small sauna, two double beds and private view veranda for $35 d. Extras include breakfast service at additional cost, mosquito nets, and a small but lovely blue lap pool.

OVER $50

If, however, you prefer the beach, consider rustic-chic **Posada La Termita** (www.posada latermita.com, $75 d) back downhill, right on the dazzling San Agustinillo beachfront. Italian-born owner Isabel Bresci offers four deluxe cabañas, with choice of one king-sized, two double, or two single beds, with private hot-water shower-bath, fan, and mosquito net. Reservations can be made through the website.

🌙 Casa Pan de Miel (about a third of a mile west of San Agustillo village, tel. 958/589-5844, casapandemiel@yahoo.com. mx, www.casapandemiel.com, $95 d, $130 q), the lifelong dream-come-true of French-born co-owner Anne Gillete, perches on its airy hilltop above the blue Pacific. Only superlatives can describe the architecturally designed amenities: spacious veranda breakfast restaurant, a blue designer pool, soft couches and chairs for sitting inside, lounge chairs and umbrellas by the pool, and panoramic ocean views east, toward San Agustinillo; south, out to sea; and west toward Mazunte's gracefully curving strand. Guests enjoy four spacious, comfortable, and artfully decorated deluxe rooms, with private view porches, hot water bathrooms, fans, a/c, and credit cards accepted, but no children under 12, please.

Innovative **Posada Rancho Cerro Largo** (ranchocerrolargomx@yahoo.com.mx, $80 s, $95 d), half a mile farther west, is the creation of builder Mario Corella, descendant of a longtime Hermosillo, Sonora, hotel family. After knocking around in the hospitality trade for several years, Mario decided to create his own version of utopia. Mario says that he wanted to "be in contact with nature and live among the community with as little impact as possible." He's done it, with a reception-restaurant and six rustically charming tile-floored, wood-and-adobe *cabañas,* furnished with hand-loomed bedspreads and opening to hammock-hung ocean-view verandas. The entire complex nestles in a summer-green and lovely hillside deciduous forest, linked by a path that meanders, between panoramic ocean viewpoints, to a gorgeously isolated, wave-washed sandy beach below. Rates include dinner and breakfast. Email for reservations (necessary in winter, highly recommended anytime). Get to Rancho Cerro Largo via the signed driveway on the Puerto Ángel–Mazunte road, four miles (6.4 km) from the Puerto Ángel bus stop.

Mazunte

Mazunte folks offer a number of lodgings, from rough beachfront *cabañas* to semideluxe architecturally designed thatched *palapas.*

$25-50

Star of the Mazunte beachfront accommodations is **🌙 Cabaña Ziga** (no email, no phone, $30 d private bath, $25 d shared bath), just west of the Turtle Museum, with 17 rooms in three floors and a palm-shaded beach-view restaurant, just above the waves. The plainly decorated, spacious, and clean tile-floored rooms come with fans and mosquito nets. As of this writing Cabañas Ziga accepts no reservations. Show up before noon to be sure you get a room, especially during the busy winter season.

Another invitingly rustic lodging on the stunning, palm-shadowed Mazunte beachfront is **Posada del Architecto** (at the far, west end of the Mazunte beach, tel. 958/583-8982, guidocco@yahoo.com.mx, reservations not accepted, $35 s or d, $4 per person dorm or camping), on Playa Rinconcito. Owners offer nine clean, *palapa*-sheltered *cabañas* with mosquito nets, fans, and private shower-baths. They also have dormitory rooms with bunks and a campground with *palapa* shelters and hammocks. Find it at the beach end of Calle Rinconcito, a block west of the bridge in Mazunte.

The fanciest accommodation in Mazunte, and sister to the Hotel La Buena Vista in Puerto Ángel, is the lovely hillside **🌙 Alta Mira Bungalows** (reserve via the Buena Vista in Puerto Ángel, tel./fax 958/584-3104, reservations@buenavista.com, www.labuenavista.com/ alta_mira, $50–60 d). Guests enjoy a beautiful

© BRUCE WHIPPERMAN

Juggling three balls might lead to four, five, or more during a long Mazunte beach stay.

ocean-view hillside setting with restaurant, the murmur of the waves, and a stepped path down to glorious Mazunte beach. The approximately 10 separate *cabañas* have comfortable rustic-chic decor, including handcrafted furniture, soft beds, hurricane lamps. Rentals include private shower-baths and mosquito nets. At this writing the Alta Mira's main drawback was low-power (solar-panel) electricity, which results in weak fans and dim light bulbs.

Get to Alta Mira Bungalows from the main through-town road. A block west of the bridge, turn toward the beach at the side road, Calle Rinconcito. Continue about a block, where you turn right at a signed uphill fork road. Continue 300 yards to Alta Mira's signed driveway on the left.

Trailer Parks and Camping

The homey **Trailer Park La Palmera Fernando's** (no telephone, $6 per person tent, $8–20 RV) has about 20 parking (big rigs possible) or camping spaces beneath a shady, tufted grove by the road at the east end of Playa Zipolite. A spirit of camaraderie often blooms among the tents and assorted RVs of travelers

from as far away as Miami, Medicine Hat, and Murmansk. RV rates get you a space for two people, including electricity and shared dump station, shower, and toilets.

Otherwise, park or camp at Zipolite's former hacienda, now new paradise ☾ **Rancho Los Mangos** RV and camping park (cell tel. 044-958/109-1316, Mex. toll-free 800/546-4693, $10 RV, $50 room, $150 bungalow). Soak in the lush tropical garden ambience, bask in the swimming pool and patio, and feast on all the mangos you can eat in season April–May. All this for $10 per person for any size RV, including electricity, water, and drainage. Also available are two deluxe two-bedroom bungalows, sleeping up to five, with living room, kitchen, and a/c for $150, and two comfortable rooms with bath and a/c for $50. Find it on the Puerto Ángel–San Agustinillo main road, at a signed driveway about half a mile past the Zipolite-Adoquín-Roca Blanca intersection.

One of Zipolite's best beach tenting spots is on the strand below Shambhala, with fine food from neighboring Restaurant Alquimista or Shambhala's restaurant uphill. The friendly

Shambhala owner, Gloria Johnson, will probably allow you to use Shambhala's showers and toilets for a small fee. Ask at the Shambhala office if it's okay to camp.

Camping is also customary on the beach in **Mazunte,** in front of Palapa Omar and Cabañas Yuri, or for a $4 per-person fee at Posada del Architecto.

FOOD

For a country place, **Puerto Ángel** has surprisingly good food, starting with the **Hotel Villa Florencia** (Blv. Virgilio Uribe s/n, tel./fax 958/584-3044, 8 A.M.–11 P.M. daily). The restaurant is right on the main beachfront street, upstairs. Lulu, the wife of the late Italian-born owner/chef, carries on his tradition, specializing in antipasti and salads ($3–5), and meat and seafood pastas ($5–12). As in any good country Italian restaurant, service is crisp and presentations are attractive. The modest wine list has, in the past, included some good old-country imports, and the pastas al dente and cappuccino rank among the best on the coast.

Most welcoming of all Puerto Ángel places to eat is the relaxingly simple restaurant at (**Casa de Huéspedes Gundi y Tomás** (uphill on the west end of Puerto Ángel's beachfront street, tel. 958/584-3068, 8 A.M.–9 P.M. daily. $4–7); see the streetside sign. Owner Gundi Ley offers hearty breakfasts, light lunches, and one or two tasty dinner entrées.

The unpretentiously elegant view *palapa* restaurant at the **Hotel La Buena Vista** (tel. 958/584-3104, 8:30–11 A.M. and 6:30–9 P.M.) is one of the best spots in town for a leisurely, intimate dinner. The menu includes salads, soups ($4), pastas ($4–7), and fresh broiled fish and meats ($7–9).

For simply good *comida casera* (home-cooked food), head straight to (**Beto's** (tel. 958/584-3011, 4 P.M.–midnight daily), two blocks west of the town center, a block uphill, past the west-side creek bridge. It's strictly a family operation, with Edilbert (Alberto) Espinosa, owner; Teresa Guzman, his mother, doing the cooking; and Felipe Guzman, his uncle, lending a helping hand. Over more than

20 years, they've barely raised their prices and have built a loyal clientele who return year after year for their tasty *ceviche* ($3) and healthy specialties, such as avocado stuffed with tuna ($4) and *pescado veracruzana* (*huachinango*, mahi-mahi, or tuna, veracruz style, $6).

For a spectacular view with late lunch or early dinner (or even just a drink), visit the family-run **Restaurant Rincón del Mar** (on the west-side headland overlooking the bay, 4–10 P.M. daily Dec. 15–Easter). Follow the *andador* toward the beach from the beachfront Avenida Uribe bridge, just west of the naval compound. At the restaurant sign, follow the stairway up the rocky headland. The star of the show (aided by a husband-daughter team) is the wife, Mari, who crafts a short but tasty menu of soups and salads ($3–5), pastas ($4–7), seafood and meats ($5–12).

Zipolite also has some good eating places. For tasty macrobiotic-style fare and a breezy beach view, go to the restaurant at **Shambhala** (on the Playa Zipolite west-end headland above the beach, 8 A.M.–8 P.M. daily). Personable owner Gloria Johnson runs a very tidy kitchen, which serves good breakfasts ($3–6), soups and salads ($3–4), and sandwiches ($3–5). No alcohol.

If you'd like a similarly healthy menu, but also with beer or wine, try **Bohemo** (noon–10 P.M. daily), Shambhala's new beachfront coffee house and café.

A regiment of satisfied patrons of (**Restaurant Alquimista** (right on the Shambhala–Lo Cósmico beachfront, tel. 958/587-8961 4–10 P.M. daily low season, noon–midnight daily high season) choose from a seemingly mile-long menu of appetizers (hummus, guacamole, $3–5), soups (onion, cream of carrot, $3–6), salads (Greek, romaine, $4–6), *tortas* (egg, ham, cheese, $3–5), fish (10 styles of fillet, $6–12), pastas (*al burro*, cream, Bolognese, $4–8), hamburgers (fish, beef, chicken, $4), and much, much more.

Beach **Restaurant San Cristóbal** (on the beach, a few steps from Zipolite's main street-*adoquín* in Colonia Roca Blanca, tel. 958/584-3191, 8 A.M.–about 9 P.M. daily) is among the best. Especially good are the breakfasts: scrambled eggs with bacon ($4), vegetable soup ($3), and hamburger with french fries ($4).

In **San Agustinillo,** longtimers like shady beachfront *palapa* **Restaurant Mexico Lindo** (at the east, Mazunte end of the beach, 8 A.M.–10 P.M. daily, closed Sept.–Oct.). Owner Fausto and his wife serve from a short but tasty menu of salads ($3), sandwiches ($2–4), tacos and tostadas ($2–4), and seafood ($5–10).

In **Mazunte,** tasty vegetarian-style goodies are the specialty at **Tanya's** (on the west end, uphill, above the cosmetics factory-store, 8 A.M.–9 P.M. daily). Besides superfresh seafood ($5–10), Tanya offers plenty of hearty juices ($2–3), salads ($3–5), and soy burgers ($3–4).

A fortunate addition to Mazunte's growing list of good restaurants is **Armadillo** restaurant and bakery (8 A.M.–11 P.M. daily high season, 3–11 P.M. daily low season, armadillo.mazunte@ yahoo.com.mx, no phone). Armadillo is the life project of a personable Mexican-French husband-wife team, who, beneath their sculpture-decorated *palapa* (he's the sculptor), offer a delicious, eclectic menu (she's the chef), including breakfasts (omelets, $3), lunch (tuna salad $4), and, for dinner, the Armadillo specialty, stuffed fish fillet ($9). Find them a block and a half down Calle Rinconcito, the street that heads toward the beach, a block west of the Mazunte bridge.

ENTERTAINMENT AND EVENTS

Puerto Ángel's entertainments are mostly spontaneous. If anything exciting is going to happen, it will most likely be on the beachfront Boulevard Uribe, where people tend to congregate during the late afternoon and evenings. A small crowd may accumulate in the adjacent restaurant Villa Florencia for coffee, talk, or something from the bar.

Sunset-watchers get their best chance from the unobstructed hilltop perch of the Hotel Ángel del Mar (atop Puerto Angel's west-side headland, or the east (Puerto Ángel) end restaurants on the beach in Zipolite, where the bars and restaurants offer something to enliven the occasion even if clouds happen to block the view.

For more lively nightlife, head west to Zipolite and Mazunte. In Zipolite, follow the youthful folks who (especially Saturdays) crowd into **Disco La Puesta** (on the Zipolite *adoquín,* 9 P.M. until the wee hours Tues.–Sat.).

Also, relax in the palm-tufted garden of the Italian-managed **Buonvento** restaurant (on the *adoquín,* at the Puerto Ángel end, tel. 958/584-3155, 6 P.M.–midnight daily). For supper, enjoy half a dozen varieties of pizza ($5–12) from 6 P.M., televised sports events, and live music Friday and Saturday and large-screen movies Sunday, both beginning at 9 P.M.

Alternatively, in Mazunte, join the regulars who relax at hangout **La Barrita** (Calle La Barrita #20, 6 P.M.–midnight nightly) with drinks and dancing (usually to recorded music) in the jardí garden-patio. Find it in mid village, on Calle Barrita, by the beach.

For additional nighttime diversions, head west to Puerto Escondido or east to Bahías de Huatulco, each about an hour by car or bus.

Hotel Ángel del Mar (hire a taxi uphill from Playa Panteón) sometimes provides music for dancing during the highest seasons, most likely between Christmas and New Year and the week before Easter.

Puerto Ángel's major scheduled event is the big **Fiesta de San Miguel Arcangel** on October 1 and 2. Then the *mascaritas* (masked children) dancers romp, carnival games and rides light up the streetfront, and a regatta of fishing boats parades around the bay.

RECREATION
Swimming and Surfing

Swimming provides cooler exercise opportunities, especially in the sheltered waters off of Playa Panteón. Off of Playa Zipolite, bodysurfing, boogie boarding, and surfing can be rewarding, depending on wind and swells. For surfing lessons ($20 for two hours) contact expert and friendly surfers Bastián and Fabián López at Casa de Huéspedes Gundi y Tomás (tel. 958/584-3068).

Be super careful of **undertow,** which is always a threat, even on calm days at Zipolite (where authorities maintain a skilled cadre of lifeguards). If

PACIFIC RESORTS

you're inexperienced, don't go out alone. Novice and even experienced swimmers have sometimes drowned at Zipolite. If you get caught in a current pulling you out to sea, don't panic. Experts advise that you simply float and paddle parallel to the beach a hundred yards or so, to a spot where the offshore current is not so severe (or may even push you back toward the beach). Alcohol and surf, moreover, don't mix. On rough days, unless you're an expert, forget it. Bring your own board, or rent one at one of the sprinkling of shops along the beach and the Zipolite *adoquín.*

Sailing and Windsurfing
If you have your own boat or windsurfing gear, sheltered **Playa Panteón** would be a good place to put it into the water, although the neighboring headland may decrease the available wind. Calm mornings at **Playas Zipolite, San Agustinillo,** or **Mazunte,** or afternoons, with more wind but rougher waves, might also be fruitful.

Snorkeling and Scuba Diving
Rocky shoals at the edges of Puerto Ángel Bay, especially just off **Playa Panteón,** are fine for casual snorkeling. **Playa Estacahuite,** on the open ocean just beyond the bay's east headland, is even better. Snorkel rentals are available on the beach, at both Playa Estacahuite and Playa Panteón.

Puerto Ángel divers enjoy a well-equipped, professional **Profundo Azul** (Deep Blue) scuba diving shop (tel. 958/584-3109, azulprofundomx@hotmail.com, www.tomzap.com/azulprofundo.html) at Playa Panteón (958/584-3437 at Zipolite), run by very experienced Juan José de Nova Reyes, known locally as "Chepe." He offers snorkel trips ($15 per person), scuba dives (two tanks, for certified scuba divers, $80), and scuba instruction, from the basics (beginners, $50) all the way up to a complete open-water advanced certification course (3–5 days, $350).

Fishing
Puerto Ángel's Playa Principal, Playa Panteón, and Playa Zipolite are the best places to bargain for a boat and captain to take you and your friends out on a fishing excursion. Prices depend on season, but you can figure on paying around $60 for a half-day excursion for three or four persons with bait and two or three good rods and reels.

During a three-hour outing a few miles offshore, a competently captained boat will typically bring in three or four big, good-eating *dorado* (mahi-mahi), *huachinango* (snapper), *atún* (tuna), or roosterfish. If you're uncertain about what's biting, go down to the Playa Principal in Puerto Ángel around 2 or 3 P.M. and see what the boats are bringing in.

Chepe, the highly experienced scuba instructor at Playa Panteón, offers fishing trips (three hours in motor *lancha* for $50, including tackle and bait, for up to four persons.

SHOPPING
Market
The biggest local market is the Monday *tianguis,* which spreads along the Pochutla main street, Highway 175, about seven miles from Puerto Ángel, one mile inland from the Highway 200 junction. It's mostly a place for looking rather than buying, as throngs of vendors from the hills line the sidewalks, even crowding into the streets, to sell their piles of onions, mangoes, forest herbs, carrots, cilantro, and *jícama.*

On other days, vendors confine their displays to the permanent Mercado 5 de Octubre, east side of the main street, between Calles 1 and 2 Sur.

In Puerto Ángel, fruit and vegetables are available (the earlier the better) at the small Puerto Ángel market, near the corner of main beachfront street Bulevar Uribe and the west-side bridge.

Handicrafts
For fine custom-made **hammocks,** visit local craftsman Gabino Silva (www.johntarleton.net/hammocks.html) at his country shop, off a jungly stretch of the road between Zipolite and San Agustinillo. He also rents two very rough *cabañas.* (However, he does have a solid seaview *palapa,* apparently orginally intended to be a restaurant, that would be fine for camping if

you have mosquito repellent.) Watch for his sign labeled Hamacas and Cabaña on the beach side of the road, 4.2 miles (6.7 km) from the Puerto Ángel village center.

A handful of handicrafts have arrived in Puerto Ángel, at **La Primavera beachware,** (on Vasconcelos, directly uphill from the pier, 9 A.M.–10 P.M. daily, tel. 958/584 3251), and at **Villa Florencia** (on Uribe, a block west of the pier, tel./fax 958/584-3044, 8 A.M.–11 P.M. daily).

In Mazunte, stop by **Artesanías Carol's** (9 A.M.–6 P.M. daily) across from the turtle museum, for a carefully selected assortment of mostly women's wear, including *huipiles,* resort wear, straw hats, shells, bathing suits, black Oaxaca pottery, interesting bamboo drinking cups, and *palos de lluvia* ("rain sticks") to restore your jangled nerves.

INFORMATION AND SERVICES
Groceries and Photo
The best-stocked grocery store on the Puerto Ángel coast is **Minisuper Alicia** (on Vasconcelos, tel. 958/584-3237, 7 A.M.–9 P.M. daily), on the right, two blocks directly uphill from the pier. Also, a few little-bit-of-everything stores in Zipolite, San Agustinillo, and Mazunte sell cheese, bread, wine, vegetables, and more.

The best local photo store is professional **Foto García** (Lázaro Cárdenas 76, tel. 958/584-0735, 8 A.M.–8 P.M. Mon.–Sat.), on the main street in Pochutla. They offer digital and film development service, and stock several film and digital point and shoot cameras and other supplies.

Money Exchange and Tourist Information
In Puerto Ángel, only a few shopkeepers change money. For example, manager Bastián López, at the Casa de Huéspedes Gundi y Tomás, changes U.S. dollars cash and travelers checks.

Otherwise, go to the banks in **Pochutla.** Best bet is **HSBC** bank (on the Pochutla main street, Lázaro Cárdenas, tel. 958/584-0699, 8 A.M.–7 P.M. Mon.–Fri., 8 A.M.–3 P.M. Sat.).

Alternatively, go to **Bancomer** (corner of Lázaro Cárdenas and Av. 3A Norte, tel. 958/584-0053, 8:30 A.M.–4 P.M. Mon.–Fri.), or, a few doors south, **Scotiabank Inverlat** (tel. 958/584-0145, 9 A.M.–5 P.M. Mon.–Fri.).

Oaxaca tourism runs a seasonal **information office** (upstairs at the foot of the Puerto Ángel pier, 9 A.M.–2 P.M. and 4–8 P.M. daily in season).

Communications
The Puerto Ángel **correo** and **telecomunicaciones** stand side by side at the Agencia Municipal (at the foot of Hwy. 175., 9 A.M.–3 P.M. Mon.–Fri.).

The Puerto Ángel **larga distancia** telephone, fax office, and **Gela Net** Internet access is on Calle José Vasconcelos (just uphill from main street Uribe, tel. 958/584-3046 or 958/584-3054, fax 958/584-3210, shenalo@hotmail.com, 8 A.M.–10 P.M. daily).

Internet access is also available in Puerto Ángel, at Puesta del Sol and Cyber café (uphill, about a block west of the Blv. Uribe bridge, 10 A.M.–9 P.M. daily).

Internet access has also arrived in Zipolite, at **Danydoquin** (tel. 958/584-3363, 9 A.M.–9 P.M. daily), with fax, copies, and public telephone, at the far (Puerto Ángel end) of the *adoquín;* likewise in Mazunte, at **Marcos Internet** (10:30 A.M.–8 P.M. daily) on the main road through town, about a block west of the turtle museum.

Health and Emergency
Puerto Ángel's **doctor** is Dr. Constancio Aparicio Juárez, who is available at the **pharmacy** (tel. 958/584-3058, 9 A.M.–2 P.M. and 5–9 P.M. daily) on Calle Villalobos, left side, half a block uphill from main street Uribe. For serious illness requiring diagnostic specialists, Dr. Juárez recommends you go to the government **Hospital Regional in Pochutla** (tel. 958/584-0204), or the **Seguro Social in Crucecita** (Bays of Huatulco, tel. 958/587-0124 or 958/587-0264).

Another option is to go to the small government **Centro del Salud** health clinic, which concentrates on preventative rather than diagnostic medicine, on the hill behind the church. Go up Vasconcelos a long curving block, go left at the first corner, and continue another block to the health center.

For police emergencies, contact the **municipal police,** uphill on Vasconcelos (tel. 958/584-3207), or call the **policía preventiva** (at the Presidencia Municipal, in Pochutla, on the town plaza, one block east of the main north-south town thoroughfare, tel. 958/584-0159).

GETTING THERE AND AWAY
By Air
Scheduled flights to Mexican destinations connect daily with airports at **Huatulco,** 19 miles (30 km) east, or **Puerto Escondido,** 44 miles (71 km) west, by road from Puerto Ángel. (For details, see *Getting There and Away* in the *Bahías de Huatulco and Vicinity* and *Puerto Escondido and Vicinity* sections of this chapter.)

By Car or RV
National highways connect Puerto Ángel to the west with Puerto Escondido and Acapulco, north with Oaxaca, and east with the Bahías de Huatulco and the Isthmus of Tehuántepec.

Highway 200 connects westward with Puerto Escondido in an easy 44 miles (71 km), continuing to Pinotepa Nacional (135 miles/217 km, three hours) and Acapulco in a total of seven hours (291 miles/469 km) of driving. In the opposite direction Bahías de Huatulco (actually Crucecita town), 28 miles (45 km) is reachable in about 45 minutes. The continuation to Salina Cruz stretches another 92 miles (148 km), or around 2.5 additional hours of driving time.

North to Oaxaca, paved but narrow and winding National Highway 175 connects 148 miles (238 km) over the Sierra Madre del Sur from its junction with Highway 200 at Pochutla. The road climbs to around 9,000 feet through cool (chilly in winter) pine forests and hardscrabble Chatino and Zapotec native villages. Fill up with gas in Pochutla. Unleaded gasoline is available at the Pochutla Pemex

stations, both on through-town Highway 175, about 300 yards toward town from Highway 200, and on the north, uphill, edge of town. Carry water and blankets, and be prepared for emergencies. The first gas station after Pochutla is at Miahuatlán, 90 miles north. Allow about eight hours behind the wheel from Puerto Ángel to Oaxaca, about seven in the opposite direction.

By Bus and Van
Virtually all long-distance bus connections must be made in Pochutla. The sole exception is one second-class Oaxaca City–bound bus that leaves Puerto Ángel nightly around 10 P.M. from the corner of Vasconcelos and Uribe, just uphill from the pier. Get your ticket at Papeleria El Globo, by the bus stop.

In Pochutla, operating out of a number of separate stations, several long-distance bus lines and two van shuttle services connect with points west, east, and north. The stations cluster less than a mile north from the Highway 200 junction along Avenida Lázaro Cárdenas, the Highway 175 main street into Pochutla.

As you enter the Pochutla business district, first you'll come to combined first-class **Omnibus Cristóbal Colón** and second-class **Sur** station on the left (at L. Cárdenas 84, tel. 958/584-0274). From there, several departures per day connect east with Huatulco at Crucecita. Some continue east, connecting with Salina Cruz and Tehuántepec, continuing to Chiapas destinations of Tuxtla Gutiérrez San Cristóbal and Tapachula, at the Guatemala border. A few buses connect north with Oaxaca via the relatively level, long (10-hour) Isthmus route, via Salina Cruz and Tehuántepec. During the dry season, buses also connect with Oaxca, via the shorter (eight-hour) trans-Sierra Highway 175. One bus continues to Puebla and Mexico City daily. A few buses also connect daily west with Puerto Escondido.

Next, **Estrella Blanca** (a few doors farther north, tel. 958/584-0380) and subsidiary-line buses (such as first-class Elite, luxury-class Turistar and Futura) connect west daily with Puerto Escondido, continuing to Acapulco, where connections are available for the entire Mexican Pacific coast, all the way to the U.S. border. They also connect east (many per day) with the Bahías de Huatulco destination of Crucecita, and Salina Cruz on the Isthmus. A few "plus" (pronounced "ploos") luxury-class buses connect daily, all the way to Mexico City, via Acapulco.

About a block farther, across the main street, **Autobuses Estrella del Valle, Autobuses Oaxaca Pacífico,** and **Fletes y Pasajes** (tel. 958/584-0138) operate out of their joint central bus station *central de autobus*. Frequent second-class and some first-class service is offered, connecting west with Puerto Escondido and Pinotepa Nacional; north with Oaxaca, Puebla, and Mexico City; and east with Huatulco. Farther north, **Atlantida** shuttle vans (at Lázaro Cárdenas 62, tel. 958/584-0116) connect north, via Highway 175, about every two daylight hours, with Oaxaca. Next door, **Eclipse** vans (tel. 958/584-0840) also offer frequent Oaxaca connections.

UPLAND EXCURSIONS FROM PUERTO ÁNGEL

Highway 175 curves its way from Puerto Ángel north, rising from the coast, continuing past a scattering of villages set in luxuriant forests, and finally climbing to cool, pine-tufted heights, where on a clear day the shining blue Pacific far below seems half a world away.

Travelers who hurry along this route find little; many of those who linger discover pleasant surprises along the way.

San Pedro Pochutla

The capital of the Pochutla governmental district was founded around 1600. One look along the busy, cluttered main street of Pochutla (pop. 30,000) reveals that it's a market town. This is most apparent on Mondays, when the side streets off the main street (Highway 175, locally known as Avenida Lázaro Cárdenas) bloom with colorful *tianguis* of vendors offering a collective mountain of merchandise.

On other days, vendors confine their piles to the formal indoor market, the **Mercado 5**

de Octubre, between Calles 1 and 2 Sur at the downtown center, on the east side of Lázaro Cárdenas.

Although most people come to Pochutla for business or to catch a bus, this town offers more than the merely perfunctory. A closer look reveals that Pochutla is really two towns rolled into one—the busy main street and the spacious, completely automobile-free central plaza and mall just one block downhill to the east.

On the west side of the plaza, the townsfolk have planted a living reminder of Pochutla, whose name comes from the Aztec-language label Pochtlán (Land of the Pochotes) for the locally plentiful *pochote* tree. You'll see a young specimen with small green leaves, five to a bunch, and spines on the trunk. People say that the *pochote* tree's edible roots sustained many starving families during times of drought and war.

Excitement mounts in Pochutla during the June 21–28 **Fiesta de San Pedro y San Pablo.** Celebrations begin with early morning masses and religious processions, then carnival rides and games, food, and fireworks. Finally, a parade of floats carries a gaggle of mysterious masked characters who climax the festivities with a traditional dance.

Even during non-festival times the nighttime plaza, illuminated with Porfirian-era streetlight globes, is doubly interesting, so much so that you may decide to stay overnight. If so, Pochutla can accommodate you with the invitingly traditional **Hotel Pochutla** (Madero 102, tel./fax 958/584-0033, $16 s, $20 d, $24 t), at the plaza's northwest corner. Owners offer 34 rooms arranged around an intimate, plant-decorated inner patio. Although many downstairs rooms are musty, upstairs they are invitingly quaint, with old-world louvered tropical-style doors, some of which open to balconies overlooking the colorful plaza scene. Rooms come with fan and private hot-water shower-bath.

Chacalapa

About nine miles (14 km) uphill from Pochutla along Highway 175, the village of San José

Chacalapa nestles in the tropical foothill forest. The village's most inviting roadside attraction is the *palapa* (**Restaurant Los Reyes** (on the west side, 7 A.M.–10 P.M. daily). Here you can pick from a long menu of soups, seafood (cocktails, fish fillets, shrimp, $3–6), *chacales* (local river crayfish), meat, tacos, quesadillas, guacamole ($3–8), *papa del horno* (baked potato), and sandwiches (hamburger, tuna, chicken, and ham and cheese, $2–4). After that, relax in the big blue pool or stroll out into the surrounding forest.

For an extended exploration, ask the friendly family owners for a guide to the nearby *cascada* (waterfall) and curative sulfur-water lagoon. Also check with Tom Bachmeir (who would be a good guide himself, see *Rancho Alegre* later in this section) or Isidro Reyes Guzmán (restaurantlosreyes@prodigy.net.mx or restaurantlosreyes@hotmail.com), the owner of Restaurant Los Reyes, for recommendations.

Along the way, your guide will help you spot, besides the locally abundant *ardillas, gavilanes,* and *aguilas* (squirrels, hawks, and eagles), some *carpinteros, tucanetas, péricos, tigrillos,* and *coatis* (woodpeckers, toucans, parrots, ocelots, and coatimundis). Your guide can also identify *plantas medicinales* (medicinal plants) in addition to the great forest trees, such as *ceiba, guanacastle, caoba,* and *macuil.*

Moreover, you may want to take a look at some of the attractive local for-sale furniture, crafted from big dried *bejuco* vines by local craftsman such as Agustén Toltepec. Ask at the Restaurant Los Reyes for directions to his house.

You may be so charmed by Chacalapa's natural delights that you want to stay overnight. If so, nearby mini-paradise **Balneario El Paraíso** ($30 d) can accommodate you. Get there from the Chacalapa village center, a few hundred yards north of the restaurant. At the *presidencia,* fork right, off the highway. Within a block, turn right again, at the Alcoholicos Anonimos sign. After exactly one mile (1.6 km) along a dirt road, turn right into the ranch gate. Here, in addition to a big 10-foot (three-meter) deep, spring-fed swimming pool, a kiddie pool, swings, slides, and a shaded

palapa for picnics, are a pair of tile-floored *cabañas* for rent, with hot-water shower-baths. Although impressive, Balneario El Paraíso's man-made amenities are only part of the attraction. Friendly owner Octavio Ramos and his wife will provide meals and are happy to show you around their forested ranch, dotted with mango and orange trees and cinnamon and other spices. Later, explore the surrounding luxuriant stream valley and forest for rewarding views of animals and birds in their natural surroundings. (*Note:* At this writing their pools were filled with water only Thursday through Sunday.)

While you're at Balneario Paraíso, be sure to visit **Rancho Alegre** (on the road, just before the Balneario, www.tomzap.com/paraiso.html). Rancho Alegre, sometimes know as Tom's Garden, is the haven of German expatriate jewelrymaker Tom Bachmeier and his Colombian wife, Nehier. If you're lucky, one of them will show you around their tropical mini-Eden, lush with bromeliads, orchids, ginger, and a wealth of zapote, cacao, coffee, and mango trees. You may contact them by mail (P.O. Box 73, San Pedro Pochutla, Oaxaca 70900).

San José del Pacífico

This is a little mountaintop town with a tremendous view, so high that the Pacific Ocean is clearly visible far below. The climate is brisk and dry, and pine-clad mountains rise all around, an ideal setting for a few days away from the tropics. What's just as good, the village has a pair of pretty fair restaurants and an invitingly rustic hotel.

Little was spared to create the (**Hotel Puesta Del Sol** (from the U.S 011-52-1-951/100-8678, in Mexico long distance 045-951/100-8678, locally 044-951/100-8678, sanjose@sanjosedelpacifico.com, www.sanjosedelpacifico.com, www.tomzap.com/sjose.html, $20 s or d, $30 t). Gardens lead downhill, past the hotel restaurant, to clean and cozy knotty-pine *cabañas* with fireplace and private hot-water shower-baths.

Food is available either at the hotel's **Restaurant Esther** (8 A.M.–8 P.M daily, $3–8) with its lovely view, or the restaurant

Rayito del Sol (Little Sunbeam) in the village nearby.

The main local diversions are natural, such as basking in the sun, hiking mountain trails to panoramic viewpoints, observing wildlife, watching spectacular sunsets, and resting or reading by the fireplace. The Puesta del Sol management arranges guided local walks and tours.

Get to San José del Pacífico by bus or car via Highway 175, either 65 miles (105 km) north of Pochutla or 81 miles (130 km) south of Oaxaca City.

Bahías de Huatulco and Vicinity

The nine azure Bays of Huatulco (ooah-TOOL-koh) decorate a couple dozen miles of acacia-plumed rocky coastline east of Puerto Ángel. Between the bays, the ocean joins in battle with jutting, rocky headlands, while in their inner reaches the ocean calms, caressing diminutive crescents of coral sand. Inland, a thick hardwood forest seems to stretch in a continuous carpet to the Sierra.

Ecologists shivered when they heard that these bays were going to be developed. Fonatur, the government tourism development agency, says it has a plan, however. Relatively few (but all upscale) hotels will occupy the beaches; other development will be confined to a few inland centers. The remaining 70 percent of the land will be kept as pristine ecological zones and study areas.

Although this story sounds sadly familiar, Fonatur, which developed Ixtapa and Cancún,

BAHÍAS DE HUATULCO AND VICINITY

To Tehuantepec, Oaxaca, Chiapas, and Guatemala

PACIFIC RESORTS

© AVALON TRAVEL

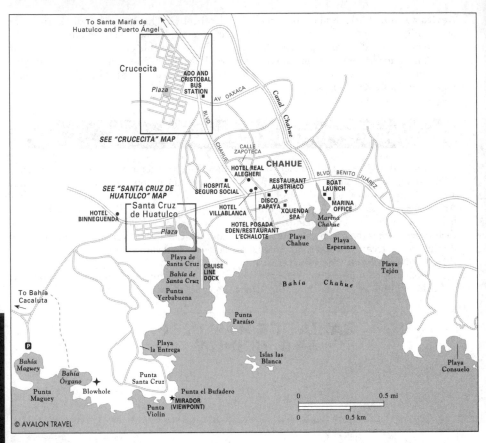

seems to have learned from its experience. Up-to-date sewage treatment was installed *ahead of time;* logging and homesteading were halted; and soldiers patrol the beaches, stopping turtle poachers. If all goes according to the plan, the nine Bahías de Huatulco and their 100,000-acre forest hinterland will be both a tourist and ecological paradise, in addition to employing thousands of local people, when complete in 2020. If this Huatulco dream ends as well as it has started, Mexico should take pride while the rest of the world should take heed.

Getting Oriented

With no road to the outside world, the Bahías de Huatulco remained virtually uninhabited and undeveloped until 1982, about the time that coastal Highway 200 was pushed through. A few years later, Huatulco's planned initial kernel of infrastructure was complete, centering on the brand-new residential service town, Crucecita (pop. 10,000), and nearby Santa Cruz de Huatulco boat harbor and hotel village on Bahía Santa Cruz.

The Bays of Huatulco decorate the coastline both east and west of Santa Cruz. To the east, a paved road links Bahías Chahue, Tangolunda, and Conejos. To the west lie Bahías El Organo, El Maguey, and Cacaluta. Of the latter three, only Bahía Maguey is accessible by paved road. El Organo and Cacaluta are accessible only with the help of a guide; the former on foot or by horseback, the latter by truck or SUV. Isolated farther west are Bahías Chachacual and San Agustín, with no road from Santa Cruz (although a good dirt road runs to San Agustín from Highway 200 near the airport).

Besides Bahía Santa Cruz, the only other bays that have been extensively developed are Chahue, a mile east, and Tangolunda, four miles east. Chahue now has a marina and a sprinkling of small-to-medium-sized, medium-priced hotels. Tangolunda has a green and lovely golf course, small restaurant/shopping complex, and six resort hotels (Las Brisas, Quinta Real, Crown Pacific, Barceló, Club Gala Resort, and Zaashila) that have all been fully operational since the mid-1990s.

(For more details, see *Exploring the Bays of Huatulco*.)

Getting Around

Frequent public **collective taxis** connect Crucecita and Bahías Santa Cruz, Chahue, and Tangolunda. Find the terminal, on Guaumuchil, two blocks east of plaza, at the corner where the boulevard heads south to Chahue. The taxis make the same trips for about $3 by day, $4 at night. No public transportation is available to the other bays. Taxi drivers are willing to drive you for a picnic to west-side bay El Maguey, or Playa Entrega (an isolated beach on Santa Cruz Bay), for about $5 one way, from Crucecita or Tangolunda; about the same to Bahía Conejos.

For an extended day trip to all road-accessible bays, figure on about $20–30 for a taxi, about $50 for a rental car. Call Thrifty (tel. 958/581-9000), Hertz (958/581-9092, 958/581-0588), or Europecar (tel. 958/581-9094, 958/581-0552).

Another option is to go by boat. The local boat cooperative (Sociedad Cooperativa Turístico Tangolunda) runs a daily excursion on the 100-passeger catamaran **Fiesta** (around 10:30 A.M., $20 per person, kids 5–9 half price) to all nine bays, including soft drinks, bilingual guide, and snacks; snorkeling is $5 extra. Reserve directly through its dock office (tel. 958/587-0081). Alternatively, tour by the similarly big catamaran **Tequila** (from the same dock, tel. 958/587-2303), or contact a travel agent such as Paraíso Huatulco (tel. 958/587-0181) or Prometur (tel. 958/587-0413).

The cooperative also rents entire boats for all-day tours for up to 10 people for about $100. Drop-off runs to the nearest beach are about $10 per boat round-trip; to the more remote, around $20–30.

Local travel agents offer other tour options: several hours of sunning, swimming, picnicking, and snorkeling at a couple of Bahías de Huatulco beaches cost around $20 per person. Tours to Puerto Ángel, Puerto Escondido, and wildlife-rich lagoons go for $30–50 per person. For reservations, call Paraíso Huatulco or Prometur (see previous paragraphs).

Another option is to get your own guide. An economical option is to hire an English-speaking taxi driver to take you wherever you want to go for several hours, or up to a whole day, for $30–50, depending on the season. Professional guides are another option.

CRUCECITA AND SANTA CRUZ DE HUATULCO

Despite its newness, Crucecita (Little Cross, pop. 10,000) resembles a traditional Mexican town, with life revolving around a central plaza and adjacent market. Crucecita is where the people who work in the Huatulco

THE HOLY CROSS OF HUATULCO

Long before Columbus, the Huatulco area was well known to the Aztecs and their predecessors. The name itself, from Aztec words meaning "Land Where a Tree (or Wood) Is Worshipped," reflects one of Mexico's most intriguingly persistent legends – that of the Holy Cross of Huatulco.

When the Spanish arrived on the Huatulco coast in the 1520s, the local native people showed them a huge cross they worshipped at the edge of the sea. A contemporary chronicler, Ignacio Burgoa, conjectured the cross had been left by an ancient saint – maybe even the Apostle Thomas – 15 centuries earlier. The cross remained as the Spanish colonized the area and established headquarters and a port, which they named San Agustín, at the westernmost of the Bahías de Huatulco.

Spanish ports and their treasure-laden galleons from the Orient attracted foreign corsairs – Francis Drake in 1579 and Thomas Cavendish in 1587. Cavendish arrived at the bay now called Bahía Santa Cruz, where he saw the cross the natives were worshipping. Believing it was the work of the devil, Cavendish and his men tried to chop, saw, and burn it down. Failing at all of these, Cavendish looped his ship's mooring ropes around the cross and with sails unfurled tried using the force of the wind to pull it down. Frustrated, he finally sailed away, leaving the cross of Huatulco still standing beside the shore.

By 1600, pilgrims were chipping pieces from the cross, so much so that in 1612, Bishop Juan de Cervantes had to rescue it. He brought the cross to Oaxaca, where he made four smaller two-foot crosses of it. He sent one specimen each to church authorities in Mexico City, Rome, and Santa María de Huatulco, head town of the Huatulco *municipio*. Cervantes kept the fourth copy in the cathedral in Oaxaca, where it has remained, venerated and visible in a side chapel, to the present day.

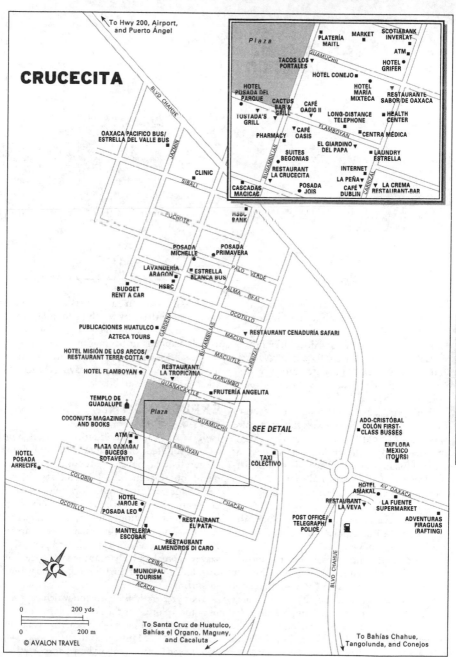

CRUCECITA

To Hwy 200, Airport, and Puerto Ángel

Plaza

PLATERÍA MAITL
MARKET
SCOTIABANK INVERLAT
ATM
HOTEL GRIFER
TACOS LOS PORTALES
GUAMUCHIL
HOTEL CONEJO
HOTEL POSADA DEL PARQUE
HOTEL MARÍA MIXTECA
RESTAURANTE SABOR DE OAXACA
CACTUS BAR & GRILL
CAFÉ OACIO II
TOSTADA'S GRILL
LONG-DISTANCE TELEPHONE
HEALTH CENTER
CAFÉ OASIS
PHARMACY
FLAMBOYAN
CENTRA MÉDICA
EL GIARDINO DEL PAPA
SUITES BEGONIAS
LAUNDRY ESTRELLA
RESTAURANT LA CRUCECITA
INTERNET
LA PEÑA
CASCADAS MAGICAS
POSADA JOIS
CAFÉ DUBLIN
LA CREMA RESTAURANT-BAR

BLVD CHAHUE
JAZMIN
SIBALI

OAXACA PACIFICO BUS/ ESTRELLA DEL VALLE BUS

CLINIC

CASCADAS MAGICAS

PUCHOTE

HSBC BANK

POSADA MICHELLE
POSADA PRIMAVERA

LAVANDERÍA ARAGON
ESTRELLA BLANCA BUS
PALO VERDE

BUDGET RENT A CAR
HSBC
PALMA REAL

OCOTILLO

PUBLICACIONES HUATULCO
GARDENIA
RESTAURANT CENADURÍA SAFARI

AZTECA TOURS
MACUIL

HOTEL MISIÓN DE LOS ARCOS/ RESTAURANT TERRA-COTTA
MACUITLE
CARRIZA

HOTEL FLAMBOYAN
RESTAURANT LA TROPICANA
GARUMBO

TEMPLO DE GUADALUPE
GUANACAXTLE
FRUTERÍA ANGELITA

COCONUTS MAGAZINES AND BOOKS
Plaza
GUAMUCHIL
SEE DETAIL

ATM
ADO-CRISTÓBAL COLÓN FIRST-CLASS BUSSES

PLAZA OAXACA/ BUCEOS SOTAVENTO
FLAMBOYAN

HOTEL POSADA ARRECIFE
COLORIN

EXPLORA MEXICO (TOURS)

TAXI COLECTIVO

OCOTILLO

HOTEL JAROJE
POSADA LEO
CHACAH

HOTEL AMAKAL
AV OAXACA

RESTAURANT LA VEVA
LA FUENTE SUPERMARKET

MANTELERÍA ESCOBAR
RESTAURANT EL PATA

POST OFFICE/ TELEGRAPH/ POLICE

ADVENTURAS PIRAGUAS (RAFTING)

RESTAURANT ALMENDROS DI CARO
CEIBA

MUNICIPAL TOURISM
ACACIA

BLVD CHAHUE

0   200 yds
0   200 m

© AVALON TRAVEL

To Santa Cruz de Huatulco, Bahías el Organo, Maguey, and Cacaluta

To Bahías Chahue, Tangolunda, and Conejos

PACIFIC RESORTS

SANTA CRUZ DE HUATULCO

hotels, businesses, and government offices live. Although pleasant enough for a walk around the square and a meal in a restaurant, and perhaps an evening at a bar or disco, it's nothing special—mostly a place whose modest hotels and restaurants accommodate business travelers and weekenders who can't afford the plush hotels near the beach.

While in Crucecita, be sure to step into the church on the plaza's west side to admire the heavenly **ceiling mural** of the Virgin of Guadalupe. The mural, the largest of Guadalupe in Mexico, is the work of local artists José Ángel del Signo and Marco Antonio Contreras, whose for-sale art is on display locally. Besides the heavenly Virgin overhead, the muralists have decorated the space above the altar with the miraculous story of Don Diego and the Virgin of Guadalupe.

The several deluxe hotels and the mostly travel-oriented businesses of Santa Cruz de Huatulco (on Bahía Santa Cruz, south, about two miles from Crucecita) cluster near the boat harbor. Fishing, tour boats, and ocean liners come and go, vacationers sun themselves on the tranquil yellow-sand Playa Santa Cruz (beyond the restaurants adjacent to the boat harbor),

while T-shirt and fruit vendors and boatmen hang around the quay watching for prospective customers. After the sun goes down, not much usually happens in Santa Cruz. Tourists quit the beach for their hotels and workers return to their homes in Crucecita, leaving the harbor and streets empty and dark.

EXPLORING THE BAYS OF HUATULCO

Isolation has left the Huatulco waters blue and unpolluted, the beaches white and clean. Generally, the bays are all similar: tropical deciduous (green July–Jan.) forested rocky headlands enclosing yellow-white coral sand crescents. The water is clear and good for snorkeling, scuba diving, sailing, kayaking, and sailboarding during the often-calm weather. Beaches, however, are typically steep, causing waves to break quickly near the sand, generally unsuitable for bodysurfing, boogie boarding, or surfing.

Your preparations depend on which bays you plan to explore. For the five developed or partially developed bays—Santa Cruz, Chahue, Tangolunda, Maguey, and San Agustín—you'll need nothing more than transportation, a hat, and sunscreen. Restaurants and stores can supply everything else.

By contrast, the four undeveloped Huatulco bays of El Organo, Cacaluta, Chachacual, and Conejos have neither restaurants, stores, drinking water, nor lots of shade; they're so pristine even coconut palms haven't gotten around to sprouting there. When exploring, bring food, drinks, hats, sunscreen, and mosquito repellent.

East Side

Bahía Chahue, about a mile from both Crucecita and Santa Cruz, is wide and blue, with a steep yellow dune above the beach, stretching to the marina jetty at the east end. With waves that break quickly near the shore, and recede with strong undertow Playa Chahue is not good for swimming, boogie boarding, or surfing. Some hotels and restaurants, and a few bars and hangouts are sprinkled along the main Boulevard Benito Juarez, but Chahue beach, three blocks beyond the boulevard, is uncrowded even on weekends and holidays and nearly empty the rest of the time.

About four miles farther east is the breezy and broad **Bahía Tangolunda.** Although hotels front much of the beach, a signed Playa Pública public access road borders the western edge of the golf course (turn right just past the creek bridge). Except for its east end, the Tangolunda beach is steep and the waves break quickly right at the sand. *Palapa* restaurants at the public beach serve food and drinks; or, if you prefer, stroll a quarter mile along the beach for refreshments at the luxurious poolside beach clubs of the Barceló and Club Gala Resort.

Over the headland about two miles farther east, **Punta Arena** (Sand Point), a forested thumb of land, juts into wide **Bahía Conejos.** Three separate steep beaches spread along the inner shoreline. The main entrance road arrives at high-duned Playa Punta Arena. Playa Tejoncito (Little Coatamundi) is beyond the rocks far to the right; Playa Conejos (Rabbits) is to the left on the other side of Punta Arena. A few palm-frond *ramadas* for shade and a

saltwater flush toilet lavatory occupy the Playa Punta Arena dune. Trees behind the dunes provide a few shady spots for RV or tent campers. (Playa Conejos is a rapidly developing residential zone. By the time you read this, most of the accessible wild dunes and beach may be occupied by houses.)

Beyond **La Bocana,** near the mouth of the Río Copalita, less than a mile farther east, a long, broad beach with oft-powerful surfing rollers (novices beware) stretches for at least a mile east. Beachfront *palapas* serve drinks and very fresh seafood and rent surfboards for about $14 per day. A spring-fed lagoon above the beach (bring your kayak) appears ripe for wildlife-viewing.

After La Bocana, the road bends inland, paralleling the **Río Copalita wildlife sanctuary,** perfect for adventurous exploring. Several operators guide visitors on river ecotours: José Aussenac, owner of Posada Michelle (tel. 958/587-0535), organizes and guides outdoor adventure-tours. Options include bird- and animal-watching walks along riverine forest trails, kayaking river rapids, rafting, and mud baths at a riverside ranch.

West Side

Bahía Santa Cruz has a pair of inviting beaches, **Playa Entrega,** and the most visited, **Playa Santa Cruz,** beyond the shops and restaurants, to the right (facing the ocean) of the boat harbor. Especially during the high winter season and weekends, kids play and vacationers improve their tans at Playa Santa Cruz, and two or three days a week cruise liners dock (and discharge hundreds of tourist ashore) at the adjacent, east side, maritime terminal dock.

Playa Entrega is a small, hidden stretch of sand slipped into the west side of Bahía Santa Cruz. It is the infamous spot where, on January 20, 1831, Vicente Guerrero, president and independence hero, was brought ashore in custody of arch-villain Francisco Picaluga and sent to be murdered in Oaxaca a few months later.

Quarter-mile-long Playa Entrega is the ideal Sunday beach, with calm, clear water and clean yellow sand. Swimming, kayaking, and often snorkeling, sailing, and sailboarding possibilities are excellent. A number of shoreline restaurants serve fresh seafood plates and drinks until around 8 P.M. daily.

Hikers and drivers **get there** via the main east-west street, Boulevard Santa Cruz, which passes the inland edge of the Santa Cruz boat harbor. Continue west, bearing left, at the Y intersection at the Hotel Binneguenda (mark your odometer) on the right. After 0.8 mile (1.3 km) the road bends left and winds uphill, past panoramic viewpoints above Bahía Santa Cruz. Follow the signs and you'll soon be at Playa Entrega.

If, instead of curving left to La Entrega, you follow the highway that continues straight ahead at the same spot, you'll be headed for the Bahías El Maguey, El Organo, Cacaluta, and Chachacual (Chah-chah-KOOAHL). The planned roads to the latter three of these four bays had not yet been completed. Until authorities get around to finishing them, land access to the Bays of El Organo, Cacaluta, and remote Chachacual will be achievable only by hikers or experienced drivers in off-road vehicles who know the myriad dirt tracks that wind through the tropical deciduous forest west of Santa Cruz. If in doubt, hire a jeep and a guide, or take a boat tour.

Bahía El Organo is closest. About 1.1 miles (1.8 km) along the highway from the Hotel Binneguenda, look on the left side for the (one-foot-high, 30-foot-long) raised concrete curb. The easy, unofficial half-mile (0.8 km) foot trail to El Organo takes off downhill through the forest from there. The beach is isolated, intimate, and enfolded by rocky shoals on both sides, and sprinkled with driftwood and green verbena vines. Stroll the quarter-mile-long beach, enjoy the antics of the spouting blowhole on the left-side shoal, and, with caution, swim beyond the close-in surf. Surf fishing appears to be fine here. Some trees behind the dune provide shade. Bring food, water, and everything else, including insect repellent.

Back out on the road, continuing straight ahead, the paved highway forks again (about 1.8 miles from the hotel). Either continue

straight ahead downhill to El Maguey, or fork right to Cacaluta. The sandy crescent of **Bahía El Maguey** is bordered by tidepools tucked beneath forested headlands. Facing a protected fjordlike channel, the Maguey beach is usually calm, nearly waveless, and fine for swimming, snorkeling, diving, and sailing. It would be a snap to launch a kayak or a rubber boat here for fishing in the bay. Beach access is on foot only, via a downhill staircase. A procession of permanent seafood *palapas* line the beach. Most days, especially weekends and holidays, picnickers arrive and banana towboats and *aguamotos* (minimotorboats) buzz the beach and bay.

Bahías Cacaluta, Chachacual, and San Agustín

The paved road that forks right toward **Bahía Cacaluta** ends at a steel barrier, about 0.7 mile (1.1 km) past the fork, at an unsigned sandy but firm track, negotiable by car, bicycle, or on foot. It continues past the barrier and winds and bumps ahead through the shady tropical forest, past two signed forks that, if you bear left all the way, will lead you to Playa Cacaluta after about 1.2 miles (1.9 km) from the pavement's end.

There, the bay spreads along a mile-long, heart-shaped beach, beckoningly close to a cactus-studded offshore islet. Swimmers beware, for waves break powerfully, surging upward and receding with strong undertow. Many shells—limpets and purple- and brown-daubed clams—speckle the beach. Surf-fishing prospects, either from the beach itself or from rocks on either end, appear excellent.

Bahía Chachacual (chah-chah-KOOAHL) past the Río Cacaluta, about four miles farther west from Bahía Cacaluta, is a sand-edged azure nook accessible only with a guide, via forest tracks.

Bahía San Agustín, by contrast, is popular and easily reachable by Pochutla-bound bus, then by the good dirt road just across the highway (one-way taxi from the highway runs about $8, *colectivo* van $2) from the fork to Santa María Huatulco (at Km 236, a mile west of the airport). After about seven miles along a firm track, accessible by all but the bulkiest RVs, bear right to road's end to a modest but very crowded village of *palapas* at the bay's sheltered west end. From there, the beach curves eastward along two miles of forest-backed dune.

Besides good swimming, sailing, sailboarding, and fishing prospects, Bahía San Agustín offers some self-contained RV or tent camping options. On your way in, follow the first of two left forks immediately before the road's end. After about a mile, you arrive at **El Playon** (Big Beach). Facilities, besides a long, lovely curving beach, include several beachfront *palapa* restaurants and several sandy lots, ripe for RV and tent camping.

Back on the entrance road, if you follow the second left fork, after a soccer field, you arrive at **El Sacrificio,** a sheltered, family-friendly beach, lapped by gentle waves, lined by *palapa* restaurants, and picturesquely decorated by big, friendly rocks.

Another choice is to turn right about 100 yards before the end of the road and explore the wild, rough, and very fishable, campable, and surfable open-ocean beach.

A few small stores and the road's-end village *palapas* can, at least, supply seafood and drinks and maybe some water and basic groceries.

Adventure Tours

José Aussenac, owner-operator of **Copalita River Tours,** (at his Hotel Posada Michelle, tel. 958/587-0535) organizes and guides outdoor adventure tours in the east-side Río Copalita wildlife sanctuary. Options include bird- and animal-watching walks along riverine forest trails, kayaking river rapids, and mud baths at a riverside ranch. Contact him for more information and reservations.

Another good choice is to go with **Cascadas Magicas** (Chacah 310, a block south of the Crucecita plaza, tel. 958/587-1470, cascadas-magicas@hotmail.com) to the luscious tropical foothill forest headwaters of the Río Copalita and hike forest trails for a refreshing swim and picnic (about $30 per person) in the waterfalls of Copallilla creek.

Alternatively, you might plan a trip with **Aventuras Piraguas** (www.piraguas.com), a rafting outfitter that guides groups, mostly during October and November. They have no office in Huatulco. They operate out of Veracruz and meet their clientele in Huatulco by appointment.

Guide

Savvy local folks recommend the services of ecologically sensitive guide **Mario Cobos** (tel. 958/587-1833, info@mariocobos.com, www.mariocobos.com). Although Mario's first love is bird-watching, he also offers fishing excursions and backcountry eco-tours. His fee begins at $50 per day, for one or two persons, with your wheels. Jeep rental (figure a minimum of about $50) is extra.

ACCOMMODATIONS

In Huatulco as in other resorts, hotels on the beach are the priciest. Tangolunda's are most expensive, Santa Cruz and Chahue hotels fall in between, and Crucecita's hotels are the cheapest. Virtually all Huatulco lodgings are of modern standard, with private baths with hot water. Many, but not all, have air conditioning, a plus, especially in the warm spring. More information about most of the hotels listed below is available through the Huatulco Hotel and Motel Association (toll-free U.S. and Canada tel. 866/416-0555, local tel. 958/581-0486, fax 958/581-0487, info@hoteleshuatulco.com.mx, www.hoteleshuatulco.com.mx).

Huatulco accommodation rates are highly seasonal. Hotels recommended below are arranged by the customary low-season rates, which rise anywhere between 20 percent and 100 percent, according to demand, during the high Christmas–New Year and Easter seasons and some *puente* (bridge) three-to-five-day holiday weekends.

Crucecita

Nearly all Crucecita lodgings are within a few blocks of the central plaza. They are generally clean, well-managed posada-style hotels, but most are without restaurants and even fewer

PACIFIC RESORTS

(none among the recommendations below) with pools.

UNDER $25

First, the economy **Posada Primavera** (Palo Verde 5, corner of Gardenia, tel./fax 958/587-1167, fax 958/587-1169, $23 s or d in one bed, $25 d or t in two beds), a few blocks north of the plaza, offers six simply furnished but clean, light, high-ceilinged upstairs rooms with bath. Windows look out onto the palmy, bougainvillea-adorned surrounding neighborhood. Rooms come with fans.

At the adjacent corner, **Hotel Posada Michelle** (Gardenia 8, tel./fax 958/587-0535, $23 s or d with fans, $35 with a/c), run by personable ecotour guide José Aussenac, offers about a dozen smallish but clean and comfortable rooms with big beds, baths, and good satellite TV. Some of the rooms are airy and light; others, although dark because of their half-mirrored windows (for privacy), do have white walls and open to a breezy, second-story walkway that leads to a pleasant, hammock-hung, shady view porch.

$25-50

A couple of blocks south of the plaza, budget-minded visitors should check out the newish **Posada Leo** (Bugambilias 302, tel. 958/587-0372 or 958/587-2601, posada-leo_hux@hotmail.com, $22 s, $25 d). The six rooms, although a bit cramped for their two double beds, are attractively tiled and furnished with hand-woven bedspreads, and have shiny modern shower-baths. All rooms come with cable TV and fans; some with a/c for $5 extra. Furthermore, guests enjoy an airy upstairs patio for reading and relaxing.

Nearby, just a block south of the plaza, find **Posada Jois** (Chacah 209, tel. 958/587-0781, joishuatulco@hotmail.com, $25–33 d), between Carrizal and Bugambilias. Past the welcoming female owner's storefront are seven differing rooms on both ground and upper floors. The most attractive are upstairs. One is semideluxe, with king-sized bed and bath; another room is for four with two double beds

and bath. There is also a pair of rooms with shared baths, all with hot water, TV, and fans. A major plus here is an inviting, shady terrace for guest use, with tropical plants and soft chairs for relaxing.

On Guamuchil, just half a block east of the plaza, the **Hotel Los Conejos** (Calle Guamuchil 208, tel./fax 958/587-0054, 958/587-0009, informacion@turismoconejo.com, www.turismoconejo.com, $30 s, $35 d) offers 10 spic-and-span rooms built around the upstairs balcony of a tranquil, intimate interior patio. The rooms are attractively decorated with ceramic tile floors, white stucco walls, and tasteful, color-coordinated curtains and bedspreads. Rooms come with choice of a/c or fans; all have cable TV, private hot-water shower-baths, Internet café, and small restaurant, but no parking.

About three blocks east from the Crucecita plaza hubbub, the **Hotel Amakal** (Av. Oaxaca 1, tel. 958/587-1500, toll-free Mex. tel. 800/667-5343, fax 958/587-2338, amakal@prodigy.net.mx, $32 s or d with fan, $35 d with a/c, credit cards accepted) offers semideluxe, modern-standard rooms at reasonable prices. A stairway from the small, spartan lobby leads upstairs to 26 clean, light, white-tile-floored, invitingly decorated rooms with modern-standard baths. With street parking only.

Two blocks south of the plaza, at the corner of Colorin, **Hotel Jaroje** (hah-RO-hay; Bugambilias 304, tel./fax 958/583-4801, jaroje@yahoo.com.mx, $40 d) offers 12 comfortable rooms, simply but attractively decorated with color-coordinated drapes, bedspreads, and shiny-tiled baths, and include a/c, cable TV, and breakfast.

The owner of the Restaurant Sabor de Oaxaca has turned profits into investment in lovely **Hotel María Mixteca** (Guamuchil 204, tel. 958/587-2336 or 958/587-2337, fax 958/587-2338, andrea100@prodigy.net.mx, www.travelbymexico.com/oaxa/mariamixteca, $45 d), just a block east of the plaza. The 14 rooms are situated around an inviting, tranquil inner patio. Reflecting the owner's love of the Mixteca region, all rooms are named individually, mostly for Mixteca towns, such as Juquila, Tlaxiaco, and Juxtlahuaca. Rooms are high ceilinged and attractively decorated in pleasant pastels, tile, and native art. One room has a queen-sized bed, the rest have two double beds, and many have airy private balconies. Rates include a/c, cable TV, wireless Internet access, parking, and credit cards accepted.

$50-100

The **Hotel Suites Begonias** (Bugambilias 503, tel. 958/587-0390, reservaciones@hotelbegonias. com, $55 s or d, credit cards accepted), at the southeast plaza corner, offers a semideluxe, family-run alternative. The rooms, although clean and comfortable, have motel style walkways passing their windows, decreasing privacy. Rates for the 13 rooms include fan, a/c, and TV.

A very worthy addition to Crucecita's deluxe lodging options is the new, refined **【 Hotel Mision de los Arcos** (Gardenia 902, tel. 958/587-0165, fax 958/587-1903, info@misiondelosarcos.com, www.misiondelosarcos.com, $55–65 d), a block north of the plaza's northwest corner. Owners offer 14 spacious, rustic-chic white-and-beige-motif rooms and suites. Walls are pleasingly white, with accents in beige tile. Guests in many rooms enjoy views toward the leafy park next door. Some rooms have airy balconies and/or private patios. Rooms all come with large luxurious baths, cable TV, a/c, credit cards accepted, excellent restaurant downstairs, but street parking only.

Santa Cruz

Although no Santa Cruz hotels are actually on the beach, they all have inviting pool patios on their own grounds and are within a five-minute walk of the lovely golden strand of Playa Santa Cruz.

$50-100

Consider the worthy and inviting 63-room **Hotel Marina** (Tehuántepec 112, tel. 958/587-0963 through -0968, fax 958/587-0830 hotelmarinaresort@yahoo. com, www.hotelmarinaresort.com, $75 d), that perches on the east side of the Santa Cruz harbor-marina. Rooms are comfortable and deluxe, and come with phones, a/c, cable TV, bar, restaurant, inviting pool patio, parking; credit cards accepted.

Another attractive option is the renovated **Hotel Marlin** (Paseo Mitla 107, tel. 958/587-0055, toll-free Mex. tel. 800/712-7373, fax 958/587-0546, hmarlin@ prodigy.net.mex, www.oaxaca-mio.com/ marlin.htm, $75 s or d), only two blocks from the beach. From street level, the small lobby leads to an appealingly intimate coral-hued inner pool patio and adjacent restaurant, enfolded by three stories of accommodations. Upstairs, the 29 rooms are thoughtfully decorated with colorful bedspreads, floor-length drapes, attractive, rustic tile floors, and deluxe modern-standard bathrooms. Rooms come with a/c, cable TV, phones, beach club, but no parking; credit cards accepted.

On the main Boulevard Santa Cruz, a block inland from the boat harbor, the popular long-time **Hotel Castillo Huatulco** (Blv. Santa Cruz 303, tel. 958/587-0135 or 958/587-0144, toll-free Mex. tel. 800/227-8489, fax 958/587-0131, ventas@hotelcastillohuatulco.com, www.hotel castillohuatulco.com, $78 d) offers a recommendable alternative. Its 106 white stucco and tile neo-colonial-motif rooms are deluxe, comfortable, and high-ceilinged. Amenities include, phone, cable TV, a/c, palmy pool patio, restaurant, beach club, parking; credit cards accepted. Ask for a discount, especially during times of low occupancy.

Three blocks west of the Santa Cruz harbor and beach stands the distinguished **Hotel Meicer Binneguenda** (Blv. Santa Cruz 201, tel./fax 958/587-0078, Mex. toll-free tel. 800/581-9996, binniguenda@prodigy.net. mx, www.meicerhotels.com, $95 s or d). Neocolonial arches, pastel stucco walls, and shiny copper and ceramics handicrafts decorate the interiors, while in the adjacent leafy patio guests sun themselves around the elaborate cascade pool. Upstairs, the colonial-chic rooms are spacious, comfortable, and equipped with phones, cable TV, a/c, modern-standard bathrooms, restaurant-bar and beach club. Rates for the approximately 140 rooms include parking; credit cards accepted. Request a discount package (*paquete;* pah-KAY-tay), especially during times of low occupancy.

(*Note:* During recent years, the Hotel Binneguends has been promoting all-inclusive group-rate packages during weekends and holidays. As a consequence, they close down their refined regular restaurant and serve mass buffets adjacent to the pool patio to crowds of tourists. Best ask if their regular (à la carte) restaurant will be open during your planned stay.)

Chahue

The Bahía Chahue vicinity has, in recent years, acquired a number of new hotels that dot the mostly undeveloped land a few blocks from the beach. At present, however, underdevelopment and isolation make Chahue a less attractive beach neighborhood than either Santa Cruz or Tangolunda. Nevertheless, if you can get a low promotional rate, you might consider staying at one of the hotels recommended here.

$50-100

A block inland from the bayfront boulevard, about four blocks from the beach, find the semideluxe **Hotel Real Aligheri** (Calle Zapoteco, tel. 958/587-1242, toll-free Mex. tel. 800/737-0783, fax 958/587-1243, hrealigheri@prodigy.net.mx, www.oaxaca-mio.com/hrealaligheri.htm, $55 d). It offers about 20 clean, comfortable rooms with pool, a/c, cable TV, and beach club access.

Nearby, on the same quiet side street, my hurrahs go out to the petite █ **Posada Eden Costa** (Calle Zapoteco, tel./fax 958/587-2480, info@edencosta.com, www.edencosta.com, $60 d), behind the larger Hotel Villablanca. Here the husband-wife owners—he's French, she's Southeast Asian—set the international theme. The nine rooms and three kitchenette suites, all with a pair of double beds, are simply beautiful, with rustic-chic tiled floors and gorgeous *talavera*-accented bathrooms. Rooms come with cable TV, fans, attractive pool patio, and the top-pick on-site restaurant L'Echalote.

Not so charming, but nevertheless very recommendable next door is the relaxing **Hotel Villablanca Huatulco** (Blv. Benito Juárez, corner of Zapoteco, tel. 958/587-0606, toll-free Mex. tel. 800/712-7757, toll-free U.S. tel. 888/844-7429, toll-free Canada tel. 877/219-9631, fax 958/587-0660, hotelvillablanca@prodigy.net.mx, www.hotelesvillablanca.com.mx, $90 s or d). Hotel Villablanca guests, mostly upper and middle-class Mexican weekenders, enjoy simply but comfortably furnished semi-deluxe rooms and junior suites. Amenities include attractively rustic tiled floors, blue curtains and bedspreads, modern-standard baths, and private balconies overlooking a palmy pool-patio. Two kids under 12 with parents are free; third night is customarily free. All rooms come with air-conditioning, phones, cable TV, restaurant-bar, beach club, but street parking only.

Tangolunda

Several luxury resort hotels spread along the Tangolunda shoreline. The Hotel Las Brisas dominates the sheltered western side-bay, with four stacklike towers that make the place appear, from a distance, like a big ocean liner. As you move east, next comes the elegant Hotel Quinta Real, perching atop its bayview hillside. The Hotel Barceló and Club Gala Resort stand side by side on the bay's inner recess next to the golf course. The Camino Real Zaashila Resort spreads gracefully to its east-end cove, while in the middle, away from the beach, the gleaming white Crown Pacific stair-steps up the hillside.

The emphasis of all Tangolunda resorts is on facilities, such as multiple pools, bars, and restaurants, full wheelchair access, live music, discos, shows, and sports such as tennis, golf, sailing, kayaking, sailboarding, snorkeling, diving, and swimming. Other amenities may include shops, baby-sitting, children's clubs, and Spanish and arts and crafts instruction.

$100-200

Of the Tangolunda luxury hotels, both the most economical and with some of the most spacious rooms is the **Hotel Crown Pacific**

(Blv. Benito Juárez 8, tel. 958/581-0044, toll-free Mex. tel. 800/711-0044, fax 958/581-0221, reservaciones@crownpacifichuatulco.com). Despite its lavish facilities, the major drawback of the Crown Pacific is that it's not actually on the beach: guests must either walk or shuttle a couple of blocks to the beach club. Although standard rates are about $150 per person, bargain packages can run as low as $100 per person, low-season double occupancy, including all meals, drinks, sports, kid's miniclub, and in-house entertainment, all with a/c. During high winter season season and holidays, the same costs about $200 or more per person.

The **Club Gala Resort Huatalco** (Blv. Benito Juárez 4, tel. 958/583-0400, 958/581-0220, toll-free Mex. tel. 800/712-7401, fax 958/581-0220, infohux@galaresorts.com.mx, reservhux@galaresorts.com.mx, www.galaresorts.com.mx, $125 per person all inclusive), originally built and operated by the competent Mexican Club Maeva chain, ranks among Mexico's better all-inclusive resorts. The beach setting is gorgeous, the tile floors in the halls and rooms shine, and bright bedspreads, immaculate bathrooms, and private oceanview balconies grace the accommodations. Kids seven years or under go free; 8–11 half price.

The **Barceló Huatulco** (Blv. Benito Juárez, tel. 958/581-0039, toll-free U.S./Can. tel. 800/227-2356, fax 958/581-0113, reservas@barcelohuatulco.com, www.barcelohuatulco.com, $125 per person all inclusive), originally a Sheraton hotel, is now a worthy member of the worldwide Spanish Barceló chain. Rooms are comfortable, deluxe, and decorated in soothing pastels, with private bay-view balconies, phones, cable TV, and a/c. All lodging, food, drinks, and in-house entertainment are included. Kids 2–12 stay for about $55.

Perched at the west end of Bahía Tangolunda, the **Hotel Las Brisas Huatulco** (Lote 1, tel./fax 958/583-0200, fax 958/583-0240, toll-free Mex. tel. 800/227-4727, toll-free U.S./Can. tel. 888/559-4329, lasbrisas.huatulco@brisas.com.mx, www.brisas.com.mx, $150 s or d), formerly Club Med, is now owned and operated by the highly respected Mexican Las Brisas hotel chain. The place is huge, spreading from its grand open-air lobby, from which carts ferry guests to hundreds of spartan-deluxe view rooms equipped with all modern amenities. Hotel facilities include many sports, three pools, gym, secluded beaches and coves, kiddie activities, and much more. Two kids under 12 go free with parents; breakfast is included.

OVER $200

If the **Camino Real Zaashila Huatulco** (Blv. Benito Juárez Lote 5, tel. 958/583-0300, toll-free Mex. tel. 800/910-2300, toll-free U.S./Can. tel. 800/722 6466, fax 958/581-0461, zaa@caminoreal.com.mx, zaares@prodigy.net.mx, www.caminoreal.com, $300–450 d) hasn't yet gotten an architectural award, it should soon. Builders have succeeded in creating a modern luxury hotel with an intimate feel. This begins right at the reception, a plush round *palapa*, where arriving guests are graciously invited to sit in soft chairs while being attended to by personable clerks, who are also seated, behind rustic, designer desks. Outside, you walk to your room through manicured tropical gardens, replete with gurgling fountains, splashing brooks, and cascading, green lawn terraces. If the Zaashila has a drawback, it's in some of the 148 rooms, which, although luxurious and comfortable, are entirely tile-floored and could use more color and warmth. However, the arrangement of separate units, nested like a giant child's building blocks, resembles a space-age Hopi Native American pueblo, each unit uniquely perched among the whole, affording much privacy and light, especially in upper-floor units. Outside, a few steps downhill, past the big, meandering blue pool, comes the superb beachfront: acres of luscious, billow-washed yellow sand, intimately enclosed between wave-sculpted rocks on one side and a jungly headland on the other. Some units have their own little private pool; all have access to water sports, tennis, golf, and three restaurants.

Playa Conejo

A personable North American couple, Richard and Brooke Gazer, have built **Villa Agua Azul** (overlooking Playa Conejos, tel.

958/581-0265, guarei@hotmail.com, www
.huatulco.com.mx/aguaazul, $130–150 s or
d year-round), with six elegantly lovely and
comfortable guestrooms, into their home. The
luxuriously private accommodations stair-step
down from the main house to an airy ocean-
vista garden pool patio. Rates include a hearty
breakfast. For the Christmas–New Year holiday, add 25 percent; with fans and a/c, non-
smoking adults 18 and over only, and a short
downhill walk to a private, intimate beach.

Camping

Authorities permit tent camping and RV parking at some of the Bahías de Huatulco. Self-
contained RV parking or tenting is allowed in
the big Bahía Tangolunda public beach access
lot for about $2 per person per day. Although
the beach is beautiful and the partly palm-
shaded lot is pleasant enough, facilities are limited to toilets and cold-water showers. Get there
along the road along the beach to Tangolunda.
Turn right at the signed Playa Pública public
access road bordering the western edge of the
golf course.

Other Huatulco beaches, such as Playa El
Maguey, may be available for RV or tent camping. For more information, visit the **Huatulco
National Park office** (adjacent, beach side,
to the boat harbor, Santa Cruz de Huatulco,
tel. 958/587-0446, reservations booth 8 A.M.–
noon daily, administration office 9 A.M.–2 P.M.
and 4–6 P.M. Mon.–Fri.), both of which issue
camping permits *(permisos).*

FOOD

Aside from the Tangolunda hotels, most of the
good Huatulco eateries are either on or near
the Crucecita plaza.

Breakfast, Snacks, and Bakery

For inexpensive homestyle cooking, try the *fondas* at the Crucecita *mercado* (market), between
Guamuchil and Guanacastle, half a block off
the plaza.

The market stalls are good for fresh fruit during daylight hours, as is the **Frutería Angelita**
(just across Guanacastle, 7 A.M.–9 P.M. daily).

Also nearby, the **Panadería San Alejandro**
(at the southeast plaza corner of Flamboyan
and Bugambilias, tel. 958/587-0317,
7 A.M.–10:30 P.M. daily) offers mounds of
scrumptious baked goodies.

The crowd of satisfied customers will lead
you to Crucecita's best-bet snack shop, **Los
Portales Taco and Grill** (corner of Guamuchil
and Bugambilias, right on the plaza, tel.
958/587-0070, 8 A.M.–2 A.M. daily). Breakfasts
($2–4), a dozen styles of tacos ($2–4), Texas
chili (or, as in Mexico, *frijoles charros*—cowboy
beans, $2), and barbecued ribs ($5) are the specialties. Beer is inexpensive, to boot.

For a relaxing drink or a sandwich in Santa
Cruz, go to the **Cafe Huatulco** (at the bandstand in the shady Santa Cruz town plaza, a
block west of the marina embarcadero, tel.
958/587-1228, cafehuatulco@hotmail.com,
8 A.M.–10 P.M. daily). The mission of the
friendly owner, Salvador López de Toledo,
and his wife (who operates the kitchen) is to
promote the already well-deserved popularity
of Huatulco's mountain-grown coffee, which
they grind fresh daily for their good cappuccinos and café lattes. Furthermore, Salvador is a
good source of information on Huatulco coffee and the mountain *fincas cafeteleras* (coffee
farms) where it's grown.

Restaurants

The refined sidewalk atmosphere of **Cafe Oasis**
(at the southeast plaza corner, Bugambilias
and Flamboyan, tel. 958/587-0045, 8 A.M.–
midnight daily) has made it Crucecita's plaza-
front restaurant of choice. Beneath cooling
ceiling fans, customers watch the passing plaza
scene while enjoying a full bar and a professionally prepared and served menu of breakfast
($4–6), good espresso, fruit and salads ($2–5),
hamburgers ($3–5), Mexican and international
specialties ($5–10), and much more.

Lovers of fine Italian cuisine can't miss enjoying a meal at Crucecita's class-act restaurant, **El Giardino del Papa** (The Pope's
Garden, Flamboyan 204, tel. 958/587-1763,
2 P.M.–midnight daily), brainchild of owner
Rossana Pandolfini, of Amalfitano, Italy, and

chef Mario Saggese of Salerno. Mario, who was once the pope's bodyguard, immigrated to Mexico to follow his passion for cooking. Rossana asked Mario to come to Huatulco because she craved pasta al dente the way it's "supposed to be" in the old country. Although Mario's suggestions include calamari criollo ($12), scampi al brandy ($15), *insalata* Mediterrenea ($5), and spaghetti a la Mario ($12), whatever you get will be tasty. Call for reservations, especially during the winter. Find the restaurant one block west of the plaza's southwest corner.

Diagonally across the plaza, half a block north of the plaza's northwest corner, step into the cool, airy interior of **Restaurant Terra Cotta** (at the Hotel Misión de los Arcos, Gardenia 902, tel. 958/587-0165, 8 A.M.–11 P.M. daily). Kick back and enjoy the leafy green bay-window view while you choose from a list of tasty breakfasts (eggs any style $3.50, omelets $4, waffles $3), salads (caesar $6), baguettes (barbequed pork loin $7), and Mexican specialties (*mole negro* on chicken $8, baby back ribs with luscious tamarind sauce $10).

A worthy new addition to the Crucecita plaza-front restaurant options is **Tostada's Grill** (on the south side, tel. 958/587-1697, 7 P.M.–midnight daily). Although it offers plenty of good soups, salads, and pastas ($3–6), the house specialties come hot off the grill: barbecued ribs ($9), whole lobster ($14), surf and turf brochette ($11), and barbecued snapper, tuna, or *dorado* ($10).

Good, economically priced, local-style food in an open-air, TV-free setting is the specialty of refined but relaxing **Restaurant La Crucecita** (501 Bugambilias, corner of Chacah, tel. 958/587-0906, 8 A.M.–11 P.M. daily), one block south of the plaza. A platoon of loyal local customers arrives daily to enjoy the afternoon five-course *comida corrida*. Pick an entrée (such as *guisado de res, costilla en mole verde*, or *chiles rellenos*) and you get bottomless fruit *agua* (choice of lemon, orange, jamaica, pineapple), soup, rice, cooked veggies or salad, and dessert, all for $5. The *comida* is served between noon and about 4:30 P.M.

For late lunch or *comida*, local folks crowd into the airy *palapa* of **Restaurant Almendros di Caro** (on Ocotillo, just west of Carrizal, three blocks south, one block east of the plaza's southeast corner, tel. 958/587-0645, 8 A.M.–8:30 P.M. daily), life project of friendly Carina Enriquez Gutiérrez. Here, the big draw is the four-course set lunch, but with plenty of options. Choose your soup, main plate (of pasta, or meat, or seafood, or *antojito*), and you get rice, a drink, and dessert thrown in, all for $5. Also good for breakfast.

Fine dining in Huatulco has received a big boost at **Restaurant L'Echalote** (on Calle Zapateco behind the big Hotel Villablanca in Chahue, tel. 958/587-2480, info@eden-costa.com, 2–11 P.M. Tue.–Sun.). Although the cooking of owner-chefs Thierry Faivre and his Laotion wife, Tina, derives from an entire world of cuisine experience, their creations invariably come with a French touch. Ask Thierry to put on Edith Piaf and it will be better than Paris. Everything they serve is good, from the soup (*caldo camarón* $9), salad with goat cheese ($7), and Thai fondue for two ($22). *Vive la France!* Reservations highly recommended.

Restaurant Austriaco (1:30–11 P.M. Mon.–Sat.) of chef Manfred Gruber embellishes the growing Huatulco fine-food tradition. His eclectic and variable menu often includes Grecian- or Tuscan-style salad ($5); *gulasch* (beef stew), Viennese-style *schnitzel* (veal or pork cutlet), Asian chicken, *filete de mero* (sea bass), *sauerbraten* (sausage with pickled cabbage), *rinz roladen* (rolled steak), all $6–10; and apple strudel ($3). Yum. Find Austriaco at Plaza Chahue, on the street-front, 100 yards east of high-profile disco Papaya.

ENTERTAINMENT
Nightlife

Huatulco entertainments center on the Crucecita plaza. Although the hubbub cools down on weekdays and during low season (and hot clubs seem to change as often as the Huatulco breeze), many spots heat up significantly during the winter high season.

PACIFIC RESORTS

A growing platoon of visitors and local expatriates gather for a little bit of Ireland in Huatulco at **Café Dublin** (Calle Carrizal, noon–after midnight daily low season, 6 A.M.–2 A.M. daily high season), a block east and half a block south of the Crucecita plaza's southeast corner. Good imported beer, Irish coffee, spaghetti and meatballs, hamburgers, satellite TV, and good fellowship keeps the customers happy. In a cozy upstairs room, patrons settle in for the evening, socializing, enjoying recorded music, and watching videos.

Next door to the Café Dublin is the very worthy low- to medium-volume jazz, guitar, and vocal nightspot **La Peña** (Carrizal 504, cell 044-958/587-6986, 7–11 P.M. Mon.–Sat.).

One of the longest lasting Crucecita nightclubs is the **La Crema Restaurant-Bar** (on Carrizal, across from Café Dublin and La Peña bar, tel. 958/587-0702, 6 P.M.–2 A.M. Tues.–Sun.). In high season, it's open nightly, with food and drink, videos, flashing lights, and high-volume *salsa* music for dancing.

A pair of promising new nightspots have opened up in Chahue. The original was the cleverly decorated disco **La Mina** (in the basement of the Hotel Real Aligheri, on Zapoteco, about a block north of main Boulevard Benito Juárez, tel. 958/587-1242), fixed up to resemble a coal mine. Programs include mostly salsa, tango, and 1970s and 1980s rock.

Newer and hotter is **Disco Papaya** (on main east–west Bulevar Benito Juárez, beach side, approximately two blocks east of the intersection to Crucecita, tel. 958/587-2589, 9 P.M.–3 A.M. Thurs.–Sat.).

Sunset Cruise, Live Music, and Tourist Shows

Lovers of quieter diversions might enjoy going on a wine, snack, and soft-music sunset cruise on the sailboat **Luna Azul** (tel. 958/587-0509). For higher-volume entertainments with your sunset view, go by the catamaran **Tequila** (tel. 958/587-2303) from the Santa Cruz boat harbor.

The **Club Gala Resort** in Tangolunda is one of the most reliable sources of hotel nightlife.

Live music often plays before dinner (about 6–8 P.M.) in the lobby bar, and "Gala Night" tourist buffet and shows rev up at least weekly year-round. Contact a travel agent or call the hotel directly (958/583-0400) for details and reservations (about $55 per person, including everything). Other hotels, such as the Crown Pacific (tel. 958/581-0044) and Barceló ("Caribe Tropical" and "Broadway" nights, tel. 958/587-0055) may also offer similar buffet and show entertainments in season.

SPORTS AND RECREATION
Swimming, Snorkeling, and Scuba Diving

Swimming is ideal in the calm corners of the Bahías de Huatulco. Especially good swimming beaches are at **Playa Entrega** in Bahía Santa Cruz and **Bahía El Maguey.**

Generally clear water makes for rewarding snorkeling off the rocky shoals of all of the Bays of Huatulco. Local currents and conditions, however, can be hazardous. Novice snorkelers should go on trips accompanied by strong, experienced swimmers or professional guides. Although rentals are generally available, best be prepared with your own equipment.

Huatulco scuba divers enjoy the services of well-equipped and professional **Hurricane Divers** scuba shop (tel. 958/587-1107, email@ hurricanedivers.com, www.hurricanedivers .com, 9 A.M.–6 P.M. Mon.–Fri., 9 A.M.–4 P.M. Sat.), in the small complex between the Santa Cruz main beach and boat harbor. They start novices out with a pool mini-course, followed by a three-hour ($95) resort dive in a nearby bay. Snorkelers go for about $60, with good equipment furnished. Hurricane Divers' (PADI) open-water certification course takes about four days and runs about $340, complete. With your open-water certificate, you are qualified for the advanced (two-tank $120) dives. After that, you may be ready for more advanced trips, which might include local shipwrecks, night dives, and marine flora, fauna, and ecology tours.

Alternatively, try very experienced (since 1988 in Huatulco) **Buceos Sotavento,** which offers similar (PADI) services. Contact them at the Plaza Oaxaca complex (upstairs, shop #18, on the Crucecita plaza, southwest corner of Flamboyan and Gardenia, tel./fax 958/587-2166, scubasota@hotmail.com, www.tomzap.com/sotavento.html) or in Tangolunda (across from the Hotel Barceló, tel. 958/581-0051, cell tel. 044-958/587-7441).

Fishing and Boat Launching

The local boat cooperative **Sociedad Servicios Turísticos Bahía Tangolunda** takes visitors out for fishing excursions from the Santa Cruz boat quay. Contact them at their ticket office (for catamaran *Tequila*, tel. 958/587-2303) at the Santa Cruz boat dock.

For a launch with two lines and bait, figure on paying about $25/hour, for a minimum five-hour excursion. For big-game fishing, rent a big 40-foot boat, with lines for several persons, for about $250. More reasonable prices might be obtained by asking around among the individual fishermen at the Santa Cruz boat harbor or the village at San Agustín.

For example, you can go fishing deluxe in the 33-foot motor yacht *Fortuna* (tel. 958/581-0491 or 958/587-1381, toll-free Mex. tel. 800/624-6161, fortunahuatulco@msn.com), with about four lines and room for about six. Organize a party and rent the whole boat for about $450 per day. Individuals can book for about $80 a day during high season, depending on the number of customers they have.

On the other hand, you can leave the negotiations up to a travel agent, who will arrange a fishing trip for you and your friends. You can stop afterward at a beachside *palapa*, which will cook up a feast with your catch. Save money by bringing your own tackle. Rates for an approximately three-hour trip for three run about $60 if you supply your own tackle, $120 if you don't. Contact the agent at your hotel travel desk, or an outside agent such as **Paraíso Huatulco** (in the Hotel Flamboyan on the Crucecita plaza, tel. 958/587-0181, fax 958/587-0190) or **Aventuras Huatulco** (in Plaza Conejo, on Guamuchil, half a block east of the Crucecita plaza, tel. 958/587-0054 or 958/587-1695).

Huatulco's best **boat-launching site** is at easily reachable Bahía Chahue marina, with about 40 slips and an excellent heavy-duty boat ramp. Go to the marina office (tel. 958/587-2652, 8 A.M.–3 P.M. and 4–6 P.M. Mon.–Fri.) for permission to launch ($15) and slip rental information. Slip rates run about $0.55 per foot per day (between 35 and 80 feet) at the dock. Electricity and water cost extra. Find it from the east–west Chahue beachfront boulevard, follow the sign for remolques (trailers) to the big parking lot and ramp.

Tennis, Golf, and Spa

If you're planning on playing lots of tennis, best stay at one of the Tangolunda luxury resorts, such as the Barceló or the Las Brisas. Otherwise, the Tangolunda Golf Course (tel. 958/581-0037, fax 958/581-0059) rents tennis courts for about $7/hour. The tennis courts are next to the clubhouse on the knoll at the east side of the golf course.

The breezy green **Tangolunda Golf Course** (tel. 958/581-0037, fax 958/581-0059), designed by the late architect Mario Chegnan Danto, stretches for 6,851 yards down Tangolunda Valley to the bay. The course starts from a low building complex (watch for bridge entrance) off the Highway 200–Tangolunda highway across from the sanitary plant. Greens fee runs about $80 for 18 holes, $64 for 9 holes, cart $35, club rental $17, caddy $25.

The luxury **Xquenda** (sh-QUEN-dah, "soul" in Zapotec, tel. 958/583-4448 or 958/583-4449, xquenda@huatulcospa.com, www.huatulcospa.com, 9 A.M.–6 P.M. daily) spa and athletic club, in Chahue, west side, on the Santa Cruz-Tangolunda road, offers tennis, paddle tennis, and a lap swimming pool. Spa services include massage, facials, *temazcal* ceremonial hot room, and more.

Horseback Riding

Rancho Caballo del Mar (tel. 958/589-9387, local cell 044-958/587-4886) guides horseback trips along the ocean-view forest trail that stretches from its corral through the eco-preserve zone by the Río Copalita. The four-

PACIFIC RESORTS

mile tour, which costs about $40 per person, begins at the ranch site, on the road (best go by car or taxi) on the road several miles east past Tangolunda, about a mile before (south of) Highway 200.

SHOPPING
Market and Handicrafts

Crucecita has a small traditional market (officially the Mercado 3 de Mayo) east of the plaza, between Guanacastle and Guamuchil. Although produce, meats, and clothing occupy most of the stalls, a few offer Oaxaca handicrafts. Items include black *barra* pottery, hand-crocheted Mixtec and Amusgo *huipiles*, wool weavings from Teotitlán del Valle, and whimsical duck-motif wooden bowls carved by an elderly but sharp-bargaining local gentleman.

In Santa Cruz, just west of the boat harbor, a warren of dozens of stalls offer nearly everything from T-shirts and Taxco silver to carved wooden fish and lacquerware.

Steep rents and lack of business force many local silver, leather, art, and other handicrafts shops to hibernate until tourists arrive in December. The few healthy shops with good selections cluster either around the Crucecita plaza, the Santa Cruz boat harbor, or in the Punta Tangolunda shopping complex adjacent to the Hotel Barceló (or shops in the hotel itself).

In Crucecita, one of the most reliable crafts stores is **Plata de Taxco** (9 A.M.–9 P.M. daily), next to Hotel Suites Begonias, a few doors south of the plaza's southwest corner. Here you can select from an all-Mexican assortment: shiny *barro negro* (black pottery) from the Valley of Oaxaca, pottery moon and sun faces from Tonalá, Jalisco, *talavera* ware from Puebla, *alebrijes* from Arrazola, near Oaxaca City, and lots of glistening silver jewelry from Taxco.

Alternatively, for a fine all-Taxco silver collection, especially rings, go to **Platéréa Maitl** (tel. 958/587-1223, 9 A.M.–9 P.M. daily) on the Crucecita plaza, west side, between Guancaxtle and Guamuchil.

One of the few local handicrafts workshops is the charmingly traditional **Mantelería Escobar** (Ocotillo 217, tel. 958/587-0532, 9 A.M.–8 P.M.

Mon.–Sat) at the corner of Bugambilias, three blocks south of the Crucecita plaza. This factory uses century-old looms to create lovely all-cotton *manteles* (tablecloths). Besides their own work, they also sell plenty—blouses, skirts, *huipiles*, and ceramics—from all over Oaxaca.

Another worthwhile Crucecita handicrafts option is **Artesanías Paradiso** (tel. 958/587-0268, 9 A.M.–10 P.M. Mon.–Sat., 5–10 P.M. Sun.), just past the plaza's northwest corner, on Gardenia, corner of Guarumbo. Among the many carefully selected treasures, find masks from Huazaolotitlán, black pottery from San Bartolo Coyotepec, dolls from San Miguel de Allende, *alebrijes* from San Martén Tilcajete, and a whole roomful of fetching one-of-a-kind dresses, blouses, and skirts ranging from traditional to chic.

INFORMATION AND SERVICES
Supermarket, Laundry, and Photography

The supermarket **La Fuente** (tel. 958/587-0222, 8 A.M.–10 P.M. daily), in Crucecita on east-side Avenida Oaxaca, a block east of the Pemex station, offers a large stock of groceries, an ice machine, and a little bit of everything else.

Take your washing to the **Lavandería Aragon** (8 A.M.–8 P.M. Mon.–Sat.). Find it five short blocks north of the Crucecita plaza, on Flamboyan, corner of Gardenia and Palma Real.

For quick digital and film processing and printing, go to **Foto Conejo** (tel. 958/587-0054, 9 A.M.–8 P.M. Mon.–Sat., 9 A.M.–5 P.M. Sun.), just off the Crucecita plaza, across Guamuchil from the market. Besides a photo-portfolio of the Bahías de Huatulco, the friendly owner stocks point-and-shoot cameras and both film and digital supplies and accessories.

Money Exchange

For cash, you may either use the ATMs available at all of Huatulco's banks, or go inside. In Crucecita, try long-hours **HSBC** (8 A.M.–7 P.M. Mon.–Sat.), at the corner of Bugambilias and Sibali, eight short blocks north of the plaza. Otherwise, go to **Scotiabank Inverlat** and

ATM, with shorter hours (9 A.M.–4 P.M. Mon.–Fri.), a block west of the plaza at the corner of Guamuchil and Carrizal. After hours, use either the Banamex ATM, on Carrizal a block west of the plaza a few doors north of the Hotel Grifer, or the Bancomer ATM, on the Crucecita plaza's southwest corner by the newsstand.

Other banks are in Santa Cruz: **Banamex** (tel. 958/587-0322, 9 A.M.–4 P.M. Mon.–Fri.), on the main street Avenida Benito Juárez, corner of Pochutla, exchanges both U.S. and Canadian travelers checks. **Bancomer** (tel. 958/587-0305, 8:30 A.M.–4 P.M. Mon.–Fri.), on the adjacent corner, across Pochutla, does about the same thing.

Post and Telecommunications

The Huatulco *correo* (post office, tel. 958/587-0551, 8 A.M.–8 P.M. Mon.–Fri., 8 A.M.–4 P.M. Sat.) and *telecomunicaciones* **Telecom** (tel. 958/587-0894, 8 A.M.–7 P.M. Mon.–Fri. and 9 A.M.–12:30 P.M. Sat.) stand side by side, across from the Pemex gas station on east-side Blv. Tangolunda.

For telephone, buy a **Ladatel** telephone card and use it at public telephones, or go to one of the **larga distancia** businesses on Carrizal, near the Hotel Grifer, such as **Caseta Telefónica Gemenis** (tel. 958/587-0735 or 958/587-0736, 9 A.M.–8 P.M. daily).

Internet connection is available at Cuijosnet store (Carrizal 504, between Flamboyan and Chaca, tel. 958/587-1569, 10 A M –10 P.M. daily), next to the Irish Pub.

Health and Emergency

Among the better of Huatulco private clinics is **Clínica Médico** (403 Sibali, corner of Gardenia, about eight blocks north of the Crucecita plaza, tel. 958/587-0600 or 958/587-0687), with 24-hour emergency service.

For an English-speaking, U.S.-trained doctor, go to IAMAT (International Association for Medical Assistance to Tourists) member and general practitioner **Dr. Andrés González Ayvar** (at the Hotel Barceló, tel. 958/581-0055 or cell 044-958/587-6065, 11 A.M.–1 P.M. and 8:30–11 P.M. Mon.–Sat.).

Alternatively, go to the 24-hour government **Centro de Salud** clinic (tel. 958/587-1421), on Carrizal, a block east of the Crucecita plaza, or the big modern-standard **Seguro Social** hospital (tel. 958/587-1182, 958/587-1183), in Crucecita, on the boulevard to Tangolunda, a quarter mile south of the Pemex gas station.

For routine medications, Crucecita has many pharmacies, such as **Farmacia del Centro** (plaza corner of Flamboyan and Bugambilias, tel. 958/587-0232, 8 A.M.–10 P.M. Mon.–Sat., 9 A.M.–2 P.M. and 5–10 P.M. Sun.), at street level, below the Hotel Begonias.

For police emergencies, call the Crucecita **policía** (tel. 958/587-0210), in the Agencia Municipal behind the post office, across the Tangolunda boulevard from the Pemex *gasolinera*.

Immigration and Customs

Both Migración and the Aduana are at the Huatulco airport. If you lose your tourist permit, try to avoid trouble or a fine at departure by presenting Migración with proof of your date of arrival—stamped passport, an airline ticket, or preferably a copy of your lost tourist permit—a day (or at least three hours) before your scheduled departure.

Tourist Information Offices

The Huatulco office of the **Oaxaca Secretary of Tourism** (tel./fax 958/581-0176, 8 A.M. 5 P.M. Mon.–Fri. high season only) is in the Tangolunda hotel zone, inland side, west edge of the hotel-shopping complex.

Alternatively, go to **Huatulco Municipal Tourism** (tel. 958/587-1871 or 958/587-1070, fax 958/587-1777, 9 A.M.–5 P.M. Mon.–Fri., 9 A.M.–2 P.M. Sat.,) in the Crucecita Casa de Cultura, upstairs, at the corner of Bugambilias and Ceiba, four blocks south of the plaza.

Newspapers, Books, and Magazines

The small **newsstand** (tel. 958/587-0279, 8 A.M.–10 P.M. daily) at the southwest Crucecita plaza corner stocks a number of North American magazines, such as *Newsweek,*

People, and *Scientific American,* in addition to the daily *News* from Mexico City.

Also, pick up a copy of **Huatulco Magazzine,** the handy commercial tourist booklet, at your hotel or a store or travel agent, or at the magazine's office (Cerrada de Tlacolula no. 3, tel. 958/587-0342, www.huatulco.magazzine.net), in Santa Cruz.

Ecology Association

Local ecologists and community leaders monitor Huatulco's development through their informal **Green Globe 21** association. They gather weekly at the Café Huatulco kiosk in the Santa Cruz plaza. Among the group's leaders are Ivonne Kraak of Hurricane Divers (tel. 958/587-1107) and Federico Roth, manager of the Hotel Quinta Real (tel. 958/581-0428).

GETTING THERE AND AWAY
By Air

The **Huatulco airport** (officially the Aeropuerto Internacional Bahías de Huatulco, code-designated HUX) is just off Highway 200, eight miles (13 km) west of Crucecita and 19 miles (31 km) east of Puerto Ángel. The terminal is small, with a pair of snack bars, a few handicrafts and trinket shops and a small book and magazine store, with some English-language paperback novels, and an ATM.

A number of scheduled air carriers connect with Mexican and international destinations: The most direct U.S. flight is via **Continental Airlines,** which connects daily non-stop with Houston. For information and reservations, call toll-free Mexico tel. 800/900-5000, at airport tel. 958/581-9103, or contact a travel agent.

Mexicana Airlines affiliate **Click** airlines connects daily with Mexico City, where many U.S., Canadian, and European connections are available. For reservations, call Click locally (958/581-9007), or Mexicana's office at the Plaza Chahue shopping center (tel. 958/587-0223 or 958/587-0243, or toll-free in Mexico tel. 800/502-2000). For flight information, call the airport (958/581-9008, or 958/587-9007).

A number of winter–spring seasonal charter flights connect Huatulco with U.S. and Canadian destinations, such as Toronto, Winnepeg, Calgary, Vancouver, New York, Chicago, Denver, Seattle, and many more. For more information and reservations, contact a travel agent.

Of the long-distance Mexican charter airlines, **Magnicharter** is the most frequent, connecting with Mexico City daily except Tuesday. For reservations and flight information, call the airline (tel. 958/587-1435, 958/587-1436, or 958/587-1112), or a travel agent, such as Paraíso Huatulco (tel. 958/587-0181), or Prometur (tel. 958/587-0413).

Also, experienced local light charter airline **Aerotucan** (toll-free 800/640-4148, Huatulco local tel. 958/587-2427, Oaxaca City 951/501-0530 or 951/501-0532, www .aero-tucan.com) regularly connects Huatulco with Oaxaca City, Puebla, and Veracruz.

Huatulco **air arrival** is simple and straightforward. Nevertheless, since the terminal has no hotel booking agency or money-exchange counter (although there is an ATM), come with a hotel reservation and sufficient pesos to last until you can get to the bank in Santa Cruz or Crucecita. After the typically quick immigrations and customs checks, arrivees have a choice of efficient ground transportation to town. Agents sell tickets for collective GMC Suburbans to Crucecita, Santa Cruz, and Tangolunda (about $9). A private *taxi especial* outside the airport gate only, for three, possibly four passengers, runs about $12 to the same destinations. Prices to Puerto Ángel vicinity run about double these.

Mobile travelers on a budget can roll their suitcase the couple of blocks from the terminal to Highway 200 to catch one of the frequent public *taxis colectivos* (about $1–2) headed either way to Crucecita (east, left) or the Pochutla (Puerto Ángel) junction (west, right).

A few **car rental** agents are usually on duty for flight arrivals. If they're not, make a reservation ahead of time and they will meet your flight: Call Thrifty (at airport tel. 958/581-9000, in Crucecita tel. 958/587-0010, or Mex. toll-free tel. 800/021-2277, www.thrifty.com), or Hertz (at airport tel. 958/581-9092, in Tangolunda tel. 958/581-0588, www.hertz.com), or Europecar (at airport tel. 958/581-9094, in Crucecita, tel. 958/581-0552, www.europcar.com).

By Car or RV

Paved highways connect Huatulco east with the Isthmus of Tehuántepec, west with Puerto Ángel and Puerto Escondido, and north with Oaxaca.

Highway 200, the east–west route, runs an easy 100 miles (161 km) to Tehuántepec, where it connects with Highway 190. From there, it continues northwest to Oaxaca and east to Chiapas and the Guatemala border. (A new $2 toll cutoff, fork left about five miles west of, before, Salina Cruz, cuts the time to Tehuántepec and, thence Oaxaca, by at least half an hour.)

In the opposite direction, the Highway 200 route is equally smooth, connecting Huatulco with Pochutla (Puerto Ángel), 25 miles (40 km) west, and Puerto Escondido, 70 miles (113 km), continuing to Acapulco in a long 322 miles (519 km). Allow about three hours to Tehuántepec, 1.5 hours to Puerto Escondido, and to Acapulco, a full nine hours' driving time, either direction.

Highway 175, the cross-Sierra connection north with the city of Oaxaca, although paved, is narrow, winding, and oft-potholed, with few services in the 80-mile high Sierra stretch between its junction with Highway 200 at Pochutla (22 miles west of Crucecita) and Miahuatlán in the Valley of Oaxaca. The road climbs to 9,000 feet into pine-tufted, winter-chilly Chatino and Zapotec country. Be prepared for emergencies. Allow eight hours northbound, seven hours southbound, for the entire 175-mile (282-km) Huatulco-Oaxaca trip. (You can save an hour by road Huatulco–Oaxaca by taking the new shortcut, from Highway 200, a couple of miles west of the Huatulco airport, via Santa Cruz de Huatulco and Pluma Hidalgo, to Highway 175 and thence to Oaxaca.)

By Bus

At least six long-distance bus lines connect Huatulco with destinations east, west, and north. They depart from three separate terminals in Crucecita. First-class carriers **Omnibus Cristóbal Colón (OCC), Autobuses del Oriente (ADO)** and second-class **SUR** share a new terminal (Rescadillo 108, corner Blv. Chahue, tel. 958/582-0259, toll-free Mex. tel. 800/702-8000, www.ticketbus.com.mx), three long blocks east of the Crucecita plaza and a block north of the Pemex gas station. From there, buses connect west with Pochutla (Puerto Ángel) and Puerto Escondido. Buses also connect east with Salina Cruz and Tehuántepec on the Isthmus, continuing either east to San Cristóbal las Casas and Tapachula in Chiapas, or north with Coatzacoalcos, Veracruz, and Merida. Other buses connect via the Isthmus long (10-hour) route north with Oaxaca, where some continue to Mexico City, either by the (slow route), Highway 190 via Huajuapan and Cuautla, Morelos, or by the (quick route), expressway via Tehuacán and Puebla.

Five blocks directly north of the Crucecita plaza, corner of Palma Real, a few **Estrella Blanca** (tel. 958/587-0680) affiliate buses, such as first-class **Elite,** connect west with Pinotepa Nacional and Acapulco via Pochutla, Puerto Escondido, and Acapulco, and east with Salina Cruz.

Furthermore, a few second- and first-class **Estrella del Valle** and **Autobuses Oaxaca Pacífico**(tel. 958/587-0354) buses connect daily with Oaxaca by the winding trans-sierra Highway 175 route via Pochutla. The trip is a quick eight hours. Buses depart from the curbfront, on Calle Jazmin, at the corner of Sabali, nine blocks north of the plaza.

UPLAND EXCURSIONS INTO COFFEE COUNTRY

A century before the Bahías de Huatulco development was even on the drawing board, the cooler, greener Huatulco uplands were home to a community of farmers and fruit and coffee ranchers. Bypassed by the new Highway 200 and the coastal resort development, the foothill region above the Bahías de Huatulco is a treasury of traditional Oaxaca life and natural diversions—wildlife to view, springs and waterfalls to splash in, and jungle coffee ranches to visit and explore.

The foothill destinations of Santa María Xadani and La Gloria Coffee Farm make an enjoyable day trip by car or tour. By bus, allow two days, including an overnight at the coffee farm. Along the way, nature lovers will enjoy the leafy foothill country, laced with springs and cascades gurgling through leafy, vine-hung woodland, rich with birds, mammals, and fluttering butterflies.

Ecotouring and Guides

Local tour operators guide hiking and bird-watching tours to archaeological zones, coffee farms, pilgrimage and sacred sites, springs, and waterfalls in the jungly foothill hinterland north of Huatulco. One of the most experienced and environmentally sensitive operators is **Aventuras Huatulco** in Crucecita (Blv. Guelaguetza Local 12, C-9, Sector J, tel. 958/587-1695, local cell tel. 044-958/589-3907, erastorojas@hotmail.com). They offer a range of options, from one-day walks along the Río Copalita (ruins, bird-watching by canoe, mud bath) and jungle jeep safaris and lunch at a coffee farm to jungle overnights (waterfalls, rock hieroglyphic paintings) and complete five-day excursions from Oaxaca City including much of the above.

Or try other agents, such as reliable **Servicios Turísticos del Sur** (at the Hotel Castillo, tel./fax 958/587-1211, huatulco@ prodigy.net.mx), for similar services. You might also contact your hotel tour desk or visit www.oaxaca-mio.com/huatulco/ huatulcoserviosturisticosdehuatulco.htm for many more options.

A sprinkling of jungle **coffee farms** *(fincas cafeleteras)* invite visitors. One of the best prepared is foothill **Finca El Pacifico** (in Spanish, local cell tel. 044-958/584-6094, cafepluma-hua@huatulco.net.mx), which offers cozy country lodging and hearty food, jungle nature walks, bathing in cool natural springs, and viewing their coffee processing operation. You can access them directly or through a guide or tour operator.

Santa María de Huatulco

Colonial-era Santa María de Huatulco (pop. 9,000) is the head town of the sprawling Huatulco *municipio,* which encompasses the entire Bahías de Huatulco development. Although living at the center of a mountain, jungle, and seashore domain, Santa María de Huatulco people have looked toward the emerald Sierra rising precipitously on their northern horizon. Those mountains and their foothills have traditionally been the main source of Huatulco's wealth—the aromatic produce of a host of *fincas cafetaleras.*

Taste Huatulco coffee in one of the cafés, such as the inviting, family-run **Las Flores** on the town plaza, east side. While you're on the plaza, take a stroll around; inspect the unique *ollas* (jars) made into fountains, an inviting part of the plaza decoration.

Also take a look around the **historic old market,** uniquely built on pillars in the middle of the plaza. First among your purchases should be samples of the breads for which Santa María is famous: **Pan Yemo** (egg bread), **Pan de los Muertos** (especially popular around Día de los Muertos, November 1–2), and **Pan Tarazón** (in long loaves).

Be sure to step inside the old town church, the **Templo de Nuestra Señora de la Concepción.** Inside above the altar you'll find the Señora, and in the transept chapels a pair of mysterious, venerated objects. In the left chapel stands the **Señor de Misericordias,** an image that turned up strangely in Santa Cruz de Huatulco in the 17th century, and which people have worshiped ever since. Additionally, in the right chapel is one of the four remnant copies of the **Santa Cruz de Huatulco** (Holy Cross of Huatulco), carved from the enigmatic ancient seashore cross in 1612 and sent by the Bishop of Oaxaca, Juan de Cervantes.

Huatulco's plaza front is generally sleepy (and especially tranquil during the cool of the evening) except during fiestas and market days. The town celebrates three main fiestas. The first is on the fourth Friday of Lent (23 days after Ash Wednesday, usually in March), when folks celebrate the Señor de Misericordias. Good Friday, two days before Easter Sunday, is the Fiesta de la Santa Cruz de Huatulco. The December 8–11 fiesta honors Nuestra Señora de la Concepción. The weekly **market days** are Saturday and Sunday, when vendors' *tianguis* decorate the center of town, about three blocks south of the plaza.

If you decide to linger, a pair of small Santa María hotels can accommodate you. Both offer basic but clean rooms with private bath for about $30 d. Check out either the **Posada del Centro** (tel. 958/581-4034, $30 d) on the north side of the plaza, just west of the church, or the homey **Posada Casquito Cuatulco** (tel. 958/581-4046, 30 d), on the main cross street, to the left, as you enter town from Highway 200.

The prosperity of the local folks supports a sprinkling of good down-home restaurants. Besides the previously mentioned plaza front restaurant **Las Flores,** you can sample the excellent seafood served at **El Perro de Agua** (8 A.M.–8 P.M. daily, $5–10), on Juárez at the south edge of town. Furthermore, local folks also strongly recommend the relaxed mountain-view **Restaurant Caramba** (tel. 958/581-4094, 7 A.M.–7 P.M. daily, $5–10) for Huatulco country specialties.

By car, get to Santa María de Huatulco by driving several miles north of Highway 200, via the side road at Kilometer 238, about a mile (1.6 km) west of the Huatulco airport entrance. By *colectivo*, get there from Crucecita (bus stop a block east of the Crucecita plaza) or the Pochutla Highway 200 crossing. If necessary, transfer to a second bus at the side road to Santa María de Huatulco, at Kilometer 238, about a mile (1.6 km) west of the Huatulco airport or about 17 miles (27 km) east of the Pochutla crossing.

Pluma Hidalgo

This mini-metropolis of Oaxaca's southern Sierra owes its fame to the excellent coffee, produced by a competent cadre of local *fincas cafeteleras* sprinkled in the cool vine-hung mountain forests that surround the town. The original impulse for Oaxaca coffee growing dates back to President Benito Juárez's efforts to encourage upcountry coffee growing and shipping via the newly built port of Puerto Ángel around 1870. Although the shipping is now all by highway, the deep, rich flavor of Pluma Hidalgo coffee is prized by brew fanciers all over Mexico and the world.

SIGHTS

The town of Pluma Hidalgo (pop. 3,000, elev. 4830 feet/1470 meters) nestles on a lush mountainside 16 miles (26 km) by paved road uphill from Santa María de Huatulco. The name "Pluma" originates with the feather-like cloud (thus "plume") that often forms over the verdant ridge above the town.

The main town-center sights are the plaza, the colonial-era church and the town market, best on Sundays. Just below the market on the north side is one of the most unusually picturesque basketball courts in Mexico. From anywhere on the court (which is fenced in by netting so the ball will not get lost over the adjacent cliff) expansive vistas spread, both up to the Sierra summit and down-valley to the Pacific shore.

The must-do Pluma Hidalgo activity is visiting a coffee farm. On the plaza, on the left as you face the church, is **Abarrotes Ulilsis** (Plaza Principal 2, tel. 958/525-8091 or 958/589-8721, in Spanish), the store of coffee grower and dealer Filadelfo Ramirez Ordaz, who sells top-quality organically-grown Pluma coffee for about $5 per half-kilo bag, as well as his locally made coffee liquer. If he's available, Filadelfo offers to drive visitors out to the coffee plantation area via one of his very old rickety trucks. Best make (or ask your hotel desk clerk to make) an appointment with Filadelfo.

A safer (albeit less thrilling, given the road conditions) route would be to visit the coffee *fincas* on foot. Beginning at the plaza, walk past the Posada Isabel hotel and continue downhill along the road to the *panteón* (cemetery). From the cemetery you can enjoy views in three directions across lush mountain-framed river valleys. Past the cemetery, the downhill road leads two miles (three km) through coffee farms, marked by the shiny dark-green-leafed coffee bushes beneath the shady overhead forest canopy. At valley bottom, arrive at a river and a high 200-foot (60-meter) gushing cascade on your left.

After a cooling dip in the pond beneath the waterfall and perhaps a picnic lunch, visit the **Tres Cruces** coffee *finca* (9 A.M.–noon, Mon.–Fri.) a fraction of a mile back uphill. There you can see where the coffee pickers bring the harvested beans and watch the beans getting weighed and recorded in the logbook by the overseer, and then washed and set out to dry. Other *fincas* that you may visit in the area are La Providencia, San Francisco, and Margaritas. Be sure to wear long pants and carry insect repellent to deter mosquito and no-see-um attacks.

PRACTICALITIES

For a Pluma overnight, consider new **Hotel Posada Isabel** (Calle Guerrero, tel. 958/525-8113, joesue24-7@yahoo.com, $20 s, $25 d). The Posada Isabel, located just southwest of the church, offers six clean rooms, some with view balconies, and all with two double beds and private shiny-tile hot-water bathrooms, with TV and parking.

Also, friendly family-owned **Restaurant Luria** (Av. Hidalgo 16, tel. 958/525-8022, $10 s, $15 d) rents three rooms—two with two double beds, the other with one double bed—above the restaurant. Rooms are spartan but clean, with cross ventilation and private tiled bathrooms, with fans and hot water.

Furthermore, Restaurant Luria (6 A.M.–9 P.M. daily) offers hearty Mexican country specialties. Besides Mexican breakfasts, food offerings often include chicken smothered in *mole negro, mole coloradito* (spicy chile usually over pork or chicken), or *estofado* (meat and vegetable stew), all for about $4.

Alternatively, try plaza-front **Restaurant La Flor del Café** (Calle Guerrero 1, 6 A.M.–9 P.M. daily, $3–6), which offers traditional Mexican plates, such as *guisado de res* (beef stew) and *chilaquiles* (spicy baked tortillas and cheese).

Both Internet access ($1/hour) and public telephones are available at **Papelería Janice** (Independencia 8) on the plaza. The Pluma Hidalgo doctor is **Víctor Vásquez Ramírez** (tel. 958/525-8016). Besides medical consultations, he also furnishes essential remedies and prescription drugs from his small pharmaceutical supply.

Get to Pluma Hidalgo from the coast via Santa María de Huatulco. *Colectivos* leave frequently from the Santa María town center ($1.50 per person); taxis run about $15 for up to five people. By car, follow the (Highway 178) Pluma-marked sign left at the Santa María de Huatulco town center; pass over a scenic mountain-framed river just outside of town. Continue half an hour (16 miles/26 km) uphill to the Pluma Hidalgo right-hand turnoff. Pass the soccer field and continue a fraction of a mile to the town-center church and plaza.

You can also access Pluma Hidalgo from the Oaxaca–Pochutla Highway 175, by either bus or car. Follow Highway 175 north from Pochutla. About six miles (nine km) past Loxicha (a total of about 20 miles/33 km from Pochutla), go right at the Highway 178 intersection. Continue about five miles (eight km) to the Pluma turnoff on the left.

Santa María Xadani

This gently sloping hillside village (pop. 1,000) is tucked in a luxuriantly forested Río Zimatan valley (about 13 miles/21 km from Hwy. 200). Xadani (shah-DAH-nee) is distinguished by its five separate social orders: adults, kids, dogs, pigs, and chickens. The town pride is the **church** (at the village's upper end), dedicated to village patron the Virgen de la Concepción, whom townsfolk, joined by many outsiders, celebrate in a big fiesta climaxing on August 15.

Nearby sights include the **Cascada del Llano Grande** (waterfall) of the Río Copalita, an *ojo de agua* (spring), **Encanto**, warm on one side and cool on the other. Farther afield, one-day tours by taxi or your own car could include the spectacular **Cascada del Diablo** (Devil's Waterfall).

For a local guide (Spanish-only), ask for

friendly resident **Gregorio Cruz Cruz,** preferably at least a day or two ahead of time. Write to him at Gregorio Cruz Cruz, Domocilio Conocido, Santa María Xadani, Pochutla, Oaxaca 70999; or better, leave a message for him in Spanish at his sister-in-law's telephone, 958/587-9730.

If you're going to stay a while, Xadani offers basic services, including a pharmacy, private doctor, and a *centro de salud.*

If you can, time your arrival for Sunday morning to coincide with the *tianguis.*

La Gloria Coffee Farm

About five miles (eight km) past Xadani, you'll arrive at El Llano (YAH-noh), the site of La Gloria, a little German farm in the jungle. The parents of La Gloria's owner-operator Gustav Sherenberg arrived from the wreckage of World War II, seeking a new life in Mexico. The dream that they carved out remains with Gustav (now Gustavo), who, with his son Max, continues to improve on it.

The centerpiece, a Saxony-style whitewashed farmhouse and its antique furnishings—polished oak wall telephone, heirloom old-world sideboard, 1940s-vintage shortwave radio—endure for guests to admire and enjoy.

The build-up is a tour around the farm, which you should do not long after arrival. Along the path, you'll see acre after acre of green shiny-leafed coffee bushes beneath a canopy of great giants of the forest—*ceiba, caoba,* and Juan Diego trees. At the far point of the walk, the farm's sustaining source, a crystal-line spring, wells up from a rocky bed. On the way back, the path winds beneath both wild and cultivated trees hung with exotic fruits—brown *mamey,* green *zapote,* and the other-worldly *piña anona.* Near the farmhouse, don't miss the *mariposario* (butterfly house) and the herb garden, with familiar cilantro, *yerba buena, yerba santa,* and half a dozen others you probably have never heard of. The fun climaxes at breakfast or dinner with the family around the great hardwood dinner table, big enough for a dozen.

The Sherenberg (actually Sherenberg-Noyola)

family (Apdo. Postal 220, Bahías de Huatulco, Oaxaca 70989, local cell 044-958/589-5041, long distance tel. 958/589-5041, lagloria@hispavista.com) invites you to enjoy their farm with them, either for a day, including lunch, or overnight, including comfortable, cozy jungle-*cabaña* lodging with lunch, dinner, and breakfast included. Expect to pay about $50 per person for an overnight with food, $20 for lunch and tour only. For more information, visit www.tomzap.com/lagloria.html.

The easiest way to get to Xadani and the La Gloria coffee farm is by guide or tour from Huatulco. See *Ecotouring and Guides* in this section.

If you're going independently, Xadani is accessible via the signed side road on the north side of Highway 200, seven miles (11.4 km) west of the Río Copalita bridge and **Copalita** village (store, *palapa* restaurants, basic hotel, long-distance telephone, 41 miles/66 km east of Pochutla, 74 miles/119 km west of Salina Cruz).

If by car, set your odometer as you turn off the highway. Continue immediately through a Zimatán village (which has a store with unleaded gasoline) along a good gravel road, paralleling the gorgeous vine-hung, butterfly-decorated Río Zimatán valley. Continue through Xadani to the church (12.7 miles/20.4 km). Proceed, bearing left around the right rear side of the church, then straight ahead another 5.4 miles (8.7 km) to La Gloria Coffee Farm.

By bus, take a long-distance or local *colectivo* from Pochutla or Crucecita, which may take you at least to Copalita, or even to the Xadani Highway 200 turnoff. From there, you can catch a taxi or a truck ride (offer to pay) to Xadani, thence to La Gloria.

EAST TOWARD THE ISTHMUS: CHONTAL COUNTRY

The approximately 90-mile (145-km) Highway 200 stretching east from Huatulco to Salina Cruz is easy to travel, and consequently can pass swiftly without a pause. This, however, would be a pity, for you'd miss a whole swath of interesting and beautiful country—curving sandy beaches, wildlife-rich lagoons,

PACIFIC RESORTS

and colorful Chontal villages and markets— along the way. Instead, take a leisurely drive and plan to make some stops along the way.

Santiago Astata

Astata (pop. 7,000) is near the midpoint (about 47 miles/76 km) between Huatulco and Salina Cruz. This village is the closest thing to a metropolis along this part of the coast. The townsfolk proudly display their Chontal heritage with the big announcement *Nañoje faá loj pijeda* (Welcome to Santiago Astata) over the town entrance road.

By far the best time to arrive is during the Saturday *tianguis,* when the townspeople are so busy buying and selling that they are less likely to notice a few camera-toting visitors.

Folks will be even less self-conscious (and so distracted that they might not mind having their pictures taken) during the big local **Fiesta del Señor de Piedad** on the second Friday of Lent (second Friday after Ash Wednesday), usually in late February or March.

Even if you don't arrive during any fiesta, you should still take a look inside the church, where you'll find both of the town patrons, Santiago (on horseback, with sword in hand) and the Señor de Piedad.

Another favorite town diversion is splashing in the **community spring,** known locally as the *aguaje* (ah-GOOAH-hay). Besides all the fun, folks venerate their spring with a small chapel, **La Capilla de la Rosa Mística.** Find it at the roadside a block or two west of the town entrance arch. Afterward, enjoy a snack at one of the several *comedores* by the town highway crossing.

For those in need of basic **services,** Astata has a a pharmacy, with Doctor and Doctora Roberto and Rolanda Herrera in charge, and a public telephone (tel. 995/522-4070), all along the main ingress road, near the church and plaza. You can call the public phone— one of the only phones in town—to contact the doctors.

San Pedro Huamelula

If you missed Astata's Saturday market, you can get in on Huamelula's market on Thursday by following the signed inland side road from Highway 200, just a fraction of a mile east of Astata. After about three miles (five km), as you enter Huamelula town, you pass a number of schools, including Alma Chontal (Chontal Soul) primary school, a secondary school, and Colegio de Bachilleres del Estado de Oaxaca (Oaxaca State College).

Go through town (stores, a few *comedores,* pharmacy, doctor) to the old but restored bright birthday-cake yellow-and-blue church, **Templo de San Pedro.** Inside, the same bright yellow and blue continues, right up to the altar, presided over by a very antique Saint Peter. In the right transept chapel, pay your respects to an even older Santa Lucia in the glass case.

Here, the usually serene atmosphere shifts to raucous and jubilant during the June 25–26 **Fiesta de San Pedro.** Processions, fireworks, food, carnival rides, and games climax in traditional dances, including the popular Danza de los Los Turcos (Dance of the Turks).

East to Salina Cruz

The sights along the eastern stretch past Astata are mostly natural, including mangrove-tufted lagoons, palmy beaches, and breezy viewpoints. What follows is a summary of some ripe possibilities to anticipate along the way. Measure mileage east from Astata or west from the Highway 200 and Trans-Isthmus Highway intersection at the north edge of downtown Salina Cruz.

Moving east from Astata, arrive at the **Laguna Colorada** dirt side road (from Astata east 7 miles/11 km, from Salina Cruz west 41 miles/66 km). The dirt road leads a few miles along the west edge of a glassy, wildlife-rich mangrove lagoon to a beach.

Another several miles along (east 19 miles/31 km, west 29 miles/47 km), another wildlife-rich mangrove lagoon, **Laguna Garrapatera,** is visible from the highway at Kilometer 348. A wave-washed white sandspit borders the lagoon on the ocean side. The lagoon looks fine for kayaking or rubber rafting, and the beach could be great for camping if you can get to it.

At Kilometer 349, Highway 200 rises to a

viewpoint overlooking the idyllic green **Río Bamba Valley** (east 20 miles/32 km, west 28 miles/45 km). Several miles farther (east 31 miles/50 km, west 17 miles/27 km) arrive at the dirt road turnoff to surfing and seafood-*palapa*-restaurant **Playa Cangrejo** (Crab Beach).

Next, pass **Morro Mazatán** town (east 36 miles/57 km, west 13 miles/21 km). Finally, arrive at the signed dirt side road to **Playa Brasil**, which has a great oceanfront breeze-blown sand hill on its west end (east 41 miles/65 km, west 8 miles/13 km).

Puerto Escondido and Vicinity

Decorated by intimate coves and sandy beaches, and washed by jade-tinted surf, Puerto Escondido enjoys its well-deserved popularity. Despite construction of a jet airport in the 1980s, Puerto Escondido remains a place where most everything is within walking distance, no high-rise blocks anyone's sunset view, and moderately priced accommodations and good food remain the rule.

Puerto Escondido (Hidden Port) got its name from the rocky Punta Escondida that shelters its intimate half-moon cove, which perhaps would have remained hidden if local farmers had not discovered that coffee thrives beneath the cool forest canopy of the lush seaward slopes of the Sierra Madre del Sur. They began bringing their precious beans for shipment when the port of Escondido was established in 1928.

When the coast highway was pushed through during the 1970s, Puerto Escondido's then-dwindling coffee trade was replaced by a growing trickle of vacationers, attracted by the splendid isolation, low prices, and high waves. With some of the best surfing breaks in North America, a permanent surfing colony soon was established. This led to more nonsurfing visitors, who, by the 1990s, were arriving in droves to enjoy the comfort and food of a string of small hotels and restaurants lining Puerto Escondido's still-beautiful but no longer hidden cove.

Getting Oriented

Puerto Escondido (pop. 55,000) seems like two towns separated by Highway 200, which runs along the bluff above the beach. The upper town is where most of the local folks live and go about their business, while in the

town below the highway most of the restaurants, hotels, and shops spread along a single, touristy, beachfront street mall, **Avenida Pérez Gasga**, (known locally as the *adoquín,* ah-doh-KEEN), where motor traffic is allowed only before noon. In the afternoon chains go up, blocking cars at either end.

Beyond the west-end chain, Pérez Gasga leaves the beach, winding uphill to the highway, where it enters the upper town at the *crucero,* Puerto Escondido's only signaled intersection. From there, Pérez Gasga continues into the upper town as Avenida Oaxaca, National Highway 131.

Getting Around

In town, walk or take a taxi, which should run no more than $3 to anywhere. For longer excursions, such as to Lagunas Manialtepec and Río Grande (near National Park Lagunas de Chacahua, westbound), and as far as Pochutla (near Puerto Ángel, eastbound), ride one of the very frequent *urbano* buses that stop at the *crucero,* or rent a car from **Budget** (tel./fax 954/582-0312 or 954/582-0315, budget33@ hotmail.com) or Economica Rent-a-Car (tel. 954/582-2557).

Safety Concerns

Occasional knifepoint robberies and muggings have marred the once-peaceful Puerto Escondido nighttime beach scene. Walk alone and you invite trouble, especially along Playa Bachoco and the unlit stretch of Playa Principal between the east end of Pérez Gasga and the Hotel Santa Fe. If you have dinner alone at the Hotel Santa Fe, avoid the beach by returning

© AVALON TRAVEL

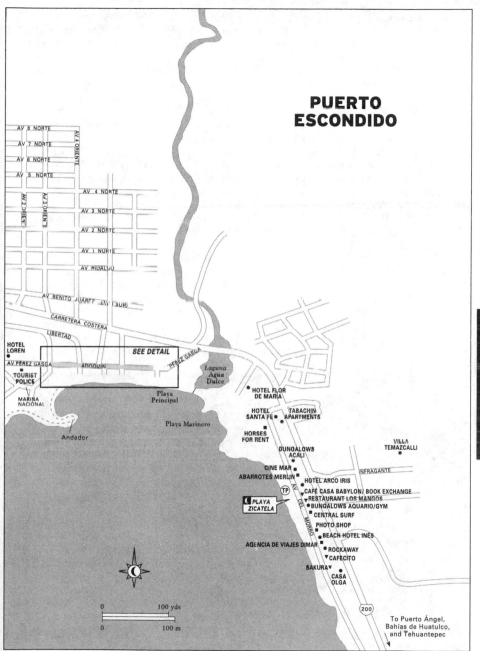

PUERTO ESCONDIDO

AV 8 NORTE
AV 7 NORTE
AV 6 NORTE
AV 5 NORTE

AV 4 ORIENTE

AV 4 NORTE
AV 3 NORTE
AV 2 NORTE
AV 1 NORTE
AV HIDALGO

AV 2 ORIENT
AV 3 ORIENT

AV BENITO JUÁREZ (AV 1 SUR)

CARRETERA COSTERA

LIBERTAD

HOTEL LOREN

SEE DETAIL

PÉREZ GASGA

AV PÉREZ GASGA   ADOQUIN

TOURIST POLICE

MARINA NACIONAL

Laguna Agua Dulce

Playa Principal

HOTEL FLOR DE MARÍA

Playa Marinero

HOTEL SANTA FE   TABACHÍN APARTMENTS

Andador

HORSES FOR RENT

BUNGALOWS ACALI

VILLA TEMAZCALLI

CINE MAR

ABARROTES MERLIN

INFRAGANTE

HOTEL ARCO IRIS

TP   CAFÉ CASA BABYLON/ BOOK EXCHANGE
RESTAURANT LOS MANGOS

PLAYA ZICATELA   BUNGALOWS AQUARIO/GYM

CENTRAL SURF

AV DEL MORRO

PHOTO SHOP

BEACH HOTEL INÉS

AGENCIA DE VIAJES DIMAR

ROCKAWAY

CAFECITO

SAKURA

CASA OLGA

200

0   100 yds
0   100 m

To Puerto Ángel,
Bahías de Huatulco,
and Tehuantepec

PACIFIC RESORTS

by taxi or walking along the highway to Pérez Gasga back to your hotel.

Fortunately, such problems seem to be confined to the beach. Visitors are quite safe on the Puerto Escondido streets, often more so than on their own city streets back home.

BEACHES AND ACTIVITIES

Puerto Escondido's bayfront begins at the sheltered rocky cove beneath the wave-washed lighthouse point, Punta Escondida. The shoreline continues easterly along Playa Principal, the main beach, curving southward at Playa Marineros, and finally straightening into long open-ocean Playa Zicatela. The sand and surf change drastically, from narrow sand and calm ripples at Playa Principal to a wide beach pounded by gigantic rollers at Zicatela.

Playa Principal

The best place to appreciate Puerto Escondido is not from the cluttered *adoquín*, but from one of the shady restaurants (such as Los Crotos or Junto del Mar), that front Playa Principal. It's here that Mexican families love to frolic on Sunday and holidays and sun-starved winter

vacationers doze in their chairs and hammocks beneath the palms. The sheltered west side is very popular with local people who arrive afternoons with nets and haul in small troves of silvery fish. The water is great for wading and swimming, clear enough for casual snorkeling, but generally too calm for anything else in the cove. However, a few hundred yards east around the bay the waves are generally fine for bodysurfing and boogie boarding, with a minimum of undertow. Although it's not a particularly windy location, sailboarders do occasionally bring their own equipment and practice their art here. Fishing is fine off the rocks or by small boat, easily launched from the beach. Shells, generally scarce on Playa Principal, are more common on less-crowded Playa Zicatela.

Playa Marinero

As the beach curves toward the south, it increasingly faces the open ocean. Playa Marinero begins about 100 yards from the "Marineros," the east-side rocky outcroppings in front of the landmark Hotel Santa Fe. The rocks' jutting forms are supposed to resemble visages of grizzled old sailors. Here the waves can be rough.

Take a seat for breakfast and soak in the morning Playa Principal ambience.

Swimmers beware: Appearances can be deceiving. Intermediate surfers practice here, as do daring boogie boarders and bodysurfers.

Turn around and gaze inland at the giant Mexican flag, waving in the breeze on the hill above the east-side beach. At dawn every rainless day soldiers of the 54th infantry battalion raise the colossal banner, which measures about 82 by 59 feet (18 by 25 meters) and is so heavy that it takes a dozen of them to raise it.

Playa Zicatela

Past the Marinero rocks you enter Mexico's hallowed ground of surfing, Playa Zicatela. The wide beach, of fine golden-white sand, stretches south for miles to a distant cliff and point. The powerful Pacific swells arrive unimpeded, crashing to the sand with awesome, thunderous power. Both surfers and nonsurfers congregate year-round, waiting for the renowned Escondido "pipeline," where grand waves curl into whirling liquid tunnels, which expert surfers skim through like trains in a subway. At such times, the spectators on the beach outnumber the surfers by as much as 10 or 20 to one. Don't try surfing or swimming at Zicatela unless you're an expert.

West-Side Beaches: Manzanillo, Carrizalillo, and Bachoco

About a mile west of town, the picture-postcard little blue bays of Bahía Puerto Angelito and Bahía Carrizalillo nestle beneath the seacliff. Their sheltered gold-and-coral sands are perfect for tranquil picnicking, sunbathing, and swimming. Here, snorkeling and scuba diving are tops, among shoals of bright fish grazing and darting among the close-in coral shelves and submerged rocky outcroppings. Get there by launch from Playa Principal or by taxi. On foot (take a sun hat and water) follow the street that heads west from Pérez Gasga, uphill across from the Hotel Nayar. Continue to the second street on the left, Avenida 1 Poniente, turn left and go a long block to Avenida 5 Sur. Turn right and continue straight ahead for about a half mile to Bahía Puerto Angelito, which shelters **Playa Manzanillo** at its inner edge. Follow

the stairstep down the cliff. Even more pristine **Bahía Carrizalillo,** a petite strip of golden sand with a few *palapa* restaurants, is another mile farther west.

Playa Bachoco, yet another mile farther west, down the bluff from the Hotel Posada Real, is a long, scenic strip of breeze-swept sand, with thunderous waves and correspondingly menacing undertow. Swimming is much safer in the inviting pool of the adjacent Hotel Posada Real beach club.

If you're strong, experienced, and can get past the breaking waves, snorkeling is said to be good around the little surf-dashed rocky islet 100 yards offshore.

Although Playa Bachoco's un-sheltered nooks appear inviting for beach camping, local people don't recommend it because of occasional *rateros* (thugs and drunks) who roam Puerto Escondido beaches at night.

Beach Walking

The *andador* (concrete walkway), which circles the lighthouse point, provides a pleasant, breezy afternoon (or sunset) diversion. From the west chain, follow the street, Marina Nacional, that heads toward the beach. Immediately on your left, stairs head down onto the beach cove, where, on the rocks that shelter the cove, at the Capitania del Puerto building, the *andador* heads left along the rocks. It continues, above the spectacularly splashing surf, for about half a mile. Return by the same route, or loop back through side streets to Pérez Gasga.

For a longer walk, you can stroll as far out of town along Playa Zicatela as you want, in outings ranging from an hour to a whole day. Avoid the heat of midday, and bring along a sun hat, shirt, drinks, and snacks (and perhaps sunglasses) if you plan on walking more than a mile past the last restaurant down the beach. Your rewards will be the acrobatics of surfers challenging the waves, swarms of shorebirds, and occasional finds of driftwood and shells. After about three miles you will reach a cliff and a sea arch, which you can scamper through at low tide to the beach on the other side, **Playa Barra de Colotepec.**

PACIFIC RESORTS

Playa Barra de Colotepec's surf is as thunderous as Zicatela's and the beach even more pristine, being a nesting site for sea turtles. The beach continues for another mile to the jungle-fringed lagoon of the Río Colotepec where, during the dry winter season, a host of birds and wildlife, both common and rare, paddle and preen in the clear, fresh water.

You could break this eight-mile round-trip into a pair of more leisurely options: Hike A could cover Zicatela only. On Hike B you could explore Playa Barra de Colotepec and the Laguna de Colotepec by driving, taxiing, or busing straight to La Barra, the beach village just west of the Río Colotepec. Access is via the signed side road just before (west of) the Río Colotepec bridge.

Boat Tours

Travel agencies; the local boat cooperative, **Sociedad Cooperativa Turística Nueva Punta Escondida;** and some individual boatmen offer trips for parties of several passengers right from the main town beach. The minimum one-hour trip takes you for a look at a number of sandy little coves west of town, including Carrizalillo (Little Reeds), Puerto Angelito and its beach, Playa Manzanillo (Little Apple), Coral, and Puesta del Sol (Sunset). Take drinks, hats, sunscreen, and sunglasses, and don't go unless your boat has a sunroof. Trips can be extended (about $15 per additional hour) to your heart's content of whale-, dolphin-, and turtle-watching, beach picnicking, snoozing, and snorkeling. For more details, visit www.tomzap.com/pe-coop.html.

Alternatively **Omar's Sportfishing** (local cell 044-954/559-4406, long distance 045-954/559-4406, omarsportfishing-1@hotmail.com, or dolfamily@hotmail.com) offers excursions, including dolphin-, whale-, and turtle-watching. You can find Omar on the beach at Puerto Angelito. For more information, visit www.tomzap.com/omar.html.

ACCOMMODATIONS

The successful hotels in Puerto Escondido are appropriate to the town itself: small, moderately priced, and near the water. They dot the beachfront from Playa Zicatela around the bay and continue up Av. Pérez Gasga to the highway. Most are either on the beach or within a stone's throw of it, which makes sense, because it seems a shame to come all the way to Puerto Escondido and not stay where you can soak up all the scenery.

Rates for the hotels, all recommended below, are listed in ascending order of customary low season room rates. These prices, unless noted, are in effect most of the year, except for high season (Christmas–New Year, Easter, some long weekend holidays, and sometimes July and August).

Perez Gasga-*Adoquín*
UNDER $50

Moving downhill, from the highway, first find the immaculate, best-buy **❰ Hotel San Juan** (Felipe Merklin 503, tel. 954/582-0518, fax 954/582-0612, sanjuanhotel@prodigy.net.mx, www.sanjuanhotel.com.mx, $25 s or d, $32 t). For those who like saving money and don't mind (or would enjoy) a ten-minute downhill walk to the beach, this is the place. Rooms, in four levels, enclose an intimate inner pool patio. They are squeaky clean and invitingly furnished with wall paintings, reading lamps, and color-coordinated drapes and bedspreads. Amenities include private hot-water shower-baths, fans, in-house wireless Internet access, morning coffee, restaurant, and parking. For a splurge, add $13 for a/c with a luxuriously private ocean-view balcony.

Right on the beach amid the tourist-mall hullabaloo is the enduring **Hotel Las Palmas** (Av. Pérez Gasga s/n, tel. 954/582-0230, fax 954/582-0303, $15 s, $30 d, 45 t). Its main plus is the palmy, vine-strewn patio where you can sit for breakfast every morning, enjoy the breeze, and watch the boats, the birds, and families frolicking in the billows. The big drawback, besides sleepy management and no pool, is lack of privacy. Exterior walkways pass the room windows, which anyone can see through unless you close the curtains, which unfortunately makes the (fan-only) rooms dark and hot. This doesn't seem to bother the legions of return customers, however, since they spend little time in their rooms anyway. There are 40 smallish rooms and a restaurant; credit cards not accepted.

The popular **Hotel Loren** (Av. Pérez Gasga 507, tel. 954/582-0057, fax 954/582-0591, $30 s or d, $41 t), downhill just two blocks from the beach, offers approximately 30 rooms spread through two three-story buildings. Guests in the front-building rooms enjoy private, ocean-view balconies. (However, all rooms, especially the bathrooms, could use a good scrubbing). The good news is the hotel's inviting blue pool patio and the short five-minute walk to the beach. Reserve a *cuarto con vista* in the front-building view room. Reservations are often necessary, especially in the winter. The rooms are basic but comfortable. Add $10 for a/c; with parking and credit cards accepted.

The **Hotel Rincón del Pacífico** (Av. Pérez Gasga 900, tel. 954/582-0056 or 954/582-0193, fax 954/582-1812, reservaciones@rincondelpacifico.com.mx, $32 s, $40 d, $48 t with fan only, $56, $70, and $84 with a/c, $100 larger suites), next door to the Hotel Las Palmas, offers about the same. The two tiers of clean, comfortable rooms enfold a shady patio that looks out onto the lively beachfront. As at the Hotel Las Palmas, you must draw drapes for privacy in the hotel's glass-front rooms. This is nevertheless a very popular hotel. Reserve early. Ask for a discount during low-occupancy season (May–June and Sept.–Oct.). Amenities include TV, a/c, and restaurant; credit cards accepted (but not American Express), but no parking nor pool.

Although it's not right on the beach like its neighbor hotels Las Palmas and Rincón del Pacifico across the *adoquín* walkway, the rooms of the ◖ **Hotel Casa Blanca** (Av. Pérez Gasga 905, tel. 954/582-0168, fax 954/582-3120, imariabc@hotmail.com, www.ptohcasablanca.com, $28 s and $40 d) are larger, cooler, and much more private. Some rooms even have private balconies, fine for people-watching on the street below. Guests report that noise is not a problem since cars and trucks are banned on Gasga noon–7 A.M. Other amenities include

a shelf of used paperback books, and, beyond the graceful arches that border the lobby, a petite, inviting pool and patio. The 21 clean, comfortable rooms have fans, private hot-water shower-baths, and credit cards accepted, but no parking.

Also perched on the same view hillside as the Hotel Loren, three blocks above the beach, the 1960s-genre **Hotel Nayar** (Pérez Gasga 407, tel. 954/582-0113, fax 954/582-0319, hotel_nayar@hotmail.com, www.oaxaca-mio.com/hotelnayar.htm, $41 s, $48 d, $51 t) spreads from its inviting pool patio past the reception to a viewpoint restaurant. Its spacious, simply but comfortably furnished air-conditioned rooms include reading lamps, hot-water shower-baths, fans and a/c, and in-house wireless Internet connection.

$50-100

Tucked in its own corner, away from the tourist mall bustle, the compact ◖ **Le P'tit Hotel** (at the west-end intersection of Soledad and the *adoquín*, tel. 954/582-3178, michelkobryn@tutopia.com, www.oaxaca-mio.com/leptit.htm,

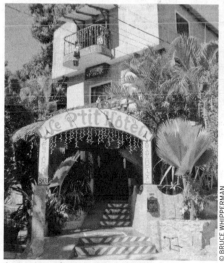

A number of modest but inviting hotels sprinkle the Puerto Escondido *adoquín* beachfront walkway.

© BRUCE WHIPPERMAN

PACIFIC RESORTS

$50 s or d, $65 with a/c, $10 per extra person) offers an attractive lodging option. Personable French-born owner-builder Michel Kobryn offers 16 rooms and thatched south-seas-style bungalows, all lovingly adorned with colorful tile, original wall art, decorator reading lamps, and sparkling bathrooms. Amenities include cable TV, restaurant, wireless Internet, inviting small pool patio, and credit cards accepted.

Back uphill, two blocks below the highway on a short side street off Pérez Gasga, is the **Hotel Paraíso Escondido** (Calle Union 1, tel./ fax 954/582-0444, $65 s or d). A tranquil colonial-chic refuge, the hotel abounds in unique artistic touches—Mixtec stone glyphs, tiny corner chapels, stained glass, and old-world antiques—blended into the lobby, corridors, and patios. The two levels of rooms nestle around a lovely view pool and restaurant patio. The rooms themselves are large, with view balconies and designer tile bathrooms, wrought-iron fixtures, and handcrafted wooden furniture. Very popular with North American and German winter vacationers; get reservations in early. The 24 rooms include a/c, pool, kiddie pool, and parking, but credit cards not accepted.

Playa Zicatela

Beach lovers and surfing enthusiasts enjoy staying on Playa Zicatela, the creamy strand that stretches east and south of the busy *adoquín*. Here, folks relax, in street-side cafes and restaurants and strolling and sunning on the beach as they watch the surfers conquer (or try to conquer) Zicatela's awesome, oft-thunderous open-ocean waves.

UNDER $50

Three long blocks south along Playa Zicatela stands the very economical and tidy "surfer village" **Rockaway** (Av. del Morro, tel. 954/582-0668, rockhomemx@yahoo.com, www.mexonline.com/rockaway.htm or www .hotelrockaway.com, *cabañas* $12 s, $20 d, $34 q, rooms $30 s, $47 d, 54 t), a fenced-in cluster of about 10 clean, concrete-floored bamboo and thatch *cabañas*. Plainly decorated but clean, spacious, and fan-equipped, they sleep up to four and come with private showers and toilets, mosquito nets, and shady, hammock-hung front porches. An inviting, leafy pool patio occupies the center, while a squad of new air-conditioned rooms stands to one side. Weekly or monthly discounts are negotiable; with parking.

Back at Playa Zicatela's north-end beginning, find ❰ **Bungalows Acali** (Av. del Morro, tel. 954/582-0754, casadanycarmen@escondido. com.mx, $30 s, $32 d, $38 t, $50 with a/c). Here, a small colony of rustic *cabañas* clusters around a blue pool in a banana, palm, and mango minijungle. The *cabañas* themselves, like a vision out of a south-seas tale, are built with walls made of sticks (non-see-through) and sturdy plank floors, raised above ground level. Rentals are clean, fan-equipped, with mosquito nets and good bathrooms. Rooms have fan, hot-water shower, small refrigerator, and parking; credit cards accepted.

Additionally, Acali offers three rustic hammock-hung, sunset-view kitchenette bungalows perched on its leafy bamboo- and mango-decorated hillside for about $36 for one to four, fan only; $70 with a/c.

About two long blocks south down the beach comes **Beach Hotel Inés** (Av. del Morro, tel. 954/582-0416, fax 954/582-0792, info@hotelines.com, $25–120 d), the life project of German expatriate Peter Voss and his daughter, Inés. Their 45 units occupy the palmy periphery of a lush, pool-café-garden layout, which climaxes with an attractive, stuccoed, two-story complex of rooms at the back side. At the shady poolside tables, longtime repeat guests linger for coffee and conversation after late-morning breakfasts, stroll the beach in the afternoon, and return for a balmy sunset happy hour. Other days they sunbathe au naturel or relax in the petite but luxurious health club, which provides massage and hot tub. Most of the rentals are hotel-style rooms, in deluxe and superdeluxe grades, with clean, light interiors, comfortable furnishings, and well-maintained bathrooms. They rent four levels of accommodation, from smallish, but comfortable, hotel-style rooms to larger cabañas, deluxe apartments, and large super-deluxe suites.

© BRUCE WHIPPERMAN

Most Playa Zicatela hotels, such as the Beach Hotel Inès, welcome guests with a palmy interior pool-patio.

Tucked only a block inland from the beach, at the far south end of the Zicatela development, is **Casa Olga** (Av. del Morro, olga_hmex@yahoo.com.mx, no phone, $30 s, $35 d, $60 q) that the friendly Mexican owner likes to call "your home away from home." And yes, it could easily be, with five attractively decorated, comfortable rooms on hammock-hung porches overlooking a lovely green lawn, garden and blue swimming pool. The upper-story rooms, with two and three beds, are the most invitingly private, with airy ocean view and awning-draped shade. All have private hot-water shower-baths, fans, and use of an outdoor kitchen adjacent to the pool-patio.

$50-100

It's easy to miss the **Hotel Flor de María** (at Primera Entrada Playa Marinero, Colonia Marinero, tel. 954/582-0536, fax 954/582-2617, pajope@hotmail.com, www.mexonline.com/flordemaria.htm, $37–60 d), tucked on a quiet side street above east-side

Playa Marinero. That would be a pity, for the Flor de María is an attractive, reasonably priced hotel, half a block from the beach. Rooms rise in two stories around a tranquil, leafy interior patio. At rooftop, a breezy sundeck-bar, with a small but inviting pool and a hammock-hung *palapa,* overlooks a beach-and-bay vista. The approximately dozen immaculate deluxe rooms are simply but thoughtfully decorated, each with two double beds with flowery violet covers and modern-standard hot-water shower-baths. Additionally, the hotel offers a pair of similarly inviting but more spacious second-floor ocean-view suites and a very good restaurant.

Head about three blocks south along Av. del Morro, which runs along Playa Zicatela, to the three-story **Hotel Arco Iris** (Av. del Morro s/n, Colonia Marinero, tel./fax 954/582-1494, 954/582-0432, arcoiris@hotel-arcoiris.com.mx, www.hotel-arcoiris.com.mx, $50 s, $60 d). A flowery, shady green garden surrounds the hotel, leading to a gorgeous rear pool and patio. For those who love sunsets, sand, and waves (and don't mind their sometimes insistent pounding), one of the spacious, simply furnished top-floor view rooms might be just the ticket. The Arco Iris's proximity to the famous Puerto Escondido "pipeline" draws both surfers and surf-watchers to the third-floor restaurant La Galera, which seems equally ideal for wave-watching at breakfast and sky-watching at sunset.

OVER $100

Puerto Escondido's class-act hostelry is the (Hotel Santa Fe (Av. del Morro, Playa Marinero, tel. 954/582-0170 or 954/582-0266, fax 954/582-0260, from U.S. toll-free tel. 888/649-6407, Mex. toll free tel. 800/712-7037, info@hotelsantafe.com.mx, www.hotelsantafe .com.mx, $126–223 d). Built in pleasing neocolonial style, with gracefully curving staircases, palm-shaded pool patios, and flower-decorated walkways, the Santa Fe achieves an ambience both intimate and luxuriously private. Its refined but relaxed restaurant, wonderful for morning oceanview breakfasts, serves a delicious menu, featuring a number of traditional Oaxacan specialties.

The accommodations—spacious, high-ceilinged and comfortable—are thoughtfully appointed with hand-painted tile, rustic wood furniture, and regional handicrafts. Moreover, the recently added room wing has enhanced the hotel's ambience, with a new airy and tranquil elevated view pool patio that connects gracefully with the original hotel section. The approximately 50 accommodations come in standard, junior, and master suite grades; an additional 10 kitchenette bungalows sleeping four; kids under 12 free. All accommodations come with a/c, phones, parking, and credit cards accepted, but no TV.

Apartments and Long-Term Rentals

If you're planning on a stay of two weeks or more, you may be able to save money and yet have all the comforts of home in an apartment rental. First look over the classifieds in the English-Spanish newspaper El Sol de la Costa (tel./fax 954/582-2230, elsol@escondido.com.mx, www .elsoldelacosta.com), edited by Warren Sharpe.

Also check with local realtors; the best for rentals is Vicki Cole of Zicatela Properties (tel. 954/582-2495, info@zicatelaproperties. com, www.zicatelaproperties.com). Vicki also provides help—real-estate matters, immigration papers, residency—for newcomers.

Alternatively, for rentals, you might also contact Nolan Van Way, of PEP Realty (tel. 954/582-0085, nvpep@yahoo.com, www .pep-realty.com).

Trailer Park, Camping, and Hostel

Occasional muggings and robberies on the beach have eliminated virtually all camping on Puerto Escondido beaches (with the possible exception of Easter week, when such large crowds flock into town that they spill onto the beaches).

Nevertheless, beachfront camping space is available in small, palm-shaded trailer park Palmas de Corté (once closed, now reopened, at the east side of Puerto Escondido's Playa Principal, half a block downhill from the chain, no telephone, cortes@ptoescondido. com.mx, $15–25 for Rvs, $5 per person for tents). Facilities include security fence, night watchman, brand-new showers and toilets, all hookups, and room for about a dozen RVs and maybe some tents.

A good alternative for tenters and hostelers is Shalom Hostel (in Rinconada subdivision, west side of town, on the east end of Calle Benito Juárez, tel. 954/582-3234, rigeloo@ yahoo.com, $5 per person tents, $10 per person cabañas, $6 per person dorm). Besides tenting in their shady, green back garden, with heavenly pool-patio, they offer rustic cabañas with shared baths and dorm beds for $6, with snack restaurant and parking out front.

For central location, the best hostel-type choice seems to be Hotel and Youth Hostel Mayflower (tel. 954/582-0367, fax 954/582-0422, minnemay7@hotmail.com, www.tomzap.com/mayflower.html, rooms $35 d, dorm $9 per person). Find it half a block uphill on Andador Libertad, the stairstepped walkway a block east of the adoquín's west end. Here you can choose from 14 plain but clean hotel rooms with bath or hostel dorm beds.

Extras include communal kitchen, Internet access, and lots of local information.

Alternatively, nearby, you might consider the smaller, bare-bones but clean **Hostal Puerto Escondido** (tel. 954/582-3455, hostalpuertoescondido@hotmail.com, www.mexonline.com/pehostal.htm, $5 per person), also on Andador Libertad within a block of the *adoquín*. Facilities (communal kitchen and Internet access) are spare, but the price is right.

FOOD
Breakfast and Snacks
Mornings you can enjoy breakfast with the baked offerings of Carmen's pastry and coffee shop restaurant **Cafecito** (on Zicatela beach, south end, half a block south of Rockaway next to Bungalows Acuario, 6 A.M.–10 P.M. Wed.–Mon.). Here, you can savor a cappuccino and one of her goodies as you watch the surfers conquering the waves.

Carmen has aquired some competition at **Baguettería Vivaldi** (middle of beachfront Av. Pérez Gasga, across the street from the Hotel Casa Blanca, tel. 954/582-0800, 7:30 A.M.–11 P.M. daily), the labor of love of friendly Jenny Sinnhuber, who, besides lots of homemade bread, serves a wide selection of delicious breakfasts and sandwiches for lunch.

You can also get your day started right with breakfast, while watching the beachfront scene, at leafy **Restaurant Los Crotos** (on the *adoquín*, west end). See *Upper Town and Adoquín* for details.

Upper Town and *Adoquín*
Many of Puerto Escondido's good restaurants line the *adoquín*. One major exception is immaculate, strictly home-cooking-style (**Margaritas** (Ave. 8 Norte, few doors east of Calle 2 Poniente, tel. 954/582-0212, 8 A.M.–6 P.M. daily), where all you need is to love good Mexican food. Find it in the upper town, near the market. Although the long country menu, including eggs in several styles ($3), tacos, tamales, and quesadillas ($2–3), fish and shrimp any style ($6–10), and broiled

steaks ($8–12) reveals nothing unusual, everything arrives at your table delicious. The day's main event is the *comida corrida* set lunch. You get all of this for $3.50: entrée (for example, savory beef or pork *guisado* stew, or *mole* chicken, or chiles rellenos), dessert, and drink, chosen from a half dozen delicious fruit *aguas* (strawberry, lemonade, melon, orange, and more).

Back down on the *adoquín*, **Restaurant La Galería** (just inside the west end chain, on the inland side of Pérez Gasga, tel. 954/582-2039, 8 A.M.–midnight daily, $5–12) usually has customers even when most other eateries are empty. The reason is the excellent Italian fare—crusty, hot pizzas, rich pastas and lasagna, bountiful salads, and satisfying soups—which the European-expatriate owner puts out for her batallion of loyal customers.

For refined beachfront ambience, try the excellent, airy **Restaurant Junto del Mar** (right on the beach, just inside the *adoquín* west end chain, tel./fax 954/582-0025, 8 A.M.–11 P.M. daily, credit cards accepted). The menu offers good breakfasts—rich bottomless coffee, fresh fruit, omelets, and French toast ($2–5)—plus many delectable lunch and dinner options. Specialties include shrimp-stuffed fillets ($9), lobster and shrimp brochettes ($11–14), and whole garlic-stuffed fish ($9). Mornings are brightened by the always-changing beach scene; evenings, the setting turns romantic, with soft candlelight and strumming guitars.

Breakfast patrons at beachfront **Restaurant Los Crotos** (a block farther east, tel. 954/582-0025, open daily 8 A.M.–11 P.M., $4–12) sit at shady view tables, enjoying the fascinating morning beachside scene. Later, at lunch and dinner, back beneath the luxuriously breezy, palm-fringed *palapa*, the house specialties—jumbo shrimp, broiled lobster, and superfresh pompano, attractively presented, competently served, and delicious—seem like an added bonus.

Two blocks farther east, just outside the east-end chain, try the tasty creations ($7–14) of owner-chef Bendito, at his completely unpretentious (**Restaurant Bendito** (tel. 954/588-2186, 8 A.M.–midnight daily). Make up a party and enjoy sampling his delicious Napoli-style specialties, such as spaghetti puttanesca ($5), spinach raviolis ($5), mushroom fettuccine ($7), and pizza *zavarieta* ($8).

Playa Zicatela

If you have dinner at the restaurant of the 〔 **Hotel Santa Fe** (Av. del Morro, Zicatela side of the bay, tel. 954/582-0170, 7:30 A.M.–11 P.M. daily), you may never go anywhere else. Savory food, impeccably served beneath a luxurious *palapa* and accompanied by softly strumming guitars, brings travelers from all over the world. Although everything on the menu is delicious, the restaurant is proudest of its Mexican favorites, such as rich tortilla soup ($4), bountiful plates of chiles rellenos ($9), and succulent snapper, Veracruz style ($11).

Restaurant Mangos (farther south, on Zicatela beach, next to Hotel Acuario, tel. 954/582-3805, 8 A.M.–midnight daily) packs in a steady stream of youthful customers, with a long menu of innovative breakfasts (crepes, three-egg omelets, $4), salads (plenty of alfalfa sprouts, $3–5), sandwiches (*cuerno*, large horn croissant, $5), and Mexican specialties (fish-stuffed chiles rellenos, $6).

Farther south a few block, past Hotel Rockaway, **Restaurant Cafecito** (tel. 954/582-0516, 6:30 A.M.–10 P.M. daily) is headquarters for a loyal platoon of local surfers and Canadian and American residents who crowd in for bountiful breakfasts ($3–5), hamburgers ($3–4), and fresh seafood plates ($6–8). (Unfortunately, Cafecito's popularity is both a boon and burden, when the customer crowd is sometimes simply too large and noisy for both comfort and good service.)

Customers at **Sakura** sushi bar and Japanese restaurant (on Zicatela, south end, past Cafecito, cell tel. 044-954/559-0239, 8 A.M.–11 P.M. daily) enjoy a menu so correct that it seems straight out of the owner's Yokohama hometown. He offers a trove of delectable options, such as *miso* soup ($2), *wakame* (seafood salad, $4), chicken *teriyaki* ($6), vegetable *tempura* ($5), and *teppanyaki* ($5–10). *Daijobu des neh!* (Wonderful!)

ENTERTAINMENT AND EVENTS

Nightlife

The amusements along the *adoquín* mall are Puerto Escondido's prime after-dinner entertainment source. By around 9 P.M., some people get weary of walking and, since there are few benches, begin sitting on the curb and sipping bottles of beer near the west-end chain.

The main attraction of curb-sitting is watching other people sitting on the curb, while listening to the music blasting nightly from the open-air bars of **Blue Station** and **Wipe Out,** nearby. The music is so loud that little can be gained except hearing impairment by actually taking a seat in the bars themselves.

For those who prefer to gyrate to the beat of *adoquín* discos, besides Wipe Out and Blue Station, go to the **Los Tres Diablos** in the middle of the *adoquín* across from the Hotel Las Palmas.

For softer musical offerings, check out the guitarists who play evenings at the Hotel Santa Fe Restaurant Bar, and/or the **El Son y La Rumba** nightclub, with Mayka Y Amigos, entertaining nightly in season, also on the *adoquín*.

For more entertainment suggestions, ask friendly **Gina Machorro** (tel. 954/582-0276, 954/582-1186, ginainpuerto@yahoo.com), who staffs the Pérez Gasga information booth.

Sunsets and Happy Hours

Many bars have sunset happy hours, but not all of them have good sunset views. Since the Oaxaca coast faces south (and the sun sets in the west), bars and restaurants along west-facing Playa Zicatela, such as Hotel Santa Fe, Hotel Arco Iris, Sakura, and Restaurant Cafecito, are the only ones that can offer unobstructed sunset horizons.

If, on the other hand, you prefer solitude, stroll the bayfront *andador* (walkway) that begins on the Playa Principal, west side, on the rocks by the Capitán del Puerto office. It leads west, past a succession of breezy sunset viewpoints above the waves, about a half mile, to steps that continue uphill to city streets near the lighthouse.

Festivals

Puerto Escondido pumps up with a series of fiestas during the low-season (but excellent for vacationing) month of November. Scheduled Fiestas de Noviembre events invariably include surfing and usually sportfishing, cooking, and beauty contests, and notably, the dance festival, **Fiesta Costeño,** when a flock of troupes—from Pochutla, Pinotepa Nacional, Jamiltepec, Tehuántepec, and more—perform regional folk dances.

Visitors who hanker for the old-fashioned color of a traditional fiesta should be sure to arrive in Puerto Escondido by December 8, when seemingly the whole town takes part in the fiesta of the **Virgen de Soledad.** Besides being the patron saint of the state of Oaxaca, the Virgen de Soledad is also protectress of fishermen. To honor her, around 3 P.M. the whole town accompanies the Virgin by boat out to the bay's far reach, and then returns with her to the church plaza for dancing, fireworks, and bullfights.

If you can't be in Puerto Escondido in time to honor the Virgin in December, perhaps you may be able enjoy either Puerto Escondido's **Carnaval** or take a day trip a couple of hours west of Puerto Escondido to enjoy the more traditionally colorful native Carnaval fiestas at one of the small towns around Pinotepa Nacional, with parades, fireworks, and masked traditional dances, on the weekend before Ash Wednesday, the beginning of Lent. (See *Festivals* in the *Pinotepa Nacional and Vicinity* section of this chapter.)

For more nightlife suggestions, see friendly **Gina Machorro** (tel. 954/582-0276, 954/582-1186, ginainpuerto@yahoo.com), who staffs the Pérez Gasga information booth.

SPORTS AND RECREATION
Surfing, Snorkeling, and Scuba Diving
Although surfing is de rigueur for the skilled in Puerto Escondido, beginners usually learn by starting out with bodysurfing and boogie boarding. Boogie boards and surfboards are for sale and rent ($7/day) at a few shops along the *adoquín* and Zicatela beach.

The most experienced is **Central Surf** (tel. 954/582-2285, www.centralsurfshop.com, 9 A.M.–2 P.M. and 4–7 P.M. daily in high season), which also offers surfing lessons on Playa Zicatela at Bungalows Acuario.

Beginners practice on the gentler billows of **Playa Principal** and adjacent **Playa Marinero** while advanced surfers go for the powerful waves of **Playa Zicatela,** which regularly slam foolhardy inexperienced surfers onto the sand with backbreaking force.

Local aficionados organize **surfing tournaments** during the summer–fall surfing season. Dates depend on when the surf is up. For information, it's best to contact friendly **Gina Machorro** (tel. 954/582-0276, 954/582-1186, ginainpuerto@yahoo.com), who staffs the Pérez Gasga information booth.

Clear blue-green waters, coral reefs, and swarms of multicolored fish make for good local snorkeling and diving, especially in little **Puerto Angelito** and **Carrizalillo** bays just west of town. A number of *adoquín* stores sell serviceable resort-grade snorkeling equipment.

A professional dive shop, **Aventura Submarina** (Av. Pérez Gasga 601 A, local cell tel. 044 954/582-2353, asubmarina@yahoo.com.mx, 9 A.M.–2 P.M.), at the west-end stop sign, has gained a foothold in Puerto Escondido. It's run by friendly veteran PADI instructor Jorge Pérez Bravo. Introductory lesson, including one offshore dive, runs about $80, including equipment. For certified (bring your certificate) open-water divers, a one-tank night dive costs about $60, a two-tank day dive, about $120.

Alternately, check out equally professional **Puerto Dive Center** (a block farther east, at the corner of Libertad steps, across from the HSBC ATM, local cell tel. 044-954/102-7767, info@puertodivecenter.com, www.puertodivecenter.com).

Sportfishing
Puerto Escondido's offshore waters abound with fish. Launches go out mornings from Playa Principal and routinely return with an assortment including big tuna, mackerel,

snapper, sea bass, and snook. The sheltered west side of the beach is calm enough to easily launch a mobile boat with the help of usually willing beach hands.

The local **Sociedad Cooperativa Turística Nueva Punta Escondida** (www.tomzap.com/pe-coop.html), which parks its boats right on Playa Principal, regularly takes fishing parties of three or four out for about $25 an hour, including bait and tackle. Check with boatmen right on the beach, or at their Restaurant Pescador, at the west end of the main town beach (where they will cook up a dinner of the fish you catch).

Individual captains also offer sportfishing excursions. Check out highly recommended **Capitán Carlos Guma** (tel. 954/582-1303, local cell tel. 044-954/102-4090, guerra445@hotmail.com). He has a 25-foot boat, fine for catching big, fine-eating *dorado* (mahi mahi), tuna, and *pez gallo* (roosterfish). He charges $25 per hour, four-hour minimum.

Alternatively **Omar's Sportfishing** (local cell tel. 044-954/559-4406, omarsportfishing-1@hotmail.com) offers fishing excursions, for about the same prices, bait and tackle included. You can find Omar on the beach at Puerto Angelito.

Additionally, travel agencies, such as **Viajes Dimar** (Av. Pérez Gasga 905, tel. 954/582-0734 or 954/582-1551, in Zicatela tel. 954/582-2305, viajesdimar@hotmail.com), arrange fishing trips.

Gym and Tennis

The **Acuario Gym** (on Playa Zicatela, at the Bungalows Acuario, tel. 954/582-0357) has a roomful of standard exercise equipment. Single visits run about $3, one-month passes $18.

Probably the only tennis courts in town available for public rental ($12/hour, daytime only) are at the **Hotel Posada Real** (tel. 954/582-0133). Call for a reservation.

Walking, Jogging, and Horseback Riding

Playa Zicatela is Puerto Escondido's most interesting walking course. Early mornings, before the heat and crowds, are good for jogging along the *adoquín*.

Avenida del Morro, which parallels Playa Zicatela, is good for jogging, best during early morning or late afternoons when it isn't too hot. (For more walking details, see *Beach Walking* earlier in this chapter under *Beaches and Activities*.)

Ease your hiking by riding horseback along Playa Zicatela. Rentals are available on the beach in front of Hotel Santa Fe for around $20 per hour.

SHOPPING
Market and Handicrafts

As in most Mexican towns, the place to begin your Puerto Escondido shopping is the local **mercado** (Av. 10 Norte), one long block west of the electric station on upper Avenida Oaxaca. Although produce occupies most of the space, a number of stalls at the south end offer authentic handicrafts. These might include Guerrero painted pottery animals; San Bartolo Coyotepec black pottery; masks from Guerrero and Oaxaca with jaguar, devil, and scary human-animal motifs; the endearing multicolored pottery animals from Iguala and Zitlala in Guerrero; and beautiful crocheted *huipiles* from San Pedro Amusgos.

Back downhill on the *adoquín,* the prices increase along with the selection. Perhaps the most fruitful time and place for handicraft shopping is during the cooler evenings, within the illuminated cluster of crafts stalls just beyond the *adoquín* east-end chain. Among the finest bargains that, with effort, you will find are the gorgeous handwoven rugs and serapes from Teotitlán del Valle and Santa Ana del Valle near Oaxaca City. The highest-quality examples are the most tightly woven—typically about 20 strands per centimeter (50 per inch).

Oaxaca's venerable jewelry tradition is well represented at the very professional **Oro de Monte Albán** (Av. Pérez Gasga, low season, tel. 954/582-0530, 10 A.M.–2 P.M. and 6:30–10:30 P.M. Mon.–Sat., closed Sun.), ocean side, inside the west-end chain. Here are authentic museum-grade replicas of the celebrated Mixtec-style trove discovered in Monte Albán's Tomb 7.

The Uribe silversmithing family well represents Taxco tradition at its **Platería Ixtlán** (tel. 954/582-1672, 10 A.M.–10 P.M. Mon.–Sat.), a few doors east. Choose from a host of fetching floral, animal, and abstract designs, in silver and turquoise, garnet, jade, and other semi-precious stones.

INFORMATION AND SERVICES
Groceries
Abarrotes Lupita (10 A.M.–11 P.M. daily), a fairly well-stocked small grocery, offers meats, milk, ice, and vegetables. Out on Playa Zicatela, a few stores, such as **Abarrotes Merlin** (tel. 954/582-1130, 8 A.M.–11:30 P.M. daily), offer a modest grocery and wine selection.

Photography
Foto Express Figueroa (on Av. Pérez Gasga next to Viajes Dimar, tel. 954/582-0526, 9 A.M.–9 P.M. daily) offers fast photofinishing, Kodak color print and slide film, and digital services, supplies, and a moderate stock of accessories, including point-and-shoot cameras.

On Playa Zicatela, **Centro Photografico** (tel. 954/582-3307, 9 A.M.–9 P.M. Mon.–Sat., 10 A.M.–7 P.M. Sun.) offers a modest selection of film, cameras, accessories, and color and black-and-white developing and printing services.

Tourist Information Offices
Most months of the year, Oaxaca tourism sparkplug Gina Machorro staffs an **information booth** (on the *adoquín,* tel. 954/582-1186, 954/582-0276, ginainpuerto@yahoo.com, 9 A.M.–2 P.M. and 4–6 P.M. Mon.–Fri.), just inside the west-end chain. Gina also gives a **walking tour** of Puerto Escondido, including the Puerto Escondido archaeological zone.

Otherwise, you can consult the well-informed *oficina de turismo* staff (tel./fax 954/582-0175, 8 A.M.–3 P.M. Mon.–Fri.), who distribute a map of Oaxaca. They are located just off Highway 200, in the little office on the beach side of the highway, a couple of blocks east of the airport Pemex gas station.

Spanish Instruction
The very experienced Puerto Escondido **Language Institute** (tel. 954/582-2055, info@puertoschool.com, www.puertoschool.com) offers private or group lessons, homestays, tours, rock climbing, and more, across the highway from Cruz Azul cement store, above Playa Zicatela.

Alternatively, you might check out either **Maress Spanish School** (Avenue 2a, Norte, tel. 954/582-4159, local cell tel. 044-954/544-3658, www.puertospanish.com) or **Méndez Spanish School** (Marsopas 36 and 37, west-side Rinconada district, cell tel. 044-954/108-6942).

Furthermore, at least two individual teachers offer **Spanish lessons:** Sheila Clarke (tel 954/582-0276, Dec.–Feb. and June–Aug. only) and Yolanda Park (tel. 954/582-0837).

Publications, Movies, and Library
One of the few local outlets of English-language newspapers or magazines in Puerto Escondido is **Publicaciones Fabian** (tel. 954/582-1334, 8 A.M.–9 P.M. Mon.–Sat.) in the uphill town, corner of main-street Avenida Oaxaca and Calle 1 Norte. Usually available are the daily Mexico City *News* and magazines such as *Time, Newsweek,* and *Scientific American* and maybe some new paperback novels.

The local English-Spanish tourist newspaper, **El Sol de la Costa,** provides a load of useful information, including community events listings, informative cultural features, emergency numbers, apartment rental listings, and many service advertisements. Pick up a free copy in one of its many advertiser-businesses along the *adoquín.* If you can't find a copy, contact editor Warren Sharpe (tel. 954/582-2230, elsol@escondido.com.mx, 9:30 A.M.–4 P.M. Mon.–Fri., 9:30 A.M.–2 P.M. Sat.).

English-language books are available in at least three spots in Puerto Escondido. On Playa Zicatela there's the used-paperback **Book Exchange** (at Café Casa Babylon, next to the Bungalows Acuario) as well as **Cine Mar** (near the south end of Playa Zicatela, tel. 954/100-3656, 10 A.M.–11 P.M. daily except Wed.). Cine Mar's friendly proprietor, Paul Yacht, lives out his bliss selling and exchanging used and new books and renting, selling, and screening videos. Two screenings, of hits such as *Atonement, There Will Be Blood,* and *Diving Bell and the Butterfly,* begin at 7 P.M. daily.

Furthermore, a **lending library** (in the west-side Rinconada district, on east–west Avenida Benito Juñez, 10 A.M.–2 P.M. Mon., Wed., and Sat.) is maintained by the International Friends of Puerto Escondido (IFOPE). Contact Sheila Clarke (tel. 954/582-0276) or the IFOPE hotline (local cell tel. 044-954/540-3816) for more information.

Money Exchange

Banamex (Pérez Gasga 314, tel. 954/582-0626, 9 A.M.–4 P.M. Mon.–Fri., 10 A.M.–2 P.M. Sat.), with ATM, uphill from the Hotel Nayar, changes U.S. and Canadian cash and travelers checks. Moreover, **HSBC** (Av. 1 Norte in the upper town, tel. 954/542-1825, 8 A.M.–7 P.M. Mon.–Sat.) also changes money. You can also use the HSBC 24-hour ATM, around the mid-point of the *adoquín,* next to the Hotel Las Palmas.

After bank hours, the small **casa de cambio** (money exchange, tel. 954/582-1928, 10 A.M.–2 P.M. and 5:30–9 P.M. Mon.–Sat., 10 A.M.–2 P.M. Sun.) on Pérez Gasga, next to the Hotel Casa Blanca, also exchanges cash and travelers checks. Another *casa de cambio* (tel. 954/582-0592, 9 A.M.–7 P.M. Mon.–Sat.), on Playa Zicatela next to Bungalows Acuario, offers similar services.

Communications

The *correo* (tel. 954/582-0959, 8 A.M.–3 P.M. Mon.–Fri., 9 A.M.–1 P.M. Sat.) and *telégrafo* (tel./fax 954/582-0232, 8 A.M.–7:30 P.M. Mon.–Sat., 9 A.M.–noon Sun.) stand side by side on Avenida 7 Norte, corner Avenida Oaxaca, seven blocks into town from the *crucero.*

For local and long-distance telephone, buy a Ladatel public telephone card at one of many *adoquín* stores and use it in street telephones. First dial 001 for calls to the United States and Canada, and 01 for long-distance calls within Mexico.

On Playa Zicatela, use either the public street phones, or the public long-distance telephone at the desk of the Bungalows Acuario.

Beware of certain prominently situated "Call Home Collect" or "Call Home with Your Credit Card" telephones. Tariffs on these phones can run $10 or more per minute, with a three-minute minimum, costing $30 whether you talk three minutes or not. Ask the operator for the rate; if it's too high, take your business elsewhere.

Internet connection, fax, and long-distance telephone are available at **Coffee Net** (tel. 954/582-0797, 11 A.M.–10:30 P.M. daily), across from the HSBC ATM in the middle of the *adoquín.* Also, on Playa Zicatela, Internet access is available at the store next to the Bungalows Acuario (tel. 954/582-1026, 9 A.M.–11 P.M. daily).

Health and Emergencies

If you need a doctor, go to the small **Sanatorio del Carmen** (tel. 954/582-1876 or 954/582-0174), three blocks west of the *crucero,* uphill from the highway on Calle 3 Poniente between Calles 2 and 3 Norte. There are a number of doctors, including general practitioners, and specialists, such as pediatrician, family medicine, opthamologist, and internist, plus a pathology laboratory.

You could also consult with English-speaking general practitioner **Dr. Mario Francisco de Alba** (tel. 954/582-3581, cell 044-954/588-4018), on the *adoquín* outside the east-end chain, at his pharmacy San Lucas.

Another option is the 24-hour government *centro de salud* (Av. Pérez Gasga, tel. 954/582-2360), below the Hotel Nayar, by Banamex.

Get over-the-counter remedies and prescriptions at one of the good tourist-zone pharmacies, such as the 24-hour **Farmacia La Moderna** (tel. 954/582-0698 or 954/582-2780, 24 hours daily) of Dr. José Luis Esparzar, on

Gasga a block below the *crucero;* or **Super Farmas** (tel. 954/582-0112, 8 A.M.–11 P.M.), on the *adoquín* across from Hotel Las Palmas.

For **police** emergencies, call the municipal police (tel. 954/582-0498), or go to the headquarters in the Agencia Municipal on Highway 200, about four blocks west of the Pérez Gasga *crucero.* Alternatively you can contact the state police (tel. 954/582-1023) on Avenida Pérez Gasga, opposite the Hotel Loren. For fire emergencies, call the *bomberos* (local cell tel. 044-954/5540-3816) or the police (see above).

Community Organizations and Projects

The grassroots **International Friends of Puerto Escondido** (IFOPE, ifope@hotmail .com, www.tomzap.com/ifope.html) welcomes Puerto Escondido newcomers with information and assistance, a lending library, and educational and social events. Also check their monthly meeting date (at this writing, at 10 A.M.–noon, on the second Saturday of each month,

at the Hotel Fiesta Mexicana, in the Bachoco subdivision, west of town) in the meetings section of the local *El Sol de la Costa* newspaper.

One of IFOPE's most helpful activities, especially for Puerto Escondido visitors, is the **Emergency Response Team** (local cell tel. 044-954/540-3816) staffed by English-, German-, Spanish-, French , and Italian-speaking volunteers who help foreigners in trouble. For more information contact IFOPE's sparkplugs, Vicki Cole (tel. 954/582-2495, zicatela_properties@yahoo.com, www.zicatelaproperties .com) and Nolan Van Way (tel. 954/582-0085, nvpep@yahoo.com, www.pep-realty.com), both local real estate agents.

One of the major ongoing projects of the local ecological organization, **Eco Escondido** is the recycling plant at the Hotel Acuario on Playa Zicatela, directed by community leaders Alejandro Villanueva and Hector Marshelli. For more information, contact Gina Machorro (tel. 954/582-0276, 954/582-1186, ginainpuerto@yahoo.com) at the *adoquín* west-end information booth. Or, if you want to pitch in,

© BRUCE WHIPPERMAN

Turtle rescue volunteers are finally rewarded by seeing hundreds of hatchlings return to the ocean from Playa Zipolite.

drop by the hotel, about a quarter-mile (a half km) south of the *adoquín*'s east end.

Locally grown eco-projects well worth visiting are the two reptile sanctuaries east of Puerto Escondido. For details, see *Excursions East of Puerto Escondido* in the *Excursions from Puerto Escondido* section of this chapter.

Another nearby eco-project is the famously successful 20-year-old **turtle sanctuary** at Playa Escobillo (at Hwy. 200 Kilometer 181, tel. 958/589-5908, 958/587-9306, santuarioescobillo@yahoo.com), about 20 miles (32 km) east of Puerto Escondido. There, a cadre of SEMARNAT (Secretariat of Marine Natural Resources) professionals and volunteers are rescuing, hatching, and have returned many hundreds of thousands of baby turtles to the ocean during the past 20 years. They welcome visitors with tours, a restaurant, campground, and rustic beachfront *cabaña* lodging.

Meditation and Massage

Healing is the mission of partners Patricia Heuze and Alejandro Villanuevo, who operate **Villa Temazcalli** (tel. 954/582-1023, ptetemazcalli@yahoo.com, www.temazcalli.com) meditation and massage center, on the west end of town, in Colonia Láazaro Cárdenas, on Avenida Infragante, two blocks uphill from the highway. Facilities include rustic hot baths, an indigenous-style *temazcal,* and massage room in an invitingly tranquil tropical garden setting. Prices run about $55 each for massage and the hot tub, and about $25 for one, $50 for two, and $60 for three, for the *temazcal.*

Travel Agent and Car Rental

One of the most respected travel agents in town is **Viajes Dimar** (Av. Pérez Gasga 905, tel. 954/582-0734 or 954/582-1551, in Zicatela tel. 954/582-2305, viajesdimar@hotmail.com). They offer a wide range of travel services, especially eco-tours, air and bus tickets, fishing excursions, and more.

Rent a car at **Budget Rent a Car** (tel. 954/582-0312, budget33@hotmail.com) on Calle Juárez, beach side of Highway 200, in the Bachoco suburb by the airport.

Alternatively, try **Economica Rent-a-Car** (Las Brisas 7, tel. 954/582-2557) on the downhill street, from Highway 200, at the south end of Playa Zicatela development.

Laundry

Get your laundry done at the **Lavandería Pérez Gasga** (tel. 954/540-5617, 8 A.M.–8 P.M. Mon.–Sat., 8 A.M.–5 P.M. Sun.) by Banamex, about two blocks uphill from the west-end chain.

GETTING THERE AND AWAY
By Air

The small jetport, officially the **Aeropuerto Puerto Escondido** (code-designated PXM), is just off the highway a mile west of town. The terminal, only a plain waiting room with check-in desks, has no services save a small snack bar. Out in front, *colectivos* to hotels in town run $3 per person. Arrivees with a minimum of luggage, however, can walk a block to the highway and flag down one of the many eastbound local *colectivos,* which all stop at the main town highway crossing. Arrive with a hotel in mind (better yet a hotel reservation in hand), unless you prefer letting your taxi driver choose one, where he will probably collect a commission for depositing you there.

Although car rental agents may not routinely meet flights, they will meet you if you have a reservation. Contact **Budget** (tel. 954/582-0312 or 954/582-0315, budget33@hotmail.com).

Be prepared to pay the $12 international departure tax, or its Mexican peso equivalent, if your ticket doesn't already include it. If you lose your tourist card, avoid trouble or a fine by taking your passport and some proof of your arrival date (such as a stamped passport, a copy of your lost tourist card, or an air ticket) to **Migración** at the airport (tel. 954/582-3369), for help *before* your day of departure.

A few regularly scheduled flights connect Puerto Escondido with other Mexican destinations.

Mexicana Airlines affiliate carrier **Click Airlines** (tel. 954/582-2023, 954/582-2024, or toll-free Mex. tel. 800/112-5425 or

800/282-6262) connects daily with Mexico City.

If the above flight cannot take you where you want to go, try **Aerovega** (tel./fax 954/582-0151, cell tel. 044-954/588-0062, in Oaxaca City tel. 951/515-4982, aerovegaoax@hotmail.com, aerovegapto@hotmail.com, www.oaxaca-mio.com/acrovega.htm), the dependable local air-taxi service.

Alternatively, charter airline **Aerotucan** (tel./fax 954/582-3461, in Oaxaca City tel. 951/501-0530 or 951/501-0532, or toll-free Mex. tel. 800/640-4148, info@aerotucan.com.mx, www.aerotucan.com.mx) routinely runs Oaxaca–Puerto Escondido flights, depending upon passenger demand.

Puerto Escondido is also accessible via the Puerto Ángel–Huatulco airport, one hour east by road. (See the *Bahías de Huatulco and Vicinity* section earlier in this chapter.)

By Bus

Several long-distance bus lines serve Puerto Escondido from the new bus station on Highway 131 uphill, a mile beyond the north edge of town. Some offer first-class service. **Estrella Blanca** (tel. 954/582-3878 or 951/582-0086) and subsidiary lines (luxury and first-class Elite and Futura and others) travel the Highway 200 Acapulco–Isthmus route. More than two dozen daily *salidas de paso* come through en route both ways between Ixtapa and Zihuatanejo, and Acapulco and Pochutla, Huatulco (Crucecita), and Salina Cruz. Additionally, a few departures also connect north with Mexico City, via Acapulco.

Cooperating lines **Autobúses Estrella del Valle** and **Autotransportes Oaxaca Pacífico** (tel. 954/582-0050) provide both first- and second-class connections east with Pochutla. Some of these buses continue north past Pochutla, connecting with Oaxaca City and Mexico City, via Highway 175.

Both **Autobúses Estrella Roja del Sureste** (tel. 954/582-0603) and **Linea Dorada**, formerly La Solteca, second-class bus lines connect north with Oaxaca City (with some departures

via pilgrimage town Juquila) along Highway 131 direct from Puerto Escondido.

An additional pair of second-class bus lines, **Transportes Oaxaca-Istmo** and **Fletes y Pasajes**, connect east, via Highway 200, with Pochutla, Huatulco (Crucecita), and Salina Cruz, Tehuántepec and Juchitán.

Operating from their own separate station, on Hwy 200, half a block west of the Crucero signal, **Cristóbal Colón** (OCC) and **Autobuses del Oriente** (ADO) (tel. 954/582-1073), the other major first-class bus lines provide broad service east, northeast, north and northwest. From Puerto Escondido, they serve the Oaxaca east coast and Isthmus, connecting all the way east to to San Cristóbal las Casas in Chiapas and Tapachula, at the Guatemala border, and north with Coaztacoalcos and Veracruz on the Gulf of Mexico, and northeast with Cancun on the Mexican Caribbean. Intermediate destinations include Pochutla, Huatulco (Crucecita), and Salina Cruz. At Pochutla and Salina Cruz, passengers can transfer to Cristobal Colón Oaxaca City–bound buses. One of these continues, northwest, via Puebla, to Mexico City (both Tapo and Norte terminals).

By Car or RV

National Highway 200, although sometimes winding, is generally smooth and uncongested between Puerto Escondido and Pinotepa Nacional (89 miles/143 km, 2.5 hours) to the west. From there, continue another 160 miles (258 km/4.5 hours) to Acapulco. Fill up at Puerto Escondido before you leave, although gasoline is available at several points along the routes.

Traffic sails between Puerto Escondido and Puerto Ángel, 44 miles (71 km) apart, in an easy hour. (Actually, Pochutla is immediately on the highway; Puerto Ángel is an additional six miles to the right, downhill from the Pochutla junction.) Puerto Ángel is alternatively accessible via the very scenic paved (but sometimes potholed) shortcut, via the minisorts of Mazunte and Zipolite, from Highway 200, at San Antonio village, Kilometer 198. Santa Cruz de Huatulco Is an easy 27 miles (45 km) farther east from the Pochutla junction.

To or from Oaxaca City, all paved but sometimes roughly potholed National Highway 131 connects directly north, along main street Avenida Oaxaca, via its winding but spectacular 158-mile (254-km) route over the pine-clad Sierra Madre del Sur. The route, which rises 9,000 feet through Chatino foothill and mountain country, can be chilly in the winter and has few services along the lonely 100-mile middle stretch between San Gabriel Mixtepec and Sola de Vega. Take water and blankets, and be prepared for emergencies. Allow about nine hours at the wheel from Puerto Escondido, eight hours the other way, from Oaxaca City. Fill up with gasoline at the airport Pemex stations on either end before heading out. Unleaded gasoline is consistently available only at the Sola de Vega Pemex *gasolinera* en route.

EXCURSIONS FROM PUERTO ESCONDIDO

Whether you go independently or by escorted tour, outings away from the Puerto Escondido resort can reveal rewarding glimpses of flora and fauna, local cultures, and idyllic beaches seemingly half a world removed from the *adoquín* tourist hubbub. For escorted tour suggestions, see *Tours* at the end of this section.

Farthest afield, to the west of Puerto Escondido, are the colorful festivals, markets, and handicrafts of the indigenous Mixtec towns of **Jamiltepec** and **Pinotepa Nacional** and the crystalline beaches and wildlife-rich mangrove reaches of the **Parque Nacional Lagunas de Chacahua.** To the east lie the hidden beaches of **Mazunte, Zipolite,** and the picture-book **Bahía de Puerto Ángel,** with its turtle museum, au naturel sunbathing on Playa Zipolite, and very accessible off-beach snorkeling at Puerto Ángel. A bit farther beckon the nine breezy Bahías de Huatulco, ripe for swimming, scuba diving, wildlife-viewing, biking, and river rafting. For details of all of the above out-of-town sights, refer to the corresponding sections of this chapter.

Closer at hand, especially for wildlife lovers and beachgoers, are the jungly lagoons and pristine strands of the west-side **Laguna Manialtepec,** the nearby hot springs and Chatino sacred site of **Atotonilco,** and a duo of home-grown **animal conservation sanctuaries.**

Laguna Manialtepec

Sylvan, mangrove-fringed Laguna Manialtepec, about 10 miles west of Puerto Escondido, is a repository for Pacific Mexico wildlife. Unlike Lagunas de Chacahua, Laguna Manialtepec is relatively deep and fresh most of the year, except occasionally during the rainy season when its main source, the Río Manialtepec, breaks through its sandbar and the lagoon becomes a tidal estuary. Consequently lacking a continuous supply of ocean fry for sustained fishing, Laguna Manialtepec has been left to local people, a few Sunday visitors, and its wildlife.

Laguna Manialtepec abounds with birds. Of the hundreds of species frequenting the lagoon, 40 or 50 are often spotted in a morning outing. Among the more common are the olivaceous cormorant and its relative the anhinga, and herons, including the tricolored, green-backed, little blue, and the black-crowned night heron. Other common species include ibis, parrots, egrets, and ducks, such as the Muscovy and the black-bellied whistling duck. Among the most spectacular are the huge great blue herons, while the most entertaining are the northern *jacanas,* or lily walkers, who scoot across lily pads as if they were the kitchen floor.

Manialtepec tours are conveniently arranged through travel agencies in Puerto Escondido. Although most of these advertise so-called "ecotours," a pair of genuine very worthwhile ecotours are led, respectively, by Canadian ornithologist Michael Malone and his equally professional student, known simply as "Lalo." (For details see *Tours* at the end of this section.)

If, however, you prefer to organize your own Manialtepec excursion by bus or car, you might find yourself tempted to linger—Manialtepec is ripe for kayaking, boating, and RV and tent camping along its mangrove- and palm-decorated shoreline. A handful of shady restaurant and lodging compounds along the shore offer the essentials for a week of Sundays in paradise.

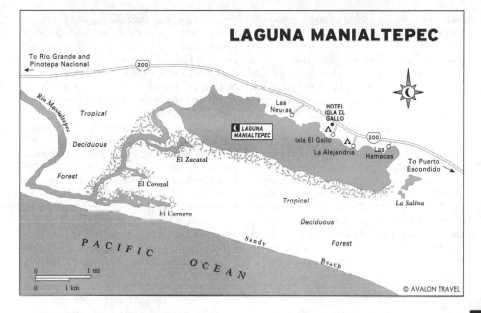

LAGUNA MANIALTEPEC

© AVALON TRAVEL

Laguna Manialtepec Mini-Resorts

One of the better organized of these resorts is **Las Hamacas,** at the lake's eastern end near the Kilometer 126 marker, about 10 miles (16 km) west of Puerto Escondido. The owners have gotten off to a good start in creating their version of paradise, with a mini-farm of ducks, goats, sheep, cattle and rabbits, a lakeshore *palapa* restaurant (entreé $3–8), kayak rentals ($20 per day), and lagoon tours.

One kilometer farther west is the sleepy little family-run pocket Eden of **La Alejandria,** (local cell tel. 044-954/550-2873, $10–15 RVs, $15 *cabañas*), which nestles along its 100 yards of lakefront, shaded by palms and great spreading trees. It's so idyllic that the *Tarzan* TV series picked La Alejandria for its setting, adding a rustic lake tree house (now destroyed by hurricanes) to the already gorgeous scene. Embellishing all this is a homey restaurant/bar, screened-in from bugs, decorated with animal trophies, and reminiscent of an old-time East African safari lodge.

La Alejandria rents about six palm-shaded RV spaces with electricity and water (be prepared with your own long extension and hose) for about $10, $15 with electricity. Camping spaces also go for the same prices. They also rent some very rustic South Seas *cabañas* for about $15; check for mildew and see if everything is working before moving in, however.

Another kilometer west of La Alejandria is lakefront restaurant and dock **◖ Isla El Gallo** (tel. 954/588-7280, 954/588-3650), perfect for a day or a week exploring the lagoon. At least stop for lunch at the restaurant, then follow up on more local options, such as snoozing in a hammock, volleyball, swimming, kayaking, and bird-watching along the mangrove-decorated shoreline, launching your own canoe or boat ($5), or hiring one of El Gallo's boatmen to take you on a lagoon excursion from the dock.

If you decide to linger, Isla El Gallo offers 18 modern, invitingly furnished lakefront **hotel** rooms ($46 s or d, $50 t, $55 q). The lower rooms' windows, unfortunately, don't open for fresh air. Ask for one of the upper-floor rooms, with doors opening to private balconies and lake views. Tariffs include hot-water shower-baths and a/c.

Aguas Termales Atotonilco

Also on the west side, a few miles west of Laguna Manialtepec, the Atotonilco hot springs, a Chatino sacred site, provides an interesting focus for a day's outing. The jumping-off point is the village of San José Manialtepec, about half an hour by bus or car west of Puerto Escondido.

At the village, you should hire someone to show you the way up the semi-wild canyon of the Río Manialtepec. The trail winds along cornfields, beneath forest canopies, and past Chatino native villages. Finally, you arrive at the hot spring, where a clear bathtub-sized rock basin bubbles with very hot (bearable for the brave), clear sulfur-smelling water.

Get there by tour, or driving or busing to the Highway 200 turnoff for San José Manialtepec, around Kilometer 116, just east of the Río Manialtepec bridge. Village stables provide horses and guides to the hot springs. It's a very easy two-mile (three-km) walk, except in times of high water on the river, which the trail crosses several times.

Excursions East of Puerto Escondido

A pair of **grassroots conservation projects** on Puerto Escondido's east side are well worth a visit. First, just a few miles east of Puerto Escondido, in Barra de Colotepec, just after (east of) the big Río Colotepec bridge, visit the **Producción Ecoturístico Colotepec** (tel. 954/588-7376 or 954/582-0720, 8 A.M.–5 P.M.) turtle, iguana, and crocodile sanctuary of Galo Sánchez. Galo, his wife, family, and neighbors started with a beachfront turtle rescue effort that now includes crocodiles and iguanas. Their aim is to return all of the endangered creatures that they are nursing to the wild. They're happy to receive visitors daily, and ask a nominal donation of about $1 per person; if you can afford more, give it. Get there either by car or *colectivo* from the Puerto Escondido highway crossing. About four miles (6.4 km)

east of town, just after the big Río Colotepec bridge, turn right onto the side road to the village. Continue about 0.4 mile (0.6 km) straight ahead to Galo's house on the left side.

A more mature but equally laudable effort has been mounted by Marcelino López Reyes at his **Iguana and Land Turtle Nursery** about half an hour by car or bus east of Puerto Escondido. Marcelino, a veterinarian, has been working for about 15 years at the nearby government turtle-hatching station at Escobillo, helping to hatch and return about 1,000,000 *laut* (leatherback), *golfina* (olive ridley), and *carey* (hawksbill) turtles to the wild. For the same number of years, friendly Marcelino has also devoted himself to his personal mission: to restore local populations of iguanas and land turtles. Although a hurricane nearly demolished his operation, he's back up and running, with dozens of healthy reptilian residents in a big outside enclosure. Besides the green *iguana verde (Iguana iguana),* and black *iguana prieta (Ctenosaura pectinata),* he's also restoring two local species of endangered land turtles, the *tortuga del monte (Rinoclemys pulcherrima),* and the *tortuga sabanera (Rinoclemys Ruvida).* Don't miss visiting him (watch for the *criadero iguana* sign), at the east side of the Río Coazoaltepec bridge about 21 miles (34 km) east of Puerto Escondido, or 23 miles (37 km) west of Puerto Ángel–Pochutla. The best time to find him there is around 5 P.M., after work on weekdays. If he's not there, one of his young assistants will probably be on hand to show you around. He appreciates a donation of about $1 or more if you have it.

Tours

Puerto Escondido agencies and guides conduct outings to all of the above and more. The **Hidden Voyages Ecotours** of the Canadian husband-wife team of Michael Malone and Joan Walker (he's an ornithologist; she's an artist-ecologist) lead unusually informative tours seasonally, December through March. Besides their excellent bird-watching and animal-viewing boat tour at Laguna Manialtepec, they also offer a Lagunas de Chacauhua wildlife tour and a sunset tour. Their trips run about $40–65 per day, per person, depending on amenities. Contact them in Puerto Escondido December 1–April 1 through the competent Viajes Dimar travel agency (Av. Pérez Gasga 906, tel. 954/582-0734, 954/582-1551 or 954/582-2305, viajesdimar@hotmail.com or michael@peleewings.ca). In the off season, contact them in Canada (tel. 519/326-5193). For more information, visit www.wincom .net/~pelewing/hvecotur.html.

Other Dimar tours include a full-day jaunt east to the turtle museum at Playa Mazunte, continuing to Playa Zipolite, where you can stop for lunch and an afternoon of snorkeling around Puerto Ángel. Evenings during the dark of the moon, trips can include night snorkeling when algae coat everything underwater with an eerie bioluminescent glow. The cost runs about $50 per person. Additionally, they offer an all-day hiking, picnic, and swimming excursion at a luxuriously cool mountain river

and cascade in the sylvan Sierra Madre foothill jungle above Pochutla for about $50 per person, or $95 for two days, one night (minimum four persons).

Alternatively, you could also try one of the excellent tours guided by very experienced and well-equipped **Lalo Tours** (tel. 954/582-2468, laloecotours@hotmail.com or laloecotours1@ yahoo.com.mx, www.lalo-ecotours.com). Their several tours (full day tours about $45 per person, half-day $25) include Laguna Manialtepec bird-watching by boat or kayak; bird-watching by footpath in Laguna Manialtepec's barrier sandbar forest; an ocean sunset cruise; and a fascinating night exploration by boat of the ghostly glow of Laguna Manialtepec's phosphorescent waters.

For more guides and tour providers, check with your hotel desk, the local tourist newspaper *El Sol de la Costa*, or visit www.tomzap.com (and click on Oaxaca, then Puerto Escondido, then Tours).

Upland Excursion into Chatino Country

Head north from Puerto Escondido along Highway 131 and you enter the homeland of the Chatino people, who have lived quietly in their remote mountain hamlets longer than anyone can remember. Long neglected and little studied by historians and anthropologists, the Chatinos are now increasingly learning of their distinguished past and appreciating the value of their traditional language and customs.

In the old days, the only reason most outsiders ever came to Chatino country was the miraculous Virgin of Juquila, celebrated every December by adoring crowds who overflow Juquila's dozen-odd hotels and bed down in doorways, cars, buses, and the surrounding mountain forest, just to push their way to within 50 feet of the tiny, frail, beloved figurine.

Nopala people tell another story altogether. Theirs is the former domain of the great Chatino kings, whose history is just beginning to be uncovered by scholars. Nopala is also an important

center of coffee production, surrounded by dozens of *fincas cafeteleras*, which in February and March harvest and roast a trove of fragrant beans for local, national, and international consumption.

An important consequence of the *fincas cafeteleras* is that they've sparked a renaissance of ecological awareness throughout Oaxaca's entire southern Sierra. Many growers have found markets for their produce among environmentally-aware European and North American buyers, who prefer to buy coffee organically grown, without pesticides and herbicides, just exactly as the local growers have done since coffee was first introduced among Chatino people during the late 19th century.

Encouraged by their contacts with outside eco-activists, certain coffee farm owners and other ecologically aware local entrepreneurs have begun to offer tours, food, and lodging to visitors, who are trickling into Nopala in ever-increasing numbers.

SANTOS REYES NOPALA

Nopala (pop. 6,000, elev. 2,000 feet/600 meters) is tucked into the upper valley of the Río Manialtepec, the heartland of Chatino country. Archaeologists reckon that the Chatino people have been living there for at least two thousand years. Stelae found at the nearby Cerro La Iglesia archaeological site resemble the famous Olmec-style *danzantes* of Monte Albán and are generally believed to date from the same period, around 500 B.C.

Nopala's townspeople nevertheless live very much in the present, enjoying a bit of the profits from their home-grown coffee. The government, moreover, has provided them with a generous sprinkling of schools: *primarias*, a *secundaria*, and, for the university-bound, a *preparatoria*, unusual for such a small, out-of-the way town. Afternoons in town, you can immediately see the positive effect of all this: hundreds of smartly dressed, bright-eyed schoolchildren trooping home after their classes are done.

Part and parcel with the increased emphasis in education, Oaxaca's unique new Usos y Costumbres law is having a significant local effect. No political parties, hubbub, or vote payoffs are necessary. A simple town-hall vote of the assembled citizenry is now sufficient to place Nopala's *presidente municipal* in office.

Sights

Nopala, Land of the Nopales in the Aztec language (which translates to La B'ya in Chatino), is a pretty little place, perched on a hill surrounded by green mountains. You can best appreciate all this by climbing the stairs (as a formality, ask the policeman on the porch if it's OK) to the top floor of the *palacio municipal,* just uphill from the main-plaza market. On the south (sunny side) rises **Cerro de Atole,** with the cross on top, where everyone climbs on February 24, the Día de la Bandera (Day of the Flag), and feasts upon the view, including the blue Pacific.

The name of the mountain, from *atole,* a nourishing Mexican drink made from corn, comes from the time when every house in town was a *jacal,* or thatched hut. In those days, building a new house was a community affair,

---

TROUBLE IN CHATINO COUNTRY

Juquila's bustle appears so focused by the constant flow of faithful that you might think that the Virgin is all that Juquila is about. Beneath the busy surface, however, lies a complex network of personal relationships held together by political, business, kinship, and *compadrazgo* ties.

In the recent past, this tight social system, fueled by a communal forest property boundary dispute between Juquila and the rival town of Yaitepec, led to a local war that in some years resulted in hundreds of shootings, knifings, and machete slashings. Scores of Juquila and Yaitepec men bear scars of such violent encounters.

Fortunately, however, peace seems to have come to Chatino country, with the shaking of hands over a government-brokered pact in late 1998, fixing the boundary between Juquila and Yaitepec. For a fascinating in-depth look into Chatino social relationships and this dispute, check out James Greenberg's book, *Blood Ties: Life and Violence in Rural Mexico.*

---

when all the neighbors would climb the Cerro de Atole to gather the *pasto* (grass) for the new house's roof. When the work was all done, the owner would reward his friends with a party, which would include plenty of *atole.*

On the opposite side, toward the northwest, notice the apparent gash below the mountain summit, which rises perhaps three miles (five km) beyond the town limits. That's the big **Cascada de San Juan Lachao** (about six miles/10 km, by road), a waterfall that's a locally popular place for cooling off on a hot day. To the right of that, approximately due north, rises **Cerro La Iglesia** (a steep, one-hour hike), named for the ruined fortified city, an important archaeological site, halfway down its flank. A bit farther to the right (east) of that, also halfway down yet another jungle-clad mountain, you can just make out some of the buildings of **Finca Costoche** (half-hour hike), a locally prominent coffee farm named for the jaguarundi, a wildcat and ferocious chicken-eater common in these parts.

In the northeast foreground, to the right behind the plaza-front buildings, you may be able to make out the mossy, colonial-style facade of the venerable **Templo de Los Reyes Santo Magos** (Church of the Holy Magi Kings), now replaced by the new church on its left. From here, townsfolk hold their yearly patronal festival for three days centering on El Día de Los Reyes, January 6. Invariably, townsfolk will enjoy a big party, including fireworks, a *calenda* (procession) carrying the images of their patron kings, and the town's favorite dances. These include the Guajolote (offering of the turkey) and Las Chilenas, a courtship dance not unlike the renowned Jarabe Tapatía, the so-called Mexican Hat Dance of Guadalajara.

Also in the foreground, to the east, you can see the redbrick decor of the one-of-a-kind **Hotel Palacio Chatino,** the town's most prominent hotel, labor of love of Dr. Elfego Zurita.

As you make your way down atop the *palacio municipal,* be sure to take a close look at the several stelae embedded into the upper-floor and stairwell walls. Archaeologists, who dug them up at Cerro La Iglesia, believe them to represent Chatino high priests or kings, dating from about 500 B.C. If you look carefully around the bases, you'll see some yet-to-be-deciphered name-dates, presumably of the personages represented. Notice that the upstairs figures have their arms folded over their chests, as in a burial, while the one in the middle of the stairwell is a priest in the act of human sacrifice, holding an obsidian knife in his right hand and a (gulp!) human heart in his left. (*Note:* Plans are afoot in Nopala to open a new museum to display their artifacts; there's a chance that the aforementioned stelae may move to the new museum, on the north side of the plaza.)

Accommodations

Nopala is ready for visitors, with a pair of comfortable hotels and at least three acceptable *comedor* restaurants. The economical lodging choice is **Hotel Palacio del Chatino** (Hidalgo 55, tel./ fax 954/586-0000, $20 s, $30 d), whose bright red-and-white brick decor you probably already saw from atop the *palacio municipal.* The physician-owner has polished his little six-room hotel (three on top and three on the bottom, all around an interior garden) into a first-rate establishment. Rooms are clean and comfortably furnished with hot water, fans, and big double beds. The upper ones especially have plenty of air and light and look out on valley and mountain views on two sides. They're hard to beat, especially this far out in the country. Reserve ahead through the owner, Dr. Elfego Zurita.

The other lodging is the **Posada Nopala** (Prolongación Calle Hidalgo s/n, tel. 954/586-0032, tabachinpaul@gmail.com, www.tabachininfo.com, $90 d), owned by American Pablo (Paul) Nunn Cleaver, also owner of Tabachín Apartments on Playa Zicatela in Puerto Escondido. Posada Nopala's hacienda garden-style layout consists of four luxuriously built rooms complete with charming baroque architectural details, including carved solid-hardwood doors. These rooms share one elaborately luxurious onyx and tile bathroom. Another, larger house, which includes the dining room and the owner's quarters, has two similarly elaborately decorated rooms with their own baths. Amenities include a big orchard in the back with all the mandarin oranges and mangos you can eat (in season). Reserve through the owner, Pablo Nunn Cleaver, in Puerto Escondido (Apartmentos Tabachín del Puerto, Av. del Morro s/n, tel. 954/582-1179 or 954/582-1664) or in Nopala at Posada Nopala. Ask Pablo about Nopala tour arrangements, including local sights and coffee farms.

Food

Nopala can supply you with plenty of local-style food. If you want, start at the big **market,** which operates every day but is even bigger on *tianguis* days, Saturday and Sunday. The hundreds of native Chatino women flood into town in bright *traje* with their loads of *calabazas* (gourds), *cal* (lime or quicklime), *camote* (candied root, like sweet potato), *guajalotes* (turkeys), and much more.

If you'd rather not prepare your own dinner, pick out the goodies you want at the clean *fondas* upstairs, in the building opposite the *palacio municipal* on the plaza's east side. Fonda **Magali** is especially recommended by guide Frédy (see below).

Or if you'd rather, go to one of the more formal *comedores,* such as the **Sarita** (on hidalgo, about two blocks downhill from the market, 8 A.M.–5 P.M. daily, $3–5); or for pizza, go to pizzeria **Kore's** (on Iturbide, downhill from the plaza, noon–9 P.M. daily, $4–10), next to Frédy's photo shop.

Information and Services

Nopala's key service establishments are clustered right around the inviting, shady central plaza. Uphill, to the left of and facing the *presidencia municipal,* is the *correo* (9 A.M.–3 P.M. Mon.–Fri.) and the *telégrafo* (tel. 954/586-0079, 9 A.M.–3 P.M. Mon.–Fri.), across the street adjacent to the basketball court, for fax and money orders.

At the end of the alley adjacent to the post office is Dr. Zurita's **Farmacia "Willey"** (tel./ fax 954/586-0000, 8 A.M.–9 P.M. daily). The *larga distancia* (tel./fax 954/586-0000) telephone office is at the hotel Palacio del Chatino reception, behind the pharmacy.

While in town, be sure to contact personable, well-informed local photographer and guide **Frédy Zárate,** who likes to show people around town. Farther afield, he can take you on excursions to local sights, such as the San Juan Lachao waterfall, the Cerro La Iglesia archaeological site, a coffee farm, and more. Expect to pay about $25 per day for his services. He speaks Spanish only, however; if necessary bring someone along to interpret. Contact him ahead of time at his house (corner of Zaragoza y Itúrbide, tel. 954/586-0043, 954/586-0193).

Getting There and Away

Get to Nopala from Oaxaca City by second-class buses **Estrella Rojo del Sureste** or **Solteca** (or **Transol**) from the *camionera central segunda clase* at the Mercado Abastos (take a taxi) on Oaxaca City's south side. From Puerto Escondido, go by the same bus lines, from the central bus station on Highway 131 (tel. 954/582-0603) at the northern edge of town. *Note:* Long-distance buses from either Oaxaca City or Puerto Escondido do not go all the way to Nopala. Get off at San Gabriel Mixtepec and take a taxi or catch a ride from a truck or local *colectivo* the remaining seven miles (12 km, see driving directions below) to Nopala.

By car or RV from Oaxaca, drive the paved but often potholed Highway 131 south 120 miles (194 km, figure around six hours for safety) to San Gabriel Mixtepec. In the middle of town, where the road cuts sharply left, continue straight onto the paved side street to Nopala. Continue another seven miles (12 km) along a good but curvy paved road to Nopala.

In the opposite direction, from Puerto Escondido, drive 27 curving, sometimes bumpy, uphill miles (44 km) north along Highway 131 to San Gabriel Mixtepec. In the middle of town, when the road makes a sharp turn right, go left at the paved side street. Continue another seven miles (12 km) along a paved but winding road to Nopala. Allow about an hour and a half for a safe trip.

Excursion to Santa Magdalena Tiltepec

Santa Magdalena Tiltepec (pop. 4,000) is a very modest town perched on a hillside a few miles south of Nopala. A roadside sign a couple of miles before Nopala along the San Gabriel–Nopala road invites visitors to come see the local *artesanías alfarerías* pottery handicrafts. The products, made by both men and women, are rustically attractive low-fired hand-coiled vases, jugs, and *comales* (griddles) in a handsome brown, enhanced by quizzically unique black markings. A number of potters are happy to demonstrate their wares. I stopped in at the house of Señora Ceriales Rojas, on Calle Buena Vista, a few doors uphill from the road's-end town plaza. Señora Ceriales also recommended the work of others, including Jeremia Ríos, Margarita López, and her relative, prizewinning Hipolyta Rojas.

SANTA CATARINA JUQUILA

Much of the life in the Chatino mountain town of Juquila (hoo-KEE-lah, pop. 25,000) revolves around its renowned patron, the Virgin of Juquila, the object of adoration for multitudes who begin converging on the town around the first of December.

The reason for all the hubbub is a small, frail figurine scarcely more than a foot tall, which was donated to Juquila by a priest, Father Jordán de Santa Catalina, of the neighboring town of Amialtepec, in 1713. Father Jordán feared that the image, which was already locally adored, deserved a more secure home than his rude *jacal*.

The love the faithful show for the Virgin of Juquila has grown over the centuries. Somehow, she strikes chords of sympathy in the hearts of Mexicans, perhaps partly because of her frailty and also because she's a simple figurine of a native woman, not unlike a pre-conquest goddess idol.

She was first revered by the Chatino people of Amialtepec during the 16th century when she resided in the town church. But in 1633, the entire town of Amialtepec burned down, and one of the sole remembrances left intact was the Virgin, who from that point forward became a symbol of hope for Chatino people.

◖ Santuario de Nuestra Señora de Juquila

The Juquila town plaza, half a block uphill from the terminus of Avenida Antonio Valdez, the entrance drive into town, is the place to appreciate Juquila and the town's beloved patron. Getting there requires some doing, however, especially during festivals. If you're driving, park your car in the lot of the Hotel del Carmen (on

Local *vaqueros* honor the Virgin of Juquila with a ceremonial highway procession on horseback.

the right-hand side of Valdez, half a block before the plaza) and check in at the desk or order breakfast or lunch, if the restaurant is open. If busing, walk or ride a taxi from the Juquila station about a mile (1.6 km) ahead along Valdez to the plaza.

The baroque shrine-church, the Santuario de Nuestra Señora de Juquila, faces approximately east (unusual for Mexico, where most churches face west). If you face west, toward the church, the *palacio municipal* stands on your left, on the plaza's south side. On your right (north), sloping below the plaza level, stands the town market. Main plaza-front business street Calle Benito Juárez runs south to your immediate left, while on your immediate right, the same thoroughfare continues north as Calle Revolución, where *tianguis* spread on Saturday and Sunday.

Step inside the church, where the tiny Virgin stands above the main altar, surrounded by flowers and encircled by a halo of blue fluorescent light. Multiple copies of the Virgin rest to one side of the main altar, while in a right-hand chapel, other copies, hung with *milagros* (wish medals), preside above a host of flickering candles.

Back in the nave, the faithful continuously arrive and quietly seat themselves in the pews, while others kneel before the altar, gazing at the Virgin. The diminutive figure is decorated with a pearl-garnished silk cape. Her face is of brown complexion, and upon her head rests a regal, native-style headdress. In front of the altar stand boxes for donations and personal letters to the Virgin.

◖ La Capilla del Pedimento

Despite the supernumerary virgins in the plaza church itself, another nearby hilltop shrine, locally known as La Capilla del Pedimento, also draws multitudes of pilgrims. You'll find it near the clutter of roadside stalls about three miles (five km) back, east along the highway out of town.

At the stalls you can purchase nearly everything from food, drinks, and religious pictures and reproductions of the Virgin to *milagros,* candles, and flower gifts for her. Collect your offerings and follow the human flow north of the highway about a quarter mile to the small summit chapel.

There you'll see a larger ceramic reproduction of the Virgin in a pink silken robe, heavily hung with *milagro* medals. For an appreciation of the annual mountain of adoration that the Virgin receives, stroll around behind the chapel and marvel at the pile upon pile of offerings, far too numerous to count or save, left by untold thousands of pilgrims.

Other commonly visited sights not far away from Juquila include the old Chatino center of **Amialtepec** and the spectacular 165-foot (50-meter) **Cascada Chorro Conejos.** Ask at your hotel desk for a guide to show you the way.

Accommodations

Juquila's probable best-bet hotel is the **Hotel del Carmen** (Antonio Valdez s/n, tel./fax 954/524-0004, $32 s or d, $40 d or t), at the town center. With an entrance driveway leading to a big rear parking lot, this is an especially convenient option for drivers in congested Juquila. The approximately 40 rooms are clean and mostly semi-deluxe, with hot-water shower-baths, TV, good (seasonal only) restaurant, and parking. Some rooms are better than others. Check the mattress before moving in.

Other cheaper options are available around the plaza half a block uphill. The best of these is probably the homey, family-run **Posada los Ángeles** (Calle Benito Juárez 2, Barrio Grande, tel. 954/524-0073, $27 s or d with one bed, $28 d, $35 t with two beds), at the plaza's southeast corner. The approximately 20 rooms are clean, simply furnished, and well-maintained, with shaded (as opposed to bare-bulb) lamps. Rooms vary; if possible, get one with a balcony, plaza-front view.

If Posada los Ángeles is full, try the **Hotel Juquila Plaza** (Av. Revolución 4, tel. 954/524-0066, $25 s or d, $34 t), on the plaza, right in front of the church. Rooms, although clean enough, aren't as thoughtfully furnished or as well-maintained as the Posada del Ángel. Some, however, have plaza-front views. All rooms have hot-water shower-baths and parking.

If the rush of pilgrims has filled all the above accommodations, you can try others downtown, among them the **Hotel San Nicolas** (Calle Antonio Valdes s/n, tel. 954/524-0120, $32 s or d), and the **Hotel La Conchita** (Calle Hidalgo s/n, tel. 954/524-0015, $25 s or d in one bed, $37 d in two beds), below and behind (southwest of) the church.

Food

Several sources around the plaza offer things to eat. For fruits and vegetables, go to the market on the plaza's north side. A convenient grocery source is **Abarrotes El Centro** (tel. 954/524-0060, 8 A.M.–10 P.M. daily), on the plaza's northeast corner across Revolución from the market. Hearty country-style food, always wholesome if hot, is available at *fondas* in the market.

The few good restaurants are mostly confined to the hotels. Fanciest in town is the restaurant in the **Hotel del Carmen** (tel. 954/524-0004, about 7:30 A.M.–10 P.M. seasonally, $3–7), on Antonio Valdez half a block north of the church, with a good standard menu of soups, sandwiches, meats, poultry, and Mexican specialties.

For a homier option, go to the restaurant **❰ La Angelita** (tel. 954/524-0073, 7 A.M.–10 P.M. daily, $2–5), in the Hotel Posada los Ángeles, opposite the church on the plaza's northeast corner. Here, the friendly female hotel owner supplies patrons with tasty local-style *desayunos, comidas,* and *cenas* (breakfasts, lunches, and suppers).

Festivals

The big Saturday and Sunday *tianguis,* spreading from the northeast corner of the plaza, is Juquila's main regular event. It swells to a 15-day marathon blowout during the December **Fiesta de la Virgen de Juquila.** The celebration begins quietly in late November with early-morning masses and religious processions; builds with a street carnival, floats, and fireworks; and climaxes around December 8 with traditional and modern dances, tapering off after the December 12 Virgin of Guadalupe festival.

Shopping

Stalls on Revolución past the plaza's northeast corner offer a variety of local handicrafts and food delicacies. Handicrafts include embroidered *huipiles, cinturones* (belts), *manteles* (tablecloths), and *servilletas* (napkins). Foods include coffee, coconut candy, and *panela* (brown sugar).

Stands near the church offer a wealth of old-time religious souvenirs. The Hotel del Carmen sells attractive replicas of the Virgin of Juquila.

Services

Juquila, the capital of the big southern Sierra Juquila governmental district, offers some basic services (but unfortunately no bank as of this writing). The *correo* and the *telecomunicaciones* (tel. 954/524-0023, both 9 A.M.–3 P.M. Mon.–Fri.) are in the rebuilt *palacio municipal,* south side of the plaza. A public telephone office, **Caseta Lidia** (tel. 954/524-0192, 7 A.M.–9 P.M.), inside at the rear of the market, offers long-distance and public fax service.

For routine medicines and drugs, try the plaza-front **Farmacia Dolores,** opposite the church. If you get sick, follow the recommendation of your hotel desk or hire a taxi to take you to the local **Hospital Civil.** Alternatively, near the plaza, consult with general practitioner **Dr. José Luis Zavaleta,** on Revolución, uphill side, at two locations: either at his **Clinica San Juanito** (104 Chapultepec, tel. 954/512-2875) or his office (on the second floor above Abarrotes Zavaleta, tel. 954/524-0237), directly across the plaza from the church.

Getting There and Away

Juquila is accessible from the coast, north via paved but sometimes potholed Highway 131, the main north–south street through Puerto Escondido. Fill up with gasoline, then follow the winding 55-mile (88-km) route, climbing to the cool, 8,000-foot (2,400-meter) summit to El Vidrio crossing (gas station and rough truck-stop *comedores*). There, drivers fork left and continue another 19 miles (30 km) west to Juquila. For safety, allow about 3.5 hours for the entire curvy uphill trip.

The same is approximately true heading

south from Oaxaca City. Fill up with gasoline at the airport Pemex station south of town and continue to about two miles (three km) south of Coyotepec, where you fork right on to Highway 131. Continue, winding uphill and down, past Sola de Vega (roadside hotel, restaurant, and unleaded gasoline) to the El Vidrio summit crossing (103 miles/166 km). Turn right at the fork and continue the remaining mostly paved but sometimes bumpy 19 miles (30 km) west to Juquila.

A pair of long-distance second-class bus lines serve Juquila from both Oaxaca City and Puerto Escondido. From the Oaxaca City *camionera central segunda clase* near the west-side Abastos market, ride either **Solteca (Transol)** or **Estrella Roja del Sureste** to Juquila. The same lines connect with Juquila from the Puerto Escondido central bus station (tel. 954/582-0603). *Note:* Not all buses make the 19-mile (30-km) detour to Juquila from the El Vidrio crossing. In such a case, get off the bus at El Vidrio and catch a local *colectivo* for the remaining 19 miles.

Parque Nacional Lagunas de Chacahua

The Parque Nacional Lagunas de Chacahua spreads for about 20 miles of open-ocean beach shoreline and islet-studded jungly lagoons midway between Pinotepa Nacional and Puerto Escondido. Tens of thousands of birds typical of a host of Mexican species fish the waters and nest in the mangroves of the two main lagoons, Laguna Pastoría on the east side and Laguna Chacahua on the west.

The fish and wildlife of the lagoons, overfished and overhunted by local people during the 1970s and 1980s, are now recovering. Commercial fishing is now strictly licensed. Crocodiles were hunted out during the 1970s, but the government is restoring them with a hatchery on Laguna Chacahua.

For most visitors, mainly Mexican families on Sunday outings, access is by boat, except for one unpaved road (passable in the dry season; marginally so in the wet). From east-side Zapotalito village, the local fishing cooperative offers full- and half-day boat excursions to the beaches, Playa Hermosa on the east side and Playa Chacahua on the west.

EXPLORING LAGUNAS DE CHACAHUA

Zapotalito, on the eastern shore of Laguna Pastoría, is the sole quick access point to the Lagunas de Chacahua. Get there from the Zapotalito turnoff at Kilometer 82, 51 miles

(82 km) from Pinotepa and 41 miles (65 km) from Puerto Escondido. (Taxis and local buses run from Río Grande all the way to Zapotalito on the lagoon, while second-class buses from Puerto Escondido and Pinotepa Nacional will drop you on the highway.)

From the Zapotalito landings, the fishing cooperative, Sociedad Cooperativa Turística Escondida, enjoys a monopoly for transporting visitors on the lagoons. The boatmen used to make their livings fishing; now they mostly ferry tourists. Having specialized in hauling in fish, they are generally neither wildlife sensitive nor wildlife knowledgeable. Canopied powerboats, seating about 10, make long, full-day trips across the lagoon to lovely Playa Chacahua and village, for about $70 per boat. Cheaper (about $30) half-day excursions take visitors to nearby **Playa Cerro Hermosa** at the mouth of Laguna Pastoría for a couple of hours' beach play and snorkeling—if you bring your own snorkeling gear. On the other hand, you can save yourself $30 and drive, taxi, or walk the approximately two miles along the shoreline road from Zapotalito to Playa Cerro Hermosa. Here you'll find a lovely open-ocean beach good for surf-fishing, beach sports, and camping, a wildlife-rich lagoon mangrove wetland, and several *palapa* restaurants.

A much cheaper option for crossing the lagoon to Playa Chacahua is to go like the local

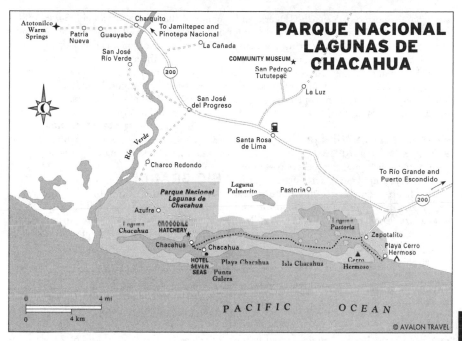

PARQUE NACIONAL LAGUNAS DE CHACAHUA

people do: Take the *colectivo* boat (less than $2) that leaves every two hours. It drops you at the Chacahua island dock, from which you can ride a truck (also less than $2) to Chacahua village.

(*Note:* There are two Chacahua villages, on opposite, east and west, sides of Laguna Chacahua. To distinguish them, I label them east-Chacahua and west-Chacahua, respectively.)

Another cheap route to Playa Chacahua is to drive, taxi, or ride a truck south from San José del Progreso, on Highway 200, about 15 miles west of the Zapotalito turnoff. The route, unpaved but passable even in rain, starts from the center of San José del Progreso the village and extends a total of about 14 miles (23 km). It leads south about five miles (eight km) to Charco Redondo village, where you jog right onto the elevated levee road. Continue another five miles (eight km) to El Azufre, where you fork left and continue another four miles (six km) to west Chacahua village (pop. 1,000), with a few stores, *palapa* restaurants, the crocodile

hatchery, and a boat landing. Stores offer secure parking for about $2 per day. The boat crossing to Playa Chacahua and the east-Chacahua village on the opposite side costs $1 per person.

The **crocodile hatchery** is at the west-Chacahua village, on the west side of the lagoon, home to a small community of *costeño* families, a run-down hotel, a few stores and some lagoonside *palapa* restaurants. Past the rickety crocodile caretaker's quarters are a few enclosures housing about 100 crocodiles segregated according to size, from hatchlings to six-foot-long toothy green adults.

Boat Excursion to Chacahua

The more expensive, but quick, full-day private excursion to Playa Chacahua, about 14 miles (23 km) distant, unfortunately necessitates a fast trip across the lagoon. It's difficult to get the boat operators to slow down. They roar across broad Laguna Pastoría, scattering flocks of birds ahead of them. They wind among the islands, with names such as

Escorpión (Scorpion), Venados (Deer), and Pinuelas (Little Pines), sometimes slowing for viewing multitudes of nesting pelicans, herons, and cormorants. They pick up speed again in the narrow jungle channel between the lagoons, roaring past idyllic, somnolent El Corral village, and break into open water again on Laguna Chacahua.

East-Chacahua Village and Playa Chacahua

The excursion climaxes at the east-lagoon half of Chacahua village across the estuary. The main attraction here is **Playa Chacahua,** lovely *because* of its isolation. The unlittered golden-white sand, washed by gently rolling waves, seems perfect for all beach activities. You can snorkel off the rocks nearby, fish in the breakers, and surf the intermediate breaks that angle in on the west side. Once only a few, now many, *palapas* crowd the beach, offering food, drinks, and lodging. Don't miss María's enchiladas. Moreover, for beachcombers, wild-life-viewers, and backpackers (who carry their own water), the breezy, jungle-backed beach spreads for 10 miles both ways.

The original and still most popular lodging here is the **Restaurant and Hotel Siete Mares** (Seven Seas, tel. 954/588-1340, $25 d) tourist *cabañas*. The approximately 20 *cabañas* occupy Chacahua's choicest location. Half of them face the beach, while the other half face the lagoon. For more privacy and tranquility, choose the latter. Rooms come with fan and private shower and toilet. The Siete Mares's added bonus is friendly owner Doña Meche's restaurant (8 A.M.–9 P.M. daily, $3–8), which keeps satisfied customers returning year after year.

Furthermore, Doña Meche's son Reynaldo and daughter Juana also rent *cabañas*. Both are on the lagoon-front, away from beach. As you walk north along the lagoon-front, Reynaldo's *cabañas,* **Los Almendros** (named for the surrounding almond grove, $25 d), come first. Reynaldo also arranges lagoon wildlife-viewing boat tours, for about $25 per person.

Juana's accommodations, which she has

named **Cabañas Delfines** (tel. 954/588-3800, $25 d with fan, $35 d with a/c), are a few steps farther north. She is proud of her lodgings, which she claims are the most deluxe of all Chacahua. She also welcomes tenters to her campground for $3 per person per night, including hammock-hung *palapa* shelters and showers.

Also, some groceries and fruits and vegetable are available at **Abarrotes Nayeli** store (8 A.M.–9 P.M. daily), on the lagoonfront, between Juana's and Reynaldo's *cabañas.*

RÍO GRANDE

Río Grande (pop. 15,000), five miles (eight km) east (Puerto Escondido side) of the Lagunas de Chacahua–Zapotalito access road, is a transportation, supply, and service point for the region. Right on the highway are *abarroterías* (groceries), pharmacies and doctors, and Ladatel card-operated street telephones.

The downscale **Hotel Río** (Av. Puebla, tel. 954/582-6033, $15 s, $20 d with fans, $25 d with fan and a/c) is the two-story building off the highway's north side, at the west end of town. It offers two floors of 22 plain but clean rooms, encircling a spacious parking courtyard. All have private baths, but tepid (not hot) water.

On the highway corner, across the street, the homey, family-run **Restaurant Río Grande** (8 A.M.–9 P.M. daily) provides hearty meals, especially a daily four-course (soup, rice, entrée, and dessert) *comida corrida* for about $4.

On the east edge of town, the once-inviting but now somewhat-neglected **Hotel Paraíso Río Grande** (Carretera 200, tel. 954/582-6196, $15 s, $20 d, $25 t with fan, $20 s, 25 d, $30 t with a/c) offers a big swimming pool (if it's in working order) and a kiddie pool in a spreading grassy patio, plus large brick-and-tile rooms with either fans or air-conditioning. The 20 rooms (check for mildew) come with fan and TV; $5 more for air-conditioning. The hotel's soaring, classically vaulted ceilings and elegant brick arches flow from the expertise of its friendly and articulate architect builder. His life project has been to first build, and now extend, the hotel, using unreinforced brick and concrete only, not unlike ancient Roman buildings, but with the addition of innovative new designs.

Balneario-Restaurant and Hotel Las Delicias

This grassy palm- and *palapa*-shaded balneario (Carretera 200, Km 107, local cell tel. 044-954/559-2430, 8:30 A.M.–7 P.M. daily) provides a relaxing food and lodging option not far from Lagunas de Chacagua only a few miles east of Río Grande. For about $5 entrance per person, families can stay the whole day, enjoying a big blue pool, kiddie pool, playground equipment, and plenty of shady room to run around within a fenced garden park. The restaurant serves from a long, very recognizable menu, with lots of breakfast ($3–5) and seafood ($7–10) selections. The several newish hotel rooms ($30 d with fan, $35 d with a/c), located in a row along the quiet side, away from the highway, are modern, simply decorated, and clean and comfortable, all with private hot-water shower-baths. If you're arriving on a weekend or holiday, best reserve a few days ahead of time.

Roca Blanca

Travelers hankering for an afternoon or a few tranquil days on the beach can have it at Roca Blanca (White Rock), tucked on the shoreline about six miles (10 km) east of Río Grande or 22 miles (36 km) west of Puerto Escondido. Here, a few rustic *palapa* restaurants front a long curving beach of yellow-white sand, washed by gentle rollers. Islet Roca Blanca perches picturesquely offshore, softening the Pacific swells. On the west side, a lagoon, backed by a scenic jungle of rocky outcroppings, provides shelter for kiddie play and often some impromptu *palapas* that await restoration by new occupants.

If you want to stay, but arrive unequipped for camping, check out the adjacent *cabañas*. Here, about $10 gets you a petite round thatched wooden house with a bed for two, with showers and toilets in an adjacent concrete building. There are also a lot for parking self-contained RVs and a lagoon-side beach good for setting up a tent, and kayaking or rubber-boating either in the ocean or the lagoon. Be prepared with bug repellent, especially around sunset. For more information, check with the owner, Andres López Solano (tel. 954/582-6328), in Río Grande.

SAN PEDRO TUTUTEPEC

Tututepec ("Hill of the Birds" in the Aztec language, pop. 10,000) is a locally important town that perches on the breeze-cooled heights about five miles (eight km) inland from Highway 200. Get there by turning north (right), westbound, at the signed side road at Santa Rosa de Lima, 45 miles (72 km) west of Puerto Escondido (or 44 miles/71 km east of Pinotepa Nacional). After about two miles (three km) from the highway, turn left at the fork, which leads a few more miles uphill to Tututepec and ends at the town plaza.

Few local residents appear aware of their town's proud tradition as the only Oaxaca kingdom that withstood the 15th-century Aztec invasion and remained independent at the time of the conquest in 1522. Today's residences are built perfunctorily on the same hilltops where Tututepec's kings raised their pyramids and temples.

Community Museum

Nevertheless, a trove of excavated remains give clues to Tututepec's past splendor. Find these in the airy new community museum, **Yucosaa** (the local Mixtec-language name for Tututepec, in the town center, a half block from the central plaza, tel. 954/541-0310, 10 A.M.–2 P.M. daily).

Inside the museum's luxuriously spacious interior, volunteers preserve Tututepec's treasured artifacts, including a fascinating collection of antique animal-motif pottery *silbatos* (whistles), a host of fetching animal figurines, and a treasury of exquisite polychrome tripod pottery. The museum also displays a number of massive ancient monoliths—of the goddess of fertility, a pair of Quetzalcoatl-like serpents, and a headless jaguar—carved in styles reminiscent of Teotihuacán and Tula (Land of the Toltecs). *Note:* Since the museum is staffed by volunteers, visitation hours may vary from the announced schedule. Best telephone the *presidencia municipal* (in Spanish, tel. 954/541-0016 or 954/541-0017) ahead of time and verify the schedule and/or make an appointment for a museum visit.

While you're in town, you might climb the concrete stairs leading uphill from the west side of the town plaza to the hilltop mini-park and take a look inside the town church. On the altar is the image of St. Peter, the town patron (who, however, is not the object of the main local festival, which is the Fiesta de Candelaria, around February 2).

Food and Services

While you're in Tututepec, you can avail yourself of reliable eating places and a number of services located in the vicinity of the town plaza. These include *comedor* Petra Soriano for cooked food, and a couple of *abarroterías* for groceries, fruit, and vegetables. Nearby services include a *correo, telecomunicaciones* (both 9 A.M.–3 P.M. Mon.–Fri.), and a *centro de salud.* Gasoline is available at the Pemex station on Highway 200, not far east of the Tututepec turnoff.

CHARQUITO ATOTONILCO WARM SPRINGS

About 10 miles (16 km) west of the Tututepec side road, Highway 200 passes over the **Río Verde,** Oaxaca's grand river, which funnels the entire runoff from Oaxaca's central valley into the Pacific a few miles downstream. West of the river, near the Kilometer 48 marker, just over a half mile (one km) west of Charquito village, turn left at the Guayabo-labeled side road for Atotonilco hot springs and sacred site.

If driving, set your odometer at the turnoff. Continue through Guayabo (2.1 miles/3.4 km), Patria Nueva (2.8 miles/4.5 km), and a shallow river bed (about a foot and a half deep during the rainy season) to the warm spring at 4.2 miles (6.8 km).

This source of warm, sulfury, curative water has been used and revered by untold generations of local people. Folks have built a small chapel on the hill above the pair of springs. The first spring is to the right, below the road, beneath an immense, spreading *guanacastle* tree, and the second is marked by a wide, waist-deep riverbank bathing pool.

A continuous stream of mostly local people bathe here, especially on Sundays and holidays. If you've got extra time, this might be an interesting place to set up a tent or park your RV for a few days (at a respectful distance from the springs themselves; as a courtesy, ask if it's OK to camp). Unless you're under three, *do not bathe nude.* Please respect local custom by wearing at least a modest bathing suit while using the springs.

On the slope above the springs, pay your respects inside the small chapel, dedicated to the **Virgen de los Remedios.** Here, at the altar, people give "thanks to the virgin for the hot waters that have been provided."

West to the Mixtec Coast

In reality, the Costa Chica (Little Coast), which includes the Oaxacan Pacific coast west of Puerto Escondido and the adjoining state of Guerrero coast all the way to Acapulco, isn't very little. Highway 200, heading out of Puerto Escondido, requires approximately 300 miles (480 km) to traverse it.

From Puerto Escondido, you head northwest, first passing settlements such as San José Manialtepec, on the southern fringe of Chatino-speaking country. Next, you pass the wildlife refuges of Laguna Manialtepec and Parque Nacional Lagunas de Chacahua and continue into the Mixtec coast (Mixteca de la Costa) past its main towns of Tututepec, Jamiltepec, and Pinotepa Nacional.

To many native people of Oaxaca's Costa Chica, Spanish is a foreign language. A large fraction of the *indígenas*—Chatino, Mixtec, and Amusgo—live in remote valleys and foothill villages, subsisting as they always have on corn and beans, without sewers, electricity, or paved roads. Those who live near towns often speak the Spanish they have learned by coming to market. In the Costa Chica town markets, you will brush shoulders with them—men, sometimes in pure-white cottons, and women in colorful embroidered *huipiles* over wrapped hand-woven skirts.

Besides the native Mexicans, you will often see African Mexicans—*morenos* (brown ones)—known as *costeños* because their isolated settlements are near the coast. Descendants of African slaves brought over hundreds of years ago, the *costeños* subsist on the produce from their village gardens and the fish they catch.

Costa Chica *costeños* and *indígenas* have a reputation for being unfriendly and suspicious. If true in the past (although it's certainly less so in the present), they have had good reason to be suspicious of outsiders, who in their view have been trying to take away their land, gods, and lives for 300 years.

Communication is nevertheless possible. Your arrival might be the event of the week for the residents of a little foothill or shoreline end-of-road village. People are going to wonder why you came. Smile and say hello. Buy a soda at the store or *palapa*. If kids gather around, don't be shy. Draw a picture in your notebook. If a child offers to do likewise, you've succeeded.

SANTIAGO JAMILTEPEC

About 68 miles (109 km) west of Puerto Escondido and 18 miles (30 km) east of Pinotepa Nacional stands the hilltop town of Jamiltepec (hah-meel-teh-PAYK). Two-thirds of its 20,000 inhabitants are Mixtec, who preserve a still-vibrant indigenous culture. A grieving Mixtec king named the town in memory of his infant son, Jamily, who was carried off by an eagle from this very hilltop.

Around Town

The central plaza, about a mile (1.6 km) from the highway (follow the signed side road north), stands at the heart of the town. You can't miss it, because of the proud town plaza–front clock

(and sundials) and the market, always big but even bigger and more colorful on Thursday, the day of the traditional native *tianguis,* when a regiment of campesinos crowd in from the Jamiltepec hinterland.

Moreover, several big festivals are instrumental in preserving local folkways. They start off on New Year's Day and resume during the weeks of Cuaresma (Lent), usually during February and March. Favorite dances, such as Los Tejerones (Weavers), Los Chareos, Los Moros (The Moors), and Las Chilenas, act out age-old events, stories, and fables. Los Tejerones, for example, through a cast of ani-mal-costumed characters, pokes fun at ridicu-lous Spanish colonial rules and customs.

Soon after, Jamiltepec people celebrate their very popular pre-Easter (week of Ramos) festival, featuring neighborhood candlelight processions accompanied by antique 18th-century music. Hundreds of the faithful bear elaborate wreaths and palm decorations to the foot of their church altars on Domingo de Ramos (Palm Sunday).

Later, merrymaking peaks again, between July 23 and 26 during the Fiesta de Santiago Apóstol (Festival of St. James the Apostle) and on September 11 with a festival honoring the Virgen de los Remedios. All this celebrating centers in the town church, the **Templo de Santiago Apóstol,** destroyed by a 1928 earthquake but brilliantly restored from 1992 to 1999, using the same method as the original Dominican padres, who supervised the 16th-century construction of mortar, strengthened with egg yolks. Take a look inside, where the town patron Santiago (St. James, sword in hand) and the Virgen de Los Remedios (Virgin of the Remedies) preside above the altar.

Regardless of the festivals, Jamiltepec at midday is a feast of traditional sights and sounds, accessible by simply strolling around the market and side streets. For an interesting side excursion, take a stroll to some of the local **ojos de agua** (community springwater sources). From the plaza's northeast side, head east, downhill, along Calle 20 de Noviembre. After about a block, you'll arrive at a covered *pileta* (basin) built into the hillside rocks on the left, where folks fill bottles and jars with drinking water. Continue downhill another couple of blocks to *ojo de agua* **El Aguacate,** where another covered basin, on the left, supplies drinking water, while a cluster of folks wash clothes and bathe in a natural spring beneath an adjacent shady roof.

If you're interested in a more spectacular water diversion, follow the gravel road by local minibus or car north out of town about 15 miles (25 km) to the **cascada** in the foothill country near San José de las Flores village.

Shopping

Jamiltepec is well worth a stop if only to visit its market handicrafts shops, such as **Yu-uku Cha-kuaa** (Hill of Darkness) of Santiago de la Cruz Velasco. Personable Santiago runs his shop at the Jamiltepec plaza market because the government cluster of shops (Centro Artesanal de la Costa, on the highway) was closed down, victim of a dispute over control. The local Mixtec artisans wanted to manage their own handicrafts sales, while the regional branch of the INI (Instituto Nacional Indigenista) preferred to manage instead. The Mixtecs stuck together and refused to bring their handicrafts, closing the government operation.

Some of those crafts—masks, *huipiles*, carvings, hats—occupy the shelves and racks in Santiago's shop on the market's northeast side (ask for Santiago by name), open until about 4 P.M. His home (where he also sells handicrafts) is located on main street Avenida Principal at Francisco Madero, by *seguro social,* the government health clinic (turn off at the highway sign). If you don't want to miss him, write Santiago at Av. Principal, Esquina Fco. Madero, Barrio Grande, Sec. 5, Jamiltepec, Oaxaca 71700.

Practicalities

Jamiltepec, capital of the Jamiltepec governmental district, has a number of basic hotels, restaurants, and services (but not yet a bank) near the town plaza. For an overnight, take a look at the **Hotel Díaz** (Hidalgo 4,

tel.958/582-9103, fax 958/582-8050, $10 s, $14 d) at the northeast plaza corner. It offers a dozen clean, basic rooms around an airy upstairs patio, with fan and private bath (but room-temperature water only). (If the Hotel Díaz is full, take a look at the **Hotel Maris** (tel. 954/582-8042, $17 d) or **Hotel Pérez** (tel. 954/582-8249, $20 d), both on Calle Josefa O. Domínguez nearby.

Additionally, out on the highway, at the west edge of town, consider Jamiltepec's newish, semi-deluxe **Hotel Mirador** (tel. 954/559-2448, $18 s or d in one bed, $25 d with two beds with fan, $20 s or d in one bed, $30 d in two beds with a/c), perched on a view hillside, next to Highway 200. Fine for an overnight, the Mirador offers about 15 comfortable (if a bit dark) rooms. All with hot-water shower-baths, parking and an acceptable restaurant.

For medicines and drugs, go to **Farmacia del Perpetuo Socorro** (Pharmacy of Perpetual Relief, Hidalgo 2, tel. 954/582-9046, 8 A.M.–8 P.M. daily), next to Hotel Díaz, at the plaza's northeast corner, run by a team of friendly sisters. If you need a doctor, they recommend either **Dr. Manuel Mota,** on Highway 200, in town barrio Sección 4, or the *seguro social* hospital with 24-hour emergency service, in town barrio Las Flores.

WEST OF JAMILTEPEC
◖ Huaxpáltepec Pre-Easter Fair

For 20 miles (32 km) west of Jamiltepec, Highway 200 stretches through the coastal Mixtec heartland, intriguing to explore, especially during festival times. The population of San Andres Huaxpáltepec (oo-wash-PAHL-tay-payk), about 10 miles east of Pinotepa, sometimes swells from about 4,000 to 20,000 or more during the three or four days before the day of Jesus the Nazarene, on the fourth Friday of Lent (or in other words, the fourth Friday after Ash Wednesday). The entire town spreads into a warren of shady stalls, offering everything from TVs to stone metates. The purchase of a corn-grinding metate, which, including *mano* stone roller, sells for about $25, is as important to a Mixtec family as a refrigerator is to an American family. A Mixtec husband and wife usually examine several of the concave stones, deliberating the pros and cons of each before deciding.

The Huaxpáltepec Nazarene fair is typical of the larger Oaxaca country expositions. Even the highway becomes a lineup of stalls; whole native clans camp under the trees, and mules, cows, and horses wait patiently around the edges of a grassy trading lot as men discuss prices. (The fun begins when a sale is made, and the new owner tries to rope and harness his bargain steed.)

Huazolotitlán

At nearby Santa María Huazolotitlán (ooah-shoh-loh-teet-LAN, pop. 3,000) several resident woodcarvers craft excellent **masks.** Local favorites are jaguars, lions, rabbits, bulls, and human faces. Given a photograph (or a sitting), one of them might even carve your likeness for a reasonable fee (figure perhaps $40–60). Near the town plaza, ask for Che Luna, Lázaro Gómez, or Idineo Gómez, all of whom live in the town barrio Ñií Yucagua.

Textiles are also locally important. Look for the colorfully embroidered animal and floral motif *huipiles, manteles,* and *servilletas* (native smocks, tablecloths, and napkins). You might also be able to bargain for a genuine heirloom *pozahuanco* for a reasonable price.

Besides all the handicrafts, Huazolotitlán people celebrate the important local **Fiesta de la Virgen de la Asunción** around August 13–16. The celebrations customarily climax with a number of favorite traditional dances, in which you can see why masks are locally important, especially in the dance of the Tiger and the Turtle. The finale comes a day later, celebrated with the ritual dance of the Chareos, dedicated to the Virgin.

Get to Huazolotitlán in about two miles along the paved (but oft-potholed) road that forks south uphill from Highway 200 in Huaxpaltepec. Drive, hitchhike (with caution), ride the local bus, or hire a taxi for about $3.

PINOTEPA NACIONAL AND VICINITY

Pinotepa Nacional (pop. 50,000, 90 miles/145 km west of Puerto Escondido, 157 miles/253 km east of Acapulco) and its neighboring communities comprise the hub of an important coastal indigenous region. Mixtec, Amusgo, Chatino, and other peoples stream into town for markets and fiestas in their traditional dress, ready to combine business with pleasure. They sell their produce and crafts—pottery, masks, handmade clothes—at the market, then later get tipsy, flirt, and dance.

So many people asked the meaning of their city's name that the town fathers wrote the explanation on a wall next to Highway 200 on the west side of town. Pinotepa comes from the Aztec-language words *pinolli* (crumbling) and *tepetl* (mountain)—thus "Crumbling Mountain." The second part of the name came about because, during colonial times, the town was called Pinotepa Real (Royal). This wouldn't do after independence, so the name became Pinotepa Nacional, reflecting the national consciousness that emerged during the 1810–1821 struggle for independence.

The Mixtecs, the dominant regional group, disagree with all this, however. To them, Pinotepa has always been Ñií Yo-oko (Little Place). Only within the town limits do the Mexicans (mestizos), who own most of the town businesses, outnumber the Mixtecs. The farther from town you get, the more likely you are to hear people conversing in the Mixtec language, a complex tongue that uses a number of subtle tones to make meanings clear.

Getting Oriented

On Pinotepa's west (Acapulco) side, Highway 200 splits into the town's two major arteries, which rejoin on the east (Puerto Escondido) side. The north, west-bound branch is called Aguirre Palancares; the south, east-bound branch, the more bustling of the two branches, passes between the town-center *zócalo* and church and is called Avenida Porfirio Díaz on the west side and Avenida Benito Juárez on the

POZAHUANCOS: OAXACA'S SARONGS

To a coastal Mixtec woman, her *poza-huanco* (wraparound skirt) is a lifetime investment symbolizing her maturity and social status, something that she expects to pass on to her daughters. Heirloom *pozahuancos* are of hand-spun thread, dyed in several shades. Women dye them by hand, always including a pair of necessary colors: a light purple *(morada)* from secretions of tidepool-harvested snails, *Purpura patula pansa;* and silk dyed scarlet red with cochineal, a dye extracted from the scale insect *Dactylopius coccus,* cultivated in the Valley of Oaxaca. Increasingly, women are weaving *pozahuancos* with synthetic thread, which has a slippery feel compared to the hand-spun cotton. Consider yourself lucky if you can get a traditionally made *pozahuanco* for as little as $100. If someone offers you a look-alike for $20, you know it's an imitation, made of machine-made polyester thread and synthetic dyes.

east. The main north–south street, Avenida Pérez Gasga, runs past both the church front and the *presidencia municipal,* which faces east, toward the town plaza.

C Pinotepa Market

Highway 200 passes a block north of the main town market, by the big, fenced-in secondary school, on the west side, about a mile west of the central plaza. Despite the Pinotepa market's oft-exotic goods—snakes, iguanas, wild mountain fruits, forest herbs, and spices—its people, nearly entirely Mixtec, are its main attraction, especially on the big Monday market day. Men wear pure white loose cottons, topped by woven palm-leaf hats. Women wrap themselves in their lovely striped purple, violet, red, and navy blue *pozahuanco*—saronglike, horizontally striped skirts. Many women carry atop their heads a polished

tan *jicara* (gourd bowl), which, although it's not supposed to, looks like a whimsical hat. Older women (and younger ones with babies at their breasts) go bare-breasted with only their white *huipiles* draped over their chests as a concession to mestizo custom. Others wear an easily removable *mandil,* a light cotton apron-halter above their *pozahuancos.* A few women can ordinarily be found offering colorful *pozahuancos,* made with cheaper synthetic thread, for about $30. The women told me that traditional all-handmade *pozahuancos* (handspun, hand-sewn, and hand-dyed with naturally gathered pigments) are more commonly available in outlying market towns, notably Pinotepa Don Luis (see *Excursions North of Pinotepa* later in this chapter).

Festivals

Although the Pinotepa market days are big, they don't compare to Semana Santa (the week before Easter). People get ready for the finale with processions, carrying the dead Christ through town to the church each of the seven Fridays before Easter. The climax comes on Viernes Santa (Good Friday), when a platoon of young Mixtec men paint their bodies white to portray Jews, and while intoning ancient Mixtec chants shoot arrows at Christ on the cross. On Saturday, the people mournfully take the Savior down from the cross and bury him, and on Sunday gleefully celebrate his resurrection with a riot of fireworks, food, and folk dancing.

Although not as spectacular as Semana Santa, there's plenty of merrymaking, food, dancing, and processions around the Pinotepa *zócalo* church on July 25, the day of Pinotepa's patron, Santiago (St. James).

Accommodations

The motel-style **Hotel Carmona** (Av. Porfirio Díaz 127, tel. 954/543-2322, $25 s, $30 d in one or two beds, $35 t with fan, $35 s, $45 d, $50 t with a/c), about three blocks west of the plaza, offers three stories of clean, not fancy but comfortable basic rooms and a big backyard garden with pool and sundeck. For festival dates, make reservations. The 50 rooms come with TV and parking.

If the Carmona is full or too pricey for you, check the two high-profile newer hotels, Pepe's and Las Gaviotas, on the north side of the highway on the west side of town. Of the two, **Pepe's** (Carretera Pinotepa Nacional–Acapulco Km 1, tel. 954/543-4347, fax 954/543-3602, $20 s, $25 d with fan, $26 s, $34 d with a/c) is the much better choice. It offers 35 spacious semi-deluxe rooms, with good TV, hot water, restaurant, and parking. A few doors farther west, the rooms at **Hotel Las Gaviotas** (tel./fax 954/543-2838, fax 954/543-2056, $20 d with fan, $30 d with a/c) come with TV and parking.

Third choice goes to clean **Hotel Marisa** (Av. Juárez 134, tel. 954/543-2101 or 954/543-3190, $18 s or d in one bed, $24 d or t in two beds with fan, $33 s or d in two beds, $35 t with a/c), downtown on the highway, north side of the street, all with TV and parking.

Campers enjoy a tranquil spot (best during the dry, calm, clear-water late fall–winter–spring season) on the **Río Arena** about two miles east of Pinotepa. Eastbound, turn left just after the big river bridge. Continue a few hundred yards, past a pumphouse on the left, to a track that forks down to the riverbank. Notice the waterfall cascading down the rocky cliff across the river. You will sometimes find neighbors in RVs or tents. Beneath the abandoned Restaurant La Roca (now just a rock-wall ruin), poor but friendly sand gatherers sift through sand on the riverside, planning to sell it to construction sites. A few hundred yards up, the smooth stream is excellent for kayaking (if you have some way of returning back upstream). *Note:* Lately the sand gatherers have pre-empted much of the east bank space. You might find more room to spread out on the opposite riverbank. Get there just west of the bridge, by following the dirt track downhill along the southwest riverbank.

Food

For a light lunch or supper, try the very clean family-run **Burger Bonny** (tel. 954/543-2016, 11 A.M.–10 P.M. daily), at the southeast corner of the main plaza. Besides six varieties of good hamburgers, Burger Bonny offers *tortas,* tacos, french fries, hot dogs, microwave popcorn, fruit juices, and *refrescos* ($1–4).

Also worthy is traditional-style **❖ Fonda Toñita** (7 A.M.–9 P.M. Mon.–Sat.), a block north of the churchfront, at the corner of Aguirre Palancares. Local folks flock here for the hearty afternoon *comida* (pick the entrée, and you get rice and tortillas thrown in free, $4); it's also good for breakfast ($2–4).

Third restaurant choice goes to **Tacos Orientales** (6–11 P.M. daily), with 15 styles of tacos, from fish to *carnitas,* three for $2.50. Find it on Pérez Gasga, half a block north of the churchfront.

On the other hand, consider *marisquería* **Peñitas** (8 A.M.–midnight daily), next door, which specializes in fresh seafood however you like it: fried, baked, breaded, *al mojo,* and more ($5–8).

For a quick and convenient on-the-road breakfast, lunch, or dinner ($3–6), stop by the restaurant of high-profile **Pepe's Hotel** (tel. 954/543-4347, 8 A.M.–10 P.M. daily) west of town.

Services

For the freshest fruits and vegetables, visit the town market any day, although it's biggest on Monday. For film and film processing, step in to **Arlette Foto** (tel. 954/543-2766, 8 A.M.–8 P.M. Mon.–Sat., 8 A.M.–3 P.M. Sun.) near the plaza's southwest corner.

Exchange money over the counter or use the ATM at all Pinotepa banks. Try **Bancomer** (tel. 954/543-3022 or 954/543-3190, 8:30 A.M.–4 P.M. Mon.–Fri.), corner of Díaz and Progreso, two blocks west of the plaza; or **Banamex** (954/543-3022, 9 A.M.–4 P.M. Mon.–Fri., across the street); or long-hours **HSBC** (tel. 954/543-3949 or 954/543-3969, 8 A.M.–7 P.M. Mon.–Fri., 8 A.M.–3 P.M. Sat.), also on Avenida Progreso, but across Porfirio Díaz and uphill a block from Bancomer.

Find the *correo* (tel. 954/543-2264, 8 A.M.–7 P.M. Mon.–Fri.) about half a mile west of downtown, a block past Hotel Pepe's and across the street. Find the *telecomunicaciones* office one block north of the plaza church, on Avenida Pérez Gasga (tel. 954/543-2019, 8 A.M.–7:30 P.M. Mon.–Fri., 9 A.M.–noon Sat.– Sun.). For telephone, use Ladatel card-operated street telephones, or go to the long-hours *larga distancia* Lada Central telephone and fax office (tel. 954/543-2547), on the plaza, south side. A few doors away, answer your email at **Switch Internet** store (8 A.M.–9 P.M. daily).

For a doctor, go to the 24-hour **Clínica Rodriguez** (Aguirre 503 Palancares, tel. 954/543-2330), one block north, two blocks west of the central plaza churchfront. Get routine medications at one of several town pharmacies, such as the 24-hour **Super Farmacia** on Díaz, a block west of the central plaza churchfront.

Getting There and Away

By car or RV, Highway 200 connects west to Acapulco (160 miles/258 km) in an easy 4.5 hours' driving time. The 89-mile (143-km) eastward connection with Puerto Escondido can be done safely in about 2.5 hours. Additionally, the long 239-mile (385-km) Highway 125–Highway 190 route connects Pinotepa Nacional to Oaxaca, via Putla de Guerrero and Tlaxiaco (136 miles/219 km). Although winding most of the way and potholed at times, the road is generally uncongested. It's safely driveable in a passenger car with caution, from Pinotepa to Oaxaca City (nearing Oaxaca City, at Nochixtlán, exit Hwy. 190 and follow the *cuota autopista,* toll expressway) in about eight hours (under dry conditions) at the wheel, and seven hours in the reverse, downhill, direction from Oaxaca City.

By bus, from the new **Camionera Central** (Central Bus Station), about half a mile west of downtown, several long-distance bus lines connect Pinotepa Nacional with destinations north, northwest, east, and west. Dominant line **Estrella Blanca** (tel. 954/543-3194), via subsidiaries Turistar, Elite, Futura, Gacela, and Flecha Roja, offers several daily first- and second-class *salidas de paso* (departure

buses passing through): west to Acapulco, Zihuatanejo, Lázaro Cárdenas, and Mexico City; and east to Puerto Escondido, Pochutla (Puerto Ángel), Bahías de Huatulco, and Salina Cruz.

Other independent, mostly second-class lines also operate out of the same terminal. **Fletes y Pasajes** (tel. 954/543-6016) connects with inland points, via Putla de Guerrero, Tlaxiaco, and Teposcolula along Highway 125, continuing along Highway 190 via Nochixtlán, to Oaxaca City. **Estrella del Valle** (tel. 954/543-5476) also connects with Oaxaca City, but in the opposite direction, via Highway 200 east to Puerto Escondido and Pochutla (Puerto Ángel), thence north along Highway 175, via San José del Pacifico and Miahuatlán, to Oaxaca City. On the other hand, second-class **Estrella Roja del Sureste** (tel. 954/543-6017), in addition to connecting with Oaxaca via Pochutla, thence over the sierra via Highway 175, also connects with Oaxaca, first following Highway 200 to Puerto Escondido, thence turning inland, north, along Highway 131, over the sierra, via El Vidrio (Juquila) and Sola de Vega, to Oaxaca City.

A welter of local buses connect with dozens of nearby towns and villages, from a streetside terminal downtown, north side of Aguirre Palancares, half a block north and half a block east of the plaza churchfront. Destinations include Jamiltepec, Huazolotitlán, Pinotepa Don Luis, San Juan Colorado, Cacahuatepec, San Pedro Amusgos, and many more.

EXCURSIONS NORTH OF PINOTEPA

The local patronal festival year begins early, on January 20, at **Pinotepa Don Luis** (pop. 5,000), about 15 miles, by back roads, northeast of Pinotepa Nacional, with the uniquely Mixtec festival of San Sebastián. Village bands blare, fireworks pop and hiss, and penitents crawl until the finale, when dancers whirl the local favorite dance, Las Chilenas.

Yet another exciting time around Pinotepa Nacional is during **Carnaval,** when nearby communities put on big extravaganzas.

Pinotepa Don Luis, sometimes known as Pinotepa Chica (Little Pinotepa), is famous for the wooden masks the people make for their big Carnaval. The celebration usually climaxes on the Sunday before Ash Wednesday, when everyone seems to be in costume and a corps of performers gyrates in the traditional dances: Paloma (Dove), Tigre (Jaguar), Culebra (Snake), and Tejón (Badger).

Pinotepa Don Luis bubbles over again with excitement during Semana Santa, when the faithful carry fruit- and flower-decorated trees to the church on Good Friday, explode Judas effigies on Saturday, and celebrate by dancing most of Easter Sunday.

San Juan Colorado, a few miles north of Pinotepa Don Luis, usually appears as just another dusty little town until Carnaval, when its festival rivals that of its neighbors. Subsequently, on November 29, droves of Mixtec people come into town to honor their patron, San Andres. After the serious part at the church, they celebrate with a cast of favorite dancing characters such as Malinche, Jaguar, Turtle, and Charros (Cowboys).

Amusgo Country

Cacahuatepec (pop. about 5,000, on Hwy. 125 about 25 miles north of Pinotepa Nacional) and its neighboring community San Pedro Amusgos are important centers of the Amusgo people. Approximately 20,000 Amusgos live in a roughly 30-mile-square region straddling the Guerrero–Oaxaca state border. Their homeland includes, besides Cacahuatepec and San Pedro Amusgos, Ometepec, Xochistlahuaca, Zacoalpán, and Tlacoachistlahuaca on the Guerrero side.

The Amusgo language is linguistically related to Mixtec, although it's unintelligible to Mixtec speakers. Before the conquest, the Amusgos were subject to the numerically superior Mixtec kingdoms until the Amusgos were conquered by the Aztecs in A.D. 1457, and later by the Spanish.

Now, most Amusgos live as subsistence

the colorful and delicate hand embroidery of San Pedro Amusgos

© BRUCE WHIPPERMAN

farmers, supplementing their diet with occasional fowl or small game. Amusgos are best known to the outside world for their lovely animal-, plant-, and human-motif *huipiles,* which Amusgo women always seem to be hand-embroidering on their doorsteps.

Although Cacahuatepec enjoys a big market each Sunday, that doesn't diminish the importance of its big Easter weekend festival, as well as the day of Todos Santos (All Saints' Day, November 1), and Día de los Muertos (Day of the Dead, November 2), when, at the cemetery, people welcome their ancestors' return to rejoin the family.

San Pedro Amusgos celebrations are among the most popular regional fiestas. On June 29, the day of San Pedro, people participate in religious processions, and costumed participants dressed as Moors and Christians, bulls, jaguars, and mules dance before crowds of men in traditional whites and women in beautiful heirloom *huipiles.* Later, on the first Sunday of October, folks crowd into town to enjoy the traditional processions, dances, and sweet treats of the fiesta of the Virgen de la Rosario (Virgin of the Rosary).

Even if you miss the festivals, San Pedro Amusgos is worth a visit to buy *huipiles* alone. Three or four shops sell them along the main street through town. Look for the sign of **Trajes Regionales Elia** (tel. 954/582-8697, 9 A.M.–6 P.M. daily), the little store run by sprightly Elia Guzmán when she's not in Oaxaca City. Besides dozens of beautiful embroidered garments, she stocks a few Amusgo books and offers friendly words of advice and local information.

EXCURSION SOUTH OF PINOTEPA

If you hanker for a little sea breeze and the murmur of the waves, spend a day or a week at **Playa Corralero,** about 18 miles (28 km) south by a paved but potholed, finally sandy but smooth road. Get there by car or the *camionetas* (passenger trucks) that head south on the street one block west from the Hotel Carmona. Along the way, in the beginning, you'll pass rolling tropical forest country, partially tamed to corn and cattle.

About 12 miles (19 km) from Pinotepa, the road forks. The left, paved branch continues to Laguna Corralero village, a pleasant small town (pop. 2,000) of fisherfolk on the tidal estuary lagoon. Hikers could probably bargain with a boatman at the village to ferry them across the lagoon to the open ocean channel and beach (say *"Ramada Guelaguetza, por el mar"*).

Otherwise, hikers should get off the truck at the fork and walk or hitchhike the right-fork road the additional six miles (9.6 km) to the beach *ramadas.* Drivers should likewise turn right at the fork. Along the way, you pass through a thick prickly pear cactus mini-forest along the beach. Finally, you arrive at the beachfront *ramada* restaurants beside a jetty and broad channel, which a dredge keeps open for fishing boats.

The beach itself is of coarse yellowish sand, rather steep, with the consequent undertow. Waves, which don't appear good for surfing, break strongly and quickly close to shore. The same conditions, however, make the beach perfect for **surf fishing.** If you prefer solitude and don't mind a few cows for company, you can set up camp along the wide, grassy dune and camp most anywhere for four miles (6.4 km) before the *ramadas.* (*Note:* On the sand, use four-wheel drive with caution; if not, be very careful to avoid getting stuck, which might happen even with four-wheel drive.)

On the other hand, if you prefer company, park or tent near the road's-end *ramadas.* The *ramada* **Guelaguetza,** nearest the beach, run by the friendly López Herrera family, will provide you with plenty of economical fish dinners and *refrescos,* plus shade for your vehicle and/or tent.

THE MIXTECA

The Mixteca, the homeland of the Mixtecs, Oaxaca's "People of the Clouds," spreads over an immense domain encompassing the state's entire northwest, stretching northward from the tropical Pacific coast over the high, cool pine-tufted Sierra to the warm, dry "Land of the Sun" along Oaxaca's northern border. The Mixteca's vastness and diversity have led Oaxacans to visualize it as three distinct subregions: the Mixteca Alta, Mixteca Baja, and Mixteca de la Costa. These labels reflect the geographical realities of the Mixteca's *alta* (high) and *baja* (low) mountains and the tropical Pacific *costa* (coastal plain and foothills).

The Mixteca Alta comprises the Mixteca's highest, coolest country—all or part of the governmental districts of Nochixtlán, Coixtlahuaca, Teposcolula, and Tlaxiaco.

The Mixteca Baja includes, on the other hand, the warm, dry districts of Huajuapan, Silacayoapan, and parts of Juxtlahuaca along Oaxaca's northern frontier. The Mixteca de la Costa lies south of all this, encompassing the tropical coastal districts of Putla and Jamiltepec on Oaxaca's southwest border.

This chapter traces a counterclockwise circle route through the Mixteca, northwest from Oaxaca City. First, we arrive in Nochixtlán, scarcely an hour from Oaxaca City, and use it as a base for exploring the hidden delights of the southern Mixteca Alta. Next, the route continues north through country renowned for its exquisite and monumental Dominican churches, then on to the warm, sunny Mixteca Baja country around Huajuapan de León. There, our journey curves through the scenic

© AVALON TRAVEL

HIGHLIGHTS

◖ Tilantongo and Monte Negro Archaeological Zones: Monte Negro, with its "main street" lined with the remains of stone patrician homes, makes a memorable one-day excursion for adventurers (page 220).

◖ The Valley of Apoala: This bucolic, spring-fed, mountain-rimmed Oaxacan Shangri-La, replete with scenery and legends, deserves at least an overnight (page 221).

◖ Templo y Ex-Convento de San Pedro y San Pablo: The newly restored gargantuan *capilla abierta* (open chapel), for a service for 10,000 acolytes, crowned the Dominican padres architectural efforts in Oaxaca (page 229).

◖ Puente Colosal and Huerta de Juquila: Scramble a mile downhill into a hidden box canyon and explore one of the world's tallest natural bridges, decorated by giant, yet-to-be-deciphered Mixtec petroglyphs (page 239).

◖ Cerro de las Minas Archaeological Zone: A high point of your Mixteca visit will most likely be the chance to climb to the top of the regal pyramids and stroll the broad stately plazas of this archaeological zone (page 243).

◖ Santo Domingo Tonalá: This village is worth a visit, both for the 16th-century Templo de Santo Domingo, and the lovely cypress grove behind it (page 253).

◖ Laguna Encantada: This legendary spring-fed lagoon is deep, cold, and crystal-clear emerald green. It's set at the foot of a towering mountain with picture-perfect gnarled *ahuehuete* cypresses inhabiting its banks (page 256).

◖ Tlaxiaco Saturday *Tianguis*: This native market, with its winding, awning-draped stalls of scarlet tomatoes, deep green cucumbers, bright yellow *calabazas*, lilies, roses, and marigolds, may be Oaxaca's most colorful (page 261).

LOOK FOR ◖ TO FIND RECOMMENDED SIGHTS, ACTIVITIES, DINING, AND LODGING.

THE MIXTECA

back door to the Mixteca Alta—the cool, verdant roof of Oaxaca.

PLANNING YOUR TIME

The Mixteca is a large and fascinating region, rich in history and natural wonders, quickly accessible by tour, bus, or car from Oaxaca City. Your interests, of course, will show you how to use your time. If you have only a day, you can get a quick glimpse of the Mixteca on a day trip, visiting the grand restored 16th-century Dominican churches at Yanhuitlán and Teposcolula and returning to Oaxaca City in the afternoon. If you add a day for a Friday overnight in Tlaxiaco, you could soak in the sights and sounds of the big, colorful **Tlaxiaco Saturday *tianguis*** before returning back to Oaxaca City.

Add two days to the above and you'll have time en route to Yanhuitlán for a rewarding two-day side-trip from Nochixtlan for a hotel or camping overnight in the lovely, rustic **Valley of Apoala.** Here you can soak in Apoala's tranquil, bucolic ambience while exploring the limestone Cave of the Serpent, the towering canyon of the Two Colossal Rocks, and the Tail of the Serpent waterfall.

With a week to spend, you could enjoy a grand circle tour of the Mixteca. It would be best to synchronize your trip with the vibrant markets (Fri. Juxtlahuaca, Sat. Tlaxiaco) along the way. You can do this by heading north from Oaxaca City on Monday, overnighting in Apoala as described above, then continuing northeast for an overnight or two in Huajuapan, capital of the Land of the Sun, the Mixteca Baja. Here you'll find a charmingly refined city around a lovely central plaza, dotted with comfortable hotels and good restaurants. The town's sights could begin with the market and continue to the monumental pyramids of the **Cerro de las Minas Archaeological Zone** north of town. A rewarding day trip out of Huajuapan would include the lovely green Valley of the Río Mixteco and a visit to the pilgrimage town of San Pablo and San Pedro Tequixtepec and community museum that highlights the fascinating, but as yet untranslated, *Ñuiñe* glyphs.

Thursday, continue your tour by heading south to **Santo Domingo Tonalá** for a visit to the town's great grove of ancient *sabino* trees and a walk into the nearby Boqueron (Big Mouth) of the spectacular canyon of the Río Mixteco. Continue south for an overnight at Juxtlahuaca; on Friday, stroll the fascinatingly rich native market and marvel at the emerald-green **Laguna Encantada** spring-fed lake. Spend the night in Tlaxiaco, and on Saturday take in the grand market, the cathedral, and the unmissable Botica la Parroquia antique pharmacy.

On Sunday, return back to Oaxaca City, with stops in Teposcolula and Yanhuitlán, as described above.

© BRUCE WHIPPERMAN

Laguna Encantada

Northwest from Oaxaca City

NOCHIXTLÁN

Nochixtlán (noh-chees-TLAN, pop. 13,000), bustling capital of the governmental district of Nochixtlán, is interesting for its colorful market and festivals and especially as a jumping-off point for exploring the wonders of the idyllic mountain valley of Apoala and the remains of the ancient Mixtec kingdoms of Tilantongo and Yucuita.

Sights

Nochixtlán town itself spreads out from its plaza, which is directly accessible from Highway 190, from the Oaxaca side by north–south street Calle Progreso and, from the adjacent, Tamazulapan side, by east–west Calle Porfirio Díaz. The streets intersect at the northwest corner of the central plaza. From there, you can admire the distinguished 19th-century twin-towered **Templo de La Asunción** rising on the plaza's opposite side. Adjacent, to the right of the church, the *presidencia municipal* spreads for a block along Calle Hidalgo. At the plaza's northeast side is the big market, which expands into a much larger *tianguis* on Sunday, when campesinos from all over northwest Oaxaca crowd in to peruse, haggle, and choose from a small mountain of merchandise.

The major patronal **fiesta,** celebrating Santa María de La Asunción, customarily runs between August 1 and 21, climaxing around August 15. Merrymaking includes *calendas* (religious processions), *marmotas* (giant dancing effigies), *mascaritas* (dancing men dressed as women), nearly continuous fireworks, a blaringly loud public dance, and a carnival of food, games, and rides that brightens the entire central plaza.

Accommodations

Nearly everything you'll need is on or near the plaza, including one of the town's four recommendable hotels. First consider the smallish but refined downtown choice, **Hotel Roma** (Morelos 34, tel./fax 951/522-0219, $25 s, $35

d in one bed, $40 d, t, or q in two beds), on a quiet side street. Friendly husband-wife owners offer eight immaculate, mostly windowless but invitingly decorated (with bedside reading lamps) rooms, with hot-water shower-baths, TV, fans, but no credit cards accepted.

Alternatively, for more room and air, check out the loosely run but family-friendly **Hotel Santillan** (Porfirio Díaz 88, tel./fax 951/522-0351, norbertpcl@hotmail.com, $15 s, $20 d in one bed, $25 d in two beds, $30 t), on the highway's west (Tamazulapan) side, convenient for drivers and RVers. The motel-style rooms are arranged in an L-shaped, two-story tier around a spacious inner parking lot, with kiddie pool and patio garden. Additional amenities include a volleyball/basketball court and a pair of shady picnic *palapas*. Upper rooms, probably the best choice, are plainly furnished, but light. All come with hot-water shower-bath, parking, and a family-run restaurant, and proximity (half a block west of) the Cristóbal Colón–Sur bus station. (Details, however, are not the family's strong point. Inspect your room to see if all is in order and repaired before moving in.)

Right across from the main bus station, check out the brand-new **Hotel San Antonio** (Porfirio Díaz 112, $20–40 s or d), too new for a phone at this writing. The 25 deluxe rooms, invitingly furnished in beige-tone bedspreads and drapes, with shiny hot-water bathrooms and spacious modern-standard wash basins and commodes, are stacked in three stories above bottom-floor parking garage. More expensive rooms come with king-size bed and whirlpool tub.

On the diagonally opposite, Oaxaca, side of town, find the newish **Hotel Juquila** (Carretera Oaxaca Km 1, tel. 951/522-0581, $25 s or d in one bed, $30 d or t in two beds) on the highway, Oaxaca side, about half a mile (one km) from the center of town, a few doors from the ADO bus stop. The hotel's name comes from the owner's devotion to the

Virgin of Juquila, for whom he keeps a candle burning in front of a picture of the Virgin on the hotel front desk. Upstairs, the rooms are sparely decorated but very clean. Many are dark, however. Ask for one with *mas luz* (more light). Rooms all come with TV, hot-water showers, and a restaurant downstairs. If you're sensitive to noise, be prepared with ear plugs; the passing trucks and buses may be a problem here.

Food

Nochixtlán offers a sprinkling of budget meal and bakery options. For wholesome (if they're hot) country-style meals, go to the *fondas* in the market, on the north side of the plaza.

Evenings the action spreads to the market streetfront, across from the church, where a line-up of stalls does big business serving a small mountain of tacos, *tortas,* quesadillas, and especially the Oaxaca specialty, *tlayudas:* giant pizza-sized crisp tortillas loaded with everything from beans and cheese to spicy *chorizo* sausage, cabbage, boiled eggs and more ($3–6).

Freshly baked offerings are plentiful at the **Panadería Plaza** bakery (on Díaz, 7 A.M.–9:30 P.M. daily), a block and a half west of the plaza.

Huge pizza-like *tlayudas* are a Nochixtlán specialty.

For restaurant-style ambience go to standby **Restaurant Claudia** (and Internet store, along the block just west of the plaza, tel. 951/522-0190, 9 A.M.–11 P.M. daily, $3–5), one of the better family-style eateries on Díaz. It's open for *desayuno* (breakfast), *comida* (lunch), and *cena* (supper), when you can answer your email or stay up and watch the late-night movie with the family owners.

Alternatively, try **Restaurant Uruapan** (at southwest corner of Díaz and Hwy. 190, tel. 951/522-0495, 8 A.M.–9:30 P.M. daily, $3–5). Offerings include especially good Mexican-style breakfasts, with fruit ($2–4), a hearty afternoon four-course *comida* with tasty entrée such as *guisado de res* (savory beef stew), with soup, rice, and dessert included ($4–5), and à la carte omelets, tacos, quesadillas, tamales, and much more for supper ($3–5).

Information and Services

Travel agents are often willing sources of information; drop into **Viajes Gran Via** (tel. 951/522-0414, 8 A.M.–8 P.M. Mon.–Sat.), four blocks west of the plaza, south side of Diáz.

Find the **correo** (tel. 951/522-0309, 8 A.M.–3 P.M. Mon.–Fri.) at the plaza's southwest corner, west end of the *presidencia municipal.* Skip uphill east, half a block past the *presidencia,* to *telecomunicaciones* (tel. 951/522-0053, 9 A.M.–3 P.M. Mon.–Fri., 9 A.M.–12 noon Sat., at the corner of Hidalgo and Reforma).

For economical local or long-distance telephone access, buy a widely available Ladatel telephone card and use it in one of the several downtown street telephones. Otherwise, use the long-distance phone at Porfirio Díaz 47 (tel. 951/522-0618) and five doors from the plaza's northwest corner (of Díaz and Allende). Furthermore, Internet access is available at the Restaurant Claudia, across Díaz.

Stock up with pesos at **Bancomer** (tel. 951/522-0154, 8:30 A.M.–4 P.M. Mon.–Fri.), in the middle of the plaza's west side, with a 24-hour ATM.

A number of attractive all-Oaxaca handicrafts are for sale at the small **Tradición Santiago** (Díaz 49, tel. 951/522-0294, 9 A.M.–9 P.M. daily). Offerings include fetching embroidered *huipiles* from remote source villages (such as Yalalag and Tehuacán), genuine home-grown Oaxaca *mescal,* and the famous green pottery from Atzompa.

Simple over-the-counter remedies and prescriptions are available at the big well-stocked drug store, **Farmacia San Luis** (tel. 951/522-0484, 7 A.M.–11:30 P.M. daily) at the plaza's northwest corner.

As for doctors, go to the highly recommended **Doctora Oralia Vásquez Morales** (next to Hotel Romaña, 951/522-0153), a family medicine specialist. Alternatively, you can visit the **Centro de Especialidades,** of José Manuel Sosa Bolanos, M.D. (Melchor Ocampo 12, tel. 951/522-0594, 9 A.M.–7 P.M. Mon.–Sat.).

For police and fire emergencies, dial 951/522-0430, or go to the *policía municipal,* at their plaza-front station, at the east end (across from the church) of the *presidencia municipal.*

Getting There and Away

Several long-distance bus lines serve

© BRUCE WHIPPERMAN

Nochixtlán. First-class **Autobuses del Oriente** (ADO) and **Omnibus Cristóbal Colón** (OCC) and second-class **Sur** (operating jointly out of their west-side station on Díaz, Hwy. 190, tel. 951/522-0387), provide broad service southeast with Oaxaca City; northwest with the Mixteca Baja (Tamazulapan, Coixtlahuaca, Huajuapan), continuing to Puebla and Mexico City; and west with Teposcolula, Tlaxiaco, Juxtlahuaca, Putla, and intermediate points in the Mixteca Alta.

Additionally, second-class **Fletes y Pasajes** (on Díaz, directly across the highway from ADO-OCC-Sur, tel. 951/522-0585) offers connections northwest with Mexico City via Tehuacán and Puebla.

Enterprising **Transportes Turísticos de Nochixtlán** (Díaz 72, tel. 951/522-0503), on the west-side highway, offers fast and frequent Suburban van rides to and from Oaxaca City (6 A.M.–9 P.M. daily, $15). In Oaxaca City, contact them downtown (Galeana 222, tel. 951/514-0525). They also rent Suburban station wagons for $15 per hour; negotiate for a cheaper daily rate. This would be especially handy for a family or group visit to Apoala.

Drivers can cover the 50 miles (80 km) from Oaxaca City in an easy hour via the *cuota autopista*. If you want to save the approximately $6 car toll (more for big RVs and trailers), figure about two hours via the winding old Highway 190 *libre* route.

YUCUITA, TILANTONGO, AND MONTE NEGRO: FORGOTTEN KINGDOMS
Yucuita

Yucuita (pop. 500) was once far more important than it is today. It started as a village around 1400 B.C., then grew into a town of 3,000 inhabitants around 200 B.C., about the same time that early Monte Albán was flourishing. Later, by A.D. 200, it lost population and became a center secondary to Yucuñudahui, several miles north.

The claim to fame of drowsy, present-day Yucuita, about five miles (eight km) northwest of Nochixtlán, is that it sits atop the old

Yucuita, one of the Mixteca's largest and most important (but barely explored) archaeological zones. City officials received donations of so many artifacts that they had to organize a small community museum to hold them. Local volunteers offer, when possible, to open it up for any interested visitor. (Drop by the *presidencia municipal* before noon, preferably on a weekday, early enough to arrange a visit.)

Inside, your guide might point out (in Spanish) interesting aspects of the collection (mostly pottery): 2,000-year-old turkey eggs, human-effigy censers and bowls, thousand-year-old *manos* and *metates*, just like those used today, and a platoon of small, toy-like figurines. The most intriguing piece in the museum is a carved stone relief of a seated figure, appearing Olmec-influenced, holding what looks like a bunch of flowers. Maybe this is related to the meaning of Yucuita, which in Mixtec means Hill of Flowers.

Perhaps your guide will have time to show you around town. In any case, be sure to explore the **Yucuita archaeological zone** by climbing the reconstructed steps (fast becoming part of the ruins themselves) next to the paved through-town highway, about a mile (1.6 km) south of the town plaza. If you're agile and adventurous, you can enter the site via a dry **tunnel** that runs about 100 feet (30 meters) from the entrance steps to a big opening and then continues another hundred feet to a final opening, where you can lift yourself out. (*Warning:* Carry a flashlight and a stick to spot and ward off pests, such as scorpions and rattlesnakes, in time to back out. If this scares you, don't try the tunnel.)

Aboveground, what you mostly see is an expansive corn and bean field littered with the stones from the walls and foundations of ancient Yucuita. Pottery shards are common—the colored ones especially stand out. A couple hundred feet to the south of the tunnel opening, inspect the partly reconstructed temple mound with an unfinished stairway and four belowground chambers. Archaeologists say that the entire site, elongated along a north–south axis, is riddled with buried structures, whose remains extend beyond the high hill (the original Hill of Flowers) to the north.

If possible, coordinate your Yucuita visit when the ordinarily sleepy town is at its exciting best during the **Fiesta de San Juan Bautista,** June 22–24. Many folks return home to Yucuita from all over Mexico and the United States for reunions and to once again enjoy country delicacies, dance the favorite old dances, honor San Juan with grand floral processions, and thrill to rockets bursting and showering stars overhead. (If you can't come in June, then come for the equally popular fiesta to honor the beloved Virgin of Guadalupe around December 18.)

GETTING THERE

Reach Yucuita via minibus from Calle Porfirio Díaz, in front of the Nochixtlán market, or on Highway 190, northwest side of town. Drivers, head northwest on Highway 190 from Nochixtlán. Continue straight ahead along the old Highway 190, *not* the *cuota* expressway, toward Huajuapan. Pass the gas station and continue for about two miles (three km) until you see a signed right turnoff to Yucuita. Southbound drivers, on old Highway 190, watch for the signed left turnoff to Yucuita before Nochixtlán. If you reach the Pemex *gasolinera,* before the *cuota* expressway, you have gone too far. Turn around and look for the signed Yucuita right turnoff.

◖ Tilantongo and Monte Negro Archaeological Zones

The Tilantongo archaeological zone is the town itself (pop. 4,000), which sits smack on top of storied ancient Tilantongo. In the old days, around A.D. 1050, Tilantongo was the virtual capital of the Mixteca, ruled by the ruthless but renowned Mixtec king 8-Deer of the Tiger Claws. Carved stones built into the Tilantongo town church wall attest to Tilantongo's former glory.

The town government (tel. 951/510-4970, cca_tilantongo@hotmail.com) commissioned a

Regal, columned palace-houses speak of Monte Negro's distinguished past as a commercial and ceremonial center.

mural, now on the outside wall of the *presiden- cia municipal,* which dramatically portrays the legendary Mixtec Flechador del Sol (Bowman of the Sun) and copies of pages from the Codex Nuttall, a pre-conquest document in blazing color that records glorious events in Mixtec pre-conquest history. See if you can identify 8-Deer (hint: look for the very pictorial 8-Deer hieroglyph) on one of the Codex pages repro- duced in the mural.

At least as important and more rewarding to explore is the much older Monte Negro archae- ological zone atop the towering, oak-studded **Monte Negro** (Black Mountain) visible high above Tilantongo. A graveled road, passable by ordinary cars, easier for higher-clearance trucks or jeep-like vehicles, allows access to the top in about an hour. If you have no wheels, you may be able to get a taxi driver to take you up there. If not, perhaps someone with a car might accept the job. Fit hikers should allow about three hours for the five-mile (eight-km) uphill climb, two hours for lunch and exploring the site, and two hours for the return. Take plenty of water, wear a hat and strong shoes, and use a good sunscreen. You must obtain permission from authorities at the *presidencia,* who require that a local guide (whom they will furnish, fee about $10, plus lunch) accompany you.

Monte Negro flourished about the same time as early Monte Albán, from about 500 B.C. to 0 B.C. The 150-acre hilltop zone is re- plete with ruined columned temples, raised residences of the elite (complete with inner patios), ceremonial plazas, and a ball court, all aligned along a single avenue. Monte Negro's long, north–south orientation is reminiscent of Monte Albán, although its structures are not as grand. For reasons unknown, Monte Negro, like Monte Albán, was abandoned during the Late Urban Stage, around A.D. 800. All that remains are the old city's stone remnants, while its descendants still husband the land you see in all directions from the breezy hilltop. Some of what surrounds you is thick oak forest; other parts are fertile terraced corn and bean fields, while much, in mute testimony to the passage of time, is tragically eroded.

FOOD AND ACCOMMODATIONS

A friendly, enterprising lady offers food and ac- commodation in Tilantongo. **Señora Teresa** (tel. 951/505-4457) serves breakfast, lunch, and dinner ($3–5) and rents a sparely fur- nished room or two ($10) in her modest house, located behind the *presidencia,* steeply uphill two blocks, on the left.

Tilantongo authorities tell me that they are planning *cabaña* accommodations as part of their new ecotourism program.

GETTING THERE

Bus passengers can go by the Tilantongo– Nochixtlán bus, which makes the trip about **three times** a day from Calle Porfirio Díaz, in front of the Nochixtlán market. Drivers, follow Highway 190 (old *libre* route) to the Jaltepec paved turnoff about eight miles (13 km) south- east (Oaxaca City direction) from Nochixtlán. Mark your odometer at the turnoff. The road is paved to the Jaltepec plaza (5.1 miles/8.2 km), where you turn right. The road is dirt and gravel, often rough, after that. Follow the Tilantongo (or Teozocoalco) signs. Turn left at a church (10.8 miles/17.7 km) at Morelos villages, and right after a river bridge (14.8 miles/23.8 km). (*Note:* The riverfront at the bridge would make a lovely picnic or overnight camping spot, beneath the shade of the grand old *sabino,* especially during the dry, clear- water fall–spring–summer season.) You'll pull up to the Tilantongo plaza after 18 miles (29 km) and about an hour of steady bumpy driving.

🄲 THE VALLEY OF APOALA

It's hard to describe the valley of Apoala, tucked in the mountains north of Nochixtlán, with anything less than superlatives. A fertile, terraced, green vale nestles beneath towering cliffs far from the noise, smoke, and clutter of city life. Apoala is no less than a Oaxacan Shangri-La—a farming community replete with charming country sights and sounds such as log-cabin houses, men plowing the field with oxen, women sitting and chatting as they weave palm-leaf sombreros, dogs barking, and burros braying faintly in the warm dusk. The spring-

© BRUCE WHIPPERMAN

Log cabin houses are the dwelling of choice in the rustic Valley of Apoala.

fed river assures good crops; people, consequently, are relatively well off and content to remain on the land. They have few cars, almost no TVs, and few, if any, telephones.

What's more, the local folks are ready for visitors. I arrived at a string stretched curiously across the narrow gravel entrance road. I realized that there must be a good reason for this, so I stopped instead of just barging in. The explanation is that the local folks want to tell you about the wonders of their sylvan valley. The entrance fee is about $5 per group, including guide (an absolute must).

Exploring Apoala

The tour, which takes about two hours, begins at the **Cave of Serpent,** translated from the local Mixtec dialect, which all townsfolk speak. Just before the cave, you pass a crystalline spring welling up from the base of a towering cliff. This spring supplies a large part of the Río Apoala flow, which ripples and meanders down the valley and which folks use to keep their fields green. Another major (and

more constant) part of its flow wells up from beneath a huge rock across the creek, below the cave entrance.

Entering the cave, be careful not to bump your head as you descend the tight, downhill entrance hollow. Immediately, you see why your guide is so important: He carries a large battery and light to illuminate the way. In the first of the cave's two galleries, bats flutter overhead as your guide reveals various stalactites and then flashes on the subterranean river gurgling from an underground dark lagoon, unknown in extent. What *is* known, however, is that the water from the lagoon arrives at the springs at Tamazulapan, more than 30 miles (50 km) away. Someone long ago dropped some oranges into the cave lagoon in Apoala, and they bobbed to the surface later in Tamazulapan.

In the other cave gallery (careful, the access is steep and slippery), the light focuses on a towering stalagmite capped by a bishop's visage, complete with clerical miter and long beard. On the other side, you see a stalactite shaped exactly like a human leg.

After the cave, you'll head up-valley between a pair of cliffs that tower vertically at least 500 feet (150 meters). If you speak Spanish or have someone to interpret, be sure to ask the guide to explain the names and uses of the *plantas medicinales* (medicinal plants) along the path. Every plant, even the notorious *mala mujer* (bad woman), which your guide can point out, seems to have some use.

Soon, above and to your left, you'll see the towering 2,000-foot (600-meter) burnt-yellow rampart, **La Peña Donde Murió El Aguila con Dos Cabezas** (The Rock Where the Eagle with Two Heads Died). No kidding. It seems that, once upon a time, a huge eagle that actually had two heads lived in one of the many caves in the rock face. The problem was, it was killing too many lambs, so one day one of the villagers shot it. The Eagle with Two Heads, however, lives on in the community memory of Apoalans.

Finally, after about 20 minutes of walking and wondering at the natural monuments towering around you, the climax arrives: a

THE LEGEND OF THE FLECHA DEL SOL (ARROW OF THE SUN)

Once upon a time, the Mixtec warrior chief Yaconooy arrived with his soldiers in present-day Valley of Nochixtlán, looking for land for his people to settle and grow their crops. He found the place deserted, except for a brilliant sun in the sky overhead. Spoiling for a fight, but with no one to battle, Yaconooy shot an arrow at the sun, and wounded it. The Sun's blood colored the horizon, the clouds, and the sky. With this victory over the sun, Yaconooy founded his dynasty, which prospered from his capital, the regal but now-ruined city atop Monte Negro, the Black Mountain, near the modern town of Tilantongo.

The fresco at Tilantongo City Hall illustrates how the Mixtecs came to settle in the present territory of Oaxaca.

© BRUCE WHIPPERMAN

---

narrow, river-cut breach in the canyon, like some antediluvian giant had cut a thin slice through a mountain of butter. The slice remains, between a pair of vertical rock walls called **Las Dos Peñas Colosales** (The Two Colossal Rocks).

The grand finale, down-valley about a mile (1.6 km), is the waterfall **Cola del Serpiente** (The Serpent's Tail). You walk down a steep forested trail that looks out on a gorgeous mountain and valley panorama. At the bottom, the Río Apoala, having already tumbled hundreds of feet, pauses for spells in several pools, and finally plummets nearly 300 feet (90 meters) in a graceful arc to an emerald green pool surrounded by a misty, natural stone amphitheater.

Local Guides

If you'd like a guide for more local exploring, contact very knowledgeable and personable **Leopoldo Guzman Alvarado,** who, if he can't guide you himself, will find someone who can, such as youthful **Oswaldo López Jiménez.** To contact them in advance, leave a message via

the Apoala satellite phone: Dial long distance 01-55/5151-9154.

Accommodations and Food

Camping, by self-contained RV or tent, would be superb here. The community has set aside a choice grassy riverside spot, across the river from the cave at the upper end of town, heavenly for a few days of camping. The tariff, payable at the *cabaña* (see below) is about $15 per day per group. Clear, pristine spring water, perfect for drinking, wells up at the foot of the cliff at road's end nearby. Wilderness campers can choose among more isolated spots upstream, ripe for wildlife-viewing. (Swimming, however, is only permitted downstream from the village, preferably at the foot of the waterfall. Always swim with a bathing suit on, however; skinny-dipping is locally disapproved.)

Non-campers shouldn't miss staying in Apoala's fine *cabaña ecoturística* ($15 per person) where you probably first met your guide. This is a model of Oaxaca's improved second-generation government-built, locally managed

THE MIXTECA

tourist accommodation. Besides three very clean and comfortable modern-standard rooms with either one or two double beds it features a light, spacious solarium–sitting room–snack café, serving water, beer, and sodas, as well as breakfast, lunch, and early supper.

Guests can also eat their own food there. If you do, bring your own food, since Apoala has only one basic store, the Conasupo (grocery only, no fruit or veggies, 9 A.M.–4 P.M. Mon.–Fri. except Wed.). In emergency, go to the very modest *abarrotes Juana* (grocery), behind the *cabaña ecoturística*, which furnishes basic meals and a few food supplies.

Overnight reservations are strongly recommended. Reserve directly with Apoala through their satellite phone connection (in Mexico long-distance tel. 01-55/5151-9154; in Mexico City, simply dial as a local call: 5151-9154; from the U.S. tel. 011-52-55/5151-9154). Alternatively you can get information and lodging reservations in Oaxaca City at the government alternative tourism office (Murguia 206, up the driveway, in the back, tel. 951/516-0123, info@aoaxaca.com, www.oaxaca.travel/alternativo).

Getting There

Like Shangri-La, Apoala isn't easy to get to. Bus passengers have it easiest. The Apoala community provides an Apoala-marked *colectivo* ($4), which leaves from Calle 2 de Abril near the corner of Morelos (a block north of the plaza's northeast corner). At this writing, the bus departs at noon Wednesday–Monday, arriving in Apoala around 3 P.M. It departs Apoala for Nochixtlán on the same days at around 6:30 A.M., at 4 A.M. on Sunday. Check locally for the Apoala bus schedule with stores or bus or truck drivers parked along 2 de Abril. To check in advance, call the Apoala satellite phone number: Dial long distance 01-55/5151-9154. Otherwise, taxis and passenger trucks make the same trip hourly until about 5 P.M. from the same spot. The truck fare typically runs $4–6.

For drivers, the 26-mile (42-km) rough dirt and gravel road is a challenge, especially in an ordinary passenger car. The route heads north from downtown Nochixtlán; turn left from Calle Porfirio Díaz (the street that borders the plaza's north side) at the street just past (east) the market. Follow the road signs all the way.

Trucks, vans, and VW Beetles carry nearly all the traffic to Apoala, although a careful, experienced driver in an ordinary car could usually complete the trip with minimal damage. The ideal vehicle (which I've driven three times) would be a high-clearance Jeep-like truck or sport-utility vehicle, with tough tires. Four-wheel drive, not necessary under dry conditions, would be mandatory in rain. Under dry conditions, lighter, maneuverable campers and RVs could make it; large rigs would be marginal at best, because of the narrow, steep, rocky, and winding descent into Apoala Canyon.

Dominican Route South

Of the four missionary orders—Franciscans, Jesuits, Augustinians, and Dominicans—who established an important presence in New Spain, the Dominicans were dominant in Oaxaca. Hernán Cortés had barely begun to resurrect Mexico City from the rubble of old Tenochtitlán when a stream of Dominican padres was heading southeast to Oaxaca. For the next three centuries, until republican reforms forced many of them from Mexico during the latter 1800s, the padres earnestly pursued the spiritual thrust of Spain's two-pronged "God and Gold" mission in the New World. The Dominicans converted, educated, protected, and advocated for Oaxaca's native peoples, often in conflict with brutal and greedy Spanish soldiers and colonists.

The Dominicans' legacy remains vibrant to this day. More than 90 percent of Oaxacans consider themselves Catholics, and lovely old Dominican ex-convent/churches decorate the Oaxacan countryside. Some of these outstanding venerable monuments—notably at **Yanhuitlán, Teposcolula, Tlaxiaco,** and **Coixtlahuaca**—grace the Mixteca Alta, not far from the modern town of Tamazulapan, making it a natural base for extended exploration of what has become known as Oaxaca's Dominican route. The Dominican route's more isolated (but very intriguing) northern section—north and west of Tamazulapan—is usually explored via the *autopista* that connects with Coixtlahuaca, from Nochixtlán and Oaxaca City (for details, see the *Dominican Route North* section).

TAMAZULAPAN AND VICINITY

Tamazulapan (tah-mah-soo-LAH-pahn, pop. about 20,000), partly by virtue of its crossroads position on the National Highway 190, has outgrown its more venerable, but isolated, neighbor towns and become the major service and business center for the Teposcolula district. You know you're in Tamazulapan immediately as you pass its town plaza, which proudly

displays a semicircular columned monument right by the highway in honor of Benito Juárez, "Benemérito de las Américas." Upon reflection, nothing seems more appropriate directly on the Pan-American Highway.

Sights

As you stand on the edge of the highway (locally known as Carretera Cristóbal Colón) looking at the Benito Juárez monument, you'll be facing approximately north. The noble, portaled *presidencia municipal* will appear straight ahead behind the square, the **Plaza Constitución.** To your right, beyond the storefronts along plaza-front Calle Independencia rise the ruddy cupolas of the 18th century Dominican **Templo de la Natividad.** Bordering the plaza on your left are the stores and services along Calle Juárez.

Walk a block east and step into the cool calm of the venerable Dominican church which, although large and harmoniously decorated, is not architecturally comparable to the masterpieces at Coixtlahuaca, Yanhuitlán, and Teposcolula. What is unique, however, are the two images on the altar, both illuminated. The

TAMAZULAPAN

To Balneario Atonaltzin, and Tepelmeme

MULTIPAC

POST OFFICE
TELECOM
OBREGÓN

Market

F. JARABIA

PRESIDENCIA MUNICIPAL

HIDALGO

HOTEL CASA PERLA MIXTECA

PROVEEDORA
CONSTITUCIÓN
Plaza Constitución
INDEPENDENCIA
2 DE ABRIL

PROGRESO

RESTAURANT MAR Y TIERRA

HOTEL PUERTO MEXICO

HOTEL DOM PEDRO

SNACKS

TEMPLO DE LA NATIVIDAD

To Tejupan, Hwy 125, Teoposcolola, Yanhuitlán, and Oaxaca

190

CARRETERA INTERNACIONAL CRISTÓBAL COLÓN

190

To Huajuapan and Mexico City

RESTAURANT NOEMI
ZARAGOZA

INTERNET BIN@RY
CRISTÓBAL COLÓN BUS/ SUR BUS

LONG-DISTANCE TELEPHONE/ FAX

DR AGUILAR AGUAS/ PHARMACY

HIGHWAY POLICE

RESTAURANT COQUI

DRA JOSEFINA CLEMENTE/ FARMACIA IDEAL

0   100 yds

0   100 m

ALLENDE

LAVANDERÍA DELIJ

© AVALON TRAVEL

THE MIXTECA

bottom figure is an unusual reclining figure of Jesus in what appears to be a transparent casket. This figure is locally paraded and celebrated, along with food, games, dancing, and a basketball tournament, in a festival culminating on May 3, El Día de la Cruz.

Above the figure of Jesus is the petite town patron, La Virgen de la Natividad (The Virgin of the Nativity), whom townsfolk celebrate in a fiesta culminating on September 8. As you retrace your steps, exiting through the church garden, you pass the old Dominican convent on the left, in a state of advanced decay.

Tamazulapan townsfolk love their **Balneario Atonaltzin.** You'll see why if you drive, taxi, or walk the 1.5 miles (2.5 km) north along the road to Tepelmeme (plaza-front Calle Independencia). Soon after a bridge, you'll see the *balneario* (9 A.M.–6 P.M. daily, $3 for adults, $2 for kids) on the right. This spot would be a merely typical Sunday family bathing resort if it were not for its crystalline, naturally disinfected sulfurous springs. The waters gurgle up, cool and clear, from a pair of sources in the rocky cliff behind the Olympic double-size pool—a lap swimmer's delight (except on Sundays and holidays, when it's filled with frolicking families). Besides the big main pool, there are two kiddie pools, a local-style restaurant, volleyball, dressing areas, and a few picnic tables. The *balneario* also invites overnight tent-camping and self-contained RV parking, for about $2 per person ($5 total, including the general admission fee).

Two lesser-known but nevertheless interesting spots are the nearby **ojo de agua** swimming hole and the **Xatachio** (shah-TAH-cheeoh) archaeological zone. The *ojo de agua* (literally, eye of water), a general term for a natural spring or source of water, is about 300 feet (90 meters) back from the *balneario* toward town, on the right, below the creek bridge. Step toward the ruined building on the right and you'll see the creek cascading into a big blue pool. Before the Balneario Atonaltzin was built, this was a popular swimming hole. Today, the water appears much less than pure, since it's mostly

used by families for washing clothes. Although the steep riverbank near the bridge is nonnegotiable, you can get down to the water via a path to the right around the ruined building, through the brush, up some stone steps, and down again to the creek.

The unexcavated **Xatachio archaeological zone** is accessible via the dirt side road on the left just past the Balneario Atonaltzin. You'll first spot the zone as a brush-covered hill (actually a former ceremonial pyramid), about half a mile (one km) away on the left. *Note:* Do not try to explore the site on your own. The site lies on communal land, and people are rightly suspicious of possible artifact looters. Go to the *presidencia municipal* on the plaza and ask for permission (preferably through a local spokesperson, such as the owner or manager of your hotel); offer to pay someone (approximately $15) to act as a guide for a couple of hours. Any artifacts you might stumble upon are legally the joint property of the INAH (National Institute of Archaeology and History) and the local community.

Tejupan

If you have time, stop for a few minutes for a look inside the relatively humble, but nevertheless worthy, Dominican church and ex-convent at Tejupan (Tay-HOO-pahn) in the Tamazulapan valley, a 15-minute drive east (Oaxaca City direction) from Tamazulapan. Tejupan is a sleepy farming town, basking in its past glory, visibly represented by its noble, multi-portaled *palacio municipal* and the distinguished 17th-century Dominican **Templo y Ex-Convento de Santiago Apóstol,** across the street. Memorable inside the church is the pretty pink transept chapel, left side, dedicated to the Virgin of Guadalupe. The ex-convent section, in severe need of repair, stands to the right of the church front entrance.

Get to Tejupan by bus, taxi, or car via the signed side road off Highway 190 about seven miles (11 km) southeast of Tamazulapan, or about eight miles (13 km) northwest of the Highway 190–Highway 125 junction northwest of Yanhuitlán.

Accommodations

Of Tamazulapan's acceptable hotels, most prominent is the four-story **Hotel Dom Pedro** (Cristóbal Colón 24, tel./fax 953/533-0019, $16 s or d in one bed, $18 d in two beds, $20 t), a few doors north of the plaza. The 25 plain but clean upstairs rooms (no elevator) come with toilets and hot-water showers, TV, parking, a basic restaurant downstairs, but no phone except the long-distance phone at the hotel desk. Credit cards are not accepted.

Although **Hotel Puerto Mexico** (a few doors farther north at Cristóbal Colón 12, tel. 953/533-0044, $12 s, $22 d, $25 t) appears humdrum from the outside, guests enjoy an inviting tropical patio blooming with leafy banana trees. Rooms are clean and carpeted but have the almost universal Mexican small-town bare bulb hanging from the middle of the ceiling. Bring your own clip-on lampshade. Amenities include hot-water showers, parking, TV, and a pretty fair restaurant downstairs, but no phones. Credit cards are accepted.

The star of Tamazulapan hotels is the deluxe, newish 🄲 **Hotel Casa Perla Mixteca** (Calle 2 de Abril 3, tel./fax 953/533-0280, toll-free Mex. tel. 800/717-3956, $28 s, $33 d, and $39 t). A major plus here is the hotel's quiet location, removed from the noisy highway truck traffic. Take your pick of 10 designer-decorated rooms, with rustically lovely tile floors, hand-woven bedspreads, reading lamps, and shiny bathrooms with hot-water showers.

Food

For inexpensive prepared food, try the *fondas* inside the market and the nighttime taco stands or one of the several sit-down snack bars along the highway by the plaza.

As for restaurants, although the Hotels Dom Pedro and Puerto Mexico offer breakfast, lunch, and dinner, you might do better by walking a few steps to 🄲 **Restaurant Noemi** (Cristóbal Colón 12, tel. 953/533-0595, 7 A.M.–9 P.M. daily, $2–6) between the two hotels. The grandmotherly owners puts out Mexican home-style breakfasts, lunches, and suppers, including savory *café de la olla* (pot-brewed coffee, with cinnamon).

Another good choice is **Restaurant Mar y Tierra** (tel. 953/533-0045, 8 A.M.–10 P.M. daily, $4–12), between the Hotel Dom Pedro and Restaurant Noemi. In a relaxingly airy patio location, patrons select from a long menu of breakfasts ($2–4), soups, salads, pastas, seafood, and meat ($4–12) and suppers of Mexican specialties ($2–5). They also serve a selection of good beers and wines from their bar.

You'll also do quite well at the clean, highway-front **Restaurant Coqui** (KOH-kee, Cristóbal Colón 57, tel. 953/533-0109, 6 A.M.–9 P.M. daily), a block and a half east from the plaza. Although she'll cook nearly anything you want, the friendly owner is best at Oaxacan country delicacies, such as chiles rellenos, enchiladas *tasajos* (beef enchiladas), and Oaxacan tamales, all covered with plenty of *mole negro*.

Shopping

You can buy groceries and fruits and vegetables at either the town market (biggest on Wednesday) behind the *presidencia*, or at one of the plaza-front *abarroterías*, such as **Casa de Santiago** (Constitucion 6, west side, tel. 953/533-0015, 8 A.M.–2 P.M. and 4–9 P.M. daily).

The market, especially during the big Wednesday *tianguis*, can be a good spot for local indigenous handicrafts shopping. Items might include pottery and palm-leaf woven goods such as *tenates* (tump-line baskets), *petates* (mats), and soft woven Panama hat-like sombreros.

Services

Tamazulapan provides a number of basic services along the blocks near the plaza. Be sure to arrive with a good supply of pesos (from banks in Nochixtlán, Tlaxiaco, or Huajuapan) or U.S. dollars that you may be able to exchange in local stores or at your hotel.

The *correo* (8 A.M.–3 P.M. Mon.–Fri.) is one block north, behind the *presidencia* and

THE MIXTECA

the market, on Obregón, a few doors west of the corner of Independencia. A few doors east of the post office, *telecomunicaciones* (corner of Independencia and Obregón, tel. 953/533-0113, 9 A.M.–3:30 P.M. Mon.–Fri.) offers public telephone, money order, and fax. On the same street, you can send a fast, secure mailing via **Multipac** courier service (Obregón 2, 9 A.M.–3 P.M. Mon.–Fri. 9 A.M.–noon Sat.).

For telephone service, go to the *larga distancia* across the highway from the plaza, or one of the three or four Ladatel card-operated public phones sprinkled along the highway and near the plaza. Answer your email at Internet store **Bin@ry** (on the highway, across from the Hotel Dom Pedro, tel. 953/533-0070, 9 A.M.–11 P.M. daily).

Two doctors offer consultations and medicines at their highway-front pharmacies. Choose either **Dra. Josefina Clemente** (on the highway directly opposite the plaza, tel. 953/533-0224, pharmacy 8 A.M.–9 P.M., consultations 4–8 P.M. Mon.–Fri.,) at her Farmacia Ideal, or **Dr. Aguilar Aguas** (a block and a half east at Cristóbal Colón 43, tel. 953/533-0084, noon–6 P.M. Mon.–Fri.).

For a police emergency, go to the Delegación de Transito highway police, on duty 24 hours, half a block east and across the highway from the plaza, or call 953/533-0472. Alternatively, you can contact the municipal police at the *presidencia municipal* (tel. 953/533-0017).

Get your laundry done at handy **Lavandería Delij** (9 A.M.–8 P.M. daily except Sun.), on Zaragoza, a block and a half uphill from the Hotel Puerto Mexico on the highway.

Getting There and Away

Bus lines **Omnibus Cristóbal Colón** and **Sur** (across from the plaza, tel. 953/533-0699) operate jointly out of their highway-front station. Their buses connect southeast with Oaxaca City (transfer at Nochixtlán); northwest via Huajuapan with Cuatla (Morelos), and Mexico City; and southwest with Teposcolula, Tlaxiaco, Juxtlahuaca, and Putla, where you can transfer to a bus headed for Pinotepa Nacional on the Pacific coast.

For drivers, via Highway 190, Tamazulapan is approximately 84 miles (133 km) or two hours northwest of Oaxaca City, and 25 miles (41 km) or 45 minutes southeast of Huajuapan. By paved secondary road via Tejupan, Tamazulapan is 22 miles (34 km) or 45 minutes west of Coixtlahuaca; via paved Highway 190–Highway 125, it is 22 miles (36 km) or 45 minutes north of Teposcolula.

Dependable van service provides connections south with Oaxaca, and north with Huajuapan. Reserve and buy tickets at their small office at the Restaurant Mar y Tierra (tel. 953/533-0705), just north of the Hotel Dom Pedro. Other vans, which connect with southern Mixteca destinations of Teposcolula and Tlaxiaco, stop across the street.

TEPOSCOLULA

Although smaller in population than Tamazulapan, Teposcolula (pop. 5,000) continues to outrank it as district capital, a distinction it gained way back in 1740. Its history, however, reaches back much farther. When the Spanish arrived in the 1520s, they found well-established Mixtec towns on the hillsides above a beautiful lake-filled valley. They drained the lake for farmland and moved the population down to Teposcolula's present location. Abiding by common practice, the Spanish kept the Mixtec name, Teposcolula (Place Surrounded by Springs), tacking on the Catholic patronal title San Pedro y San Pablo. This produced a name so long that practically no one refers to the official San Pedro y San Pablo Teposcolula. People, however, still remember the old preconquest settlements on the hillsides. The old palace and temple foundations still stand, as El Fortín (The Fort) on the uphill slope behind the town and Pueblo Viejo (Old Town) on the pine-clad hilltop across the valley.

Orient yourself by standing (or imagining you're standing) on the sidewalk on the through-town highway, facing the tree-shaded town plaza. North will be straight ahead, toward the cartoon-bright, repainted *presidencia municipal* on the far side of the plaza. The main streets are 20 de Noviembre (the highway), Madero (along the plaza's left, west side), and Iturbide (along the plaza's right, east side). Diagonally on your left stands the renowned Templo y Ex-Convento de San Pedro y San Pablo.

🄲 Templo y Ex-Convento de San Pedro y San Pablo

Most visitors head right over to the venerable 1538 Dominican church and ex-convent, one of Oaxaca's most important, not only for its historical significance, but also for its monumental architecture, much of which you can view from the exterior by walking around to the church's back (west) side. Here rises the famous recently restored **Capilla Abierta** (Open Chapel), with massive, soaring arches and gigantic buttresses. Visitors often wonder why such a huge outdoor chapel was needed right next to an equally massive indoor church. The adjacent grassy expanse provides the reason. It's the **atrium,** the extension of the outdoor

chapel, the largest in Mexico, where the Dominican builders imagined 10,000 native faithful (so numerous that they were not allowed inside) gathering for mass. Although their vision was fulfilled for a span of perhaps a generation after the conquest, European diseases had decimated the Mixtec population by 1600, leaving the huge expanse, equal to three football fields, forever empty.

Walk inside the church and you'll see the original towering gilded **retablo,** which was removed from behind the altar and placed on the left side of the nave. Straight ahead, replacing it in the apse, behind the altar, rises a cheerier, simpler facade of saints, angels, and gilded flowers, that surrounds the diminutive town patron, the **Señor de Vidrieras** (literally "Lord of the Glass Box"), visible from within his protective, glass-paned compartment. And, finally, above all the glitter, high over the altar, presides the omnipresent, all-seeing eye of God.

© BRUCE WHIPPERMAN

THE MIXTECA

The celebrated Capilla Abierta (Open Chapel) graces the grand, grassy atrium of Templo y Ex-Convento de San Pedro y San Pablo.

Local people celebrate their Señor de Vidrieras in a big eight-day festival culminating on the first Friday of Lent (Cuaresma). Events include traffic-stopping processions, pilgrimages, a flower parade, plenty of fireworks, crowning of a queen, floats, bull roping and riding, and a big community dance.

Find the door to the **ex-convent** (9 A.M.–5 P.M. daily) at the rear of the nave. The ex-convent serves mostly as a museum of paintings by noted 16th-century artists Andrés de la Concha and Simón Pereyns. As you walk, see if you can recognize the functions—refectory (dining), kitchen, chapel, cloister, monks' cells (upstairs)—of the various rooms that you pass by or through. (See the sidebar *Building Churches* in *The Valley of Oaxaca* chapter.)

During your visit, at the end of the refectory (monks' dining hall) be sure to see the fresh, very recognizable modern or restored painting of Jesus with wounds, at the right hand of a very youthful God the Father, with the Holy Spirit (in the form of a radiant dove) above them. In the middle of the refectory, also notice the interesting painting of St. Michael the Archangel, dangling a fish. Also, around the cloister, note the paintings that depict the baptism, school days, mission, and dreams of Santo Domingo.

Archaeological Sites and Casa de la Cacica

If you're interested in historic ruins, you might inquire at the *presidencia municipal* for a guide to lead you to the **El Fortín** and **Pueblo Viejo** archaeological sites. (*Note:* Don't try to go to these sites without permission, since local folks are rightly suspicious of strangers poking around their archaeological zones.)

A close-in, handsomely restored site that you can visit without permission is the Casa de la Cacica (kah-SEE-kah, House of the Chiefess). Walk west about three blocks along the street heading due west from the middle of the church's huge grassy atrium. The street ends at a school, and on the right is the Casa de la Cacica.

The building is unique, for it is one of the few restored stone structures built by the Spanish specifically for indigenous nobles. The Spaniards' motivation was probably to concentrate and thus more easily control the local Mixtec population, who were living in dispersed hillside settlements when the Spanish arrived. They built a house and evidently persuaded the local *cacica* to live there, hoping that her people would follow her. Presumably, the House of the Chiefess will eventually become a museum or community cultural center, or both.

Finally, before you leave town, be sure to visit the **carcel** (jail) at the *presidencia* on the plaza. There, the prisoners make and sell handicrafts, such as leather belts, leather-covered mescal flasks, and miniature-shoe key rings.

Accommodation and Food

Teposcolula's first hotel (at least in recent times), the **Hotel Juvi** (tel. 953/518-2064, $13 s, $16 d in one bed, $17 d in two beds, $19 t, $22 q) now makes an overnight stay possible. The hotel's layout remains unique—12 rooms around a parking courtyard containing the last remnant, a grain storage crib, of the ancient family homestead. Children of the original ancestors have built a brand-new, sparely furnished (but clean) lodging, with bare, correctly country Mexican fluorescent bulbs to go with the shiny new bathroom fixtures.

You can buy basic food supplies at a plaza-front *abarroterías*, a bakery *(panadería)* (on Iturbide, a block behind the *presidencia municipal,* tel. 953/537-8683, 8 A.M.–8 P.M. daily) or treat yourself to a hearty afternoon *comida* at the town's good (but pricey) **Restaurant Eunice** (tel. 953/518-2017, 8 A.M.–8 P.M. Sun.–Fri., $4–6), a block behind the east side of the *presidencia municipal.*

Alternatively, go to the modest but clean **Temita** (1–9 P.M. daily, $3–6) restaurant, a block east (Oaxaca direction) of the plaza, by the Cristóbal Colón–Sur bus station.

Information and Services

If you're sick, consult Dr. Brigido Vidal in his **Farmacia Nelly** (on the plaza-front east side,

by the highway, tel. 953/518-2072, 9A.M.–
2P.M., 5–9 P.M. Mon.–Sat.). Alternatively,
go to the **Centro de Salud** (doctor available
8 A.M.–2 P.M. and 4–6 P.M. daily, 24 hours in
emergency)—follow Calle Madero, uphill, past
the *presidencia municipal's* west end. After two
blocks, turn left, west, and continue three long
blocks to the *centro de salud*, on the right.

For police or fire emergencies, contact the
police at the *presidencia municipal,* north side
of the plaza.

To mail a letter, make a phone call, or use
a fax, go to the *telégrafo* (on Madero, upstairs,
half a block north of the plaza's northwest corner, tel. 953/512-0057), or the *correo* (downstairs, both open 9 A.M.–3 P.M. Mon.–Sat.).
After hours, go to the *larga distancia* office (tel.
953/518-2088, 7 A.M.–10:30 P.M. daily) across
the highway from the plaza.

Getting There and Away

Bus transportation to and from Teposcolula
is easy and frequent. Bus passengers arrive at
and depart from the bus station (Autobuses
Sur, Omnibus Cristóbal Colón, and Fletes y
Pasajes, tel. 953/518-2000) on Highway 125,
half a block east from the plaza. Buses connect southeast with Oaxaca City, north with
Tamazulapan, Huajuapan, and Mexico City,
and south with Tlaxiaco, Juxtlahuaca, and
Putla (where connections are available with
Pinotepa Nacional on the Pacific coast).

Long distance **Viajes Turísticos Tlaxiaco**
vans connect frequently with Oaxaca and
Tlaxiaco, from the small station directly across
the highway from the town plaza.

For drivers, Highway 125 runs right past
Teposcolula's town plaza, about eight miles
(13 km) southwest of its junction with the
Oaxaca City–Mexico City Highway 190.
From Oaxaca, using the *cuota autopista* (toll
expressway), drivers should allow around
two hours to safely cover the approximately
78-mile (125-km) Oaxaca City–Teposcolula
distance; add at least another hour if going
by the old *libre* route. From Tamazulapan in
the north, allow about 45 minutes for the 22
miles (36 km) via Highway 190–Highway 125

and about an hour for the 29 miles (47 km)
along Highway 125 to or from Tlaxiaco in the
south.

YUCUNAMA

Teposcolula's petite neighbor, Yucunama
(pop. 600), is attractive partly *because* of its
small size. Imagine taking a seat on a stone
bench one bright, blue summer morning in
Yucunama's flower-decorated town plaza.
Birds flit in the bushes and perch, singing,
in the trees. Now and then, someone crosses
the square and returns your *"Buenos días."* You
admire the proud, whitewashed bandstand at
the plaza center; behind it rises the old church
facade, patriotically decorated like a birthday
cake in red, white, and green. From the plaza,
cobbled streets pass rustic stone houses and
continue downhill to verdant fields, which, in
the distance, give way to lush oak and pine-
tufted woodlands.

Although it sounds too good to be true, it
isn't. Yucunama's beauty is probably one reason that Mixtec people have been living there
for at least 4,000 years. Its name, which means
Hill of Soap, perhaps reflects the town's spic-
and-span plaza, clean-swept streets, and newly
painted public buildings. It's a pure Mixtec
town, for although Yucunama is part of the
Teposcolula district, Spanish settlers never
lived here. In fact, in 1585 the all-Mixtec
townsfolk declared themselves an independent republic. Nothing came of that, but
Yucunama's people nevertheless retain their
independent spirit.

Make **Bee Nu'u** (House of the People, tel.
951/526-1455), on the plaza opposite the dignified, porticoed *presidencia municipal,* your first
stop. Best call ahead for an appointment with
a guide to open the museum for you. Lacking
this, be sure to arrive early on a weekday at
the *presidencia municipal* and ask if someone
might open the museum for you. Say (or show
them) this: *"¿Puede alguién mostrar el museo
para nosotros?"* ("Can someone show us the
museum?")

The museum's several very interesting exhibits include the original of the Lienzo

Yucunama, an *amate* (wild fig bark paper) document from the 1300s that details the 35 tribute payments of a Yucunama Mixtec noblewoman with the name-date 5-Eagle, and her first and second husbands, 12-Flower and 10-Eagle, to her father, who lived in a nearby town. In the cabinet below the *lienzo* stands a copy of the famous **Codex Nuttall** (folded like an accordion), which details, in full color, the exploits of the renowned Mixtec lord 8-Deer. Your guide may be able to provide some details (including odysseys to Coatzacoalcos on the Gulf Coast, and perhaps as far as Panama) of 8-Deer's adventures. If you don't understand Spanish, the museum is well worth bringing a friend to translate for you.

Another fascinating exhibit displays the complete remains of a robust 70-year-old noblewoman (notice her very husky leg bones) and the trove of goods recovered from her grave, one of a score of burials retrieved locally by archaeologists.

Yucunama's richness as an archaeological zone is further evidenced by the two 1996 INAH (National Institute of Archaeology and History) survey maps of the buried remains of a pair of early Classic-period (300 B.C.–A.D. 300) towns nearby. If you're strongly interested, ask at the *presidencia* and you may be able to get permission and a guide. Expect to pay $20 for a full-day guided trip; transportation is extra.

On the other hand, you can step outside the museum and guide yourself on a short stroll to a pair of nearby local sights. Walk down Calle Independencia (from the museum, follow the left side of the plaza, past the *presidencia*) about three long blocks east to the picture-perfect **town fountain,** fed by the old town aqueduct. You may see women doing the day's laundry in the adjacent arched public washhouse basins. A block south and a couple more blocks downhill east, at the end of Calle Libertad, you can marvel at Yucunama's oldest resident, the gigantic 1,000-year-old **Tule,** or *ahuehuete* tree (Mexican cypress, *Taxodium mucronatum*), a distant cousin of the California redwood. If you get lost, you can identify El Tule by its

tall, bushy green silhouette, or mention El Tule (TOO-lay) to anyone.

Festivals

You'll have even more fun if you arrive during one of Yucunama's festivals. The biggest is the patronal **Fiesta de San Pedro Mártir de Verona,** which culminates on April 29. Festivities begin on April 26 with a *calenda* (procession) and plenty of *mescal, aguardiente,* and *pulque* for those so inclined. Sometimes town men dress up like women and perform the dance of the *mascaritas* (little masks). The fun continues with more processions, plenty of flowers, food, fireworks, masses, and a dance on April 29.

Other especially festive times in Yucunama include the fiesta of the Virgen del Rosario (first Sunday in October), El Día de los Muertos (Day of the Dead, November 1 and 2), and the Christmas Eve procession, where everyone in town accompanies the infant Jesus to the church, then watches (or does) the traditional dance of the Pastor y Pastorela (Shepherd and Shepherdess).

Getting There and Away

Yucunama is about six miles (nine km) northwest of the Highway 125–Highway 190 intersection. Drivers, follow the signed graded gravel road that takes off from the north corner of the intersection. By bus, ride a Cristóbal Colón, Sur, or Fletes y Pasajes bus to the Highway 125–Highway 190 intersection, then hike the six miles (nine km) or ride a *colectivo* van or truck from there. A number of snack stands and small stores at the intersection can provide water and food.

YANHUITLÁN

It sometimes seems a miracle that the Dominican padres, against heavy odds and isolated as they were in the far province of Oaxaca, were able to build such masterpieces as their convent and church in Yanhuitlán. Upon reflection, however, their accomplishments seem less miraculous when you realize the mountain of help the padres received.

When Father Domingo de la Cruz began the present church, in 1541, Yanhuitlán retained the prosperity and the large skilled population that it had when it was a reigning Mixtec kingdom prior to the arrival of the Spanish. For a workforce, de la Cruz used the labor of thousands of Mixtec workers and artisans, who deserve much of the credit for the masterfully refined monuments that they erected.

And monuments, indeed, they still are. Approaching Yanhuitlán from the northwest, the road reaches a point where the entire Yanhuitlán Valley spreads far below. In the bright afternoon sun, the white-shining, massively buttressed Yanhuitlán church and adjacent atrium (now soccer field), big enough for 15,000 indigenous faithful, dwarfs everything else in sight.

Up close, you see why. The building's exquisitely sculptured Renaissance facade towers overhead, making those standing on the front steps appear like ants. A graceful semicircular arch frames the entrance, while in the niche to the left stands the robed St. Francis of Assisi. In the right niche, Santa Margarita de Alacoque occupies the position customarily reserved in Dominican church facades for Santo Domingo de Guzmán, the Dominican order's revered founder. Santo Domingo is nevertheless present. Directly above the front portal, a masterful relief of Holy Mother Mary shelters a diminutive Santo Domingo and Santa Catarina de Siena, like small children, beneath her cape.

The church, officially the **Templo y Ex-Convento de Santo Domingo de Guzmán,** is as much a museum of national treasures as it is a place of worship. In fact, it is divided so: The ex-convent, which you enter on the right, has been converted to a **museum** (9 A.M.–3 P.M. daily). Inside, you begin to appreciate the gigantic proportions of the place as you circle the cloister, passing beneath ponderous but delicately designed arches that appear to sprout and spread from stone cloister columns like branches from giant trees. On the stairway leading upstairs at the cloister's corner, don't miss the mural of Jesus dressed

© BRUCE WHIPPERMAN

Templo y Ex-Convento de Santo Domingo de Guzmán

like a 16th-century dandy except for his bare feet and the little angel perched on his shoulder.

The nave glows with golden decorations. Overhead, stone rib arches support the ceiling completely, without the need of columns, creating a single soaring heavenly space. Up front, above the altar, Santo Domingo presides, gazing piously toward heaven, his forehead decorated by a medallion that appears remarkably like a Hindu *tilak*. Before you exit, take a look by the front door for the dramatic painting of Jesus, whip in hand, driving the money changers from the temple.

Get to Yanhuitlán, on Highway 190, by Sur, Fletes y Pasajes, or Omnibus Cristóbal Colón bus. By car, head 12 miles (19 km) north along Highway 190 from Nochixtlán (62 miles from Oaxaca via the toll expressway, allow an hour and a half), or 23 miles (37 km) south from Tamazulapan.

THE MIXTECA

Dominican Route North

This corner of the Mixteca hides a treasury of undiscovered gems, just right for adventurers hankering to follow the road less traveled. First, make sure you spend some time at the grand old Dominican church at Coixtlahuaca, the Templo y Ex-Convento de San Juan Bautista. Then continue north to the hamlet of San Miguel Tequixtepec to contemplate the ancient (1590) stone bridge, the community museum's mammoth fossils, continue on a prehistoric rock painting excursion, and finally enjoy an overnight in Tequixtepec's cozy community-built *cabaña* lodging. Carry on north to Tepelmeme de Morelos and culminate your adventure by boulder-hopping down into a tropical canyon to the astonishingly grand Puente Colosal.

COIXTLAHUACA

Coixtlahuaca (koh-eeks-tlah-OOAH-kah, pop. 3,000), although the capital of an entire governmental district encompassing a significant fraction of the Mixteca Baja's *municipios,* is a modest town even by Oaxaca standards. Before the conquest, it was a powerful Chocho-speaking (Chocholteco) chiefdom, so strong that in the 1400s the Coixtlahuaca warriors stopped the invading Aztecs, forcing them to detour through Tlaxiaco. During colonial times and through the 19th century, Coixtlahuaca continued to be an important Chocholteco market center. But depopulation by emigration and increased education and literacy in Spanish have reduced the number of Chocho speakers to a handful of elderly folks in the surrounding countryside.

Most visitors enter Coixtlahuaca by the *cuota autopista* from Oaxaca City. Just inside the edge of town, a big sign on the left marks the road north to San Miguel Tequixtepec. Straight ahead a couple more blocks, most drivers turn right on Independencia, the main town street. Nearly all stores and services are spread along Independencia, which continues several blocks past the town plaza and then the church, both above and to the left of the street. Bus passengers will arrive at the Autobuses Sur station, on Independencia, in the town center.

Sights

Coixtlahuaca's past importance is reflected in its grand church, the **Templo y Ex-Convento de San Juan Bautista,** one of Oaxaca's largest. Inside, its nave stretches to the proportions of a grand European cathedral, its vault soaring overhead, supported by a delicate network of brilliantly painted colored stone arches. Dominican friar Francisco Marín, Coixtlahuaca's first vicar, was the moving force behind all this grandeur, initiating construction in 1546. Although the Reforms forced closure of the convent in 1856, the Dominicans continued to run it as a church until 1906, when locally based "secular" clergy took over.

In addition to its robust proportions, the

the massive but lovely church at Coixtlahuaca

church has much of interest. As you enter, notice the dark-complexioned image of African padre San Martín de Porres, in a friar's robe, on the right. Farther into the nave, gaze overhead and admire the whirling, rainbow-hued floral designs, lovingly executed by long-dead native artists. All are original, although time and recent replastering have erased much that you don't see. On the right, take a look at the unusually large side altar to the Virgin of Guadalupe and continue to the main altar, where St. John the Baptist, Coixtlahuaca's patron saint, presides at the foot of the towering, gilded *retablo* (altarpiece).

The town is mostly quiet, except for fiestas, which include the patronal festival of San Juan Bautista, around June 24, and the festival of the Señor del Calvario (Lord of Calvary), during the last half of May. The fiestas include processions, carnival games, traditional food, the hazardous *jaripeo*, and the Jarabe Chocholteco traditional Coixtlahuaca courtship dance.

Accommodations and Food

The only hotel along the expressway between Nochixtlán and Tehuacán, Puebla, is the local **Hotel Marina Sol** (Calle Independencia s/n, no telephone, $15 d). Although it has been neglected in recent years, renovations are in the works. The owner's motivation is most likely the ongoing renovation of the church across the street and the lavish *parador turístico* (tourist center), recently built (but not yet operating at the time of this writing).

Although the Hotel Marina Sol's rooms have been of the basic bare-bulb variety, they're clean and spacious, with shower-bath and hot water. Summer humidity, however, has, in the past, caused the rooms to accumulate mildew. If so, beds will need fresh linens; don't hesitate to request them before moving in. Guests additionally enjoy a tranquil (but neglected) garden setting, decorated with statuesque green Roman cypresses, and a countryside-view deck behind the reception. (You may have to ask around for the manager, who has been present only when guests were expected. If you can't find the manager, or the rooms

are unacceptable, best lodge in San Miguel Tequixtepec, a few miles north.)

As for food, Coixtlahuaca has two or three ordinary *comedores* and taco shops on Independencia, plus the highly recommendable **Restaurant Blanquita** downhill on the entrance road from the expressway, a block below the north road to San Miguel Tequixtepec. Blanquita is open for breakfast (good *huevos a la Mexicana*, $2.50) when the first customer knocks on the door in the morning. Other specialties include *guisado de res* (beef stew, $2.50) for *comida* and quesadillas (two for $2) for *cena*.

Another Coixtlahuaca pleasant surprise is the **Frutería Juquilita** fruit store (8 A.M.–8 P.M. daily) on the street above the town plaza and *presidencia*.

Furthermore, some stores also offer a pair of renowned Coixtlahuaca baked specialties: *menudencia* rolls—big, brown, and not too sweet, sprinkled with a bit of sesame—and pancake cubes, made with alcoholic *pulque* instead of water.

Information and Services

Other services along Independencia include a combined *farmacia–larga distancia*, La Lupita. At the town plaza, a few blocks east, before the church, next to the plaza-front library, find the *telégrafos* (9 A.M.–3:30 P.M. Mon.–Fri.) for fax and money orders. Also find a *correo* (9 A.M.–3:30 P.M. Mon.–Fri.) nearby. Additionally, there is a *centro de salud* tucked on the side street, between the town plaza and the church grounds.

For handicrafts shoppers, **Artesanías del Sur** store (Independencia 20, tel. 953/503-5475), next to the bus station, offers a fetching collection of locally-crafted pottery, woven palm baskets, sombreros, wooden toys and trinkets, and more.

Getting There

Get to Coixtlahuaca from the Oaxaca City first-class bus terminal by Sur bus via Nochixtlán. Depart Coixtlahuaca from the bus terminal on Independencia, via first- and second-class Sur buses that connect east with Nochixtlán (thence Oaxaca City), south with Tlaxiaco via

THE MIXTECA

Teposcolula, and north with Mexico City via Puebla.

Drivers from Oaxaca City simply follow the *cuota autopista* north approximately 70 miles (113 km), 80 minutes, to Coixtlahuaca. From Tamazulapan, Yanhuitlán, or Teposcolula, drivers get to Coixtlahuaca via the paved road east from the Highway 190 junction at Tejupan, south of Tamazulapan, continuing an easy 15 miles (24 km) to Coixtlahuaca.

SAN MIGUEL TEQUIXTEPEC

Tequixtepec is the Aztec translation of the town's original Chocho name, Jna Niingui (Hill of the Conch). Local legend says that Tequixtepec was the site of a now-lost temple dedicated to the god of the conch.

The local region comprises the *municipio* of San Miguel Tequixtepec; once rich, fertile, and thickly populated, it has fallen on hard times. Overgrazing, tree cutting, and selling the stones from the old irrigation terraces have degraded the Tequixtepec region into a semi-desert. Many hills are half-eroded, bare stone. Some good land exists at the stream bottoms, but many people are discouraged by such hardscrabble farming. Most residents leave to work for a year in Oaxaca City, Mexico City, or the United States, then come back and live for three or four years on their earnings. The population has dwindled from 3,000 around 1900 to perhaps 400 now.

It turns out, however, that San Miguel Tequixtepec is a village with grit. It shows in the people and their efforts to reverse their fortunes. A major moving force behind the local folks' determination is personable community leader Juan Cruz Reyes, who spearheaded the remodeling of a ruined schoolhouse into a working museum, now a focus for showing off Tequixtepec's valuable touristic assets: a graceful 1909 *presidencia municipal,* a dignified 18th-century church, woven-palm handicrafts, and, in the vicinity, a colonial-era fossil bridge and prehistoric rock paintings.

Sights

If you arrive heading north along the road

from Coixtlahuaca, after about five miles (eight km) you cross a creek bridge, where you can gaze upon an adjacent crumbling early colonial-era **stone-arched bridge.** It's a remnant of Tequixtepec's glory days, when merchants marketed small fortunes of locally grown silk and red cochineal dye. Tequixtepec tradition says that one such merchant, Don Diego de San Miguel, built the bridge around 1590 to easily transport his valuable silk and cochineal to the formerly big market in Coixtlahuaca. (Although still crossable on foot at this writing, the old bridge is in bad shhape. Hopefully, it will be restored before it falls victim to one of Oaxaca's frequent earthquakes.)

At the town plaza two miles (three km) farther north, make your first stop at the **community museum.** If available, a volunteer will show you the exhibits of local historical lore, fossils (notably, a huge mammoth tusk), local archaeological finds, and handicrafts. (If the museum is closed, ask around to see if someone, such as Juan Cruz Reyes, might be available to open it up for you.)

If you've made a prior appointment (see *Guides* later in this section), volunteers will be available to show you around the town, probably starting at the town church, the **Parroquia de San Miguel Arcángel,** built of locally quarried rose *cantera* stone and finished in 1766. The vases you see topping the churchyard fence are from Atzompa, near Oaxaca City, and are always ready to be filled with flowers during the town's festivals. Foremost is the big September 27–29 town patronal fiesta in honor of San Miguel. Highlights include traditional dances, such as the Cristianos y Moros (Christians and Moors), each of the festival days. Other important fiestas are celebrated on Palm Sunday (Domingo de Ramos) and Sábado de Gloria (the Saturday before Easter Sunday), when people, for the occasion called *mecos,* don masks and do a kind of adult trick or treat. They go from store to store, asking for something to drink and dancing with whomever is present. Yet another important day in Tequixtepec is Sunday, when, between 3 and 4 P.M., teams face off for a game of *pelota mixteca,* the local version of the ancient Mesoamerican ball game.

As you walk around town, be sure to ask your guide to take you to someone who is weaving palm leaves. This won't be difficult, since everyone appears to be doing it during most of their waking hours. Townsfolk gather and sun dry the leaves of the little local wild palms, which they craft into a number of useful items, notably mats, grain bags, rope, and sombreros. Although their reward (about $0.25 for a sombrero) is pathetically small, at least the raw materials are free and everyone seems to have plenty of time on their hands. This is especially true during the hot (February–June) dry season, when people do their weaving in cool, backyard *cuevas* (caves), most often in the company of others, when work becomes a party.

Something else you shouldn't miss during your around-town walk is a traditional *temazcal* (ritual hot room). Many local traditional curers have built *temazcales* of stone in their backyards for healing, especially for women after childbirth.

Finally, if the season is right, don't miss sampling a *tuna* (cactus apple). Simply pluck one from the leaf-tip of the many neighborhood nopal (prickly pear) cactuses. If it's red and ripe, you'll be in for a sweet, delicious treat.

Guides

It is best to have made an appointment before arriving at the Tequixtepec museum. Call the Tequixtepec long-distance phone (tel. 953/503-5407, in Spanish) directly. If your Spanish is rusty, ask a friend or your hotel desk clerk to do it for you. Leave a message (or a fax: ask for *"tono fax, por favor"*) telling your arrival time. Either Juan Cruz Reyes or another of the museum committee members should reply. You can also contact them weeks ahead of time by writing to the Museo Comunitario, Juan Cruz Reyes, Presidente, Domocilio Conocido, San Miguel Tequixtepec, Oaxaca 79360.

Even if you arrive unannounced (but by noon) you still might be able to hire a guide (Spanish-speaking only) to lead you to the rock paintings for a modest fee, perhaps $20. If not Juan Cruz himself, Nazario Zacarias Zacarias, Jacobo Cruz Gúzman, and Joventino Cruz Cruz are all capable and competent.

Hieroglyphic Rock Painting Excursion

Farther afield, but well worth a day's time for travelers interested in antiquities and the great outdoors, are the local *pinturas rupestres* (rock paintings), which adorn the walls of a nearby river canyon. The jumping-off point, for which you certainly will need a guide, is Rancho La Barrete, a few miles from town, where a rocky but easy trail heads down into a shallow canyon, the Arroyo Palo Solo Arroyo, of the local Río Grande.

As you descend, keep quiet and keep your eyes peeled for armadillo, coyote, deer, fox, skunk, wild turkeys, or any of a host of bird species. Your immediate destination is the **Cueva de la Iglesia**—a sacred site where

© BRUCE WHIPPERMAN

Temazcales, sauna-like hot rooms, are used by women for recovery after childbirth and to treat common ailments.

THE MIXTECA

children used to be baptized on a large flat rock below the cave. In the cave above, you can see an eagle's nest; nearby is a prehistoric painting dubbed the "alligator man."

Farther down the canyon, climb over a low ridge and cross an often-dry tributary, the Río Seca. Soon you pass Peña Pirul and Peña Amarillo, a pair of painting-decorated cliff faces pocked with caves, and, above, ancient walls and irrigation terraces. Finally, after passing through a forest of moss-draped trees, comes the climax, the **Peña de los Guerreros** (Rock of the Warriors), adorned with plumed figures carrying shields and feathered lances.

Practicalities

Tequixtepec townsfolk, with government help, have built a pair of comfortable *cabañas* (tel. 953/503-5407, $6 per person) on the town plaza, adjacent to the *presidencia municipal*. Each has bunk beds and hot-water showers for overnight visitors. Bring your own towel and soap. Moreover, you can camp by tent or self-contained RV, for which it would be no problem to obtain permission from the generally hospitable townsfolk. Ask Juan Cruz Reyes or one of the other museum volunteers. Call the Tequixtepec number, tel. 953/503-5407, for *cabaña* reservations (although they will not generally be necessary).

If the above fails, you might contact the **Oaxaca Alternative Tourism department** in downtown Oaxaca (Murguia 206, up the driveway, in the back, tel. 951/516-0123, info@aoaxaca.com, www.oaxaca.travel/alternativo) for information and reservations.

Basic fruits, vegetables, and foodstuffs are available at a pair of grocery stores, one of which also runs the long-distance telephone. It's on the corner across the main street, half a block south from the museum. The other, a block north, is run by the friendly sisters Elvia and Cari Córdoba Reyes. Given half a day's notice, the sisters will also cook hearty, wholesome, reasonably priced meals for you.

Getting There

From Oaxaca, get to Tequixtepec by bus via Nochixtlán and Coixtlahuaca. From the Oaxaca City first-class terminal, ride a bus, such as Sur or Cristóbal Colón, to Nochixtlán. Continue via Sur to Coixtlahuaca, where you can catch a *colectivo* north the seven miles (11 km) to Tequixtepec.

Bus passengers can also get to Coixtlahuaca, thence Tequixtepec, from Tamazulapan, by the Sur bus line, via the paved road through Tejupan.

For drivers, access to Tequixtepec is also best through Coixtlahuaca. From Oaxaca City, simply follow the *cuota autopista* north approximately 70 miles (113 km), 80 minutes, to Coixtlahuaca, and continue another seven miles (11 km) north via the signed gravel road (that forks left as you enter Coixtlahuaca) to Tequixtepec.

From Tamazulapan, Teposcolula, or Yanhuitlán, access is best via the paved road that intersects Highway 190 at Tejupan, from which Coixtlahuaca is an easy, scenic 15-mile (24-km) half-hour drive.

TEPELMEME DE MORELOS

Before the Spanish conquest, Tepelmeme de Morelos (pop. 1,600), eight miles (13 km) north of Tequixtepec, was a semi-independent chiefdom, a tributary of Nochixtlán, at times allied with neighboring Mixtec and Ixcatec chiefdoms. The Mixtec connection was so strong that anthropologists sometimes speak of pre-conquest Tepelmeme as a fused Mixtec-Chochotec culture. Tepelmeme's earliest Christian church, founded by the Dominican missionaries not long after the conquest, was built over an earlier Mixtec-style temple at the same spot where the present church stands on the town plaza.

Despite Spanish dominance, Tepelmeme's Chocho-speaking rulers retained influence over their people into the 18th century. At that time, during the 80 years until 1743, their dynasty was united with the Ixcatec kingdom of Ixcatlán, to the northwest. The great majority of Tepelmeme people continued to speak Chocho until around 1900, when improved education and Spanish literacy began to reduce the number of Chocho speakers to the small group of elderly folks who still speak it.

The present town appears to be the rival metropolis of the Coixtlahuaca district, sometimes overshadowing the district capital in hustle and bustle. The source of Tepelmeme's prosperity is its relatively fertile valley soil, not nearly as eroded as many other Mixteca communities. Some farmers, consequently, have money for wells, pumps, and electricity for irrigation. A number are prosperous enough to even own tractors.

Sights

Tepelmeme, laid out along a north–south axis, has two town plazas. The more formal of the two, a *jardín* with grass and a promenade-encircled bandstand, borders the church on its east side and the *presidencia municipal* on the south. Further south, behind the *presidencia*, is the town's real heart—the scruffy but seasonally busy market plaza.

Unfortunately, the community museum, **Niace** (nee-AH-say), which in Chocho means Mountain of Honey, has been closed in recent years. You might check with the town officials at the *presidencia* (tel. 953/506-6149 or 953/506-6143) to see if the museum has reopened. If so, you will have the pleasure of seeing the museum's collection, mainly artifacts, including a huge ceremonial conch shell uncovered from one of the region's several excavated archaeological sites. Most prominent are the copies of the ancient but sophisticated glyphs painted on the cliff face at the awesome Puente Colosal natural bridge.

Townsfolk built the *jardín*-front church, the newly restored **Templo de Santo Domingo de Gúzman,** in 1769 to replace an earlier, conquest-era church. Community adoration culminates here during the major August 1–4 festival in celebration of Santo Domingo. Folks mark his memory with pilgrimages, processions, baptisms, confirmations, fireworks, and a big carnival.

Inside, don't miss the right transept chapel, dedicated to the Sacred Heart of Jesus. Here, you'll find several intriguing banners, one for each of the town's *mayordomías,* the community organizations separately responsible for Tepelmeme's 10 yearly religious festivals. The pervasive influence of the *mayordomías* is visible, both separately during the individual festivals

that they each organize, and collectively, on the first Friday morning of each month, when their dozens of members, representing virtually all the town's families, gather to parade their five respective banners around the *jardín.*

◖ Puente Colosal and Huerta de Juquila

With a prior appointment, a Tepelmeme guide (call the Tepelmeme *presidencia,* tel. 953/506-6149 or 953/506-6143) will be available to escort you (13 miles/21 km) to the point of departure for the two-mile (three-km), two-hour round-trip hike down a forested boulder-strewn creek bottom to Puente Colosal. Here it appears as if a glacier era lake once filled a deep limestone box canyon. Over eons, the water gradually dissolved the limestone, finally scooping out a yawning, 200-foot-high (60-meter-high) tunnel through a towering mountain ridge. The result is spectacular Puente Colosal, probably the world's tallest natural stone bridge.

Puente Colosal has most certainly inspired awe in human visitors for thousands of years. Some inscribed their presence, in both primitive rock paintings and refined (probably city-state stage A.D. 1000–1500) Mixtec glyphs, graphically painted on Puente Colosal's stone face. Someday, when archaeologists finally crack the ancient Mixtec code, humanity will know what Puente Colosal inspired them to record for posterity on its stark bedrock walls.

Get there—by permission only, through the Tepelmeme municipal authorities—accompanied by a local guide. A rugged, high-clearance vehicle is necessary for the last few miles of this route: Mark your odometer at the Tepelmeme town center. Head north through town to the expressway entrance (1.2 miles/2 km). Continue north to the expressway bridge, Puente La Unión (six miles/9.6 km). With caution, just before the bridge, exit left at the unofficial dirt driveway. Cross back over the expressway via the bridge, then, after a fraction of a mile, turn right (6.3 miles/10 km) at the T at Ranchería La Unión. At mile 8.3 (13.4 km), turn left at another T, at Ranchería Puerto Mixteco. Continue down a mountain-rimmed farm valley past a hillside spring and small dam at Rosario (10.4 miles/16.7 km). Continue down-canyon via the increasingly rough track to road's end (13.5 miles/21.7 km) and the accommodations cabañas. Puente Colosal is at the downstream end of the canyon. Scramble downhill via a steep trail to the shady stream bottom, then boulder-hop the remaining mile and a half (2.4 km). Although the stream bottom is usually dry, **beware of possible flash flooding** from upstream thunderstorms. Take a hat, binoculars, camera, strong shoes, and drinking water.

Well-equipped wilderness backpackers might enjoy spending an overnight or two beneath Puente Colosal's grand, sheltering rock ceiling. The environs are ripe for wildlife-viewing, expert-grade vertical rock climbing, and exploring past Puente Colosal's downstream portal, where the stream bottom continues into a lush semitropical mountain-walled wild valley.

Even more remote is the locally famous and idyllic **Huerta de Juquila** grove and waterfall. Access, strictly by museum- or municipal-approved guide only, is also north of Tepelmeme via the expressway to Puente La Unión. In this case, however, you turn left at the T (see Puente Colosal directions) at Ranchería La Unión. The route continues another 18 miles (29 km) into the mountainous backcountry on foot or by horseback. The key intermediate destination is Mahusipan village (jeep-accessible, at 13 miles/21 km), where you continue on foot or by horse approximately another five miles (8 km) to Huerta de Juquila.

Practicalities

For accommodation, Tepelmeme offers *cabañas* near the road's end, on the way to Puente Colosal. Reserve by leaving a message at the Tepelmeme *presidencia municipal*

(tel. 953/506-6149 or 953/506-6143) specifying how many in your party and when you'll be arriving. If this fails, contact the government alternative tourism office in Oaxaca City (Murguia 206, up the driveway, in the back, tel. 951/516-0123, info@aoaxaca.com, www.oaxaca.travel).

Tepelmeme has a sprinkling of basic grocery stores and restaurants. Get groceries, fruits, and vegetables at the small mini-super Lupita (about three blocks north of the town plaza, past the river bridge, 8 A.M.–9 P.M. daily). Wholesome cooked breakfast, lunch, and dinner is available at **Cafetería Germel** (8A.M.–8 P.M. Mon.–Sat., $3–6), near the *presidencia*.

For stamps and letter-mailing, go to the *correo* (by the museum on the market plaza's north side, 5–7 P.M. Mon., Wed., and Fri.). If you're ill, go to the *centro de salud*, at the *jardín* southeast corner, between the *presidencia* and the church. You can also make long-distance phone calls at the little *larga distancia* at Lupita grocery, three blocks north of the jardín, past the bridge, before the Sur bus station.

Getting There

Get to Tepelmeme by bus, from Oaxaca City, by Sur bus via Nochixtlán (where you might have to transfer to a Coixtlahuaca-bound bus.) From Coixtlahuaca, you should continue via *colectivo* van or truck the eight more miles (13 km) north to Tepelmeme.

Drivers, from Oaxaca City drive north two hours, approximately 85 miles (137 km), via the *cuota autopista* to the Tepelmeme exit. From Tamazulapan, drivers head along Calle Independencia, which becomes the gravel road leading directly to Tepelmeme (via Teotongo and Ihuitlán). Figure about an hour and a half of relatively easy, but sometimes bumpy, driving for the 27-mile (43-km) trip.

The Mixteca Baja: Land of the Sun

Although its name implies a lowland, the Mixteca Baja is high, seasonally dry, but sunny country. It comprises the 3,000- to 5,000-foot (900- to 1,600-meter) mountain valley and plateauland of northwest Oaxaca. Before the conquest, this land was richer and much more densely populated than today. Irrigated stone-terraced fields graced the hillsides and busy market towns supported large populations of Mixtec-speaking people in the fertile valleys. However, after the conquest, the Spanish soldiers and settlers forcibly congregated the indigenous people into more controllable villages and introduced sheep and goats, which quickly ate up much of natural grassland. Their way of life changed forever, the people abandoned most of their irrigated fields, and their terraces fell into ruin.

Now, however, the people of the Mixteca are making a comeback; they are replanting their fields and rebuilding their their terraces. Furthermore, they offer a modicum of hotels and restaurants and a sprinkling of community museums. These smooth the way for visitors to enjoy the wonders of their land, which vary from natural beauty—crystalline springs, stalactite-hung limestone caves, grand cool groves of ancient *sabino* (Mexican cypress) trees, wildlife-rich river canyons—to the exotic color and bustle of indigenous markets, the mystery of ancient ruined cities, and the fascinating puzzle of the yet-to-be deciphered glyphs of the pre-Columbian Ñuiñe language.

HUAJUAPAN DE LEÓN AND VICINITY

Huajuapan de León (pop. 50,000), with good hotels, restaurants, and many services, makes a comfortable base for enjoying the intriguing corners of the northern Mixteca Baja. Day trips north, via the Tehuacán road, open the fertile, green vale of the Río Mixteco with its colorful hamlets, venerable churches, and ancient archaeological sites. Similarly, excursions south, along the high road to the Mixteca Alta,

reveal a wealth of hiking, camping, boating, and fishing opportunities.

What's even better is that the town itself has much to offer. For first-time arrivals, untouristed Huajuapan de León is a pleasant surprise. The town center—plaza, church, and *presidencia municipal*—is removed a few blocks south of the Highway 190 clutter and bustle. Although the present town dates only from colonial times, the surrounding region, which city hall boosters call Tierra del Sol (Land of the Sun), has been inhabited for many millennia. The extensive Cerro de Las Minas (Hill of the Mines) archaeological zone, just a mile (1.6 km) north of the present town, was a ceremonial, market, and governmental center for thousands of inhabitants during its apex, around A.D. 500. It was excavated and partially restored during the late 1980s.

Huajuapan (a tongue twister; say ooah-WAH-pahn) put itself on the map during Mexico's War of Independence. After two years of seesaw rebellion, national attention focused on Huajuapan, where *insurgente* Valerio Trujano was leading local forces in blocking the advance of a well-disciplined royalist force. Inspired by faith in their patron saint, El Señor de los Corazones (The Lord of the Hearts), the Huajuapan fighters resisted a royalist siege of 111 days, until relieved by Independence hero General José María Morelos on June 23, 1812.

Later, in the early 1820s, Huajuapan's favorite son, Antonio de León (thus, Huajuapan de León) played a crucial role in securing Mexican Independence. He was among the first leaders in conservative Oaxaca to support Agustín de Iturbide's Plan de Iguala, which finally freed Mexico from Spain. Later, León headed the fight against Iturbide when he proclaimed himself emperor and dissolved Congress. León (by then a general at the age of 29) and Nicolas Bravo captured Oaxaca City for republican forces on June 9, 1823.

CERRO DE LAS MINAS

To Mexico City
COLONIA RÍO BALSAS

To Río Mixteco Valley, Puebla, and Mexico City

COLONIA EL CALVARIO

COLONIA TEPEYAC

MAP AREA

COLONIA SANTA CRUZ

COLONIA LOS PRESIDENTES

CLINIC

TELECOM

POST OFFICE

COLONIA LA PROVIDENCIA

Río Mixteco

HOTEL CASABLANCA

To Oaxaca

0   0.5 mi
0   0.5 km

CRISTÓBAL COLÓN/ADO

FLETES Y PASAJES BUS

SUR BUS

BRAVO

HUAJUAPAN DE LEÓN

NECTAR ZAPOTECO

AUTOBUSES BOQUERÓN

FARMACIA AHORRO

★ MUSEO REGIONAL

CONSTITUCIÓN

VALERIO TRUJANO

ARTESANIAS DE PALMA

HOTEL PLAZA DEL ÁNGEL

NATURAL FOOD

NUYOÓ

BAKERY

PRODINETPC.COM

HOTEL TESORO DE MICHAPA

INTERNET

HOTEL COLÓN

COLÓN

ZARAGOZA

To Market Tianguis (Saturday)

FOOD STANDS

FARMACIA REYES

BENITO JUAREZ MARKET

TACO STANDS

CATHEDRAL

HIDALGO

BANAMEX

CAPILLA DEL SEÑOR DE LOS CORAZONES

MADERO

PALACIO MUNICIPAL

DE LEÓN

Plaza Antonio León

DIAZ

RESTAURANTE AJO Y CEBOLLAS

HSBC

CAFÉ PASTICEL

KONICA PHOTO

MONEY EXCHANGE/FED EX

TURISMO "OH TIERRA DEL SOL"

BANCO SANTANDER SERFIN

ANTONIO

GALINDO

RESTAURANT AND HOTEL GARCIA PERAL

AQUILES

SERDÁN

HOTEL LAREDO

PORFIRIO

REFORMA

URRUTIA

LAVANDERÍA EASY

BIG BITE BURGER

TEMPLO EXPIATORIO

VAZQUEZ

0   100 yds
0   100 m

© AVALON TRAVEL

The Plaza

The town's choice people-watching spot is the tranquil, old-fashioned town plaza, **Plaza Central Antonio de León**, bordered by the *presidencia municipal* on its west side. On the plaza's north side stands a distinguished bronze statue of General Antonio de León (1794–1847). Also on the north side, across the street from the plaza, rise the twin spires of the late-19th-century **Catedral de la Virgen de Guadalupe**. A major plaza-front thoroughfare is Antonio de León, on the west side, which becomes Valerio Trujano as it continues north to its highway crossing. On the plaza's east side runs Avenida Porfirio Díaz, which jogs around the back side of the cathedral, becoming Avenida Nuyoo (noo-YOH-oh) as it heads north to the highway.

The plaza's major source of early-evening entertainment is the army of birds, mostly black grackles, who around sunset head from all directions straight for the big, bushy plaza trees. For about an hour, they flutter, cackle, and squabble for perches until they finally settle down for the night.

Stroll over for a look inside the cathedral. For Mexico, this is a new church. Earthquakes repeatedly damaged the previous structures occupying the site since colonial times. The present church, built in the late 1800s, was so severely damaged by earthquakes that it had to be extensively rebuilt and earthquake-proofed in the 1960s. But for the people of Huajuapan, it's not the building but what it contains that counts.

Inside, a brilliantly illuminated Virgin of Guadalupe occupies the main front altar, while in the right-side chapel, the **Capilla del Sagrario del Señor de los Corazones,** a painted celebration of baroque glitter climaxes in the beloved, dark-complexioned Señor hanging limply above the altar. On auspicious days, the faithful arrive in a near-continuous stream to pay their respects. As you leave, look on the wall in the small sub-chapel on the left, just outside the door, for the heart festooned with little metal *milagros* (wish offerings), which beseeching pilgrims have left for the Señor.

[Cerro de las Minas Archaeological Zone

Be sure to spend at least an hour investigating the remains of Cerro de las Minas, a major urban-stage (A.D. 300–800) Mixtec town. Artifacts uncovered on this hill just north of town during the 1980s demonstrate characteristics of so-called *Ñuiñe* glyphs, which archaeologists recognize as one of the five unique writing systems of ancient Mesoamerica.

Similar finds unearthed at contemporaneous Mixteca Baja ruined cities, such as Tequixtepec, Chazumba, Miltepec, Suchitepec, Lunatitlán, and Mixtlahuaca, led archaeologists to name the style by the Mixtec label, *Ñuiñe* (nyoo-EE-nyay), for the "Hot Country," the Mixteca Baja, where they have been found.

Before charging up the hill, however, first visit the **Huajuapan Regional Museum** (Museo Regional de Huajuapan, Nuyoo 15, no phone, 8 A.M.–2 P.M. and 4–8 P.M. Tues.–Sun., www.mureh.gob.mx), half a block uphill from the church. Professionally prepared exhibits on the bottom floor give an overview and explanations of the exquisite finds at Cerro de las Minas. Upstairs is a library and beautifully displayed life-sized mock-ups—community, costumes, economics, fiestas, religion, and work—of present Mixteca Baja people. Another room exhibits a graphic post-Conquest history and culture of Huajuapan up to modern times, including a description of the interesting tradition of *tequio* (community volunteer work). The museum also sells some books of local history and culture, notably archaeologist Marcus Winter's *Cerro de las Minas* guide to the ruined city uphill.

EXPLORING THE SITE

After the museum, get to the ruins by driving, hiking, or hailing a taxi. Wear sturdy walking shoes, a hat, and take water. From the town center, follow Nuyoo north across the highway and three blocks past the uphill church.

Continue straight ahead, up a steep, rocky track and turn right to the parking lot, marked by a Zona Arqueología sign. From there, on foot, scramble uphill past the retaining wall to the highest point, **Mound 1,** on the east side.

From the top, the entire Huajuapan Valley spreads in all directions. On the south side, in the distance, rise the downtown cathedral's ruddy twin towers. Far behind them stand the cloud-draped heights of the Mixteca Alta. On the opposite, north side, flat-topped Cerro Yucunitza, the site of another hilltop ruined city, towers over the valley. Below Yucunitza's right shoulder, the Río Mixteco meanders below the high brushy hills of the Mixteca Baja.

Unrestored Mound 1, most certainly a former pyramid, slopes downhill past some reconstructed walls and stairs to a wide ceremonial courtyard. Descend Mound 1 to the courtyard. On its north side are the previously excavated Tombs 4 and 5. On the south side, a staircase descends to a smaller courtyard complex of what appear to be residential walls and patios. Continue west to **Mound 2,** a partly reconstructed ceremonial pyramid. Looking south toward town from its summit, you can view the clear outlines of a partially excavated **ball court** about a hundred yards down the slope.

Continue west, descending the regal, restored ritual staircase down the west side of Mound 2 to a grand 100-yard-square courtyard. Ahead rises **Mound 3,** a brushy hill that probably conceals yet another staircase and pyramid summit.

The visible hilltop remains of Cerro de las Minas around you were the ceremonial hub of a small city that, at its apex around A.D. 500, was home to perhaps 4,000 people whose hundreds of homes extended over scores of surrounding hillside acres. Like many of Oaxaca's forgotten cities, the city's original name has been lost over time. What archaeologists do know, however, is that, like Monte Albán and several other of Oaxaca's ancient cities, the inhabitants of Cerro de las Minas mysteriously abandoned it around A.D. 800.

Las Campanas

Las Campanas park, a lovely streamside stroll on Huajuapan's northwest outskirts, is worth at least an hour's visit. At Las Campanas, community efforts have preserved a unique natural desert-like spring and habitat, decorated with rock outcroppings and ferny, shaded nooks. Tables beneath streamside willows make for restful picnicking.

The name Las Campanas (The Bells) derives from the stalactites hanging from the ceilings of shallow, streamside caves. If struck just right, a stalactite will vibrate and ring with a soft, bell-like monotone.

(*Note:* Experienced cavers might enjoy exploring the cave complex upstream from Las Campanas. A large tree, locally known as Palo Blanco, marks the entrance. The cave extends a mile or two uphill to around Agua Dulce village. *Ordinary travelers should only attempt this led by an experienced guide.* For information and guide recommendations, check with the municipal museum director and/or the tourism office at the *presidencia municipal.*)

Las Campanas, although readily accessible, is not well marked and is easy to miss. Follow the road to Mexico City about a mile (1.6 km) west of Huajuapan town center. Las Campanas nestles in a shallow arroyo on the left, marked by an old Hotel Crystal sign about a block or two after the entrance driveway to the Universidad Tecnología de la Mixteca. If you pass a government *vivero* (nursery) on the left, you've gone too far; turn around and return one block to Las Campanas.

Shopping

If it's Saturday, the day of Huajuapan's big *tianguis,* walk to Colón, which borders the church's north side. Continue east for a block and follow Zaragoza, the street that heads diagonally northeast two long blocks to the market on the right. Besides doing your grocery shopping from stalls in the covered section, wander beneath the shady *tianguis* for your pick of the best, from mounds of luscious bananas, tomatoes, cucumbers, and squashes. During the summer and fall, you'll also see plenty of pears, peaches, guavas, and grapes. Also admire the piles of deep-red chilies and bright-yellow *flor de calabaza* (squash flower) used for flavoring soups and stews. Here and there, you'll glimpse piles of old-fashioned items, such as corn husks (for wrapping tamales), *cal* (lime or quicklime) for soaking corn, red *jamaica* (hah-MAHEE-kah) petals for delicious drinks, nopal (cactus leaves), *tamarindo* and *guaje* pods, yellow *manzanilla* (chamomile) flowers, and hunks of *panela* (brown sugar). Throughout your walk, take note that the women vendors are definitely in charge, although few wear *traje.*

You'll also find some **handicrafts.** Locally made items include red- and black-streaked pottery, in practical shapes such as *ollas* (pots), bowls, and *comales* (griddles); and stone, carved into *metates, metates* and *molcajetes* for grinding corn and chilies. Local folks also sell plenty of items woven from palm. These include sombreros, *bolsas* (purses), *petates* (mats), and *cestas* (baskets).

Although few if any local people make textiles, they do import and sell, mostly *huipiles,* from other parts of Oaxaca. You'll probably find some on Wednesday, if you look around the covered section.

A pair of small stores on Nuyoo, in the town center, offer handicrafts. First, take a look at the woven-palm treasures of the precious little **Artesanías de Palma** (Nuyoo 13, 9 A.M.–6 P.M. Mon.–Sat.), half a block uphill from the cathedral. Stop by and pick a few items from their selection of old-fashioned dress-up costumes, cowboy hats, and *calabazas* for carrying water. Uphill, across Nuyoo from the museum, the **Nectar Zapoteco** mezcal shop (Nuyoo 20, 8 A.M.–10 P.M. daily) also stocks some attractive Valley of Oaxaca handicrafts. These include pottery from Atzompa and Coyotepec, leather, and mezcal, in dozens of flavors.

Accommodations
UNDER $25
The budget hotel choices (none of which accept credit cards) dot the downtown, along Nuyoo and Colón, near the second-class bus stations. **Hotel Colón** (Colón 10, tel./fax 953/532-0817 or 953/532-1860, $15 s or d, $22 d with cable

TV, $30 t), on the north side of the church, is probably the best super-budget choice. It offers about 20 clean but smallish dark rooms, with hot-water shower-baths, around a parking patio, with *gratis* songs from the owner's many birds, and a restaurant on site.

Another recommendable budget choice is the **Hotel and Restaurant El Tesoro** (Nuyoo 7, tel. 953/532-0895, $13 s or d, $17 s or d). Choose from around 20 basic rooms with bath around an inviting plant-decorated restaurant patio, also embellished by birdsong. Here, clean but small rooms, with TV, are set back from the busy street and consequently insulated from traffic noise.

For another economical choice, take a look at **Hotel Laredo** (just a block south of the plaza, at Antonio de León 13, Colonia Centro, tel. 953/532-0402, $19 s or d, $26 d or t in two beds). The 40 rooms, stacked in three levels around a parking courtyard, are plain and less than immaculate. If not acceptable, ask them to clean up what's wrong before paying. Amenities include bath, fan, parking, and a passable restaurant.

$25-50
High marks go to suburban resort-style **Hotel Casa Blanca** (Amatista 1, Colonia Sta. Teresa, tel. 953/532-0779 or 953/532-9364, fax 953/532-0979, $35 s or d in one bed, $44 d in two beds, $50 t, add $5 for a/c), on Highway 190, Oaxaca City side, about a mile (1.6 km) east of downtown. This is a comfortable option for drivers anxious to avoid downtown traffic and save money. The Casa Blanca's 70 semideluxe rooms, in two-story wings scattered through a spacious garden complex, are carpeted and comfy. (Details, however, are not the hotel's strong suite; make sure that everything is working before moving in.) Amenities include hot-water baths, cable TV, fans, relaxing pool-patio, a good restaurant, parking, phones, and credit cards accepted.

If you want to stay downtown, but can't find anything else, you can settle for a night in the **Hotel Plaza del Ángel** (Valerio Trujano 22, tel./fax 953/532-0851). Although not much to

THE MIXTECA

look at from the outside, the Ángel has carpeted, and therefore quiet, hallways. Rooms, plain but clean, have baths. Rates run $25 s, $33 d, $45 t, with TV, fans, parking, but no phones nor credit cards accepted.

OVER $50
Visitors who enjoy soaking up Mexico should choose the immaculate, class-act ◖ **Hotel Garcia Peral** (Porfirio Díaz 1, tel. 953/532-0777 or 953/532-0742, fax 953/532-2000, hotelgarcia_peral@yahoo. com, www.hotelgarciaperal.com, $47 s, $58 d), by the central plaza. The 37 rooms in three floors surround an inviting pool patio blooming with tropical plants and birdsong. Rooms are comfortably furnished, with beige bed covers, reading lamps, attractively rustic tile floors, and modern-standard bathrooms. Amenities include fans, a good restaurant-bar, pool and sauna; credit cards accepted. Parking is street-front, but secure, right in front of the hotel reception.

Food
Huajuapan's best grocery, vegetable, fruit, and economy meals source is the downtown **Mercado Benito Juárez,** west, across de León, from the plaza's northwest corner. For wholesome cooked specialties, visit the airy **andador de fondas** walkway that on the Benito Juárez market's north side.

On the other hand, health food fanciers can get plenty of honey, grains, juices, soya, vitamins, supplements, granola, and yogurt at **Natura** (Nuyoo 18, tel. 953/532-2538, 9 A.M.–9 P.M. Mon.–Sat.), a block uphill from the cathedral. Satisfy your hankering for cake, pie, and cookies at the bakery, **Espiga de Oro,** nearby at Nuyoo 9, half a block uphill from the cathedral.

The town center abounds with wholesome cooked food. For inexpensive snacks and meals, try the **taco stands,** on the corner northwest of the church. On the other hand, cross Colón and walk up Nuyoo a few doors and step into the sheltered patio of the hotel and **Restaurant El Tesoro de Michapa**

(Nuyoo 7, tel. 953/532-0895, $4–8). Here, you can enjoy a good home-cooked meal accompanied by the melodies of the owner-chef's pet tropical birds. Alternatively, across the street, you can do plenty of wholesome local-style eating at the **Restaurant El Dorado** (Nuyoo 8, 8A.M.–9 P.M. daily, $3–6), a few steps uphill from the corner of Colón.

A cluster of good restaurants serve customers on the east-side plaza-front. For refined dining, try the airy restaurant of the ◖ **Hotel Garcia Peral** (tel. 953/532-1532, 8 A.M.–10:30 P.M. daily). Pick from the long menu of a little bit of everything, from cream of asparagus soup ($4) and club sandwiches ($4) to shrimp salad ($4), filet mignon ($13), or enchilada Oaxacan style, smothered in black mole sauce ($6).

Relaxing courtyard ambience, quiet music, and genteel conversation draw a steady stream of middle- and upper-class patrons to **Cafetería Pasticel** (on Díaz next to HSBC, tel. 953/532-2161, 8 A.M.–11 P.M. daily), on the plaza's east side. Here, diners start off the day with Oaxaca espresso coffee and hearty breakfasts (hotcakes, eggs, $2–4), and enjoy lunches and suppers of American-style sandwiches (hamburgers, hot dogs, and club $2–4) and hearty Oaxacan-style specialties (chicken enchiladas, *chilaquiles,* tacos $2–5).

You enjoy both good food and a superbly airy plaza-front sunset-view perch above the traffic at **Restaurant Ajos y Cebollas** (Garlic and Onions, tel. 953/532-0795, 8 A.M.–midnight daily), upstairs from the HSBC. Choose from a very recognizable Mexican-style menu of breakfasts, soups, salads, and pastas ($3–4), and seafood and meats ($5–10).

Information and Services
A number of banks around the plaza, all with ATMs, change money. Best for its long hours is **HSBC** (on Díaz, tel. 953/532-0169, 8:30 A.M.–7 P.M. Mon.–Sat.), at the plaza's northeast corner, south of the church.

If somehow HSBC isn't satisfactory, walk a block to **Banco Nacional de Mexico** (Banamex, tel. 953/532-1282, 9 A.M.–4 P.M. Mon.–Fri.), at the plaza's northwest corner; or

Banco Serfin (corner of de León and Galindo, tel. 953/532-0424, 9 A.M.–4 P.M. Mon.–Fri., 10 A.M.–2 P.M. Sat.), a long block south of Banamex.

To get to the *correo* (5 de Febrero 16, on the south side, tel. 953/532-0692, 8 A.M.–4 P.M. Mon.–Fri., 9 A.M.–1 P.M. Sat.) from the plaza's southwest corner, walk south on de León three blocks to 5 de Febrero; turn right and continue another two blocks to the post office on the left side of the street. The *telecomunicaciones* (with money orders, telephone, and fax) is on Galindo, between Hidalgo and Matamoros, southwest of the plaza. From the plaza's southwest corner, walk a block south, turn right at Hidalgo, and walk a block and a half.

Long-distance telephone and fax are readily available at the money exchange, Federal Express, and copy shop (on the plaza, west side, tel. 953/532-2908, 9 A.M.–5 P.M. Mon.–Fri., 9:30 A.M.–2:30 P.M. Sat.–Sun.).

Internet connection is available at **Prodinetpc.com** (Nuyoo 12A, tel. 953/532-2724, 9 A.M.–10 P.M. daily).

If you get sick, one of the best places to go for a doctor is the **Centro de Especialidades de la Mixteca** (Zaragoza 24, tel. 953/532-1355, consultations 9A.M.–8 P.M. Mon.–Sat.), across from the town market three blocks west of the plaza. It has about 15 specialists on call, from gynecologists and pediatricians to internists and a cardiologist.

For routine remedies and prescriptions, go to one of the several pharmacies near the plaza, such as **Farmacia San Jorge** (on Colón, behind the church, tel. 953/532-1399, 8 A.M.–11 P.M. daily), or its second branch (Nuyoo 20, half a block north from the church, tel. 953/532-1123 or 953/532-1584, 8 A.M.–11 P.M. daily).

Although Huajuapan has a city *turismo* office on the upper floor of the *presidencia municipal* at the west side of the plaza, you might get more good information by consulting friendly José Flores Cubas, owner of the **Turismo "Oh Tierra del Sol"** (at the plaza's southeast corner, tel. 953/532-4555, fax 953/532-2656, ohtierradelsol@hotmail.com, 9 A.M.–8 P.M Mon.–Sat.).

Get your wash done at **Lavandería Easy** (8 A.M.–8 P.M. Mon.–Sat., 9 A.M.–6 P.M. Sun.), on Hidalgo, one block west, one block south from the plaza's southwest corner.

Getting There and Away

Several first- and second-class bus lines operate out of various terminals, providing direct connections with many Oaxacan and national destinations. The busy all-first-class terminal (tel. 953/532-9309), six blocks north of the plaza at the Highway 190 intersection with Nuyoo, is the center for **Cristóbal Colón, Autobuses del Oriente (ADO), Sur,** and **Autobuses Unidos (AU)** ticket sales, arrivals, and departures. Principal connections, including many intermediate destinations, are southeast with Nochixtlán and Oaxaca City; south via Highway 15 and Tonalá with Juxtlahuaca, where you can transfer on to Tlaxiaco, Putla, and Pinotepa Nacional; and northwest with Puebla and Mexico City.

Second-class **Fletes y Pasajes** (on the highway, across the street, west from the ADO station) offers a broad range of connections in Oaxaca, approximately the same as Sur.

Some second-class bus and van stations are scattered along Nuyoo, along the blocks north of the cathedral. **Sur** (at the corner of Bravo and Nuyoo, tel. 953/532-5631) offers connections southeast, including a swarm of intermediate destinations, with Tamazulapan, Nochixtlán, and Oaxaca City; south with Juxtlahuaca, Putla, and Tlaxiaco; north with Puebla; and northwest with Cuautla, Morelos, and Mexico City Tapo and Airport.

A second, smaller line, **Boqueron** (Nuyoo 21, no telephone) offers connections along the north–south Tonalá–Juxtlahuaca–Putla route all the way to Pinotepa Nacional, on Oaxaca's Pacific coast.

Furthermore, **Autobuses Erco** (Linea Oro, Nuyoo 19) offers first-class express connections with northern destinations of Izucar de Matamoros, Tlapa de Comonfort, Cuernavaca, Puebla, and Mexico City.

In addition, long-distance *colectivo* van transportation is available via **Servicios**

Turísticos Lázaro Cárdenas (on Nuyoo, east side, about half a block north of the church). Service includes south and southeast destinations of Oaxaca City, Tonalá, Juxtlahuaca, and Tlaxiaco.

Drivers have their pick of four major paved highways radiating from Huajuapan. Northwest, Highway 190 connects with Mexico City—196 miles (316 km) via Cuautla, Morelos. Two winding lanes and numerous big trucks along the way usually slow traffic along this route. Figure about seven hours under good conditions, either way. A quicker alternative is to first head northeast via Highway 125, 74 miles (118 km), two hours, to Tehuacán, Puebla. There, connect with the *cuota autopista,* which will whisk you in another three hours, via Puebla, to Mexico City.

For Oaxaca City, follow Highway 190 for 70 miles (113 km), two hours, southeast to Nochixtlán. Continue via the *cuota autopista* to Oaxaca City, another 50 miles (80 km), about one additional hour.

Drivers can also access points directly south most easily via Tonalá, along the paved (but sometimes potholed), lightly trafficked secondary road, Highway 182, which takes about two hours to Juxtlahuaca (62 miles/100 km). South of Juxtlahuaca 25 miles (40 km, one hour), at the Highway 125 junction, either head left (east) along Highway 125 another 21 miles (34 km) and one hour to Tlaxiaco, or go right (south) along Highway 125 via Putla to Pinotepa Nacional on the Pacific coast (a total, from Huajuapan, of 206 miles/332 km). Allow six hours' driving time south to the coast, four hours to Tlaxiaco.

NORTH OF HUAJUAPAN: INTO THE ÑUIÑE REGION

National Highway 125 winds north along the rural, tree-shaded valley of the Río Mixteco, passing a sprinkling of little towns, sleepy except during fiestas, when they liven up with days of processions, barbecues, and carnivals. Along this route, interest climaxes at **San Pedro y San Pablo Tequixtepec,** where townsfolk welcome visitors to explore their community museum. There, you can view the *Ñuiñe* engraved monoliths, whose cryptic inscriptions have convinced archaeologists that they represent a unique written language.

By car, starting early, you could enjoy this 75-mile (121-km) round-trip excursion in a day, allowing time for a picnic in Tequixtepec (22 miles/35 km from Huajuapan) around the midpoint. Bus travelers, head out by ADO, Sur, or AU bus straight from Huajuapan, on a Tehuacán-bound bus. Ask the driver to let you off at the Tequixtepec entrance road, where you can catch a taxi or the town *colectivo* van and ride the three miles (five km) to town. Afterward, either continue north or return to Huajuapan stopping along the way, if time allows.

Santiago Huajolotitlán

This small town four miles (6.4 km) north of Huajuapan is well known, both for its annual patronal festival and as the place where the Virgin of Guadalupe appeared in 1978. First, stop at the town church, the **Templo de Santiago Apóstol,** built between 1835 and 1840. Inside, to the right as you enter, notice the popular San Isidro Labrador, the patron of farmers, animals, and children, with his customary *yunta* (yoked pair) of oxen and a child. Folks celebrate his memory on May 15, when children bring their animals to church to be blessed.

Also, don't miss the uniquely quaint town patron, **Santiago Caballerito** (Little Saint James), mounted on a small horse, waving a big sword. His festival, celebrated July 26–29, usually includes plenty of fireworks, flowers, music, marches, and *mañanitas* (early morning masses).

Also, on the slope of Cerro del Chilar, northwest of town, is the **Capilla de la Virgen de Guadalupe,** built over the spot where a shepherd saw the Virgin in December 1978. Thousands of believers subsequently flocked to the site, now relatively unfrequented, where the chapel stands.

Río Mixteco Valley and Asunción Cuyotepeji

North of Huajolotitlán, the winding river

valley is especially lush during the cooler summer rainy season, when it's abloom with fields of vegetables, tall green corn, and waving wheat. The natural charm climaxes at the riverbank itself, decorated by groves of stately *ahuehuetes* or *sabinos*. Here and there, where the highway nears or crosses the river, pause for a stroll along the river and enjoy a spell in the company of the old shady giants.

During mid-August, you also might enjoy getting in on the fun of the **Fiesta de Santa María de la Asunción,** at Cuyotepeji, about 12 miles (19 km) north of Huajuapan. At least take a look inside the church, known for its gilded baroque main *retablo* (altarpiece), crowned by the Holy Mother ascending to heaven guided by a pair of adoring cherubs.

San Pedro y San Pablo Tequixtepec

You could easily spend your entire day at Tequixtepec (formally, San Pedro y San Pablo Tequixtepec, pop. 1,400), the head town of the *municipio* of the same name. Make your first stop at the community museum, **Memorias de Yucundaayee** (yoo-koon-dah-ah-YAY-ay, adjacent to the town *presidencia municipal,* 10 A.M.–2 P.M. and 4–7 P.M. Mon.–Thurs.), named with the town's original Mixtec label (Hill of the Standing Conch), which the Aztecs translated to Tequixtepec.

The professionally prepared exhibits display the intriguing glyph-carved monoliths, with Spanish-language explanations of their *Ñuiñe* writing style. Despite a generation of study and excavations, archaeologists still can say little about the people depicted. For now, their feathered visages remain mute to us; maybe someday experts will decipher the *Ñuiñe* glyphs and understand their messages.

The recently completed **mural** on the museum's front wall depicts the sweep of Tequixtepec history, from pre-Conquest times, through independence, civil war, and reform, clear up to the 20th century, when the tradition of the town's beloved **Señor del Perdón** began in 1917–1918.

If you have arranged a tour appointment, a

COHETES: BANGS, FLASHES, AND HISSES IN THE NIGHT

Like everyone, Mexicans love celebrations, and every one of them, humble or grand, must be accompanied by *cohetes.* Although *cohetes* literally means "rockets," folks always associate them with the myriad other booming, flaring, whooshing, banging, and whirling incendiary devices that traditionally go along with *cohetes.* And while in most of the United States, bland "Safe and Sane" fireworks are all that ordinary folks set off on the Fourth of July and maybe New Year's, the sky seems to be the limit during the seemingly innumerable fiestas that Mexicans celebrate everywhere.

One big climax of celebrating peaks during the several weeks before Easter Sunday, when folks start out with a rip-roaring Carnaval (Mardi Gras) and parade the six succeeding Friday afternoons to the cannonades of *cohetes de trueno* (thunder rockets) overhead and end up with a grand explosive bash on Easter Sunday.

Whatever the occasion, the *coheteros* (rocketeers) have plenty of tricks up their sleeves, from the familiar, colorfully brilliant *cohetes de luces* (rockets of lights) to a dozen other strictly Mexican varieties. These include *toritos,* a bull-shaped frame, decorated with papier mâché and loaded with flares and firecrackers, that some daredevil wheels or carries on his back through the crowds of merrymakers.

Sometime after that, someone usually scatters some *buscapies* (heel-chasers) that go whizzing, whirling, and shrieking under the feet of the crowd.

Finally, the *cohetero* lights up the *castillo,* a grand framework laced with pinwheels, flares, and smoke bombs, from which a spinning *corona* finally swishes skyward, scattering a trail of stars in the inky firmament overhead.

THE MIXTECA

museum volunteer will be available to take you on an extensive exploration, including a three-hour round-trip hike to **Cerro de La Caja** (Mountain of the Box), a regal hilltop ruined town. There, among other things, you'll be able to inspect a ponderous box-like monolith, inscribed with a number of graphic *Ñuiñe* reliefs, one of which includes a personage devouring a captive. Make an appointment by leaving a message, specifically for the *museo comunitario* (Abigail Moran Morales in charge at this writing), with the town long-distance *caseta* (long-distance within Mexico 200/123-7044, 200/123-7045, or 200/123-7046), or alternatively, at the government tourism office in Oaxaca City (Murguia 206, up the driveway, in the back, tel. 951/516-0123, info@aoaxaca.com, www.oaxaca.travel).

Back in town, be sure to visit the church, dedicated to the **Señor del Perdón** (Lord of Forgiveness), who is celebrated in a big regional fiesta and pilgrimage culminating on the second Friday of Lent. At that time, 20,000 people are likely to crowd into little Tequixtepec, sleeping in the plaza, the town pilgrimage shelter, and in scores of buses parked along the road into town. The object of all is to ask forgiveness from the Señor del Perdón, who presides above the church's front altar.

Before you leave, ask your guide for a demonstration of **palm weaving,** which many townsfolk do during their spare moments. Both individual weavers and the museum sell examples of woven sombreros, *petates* (mats), *tenates* (tumpline baskets), and more. Additionally, be sure to step 100 years into the past into the Porfirian-era store of grandfatherly **Faustino "Tino" Moran Castillo** in the center of town opposite the church. Here you might say a good word, make a small purchase, and enjoy a sip of his zingy homemade brandy, which Faustino claims is "very good for your health."

(*Hint:* If you happen to arrive in Tequixtepec unnanounced, Faustino is the one to see first, and can usually find someone to open the museum for you.) Furthermore, if you decide to linger in Teqiuxtepec, Faustino and his daughter Abigail are prepared for you. He offers a room in his house for $10, and given a day's notice will arrange for meals for $2.50 per person. Kindly place a reservation via the town long-distance telephone (tel. 200/123-7044, 200/123-7045, or 200/123-7046).

Santiago Chazumba

The main yearly attractions here at sleepy Chazumba, about 37 miles (60 km) north from Huajuapan, are its two major festivals, in honor of **Santiago** (July 24–26) and the **Señor de Esperanza** (Lord of Hope—the 15 days beginning on Good Friday).

The town's permanent jewel is its church, dedicated to Santiago Apóstol (St. James the Apostle). Although it seems a small miracle that such a monumental building and refined works of art can be found in such an isolated little place, it is the Chazumba townsfolk's intense devotion, rather than divine intervention, that has produced the monumentally resplendent results over centuries of effort. While inside among all the glitter, don't miss the baptismal chapel to the right of the front door, the Señor de Esperanza in the transept chapel, and Santiago above the front altar.

The Chazumba bus stop supports a few highway-side eateries. Best seems to be the **Restaurant Los Arcos** (tel. 953/525-0083, 7:30 A.M.–9 P.M. daily), where you can enjoy house specialties, such as *mole de guajalote* (turkey with *mole* sauce), *tamales de frijol* (bean tamales), and *barbacoa* (barbecued beef, pork, or chicken).

Besides food, Restaurant Los Arcos also provides a long-distance telephone and fax (tel. 953/525-0083). Moreover, in town you'll find a *correo* (across the highway, 9 A.M.–1 P.M. and 3–6 P.M. Mon.–Fri.) and a *telégrafo* (9 A.M.–3 P.M. Mon.–Fri.) for money orders and fax.

ADO and **AU** buses, which depart from the Restaurant Los Arcos, connect several times a day north with Tehuacán, Puebla, and Mexico City, and south with Huajuapan, Nochixtlán, Oaxaca City, and intermediate points.

SOUTH OF HUAJUAPAN: ALONG THE HIGH ROAD TO THE MIXTECA ALTA

This lightly traveled all-paved (but sometimes potholed) route, recently re-named National Highway 182, branches south from Huajuapan, opening a scenic back door to Oaxaca's cool, green, and culturally rich Mixteca Alta. Along the way, you'll cross rushing mountain rivers, wind through fertile farm valleys, and climb to high ridges where you can gaze back down upon it all.

Pleasant surprises along the way include boating, fishing, camping, and lakeside bungalows at **Yosocuta Reservoir** and riverside hiking and wilderness camping in spectacular **Tonalá Canyon.** A few miles farther, at colonial-era Tonalá town, you can enjoy a cool, shady walk, and a picnic in the town's grand old *sabino* grove. Finally, at the route's end, at Juxtlahuaca, enjoy the color of the grand indigenous Thursday–Friday *tianguis*, a relaxing stroll, and restful overnight camping in the pine grove beside the crystalline, emerald-green **Laguna Encantada.** With an extra three hours, you can even go for an easy but amazing walking adventure through the stalactite-hung grottoes of the **limestone cave** at nearby San Miguel de la Cueva village.

Yosocuta Reservoir

This big artificial lake, eight miles (13 km) south of Huajuapan, confined by the government-built Yosocuta dam on the Río Mixteco, rises and falls with the seasons. From February through June, the reservoir drains, nourishing irrigated crops downstream. Its level consequently falls, leaving an ugly bathtub-like lakeshore ring. However, by October, the lake usually refills to its brim, gently lapping the shoreline at **Parador Yosocuta,** the major lakeside access point.

Here, you have several choices. Lakeview restaurants offer snacks, drinks, and fresh *lobina negro* (black bass) dinners. A concession, owned by the Yosocuta town

The spacious, gradually sloping shoreline of Yosocuta Reservoir, south of Huajuapan de León, invites boat launching, tenting, and RV camping.

© BRUCE WHIPPERMAN

THE MIXTECA

fishing cooperative and managed by welcoming Sammy Martínez, offers lake tours by boat ($7–12 per party), fishing excursions ($20 an hour), boat rentals, bait, and fishing poles (for sale for about $45); launching fee for your own motorboat runs about $5.

If you decide to stay overnight, Sammy will let you set up your tent on the lakeshore or park your self-contained RV overnight in the parking lot for free. He also rents out a few comfortable lakeshore four-person duplex cabins (which he calls bungalows), with their own hot-water baths and porch-front hammock hooks, for about $13 per person nightly. Reserve by leaving a reservation message for Sammy Martínez at his tel. 953/534-8112. Alternatively you can reserve a Yosocuta bungalow in Oaxaca City at the government alternative tourism office (Murguia 206, up the driveway, in the back, 951/516-0123, info@aoaxaca.com, www.oaxaca.travel).

Furthermore, if somehow Lake Yosocuta doesn't suit you, stop instead at the **Balneario las Bugambilias** (9A.M.–6 P.M. daily, $6 adults, $3 under 12), a family paradise of pools, water slides, merry-go-round, a restaurant, and a campground. It might be crowded on Sundays and holidays. The *balneario* is located on the highway about three miles west of the reservoir.

Also along the road, you must stop for a treat at **❰ Pandadería San Marcos** (7 A.M.–8 P.M. daily), on the highway at the north edge of San Marcos village, a few miles past (north of) Yosocuta (but before the Balneario). Here, you can savor what has to be the Mixteca's, if not all of Oaxaca's, best pastries.

Tonalá Canyon

South, past a high, pine-studded ridge and pass, Highway 182 winds down to the Tonalá valley. There, 27 miles (43 km) south of Huajuapan, beneath the foot of **Puente Morelos,** a steel-arch highway bridge, the Río Mixteco issues through the deep defile of Cañon de Tonalá (known locally as El Boquerón—Big Mouth).

A trail cut into the canyon wall leads to a

A sturdy walkway leads through El Boquerón, the grand river gap of the Río Mixteco.

diversion dam about a mile (1.6 km) upstream. The trail begins at some stairs not far from the bridge's north footing. It continues spectacularly, above the river along the diversion canal, winding beneath towering 1,000-foot (300-meter) moss-mottled cliffs, green-tufted like a classical Chinese painting. At one point, a great boulder overhangs the trail; at another, a mass of ferns appears to cascade from the vertical rock wall.

At the dam, the trail ends at a small park and commemorative plaque that records that President Gustavo Díaz Ordaz came here during the late 1960s to dedicate the dam, a part of the federal Río Balsas Basin Development Project. A rough informal trail continues past the dam. After 50 downhill yards it leads to a flat spot on the right, with a bit of shade, safely above the river for camping.

For equipped and prepared wilderness adventurers, the river farther upstream, which runs about 10 miles (16 km) through a wild, deep gorge, might be heaven. Overhead, vultures and eagles soar; coyotes, foxes, and wildcats hunt along the shore; and butterflies flutter among streamside trees and wildflowers. The river, rushing and often muddy during the summer rainy season, slows to a clear, tranquil creek during the dry winter and spring. Although the Yosocuta Dam upstream probably minimizes the hazard, hikers should be aware of possible flash flooding from upstream thunderstorms.

Santo Domingo Tonalá

The sleepy farm community of Santo Domingo Tonalá (pop. 3,000) owns a pair of gems: its 16th-century Dominican-founded church and ex-convent, the **Templo de Santo Domingo,** and the lovely sylvan **sabinera** (cypress grove) behind the church. First, take a look inside the church, behind its front garden, a block north of the town plaza. Just past the entrance hangs an intriguing portrait of Angel Gabriel holding the scales of justice, deciding which of a cluster of beseeching souls will be admitted to Paradise. Farther on stands an image of the beloved African Dominican padre San Martín de Porres. The treasures climax in the right-side chapel, in a glittering, gorgeous small *retablo,* appearing as intricate as filigree and dedicated to the Holy Sacrament. Continue outside to the church's right (east) side and enjoy a turn through the garden within the old convent cloister.

You'll find the *sabinera* two blocks behind the church. Stroll around and soak in the cathedral-like loveliness beneath the old trees. Perhaps you will agree that the magnificent, gnarled old veteran *sabinos,* or *ahuehuetes,* are in their own way as magnificent as the stately old-growth groves of their cousins, the California redwoods. They certainly approach the size of redwoods. At the grove's far west (left as you enter) end, find the gnarled old grandparent of them all, 15 feet (4.5 meters) in diameter and 50 feet (15 meters) around. During your walk, you probably will notice the several small, clear rivulets running through the grove. This is no coincidence; local folks believe *sabinos* to be the most intelligent of trees; they always grow where the water flows.

If you arrive on Sunday, you might be able to see a *pelota mixteca* ball game in the field across the highway at the town entrance road. A direct descendant of the ancient Mesoamerican tradition, the modern game has players batting a big rubber ball back and forth, not unlike tennis (except without a net).

Furthermore, you're in for a treat if you arrive in early May or early August, when Tonalá wakes up for its annual festivals. Between May 1 and May 4, you can get in on the fun (dancing, cockfights, and bull roping and riding) of the **Fiesta de la Santa Cruz.** Three months later, around August 4, join Tonalá folks as they rev up again for more of the same during the **Fiesta de Santo Domingo.**

Ecotourism

What's more, Santo Domingo Tonalá has been increasingly welcoming visitors. Besides camping, hiking, and wildlife viewing opportunities in Tonalá Canyon, you can enjoy guided tours of local archaeological sites. These include a cave with **pinturas rupestres** (prehistoric hieroglyphic rock paintings), and walls of ancient crumbling temples (from a time long ago, when the local population is said to have migrated from present Chiapas state).

For information on all this, drop by the local ecotourism office (tel. 953/531-0023, in Spanish), Artemio Cruz in charge, in the Tonalá *presidencia municipal.* At this writing, Artemio told me that locals are preparing hiking trails for the guided tours, navigable either on foot or by mountain bike; and in Tonalá Canyon, a riverside campground and *cabañas* for overnight accommodations.

Accommodations and Food

Consider Tonalá's one hotel, the homey **Los Mangos** (Lázaro Cárdenas 27, tel. 953/531-0023, $15 s, $20 d in one bed, $25 d or t in two beds), marked by a tall mango tree, on the entrance road from the highway. The grandmotherly owner and her daughter offer 10 rooms beside a flowery garden and the loveliest of crimson-blossomed *tabachines* (flame trees). Check the rooms before moving in; mildew can be a problem here, especially during the rainy summer. Ask for fresh linens if necessary. All rooms have baths, with 24-hour hot water and all the mangos you can eat, in season.

For groceries and fruits and vegetables, go to well-stocked **Comercial Itzoca** (8 A.M.–8 P.M. daily) on Láaro Cárdenas, northwest corner of the plaza.

For hearty home-cooked meals, try the restaurant of the Hotel Los Mangos (8A.M.– 8 P.M. daily $2–8); or alternatively, for hot dogs, hamburgers, and *liquados* go to the **Fuente de Sodas Amilec** (9 A.M.–8 P.M. daily, $1–3) downhill on Lázaro Cárdenas, a block past the plaza.

Information and Services

Most of Tonalá's essential services are on Lázaro Cárdenas, around the town plaza. For example, if you're sick, go to the 24-hour *centro de salud,* downhill past the church. For routine medications and drugs, try the **Farmacia Diana** (9A.M.–10 P.M. daily) across the street from the *centro de salud,* or the **Farmacia Santa Cruz** (9A.M.–10 P.M. daily) a block uphill from the Hotel Los Mangos. For long-distance telephone and fax go to the *larga distancia* (9A.M.–9 P.M. daily) also on Lázaro Cárdenas, a block downhill from the hotel, on the north side of the plaza.

For lots of digital photo services, go to Foto Studio Tonala (9 A.M.–3 P.M. and 5–8 P.M. Mon.–Sat.), a block south of the plaza.

Getting There and Away

Bus passengers can reach Yosocuta, Tonalá Canyon, and Tonalá town by second-class **Boquerón** buses, either south from Huajuapan or north from Juxtlahuaca.

From Huajuapan, **drivers** should first take the Mexico City direction along Highway 190 to a signed Highway 182 Juxtlahuaca or Tonalá left turnoff, about a mile (1.6 km) west of the city center. After another mile (1.6 km) turn right at the main street, Avenida Mina, and head out another eight miles (13 km) to Yosocuta. After a total of 27 miles (43 km), arrive at Tonalá Canyon; continue another 3

miles (five km) to Tonalá town, and a total of 62 miles (100 km) to Juxtlahuaca. Heading in the reverse direction, north from Juxtlahuaca, the distances total approximately 32 miles (51 km) to Tonalá, 35 miles (56 km) to Tonalá Canyon, and 54 miles (87 km) to Yosocuta. Figure about two hours at the wheel, either direction.

SANTIAGO JUXTLAHUACA AND VICINITY

Santiago Juxtlahuaca (pop. 30,000) is the largest town and major service and governmental center for the Juxtlahuaca governmental district. It's clear why the town has prospered. It nestles in a deep, fertile valley between a pair of towering oak- and pine-studded mountain ranges. Main roads branch south, west, and north, connecting Juxtlahuaca with the outside world.

A second glance at the surrounding mountains reveals sinuous trails so steep that it's a wonder how anyone could climb them. But people do—the indigenous Mixtec- and Trique-speaking mountain people, for whom Juxtlahuaca's big *tianguis* is the focus of their week. They rise long before dawn and bundle up their merchandise—perhaps a basket packed with flowers, potatoes, or carrots; maybe they pile on a few hand-loomed bright-red-striped *huipiles.* Husband and wife sling the loads on their backs, adjust the tumplines on their foreheads, and begin the steep trek downhill, with hope that this will be a good *tianguis,* and they won't have to haul everything back uphill tomorrow night.

Sights

Orient yourself by the tall, straight-laced bell tower of the town church, the **Templo de Santiago Apóstol,** visible from all over town. The church faces the customary west, downhill. If you stand looking at the church-front, south will be on your right, north on your left. The uphill direction, toward the rear of the church, is east. Main east–west streets are Libertad, which runs along the church's north side; Porfirio Díaz, along the church's south side by the plaza; and Benito Juárez, along

© ERJCE WHIPPERMAN

Dried and salted ocean fish sell briskly at Juxtlahuaca markets, especially to folks without refrigerators.

the plaza's south side. Important north–south streets are Lázaro Cárdenas, a block behind the church, and Independencia, a block farther east, uphill.

If at all possible, schedule your Juxtlahuaca visit to coincide with its two-day *tianguis,* big on Thursday but among Oaxaca's biggest on Friday. Vendors' awnings (known in the Aztec language as *tianguis*) stretch from curb to curb, beginning at the town plaza just downhill from the church, and overflow, filling half of Juxtlahuaca's south-side streets.

The star actors of the *tianguis* are the Trique women, who proudly wear their horizontally striped bright-red wool *huipiles* over their black woolen skirts. (If you wonder why in sunny Mexico they wear wool, it's because afternoons are often cloudy and cool in Juxtlahuaca, especially during the summer and fall rainy season, and doubly so in the Triques' mountaintop villages.)

A number of Trique women congregate in the town plaza and display their for-sale homespun textiles: *huipiles,* black *enredos* (skirts),

and blouses. They don't like having their pictures taken, but several remedies exist for curing camera shyness (see the sidebar *Taking People Pictures* in the *Background* chapter).

From the plaza, plunge into the hubbub of stalls on the south-side street, Benito Juárez. Along your meandering path you'll find loads of lovely fruit many exotic tropical varieties—*anonas, guanabanas, pitahayas, zapotes* but also apples, grapes, peaches, pears, and plums in the summer.

You'll also see a fair amount of pottery, especially along Calle Lázaro Cárdenas, the north-south street that runs behind the church. Varieties include flower-painted, hard-glazed bowls, cups, and plates from Santa Rosa in the Valley of Oaxaca; green ware from Atzompa, also in the Valley of Oaxaca; and red and black jugs, plates, and bowls from Puebla. A few stalls also sell soft woven palm *tenates* and *petates* (tumpline baskets and mats), and sombreros from around Huajuapan de León.

If you're in the market for masks, go to the shop of master craftsman Alejandro Jesús

THE MIXTECA

Vera Guzmán (Lázaro Cárdenas 301 Sur, corner of Melchor Ocampo, tel. 953/554-0060 or 953/554-1424, alexvera_72@hotmail.com, alexvera_72@yuahoo.com), one block east and one block south of the plaza's southeast corner. His store is adjacent to the southwest corner grocery. He got started creating masks (devils seem to be his specialty) for local fiesta dances; now he sells to the public. His prices aren't cheap; expect to pay $60 and up. From him, however, you're getting the genuine article. If you lend him your photo, he'll even create a mask of you, for around $180.

While you're strolling around, you might take a look inside the church. Just as you enter the door, look into the small alcove on the right and you'll see the town patron, Santiago (St. James), sword in hand, on his usual white horse, but this time with a cowboy hat atop his head. Up front, above the altar, you'll see Santiago in more traditional dress. Step left, into the left transept chapel, and see the Virgen de Soledad presiding above the altar.

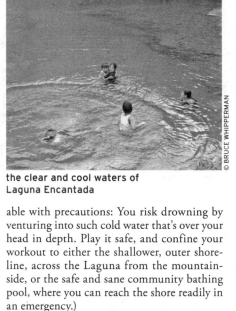

the clear and cool waters of Laguna Encantada

◧ Laguna Encantada

Yet another good reason for coming to Juxtlahuaca is Laguna Encantada (Enchanted Lagoon), a deep crystalline emerald-green lake beside the Huajuapan highway about two miles (three km) north of town. Laguna Encantada, set like a jewel at the foot of a towering mountain, is a precious asset that, besides furnishing irrigation water, supplies the adjacent communal swimming pool and picnic and camping ground. Even if you don't camp there, you should at least go for a stroll around its shoreline, made picture-perfect by the family of gnarled old *ahuehuete* cypresses inhabiting its banks.

(*Note:* So many men have drowned in Laguna Encantada's cold deep waters that legend says that Laguna Encantada has the spirit of a woman, who takes men that she likes. Notice the crosses on the inner shoreline, adjacent to the hillside, which is especially treacherous because of its steep drop-off to seemingly bottomless depths. Nevertheless, swimming in Laguna Encantada without accident is do-

able with precautions: You risk drowning by venturing into such cold water that's over your head in depth. Play it safe, and confine your workout to either the shallower, outer shoreline, across the Laguna from the mountainside, or the safe and sane community bathing pool, where you can reach the shore readily in an emergency.)

Both tent and RV camping prospects at Laguna Encantada could hardly be better. A broad cypress-shaded campground on the lake's north side provides plenty of grassy space to spread out. As a courtesy, ask the caretaker, friendly Natalia Ramos de Morales, or her husband, Francisco, who run the snack stand by the campground and the restaurant on the opposite side, if camping is OK. It always will be both allowed and free; as a courtesy, kindly buy a few tacos and drinks from them at the snack stand, and maybe even a hearty full meal, such as hamburgers, *tortas,* cappuccino, fresh fish, shrimp, and, on Sundays, scrumptious chili-garlic *mole* on roast pork ($1–4).

Natalia recommends that visitors hike up to

the top of the hill, Mogote de la Tialeja, just north of the campground. Natalia (a definite local booster) says that the Mogote, an ancient Mixtec town, is full of artifacts (which must remain in place; Mexican law forbids their removal). Artifacts or not, your reward for the 750-foot (250-meter) summit climb will be an airy, panoramic valley and mountain view.

San Miguel de la Cueva

Townsfolk of San Miguel de la Cueva (pop. 1,000), south of Juxtlahuaca, invite visitors to explore their big limestone cave. An adventurer's delight, the cave has plenty of hanging stalactites, fluttering bats, and a river that flows down from a hidden subterranean lake. Up the road, about 100 yards past the cave, is a petite pretty lake, with picnic shelters, fine for tent or self-contained RV camping. The Río Media Luna (Half Moon), which both enters and exits the tunnel-like cave, provides water (use purification tablets to be safe). A dry path continues about 300 yards through the cave to a separate exit on the north side of a small ridge. With a strong flashlight, good shoes, and a hat, you could hike it yourself, but best get permission and a guide (offer to donate $10) at the *agencia municipal* (which has flashlights) in town. Get there via the signed right-side road from Highway 15, two miles (three km) south of Juxtlahuaca. Continue about eight miles (13 km) to the hilltop town church, on the right. Go one block straight downhill to the basketball court/town plaza in front of the *agencia municipal*.

To get to the cave, turn right at the bottom of the hill, in front of the *agencia municipal*, and continue exactly one mile (1.6 kilometer) along the graded dirt road to the cave, visible downhill on the left, beyond a grassy field of big, beautiful summer lilies.

Accommodations and Food

Juxtlahuaca has several hotels, at least three of which are recommendable. Homiest is the family-run **Hotel Mixteco** (Independencia 200, tel. 953/554-0025, $9 s, $16 d, $22 t), near the corner of Libertad, two blocks behind the church. The 13 plainly furnished but clean rooms encircle a picturesque mango and lemon tree–decorated patio. Rooms come with hot-water shower-baths and parking; credit cards not accepted.

Much fancier is the brand-new **Hotel Eden** (Calle Mexico 309, tel. 953/554-0706, $24 s, $30 d in one bed, $33 d in two beds, $36 d king-sized bed, $38 t), at the corner of Morelos. Choose from three stories of 30 tastefully decorated 1990s-modern rooms, with polished wood highlights, plush maroon carpet, shiny bathrooms and built-in bed reading lamps, all with hot water, parabolic antenna TV, telephone, and wireless Internet access, but credit cards not accepted.

If both the above hotels above are full, you'll likely find a room at the **Hotel Diana** (Porfirio Díaz 300, tel. 953/554-0076, $15 s, $20 d in one bed, $30 d in two beds, $30 t), a block downhill from the plaza. The 30 basic but clean rooms come with hot-water baths, TV, hot-water showers, and parking; credit cards not accepted.

As for food, plaza-front taco stands and market *fondas* provide plenty of inexpensive local-style food. Remember: If it's hot, it's wholesome. For dessert, go to the bakery *panadería* **Guadalupana,** on Juárez, a block uphill from the plaza's southeast corner.

Market vegetable and fruit selection is super, especially during the summer. To be on the safe side, peel, cook, or scrub with soap and water any fruit or vegetable you eat. Stores such as **Estrada Fería** (on Lázaro Cárdenas, tel. 953/554-0026, 9 A.M.–9 P.M. daily), half a block south of Díaz and a block uphill from the plaza, opposite HSBC, supply basic groceries.

Juxtlahuaca people are prosperous enough to support a few restaurants. Always busy is the **Comedor Dona Tere** (behind the church on Lázaro Cárdenas, no phone, 7 A.M.–6 P.M. Mon.–Sat.), a block uphill from the plaza, by HSBC. The specialty here is a hearty afternoon four-course *comida,* typically soup, rice, stew, and dessert, for about $4.

Also acceptable is the loosely-run, long-hours, family **López Pizza** (on Lázaro Cárdenas, tel.

953/554-1213, 10:30 A.M.–10:30 P.M. daily), corner of Santa Cruz, about four blocks north of the town center, for pizza, spaghetti, calzone, hamburgers, and lettuce and tomato salad if you ask for it ($2–7).

Festivals

Local townsfolk celebrate both Santiago and the Virgen de Soledad in big festivals. Santiago's

---

EASTER CALENDAR

Although Christian religious denominations' Easter calendars vary, virtually all Western Christian churches follow the same calendar as the Roman Catholic version, universally used in Mexico. This calendar originated with the Council of Nicaea, which, in A.D. 325, set Easter as the first Sunday after the first full moon of Spring (or, more precisely, the first full moon after the Vernal Equinox, which the church authorities fixed as March 21).

The Easter season customarily kicks off with **Carnaval**, a rip-roaring party that runs the few days preceding **Miercoles de Ceniza** (Ash Wednesday), when all merriment ceases. Ash Wednesday, in turn fixed as the 46th day before Easter Sunday, occurs most often in February, and marks the beginning of **Lent**, a period of penitence and fasting. The gravity of Lent is literally rubbed in via ashes that the faithful get smeared onto their foreheads during solemn Ash Wednesday Christian church ceremonies worldwide.

In Mexico, religious processions and sober observances continue on each of the subsequent six Fridays. **Domingo de Ramos** (Palm Sunday) immediately follows the fifth Friday, and finally, after the sixth, or **Viernes Santa** (Good Friday), **Domingo Gloria** (Easter Sunday) breaks the fast of Lent as folks celebrate the risen Christ with joy and feasting.

Wikipedia explains the Easter calendar's historically interesting origin on its website at www.en.wikipedia.org/easter.

---

culminates around July 25, with a number of traditional dances: the Cristianos y Moros (a variation of the Dance of the Conquest; the Moors are the bad guys); the Chilolos (masked men, posing as women, in bells and skirts); and the town favorite, the Diablos (Devils). Much the same thing goes on during the December 8 Virgen de Soledad festival. In addition, **Carnaval** is big in Juxtlahuaca. On the four days before Ash Wednesday, the beginning of Lent, townsfolk whoop it up with the masked-dance Rubios (Blondes), a parody of the Spanish conquistadores, and the Machos dance.

Juxtlahuaca, moreover, is a center of **pelota mixteca,** the Mixtec version of the ancient Mesoamerican ball game. Although commonly played with a *hule* (natural rubber) ball, the local variation is to use a big leather ball. Players wrap their hands in thick cloth and bat the ball in a court, not unlike tennis. Local teams get ready for the yearly November 20 and February 5 tournaments nearly every afternoon in the long sandy court marked out just below the church.

Information and Services

Change money at the air-conditioned **HSBC** (on Lázaro Cárdenas behind and a block south of the church, tel. 953/554-0427 or 953/554-0428, 8 A.M.–7 P.M. Mon.–Fri., 8 A.M.–3 P.M. Sat.). If they're closed, use their ATM. If HSBC doesn't suit you, go to Juxtlahuaca's **Banamex** (on Juárez two blocks uphill from the plaza, tel. 953/554-0417, 9 A.M.–4 P.M. Mon.–Fri.), also with an ATM.

Juxtlahuaca's *correo* (8 A.M.–3 P.M. Mon.–Fri.) is on Juárez, at the southwest plaza corner. The *telecomunicaciones* (on Díaz, half a block downhill from the plaza, 9 A.M.–3 P.M. Mon.–Fri., 9 A.M.–noon Sat.) provides public fax (953/554-0044) and money orders. For after-hours long-distance phone and fax, go to either of the two private *larga distancias* on the plaza's south side.

Answer your email at **Bin@ry Internet** (on Lázaro Cárdenas, south side, corner of Libertad, tel. 953/554-0872, 9 A.M.–10:30 P.M. daily).

For travel services, go to **Micsa Agencia de Viajes** (300 Lázaro Cárdenas Sur, corner of Melchor Ocampo, tel. 953/554-0446 or 953/554-0232, 9 A.M.–9 P.M. daily), three blocks south of the church.

For photography services, film, and photographic supplies, go to the **Konica** photo shop (9 A.M.–6:30 P.M. Mon.–Sat.).

A few doctor-owned pharmacies on Lázaro Cárdenas, such as the **Farmacia Diana Luz** of Doctor Amadeo T. Chaves (tel. 953/554-0014, 9 A.M.–10 P.M.) are open long hours for consultation, prescriptions, and sales right on the spot. For hospital or emergency medical service, Juxtlahuaca has a **general hospital** (about a mile/1.6 km north of town on the Huajuapan highway, tel. 953/554-0307, 953/554-0308, or 953/554-0309).

Getting There and Away

A few long-distance bus lines connect Juxtlahuaca with various Oaxaca and national destinations. Most terminals are downhill on the highway. First-class **Sur** and **Omnibus Cristóbal Colón** buses (tel. 953/554-0181) connect via Highways 182 and 190, north with Huajuapan, continuing to Mexico City (Tapo terminal), via either Puebla (by the expressway) or Cuautla, Morelos (by Hwy. 190).

Second-class **Boquerón** buses connect south with Putla and Pinotepa Nacional and north with Tonalá and Huajuapan. Additionally, **Sur** offers many connections, including north with Huajuapan, continuing to Mexico City, and east with Oaxaca City, via Tlaxiaco, out of a **downtown station** (at the north end of Lázaro Cárdenas, corner of Progreso, tel. 953/554-0181).

Furthermore, Transportes Turísticos passenger **vans** (on Díaz, corner of Allenda, tel, 953/554-0813), a few doors downhill from the Hotel Diana, provide fast connections north, via Tonalá, with Huajuapan and Oaxaca.

For **drivers,** paved (but often potholed) mountain roads connect Juxtlahuaca with Oaxaca destinations: north with Huajuapan de León, 62 miles (100 km), 2.5 hours; south with Putla de Guerrro, via Oaxaca Highway 182 (20 miles/32 km), thence via National Highway 125 (17 miles/28 km), a total of 37 miles (60 km), in about an hour; or east, with Tlaxiaco, via Oaxaca Highway 182 (20 miles/32 km), then via National Highway 125 (30 miles/48 km), a total of 50 miles (80 km), in about two hours.

The Mixteca Alta: Roof of Oaxaca

The Mixteca Alta, Oaxaca's temperate Mixtec highland, is a land poor in gold but rich in scenic and cultural assets: Airy mountain vistas, colorful village markets, pine-scented breezes, beloved old churches, tumbling waterfalls, ancient ruins, and crystalline springs await the traveler who ventures into the Mixteca Alta.

Moreover, travel within the Mixteca Alta is not difficult. Tlaxiaco, with its hotels, restaurants, bus connections, and services, is a good base for exploring the Mixteca Alta. From Tlaxiaco, roads lead out east past cool green mountain vistas to the enigmatic ruins at Huamelulpan and Achiutla, south over the airy Chalcatongo plateau to the Cascada Esmeralda at Yosundua, and west to the friendly little Mixtec-speaking museum towns of Cuquila and San Miguel Progreso.

TLAXIACO

Asunción Tlaxiaco (ah-soon-see-OHN tlah-shee-AH-koh) is far more important than its population of about 20,000 would imply. Tlaxiaco (Place of the Ball Game) is the economic capital of the entire Mixteca Alta, a magnet for many hundreds of vendors from all over central and southern Mexico and thousands more native folks who swarm into town for the **Saturday tianguis,** second only to the big Saturday market in Oaxaca City.

THE MIXTECA

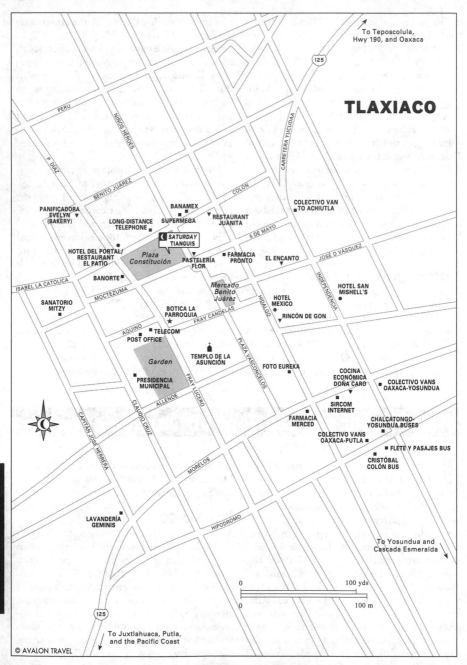

THE MIXTECA

TLAXIACO

To Teposcolula,
Hwy 190, and Oaxaca

125

PERU

NINOS HEROES

P DIAZ

BENITO JUAREZ

CARRETERA YUCUDAA

COLON

PANIFICADORA
EVELYN
(BAKERY)

BANAMEX

SUPERMEGA

RESTAURANT
JUANITA

COLECTIVO VAN
TO ACHIUTLA

LONG-DISTANCE
TELEPHONE

5 DE MAYO

SATURDAY
TIANGUIS

HOTEL DEL PORTAL/
RESTAURANT
EL PATIO

Plaza
Constitución

PASTELERÍA
FLOR

FARMACIA
PRONTO

EL ENCANTO

JOSE D VASQUEZ

ISABEL LA CATOLICA

BANORTE

Mercado
Benito
Juárez

HOTEL SAN
MISHELL'S

INDEPENDENCIA

SANATORIO
MITZY

MOCTEZUMA

BOTICA LA
PARROQUIA

HOTEL
MEXICO

RINCÓN DE GON

HIDALGO

FRAY CANDELAS

AQUINO

TELECOM
POST OFFICE

TEMPLO DE LA
ASUNCIÓN

FOTO EUREKA

PLAZA VASCONCELOS

Garden

PRESIDENCIA
MUNICIPAL

ALLENDE

FRAY LUCERO

COCINA
ECONÓMICA
DOÑA CARO

COLECTIVO VANS
OAXACA-YOSUNDUA

CLAUDIO CRUZ

CAPITAN JOSE HERRERA

SIRCOM
INTERNET

FARMACIA
MERCED

CHALCATONGO-
YOSUNDUA BUSES

COLECTIVO VANS
OAXACA-PUTLA

FLETE Y PASAJES BUS

CRISTÓBAL
COLÓN BUS

MORELOS

LAVANDERÍA
GEMINIS

HIPODROMO

To Yosundua and
Cascada Esmeralda

0   100 yds

0   100 m

125

To Juxtlahuaca, Putla,
and the Pacific Coast

© AVALON TRAVEL

Tlaxiaco, also capital of its own governmental district, was even more important in times past. During the "Order and Progress" of President Porfirio Díaz (1876–1910), Tlaxiaco's significance perhaps eclipsed even Oaxaca City. Its key position on the trade route between Puebla-Veracruz and the southern Pacific coast, as well as its large hinterland population, made Tlaxiaco the trading and supply center for much of southwest Mexico. Rich merchants and entrepreneurs, both Mexican and foreign, together with wealthy *hacendados* (landed gentry), constituted a local upper crust who, for a generation, earned Tlaxiaco the unofficial title of "Little Paris."

The Dominican missionary padres certainly understood Tlaxiaco's importance as early as 1550, when Friar Francisco Marín began building the monumental town church, the Templo de la Asunción. Scholars have identified details in the church's decorations that resemble those of the main church in the city of Caceres, Spain. This link has added a piece to one of the puzzles of Oaxaca's great Dominican churches: Where did the Dominican clerics, presumably isolated in the Oaxaca hinterlands, acquire the skill to create the masterpiece churches of Yanhuitlán, Teposcolula, Coixtlahuaca, and Tlaxiaco? The answer may lie in a previously unknown connection between the Dominican friars and the noted Rodrigo Gil de Montañon, master of Spanish Gothic–Plateresque architecture and builder of the Caceres church. (See the sidebar *Building Churches* in *The Valley of Oaxaca* chapter.)

◖ Tlaxiaco Saturday *Tianguis*

Let **Plaza Constitución,** the hub of the Tlaxiaco market, a few blocks uphill from the cluttered and bumpy through-town highway, be your key to finding your way around town. Main east–west streets Colón and 5 de Mayo run along the north and south sides, respectively, of Plaza Constitución. East of the plaza, they intersect the other main town streets, Independencia and Hidalgo, which both run north, uphill from the highway. The perfect spot to view all of this is the front porch of the

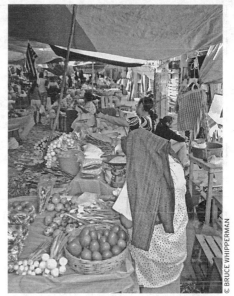

The produce at Tlaxiaco Saturday *tianguis* is among the best anywhere.

Hotel del Portal, which perches on the uphill (north) side of the plaza. From there, you'll see the town clock in the plaza foreground; and in the background, bell tower of the town church, Templo de la Asunción, a few hundred yards to the southwest. To the right of the church, behind some trees on the west side of a shady *jardín,* stands the town *presidencia municipal.*

Make sure to arrive in Tlaxiaco by noon on Saturday, in time to soak in its spreading, colorful, Saturday *tianguis.* It's fun to just wander around beneath the rainbow of awnings shading a galaxy of merchandise, both modern and traditional. Especially interesting are the time-tested handmade goods: *calabazas* (gourds) cut and carved into bowls, utensils, and musical instruments; extensive assortments of forest-gathered roots, seeds, bark, dried flowers, and nuts, ready to brew into teas to relieve dozens of illnesses; traditional clothes—hand-embroidered *huipiles* and *blusas* from all over Oaxaca—*canastas, tenates, petates* (reed baskets, palm baskets, and mats)—and soft sombreros woven from palm; and leather

MEXICAN NAMES

Nearly every Mexican, from native country folks to pure Spanish bluebloods, goes by his or her Spanish-origin names. Outsiders, confounded by long handles, such as Doña Juana María López de Díaz, wonder how Mexican names got so complicated.

The preceding "Doña Juana" example is especially complicated, because it's a typical woman's name, which is generally more complex than that of a typical man.

So, let's explain a man's name first. Take the national hero, Vicente Ramón Guerrero Saldaña. Vicente is his first given name; Ramón, the second given name, corresponds to the "middle" name in the United States. The third, Guerrero, is customarily the father's first surname, and the last, Saldaña, his mother's first surname. Only on formal occasions are men referred to with all four of their names. Simply, "Vicente Guerrero" would do most of the time.

Now, back to "Doña Juana." I threw a curve at you by introducing "Doña." It's an honorific, used as "Dame," for a distinguished woman. ("Don" is the corresponding honorific for Spanish men.)

So, skipping the honorific, women's names start out like men's: First given name, Juana; second given name, María, and father's first surname López.

Now, things get more complicated. For unmarried women, the naming is the same as for men. But when a woman gets married, she customarily replaces her second surname with her husband's first surname, preceded by "de," meaning "of." So, in the example, Juana is evidently a married woman, who has substituted "de Díaz" (her husband's first surname being Díaz) for her second surname, all adding up to "Juana María López de Díaz."

Thankfully, however, informal names for women also are simplified. Juana, above, would ordinarily shorten her name down to her first given name followed by her husband's first surname: simply Juana Díaz.

All the above notwithstanding, many Mexican women do not go along with this male-dominated system at all and simply use their maiden names as they were known before they were married.

---

cinturones, bolsas, and *billeteras* (belts, purses, and billfolds).

The added plus of all the bustle, of course, is the people, especially the native women, who really run the whole show. The men, who help transport the goods, usually stand back (and sometimes, unfortunately, get drunk) and let their spouses do the buying and selling. Perhaps the best two spots for native action are the narrow **Plaza Vasconcelos,** which heads downhill for a block from the southeast corner of Plaza Constitución, and the front steps of the church, a hubbub of native fruit and vegetable sellers.

While you're people-watching in front of the church, the **Templo de la Asunción,** take a break and step into its cool, calm interior. Although begun in 1550, the church, once a Dominican convent, has been continually modified and strengthened since that time.

Towering overhead, a network of unreinforced (no steel: all stone) Gothic arches have, amazingly, supported the entire ceiling for more than 400 years, freeing the nave from the clutter of columns and creating a heavenly, soaring space for worship, rest, and contemplation.

Tlaxiaco's patron, the Virgen de la Asunción, presides from above the altar. High above her, note the all-seeing Eye of God (which looks every bit like its counterparts that decorate many Buddhist and Hindu stupas in India and Nepal).

Townsfolk celebrate their beloved patron in a pair of annual **fiestas.** The first, the official patronal religious festival, Fiesta de la Virgen de la Asunción (accent on the "o" in "Asunción"), kicks off on August 14 and continues for two more days with processions, food, and fireworks. The second, the secular town **Fiesta de Octubre,** occurs around the third Sunday of October and includes fireworks, basketball and *pelota mixteca* (traditional ball game) tournaments, and popular dances.

Botica la Parroquia

Just across the street, north, from the churchfront, the Botica la Parroquia (8 A.M.–9 P.M. daily) is as much a museum as a pharmacy. Its 150 years of continuous operation, begun by the present owner's great-grandfather and handed down through the family, has resulted in a vast and venerable collection of antique bottles, flasks, urns, mortars and pestles, and a regiment of drawers stuffed with locally gathered barks, leaves, mosses, grasses, flowers, mushrooms, seeds, minerals, and animal parts for compounding into remedies to relieve a host of ailments. For example, you can get *siete aguas* (seven waters) for relief of *mal aire* (bad air), a folk name for a common ailment with symptoms of weakness and fever; often, but not always, modern doctors diagnose *mal aire* as malaria. You can also get *catalan* and *arnica* for aches and pains, and, for whatever else ails you, homemade herbal brandy dispensed in two-peso portions from a gallon jug on the front counter.

The present owner explains his pharmacy's history and mission: "Grandad was the town doctor. Everyone came to him when they were sick. He hand-prepared all of his prescriptions. My mom still does it."

Accommodations

UNDER $25

A block and a half west of Plaza Constitución stands the downscale old standby, the family-run **Hotel Mexico** (Hidalgo 13, tel. 953/552-0086, $10 s or d, $16 t "old" rooms, $20 s or d, $29 t "new" rooms). Rooms in "new" (private bath) and "old" (shared bath) sections surround a rambling inside patio. All of the 20-odd rooms are clean; the "old" rooms are plainly furnished, while the "new" are thoughtfully decorated with wood furnishings, attractive bedspreads, and drapes. Rooms all come with hot water available only in the morning until 11 A.M.; credit cards not accepted.

Located a few blocks southeast of the town center, the **Hotel San Mishell's** (Independencia 11, tel. 953/552-0064, $10–25 s, $20–35 d, $70 suite) offers attentive on-site family management. The 20 superior-grade rooms in a two-story wing surround an inviting inner garden patio. Inside, rooms are clean, carpeted, and thoughtfully decorated. Outside the rooms, on a shady garden-view porch, guests enjoy soft chairs for reading and relaxing. Standard-grade rooms, although clean and comfortable, occupy a two-story tier beside an adjacent parking patio. Standard-grade rooms run about $10 s, $20 d without TV, $20 s, $28 d with TV. Superior-grade rooms go for about $25 s, $28 d in one bed, $35 d in two beds. All have hot water shower-baths, TV, parking, and a breakfast restaurant, but credit cards not accepted. A super-elegant suite, fit for a king, sleeping about six, rents for $70.

$25-50

Of Tlaxiaco's hotels, the **(Hotel del Portal** (Constitución 2, tel. 953/552-0154, $20 s, $25 d in one bed, $35 d or t in two beds), at the north-side plaza-front, affords a superb vantage for soaking in the market action and exploring the colorful town center. Inside past the reception, you enter an elegantly restored grand patio, softly illuminated by an overhead skylight. The three stories of approximately 50 rooms encircle a back parking courtyard. The rooms are spartan, but clean, comfortable, and well maintained, with hot-water showerbaths, TV and parking; credit cards are not accepted.

Food

Taco stands and upstairs *fondas* at the covered **Mercado Benito Juárez** (one block south of the Plaza Constitución's southeast corner) are your best source of economical meals and snacks. Furthermore, a nearby homey sit-down *comedor,* the **Cocina Economica Doña Caro** (Morelos 13, 8 A.M.–8 P.M. Mon.–Sat.), between Independencia and Hidalgo, two blocks east and three blocks south of the plaza's southeast corner, also puts out steaming chicken, turkey, and tamales smothered in *mole,* and savory pork and beef *guisados* (stews, $4–5).

Basic groceries are available at plaza-front *abarroterías,* notably at **Super Mega** (tel. 953/552-0179, 8:30 A.M.–9 P.M. Mon.–Sat., 8:30 A.M.–6:30 P.M. Sun.), on the plaza's northeast side, two doors east of the Hotel del Portal.

Baked goods are also sold at several stalls at the Mercado Benito Juárez and at least two bakeries. Try either the **Panificadora Luisito** (corner of Díaz and Juárez, a block north of Plaza Consitución, 9 A.M.–8 P.M. daily), or the **Pastelería Flor** (on Cinco de Mayo, half a block east of the market plaza's southeast corner, tel. 953/552-0555, 9 A.M.–10 P.M. daily), with a host of delights, including chocolate, three-milk, cheese, and lemon cakes, good coffee, and hamburgers, *tortas,* and hot dogs to boot.

A sprinkling of restaurants (some very good) cater to the trickle of visitors and handful of Tlaxiaco residents who can afford to eat out. Tlaxiaco's fanciest is the **Restaurant El Patio** (in the airy inner courtyard of the Hotel del Portal, tel. 953/552-0154, 8 A.M.–9 P.M. daily). Oaxacan cuisine is the main event here; pick from a long list of appetizers, such as roasted onions with leaves of nopal ($3) or tortilla soup ($3); for a main dish, you might choose *pierna de puerco* (leg of pork) smothered in rich dark *mole* ($5), or Tlaxiaco-style tacos ($4).

Even better is the refined **(Rincón de Gon** (Aldama 1, tel. 953/552-0608, 8 A.M.–11 P.M. daily), at the corner of Hidalgo, a block east and two blocks south of the plaza's southeast corner. You can start with a choice of breakfasts, including *huevos con jamón* (ham and eggs), omelets, fruit, granola, and hotcakes ($2–5). For lunch or supper, choose from several salads ($3–5), and among entrées of fish, meat, poultry, and Mexican specialties ($6–12). Some evenings, beginning around 9, patrons enjoy relaxing instrumental music. (Unfortunately, they've acquired a TV. But to their credit, they also provide an adjacent TV-free dining room.)

For a leisurely *comida corrida* (set lunch, $4) or a bountiful à la carte selection ($3–7) on a

In the Mixteca, hardware is still largely sold in family-operated old-fashioned *ferreterias* (hardware stores).

warm afternoon, go to refined, airy restaurant ▐€ **El Encanto** (Vásquez 6, tel. 953/552-0990, 8 A.M.–9 P.M. Mon.–Sat.), a block south and a block and a half east of the main plaza's southeast corner. Find them open also for à la carte breakfast ($2–4) and *cena* (supper, $2–4).

Information and Services

Change money at Tlaxiaco's plaza-front **Banamex** (Colón 1, tel. 953/552-0166 or 953/552-0133, 9 A.M.–4 P.M. Mon.–Fri., 9 A.M.–1 P.M. Sat.). After hours, use its up-front ATM for cash.

Alternatively, go to **Banorte** (at the plaza's southwest corner, tel. 953/552-0662, 9 A.M.–6 P.M. Mon.–Fri.) for similar services and ATM.

Buy stamps or send letters at the *correo* (953/552-2126, 8 A.M.–3 P.M. Mon.–Fri., 9 A.M.–1 P.M. Sat.), on the north side of the *jardín* in front of the church. Next door, at *telecomunicaciones* (tel. 953/552-0190, fax 953/552-0465, 8 A.M.–8 P.M. Mon.–Fri., 9 A.M.–noon Sat.), you can send or receive a fax or money order.

Telephone long distance or send a fax at the *caseta larga distancia* (at the northeast plaza corner next to the Hotel del Portal, tel. 953/552-0313, 953/552-0314, or 953/552-0147, 7 A.M.–11 P.M. daily). Alternatively (and more economically) buy a commonly available Ladatel telephone card and use it to call home in the United States, Canada, or Europe ($2 for four minutes).

Answer your email and access the Internet at **Sircom Internet** (on Morelos, tel. 953/552-0063, 11 A.M.–11 P.M. daily), three blocks south of the plaza, between Hidalgo and Independencia.

If you need a doctor, ask at your hotel desk for a recommendation or contact one of Tlaxiaco's highly recommended physicians: either **Dr. Javier Noé Alavez Cervantes** at **Sanatorio Mitzy** (Moctezuma 4, a block and a half west from the plaza, tel./fax 953/552-0028); or general practitioner **Doctor Manuel López Hernádez** at the **ISSTE (Seguro Social)** clinic (on Hwy. 125, Oaxaca

City direction, about a mile east of town, tel. 953/552-0750); or surgeon **Dr. Geraldo Cruz Vela** (tel. 953/552-0210).

For nonprescription medicines and drugs, try either **Farmacia La Merced** (downhill three blocks from the plaza, at the corner of Morelos and Hidalgo, tel. 953/552-0483, 8 A.M.–9 P.M. Mon.–Sat., 10 A.M.–2 P.M. Sun.), or **Farmacia Pronto** (on Cinco de Mayo, half a block east of the plaza's southeast corner, tel. 953/552-0664, 9 A.M.–9 P.M. Mon.–Sat.).

In police, fire, or medical emergencies call the *policía municipal* (953/552-0680).

For film, development, and some digital and film point-and-shoot cameras and supplies, go to Tlaxiaco's Fuji film dealer, **Foto Eureka** (on Hidalgo, two blocks south, one block east of the plaza, tel. 953/552-0249, 8 A.M.–9 P.M. Mon.–Sat., 9 A.M.–1 P.M. Sun.).

Tlaxiaco's friendly, family-owned laundry is **Lavandería Geminis** (Capitán José Herrera 20, tel. 953/552-0708, 8 A.M.–4 P.M. and 5–8 P.M. Mon.–Sat.); find it two blocks west, three blocks south of the plaza.

Getting There and Away

A welter of taxis, local buses and minivans, and long-distance buses deposit and pick up a small army of passengers daily downhill on Highway 125, locally called Avenida Hipodromo as it runs east–west along the south edge of downtown, and Independencia after it turns north and continues along the east edge of downtown.

Long-distance service includes **Sur** and **Cristóbal Colón**, from their station at Hipodromo 24 B (tel. 953/552-0182), half a block west of the Independencia corner. There, buses connect east and southeast with Teposcolula, Yanhuitlán, Nochixtlán, and Oaxaca City; and north with Tamazulapan, Huajuapan, Puebla, Cuautla (Morelos), and Mexico City.

Also, on Hipodromo, a few doors east, second-class **Fletes y Pasajes** (tel. 953/552-0432) long-distance buses connect east and southeast with Teposcolula, Yanhuitlán, Nochixtlán, and Oaxaca City, and quickly north with Mexico City (Tapo

THE MIXTECA

terminal) by the expressway via Coixtlahuaca, Tepelmeme, Tehuacán, and Puebla.

Furthermore, a pair of good van services provide fast and frequent connections. Uphill, on Independencia, a block north of Hipodromo, **Transportes Turística Mixteca Baja** (tel. 953/552-0308) connects very frequently with Oaxaca City, via Teposcolula and Nochixtlán, south with Putla (where connections are available for the Pacific coast), and Yosundua (around noon and 6 P.M.) daily. Alternatively, reliable RAMSA vans, at Hipodromo 13, across from Cristóbal Colón, connect frequently northeast with Oaxaca City, and south with Putla.

Drivers can connect southerly, to or from Tlaxiaco, with Putla, by Highway 125 in about 47 miles (75 km) or two hours; westerly, with Juxtlahuaca via Highways 125 and 182 (50 miles/80 km) also in about two hours; and easterly with Teposcolula (26 miles/42 km) in about an hour, thence another three hours, to or from Oaxaca City.

SOUTH OF TLAXIACO

Although the glorious Cascada Esmeralda (Emerald Waterfall) at the end of the road is reason enough to venture out on this 106-mile (171-km) round-trip excursion, the sights along the way make the journey doubly enjoyable. You'll gaze at a succession of mighty pine- and oak-studded mountains, mile upon mile of green, terraced fields, and, oddly in contrast, one of the most spectacularly eroded landscapes in Oaxaca. Moreover, you'll pass more log cabins here than on a trip through all of Montana and Wyoming. And if you go on Sunday, you'll get a chance to visit a pair of busy country markets. Finally, self-contained RV or tent campers can enjoy a superbly scenic natural camping site at the dramatic top of Cascada Esmeralda. The all-paved route climbs to the top of the Mixteca Alta—the 9,000-foot (2,700-meter) cool, fertile, Chalcatongo plateau—before descending to Yosundua and the subtropical Esmeralda valley, where on a clear day, folks say, you can glimpse the blue Pacific.

The Road to Chalcatongo

Start out early (8 A.M. by bus, no later than 10 A.M. by car) because in the Mixteca (Land of the Clouds), especially in the summer–fall rainy season, sunny mornings often turn gray, drizzly, and cool by midafternoon. By bus, go from the **Unión de Transportistas Ñundeya** minibus terminal (on Hipodromo, three doors west of the Independencia corner, tel. 953/540-9894).

Drivers, mark your odometer and head south along the southern prolongation of Independencia, from the Highway 125 Independencia-Hipodromo corner. Best fill up with gasoline in town (gas on east, Oaxaca City, side only) beforehand. There is only one gas station en route, at Chalcatongo (although stores along the way do sell unleaded regular). If you want to eat well along the way, best take your own picnic, especially during the winter, when upcountry fresh fruit and veggie supplies are at low ebb.

At mile 10 (km 16), the road reaches an overlook where you can gaze down upon the **Magdalena Peñasco** valley, with erosion so dramatic that, like the scenic Badlands of Dakota, it's a sight in itself. The reason isn't so difficult to figure. Long ago, the people cut the trees for fuel and houses, then farmed the hills without contour terracing. They let sheep and goats overgraze the meadows, and when downpours began forming gullies, it was too late. Today the entire valley looks like a red, rutted devil's playground.

As you continue downhill, you'll see folks along the road weaving palm leaves, especially on Sunday, as they walk toward the weekly Magdalena Peñasco *tianguis*. Passing the town square and market, at around mile 12 (km 19), notice one of Magdalena's major public buildings—a turquoise-blue log house—on the right.

Around mile 21 (km 34), continuing through **San Mateo Peñasco,** it's difficult not to be awed by the towering stone-faced mountain on the right. In times past (or maybe even in times present) this awesomely rugged rampart, which local people call simply La Peña

(The Rock), must have been a sacred mountain, with its own Señor del Monte (Lord of the Mountain).

Today, a cross stands partway up the slope, where the villagers climb on May 3, the Día de la Santa Cruz (Day of the Holy Cross). Although arduous, the hike to the summit appears doable with effort by fit people wearing hats and sturdy shoes and carrying drinking water. Don't attempt it, however, without permission from the San Mateo Peñasco municipal authorities, who can probably suggest a guide whom you can hire to show the way.

In contrast to the eroded Magdalena valley, the surroundings of **San Pedro Molinos,** at mile 28 (km 45), appear the model of progressive farming practice. Lush valley-bottom fields give way to terraced, mid-slope gardens, which lead to a crown of thick summit forests. Molinos town is marked by its spiffy portaled *presidencia municipal.*

Farther on, at **Santa Catarina Ticúa** around mile 31 (km 50), note the uniquely picturesque three-story log house, on the right just as you arrive at the town plaza and church. Next, step across the plaza and take a look inside the brilliantly painted 18th-century church, dedicated to martyr Saint Catherine. If you're lucky, you'll arrive on November 24 or 25, when local people are celebrating Santa Catarina with processions, fireworks, sports contests, and dances. If not, at least you can admire the Mixtec pre-Columbian floral designs on the church's walls and ceiling, and maybe afterward, if it's a warm day, you might pause for a dip in the community swimming pool (if it's been maintained; it was algae-stained at my last visit) outside next to the church.

Chalcatongo

At around mile 37 (km 60), you reach high and cool, sometimes even chilly, Chalcatongo (pop. 2,000). Chalcatongo has two plazas, the first one bordered by the distinguished church, the **Templo de la Natividad,** whose patron, the Virgen de la Natividad, townsfolk celebrate with a fiesta on September 8. Chalcatongo is otherwise quiet except for Thursday, when a

regiment of local Mixtec-speaking folks and dozens of vendors from as far as Mexico City crowd in for a big country **tianguis** market.

At the second plaza, one block ahead, one block left, stands the *presidencia municipal.* Although the plazas have a few taco shops, only a few places in town serve complete, country-style meals. The best are the immaculate Restaurant El Paisano and the Restaurant El Fortín, both on the north (Tlaxiaco) side of town where, entering town from Tlaxiaco, the truck route bypass forks right. El Fortín is on the right, just before the fork.

El Paisano (around the corner, just past the Hotel 2000, 7 A.M.–8 P.M. daily) serves hearty breakfasts (*huevos a la Mexicana,* pancakes, *chilaquiles* and eggs $1–2) until noon, and a filling *comida* (pork in red *mole* $2, chiles rellenos in tomato sauce $2) until 5 P.M., and supper choices of tacos, quesadillas, eggs, and *tortas* ($2) until closing. **El Fortín,** also highly recommended locally, has similar hours and food, as does a the third restaurant choice, **El Calvario,** on the south side, at the corner of Guerrero and Insurgentes, second floor, on the highway out of town.

If you decide to stay overnight, Chalcatongo has a good family-run hotel, the **Hotel Lazo** (Cinco de Mayo 67, tel. 953/533-4061, $12 s, $18 d in one bed, $24 d in two beds, $30 t), in the south-side neighborhood. The hotel, built around an inviting interior patio courtyard, offers 24 very clean, comfortable (but smallish) rooms, with 1–3 beds and private hot-water shower bathrooms.

Yosundua and Cascada Esmeralda

Drivers lucky enough to arrive in Yosundua (at mile 51/km 82) on Sunday will probably find the way to the waterfall blocked by the big, colorful **tianguis.** Stroll around for a while, then detour downhill, then ahead, via the street that runs in front of the big church, **Templo Santiago Apóstol.** The church is dedicated to Saint James the Apostle, whom townsfolk celebrate July 23–26. Bus passengers should either hire a taxi or hike straight ahead from the Yosundua bus stop about 2.5 miles (4 km) and 1,000 feet (300 meters) downhill to the Cascada Esmeralda.

If you're hungry, stop by the clean family-run home-style **Restaurant Manantial** (Restaurant Spring, 8 A.M.–9 P.M. daily, $2–6), named for the town's crystal-clear water source, nearby. It's at the far, southeast edge of town, where the gravel road heads south to the Cascada Esmeralda.

If you miss the last bus back, you can stay at the basic but recommendable **Hotel California** ($15 s or d, $25 d in two beds), whose personable owner returned from California with a wad of cash and decided to build himself a hotel. He now has 31 mostly empty spare but clean rooms, with private hot-water shower-bath. You can't miss the place, because, except for the church, it's the biggest building (downhill two blocks on the right as you enter) in town.

Another overnight option, for people who are equipped, is to set up a tent or park their self-contained RV in the informal meadow campground at the top of the Cascada Esmeralda, at mile 53 (km 85). There, the blue-green (brown during the summer rains, however) Río Esmeralda (Emerald River) pauses a while in an inviting pool (safe only at low water) before it plunges over the cliff. The road winds another few hundred yards down a steep grade; continue on foot down a steep, short path to the foot of the falls, where you're surrounded by natural beauty. On one side, the waterfall, split into a lacy network of petite cascades, cools you with gentle spray, while on the other, far below, a grand, sun-dappled verdant valley of field and forest nestles beneath a host of sharp, soaring peaks.

EAST OF TLAXIACO

The country east of Tlaxiaco undulates over small fertile vales and green pine-forested hilltops, many crowned with the ruins of ancient buried towns and cities. Two of the largest and most interesting of those ruins are at Achiutla and Huamelulpan, not far from Tlaxiaco.

San Miguel Achiutla

The archaeological site at Achiutla (ah-shee-

YOO-tlah, pop. 1,000) is among Oaxaca's historically most intriguing, partly because it contains both pre- and post-conquest ruins. These include the remains of the earthquake-collapsed original Dominican church and a grand pre-conquest ruined complex, once the site of a renowned Mixtec oracle.

GETTING THERE

The gorgeous pine-forested mountains and lush (summer–fall rainy season) valleys you pass along the way are part of the fun of Achiutla. Bus travelers go most conveniently by the minibuses that leave for Achiutla (via Santa Caterina Tayata) from the corner of Calle Cinco de Mayo and Highway 125 (Av. Independencia) at the northeast corner of downtown Tlaxiaco. Alternatively, bargain for a taxi to take you to the Achiutla turnoff (signed Santa Catarina Tayata) about nine miles (14 km) east of town, then catch a truck from there. If so, find out the price—ask, *"¿Cuanto cuesta a Achiutla?"* ("How much to Achiutla?")—before getting on.

The road, although gravel, is easily passable by experienced drivers in ordinary cars. From Tlaxiaco, along Highway 125, drive east about nine miles/14 km, (or west from Teposcolula about 17 miles/27 km). Set your odometer at the signed Santa Catarina Tayata turnoff. After 1.2 miles (1.9 km), turn left at the fork. Continue through Santa Catarina Tayata (5.2 miles/8.4 km) and follow the left fork (5.4 miles/8.7 km). At 6.4 miles (10.3 km) pass over Río Tayata bridge and by the lovely creekside grove of ancient *ahuehuete* trees. Some of the gnarled giants, 10 feet (three meters) in diameter, must be at least a thousand years old. The adjacent creekside meadows provide good camping spots. (Bring water.) First, however, get permission (usually no problem) from the municipal authorities at Santa Catarina Tayata.

At mile 10.5 (km 17) you get the first glimpse of the old San Miguel Achiutla church on the hill straight ahead. Take a left at the T (10.8 miles/17.4 km), then right (11.2 miles/18 km) and continue straight ahead for the old church on the right, ruins on left (12.6

miles/20.3 km), and San Miguel Achiutla town at 14 miles (22.5 km).

EXPLORING THE SITE

The area of historical and archaeological interest lies on an airy, scenic hilltop west of the modern town. The present church, the antique **Templo y Ex-Convento de San Miguel Achiutla,** stands on the rise to the south of the road. It supplanted an even older church, now in ruins, on the other side of the road, probably built atop the pre-conquest oracle temple. Beyond that rises a cemetery occupying what appear to be three pre-conquest ceremonial courtyards cut, like grand stair steps, into a mountainside that rises another mile (1.6 km) to a high, breezy summit.

First, however, walk south across the broad atrium that leads to the present church. On your way, take a look at the pair of ponderous bronze bells, dated 1848, hanging from a rustic ground-level *campanario*. The Dominicans built the church probably during the 1600s, several decades after the original building was begun in 1558 across the road. The new church, dedicated to Archangel St. Michael, grew into a prosperous vicarage, surrounded by a cluster of dependent congregations. Times changed, however. The once-new church is now crumbling and nearly abandoned. Its doors open regularly only for Sunday mass at 10 A.M., after which folks lock up and return downhill for an 11 A.M. mass at the church in town.

A major exception occurs during festivals, celebrating the Sacred Heart of Jesus (June 19), **Carnaval** (Sunday, Monday, and Tuesday before Ash Wednesday), and especially the **Fiesta de San Miguel** (September 21–29), when masses fill the old church every day.

The old place is well worth a look around inside. Try finding the *sacristan* (church-keeper), who's often nearby. If you're sufficiently persuasive, he might open the door for you.

You'll find the inside completely unrestored except for the gilded, baroque main altarpiece, recently refurbished after it collapsed under its own weight. In addition to the native artists' colorful floral designs, the nave walls hold a gallery of precious 16th-century paintings. Don't miss the one showing the angel St. Michael leading a mortal into heaven. Up front, bats flit and flutter out of the baptismal chapel on the left. On the opposite side, note the unusual screened platform high on the south wall, said to have accommodated cloistered nuns who nevertheless wanted to view mass in the nave. The door on the nave's right front leads to an open courtyard, which in turn leads to the ex-convent's former working and living quarters.

Outside, across the road, the ruin of the original church probably stands atop the renowned Achiutla oracle temple. This spot abounds with legends. A Mixtec codex records that one Tilantongo queen was born from a tree in Achiutla. So powerful was Achiutla's magic that people came, believing it to be the home of an all-seeing spirit, an oracle, known then as the Corazón del Pueblo (Heart of the People), who, acting through the local priests, could portend future events. No less than the Emperor Moctezuma, when Cortés threatened his capital, sent emissaries to Achiutla. They asked that proper sacrifices be made to the oracle in return for a divination of the result of Cortés's threat. The answer was that Moctezuma's grand empire would be destroyed.

Past the ruined church, climb along paths through the ancient retaining walls, built by long-dead Mixtec masons, to the cemetery's upper levels. Gaze out toward the fertile Achiutla valley far below, encircled by a verdant crown of pine-capped mountains.

Nearby, scattered around you, the cemetery's oldest legible tombstones date from around 1900; many others, unreadably weathered and crumbling, appear much older. Buried beneath those—no one yet knows how deep or old—lie the relics of Achiutla's past.

SERVICES

Drowsy little Achiutla town downhill has a basic grocery store, a *centro de salud*, police (at the *presidencia municipal*), and gasoline, at a store at the west edge of town.

San Martín Huamelulpan

The community museum at Huamelulpan (oo-wah-may-LOOL-pahn), about a mile (two km) off Highway 125, three miles (five km) east of the Achiutla turnoff, was built partly to display the artifacts uncovered at the town's important archaeological zone. The National Archaeology and History Institute (INAH) installed the museum's archaeological exhibits in 1978. Later, the local community took over and did its own oral history project during the late 1980s, which resulted in the museum's traditional medicine displays.

Note the sign on the post on the right as you reach the town plaza. It reads, roughly: "Please stop and register at the community museum and get a guide to show you the ruins." If you arrive when the museum is closed, ask around for someone to guide you.

Huamelulpan Museum and Archaeological Zone

The museum is officially called the **Museo Comunitario Ihitalulu** (ee-ee-tah-LOO-loo), meaning "Beautiful Flower" (10 A.M.–5 P.M. Tues.–Sun.). Inside, on the left after you

---

DUENDES: SPIRITS OF MEXICO

Once upon a time, most everyone believed that the world was full of spirits that inhabited every object in creation: trees, rocks, animals, mountains, even the wind and the stars. World mythology is replete with examples, from the leprechauns of Ireland and the fairies of Mount Tirich Mir in Pakistan to the spirits who haunt old Hawaiian *heiaus* (temples) and the *duendes* of Mexico.

Such beliefs persist, especially in the Mixteca countryside. Eventually, many a campesino will take his children to his mountainside cornfield to introduce them to the *duendes*, the elfin beings who folks sometimes glimpse in the shadowed thickets where they hide from mortals.

At the upper end of his field, the campesino father addresses the *duendes*: "With your permission we clear your brush and use your water because it is necessary to nourish our corn and beans. Please allow us, for otherwise, we would starve."

Modernized city Mexicans, generations removed from country village life, often scoff at such antique beliefs. That is, until the family doctor fails to cure their weakened spouse or sick child. Then they often run to a *curandero* or *curandera* (folk healer).

"Enduendado," affliction by an angry *duende*, the *curandero* sometimes diagnoses. Often, the cure is simple and savvy: teas and poultices of forest-gathered herbs. Other

times, it is mystical, such as "purifying" by passing an egg all over the afflicted one's body to draw out the illness, and then breaking the egg into a bowl. The shape the broken yolk takes, maybe of a snake, might determine the treatment, which may be long and intricate: massage with lotions of herbs and oils, followed by a *temazcal* (sweat bath) rubdown with rough maguey fibers, all consummated by intense prayers to the Virgin of Guadalupe to force the *duende* to cease the affliction.

Many times, the folk cure fails; other times, however, it succeeds, and with enough frequency to convince millions of Mexicans of the power of the village folk healer to purge a *duende*'s poisonous spell.

© BRUCE WHIPPERMAN

Snake skins are prized for medicinal and ceremonial use by *curanderos* (native healers).

enter, you'll see the archaeological section first, with its especially notable monolith of Dzahui, the Mixtec god of rain, lightning, and thunder (akin to the Zapotec god Cocijo). Also fascinating are burial remains, including a complete skeleton and bowls for portions of water, food, and *pulque* for the afterlife. On the museum's opposite side, find the equally intriguing traditional medicine exhibit, detailing methods that *curanderos* (curers), *yerberas* (herbal healers), and *parteras* (midwives) use to treat their clients. Conditions commonly treated include *el parto* (childbirth), *el empacho* (stomach infections), *mal de aire* (shivering, and head and body aches; compare: malaria), and *el espanto* (soul loss, accompanied by severe anxiety). Displays illustrate many remedies, from herbal teas and *temazcal* hot baths to doses of chicken blood and incantations beseeching forgiveness from earth spirits.

EXPLORING THE ZONE

Leave time for a stroll around the archaeological zone. It was first visited in 1933 by Alfonso Caso of Monte Albán fame, and it has been intensively excavated and partly reconstructed by several others since the 1950s. Finds reveal that Huamelulpan was a small city occupied between 400 B.C. and A.D. 600, approximately the same epoch as Monte Albán.

The zone rambles extensively over many hundreds of acres, running north of town along an approximate east–west line. The most westerly discovered (but unreconstructed) remains lie on the high west-side **Cerro Volado** hilltop. The most intensively reconstructed portion is the so-called Church Group, near the church, a few hundred yards east beyond the town plaza and museum.

Start at the church itself, which has what appears to be a grinning pre-conquest god of death skeleton-monolith built into its right (south) wall. If you continue walking south along the road in front of the church, you will be passing the partly reconstructed **ball court,** reachable by ascending the rise to the left (east) of the road. Notice, at the

ball court's south end, the reconstructed half of its I-shaped layout. Continue east, up the second embankment, to a regal **ceremonial courtyard** climaxed on its east side with an elegant staircase and retaining walls. Climb those stairs to another level and yet another courtyard crowned by an equally elegant but smaller **ceremonial platform.**

Huamelulpan community museum volunteers lead visitors on tours of their archaeological zone, including Cerro Volado, for a fee of about $20. Arrive early and you may be able to arrange such a tour on the spot. Guides and **lodging** at Huamelulpan's tourist-house dormitory can also be reserved ahead of time by leaving a message, including time of arrival and number in your party, at the Huamelulpan long-distance telephone *caseta* (tel. 555/329-0982).

Alternatively, you may be able to make a lodging reservation and appointment through the government alternative tourism office in Oaxaca City (Murguia 206, up the driveway, in the back, tel. 951/516-0123, info@aoaxaca. com, www.oaxaca.travel).

Get to Huamelulpan by car or Tlaxiaco-bound second-class Fletes y Pasajes bus from either Oaxaca City, Nochixtlán, Tamazulapan, or Teposcolula. Get off at the Huamelulpan turnoff on Highway 125, about half an hour (13 miles/21 km) past Teposcolula. In the reverse direction, drive or ride a Fletes y Pasajes bus east from Tlaxiaco a similar 13 miles (21 km), half an hour, and get off at the Huamelulpan side-road turnoff. Continue about a mile (two km) to the museum on the town plaza.

WEST OF TLAXIACO

This is high, cool country of pine-brushed mountains, villages, and cornfields. The people are reserved but quick to return your wave and smile. They see so few outsiders that, although they try to avoid it, they can't help staring as you pass, wondering why you've come. For at least two of these communities, Santa María Cuquila and San Miguel Progreso, visitors have an immediate reason for coming: to see the community museums.

THE MIXTECA

Santa María Cuquila

The Aztecs, to whom the Cuquila (koo-KEE-lah) people were tributaries at the time of the conquest, coined the name Cuquila, which roughly translates to Snakes in the Brush. The Mixtec-speaking local people, however, previously called their village Ñu Kuiñe, which means Town of the Tiger in the local tongue.

Now, Cuquila (pop. 5,000) with the help of the government Centro de Desarollo Para los Pueblos Indígenas (www.cedei.gob.mx/cuquila) has organized a museum with a number of precious artifacts, including hieroglyph-inscribed stones found in the big archaeological zone nearby, and documents from the 1580s, such as a map of the town and several yellowed pages recording a plethora of information—town borders, officials' names, events, and perhaps even a little gossip—of early colonial days in Cuquila. The museum also displays examples of locally made present-day pottery and hand-woven *huipiles.*

The town presently runs a handicrafts store, built with the help of the American-based Amigos de las Americas (www.amigoslink .org), on the highway through town. This would be a good spot to stop and maybe see the *artesanos*—potters and weavers—at work, and/or make contacts to visit their home workshops in the village.

The museum committee is currently headed by its president, Emiliano Melchor Ayala. He and other committee members are qualified to take you on a tour (about two miles/three km, three hours round-trip, offer a donation of about $20) to their "old town" (former population about 3000) archaeological site on a hill nearby.

Archaeologists estimate that the site was occupied for about 1,300 years, from 400 B.C. to A.D. 900. The ceremonial area, consisting of the remains of a pair of royal residences, a main plaza, two tombs, and a ball court, spreads over about 25 acres. The Cuquila museum is open by appointment, which you can make, or better yet, ask your hotel desk clerk to make by calling the town long-distance telephone (tel.

953/554-0716) or the town *agencia municipal* (tel. 953/538-7051).

Get to Cuquila by local minivan, or Fletes y Pasajes or Cristóbal Colón bus from Juxtlahuaca, Tlaxiaco, or Putla. By car, Cuquila is right on Highway 125, 12 miles (19 km) west of Tlaxiaco, 35 miles (56 km) east of Juxtlahuaca, or 32 miles (51 km) northeast of Putla.

San Miguel Progreso

Two miles (three km) from the signed turn-off from Highway 125, San Miguel Progreso (pop. 3,000) welcomes visitors to its museum. The museum committee has arranged the museum displays in four different sections. First are the historic papers, such as a 1780 document defining the town limits and a copy of a 1580 *lienzo* that maps the location of buildings, roads, rivers, and town boundaries. Next comes an excellent exposition of the local wool-weaving craft, then a mock-up of a typical indigenous dwelling. An archaeological section demonstrates finds, such as stone ax blades, ceramic vases, lance points, and human burial remains, including grave offerings. A final display models the pre-conquest method of terraced agriculture.

The local area contains a number of interesting sites, enough for a whole day of exploring. These include three unexcavated archaeological zones: Lomatutaya (Where the People Rest), Tuxau (Fifteen Words), and Panteón de los Angelitos (Cemetery of the Little Angels). Also nearby are two sacred caves, where masses are celebrated on May 3, El Día de la Santa Cruz (The Day of the Holy Cross).

Time your arrival on the locally important festival dates, September 29 (Fiesta de San Miguel) or the fifth Friday of Lent (Fiesta de las Tres Caidas de Jesús), when you can get in on the fun of fireworks, food, dancing, processions, music, flowers, and carnival diversions.

To make sure that one of the museum committee members is available to show you the museum and perhaps lead you on a tour, make an appointment (or best ask your hotel desk clerk to make the appointment) through the *agente municipal,* Pedro Ramírez Enrique (tel. 953/556-4635).

Get to San Miguel Progreso by bus or car as described for Cuquila above, except that the signed side road (off of Hwy. 125) to San Miguel is about four miles (six km) past Cuquila (from Tlaxiaco) and a corresponding distance closer to Juxtlahuaca and Putla. Continue about two miles (three km) along the side road to San Miguel.

PUTLA DE GUERRERO: LAND OF WATER

After a week traveling in the cool, high Mixteca Alta, the rush of balmy moist tropical air you enjoy when entering the upland valley of Putla de Guerrero (pop. 15,000) feels like another country. Banana trees overhang the road; mangos, in season, sell for a dime apiece; the aroma of roasting coffee scents the air; and people fill their afternoons by splashing in their favorite local swimming holes.

You might want to linger a day or two and bask in the warmth. If so, Putla's colorful market and its modicum of hotels, restaurants, and services can help make your visit interesting and comfortable.

Sights

The town centers on a leafy *jardín,* about four blocks west, downhill from Highway 125. The *jardín,* bordered by the *presidencia municipal* on the south, a line of shops on the north, and the church, at its northwest corner, focuses community activity.

The colorful, bustling market, busiest on Sunday, is a block behind the *presidencia.* Here you'll find stalls offering the handmade textiles—*huipiles, rebozos* (shawls), *blusas,* and *enredos* (wraparound skirts)—for which Putla is well known. Materials vary from wool, homespun and woven by highland Trique women, to cottons, hand-embroidered by coastal Mixtecs.

Accommodations

A relaxing hotel choice in Putla is the comfortable **Hotel Beyafrey** (Guerrero 9, tel. 953/553-0294, $15 s, $20 d, $27 t), about three blocks south and two blocks west of the plaza. The approximately 30 high-ceilinged, clean rooms come with toilets and hot-water showers, fan, TV, a restaurant, big blue pool and patio around in back, and parking. Ask for a room in the quiet rear section upstairs, away from the busy street-front.

Another recommendable hotel option, convenient for bus passengers, is the newish **Hotel Plaza** (Morelos 15, tel. 953/553-0403, $15 s, $20 d in one bed, $25 d in two beds, $30 t), on the east side of town half a block below the highway. The hotel's 28 rooms surround an attractively leafy rear patio; uppers open to an inviting balcony walkway that leads to an airy street-view porch up front. (The only drawback is that room windows face the balcony, and curtains must be drawn from privacy, which renders the rooms dark.) Inside guests enjoy attractive color-coordinated pink-white decor and shiny hot-water shower-baths.

Food

You can find plenty of luscious fruits and vegetables and many inexpensive local-variety meals in *fondas* in and around the market. For groceries, try the **Abarrotería Mary Carmen** (tel. 953/553-0228, 7 A.M.–9 P.M. daily) at the southwest plaza corner across the street from the *presidencia municipal.* For a larger selection, go to **Super Mega** chain grocery (uphill a block, at the northwest plaza corner, tel. 953/553-0398, 7 A.M.–8 P.M. daily).

Start with the restaurant choices on the highway. Most inviting is **Restaurant Tito's** (next to the Cristóbal Colón bus station, tel. 953/553-1065, 10:30 A.M.–10 P.M. daily, $4–10), decorated with a gallery of paintings of sentimental old-time Putla scenes, and an airy view terrace, especially pleasant for lunch or sunset supper. You also might say a good word to the friendly travel agent–owner Tito Chaves, who's proud of his eclectic menu of salads, pasta, beef brochette, chicken fajita, and seafood (shrimp, fish, octopus).

THE MIXTECA

Also on the highway, next door, down-hill from Tito's, you can choose the clean **Abarrotes-Restaurant Velasco** (tel. 953/553-0047 or 953/553-0099, 8 A.M.–9 P.M. daily, $2–8) for breakfast, lunch, and supper.

Downhill, west, at the plaza-front, the most visible town-center eatery is the very-limited-menu (one entrée, plus tacos, eggs, *tortas*, $2–4) family-style **Comedor Familiar Gonzales** (8 A.M.–7 P.M. daily), on the corner at the north side of the basketball court, a block north of the *jardín*. (Although no salads are on the menu, ask for lettuce-tomato-avocado salad *(ensalada lechuga-tomate-aguacate)* and they'll probably be able to make it for you, $2.) If you want something fancier, go a few doors farther uphill, to refined breakfast-lunch-early supper **Restaurant Don Memo** (8 A.M.–6 P.M. Mon.–Sat., $4–10) with lots of grilled beef, chicken, and seafood choices.

Entertainment and Events

Ordinarily quiet Putla livens up during its regionally important fiestas. **Carnaval Putleco,** celebrated the Sunday, Monday, and Tuesday before *miércoles ceniza* (Ash Wednesday), is rich in traditional dances. Local favorites, nearly always performed, are Los Viejos (The Old Ones), El Macho, and Los Copala.

Later in the year, folks crowd the church-front atrium for the **Fiesta de la Natividad,** which kicks off on September 6 with a grand *calenda* and flower-decorated floats, continues with a feast of fireworks on September 7, and culminates on the following day with *peleas de gallo* (cockfights), *jaripeo,* and a big community dance.

Other times, Putla people cool off from the heat by frolicking in the Río Putla that flows past the town. You can join the fun on a hot afternoon by asking a taxi driver to take you to a *balneario* (bathing spot); one of the best is about two miles (three km) along the highway uphill from town.

Services

You'll find nearly all of Putla's basic services near the town *jardín.* Change money or use the ATM at **Bancomer** (tel. 953/553-0028, 8:30 A.M.–4 P.M. Mon.–Fri., 10 A.M.–3 P.M. Sat.), a block north from the *jardín*'s west side, across from the basketball court. Alternatively, go to **Banamex** (on Calle Oaxaca nearby, 9 A.M.–4 P.M. Mon.–Fri.); from the southeast *jardín* corner, walk two blocks east, then south (right) two blocks.

The Putla *correo* (8 A.M.–3 P.M. Mon.–Fri.) is just west, next to the *presidencia municipal,* south side of the plaza, and the *telecomunicaciones* (9 A.M.–3 P.M. Mon.–Fri., 9 A.M.–noon Sat.) is on Veracruz, a few doors north, uphill, from the *jardín* basketball court. Long-distance phone and fax are available at the *caseta* (tel./fax 953/553-0030, 8 A.M.–8 P.M. daily) on the *jardín*'s north side.

Answer your email at **Ch@velit@ Internet** (tel. 953/553-1390, 9 A.M.–10 P.M. daily), just uphill from the *jardín* basketball court.

For routine nonprescription medicines and drugs, go to the **Farmacia Ahorro** (on the *jardín*'s west side, 7 A.M.–10 P.M. daily). If you're ill, however, ask at your hotel desk for a doctor or go to see **Doctora Silvia Zarate** at her **Farmacia Popular** (at the *jardín*'s north-east corner, tel. 953/553-0252, 8 A.M.–2 P.M. and 4–8 P.M. daily). Medical consultations are also available at the **General Hospital** (tel. 953/553-0046), a block north of the *jardín*'s east side, across the street from the basketball court.

In police emergencies, call the *policía municipal* (tel. 953/553-0111).

For information and travel services go to **Agencia de Viajes Tito** (tel. 953/553-1065) of friendly Tito Chaves Garcia, on the highway next to Cristóbal Colón bus station (which Tito also manages).

Getting There and Away

A few long-distance bus lines and vans operate from stations on or near the highway and connect Putla with many Oaxaca destinations. First-class **Omnibus Cristóbal Colón** (on the highway, tel. 953/553-0163) connects south with Pinotepa Nacional and north with Mexico City, via Huajuapan and Puebla. First- and second-class **Sur** (both on the highway downhill from Cristóbal Colón, no phone; and at Sonora 34A, downtown near the Hotel Beyafrey, tel. 953/553-0350) offers both Mexico City connections via Huajuapan and Puebla and Oaxaca City connections via Tlaxiaco and Nochixtlán. Additionally, second-class **Boquerón** buses from a small terminal downhill from Cristóbal Colón connect south with Pinotepa Nacional and north by the scenic backcountry Juxtlahuaca, Tonalá route to Huajuapan.

Furthermore, vans of **Transportadora Turística Mixteca Baja** (on the highway, uphill from Cristóbal Colón, tel. 953/553-0847)

offer frequent connections with Oaxaca City, via Tlaxiaco.

For drivers, paved Highway 125 connects Putla south with Pinotepa Nacional, on the Pacific coast via 80 miles (128 km) of winding, sometimes potholed, mountain road. Allow three hours for safety. In the opposite direction, Highway 125 and Highway 182 connect Putla north with Juxtlahuaca in about 37 miles (59 km). Winding and sometimes steep grades require slow going. Allow an hour and a half uphill, an hour downhill. About the same is true for the 48-mile (77-km) connection northeast, along Highway 125, with Tlaxiaco, which, for safety, requires about two hours uphill, an hour and a half down.

THE MIXTECA

NORTHERN OAXACA

The vast, extravagantly diverse northern Oaxaca landscape encompasses three of Oaxaca's traditional geo-cultural regions: the pine-tufted northern Sierra, the fertile, tropical Papaloapan basin, and the oases of the desertlike Cañada canyonland. Here travelers ready to venture north of the Valley of Oaxaca can find their heart's content of high mountains for camping, hiking, and climbing; tropical rivers and grand, glassy lakes for fishing, swimming, and boating; crystalline springs welling from the base of emerald mountains; and country markets where people wear colorful age-old village costumes and speak ancient traditional dialects.

This chapter is organized as a grand circle tour, initially exploring the cool mountain country villages of Benito Juárez and Cuajimoloyas that perch at the first high crest north of Oaxaca City. Continuing north, deeper into the mountains, visitors will find the lushly forested, wildlife-rich country around Ixtlán and Gueletao, the beloved president Benito Juárez's northern Sierra birthplace. The route continues north, down into the luxuriantly fertile Río Papaloapan basin. Using the tropical river town Tuxtepec as a base, we explore the cultural and natural riches of the Chinantec and Mazatec ancestral homelands. The road turns west, into the high Mazateca, to Huautla de Jiménez, a mountain town made internationally famous by the hallucinogenic mushrooms of renowned *curandera* (indigenous medicine woman) María Sabina. Finally, returning west and south toward Oaxaca City, the route traces the tropical orchard oasis country of Teotitlán del Camino and Cuicatlán.

HIGHLIGHTS

◖ Balnearios Monte Flor and El Zuzul:
Refresh yourself with a swim and a picnic, and
even camping overnight, at either or both
Monte Flor or El Zuzul crystalline springs
(page 292).

◖ A Walk Along the Río Papaloapan:
Enjoy cooling off with a stroll along the river.
Take in the views and maybe even a cooling
fruit drink and lunch at a river-view *fonda* at
the Tuxtepec downtown market along the way
(page 298).

◖ El Castillo de Moctezuma: Climb the
diminutive Aztec-built pyramid (c. 1500) that
remains in an excellent state of preservation in
a Tuxtepec neighborhood park (page 299).

◖ San Pedro Ixcatlán and the Islands:
Ride an excursion boat to the charmingly rural,
all Mazatec-speaking Isla Soyaltepec and enjoy
an overnight in the charming hotel Villa del
Lago (page 305).

◖ María Sabina Mural: In Huautla de
Jimenez, be sure to visit the strangely arresting mural on the town hall, which depicts the
mission of celebrated hallucinogenic healer
María Sabina (page 311).

◖ Las Regaderas: Take an excursion outside Huautla to enjoy the cooling spray of the
Las Regaderas waterfalls, which plummet 100
feet into the wild, tumbling river (page 314).

LOOK FOR **◖** TO FIND RECOMMENDED SIGHTS,
ACTIVITIES, DINING, AND LODGING.

PLANNING YOUR TIME

You can enjoy Northern Oaxaca's charmingly
varied sights and grand scenery in an unhur-
ried circle excursion in about a week. You can
pick and choose, according to your own interests. Nature enthusiasts would be interested
especially in spending a couple of days and a
night or two exploring the limestone cave, lush
cloud forest, and mountain meadows around
Ixtlán de Juárez, perhaps tenting or lodging
in local rustic forest *cabañas*. Alternatively,
you could enjoy a bit of nearby forest walking and also have time to admire the graceful
old colonial-era churches in Ixtlán and nearby

Calpulalpan, plus the President Benito Juárez
shrine and museum, in his Guelatao birthplace, then spend an overnight in a comfy
Ixtlán hotel or forest *cabaña*.

Heading north, over the Sierra summit
and down into the lushly tropical Papaloapan
basin, be sure to stop at least for a picnic and
a swim (and maybe even a tenting or RVing
overnight) at the crystalline natural springs
Balnearios Monte Flor and/or **El Zuzul**.
Continue north to Tuxtepec for at least a day
and a night, which will give you time for a
walk along its airy riverfront, lunch at a river-
view restaurant above the market, crossing the

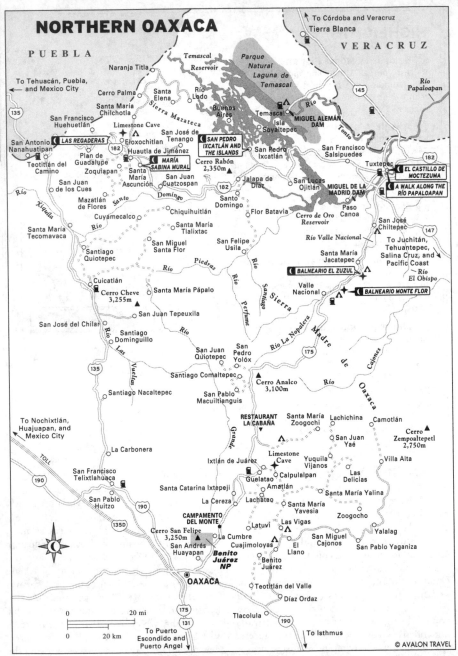

NORTHERN OAXACA

PUEBLA

VERACRUZ

To Córdoba and Veracruz
Tierra Blanca

To Tehuacán, Puebla,
and Mexico City

Naranja Titla

Temascal
Reservoir

Parque
Natural
Laguna de
Temascal

Río
Papaloapan

Cerro Palma

Santa
Elena

Río
Lodo

145

Santa María
Chilchotla

Sierra Mazateca

Buenos
Aires

Temascal

Isla
Soyaltepec

Río

Tonto

San Francisco
Huehuetlán

Limestone Cave

San José de
Tenango

MIGUEL ALEMÁN
DAM

San Francisco
Salsipuedes

San Antonio
Nanahuatipan

LAS REGADERAS

Eloxochitlan

182

Huautla de Jiménez

SAN PEDRO
IXCATLÁN AND
THE ISLANDS

San Pedro
Ixcatlán

Tuxtepec

182

Plan de
Guadalupe

MARÍA
SABINA MURAL

Cerro Rabón
2,350m

EL CASTILLO DE
MOCTEZUMA

Teotitlán del
Camino

Zoquiapan

Santa
María
Ascunción

San Juan
Cuatzospan

Jalapa de
Díaz

San Lucas
Ojitlán

MIGUEL DE LA
MADRID DAM

A WALK ALONG THE
RÍO PAPALOAPAN

San Juan
de los Cues

182

Río

Xiquila

Mazatlán
de Flores

Santo

Domingo

Santo
Domingo

Flor Batavia

Cerro de Oro
Reservoir

Paso
Canoa

San José
Chiltepec

147

Santa María
Tecomavaca

Río

Cuyámecalco

Chiquihuitlán

Santa María
Tlalixtac

San Felipe
Usila

Río Valle Nacional

Santa María
Jacatepec

To Juchitán,
Tehuantepec,
Salina Cruz, and
Pacific Coast

Río
El Obispo

Santiago
Quiotepec

San Miguel
Santa Flor

Piedras

Río

Río

Sierra

BALNEARIO EL ZUZUL

Cuicatlán

Cerro Cheve
3,255m

Santa María Pápalo

Valle
Nacional

Madre

BALNEARIO MONTE FLOR

San Juan Tepeuxila

San José del Chilar

Santiago
Dominguillo

Río

Las

San Juan
Quiotepec

San
Pedro
Yolóx

Río La Nopalera

de

175

Vueltas

135

Santiago Comaltepec

Cerro Analco
3,100m

Río

Oaxaca

Santiago Nacaltepec

San Pablo
Macuiltianguis

Grande

RESTAURANT
LA CABAÑA

Santa María
Zoogochi

Lachichina

Camotlán

To Nochixtlán,
Huajuapan, and
Mexico City

La Carbonera

Ixtlán de Juárez

Limestone
Cave

Yuquila
Vijanos

San Juan
Yaé

Cerro
Zempoaltepetl
2,750m

Villa Alta

TOLL

190

San Francisco
Telixtlahuaca

San Pablo
Huitzo

190

Santa Catarina Ixtepeji

La Cereza

Guelatao

Lachatao

Calpulalpan

Amatlán

Santa María
Yavesia

Las
Delicias

Santa María Yalina

Zoogocho

135D

CAMPAMENTO
DEL MONTE

Cerro San Felipe
3,250m

San Andrés
Huayapan

Benito
Juárez
NP

La Cumbre

Latuvi

La
Cuajimoloyas

Las Vigas

El
Llano

San Miguel
Cajonos

Yalalag

San Pablo Yaganiza

Benito
Juárez

OAXACA

Teotitlán del Valle

Díaz Ordaz

0   20 mi

175

Tlacolula

190

0   20 km

131

To Puerto
Escondido and
Puerto Angel

To Isthmus

© AVALON TRAVEL

river via the ferry and/or the hanging bridge, and exploring Tuxtepec's in-town 15th-century unrestored Aztec pyramid.

Continue west into the heartland of the indigenous Chinantec and Mazatec peoples. Spend at least a day (or better, stay on overnight at petite Hotel Villa del Lago), at picturesque hilltop lake-view Ixcatlán village. Be sure to take the boat excursion to idyllically isolated Isla Soyaltepec and island village for a bit of strolling and perhaps another overnight in an indigenous Chinantec house. Farther west, pause for at least an hour for some textile shopping at Jalapa de Díaz, where fit hikers would be challenged by a climb to the summit of the Mazatecs' holy mountain, Cerro Rabón.

Next day, farther west, climbing along and above the breathtakingly scenic, green Cañon del Río Santo Domingo, arrive in the capital of the high Mazateca, Huautla de Jiménez, home

of renowned late María Sabina of 1970s Love-Generation magic-mushroom fame. Spend a day strolling the village and vibrant indigenous market and enjoying a hike uphill to Cerro Adoración panoramic viewpoint. The next day, continuing west, downhill, stop to bask in the cool spray of **Las Regaderas** twin waterfall. Nearby, prepared adventurers might enjoy a day (or overnight two-day) exploration of the monumental Nindo-Da-Gé (Broad Spring Mountain) cavern at Eloxochitlán village.

With your grand circle tour nearly complete, coast downhill into the cactus-plumed, oasis-dotted Cañada country, for a stop at Cuicatlán, magnet for a host of Cuicatec mountain folks who crowd in daily (and even more on Sunday) for the big town market. Pause for a home-cooked *comida* at the town-favorite Boringen Restaurant before heading south, to arrive back in Oaxaca City by early evening.

Northern Sierra

The vast northern Sierra, the series of rugged mountain ranges that repeatedly rise and fall for a hundred miles, moving north from Oaxaca City, is a repository of a significant fraction of Mexico's increasingly scarce resources: unblemished pine and spruce-decorated mountain vistas, colonial-era mountain villages, and vanishing wildlife, including all of Mexico's wild cat species, from the jaguar and the ocelot to the *tigrillo* and jaguarundi. Their survival in the regions is due to the sprinkling of northern Sierra communities that carefully husband their communal lands, harvesting their lumber at only a sustainable pace and guarding their holdings against poachers.

These communities welcome visitors. Among the best prepared are Benito Juarez in the south, on the first Sierra ridge above Oaxaca City, and Ixtlán de Juárez near the northern summit. The villagers in Ixtlán de Juárez offer cozy mountain *cabaña* lodgings, campsites, and guides for exploring their lands by bicycle, foot, or car.

UP FROM THE VALLEY: BENITO JUÁREZ AND CUAJIMOLOYAS

This pair of mountain hamlets perch nearly a mile above the Valley of Oaxaca at the first towering crest of the cool, pine-tufted Sierra Juárez. The attraction here is not the towns themselves, but their gorgeous mountain environs and all that implies: great billowing clouds, summer wildflowers, cool crystalline spring water, and the scent of spruce and pine.

Furthermore, the communities and the Oaxaca government, in their effort to develop the outdoor touristic resources of the northern Sierra, offer a number of food, lodging, and outdoor activity options in Benito Juárez, Cuajimoloyas, Llano Grande, and other villages.

(*Note:* These villages are part of a local network, known cooperatively as **Pueblos Mancomunicados,** that welcomes visitors to enjoy and appreciate their wildlife-rich, pine-forested, mountain-top environment. Visitors can make accommodations and guide arrangements either directly through the communities, or more conveniently through their Oaxaca City agent, **Expediciones Sierra Norte.** See *Mountain Guide* later in this section for details.)

Sights

The modest houses and farms of Benito Juárez village (pop. 1,000) are sprinkled along a single east–west ridge-crest road. The *cabañas ecoturísticas* lodgings and the community center, **Casa del Pueblo,** with the *comedor* and a cozy fireplace, are at the east end, uphill. At that point, signs direct you toward a number of possible diversions: You have your choice of a quarter-mile *tirolesa* (a forest canopy cable ride, $3), horseback riding ($10/hr.), a stroll among the springs trickling downhill through the adjacent pine-shaded **Parque Recreativo,** or you can follow the sign marked Mirador, walking along the road (follow each uphill fork) about 1.5 miles (2.5 km) north to the *mirador* tower atop a craggy 10,300-foot-high (3,100-meter-high) perch. Here the view seems limitless. On clear days, early risers can even recognize the sunrise silhouette of Volcán de Orizaba (elev. 18,856 feet/5,747 meters), Mexico's tallest mountain, a hundred miles to the east. On the south side, steeply beneath you, spreads the central valley's verdant checkerboard of meadow, field, and pasture. On the north side, a succession of dark-green mountain ridges stretches northward until the ridges merge and become a deep-purple silhouette on the horizon. On another day, walk or get a ride about eight miles (12 km) east, past the little settlement of Los Llanos, to another viewpoint, the famous **Peña Larga,** a gigantic 50-foot (15-meter) rock where you can perch to your heart's content.

Another possibility is to follow the six-mile (10-km) *sendero peaton* (pedestrian trail) by mountain bike or on foot. The *cabañas ecoturísticas* manager rents the bikes ($10) and furnishes you with a guide ($12). For more information and *cabaña* reservations, you may contact the Benito Juárez tourism manager directly (tel. 951/545-9994), or make prior arrangements through Expediciones Sierra Norte. (See *Mountain Guide* later in this section for more details.)

Alternatively, you can simply wander around and enjoy yourself. Plenty of folks, Zapotec people (most of whom speak Spanish), are out tending their terraced cornfields, watching their cattle, and doing household chores.

Cuajimoloyas (kooah-hee-moh-LOY-ahs, pop. 1,000), four miles (6 km) east along the ridge road from Benito Juárez, is the metropolis of this part of the mountains. Besides lodging and restaurants, it has a pharmacy, health center, small grocery stores, and a telephone.

You'll be especially lucky to arrive in Cuajimoloyas during either the patronal **Fiesta de San Antonio** (June 11–14) or the **El Día de los Muertos,** which is very big locally, and stretches six days, beginning November 1 and climaxing in a whoopla of favorite traditional dances on November 5 and 6.

Your first stop should be the tourism headquarters on the right side of the road as you enter town, across from the small hotel Yacautzi (Place of the Maguey). The tourism manager can set you up with bicycles ($5/hr.), a guide ($12 for 3 hrs.), or both. Reserve in advance by leaving a message via the Cuajimoloyas tourism manager (tel. 951/524-5024).

The guided tour takes about three hours by bicycle, or about six on foot. The sights along the way customarily include **El Calvario,** a sacred spring; **Cañon del Coyote,** caves; a climb to the top of **Piedra Colorada,** a gargantuan red monolith; some waterfalls; and the **Llano del Fraile,** a sylvan wildflower-rich camping area, bisected by a trout stream.

A little farther off the beaten track, **Llano Grande** village along the same paved mountain-crest road, six miles (10 km) farther east, also welcomes lovers of the outdoors. Village offerings include rustic *cabañas,* meals, camping, bicycles, guides, and a menu of activities. These include wildlife-viewing, panoramic vistas, rappelling, and the highest local viewpoint, sacred **Yaa Tini** peak (elev. 10,600 feet/3,200 meters), where pilgrims still arrive on Easter Sunday to pay their respects to the Lord of the Mountain.

© BRUCE WHIPPERMAN

Llano Grande's new semi-deluxe *cabañas ecoturísticas* are spacious, comfortable, and fireplace-equipped.

Mountain Guide

A very convenient option is to go with well-equipped Empresa Ecoturística Comunitaria (Community Ecotouristic Enterprise), better known as **Expediciones Sierra Norte** (210 M. Bravo, Oaxaca City, tel. 951/514-8271 or 951/514-3631, sierranorte@oaxaca.com, www.sierranorte.org.mx). The personable English-speaking founder, Adriana Guzmán, and her staff work in cooperation with a network of about a dozen Sierra Norte communities, called **Pueblos Mancomunados,** that include, besides the Benito Juárez–Cuajimoloyas–Llano Grande trio, Yavesia, Latuvi, Amatlán, and Lachatao. Jointly, they have established a 60-mile (100-km) signposted hiking and mountain-biking trail network and offer accommodations in rustic village cabins and campsites.

Adriana and her staff make reservations for the cabins and help obtain access and camping permits. They also outfit and guide parties for camping, hiking, and biking outings into the mountains north of Oaxaca City,

beginning in the area around Benito Juárez and Cuajimoloyas and extending north toward the other villages. They can furnish camping gear, mountain bikes, transportation, and more.

Accommodations and Food

All three villages offer many lodging choices. The busiest and best organized is Benito Juárez, which offers an assortment of rustic but comfortable lodgings, the most economical of which is the large original tourist accommodation, still called by its original label, **Tourist Yu'u.** It accommodates about 20 persons in a dormitory hall ($12 per person), with shared toilet and hot-water showers. The facility also has several four-person bunk bed private bath guestrooms that open onto the large common hall ($10 per person). Although well-used, this is still a cozy place if you like lots of company, with a big fireplace, plenty of wool blankets, and a basic kitchen with refrigerator available for guest use. Bring your own soap and towel and, if you plan to cook, most of your own food, especially fresh fruits and vegetables. The local water is crystal pure on this mountaintop.

Additionally, Benito Juárez offers several detached private **cabañas** ($40 d, t, or q) sleeping four, with hot-water baths, fireplace, and kitchenette. For more information and reservations, call the Benito Juárez manager (tel. 951/545-9994, 8 A.M.–8 P.M. daily).

Cuajimoloyas also offers accommodations, including three duplex *cabañas* uphill above the town, and a downscale hotel, the **Yacautzi** (on the road, left side, as you enter town from Benito Juárez, $15 d rooms, $13 per person *cabañas*). Although the hotel offers five clean but unheated basic bare-bulb rooms with double bed, toilet, and hot-water shower, the three *cabañas,* a quarter mile uphill, are much cozier, each with two spacious duplex units sleeping four, with fireplace and a hot-water shower and toilet, shared by respective occupants of the duplex units. Reserve directly through the Cuajimoloyas tourism office (tel. 951/524-5024, 9 A.M.–3 P.M. and 4–8:30 P.M. daily) or through **Expediciones Sierra Norte.**

The 10 **Llano Grande** duplex *cabañas* ($45 d, $55 q) consist of five larger duplex cabins, with bunk beds for up to four, and five smaller, with double beds, for two. Hot-water showers and toilets are shared between the respective occupants of each duplex *cabaña*. Additionally, Llano Grande has recently built eight lovely, professionally built and comfortably furnished *cabañas*, with attractive bedspreads and drapes and private modern-standard shower-baths. Four of them, accommodating two persons, rent for about $45; while four larger *cabañas* each accommodate four persons and rent for about $55.

Furthermore, the Llano Grande community ecotourism office offers packages, including accommodation, meals, and a guide, for about $25 per day per person. Fireplace wood goes for $5 per load. Reserve through the village telephone (cell tel. 044-951/162-7442), or **Expediciones Sierra Norte**.

Alternatively, the whole mountaintop area is ripe for tent and some self-contained RV camping. The communities have designated at least four spots. Two walk-in-only campgrounds are close to and administered in Benito Juárez. Closest is in the **Parque Recreativo,** near the village center; and another camping site—with a view—is about 0.2 mile (0.3 km) away on foot.

Farther afield, campers may enjoy a sylvan meadow **Llano de las Tarajeas,** with campsites and good spring water. Find it a total of about ten miles (16 km) east of Benito Juárez, past Cuajimoloyas. During the summer and fall, this meandering pine-bordered meadow is decorated with a galaxy of wildflowers—lavender buttercups, red lilies, baby blue eyes, white and yellow daisies, and many more. Water comes from a pristine brook, home to some little darting fish. (Foresters have set up a small fish hatchery here, in an attempt to breed more of the little critters, some of whom have become healthy adult rainbow trout.)

To camp at Llano de las Tarajeas, reserve ($3 per person per night) with the Cuajimoloyas tourism manager (tel. 951/545-9994). **Get**

there by car, bus, or on foot. Beginning at Benito Juárez, continue four miles (6.4 km) east along the ridgeline road, through Cuajimoloyas. Continue another three miles (five km) to the Las Tarajeas sign on the left. Follow more signs another 1.8 miles (three km) to the narrow, rough driveway, only marginally passable by big RVs, on the left, to Llano de las Tarajeas.

The latter-day ecotourist influx supports a sprinkling of modest local eateries. In Benito Juárez the best is the **Casa del Pueblo** community *comedor*. In Cuajimoloyas choose between *comedores* **San Antonio** and **La Montaña,** run by friendly Gilda and Sergio Hilser; and in Llano Grande, you have *comedores* **La Curva** (good for both breakfast and groceries), **San Isidro,** and **Katy.** All are open approximately 8 A.M.–8 P.M. daily, and provide breakfasts ($2–5), afternoon comida ($3–5), and tacos, tamales, quesadillas, and hamburgers for supper ($3–5).

Campers should arrive with all food provisions in hand, especially fresh fruits and vegetables. Local stores may have only minimal supplies.

Getting There and Away

From Oaxaca City, for Benito Juárez, the most convenient option is to ride the Expediciones Sierra Norte bus; call to check departure times (tel. 951/514-8271).

Alternatively, from Oaxaca City, ride the **Sociedad Cooperativa Flecha de Zempoaltépetl** (saym-poh-ahl-TAY-paytl) bus from the Oaxaca City second-class bus terminal, headed for Cuajimoloyas (and also Llano Grande). They leave approximately six times a day for Cuajimoloyas, via Tlacolula. (They go several places, so say *"¿A Cuajimoloyas?"* before getting on.) For Benito Juárez, get off at the mountain crest, at the junction where the Benito Juárez road splits left (west). Walk or catch a ride the four miles (six km) to the Benito Juárez *cabañas* and Casa del Pueblo. *Note:* Super-fit backpackers could, alternatively, hike or thumb a ride up the car-RV route, described below, via Teotitlán del Valle.

If, however, you're in Tlacolula already, wait for the same Flecha de Zempoaltépetl bus, on the highway, at the corner across from the Tlacolula Pemex gas station and proceed as described above.

By car or RV, for experienced and fearless drivers only, it's quickest to drive to Benito Juárez via the spectacularly scenic route via Teotitlán del Valle. Turn left at the signed Teotitlán del Valle Highway 190 turnoff, about 18 miles (30 km) east of Oaxaca City. Continue straight through town, uphill on an initially bumpy road. A mile or two later, past the Teotitlán dam, the graded gravel road gets better. Ordinary cars and most RVs could negotiate it readily under dry conditions, although it might be marginal when wet. Four-wheel-drive vehicles could do it most anytime. At Benito Juárez, at mountain-top, follow the Martín Ruiz Camino street signs to Cabañas, about 0.5 mile (0.8 km) to the *cabañas ecoturísticas* and the town community center and tourism reception office (turn left half a block uphill past the *cabaña ecoturística*).

Alternatively, drivers can follow the easier but longer paved route that the bus Flecha de Zempoaltépetl takes: Heading east, at the Tlacolula Pemex station, turn left and continue about four miles (six km) to Díaz Ordaz village, where you turn left again. Continue winding uphill about 12 miles (19 km) to the mountain-top and a big road fork, at the Km 19 marker. Turn left sharply for Benito Juárez (four miles/six km); continue straight ahead for Cuajimoloyas (1.4 miles/two km) and Llano Grande (eight miles/13 km).

ALONG THE ROAD TO IXTLÁN

The high road to northern Oaxaca winds far uphill, climbing over lush, pine-clad crests and descending into deep river canyons of the Sierra Juárez, the mountainous birth-land of Benito Juárez, Oaxaca's beloved favorite son. Besides its historical and sentimental significance, the Sierra Juárez's pristine, thickly forested ridges and shadowed stream valleys are a natural garden of springs, meadows, caves, and waterfalls—a de facto wilderness refuge

for dozens of endangered species, including all of Mexico's wild cats.

The best hub for exploring the Sierra Juárez is the small town of Ixtlán de Juárez, easily reachable by bus or car, about 37 miles (60 km) north from Oaxaca City via Highway 175.

Although Ixtlán de Juárez is a worthy destination, journeys are sometimes equally memorable for the bright moments en route. The road to Ixtlán is no exception. You might uncover some pleasant surprises while lingering along the way, such as the invitingly rustic mountain restaurant and refuge Campamento del Monte, or San Andrés Huayapan and Ixtepeji, a pair of little towns with nevertheless big gems of churches.

By bus, ride a Cuenca (koo-AYN-kah) first class or ADO bus bound for Ixtlán (or Valle Nacional or Tuxtepec) from Oaxaca City's ADO–Cristóbal Colón first class station, on Highway 190 at the north side of town. Drivers, set your odometer and head out from the junction where Highway 175 splits north from Highway 190, about three miles (five km) east of the Oaxaca City center.

San Andrés Huayapan Church and Reservoir

If you have time, detour into San Andrés Huayapan (left turnoff from Hwy. 175), approximately 2.5 miles (four km) uphill from Highway 190. First of all, take a look inside the town's jewel: the distinguished, double-towered 17th-century **Templo de San Andrés.** Past the front door, admire the mural of the Last Supper in the nave and the colorful sculpture of San Andrés in the main altarpiece's central niche.

Afterward, reverse your path by taxi or car to the **Presas de Huayapan** (Dams of Huayapan) on opposite sides of the entrance road, a fraction of a mile uphill from Highway 175. The pair of dams, although built for irrigation, have created a popular, scenic recreation reservoir (prettiest during late-summer high water, when no ugly bathtub-like ring scars the lakeshore), forming petite bays in the folds of the surrounding forested hillsides.

Restaurants serve food, and concessionaires rent boats. Swimming, however, is not recommended, due to the lakeshore's steep incline.

Campamento del Monte

About 17 miles (27 km) north, you arrive at an attractive chalet-style view restaurant perched on the right (east) side of Highway 175. Although the **(Restaurant del Monte** (tel. 951/518-6139, $5–7) is certainly worth a stop (especially for fresh trout or baked rabbit, $6) all by itself, the Campamento del Monte (tel. 951/518-6139 or cell 044-951/111-2577, 9 A.M.–3 P.M. Mon.–Sat., delmontemx@hotmail.com, $15 per person, three person minimum per cabin) across the road is the main attraction. A handful of rustic cabins (at Km 27, Carretera Oaxaca–Guelatao), sprinkled in the pine-oak forest above the highway, offers tranquility and lots of fresh air in a gorgeously secluded pine-shaded setting. The family Pérez Chávez, who first built the restaurant, then the cabins, has named them individually: Toro de Silviero, Laguna Azul, Colmilla Blanco, and Luna de Octubre. Like their names, each is uniquely inviting, built with rustic wood, tile, and brick, with plenty of light, tree-framed mountain and forest vistas, a fireplace with lots of wood, an outdoor grill, hot-water shower-bath, stove, and refrigerator (although you have to furnish your own towels, bedding, and pots, pans, dishes, and utensils).

Rentals are popular, so be sure to reserve and mail a 50 percent deposit at least 10 days ahead of time. Although their literature insists on prior reservations, they do rent to drop-ins between 3 and 9 P.M. if they have a cabin available, which is likely Sunday–Thursday. Bring mosquito repellent, especially necessary early evenings during the summer wet season.

In addition to cabin rentals, the managers also welcome day visitors for about $10 per car. Tenters, RVers, and trailers are also welcome, for $15 per night, with hot-water showers and toilets provided. Diversions include picnicking, bird- and animal-viewing, and rambling through the sylvan pine- and oak-studded mountainside to local view summits.

Santa Catarina Ixtepeji

This formerly sleepy little canyon community, at the headwaters of the Río Grande, is waking up. Now, folks are welcoming nature lovers to enjoy their great outdoors. They've even established an easily accessible visitors center (tel. 951/516-7898, 9 A.M.–6 P.M. daily) on Highway 175 at La Cumbre (about a mile past Campamento del Monte), 18 miles (29 km) uphill from Highway 190.

At the visitors center, find out about the 4,000-acre (six-square-mile) Ixtepeji (eeks-tay-PAY-hee) nature preserve, with hiking and biking trails through shadowed spruce, pine, and oak forests past ferny dells and cold crystal-clear springs, a cascading waterfall, and spectacularly panoramic viewpoints. All this for $4 per person entrance fee.

Furthermore, the Ixtepeji community invites you, after a day of such exhilarating exploring, to set up your tent in their *campamento* (campground) or stay overnight in one of their six mountain *cabañas*. Each *cabaña* has three bunk beds. Hot-water shower-baths and toilets are shared. Expect to pay about $15 per person for a *cabaña*, $3 for camping. Meals are also available. For more information, log on to the Ixtepeji page on Ron Mader's super website (www.planeta.com/ecotravel/mexico/oaxaca/ixtepeji.html).

Reserve Ixtepeji accommodations through the Ixtepeji visitors center (tel. 951/516-7898) or the government alternative tourism office (206 Murguia, two blocks northeast of the central plaza between Reforma and Cinco de Mayo, tel. 951/516-0123 or 951/516-4828, fax 951/514-8501, or info@aoaxaca.com, www.oaxaca.travel).

GETTING THERE

By bus, ride a Cuenca (koo-AYN-kah) first class or ADO bus bound for Ixtlán (or Valle Nacional or Tuxtepec) from Oaxaca City's ADO–Cristóbal Colón first-class station, on Highway 190 at the north side of town. Or, hire a taxi to the intersection, three miles (five km) along Highway 190, east of downtown Oaxaca City, where Highway 175 forks north. From there, ride the **Transportes Ixtlecos** van, hourly 8 A.M.–7 P.M.; or the *colectivo* Laa Yetzi 200 yards north of the Benito Juárez statue. (Alternatively, you can ride the Transportes Ixtlecos van from Rayon 608, tel. 951/514-1104, in downtown Oaxaca.) Drivers, at La Cumbre, 18 miles (29 km) from the Highway 190 intersection, follow the signed turnoff and simply continue for about four miles (six km) down-mountain to the *cabañas*. If, however, you're driving directly to the town, best continue about five miles farther north, to La Cereza (around Mile 23/Km 37), where a gravel road leads directly downhill to the town center.

While you're there, be sure to see the beloved old **Templo de Santa Catarina,** by far the biggest building in Ixtepeji. The church's main attraction (unless you plan your visit to coincide with three days of the Fiesta of Santa Catarina, around November 25) is the towering, superb Renaissance facade. Prominent are the eight exquisitely spiraled Solomonic columns, four above and four below. Notice also the facade's empty niches, which once sheltered St. John the Evangelist, St. Nicolas, and St. Michael, until they were probably toppled by an earthquake. Nevertheless, St. Peter remains on the left, with Bible, flag, and staff, as does St. Catherine, high above, with flowing robe and sword.

AT THE SUMMIT: IXTLÁN DE JUÁREZ AND VICINITY

If a Mexican person told you that he lived in Ixtlán, you still wouldn't know where that is, for there are many Ixtláns in Mexico. The prefix *ix-* refers to *ixtle,* the Aztec word for the fibers of the maguey plant. The suffix *-tlan* means "land of," or "place of." The maguey plant is widespread in Mexico, and the Aztecs were so dominant at the time of the conquest that their names for local towns are still used today. So the many Ixtláns are all places the Aztecs named Land of the Maguey. Oaxaca Ixtlán people gave their town a unique name, by naming it Ixtlán de Juárez, after their favorite son, revered President Benito Juárez.

People don't grow much maguey around Ixtlán de Juárez anymore, nor do they grow any cochineal, cultivation of which created a number of millionaires in the vicinity. Their money built the ornate old Churrigueresque churches in Ixtlán and the neighboring town of Calpulalpan.

What Ixtlán people do grow a lot of is wood, in the thick forests coating this part of the northern Sierra. Wisely, they don't cut too much of it, so their forests remain rich habitats for many wild creatures, including all species of Mexican native cats (notably the jaguar and mountain lion), spider monkeys, and tapirs, many of which have disappeared in other parts of southern Mexico. The diversity of species is so rich in Ixtlán's woodlands that a panel of international experts convened by the World Wildlife Fund has rated the local forest as one of the world's 17 outstandingly biodiverse ecosystems. What's great for visitors is that the Ixtlán de Juárez community invites them to come see and appreciate their wild treasures through a special community-run ecotourism company.

Sights

Ixtlán de Juárez (pop. 8,000), despite being the capital of its own sprawling governmental district, feels like a village, where the main evening activity is to either watch or join the kids playing basketball on the courts in the central plaza, then get *cena* (supper) before the mom-and-pop *comedores* close around 8:30 P.M. Walk three blocks in any direction and you're in the woods. But don't worry, you won't get lost. Just let the faithful chime of the plaza-tower clock lead you back.

Likewise, the landmark plaza-front *presidencia municipal,* on the plaza's north side, can help get you oriented. Main north–south streets are Sidencio Hernández on the plaza's west side, and 16 Septiembre on the east side. Crossing those is Revolución, which runs east–west, behind the *presidencia municipal.*

Ixtlán's main in-town sight is its treasured 17th-century **Templo de Santo Tomás Apóstol,** just northwest of the town plaza, behind the faithful, very proper plaza clock. The present *templo,* started by Dominican fathers around 1640, replaced an earlier all-adobe church. Construction was completed about a century later, in 1734. The first thing to notice about old Santo Tomás is that it's made of the same light green *cantera* that you see so much of in Oaxaca City's public buildings. Ixtlán's source, however, is local.

Decorating the baroque facade's summit is a bas-relief showing the dramatic confrontation of doubting Thomas with the risen Jesus. Inside, instead of the usual one golden *retablo* behind the altar, several more decorate the nave walls, with gilded saints, angels, and masterfully pious 16th- and 17th-century oil paintings. The main *retablo*, behind the altar, shows the kneeling St. Thomas touching the chest of

BENITO JUÁREZ: MEXICO'S PRESIDENT FOR ALL SEASONS

Mexico's memory of Benito Juárez, its most revered president, is draped in legend. What's certain is that he was born on March 21, 1806, in the northern Oaxacan *municipio* of San Pablo Guelatao, at the hamlet of Santo Tomás Ixtlán. When his parents of pure Zapotec origin, Marcelino Juárez and Brigida Garcia, died tragically when Benito was three, his uncle took him in. After a quiet childhood mostly spent shepherding his uncle's flocks in the surrounding hills, Benito left for Oaxaca City in December 1818 to live with his sister, María Josefa.

For Benito, this was a lucky stroke. He became part of the Maza household, where María Josefa lived and worked as a cook. In the genteel, well-to-do Maza family surroundings, young Benito gained exposure to music, books, politics, and people – not possible for a poor boy in the country. Moreover, he met Margarita Maza, who, with the blessing of her parents, later became his wife.

While living with the Mazas, Benito immediately gained the attention of priest and bookbinder Antonio Salanueva, who, recognizing his exceptional qualities, took Benito under his wing and sent him to school in town in January 1819. With Salanueva as his patron, Benito made rapid progress. He entered Oaxaca's new Scientific and Literary Institute in August 1828 to study law. Four years later, he was a practicing attorney. He entered politics, rapidly rose from state to federal legislator, then Supreme Court judge, finally being unanimously elected governor by Oaxaca's legislature on August 12, 1849.

From a successful term as governor, Juárez returned to national prominence. He was elected Mexico's president for two separate terms, both interrupted, first by civil war during the latter 1850s and then by the French Intervention from 1862 to 1867. Victory over the French finally brought peace, and Juárez was elected president for the third time in October 1871. He toiled day and night to realize his dreams for Mexico, but he died from exhaustion on July 18, 1872.

A monument honors Benito Juárez, Mexico's sole pure indigenous president, in Tamazulapan, in the Mixteca.

© BRUCE WHIPPERMAN

© BRUCE WHIPPERMAN

The façade frieze at Ixtlán de Juárez's church of St. Thomas the Apostle depicts the dramatic confrontation of the doubting Thomas with Jesus.

the risen Jesus, the act that, according to the Gospels, removed all doubt of the resurrection's reality. Finally, before you leave, glimpse inside the baptistery, on the right side of the nave, where Benito Juárez was baptized in 1806.

If you're lucky enough to arrive between December 19 and 22, you can join the local folks in the patronal **Fiesta de Santo Tomás Apóstol.** Festivities include tying up traffic on the highway with *calendas* while bombs blast overhead, *mañanitas* (5 A.M. masses), *jaripeo* (bull riding and roping), and the Betaza traditional courtship dance.

Ecotours

Most of the natural sights around Ixtlán are on communal land, so you must make arrangements for a guide from the community-run Ixtlán ecotour agency, **Viajes Ecoturísticos Schiaa Rua Via** (Mountain Where the Clouds Are Born, Calle 16 de Septiembre, tel./fax 951/553-6075, ecoturismo_ixtlan@msn.com, www.oaxacamex.info/ixtlan, 9 A.M. 2 P.M. and 4–7 P.M. Mon.–Sat.), to accompany you.

Tours range widely over Ixtlán's spreading 48,000-acre preserve. They include bird- and animal-watching, cloud forest hikes, mountain biking, sportfishing, cave exploring, wilderness camping, and more.

All tours leave from the agency's headquarters at the northeast corner of the town plaza. Guides are competent and well trained by the agency's guiding lights and founders, biologists Norma Angélica Montes Rodríguez and Gustavo Ramírez Santiago. Expect to pay about $25 per person per day, excluding transportation. They also rent mountain *cabañas* (see *Accommodations and Food*).

With a guide, you can reach the natural sights by bus or by passenger car via Highway 175 north and the road southeast to Calpulalpan. What follows is a summary of the guided ecotour that, in the capable hands of Viajes Ecoturísticos, I enjoyed in a single day, driving my car. (Using local bus transportation, together with about 15 miles of hiking, fit travelers, accompanied by a guide, could cover the same ground in two days.)

First, follow Highway 175 north 15 miles (25 km) and turn right, uphill, onto a gravel road signed Zoogochi. Set your odometer. On the gravel road, follow the right fork at 1.5 miles (2.4 km); continue 1.2 miles, a total of 2.7 miles (4.2 km) from the highway, to a summer wildflower–carpeted grassy (but maybe too wet in the summer) meadow on the left, known locally as **Latziruetze** (Meadow of the Thistles), with good spring water and possible wilderness tenting spots in the dry winter–spring.

Continue along the same route (bear right at the first fork and left at the next two) another 2.2 miles (3.5 km) from the highway, a total of 4.9 miles (7.8 km), to **Los Pozuelos** shelter, cozy for camping (no tent needed; the sturdy roof shelters against rain). From there, you can walk the rough jeep track a quarter mile (0.4 km) uphill to the *mirador* tower, where on a clear day you can see Volcán de Orizaba (elev. 18,856 feet/5,747 meters), Mexico's highest mountain, jutting above the northern horizon.

Also from the Los Pozuelos shelter, walk the trail signed **Camino Real** and you will be following the route of long-vanished Aztec, Zapotec, and Mixtec traders who trekked between the Gulf Coast and the Valley of Oaxaca. A few hundred yards along the trail downhill (actually about 320 paces from the shelter) you'll see a big standing tree trunk on the left; at the end of a rough path about 200 feet (60 meters) downhill is a permanent spring, fine for drinking.

Around the spring, you can't help but notice the long clumps of moss hanging eerily from the trees. This is a sure sign that you're in the **cloud forest,** a remnant island of Ice Age flora, with many species, such as wild begonias (look for clusters of their small-blossomed magenta flowers), ferns, dwarf bamboo, liquid amber, and many others in common with the mountains of the southeastern United States. Here in the Sierra Norte of Oaxaca, the cloud forest covers the humid Gulf-facing northern slopes at altitudes between 6,500 and 10,000 feet (2,000 and 3,000 meters).

Next, return to Ixtlán and head out to

Oaxaca's Sierra Norte is a lushly forested landscape of pastures and deep canyons, sprinkled with small Zapotec-speaking villages.

explore a **hidden cave, spring, and waterfall** all in one. Go by the road to Calpulalpan from the southeast edge of Ixtlán. About four blocks east of Highway 175, follow the paved road past the lumber mill for three miles (five km), where, at the Cabañas sign, you turn left onto a gravel road. Continue another 0.5 mile (0.8 km) to the *cabanas* and another half mile to the cave, **Arco de Yagela.** From there the road continues another nine miles (14 km) to La Cascada (waterfall) and about 19 miles (30 km) to Los Pozuelos campsite.

Park and continue on foot downhill. Before the creek, go left at the rough trail, into the woods. After about 300 feet (90 meters), you'll be at Arco de Yagela, a cave that you approach via a yawning, stalactite-walled rock amphitheater (thus *arco,* or arc). Just inside the cave's mouth, a waterfall splashes into springs welling up from beneath the rocks. The cave itself, whose dark cavity beckons a few feet behind the waterfall, can be accessed only with an expert guide and equipment. It has not been completely explored. A small party could camp on the small, level dry space in the arc to the left of the cave mouth, or a larger party could spread out in the big open space across the creek.

Accommodations and Food

Viajes Ecoturísticos recommends the local **Casa de Huéspedes La Soledad** (Calle Francisco Javier Mina, Barrio de la Soledad, tel. 951/553-6171, $8 s, $13 d), with about 12 clean basic rooms (seven with private baths, the rest with shared bath). Reserve ahead. Get there by walking uphill, past the town plaza, two blocks; turn left at Zapata, turn right at first street, continue another block north to hotel on right.

Also recommendable is the loosely run **Hotel Casa del Cielo** (House of Heaven, Yu'u Yee'va in Zapotec, tel. 951/553-6119, $25 s or d, $30 t) on Hernández, across from the Jiménez grocery, on the right, above the street, a fraction of a block south from the plaza's southwest corner. The four rooms, with hot water, are above the back patio. Call for reservations.

Furthermore, Viajes Ecoturísticos invites

visitors to stay in their forest *cabañas* near Arco de Yagela (see *Ecotours*) a few miles out of town. The very substantial facilities include six duplex *cabañas* (tel./fax 951/553-6075, ecoixtlan@ hotmail.com, $13 per person), each of the accommodation units sleeping four, with double bed, bunk bed, and fireplace, wood included. A hot-water shower-bath and toilet is shared between each pair of duplex units. The entire complex, set in an idyllic, pine-forested stream valley, includes a common dining room serving meals, with touristic services, including mountain bike rentals and guided excursions. You can also reserve through the government alternative tourism office in Oaxaca City (Murguia 206, tel. 951/516-4828 or 951/516-0123, fax 951/514-8501, info@aoaxaca.com, www .oaxaca.travel).

Ixtlán offers several food possibilities. Stock up on fruits and vegetables during the Monday **market,** on the town plaza. Otherwise, for some fresh items and a pretty fair grocery selection, go to **Abarrotes Jiménez** (tel. 951/553-6124), just downhill from the plaza's southwest corner.

Ixtlán supports a few restaurants around the plaza. Very recommendable is **Comedor Jemima** (Sidencio Hernández 10, 6:30 A.M.–8 P.M. daily, $4–6), half a block downhill from the plaza's southwest corner. Also recommendable, on the same street, a few doors closer to the plaza corner, is **Restaurant Jiménez** (tel. 951/553-6124, 8 A.M.–8 P.M. daily, $3–8).

Another recommendable local restaurant is the newish **La Cabaña** (approximately 7 A.M.–8 P.M. daily), near the Highway 175 Km 132 marker, about 31 miles (52 km) north of Ixtlán. Inside the airy, knotty pine dining room, a small store sells basic groceries and trinkets, and a modest kitchen puts out good breakfasts (spicy *huevos a la Mexicana* $3, savory *guisado de pollo* $5, fresh trout dinner $6).

Services

Nearly all of Ixtlán's services are available near the plaza. The bank, **Banorte** (9 A.M.–4 P.M. Mon.–Fri.), at the corner of Revolución and 16 de Septiembre, a block uphill from the plaza, changes money. You can also visit the town *biblioteca* (library) next door, north side, from the bank.

The *correo* (9 A.M.–1 P.M. and 3–6 P.M. Mon.–Fri.) is also by the bank. For public fax and money orders, go to *telégrafos* (9 A.M.–3 P.M. Mon.–Fri.) at the plaza's northeast corner. After hours, you can also send a fax at the Jiménez long-distance telephone and fax, next to the Jiménez grocery (tel./fax 951/553-6097 or 951/553-6098), or buy a Ladatel card and use the street telephone out in front of the Jiménez store.

If you get sick, go to the *centro de salud* on Revolución behind the *presidencia municipal,* open 24 hours. Alternatively, consult one of the town's private doctors. Your choices are **Dr. Vicente Morales** (across Revolución from the *centro de salud,* 4–8 P.M. Mon.–Thurs.), or **Doctora Ofelia Maldonado Luis,** at her **Farmacia La Soledad** (16 de Septiembre 17A,

tel. 951/553-6003, 8 A.M.–3 P.M. and 5–9 P.M.), two blocks uphill from the plaza.

Both the *gasolinera* and the bus station are on Highway 175, about three blocks west of the plaza. Both first- and second-class Cuenca de Papaloapan and first-class ADO buses provide several daily connections south with Oaxaca City and north with Valle Nacional, Tuxtepec, and intermediate destinations. Moreover **vans,** provide several daily fast Ixtlán–Oaxaca City connections, from their terminal on Highway 175, near the Cuenca-ADO bus stop. The telephone numbers in Ixtlán are 951/553-6157 and 951/553-6289.

EXCURSIONS AROUND IXTLÁN

Calpulalpan

Little Calpulalpan (pop. 3,000) perches on its hillside about six miles (9.6 km) east along the road from Ixtlán. The town's pride is its church, the **Templo de San Mateo,** completed

The celebrated Templo de San Mateo marks the center of picturesque hillside Calpulalpan.

© BRUCE WHIPPERMAN

by the Dominicans in 1718. Ordinarily serene, the church grounds overflow with merrymakers during the **Fiesta de San Mateo,** which climaxes yearly on September 21.

The church's renovated interior soars to a magnificent wooden ceiling. Charmingly naive designs painted by early native artisans decorate the front, below the choir, while a pair of angels, following Jesus's exhortation to become "fishers of men," dangle fish from opposite sides of the front altar. Lining both side walls, several elaborate baroque *retablos* display a gallery of colorful saints and pious 18th-century oil paintings.

Uphill a few blocks from the church, the town *centro de salud* has a unique twin, the **Centro de Medicinas Tradicionales** (Center of Traditional Medicine, 9 A.M.–2 P.M. and 4–7 P.M. Mon.–Fri.), across a connecting patio. An herb-drying apparatus out front gives hints of the treatments practiced by the traditional healers inside the conventional-appearing modern white stucco building.

Guelatao town honors its native son with a bronze sculpture of Benito Juárez when he was a local shepherd boy.

Guelatao

A government-constructed monumental **Plaza Cívica** has converted this modest mountain town on Highway 175 two miles (three km) south of Ixtlán into a shrine for beloved President Benito Juárez, who was born nearby on March 21, 1806.

Juárez's timeless credo, *"El respeto al derechos ajenos es la paz"* ("Respect for the rights of all is peace"), marks the museum on the plaza, two blocks uphill from the town highway crossing. Inside, glass cases preserve a few precious mementos: a photograph, Juárez's death mask, a letter, a diary, a graduation certificate from the seminary in Oaxaca, and a model of the renowned black carriage in which Juárez for years fulfilled his duties of office, one jump ahead of his enemies.

Also on the plaza is a bronze sculpture of Juárez's mother, Brigida Garcia, and, at the *presidencia municipal,* a bust of Juárez, together with the historic letter that Juárez wrote to his ambassador in the United States, opposing the meddling of the United States in Mexican affairs.

Just north of the plaza, a shady path borders the petite spring-fed lake from which the town derives its Zapotec name, Guelatao (gooay-lah-TAH-oh), which translates as Enchanted Lagoon. On the lakeshore, see the famous sentimental bronze sculpture of young Benito, the humble shepherd boy, tending his flock.

The local community joins with the entire country in celebrating the memory of Benito Juárez, "Benemérito de las Américas" ("Hero of the Americas"). Yearly, on March 21, Mexico's president and Oaxaca's governor kick off a six-day fiesta of tournaments, fireworks, and a whirl of traditional dances by performing groups from a host of Zapotec communities.

Into the Papaloapan

Humid, tropical air, moving gently westward from the Gulf of Mexico, cools, clouds, and drops a deluge of rain on the northern slope of the Sierra Madre de Oaxaca. The water collects and cascades down the mountains, gathering into great, rushing rivers that finally deepen and wind slowly through a grand tropical lowland plain called the Papaloapan (pah-pah-loh-AH-pahn), after the river system that drains it. The Tonto, the Santo Domingo, and the Valle Nacional join near the town of Tuxtepec to form the Río Papaloapan. The rivers are the region's prime asset—at high elevations on the Sierra's northern slope, the waters nourish vast, thick forests: pine-oak at the higher elevations and a fantastically lush, tropical hardwood rain forest that spreads downhill into the valleys. There, farmers have replaced the forest with rich fields of corn and tobacco, great thickets of rubber trees, and, in the shady underlay, plantations of shiny-leafed coffee bushes. The government, moreover, has tamed and harnessed the rivers, gathering them into a pair of immense reservoirs—Temascal and Cerro de Oro—for irrigation, recreation, and electric power.

VALLE NACIONAL: LAND OF SPRINGS

As the rainwater makes its way to the valleys, it sometimes wells up as crystalline, mountain-foot springs before gathering into rushing rivers. One of the loveliest of these spring-fed rivers collects at the foot of the Sierra Chinantla, a spur of the Sierra Madre de Oaxaca. It rushes downhill past the town of Valle Nacional, where it's called the Río Valle Nacional.

Valle Nacional (pop. 10,000) is interesting mostly as a springboard to the lush valley and water country that winds north 20 miles (32 km) from its outskirts. The town itself is a commercial service center for the local *ranchos* (ranches) and *fincas* (farms). Although Valle Nacional is an important coffee-producing

center, it would be easier to get an irrigation pump here than a cappuccino. Lunch-table talk centers mostly around tobacco, coffee, and rubber prices. Although nearly everyone in town has abandoned the original Chinantec tongue for Spanish, things change on Sunday during the big weekly *tianguis*. Then, you'll most likely rub shoulders with plenty of Chinantec-speaking people, including women in colorful striped local *huipiles*.

Besides Sunday, other good times to arrive in Valle Nacional (officially San Juan Bautista Valle Nacional) are during the local fiestas: one in memory of Saint John the Baptist around June 24, and, even bigger, the **Fiesta de San José**, celebrated for three days beginning March 18. During these times, *calendas* and floats block the street, fireworks boom overhead, masses fill the church, and merrymakers dance in the plaza.

◖ Balnearios Monte Flor and El Zuzul

A pair of nearby *balnearios* (developed springs) are perfect for a relaxing afternoon picnic or a pleasant camping overnight. Idyllically lovely Balneario Monte Flor is at Cerro de Marín village, Kilometer 43, about 3.5 miles (6 km) north of Valle Nacional and about 17 miles (27 km) south of Tuxtepec. On the river side of Highway 175 northbound, watch for the small Museo Comunitario sign and rough entrance driveway on the right, at the last village *tope* (speed bump).

Downhill, below the village, under grand, spreading trees, cool, crystalline water wells up beneath a great hillside monolith into a gorgeous natural bathing pool. Kids run around, families splash in the water, chickens scratch in the grass, while downstream, women do their weekly wash. Especially on weekends and holidays, vendors set up tarps and offer soft drinks and barbecued beef, pork, and chicken.

Back uphill, in the broad grassy village commons, ask and someone may be available to open the community museum for you. (Although the keeper was out of town when I was there, folks told me that the museum displays include a collection of locally discovered archaeological artifacts.)

Good camping is available (walk downstream from the spring source a couple hundred yards) at the private paradise of friendly Diego Alonzo Francisco and his family. They offer several grassy acres shaded by big old trees, with a few chickens and turkeys pecking around, dogs, and lots of *toronjas* (grapefruit) and mangos in season.

On holidays, folks crowd in, but on any other day you'd have the place nearly to yourself. You may put up your tent, or pull in your self-contained RV, for about $4 a day. Señora Alonzo furnishes all of the drinks and home-cooked food you can eat in the adjacent restaurant. If you prefer, try your luck at fishing for *mojarra* or *pepesca* in the spring for your dinner. The family (or a neighbor) might have a spare room for the night if you have no RV or tent.

Queen of the valley's bathing springs is the local favorite, Balneario El Zuzul, a name everyone from Valle Nacional to Tuxtepec knows fondly. Part of the fun is getting there, because you have to cross the bridge over scenic, swift-flowing Río Valle Nacional. Once across, you see what the fuss is all about: a big, round, stone-edged blue pool of clear, cool spring water, which wells up from the depths for everyone's enjoyment, a perfect antidote for a hot afternoon.

Surrounding the pool is a shady, grassy park, fine for tent or RV camping. If no one seems to be in charge, you might still ask if it's OK to camp *("¿Es bueno campar?")*. You might have to look around for a while before someone understands you, because the standard dialect at El Zuzul is Chinantec. Bring your own food and drinking water (although on weekends, folks will probably be around, selling most of what you need).

Get there by driving or taking one of the *colectivo* taxis (less than $1) parked at the signed turnoff road, between Kilometers 36 and 37, about seven miles (11 km) north of

© BRUCE WHIPPERMAN

The local community welcomes visitors to enjoy the springwaters of Balneario Monte Flor.

Valle Nacional, or 15 miles (24 km) south of Tuxtepec. Continue 0.3 mile (0.5 km); turn left at the first road, and continue 0.8 mile (1.2 km) over the river bridge to Vega de Sol village on the south bank. Turn right just after the bridge and continue three blocks and turn right into the El Zuzul entry driveway.

Practicalities

Valle Nacional has one main business street, Highway 175, locally called Avenida Benito Juárez, where you'll find most basic services, except for a bank. The town plaza (which accommodates few businesses) is on the right side, northbound, approximately at the center of town.

Of the town's three hotels, the best appears to be the downscale **Hotel Valle** (Calle 2 Poniente 3, tel. 283/877-4218, $10 s or d, $15 with a/c), on a side street a few blocks south of the plaza, three doors from the highway. It offers 16 bare-bulb but acceptably clean rooms in a two-story building, with tepid-water baths. Air conditioned rooms are a plus in very warm, humid Valle Nacional.

Stores along the main street, notably **La Chinanteca,** sell plenty of luscious fruits, while *abarroterías* such as **Las Triunfada** sell lots of groceries, and a parade of *taquerias, loncherías* and *refresquerías* supply plenty more.

One of the town's best restaurants is the very clean, refined **(Desgarenes** (Juárez 29, tel. 283/877-4005, 10 A.M.–6 P.M. daily), beneath the luxurious big *palapa* on the left side of the street a few blocks north of the plaza. Open for breakfast, lunch, and early supper.

Find the *correo* and *telégrafos* (tel. 283/877-4132, 9 A.M.–3 P.M. Mon.–Fri.) at the *presidencia municipal* on the plaza. Do your telephoning at the Ladatel card–operated street telephones, on the town plaza's east side, or in front of the *presidencia.*

For a doctor, go to the 24-hour *centro de salud* (tel. 283/877-4126); turn east at the sign at the north (Tuxtepec) end of town; continue a block, off the highway.

Gasoline is available at the Pemex station, at the north end of town.

Getting There and Away

The best way to reach Valle Nacional by bus is via a Cuenca or ADO first-class bus from the first-class bus station in Oaxaca City or Tuxtepec. Get away via the bus station in the middle of town, where buses connect north with Tuxtepec and south with Oaxaca City, including many intermediate destinations. From Oaxaca City, drivers should follow federal Highway 175 about 110 miles (177 km) north, via Ixtlán, to Valle Nacional. The route, although well-maintained much of the way, except for some potholes, winds nearly continuously, with a number of steep grades along most of its length. For safety, allow about four hours at the wheel, either direction, for the entire trip to or from Oaxaca City.

SANTA MARÍA JACATEPEC

In between Valle Nacional and Tuxtepec, Jacatepec (pop. 3,000) is a village of friendly, frankly curious Chinantec-speaking folks. Well worth a stop, it's tucked on the far side of the river, once accessible only by boat or a *puente colgante* (pedestrian suspension bridge). Now, a new automobile bridge connects Jacatepec to the main road, but it's still a quiet little place, fine for a *refresco* and a stroll around town. Also, be sure to walk across the hanging bridge. You'll see it about 300 feet (90 meters) upstream from the highway bridge. If you like the place, ask around for a room for the night. Say *"¿Hay cuarto para la noche?"* and someone may be able to oblige. Like most of the houses, it will probably be a clean abode with a cement floor, surrounded by a yard full of leafy plants; it might even have a sturdy, thatched palm-leaf roof.

While you're there, take a look inside the church at the far end of the town's main street. You'll see a rare surrealistic Catholic altar, set with Jesus on the cross amid an apocalyptic landscape, with the town's patron, the Virgen de la Concepción, the only apparent ray of hope, floating above. Jacatepec is about 11 miles (18 km) north of Valle Nacional, or the same distance south of Tuxtepec.

Enliven your Jacatepec visit by arriving

during one of the community's two major festivals: on August 15, celebrating their Virgen de la Concepción, and on April 23, honoring San Jorge (St. George). Folks flood into town from all over Mexico, the United States, and Canada for tearful reunions. They honor their holy patrons with processions and *mañanitas* (devotional masses), then let loose, with carnival rides and games, plenty of old-fashioned country food, favorite old dances, and climax the whole thing by enjoying rainbows of fireworks that paint the night sky.

SAN JOSÉ CHILTEPEC

Chiltepec (pop. 3,000) is a friendly little Chinantec town with lots of thatched houses surrounded by yards abloom with bananas, red and yellow hibiscus, and crimson torch ginger. Chiltepec is a ripe prospect for an overnight, mainly because of its inviting hotel and pair of riverside *balnearios* (springs). Visitors also enjoy a sprinkling of *comedores*, especially the charmingly rustic and highly recommended *palapa* **Restaurant El Río** (9 A.M.–8 P.M. daily, $4-8). The town's modicum of services includes post office, long-distance telephone, health center, doctor, and pharmacy (Doctora Carolina Espinosa Pérez in charge).

The **Balnearios Mingo** and **Cocos** are relaxed local-style places on the winding Río Valle Nacional, with food *palapas* and plenty of shoreline for sunning, frolicking, and splashing. They're best during the warm winter-spring season, when the water is clear and inviting. During the summer rains, the high, sometimes muddy river water sends most bathers to the constantly-clear Balnearios El Zuzul or Monte Flor. Get to the Mingo from the highway by following the signed side road at the south end of town. Cocos is just off the highway; turn at the sign about a mile (1.6 km) north of town. It has plenty of grassy space beneath a palm grove, perhaps just right for tenting or parking your RV.

The hotel **Posada la Chinantla** (Benito Juárez 17, tel. 287/874-7043, $9 s, $10 d), right in the middle of town, would be fine for an overnight. Guests enjoy a shady *palapa*, with

comfortable chairs for sitting, set in a flowery garden patio. Six clean, thoughtfully decorated rooms come with hot-water baths and fans.

TUXTEPEC: RIVER COUNTRY

Tuxtepec (pop. 140,000), Oaxaca's second-largest city, is the administrative and commercial center of the rich governmental district of the same name. For at least a millennium, the town, at its strategic river-junction location, has been an important trading center. Archaeologists believe that the Popoluca people, direct inheritors of the ancient Gulf Coast Olmec mother culture, first settled Tuxtepec perhaps 2,000 years ago.

The name Tuxtepec is the Spanish version of the town's Aztec label, Tochtepec, or Hill of the Rabbits, which probably describes the town's original site, atop some low hills about a mile and a half (2.5 km) west of present downtown Tuxtepec.

At that vital spot, Tuxtepec's early Popoluca people became traders and transporters for the valuable goods—cacao, copper, cotton, feathers, gold—of upstream producers, notably the Mazatecs and Chinantecs. Both still occupy their ancestral homelands: the Mazatecs (People of Mazatlán, Land of the Deer) between the rivers Santo Domingo and Tonto, west of Tuxtepec, and the Chinantecs (People atop the Mountains) in the basin of the Río Valle Nacional, to the southwest.

The ambitious Aztec emperors, expanding their domain in the 1400s, saw strategic Tuxtepec as a key to realizing their dreams of grandeur. Aztec forces under Moctezuma I subdued Tuxtepec in the 1460s. They built a ceremonial pyramid, known locally as the Castillo de Moctezuma, which still stands in a west-side residential neighborhood.

Aztec governor-generals commanded a Tuxtepec garrison of several thousand warriors for two generations, putting down rebellions and enforcing tribute from Tuxtepec's many subject towns. The codex Mendocino recorded the yearly spoils, including: "eight hundred loads of . . . red and white blankets . . . eighty bundles of quetzal feathers . . . twenty loads of clear amber, set in gold . . . twenty loads of quartz, enameled and finished with gold . . . 200 loads of cacao . . . twenty thousand rubber balls . . . "

Hernán Cortés, almost immediately upon marching into the Aztec capital in 1519, asked Moctezuma II of his empire's source of gold. Moctezuma told him, "In Tochtepec the people wash the soil in bowls with water, and afterward, small grains of gold remain." He went on to say, "Not far from Tochtepec are some mines, said to be worked by Zapotecs and Chinantecs, who are not our subjects. If you desire to send soldiers to investigate, I will furnish emissaries to accompany them."

Cortés immediately dispatched his first gold-searching expedition outside of the Valley of Mexico, to Tuxtepec. They eventually brought back what was estimated to be 1,000 pesos' worth—perhaps a small sackful—of gold dust and small nuggets.

In late 1521, Gonzalo de Sandoval, after passing through the Valley of Oaxaca, took possession of Tuxtepec for Spain. Cortés instructed him to found a new town at Tuxtepec and name it Medellín, after the town in Spain where Cortés was born. Although the name Medellín didn't stick, Cortés persuaded the Spanish king to award him Tuxtepec as part of his Marquesate.

Tuxtepec was only a minor player in Mexican colonial and Independence history until it jumped onto the national stage in 1876 when Porfirio Díaz "pronounced" against the reelection of President Lerdo de Tejada. Díaz, a war hero and liberal ally of the revered late President Benito Juárez, threatened civil war. A group of his supporters organized in Tuxtepec, where they formulated the **Plan de Tuxtepec,** which reasserted the principles of the Reform Constitution of 1857 and invented the slogan *"¡No Reelección!"* opposing reelection of the president, a principle that remains as Mexico's law of the land to the present day.

Lerdo de Tejada, nevertheless, refused to step down. So, with the entire state of Oaxaca behind him, Díaz marched on Mexico City. Soon, Tejada fled the country and Díaz took

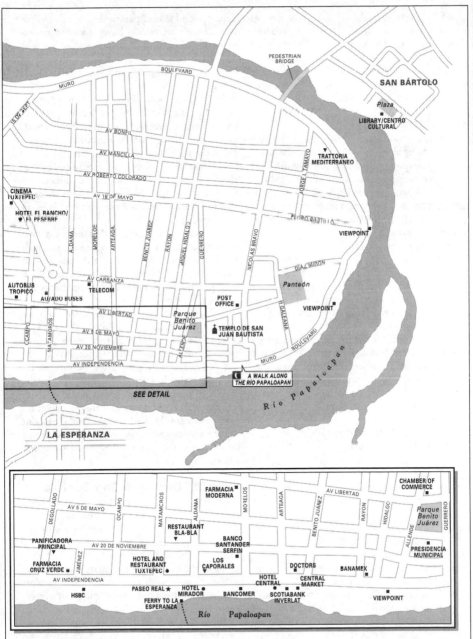

brief de facto control of the government on November 28, 1876. Shortly thereafter, Congress endorsed his action. Díaz served as legal president until 1880, as governor of Oaxaca from 1880 to 1884, then resumed the presidency, ignoring *¡No Reelección!* until revolution forced him into exile in 1911.

Orientation

Tuxtepec is a modern town that spreads for two or three miles along the steep bank of the broad Río Papaloapan, which flows nearly due east past Tuxtepec's busy downtown. The main business streets begin at the Highway 175 bridge at the west end and continue for about a mile (1.5 km) east to the town plaza. Moving away from the river, the main streets are Independencia, 20 de Noviembre, 5 de Mayo, and Libertad. A fifth street, quieter river-view boulevard El Muro, also runs parallel to the river, beginning at the east end of Independencia and gradually curving northerly, then westerly, until its course is completely reversed as it runs west along the north side of town.

Unlike most Mexican towns, Tuxtepec's main plaza, the **Parque Benito Juárez,** is not at the center of Tuxtepec, but rather at the east end, where the *presidencia municipal* and the town church, **Templo de San Juan Bautista,** face adjacent sides of the plaza.

◖ A Walk Along the Río Papaloapan

Although Tuxtepec owes its existence to the Río Papaloapan, the town has pretty much turned its back on the river ever since trucks and trains have replaced the colorful fleet of log rafts, canoes, and barges that used to carry small mountains of cotton, rubber, coffee, and lumber from the upstream hinterlands. Nevertheless, a walk along the river is an entertaining route to enjoying Tuxtepec. Avoid the heat by starting out in the morning or late afternoon from the de facto town center (judging by the hustle and bustle) at the corner of Libertad and Matamoros, three short blocks from the river, about halfway between the highway and the plaza. Here, buses arrive and depart with loads of passengers. While people wait, a host of vendors hawk a varied assortment of goods, from CDs and socks to mangos and machine screws. A number of street-front *comedores* and *loncherías* provide hearty meals and snacks.

From there, head along Matamoros toward the river. At the end, Independencia, turn left to the small riverfront square, **Paso Real,** nearly immediately on the right. Here you can enjoy the river view, the breeze, and, if it's evening, perhaps a radiant sunset mirrored on the river's glassy surface. Descend the stairs to the dock, and, for fun, ride the **riverboat** that ferries folks across to **La Esperanza** village on the opposite bank.

Continue east along Independencia two more blocks to the market (biggest on Sunday). Find the stairs (inside, on the left) and climb to the second level. Here, take a table at one of the *fondas* and enjoy a refreshment while feasting on the river view.

While at the market, be sure to visit **Artesanías Mitla** (9 A.M.–8 P.M. Mon.–Sat., 9 A.M.–2 P.M. Sun.) handicrafts shop, just inside the market's street-front central doorway entrance. Friendly proprietor Señora Anita Morales, who is actually from Mitla, in the Valley of Oaxaca, offers many fetching local woodcrafts, plus black pottery from Coyotepec. Other stores in the market you might check out are the piñata and party goods store (stalls 42 and 45), and the *huipiles* of Señora Guadalupe Gómez (stall 24).

Hanging Bridge to San Bartolo

Enjoy a scenic diversion by continuing east, to the end of the downtown at Independencia. Either on foot or by taxi, continue straight ahead along airy river-view boulevard El Muro, following (a total of about 0.5 mile/one km) along as the river bends northerly to the *puente colgante* (hanging bridge). Cross over to **San Bartolo Tuxtepec,** a sleepy village of yesteryear. Turn right at the first street and stroll up to the town *jardín* and library, where spreading, shady trees frame the view back across the river. One of the few times that San Bartolo wakes up is during its **fiesta** on August 20–24, when, besides the feasts, fireworks, processions, and masses, the town sponsors musical performances, often including marimba and local-style *música cuenqeuña*. If drowsy San Bartolo tempts you to linger, a few taco stands in the park and a sprinkling of restaurants along the main street can supply refreshments.

El Castillo de Moctezuma

This is a 15th-century unreconstructed ceremonial pyramid uncovered around 1916, now the centerpiece of a small neighborhood park in a Tuxtepec west-end suburb. Archaeologists believe that despite its *castillo* label, it was not built as a castle or fortress, but probably served as both a signal post and a ceremonial site for the populous Tuxtepec Aztec colony from around 1460 to 1520.

El Castillo rises gradually from the west side in three steps, to a height of about 25 feet (eight meters), and drops precipitously on the

After 500 years, the stones of the Castillo de Moctezuma Aztec pyramid have remained essentially undisturbed.

© BRUCE WHIPPERMAN

east side. Its surface is littered with crumbling masonry walls, which, on the north side, appear to open to a niche or tunnel.

Get there via Calle Reforma, the last street, Tuxtepec side, before the Highway 175 bridge. Turn right and continue three blocks; turn left at the T. Continue four more blocks to a big Refacciones Americano sign at Calle Ruinas. Turn right and continue one block to the park and ruins at the corner of Calles Ruinas and Tabasco.

Accommodations

Tuxtepec serves its many business visitors with a number of good hotels. Most of the fancier establishments lie along west side Bulevar Benito Juárez (the northern prolongation of Highway 175), or in the quieter neighborhoods away from the downtown. The budget accommodations, most priced under $25, are in the busy downtown either overlooking or near the river. In all cases, in warm and humid Tuxtepec, air-conditioning is worth the small extra charge.

UNDER $25

Right in the middle of town stands the attractively renovated **Hotel Mirador** (Independencia 531, tel./fax 287/875-0652, 287/875-0500, or 287/875-0797, $18 s, $20 d with fan only, $22 s or d with a/c) overlooking the river, next to the Paso Real ferry dock. Of the 51 attractively decorated rooms, reserve one of the second-floor ones, numbers 219–223, along the quieter, upper river-view corridor. Rentals all include TV, phone, hot-water bath, and parking. Credit cards are not accepted.

Another good downtown option, also occupying a choice riverfront perch, half a block east, is the **Hotel Central** (Independencia 565, tel. 287/875-0966 or 287/875-0913, fax 287/875-0801, hotelcentral@yahoo.com, $20 s, $22 d with fan only, $22 s, $24 d with a/c). Of the hotel's 24 rooms, reserve one of the three best, numbers 122, 119, and 107, along the airy upper view walkway, overlooking the river. Rooms themselves are clean and simply but invitingly decorated. All come with private hot-water baths, TV, phone, parking, and a good restaurant downstairs. Credit cards are not accepted.

Half a block west is the **Hotel Tuxtepec** (Matamoros 2, tel. 287/875-0934, illatina@ hotmail.com, $18 s or d fan only, $23 s, $27 d with a/c), a few steps off Independencia in the middle of downtown. Lacking a river-view location, the Hotel Tuxtepec management makes up for it by trying harder. Past the reception and appealingly airy street-front restaurant, the small but attractive lobby, set around a bubbling fountain, leads upstairs to 40 immaculate comfortably furnished rooms. Rentals run a reasonable, all with baths, hot water, and parking, and credit cards are accepted.

$25-50

Moving west half a mile (one km), three blocks from the highway and somewhat up the economic scale, try the renovated four-star **Hotel Playa Bruja** (Independencia 1531, tel./fax 287/875-0325, playabruja@hotmail.com, $35 s, $38 d, $42 t). The hotel's 40 clean comfortably furnished rooms rise in three stories around a small inner pool patio. Rooms all come with air-conditioning, TV, phone, parking, and a restaurant-bar. Credit cards are not accepted.

On the highway, a block from the bridge, stands one of Tuxtepec's most relaxing hotels, the spacious four-star **☾ Hotel Hacienda** (Blv. Benito Juárez 409, tel. 287/875-1500, 287/875-1621, fax 287/875-1998, hhaciendatuxt@hotmail.com, $38 s or d). Past the entrance and parking, relegated thoughtfully to the outer periphery, the reception leads to a cool, air-conditioned restaurant (with TV; ask them to turn down the volume), bordering a relaxing pool patio and shady tropical garden. The 60 semi-deluxe rooms in three-story tiers are secluded, clean, and comfortable, somewhat worn (but undergoing renovation). The most desirable rooms have small balconies overlooking the garden (ask for "*balcón con vista del jardín, por favor*"). Rates are quite reasonable for such amenities, also including air-conditioning, warm-water bathrooms, cable TV, phone, parking, but credit cards not accepted.

If everything else is full, the hotel that may have a room is the **Hotel Mesón** (Blv. Benito Juárez 1684, tel. 287/875-1200, 287/875-1359, or 287/875-1292, hotelmeson@prodigy.net. mx, $39 s or d, $43 t), on the highway about a mile (1.6 km) north of the Highway 175 river bridge. Here, the builder cleverly packed three stories of 65 rooms into a small space. The little pool, unfortunately relegated to a cramped upstairs patio, seems like an afterthought. The rooms inside, however, are clean, private, spacious, tiled, and furnished with comfortable 1980s-standard amenities. Rentals include air-conditioning, bath, cable TV, phone, restaurant-bar, wireless Internet, and parking. Credit cards are accepted.

For not many more pesos, you can stay in Tuxtepec's newest, shiniest lodging, the garden-style **☾ Hotel Villa Esmeralda** (Articulo 123 No. 74, tel./fax 287/875-5111 or 287/875-5112, hotel_villaesmeralda@hotmail.com, $48 s or d, $55 t). The Villa Esmeralda, tucked into a quiet residential neighborhood, offers immaculate semi-deluxe rooms furnished with color-coordinated bedspreads, drapes, tiled floors, and shiny modern-standard baths. An additional trio of pluses is a good restaurant, parking thoughtfully removed to the periphery, and an invitingly tranquil inner patio garden with large lap pool and adjacent kiddie pool. All this, plus air-conditioning, phone, cable TV, parking, wireless Internet, and credit cards accepted.

If the Villa Esmeralda is full, consider the nearby refined 1960s motel-style **Hotel El Rancho** (435 Blv. Avila Camacho, tel./fax 287/875-0722, 287/875-0469, or 287/875-0704, elrancho@prodigy.net.mx, $45 s or d, $53 t). The El Rancho, in a mixed residential-business neighborhood, surrounds a pleasant tropical pool and parking patio. Inside, the 49 semi-deluxe rooms are immaculate and thoughtfully and comfortably furnished. Amenities include air-conditioning, bath, cable TV, parking, a good restaurant-bar; limited wheelchair access, and credit cards accepted. The hotel's only drawback appears to be the room arrangement, on exterior corridors, where guests must unfortunately draw blinds for privacy.

Food

Tuxtepec visitors enjoy plenty of good food. The two town markets, the Mercado Flores Magón (on 20 de Noviembre, west side, two blocks from the river bridge) and the central market (on Independencia in the town center, by the river) are the best sources of groceries, fruits, and vegetables. At the central market, *fondas* upstairs serve economical, wholesome *comidas* at luxuriously airy river-view tables. Especially outstanding among the market *fondas* is (**Restaurant and Ostionería Rosy** (7 A.M.–8 P.M. Mon.–Sat., 7 A.M.–4 P.M. Sun., $3–6).

For good baked offerings, go to the **Panificadora Principal** (20 de Noviembre, tel. 287/875-0755, 7 A.M.–8 P.M. Mon.–Sat., 7 A.M.–noon Sun.), on the corner of Degollado, about five blocks from the highway; or **Petit Cafetería y Pastelería** (689 5 de Mayo, tel. 287/875-4742, 9 A.M.–8:30 P.M. Mon.–Sat., 10 A.M.–4 P.M. Sun.), nearer the center of town.

A great place to start the day is the relaxing, TV-free (**Restaurant Bla-Bla** (on 20 de Noviembre, between Morelos and Arteaga, cell 044-287/104-8570, 7 A.M.–6 P.M. daily,) in mid downtown, a block from the river. Choose from a dozen tasty breakfasts ($2–4), soups and Mexican specialties ($2–5), and poultry, seafood, meats ($4–7), and much more.

A longtime favorite downtown restaurant, famous for its local-style food and relaxed atmosphere, is town center **Caporales** (Independencia 560, upper floor, tel. 287/875-4405, 8 A.M.–6 P.M. Tues.–Sun.). Find it across the street from the Hotel Mirador. Entrées run a moderate $4–5 for breakfast, $5–10 for lunch and early supper.

Another good choice downtown, half a block west of Caporales, is the immaculate restaurant of the **Hotel Tuxtepec** (tel. 287/875-0934, 7 A.M.–11 P.M. daily), where you can enjoy a good breakfast, lunch, or supper ($3–7).

Three stars for refined ambience and attentive service go to the restaurant **El Pesebre** (435 Blv. Manuel Avila Camacho, tel. 287/875-0722 or 287/875 0469, 8 A.M. 10 P.M. daily), at the Hotel El Rancho, about a mile (1.6 km)

diagonally northwest of downtown, two blocks from throughway Bulevar Benito Juárez. Here, you can escape from the heat and the hubbub into a cool, air-conditioned TV-free atmosphere and select from a professionally prepared international-style menu of soups and salads ($3–5), sandwiches and pasta ($4–6), eggs ($2–5), and fish, fowl, and meat entrées ($4–10).

The immaculate, cheery **Restaurant Mogala** (tel. 287/875-7919, 8 A.M.–10 P.M.), at the Hotel Villa Esmeralda, is a fine place to both start and end your day. Tasty professionally prepared and served breakfasts (eggs, hotcakes, ham, bacon, fruit, $2–5), soup, sandwich, and salad lunches ($3–4), and seafood, meat, and fowl dinners ($4–7) are prepared to please even demanding palates.

One restaurant has especially ratcheted up culinary standards in Tuxtepec. Authentically prepared Italian-style specialties are the main attraction to the refined dining room of (**Trattoria Mediterraneo** (Blv. Muro 1759, tel. 287/875-8488, 1–11 P.M. Mon.–Sat., 1–10 P.M. Sun.), on the river-front boulevard, east side of town. The menu offers many fine choices. For example, start off with *prosciutto e melone* ($5), followed by *insalate caprese* ($4), and *minestrone di verdure* (vegetable minestrone, $4). Continue with the first plate, *linguini frutti di mare* (seafood linguini, $8), and finish with the second, *costolette di maile* (barbecued pork ribs, $9). Best skip dessert. Weekend reservations recommended.

Patrons at Tuxtepec's upscale restaurant–night club **La Carreta** (Blv. Benito Juárez, west of downtown, tel. 287/875-3880 or 287/875-3772, noon–1 A.M. daily) seem to do fine, especially with the chef's recommendations. For example, make up a party and share all three: *pompano enpapelada* (pompano in paper, $9), *filete de robalo* (snook fillet stuffed with shrimp, $10), and *filete tampiquena* (beef fillet, tampico-style, $9). If possible, go Thursday, Friday, or Saturday early evening to enjoy the elegant *palapa* river-view ambience and linger over after-dinner wine or margaritas until live oldies-but-goodies dance music begins at 10 P.M. Find it beyond the second traffic circle, northbound, on the east (right) side of Bulevar Benito Juárez.

Entertainment and Events

Tuxtepec's biggest party is the **Feria Tuxtepec,** which runs for about a week during late May or early June, when local people pull all of the rabbits out of their collective hat: election of a queen, grand parade of floats, horse and cowboy parade, cockfights, fireworks, a big commercial exposition, and a folkloric dance festival, including Tuxtepec's own charming **Danza de la Flor de Piña** (Dance of the Pineapple Flower).

If you're in town on July 23 and 24, during the **Fiesta de San Juan Bautista,** be sure to get in on some of the fun around the plaza, including processions, *marmotas* (dancing giants), fireworks, and a community dance.

Tuxtepec folks also make a big celebration of the **Día de los Muertos** (Day of the Dead) on November 1 and 2. At the *panteón* (cemetery) three blocks east of the plaza's northeast corner, whole families arrive in the early evening to clean up and decorate the graves with flowers, candy, candles, and the favorite foods of the deceased, then settle down for an all-night vigil.

Tropical Tuxtepec is warm year-round, and especially so during the warm spring dry season, when folks enjoy the many local *balnearios* (river swimming beaches and natural springs). Some of the best are scattered along Highway 175 south of town. (See the *Valle Nacional: Land of Springs* and *San José Chiltepec* sections earlier in this chapter.)

Information and Services

Tuxtepec has several banks, all with ATMs. The long hours of **HSBC** (805 Independencia, tel. 287/875-2211, 8 A.M.–7 P.M. Mon.– Sat.) make it a good choice. Find it between Degollado and Jiménez, about three blocks west of the town center. Alternatively, moving east, try **Bancomer** (Independencia 647, tel. 287/875-1959, 8:30 A.M.–4 P.M. Mon.– Fri.), next to the market; or **Banamex** (tel. 287/875-1974, 9 A.M.–4 P.M. Mon.–Fri.) farther east, at Independencia and Rayón.

Find the *correo* (tel. 287/875-0239, 9:30 A.M.–4:30 P.M. Mon.–Fri.) at the corner of Libertad and Nicolas Bravo, a block behind the town plaza church. *Telecomunicaciones* (tel./ fax 287/875-0202, 8 A.M.–7:30 P.M. Mon.– Fri., 9 A.M.–noon Sat.–Sun.), at the corner of Carranza and Morelos, provides public fax and money orders. (Find it by walking, from the downtown market, four blocks from the river, inland, along Morelos.)

A small platoon of **Internet** stores downtown provide email and computer services.

For nonprescription medicines and drugs, go to a *farmacia* such as **Farmacia Cruz Verde** (908 Independencia, tel. 287/875-0774), across from Banco Internacional.

Doctors are plentiful in Tuxtepec. Ask at your hotel desk for a recommendation or go to one of the several doctors downtown. Find some of them located in the office complex across Independencia from Scotiabank Inverlat. Here choices include a gynecologist (Eliseo Camacho D., tel. 287/875-3878), ophthalmologist (Julio R. Sáez), and holistic massage, equilibrium, and chakra therapist (Flores de Bach, tel. 287/875-0498 or 287/875-3239).

For more choices, or in emergency, taxi to either the **Hospital Regional Civil** (Ortiz 310, tel. 287/875-0023), corner of Calle Sebastian, or the **Hospital Seguro Social** (tel. 287/875-1366, Blv. Benito Juárez/Hwy. 175), on the town side of the river bridge.

For police or fire emergencies, contact the municipal police (tel. 287/875-3166), at the *presidencia municipal.*

The local **Cámara Nacional de Comercio** (National Chamber of Commerce, tel. 287/875-0886, 9 A.M.–2 P.M. and 5–8 P.M. Mon.–Fri., 9 A.M.–1 P.M. Sat.), at the plaza's northeast corner of Libertad and Allende, will try to answer your questions. Alternatively, travel agents, such as **Viajes Sotelo** (Morelos 118, tel./fax 287/875-2656, 9 A.M.–8 P.M. Mon.–Fri., 9 A.M.–2 P.M. Sat.), at the center of town, a block from Independencia and a block west of the market, are usually willing to answer travel-related queries.

Get your laundry done at **Lavanderia**

Lavasec (1683 Independencia, tel. 287/715-3579, 9 A.M.–2 P.M. and 4–8 P.M. Mon.–Sat., 9 A.M.–2 P.M. Sun.), downtown, far west side, two blocks from the Highway 175 river bridge.

Getting There and Away

Long-distance bus lines, from one major terminal and two minor terminals, provide many connections with both Oaxaca and national destinations.

The major station, for first-class **Autobuses del Oriente (ADO)**, first-class **Cristóbal Colón**, and mixed first- and second-class lines **Autobuses Unidos (AU)** and **Cuenca de Papaloapan (Cuenca),** is smack in the middle of downtown, three short blocks from the river, near the corner of Matamoros and Libertad. All reservations and information are available through tel. 287/875-0237, 285/875-2502.

ADO (ah-day-oh) offers broad service, covering much of southeast Mexico. Buses connect south with Oaxaca City via Valle Nacional and Ixtlán de Juárez; northwest with Orizaba, Puebla, Mexico City (Norte terminal), and Veracruz; and northeast with Minatitlán, Coatzacoalcos, Villahermosa, Campeche, Mérida, Cancún, and Chetumal, at the Belize border.

Ominbus Cristóbal Colón (OCC) buses connect southeast with Isthmus destinations of Juchitán, Tehuántepec, and Salina Cruz; and Chiapas destinations of Tuxtla Gutiérrez and San Cristóbal las Casas.

Autobuses Unidos buses connect north with Puebla and Mexico City; and southeast with Isthmus destinations of Matias Romero, Juchitán, Tehuántepec, and Salina Cruz.

Cuenca buses connect south with Oaxaca City via Valle Nacional and Ixtlán; and north and northwest with Loma Bonita, Temascal, Tierra Blanca, Orizaba, Córdoba, and Veracruz.

Additionally, **Autobuses Unidos** and **TRV** second-class buses operate out of a second terminal at the west-side Flores Magón market on 20 de Noviembre, on the downtown side of the Highway 175 ingress boulevard. Buses connect

west several times daily with Mazateca destinations of Jalapa de Díaz and Huautla de Jiménez and northwest with Temascal (Miguel Alemán dam and reservoir) and Tierra Blanca.

Small, second-class line **Autobuses Trópico** (Libertad 1215, tel. 287/875-2895), operating from a third terminal, a block and a half west of Matamoros, connects six times daily with Oaxaca City via Valle Nacional and Ixtlán.

For **drivers,** mostly good paved roads connect Tuxtepec with both Oaxaca and national destinations. Highway 175 connects south with Oaxaca City via Valle Nacional and Ixtlán, over the Sierra Madre, in about 132 miles (213 km). However, steep, winding grades can sometimes slow traffic to a crawl. Allow about five hours for safety in either direction.

Combined National Highways 147 and 185 connect Tuxtepec southeast with Tehuántepec, via Matías Romero and Juchitán. The nighttime robberies and hijackings that used to plague the lonely, northern Highway 147 leg of this route have fortunately abated. To be sure, stop at the Highway 175–Highway 147 intersection gas station to check if the highway remains secure. You can ask in Spanish, *"¿Es seguro la carretera a matías romero?"* Allow about five hours of road time, either direction, for this 189-mile (304-km) trip.

A paved, but sometimes potholed, route, Highway 182, connects Tuxtepec west with Huautla de Jiménez in the high Mazateca, via Jalapa de Díaz. Allow about three and a half daylight hours westerly, three hours easterly, for this spectacularly scenic 74-mile (119-km) top-of-the-world trip.

TEMASCAL AND MIGUEL ALEMÁN DAM AND RESERVOIR

Temascal (pop. 5,000) is the town where the Mexican government, under the leadership of President Miguel Alemán (1946–1952), began building a huge dam to control and harness the waters of the Río Tonto in 1946. The project, officially the Miguel Alemán Dam, was completed in 1955. A subsequent project, the Cerro de Oro Dam and Reservoir, was completed a generation later. The entire Papaloapan basin benefits from the two reservoirs, now connected, which provide irrigation water, low-cost electric power, and relief from flood devastation.

On the negative side, the dam's social cost was high. Many thousands of Mazatec, Chinantec, and Mixe indigenous campesino families suffered. Thousands had to be moved, some forcibly, from their land and relocated to new, unfamiliar locations.

Today, the Miguel Alemán Dam, towering hundreds of feet, just upstream from the town of Temascal, is the project's most visible reminder. It compares in magnitude with the great hydroelectric projects of the American West. Its reservoir stretches about 20 miles long and 15 miles wide (32 by 24 km) and totals about two cubic miles (eight cubic km) of water, with an average depth of around 40 feet (12 meters). The reservoir's maximum flow can generate about 500 megawatts of electric power, more than enough for the entire state of Oaxaca and nearly enough for a U.S. city the size of San Francisco.

Sights

Follow the road through Temascal town and continue another half mile (one km) uphill to a road fork. Bear right for the Temascal **embarcadero** (wharf), where *palapas* serve fresh fish *comidas* and motorboats on the shoreline wait for passengers. The lake is especially lovely considering that it's artificial. Fortunately, adequate water flows ordinarily keep the level constant and thus avoid the appearance of an ugly bathtub-like ring. From the embarcadero, the lake appears to stretch endlessly, invitingly blue and smooth, among green hills and small islands.

The **shoreline restaurants** specialize in *mojarra* (bass) and *camarón* (shrimp) dinners. Boatmen offer to take you on a two-hour *recorrido* (tour) around the lake for around $25 per boat, for up to about eight persons. Save money by doubling up with others. The prime destination, besides a number of shoreline hamlets, is Soyaltepec, one of the few villages, along with Ixcatlán, that didn't get swallowed up by the reservoir. Ask for young boatman **Alex**

The whale-shaped silhouette of Cerro Rabón, the holy mountain of the Mazatecs, looms above Cerro de Oro reservoir.

© BRUCE WHIPPERMAN

Vasquez Ramírez, or kindly **Juan Palma Mina** (who's old enough to tell you how things were here before the dam).

Besides boat rides and swimming, fishing for bass is a major local diversion. Boatmen say that the typical fish amounts to about a quarter pound, and typical catches add up to around 20 fish in a couple of hours. You can launch your own boat for free if you check with the *capitán del puerto,* at the *presidencia municipal* in Temascal; watch for the sign on the main ingress-egress street.

Parking a self-contained RV or setting up a tent is welcomed anywhere around the *embarcadero* (although level spots appear to be scarce). A small store at the road, just above the *embarcadero,* could supply water and basic food items. Better-stocked stores in Temascal could supply even more.

Before you leave, reverse your path and instead of turning left for the town, head straight along the upper-level road and take a look at the **Monument to President Miguel Alemán,** on the right before the dam. The main attraction, besides the heroic statue of Alemán, is the big mural in the open building atop the staircase. Here, government artists have tried their best to dramatize the planned benefits of the dam project. A big mural shows two contrasting worlds: before the dam, a forbidding landscape of disease, superstition, poverty, and starvation; and the bright busy modern world—natives reading, surgeons operating, scientists experimenting, engineers building, teachers teaching, farmers harvesting—after the dam.

Temascal town back below the dam bustles with plenty of *taquerias* for cooked eats, fruits, vegetables, and groceries, a *centro de salud, correo,* and *telecomunicaciones* near the *presidencia muncipal,* and Ladatel card–operated street telephones.

Getting There and Away

Second-class AU buses connect Temascal east with Tuxtepec (west-side Flores Magón market), and north, with Tierra Blanca and Veracruz.

Drivers, from Tuxtepec follow Bulevar

Benito Juárez (the northern prolongation of Highway 175). After about eight miles (13 km), turn left at the Ciudad Alemán sign. Continue approximately another half hour, or 16 miles (26 km), and turn left at the Temascal sign. After another 13 miles (21 km), continue through Temascal town to the dam, a total of 37 miles (60 km) from Tuxtepec.

◖ SAN PEDRO IXCATLÁN AND THE ISLANDS

An alternate gateway to the Miguel Alemán reservoir shoreline is through Ixcatlán, a prime spot for a country stay. The town stands at the eastern boundary of the Mazateca, where many townspeople and virtually everyone in the surrounding countryside speak Mazatec, and women wear the bright blue-and-white horizontally striped local *huipil.* A number of Ixcatlán women embroider blouses and *huipiles.* Check at the hotel for names of whom to visit. Señora Castillo makes are-to-wear cottons that she displays at Hotel Villa del Lago.

You might want to plan your visit to coincide with Ixcatlán's main festival, honoring **San Isidro Labrador** (Saint Isador the Farmer), May 13–15. The fiesta's highlight is the traditional dance La Puta Chichi (Chichi the Prostitute).

Along the Road

A major sight along Highway 182, about half an hour west of Tuxtepec, is the **Puente Pescadito,** which bridges the channel connecting the Temescal and Cerro de Oro reservoirs. *Palapa* restaurants at both ends of the bridge supply refreshments and bass dinners. Below, the riverbanks, accessible on foot or by negotiable dirt roads, are level and invite fishing for *mojarra* (bass) and RV or tent camping.

The grand lake vista spreads for miles south and north. The southern arm, Reservoir Cerro de Oro, began to fill when the **Miguel de la Madrid** dam was built downstream during the 1970s. The reservoir level rose until it finally connected with the Temescal reservoir during the mid-1990s. In joining the two reservoirs, the channel consequently also connects the drainage basins of the Río Tonto, in the north, and the Río Santo Domingo, in the south. Although the Cerro de Oro reservoir is large, with about 100 square miles (260 sq. km) of surface area, this is only a fraction of the size of the Temascal reservoir.

Past the bridge, Highway 182 leads through gently rolling pastoral country—once dense rain forest, now undulating parklike green pasture, sprinkled with palms and leafy trees. Thatched, whitewashed country houses appear atop the hills and around the bends. This is country where an unknown vehicle is an event. If you're driving, wave as you go by and the people will wave back.

Ixcatlán perches atop a long hill, surrounded by picture-perfect vistas of the verdant countryside, the deeply indented, island-dotted reservoir, and in the background, the precipitous silhouette of Cerro Rabón, the Mazatecs' holy mountain. Besides all this, Ixcatlán has an inviting small hotel, a sprinkling of country *comedores*, services, and excursions to more remote, even uninhabited, islands.

Isla Soyaltepec

If it's no later than 3 P.M., you're early enough for the trip to Isla Soyaltepec. Once a small isolated town, Soyaltepec (pop. 500) is even more isolated since the reservoir has confined it to an island where most of its friendly, frankly curious inhabitants speak only Mazatec. The only way to go is by boat, for which you can bargain (figure $15–20 for a two-hour round-trip for up to about six people) at the embarcadero on Ixcatlán's west lakeshore (below the Ixcatlán church). Beforehand, ask for boatman Fidel Alto Hermengildo, who lives in Soyaltepec, or his brother Eloy, who lives in Ixacatlán. Fidel is the Soyaltepec elementary schoolteacher and will help you find lodging if you decide to stay overnight on his island.

The six-mile (9.6 km) crossing takes about half an hour. Along the way, butterflies flutter, herons stalk their prey, and clouds billow above the mirror-smooth lake surface. On the western horizon rises the gargantuan, loaf-shaped massif of **Cerro Rabón,** often cloaked

in a blanket of clouds. You'll pass through a fleet of little islands, some with small wooded crowns, perfect for an afternoon or overnight soaking in the scenery and solitude. If you do opt for an overnight, be prepared with a tent and mosquito repellent. Have your boatman return to pick you up at an appointed time.

At Soyaltepec, climb (one hour round-trip) to the old village and church on the island hilltop. Half a dozen kids will probably accompany you. Halfway up, you scale a pre-conquest-appearing ponderous stone staircase. At the top, take a look inside the venerable (1744) church, gaze westerly over the many-island lake vista, and get a *refresco* at the hilltop store.

Accommodations and Food

◖ **Hotel Villa del Lago** (Calle Benito Juárez s/n, tel. 287/871-3090, $25 s or d) would be a pleasant surprise anywhere, but here in little, out-of-the-way Ixcatlán, it seems a small miracle. The hotel is the labor of love of its friendly owner, Patricia Sarmiento Castillo, who rents six immaculate rooms with a/c and hot-water shower-baths. She has made the hotel even more inviting with a top-level porch from which guests can enjoy Ixcatlán's dramatic lake-view panorama.

The reservoir, whose waters Ixcatlán escaped because of its hilltop perch, has brought fresh fish to Ixcatlán. A scattering of country *comedores* serve good lake bass dinners, notably the homey, clean **El Vaquero** *palapa*, (8 A.M.–8P.M. daily, $4–8) in mid-town, on main street Benito Juárez, next to the *larga distancia* sign. Best for breakfast is **El Paraíso** *palapa* (8 A.M.–8 P.M. daily, $4–8), downhill, overlooking the lake, where, besides the good food, you can feast on the luscious lake view.

Information and Services

Visitors to Ixcatlán can count on a number of basic services, including a doctor, a *centro de salud* at the town entrance, pharmacies, grocery stores, post office, and long-distance telephone.

Get to Ixcatlán by the **Autobuses Unidos** (AU) or TRV bus bound for Huautla de

Jiménez or Jalapa de Díaz from Tuxtepec's west-side Flores Magón market. Ride to the Ixcatlán side road, then taxi, catch a truck ride, or walk the four miles (6.4 km) to town.

Drivers, from Tuxtepec, turn left (west) from Highway 175 onto Highway 182 at the Jalapa de Díaz sign at the traffic circle, about three blocks north of the Río Papaloapan bridge. Continue along Highway 182 west 34 miles (about 55 km) to the signed Ixcatlán right turnoff. Continue four paved miles (six km) to town.

SAN LUCAS OJITLÁN

While on your way to or from Ixcatlán, you might detour to San Lucas Ojitlán at the signed junction, 27 miles (43 km) west of Tuxtepec and six miles (10 km) east of the Ixcatlán turnoff. Ojitlán is the *cabercera* (head town) of a medium-size Chinantec-speaking *municipio*. Its main street bustles so continuously that few stores take the customary afternoon siesta.

Ojitlán's main establishments front the town's single main street, Independencia. A good first stop would be for a cold (Jumex brand) fruit drink from the refrigerator at the friendly general store Centro Comercial del Sureste, known locally as **Tienda de Tinito** (8 A.M.–9 P.M. daily), right in the middle of town. Refreshed, from there, you could walk uphill a block or two, to the *correo* on Independencia, uphill end; or to *telecomunicaciones* (money orders and public fax), across

the street and downhill, east, from Tienda de Tinito. Or, for a doctor, walk a few blocks downhill to the *centro de salud*.

Textiles make up the principal local handicraft, mostly colorful *huipiles*, which some women weave and embroider. One of them is Juana Muñoz; many people, especially the proprietor of Tienda de Tinito, know her and can direct you to her house. If she's not home, people will most likely be able to direct you to someone else.

Ojitlán's hubbub overflows on Wednesday, the regular day of *tianguis*, when hosts of country folk, including Chinantec- and Mazatec-speaking women in their brilliant *huipiles*, flock into town.

Local excitement peaks during the big fiesta in honor of Santa Rosa, on August 28–30. Santa Rosa's popularity is a curiosity, since San Lucas, rather than Santa Rosa, is the official town patron. Community frustration over the local liturgy seems to have led to the preference for Santa Rosa. It turns out that a majority of faithful prefer the service to be in Spanish, but the local priest and the bishop in Tuxtepec insist on Latin, which no one understands.

Townsfolk do celebrate San Lucas, but with only a token fiesta. You can see evidence of the community preference inside the old church atop the hill, at the end of the main street. Behind the altar, notice the all-female cast of saints, with Santa Rosa in the middle, and San Lucas, conspicuous by his absence.

The Mazateca

JALAPA DE DÍAZ AND VICINITY: THE LOW MAZATECA

By the time you arrive at Jalapa de Díaz, you're well into Mazatec country; walk a quarter mile (0.5 km) from town in any direction and you'll hear little, if any, Spanish spoken. For women here, wearing the *huipil* is the rule rather than the exception. Local women distinguish three grades of *huipil*: everyday,

fancy, and super-fancy. The latter are beautifully crocheted all by hand, often displaying a glittering throng of birds and animals, fit for a bride.

You'd have little trouble finding Jalapa even if you had no Highway 182 to guide you. Jalapa de Díaz stands at the foot of the vertical wall of whale-shaped **Cerro Rabón** (elev. about 7,700 feet/2,350 meters), arguably Oaxaca's most uniquely prominent landmass.

© BRUCE WHIPPERMAN

The Río Uluapa issues as a pristine spring from an upstream cave.

Sights

The most colorful times to arrive at Jalapa are Thursday and Sunday, for the big country *tianguis,* when sellers' awnings cover half the town, thronging with native folks. Another good time to arrive is during either of the two patronal fiestas, in honor of San Sebastián (January 19–20) and San Antonio de Padua (June 12–13).

The **Cañon del Río Santo Domingo,** which you can begin to appreciate about five miles (eight km) up the highway from Jalapa, is one of Mexico's little-known wonders. The road climbs, rounding the foot of Cerro Rabón, and enters a vast cirque of verdant, jungle-clad ramparts on one side and the deep, plunging canyon on the other. At about 10 miles (16 km) uphill from Jalapa, you begin to cross rushing creeks, first Arroyo Blanco, then Arroyo Caballo, then finally the blue, boiling **Río Uluapa.** Walk the (sometimes steep and slippery) path to the right of the river; after about 900 feet (270 meters), follow the left fork steeply uphill. Continue about 45 minutes over rocks and beneath great, vine-hung trees

to a boulder-decorated pool, perfect for bathing (or even tenting for prepared backpackers). Above, see the river flow from a cave, as a pristine spring, then drop and tumble as a foaming waterfall and cascade.

Climbing Cerro Rabón

At first glance, Cerro Rabón appears tempting to climb. In fact, many local people do it every day. They tend fields on the mountainside and walk down to town afterward. The net rise amounts to about 6,500 feet (2,000 meters) and should be attempted only by fit hikers, with a guide, who start at the crack of dawn with good shoes, hat, food, and a jacket against cold. If the weather turns sour, go back or get shelter in someone's house. Lightning and cloudbursts up there could spell disaster. Clouds without rain are OK; they cap Cerro Rabón most of the time. This has resulted in the **cloud forest** coating the mountaintop— a Pleistocene remnant ecosystem of tree ferns, hanging moss, bright liquid amber maples, bigleafed bromeliads, and orchids.

Pack something to drink, although springs along the way should suffice for most of the water. You must get formal permission from the authorities at the *presidencia municipal,* who can probably suggest a guide, such as the experienced Antonio Bravo or his son Ángel (beekeepers who produce honey at their nearby *rancho*).

Accommodations and Food

Most of Jalapa's business establishments line the main street, Benito Juárez, which leads about a quarter mile (0.5 km) from the highway to the town plaza, bordered by the *presidencia municipal* on one side and the church, the Templo de San Sebastián, on the other.

Right in the middle of everything is the town's one lodging house, the family-run **Casa de Huéspedes Robertina** (Calle Benito Juárez s/n, tel. 287/877-2009, $15 s or d). The grandmotherly owner rents plain but clean rooms with bath down the hall.

Buy fruits and vegetables at the several curbside market stalls (which multiply into a big native *tianguis* Thursday and Sunday). Groceries are available at street-front *abarroterías,* such as **Abarrotes del Centro** (7 A.M.–8 P.M. Mon.–Sat., 7 A.M.–3 P.M. Sun.). A sprinkling of *comedores* along Juárez supply wholesome, local-style *comidas.*

For good restaurant food, try the locally recommended **Comedor Abi,** (8 A.M.–9 P.M. daily, $2–5)at the first *tope* (speed bump) on the Tuxtepec end of Highway 182 through town; or **Comedor Las Brisas** a couple of blocks farther.

Shopping

Stop at the store **Tienda Tres Hermanos** (9 A.M.–2P.M. 4–8 P.M. Mon.–Sat.), on the highway about a block (Tuxtepec direction) before the downtown entrance side road. It's named for owner Fausto's sons: Herme, Paulo, and Roberto of real name Roberto Osorio. Fausto will be happy to show and sell you examples of the lovely *manteles* (tablecloths), *rebozos* (shawls), *camisas* (shirts), and *huipiles* that he, his wife, and his friends craft.

Information and Services

For remedies, drugs, and also medical consultations, go to **Farmacia San Felipe** (tel. 287/877-2037, 8 A.M.–2 P.M. and 4–8 P.M. daily), Doctora Adriana Carrillo Gimón in charge, in the town center.

Find the town *correo* and *telecomunicaciones* (money orders and public fax) on the ground floor of the downtown *presidencia municipal,* on Benito Juárez, on the downhill side of the town plaza.

Getting There

Bus passengers get to Jalapa just as to Ixcatlán and Ojitlán. Ride second-class **Autobuses Unidos** (AU) or TRV buses east from Huautla de Jiménez or west from Tuxtepec's market Flores Magón bus terminal.

From Tuxtepec, **drivers** start out exactly as for Ixcatlán (but continue 11.5 miles/18.5 km past the Ixcatlán turnoff) to Jalapa de Díaz, a total of 44 miles (71 km) west of Tuxtepec or 32 miles (53 km) east of Huautla de Jiménez. Heading west, turn left at the town ingress road and continue about a quarter mile (0.5 km) uphill to the plaza and church.

HUAUTLA DE JIMÉNEZ AND VICINITY: THE HIGH MAZATECA

Huautla de Jiménez (pop. 20,000, elevation 6000 feet/1800 meters), tucked on a lofty Mazateca mountainside, was put on the world map during the 1960s by María Sabina, a local Mazatec-speaking *curandera* (indigenous medicine woman) who, like many others, used hallucinogenic mushrooms as part of her bag of remedies. The word somehow got out, and a small army of Love Generation devotees of hallucinogens from the United States and Europe, known locally as *gippis* (HEE-pees), quickly descended on Huautla. With them soon came a continuous stream of doctors, journalists, and anthropologists.

María Sabina seemed to enjoy her renown. She was invited far and wide to testify to the efficacy of her remedies at learned international medical conferences. But after a generation of

HUAUTLA DE JIMÉNEZ

MARÍA SABINA MURAL

POST OFFICE
ARTESANÍAS JULIETA
TELECOM
SCHOOL

PROVEEDORA DEL HOGAR

PRESIDENCIA MUNICIPAL

HOTEL OLÍMPICO

HOTEL AND RESTAURANT RINCONCITO

Market

PLAZA (BASKETBALL COURT)

TEMPLO DE LA NAVIDAD

POST BOX

CAFÉ CINEMA HUAUTLA

RESTAURANT GEMENIS

RESTAURANT ROSITA

HOTEL AND RESTAURANT JULIA

DR LÁZARO P GARCÍA

INTERNET

FARMACIA SIMILARES

ABARROTES EL SURTIDOR

PANADERÍA GIRALDA

ARTESENÍAS LARA

HOTEL 1 DE MAYO

FARMACIA DE JESÚS

RESTAURANT FAMILIAR SAN ANGEL

DR SAÚL MARTÍNEZ/PHARMACY

HUIPILES VICTORIA ENRÍQUEZ

ARTESENÍAS MAGDANI

MINISUPER TREBOL

NATURAL FOODS

FLETES Y PASAJES BUS

COLECTIVO VANS TO LOCAL VILLAGES

VANS TO OAXACA

LAUNDRY

5 DE MAYO

CUAUHTÉMOC

JUÁREZ

BENITO

GARCÍA

GONZÁLEZ

CASO

ANTONIO

To AU and TRV Bus Terminal and Hwy 182

0   50 yds
0   50 m

© AVALON TRAVEL

fame, she passed away in 1985 at the age of 90, leaving Huautla to slumber again.

Her legacy, however, remains plainly visible in Huautla today, in the several businesses and institutions that carry her name, such as the María Sabina Cultural Center, the Comedor María Sabina, and the Farmacia María Sabina.

Besides such obvious reminders, many new-generation *curanderos* carry on María Sabina's mission. Notable among them are two of her grandsons, Filongonia Garcia and Eduardo Valladares, now both middle-aged. Eduardo, who was a constant companion of his grandmother during her heyday, was asked by author Juan Garcia Carrera of his thoughts concerning death. He replied, "By offering you enlightenment, my mushrooms also resign you to the reality of death."

Orientation

Although the town itself spreads over a broad mountainside, the business and service center is concentrated mainly along a few downtown streets. Most important is the east–west Calle Benito Juárez. Addresses start at number one on Juárez and increase to the east. Just downhill from the west end of Juárez are the town market, *presidencia municipal* and the church, dedicated to the Virgin of the Nativity—all situated around the town plaza–basketball court *(cancha)*. A second street, Cuauhtémoc, downhill from the plaza, runs parallel to Benito Juárez to its intersection with a third street, Antonio Caso, which angles diagonally west, downhill from its intersection, at the east end of Benito Juárez. Highway 182 contours along the mountainside three or four blocks downhill from the town plaza.

(María Sabina Mural

Make your first Huautla stop at the Huautla town hall for a look at the dramatic mural, painted in 2007 by Mario Enrique Fernández Medina in honor of María Sabina. The mural, a dramatic panorama of the life of Maria Sabina, sweeps from left to right. Most dramatic is the panel of the deep brown face of María Sabina

who, with her hallucinogenic mushrooms, leads her clients through a transcendental window to a new, enlightened dimension. There they join with a saint-like visage of María Sabina, who, finally transformed into an eagle, cleanses (symbolized by the egg) the bodies and souls of her clients.

Inside the town hall, a modest museum displays artifacts, documents, photos, and mementos that illustrate Huautla's history from pre-Conquest through the excitement and fame of Maria Sabina's heyday to the present.

Casa María Sabina and Cerro de Adoración

El Fortín, the east-end ridgetop barrio where María Sabina lived, is revered by many Huautlecos. Her house, a simple rust-roofed white dwelling, has been unoccupied for years. It's in the neighborhood just beyond the government hospital not far from the highway. Ask for Casa María Sabina, and most likely a child will lead you there.

From there, continue to sacred site Cerro de Adoración along the path heading gradually upward along the right-hand (western) slope of the ridgetop. Your destination is just beyond the highest hill along the ridgetop, where, after a half-hour climb, you'll reach the pinnacle called Cerro de Adoración. Here, you'll find a monument with four crosses where local folks carry offerings, especially around May 3, El Día de la Santa Cruz (The Day of the Holy Cross). Besides meeting folks along the trail carrying wood or herding goats, your reward will most likely be a cool breeze and a breathtaking panoramic vista of billowing clouds and rugged peaks, sprinkled with a dozen seemingly Lilliputian villages on their slopes.

Accommodations

Newish (**Hotel Santa Julia** (Calle Cuauhtémoc 12, tel. 236/378-0586, $16 s or d, $18 s or d upstairs, $18 t) is a welcome addition to Huautla. Twenty-one spacious, clean, and comfortably furnished rooms, with hot-water shower-baths, provide the basics, with TV, parking, and restaurant. The most pleasant rooms are the upstairs rooms, some with views, on the sunny south side. Find it on the south, downhill side of the plaza. (If the Santa Julia is full, try its sister hotel, not so conveniently located, however, on the highway three blocks downhill, local cell tel. 044-236/103-5463.)

Second choice goes to **Hotel Rinconcito** (Juárez 8, tel. 236/378-0136, 236/378-0243, or 236/378-0005, fax 236/378-0674, $20 s, $23 d in one bed, $32 d, and $36 t in two beds), across Juárez from the market. Friendly husband-wife owners Leonardo Altamirano and Catalina Casamiro rent eight plain but clean rooms for, with hot-water baths. The best are in front, with views of the market below and the mountains in the distance.

Running a distant third, two blocks west, is the rough but clean **Hotel 1 de Mayo** (Juárez 30, tel. 236/378-0076, $15 s, $17 d). The three stories of approximately 20 small bare-bones rooms have hot-water baths.

If no one else has a room, the rough, extremely basic, emergency-only **Hotel Olímpico** (tel. 236/378-0107, $15 s or d, $25 t), next door, west of the Hotel Rinconcito, might have one.

Food

Go to the market for the freshest fruits and vegetables. The best grocery selection is at **Minisuper El Trebol** (Juárez 41, tel. 236/378-0027, 9 A.M.–4 P.M. and 6–9 P.M. daily), across from the Hotel 1 de Mayo.

For fresh-baked goods, try the class-act **Panadería Giralda** (2 E. Garcia González, 9 A.M.–9 P.M. daily except Wed.), on the street that angles uphill two blocks east of the Hotel Rinconcito. Find snacks, such as hamburgers, hot dogs, and *tortas,* at the stand in front of the Hotel Rinconcito, across Juárez from the market. Furthermore, good café espresso (cappuccino, latte, $1; breakfast $2; sandwiches $2) has arrived at Huautla at the former movie house, now café **Cinema Huautla** (cell 044-236/102-7252, inrock78@hotmail.com, 9 A.M.–9 P.M. daily), a few doors east of Hotel Rinconcito.

All of Huautla's several restaurants are strictly local country-style. You can expect

Open-air and immaculate streetfront market offers freshly cut pork on Huautla town's main street, Benito Juárez.

cleanliness and at least a choice of avocado, beans, *bolillos* (crunchy bread rolls), bottled water, cheese, chicken, cucumber, eggs, fruit juice, milk, pork, salsa, spaghetti, steak, tomatoes, and tortillas. A trio of acceptable eateries is on or near Avenida Cuauhtémoc. Find the homey and reliable ◖ **Restaurant Rosita** (tel. 236/378-0386, 7 A.M.–10 P.M. daily, $3–6), below the plaza's southwest corner, a few doors down the lane that angles off of Cuauhtémoc. Its airy view porch dining room is an extra plus, especially for breakfast and lunch.

Also, nearby at Cuauhtémoc 11, you might check out more basic **Restaurant Gemenis** (7 A.M.–10 P.M. daily, $3–6), or alternatively, back uphill, on the east end of Juárez, the family-run **Restaurant Familiar San Ángel** (8:30 A.M.–8 P.M. daily, $3–6).

Festivals

The most colorful times to arrive in town are during the patronal celebration **Fiesta de la**

Virgen de La Natividad (September 7–8), **El Día de los Muertos** (Day of the Dead, November 1–2), and the **Feria Comercial** (climaxing on the third Friday of Lent, 22 days before Easter Sunday). The Feria Comercial is attended by a host of villagers who crowd in from the surrounding mountains to watch their favorite traditional dances, including the Flor de Naranjo (Orange Tree Flower), Flor de Piña (Pineapple), Flor de Lis (Heaven), and Anillo de Oro (Ring of Gold). If you miss these, at least try to be present on Sunday for the big *tianguis*, when vendors' awnings fill the entire center of town.

Shopping

Huautla offers some opportunities to shop for its well-known textiles. Around the market, especially, you'll see women in handmade *huipiles* adorned with bright embroidered birds, fruits, flowers, and rainbows of pink-, yellow-, and blue-striped satin.

In addition to the *huipiles,* local women craft and decorate blouses, napkins, shirts, skirts, and tablecloths in floral and animal designs. Buy them at either market stalls, streetfront shops, or at the homes of individual craftswomen; ask Catalina Casamiro, at the Hotel Rinconcito for recommendations.

A number of streetfront shops along Juárez offer quality handicrafts. Moving east from the market, first stop should be at **Artesanías Lara** (Juárez 25, 8:30 A.M.–9 P.M.), for a bright selection of hand-embroidered dresses, skirts, *huipiles,* priced to sell.

At her shop on Juárez, just east of the Hotel 1 de Mayo, **Victoria Enriquez** (tel. 236/378-0449, 8 A.M.–4 P.M. and 6–9 P.M. daily) crafts and sells lovely *huipiles.* Furthermore, for a multicolored selection of *huipiles,* embroidered tablecloths *(manteles),* and brightly costumed dolls, continue another few doors east to **Artesanías Magdani** (Juárez 40, 8 A.M.–8 P.M. Mon.–Sat., 8 A.M.–3 P.M. Sun.).

Finally, return back to the town plaza, where on the west side, lower level, facing the church, **Artesanías Julieta** (9 A.M.–8 P.M. Mon.–Sat.) offers more handsomely embroidered huipiles, blouses, and dresses.

Services

At this writing, the Huautla HSBC bank and ATM has unfortunately closed. Hopefully it will re-open by the time you read this. If not, stock up with pesos in Tuxtepec, or at least arrive with some U.S. dollars that you could probably change at the Hotel Santa Julia or Hotel Rinconcito if you're staying there, or the Minisuper Trebol, on Juárez.

A trio of doctors maintain offices on Juárez. Moving east, first comes **Dr. Lázaro Pérez Garcia** (8 A.M.–3 P.M. and 5–8 P.M. Mon.–Sat.) and also available on call, at Juárez 12, upstairs. A block farther east, you'll find **Dr. Saul Martínez**, at his pharmacy (tel. 236/378-0257, pharmacy 9 A.M.–9 P.M. daily, consultation 9 A.M.–1 P.M. and 3–7 P.M. Mon.–Sat.), and on call 24 hours. Also find Dr. Flores Ramos at his **Farmacia Similares** (Juárez 21D, tel. 236/378-0857, 9 A.M.–3 P.M. and 5–9 P.M. Mon.–Sat.).

Nonprescription medicines and drugs are available at additional pharmacies on Juárez, such as **Farmacia de Jesús** (Juárez 16, 8 A.M.–2 P.M. and 4–8 P.M.).

The **correo** (8 A.M.–3 P.M. Mon.–Fri.) and **telecomunicaciones** (tel. 236/378-0397, 9 A.M.–3 P.M. Mon.–Fri.) stand side by side on the plaza's west side, above the shops, across the street (west) from the *presidencia municipal.*

Long-distance telephone is available at the Hotel Rinconcito (8 A.M.–9 P.M.) and three doors east, at the *larga distancia* by the bank (8 A.M.–9 P.M.).

Internet access is available at the **Digital Net** (Juárez 14A, tel. 236/378-0669, 9 A.M.–9 P.M. daily).

Photographic services, such as develop-and-print, cameras, supplies, film, and black-and-white development, have come to Huautla at **Foto Isis** (Juárez 19, tel. 236/378-0062, 9 A.M.–9 P.M. Mon.–Sat., 9 A.M.–3 P.M. Sun.).

Get your laundry reliably done at the small **lavandería** (tel. 236/378-0337, 9 A.M.–3 P.M. and 4–9 P.M.) half a block down the alley, adjacent to the Hotel Santa Julia, that runs steeply downhill from Cuauhtémoc.

Getting There and Away

Second-class **Fletes y Pasajes** buses (tel. 236/378-0406) operate out of a terminal on Calle Antonio Caso, which runs diagonally downhill from Calle Juárez. They connect west with Teotitlán del Camino, thence south with Oaxaca City via Cuicatlán; northwest with Mexico City via Tehuacán and Puebla. Furthermore, nearby, second-class **TRV** (tel. 236/378-0834) connect with Tuxtepec, and second-class **Autobuses Unidos** buses, operating from a terminal downhill by the highway, connect east with Tuxtepec via Jalapa de Díaz; and northwest with Mexico City via Teotitlán, Tehuacán, and Puebla. Local-class white **Transportes Regionales Sierra–Cañada-Teotitlán-Oaxaca** minibuses connect south with Oaxaca City via Teotitlán and Cuicatlán. Additionally, **Autotransportes Turísticos Huautla** (cell tel. 044-236/102-5548) vans connect hourly during the day with Oaxaca, from their terminal at Cuauhtémoc 23. Furthermore, from street-side, just below the downhill intersection of Cuauhtémoc and Antonio Caso, a lineup of *colectivo* vans connect with a swarm of local villages, such as Eloxochitlán and San Agustín.

For **drivers,** paved Highway 182 connects Huautla east with Tuxtepec via Jalapa de Díaz, along 76 miles (122 km) of winding but breathtakingly scenic mountain road. For safety, allow three hours eastbound, downhill, or three and a half hours westbound, uphill. In a westerly direction, Highway 182 connects Huautla east with Teotitlán del Camino in 41 miles (66 km) of paved, downhill, winding, scenic mountain road. (From Teotitlán, Hwy. 135 connects south an additional 100 miles/161 km, about 3.5 hours, with Oaxaca City.) Allow two hours downhill (westerly), 2.5 hours uphill (easterly).

Unleaded gasoline is available at the Pemex gas station on the highway a few blocks south, downhill from the town center.

EXCURSIONS AROUND HUAUTLA

The area around Huautla, a verdant, dramatically folded landscape of mountains and deep valleys, hides a number of natural wonders, the best known of which include two spectacular limestone caves and a twin waterfall.

🄲 Las Regaderas

Easiest to get to and see is Las Regaderas, a pair of waterfalls not far west along Highway 182 from Huautla. Get there by car or local *colectivo* van to Puente de Fierro, marked by a big Santa María Chicotla sign and arch, about four miles (6.6 km) west, Teotitlán direction, from Huautla. Just before the bridge, turn right and continue past the arch to a side road. Turn and continue 0.6 mile (one km) downhill to the falls.

Las Regaderas (The Showers) plummet 100 feet (30 meters) out of a jungly cliff into a wild, tumbling river. Great trees resembling California sycamores shade both banks. A steel-cable suspension walkway bridges the river next to a rustic riverside cabin. A short extension bridge accesses the cool spray at the foot of the

Shade and cool rushing water are Las Regaderas' prime assets.

© BRUCE WHIPPERMAN

falls. Some informal riverbank camping sites may be usable during low water, February–May. Security may be a problem, however. Drunkenness seems to be a major local pastime. Ask at the stores past the bridge on the highway: *"¿Es seguro acampar a las regaderas?"*

Nindo-Da-Gé

Even more spectacular is Nindo-Da-Gé (Broad Spring Mountain) cave, first explored completely in 1905, near the little town of San Antonio Eloxochitlán (ay-loh-shoh-CHEET-lahn). With a guide, you can explore several of the cave's 19 main galleries, some gigantic, some petite, in half a day. The seemingly endless procession of dripping limestone formations, which have names such as The Infernal Hill, The Fort, The Snail, and Marimba, are even more fun if you dream up your own names.

The town invites visitors to camp locally (town stores can supply food and water) and explore their cave. Recently, authorities have partially completed a road most of the way to the cave, which can be reached from town in about one mile (two km) by road, and only another half mile (one km) by foot trail.

The only obstacle to exploring the cave is the reasonable one that for safety reasons you must have a guide recommended by civic authorities. (The guide receives no money; he serves as part of his community service obligation. However, do offer a donation, perhaps about $20, in a sealed envelope, to the *ayuntamiento,* city government.)

A town committee, at this writing consisting of Isidro Beseril, Octavio Nieto, and Alonzo Nieto, is in charge. Another good person to contact for information is former cave committee member and friendly schoolteacher Professor Froilan Ríos, whose house stands on the left side of the paved road as you enter town. He recommends Alonzo and Sergio Nieto as the best guides. If you're really serious about exploring the cave, notify Alonzo and/or Sergio by leaving a message with the Eloxochitlán long-distance telephone operator

(tel. 201/250 7261), or write them (San Antonio Eloxochitlán, Teotitlan del Camino, 68530 Oaxaca), detailing your desire to visit the cave and when you're planning to arrive. Do not fail to keep the appointment. The minimum excursion requires most of a day. Arrive early and bring at least two strong flashlights (four-celled or more, with extra batteries), good-traction shoes, and enough hard hats (hard plastic construction type) for everyone.

Furthermore, the Eloxochitlán community offers a super extended adventure, a five-mile (eight km), two-day overnight, that, on the second day, continues clear through to the cave's east-end exit, at Cabaña. Your preparations must include all of the equipment above, plus food for all, including your guide, and, at least, sleeping equipment and a white-gas-powered (Coleman-style) illumination lamp, with 12 hours of fuel.

Get to San Antonio Eloxochitlán by bus or car seven miles (11 km) along the Teotitlán (west) direction on Highway 182, to the San Antonio turnoff gravel road on the right (north). Continue 4.8 miles (7.7 km) to the town church, plaza, and *presidencia municipal.*

Sotano de San Agustín

Cave enthusiasts might also enjoy hiking to the Sotano de San Agustín (Pit of San Agustín), near the village of San Agustín, on Highway 182 a few miles northeast of Huautla. The cave was only discovered during the 1990s. With a total depth of about a mile (4,800 feet/1,440 meters) and a number of long single drops (the longest at around 350 feet, 105 meters) the San Agustín cave is considered among the deepest in the world. You can reach the cave entrance accompanied by a local guide (inquire at the San Agustín *presidencia municipal*) via the steep downhill trail from near the town church. As for exploring the cave itself, only super-equipped and experienced speleologists should apply to local authorities for permission to enter.

The Cañada: Canyon Country

Shadowed from rain by mountains on all sides, the dry, tropical Cañada canyonland comprises one of Oaxaca's major geo-cultural regions. It encompasses the Cuicateca—the land of the Cuicatecs—a Mixtec-related people who, for longer than anyone can remember, have hunted and farmed their homeland's cactus-plumed canyon bottoms and temperate upland valleys. Reclusive and traditional, Cuicatec people generally venture out from their home villages only infrequently, mostly to trade at the market towns—sometimes Teotitlán del Camino, more often at Cuicatlán.

TEOTITLÁN DEL CAMINO

Just shy of Oaxaca's border with the state of Puebla stands Teotitlán del Camino (pop. 5,000), the jumping-off point for the Mazateca highlands to the east and the Cañada to the south. Teotitlán's elevation, 3,600 feet (1,100 meters), places it about a mile (1.6 km) lower and many degrees warmer than sometimes-chilly Huautla de Jiménez, in the Mazateca

highlands. Teotitlán's fortunate combination of warmth, sunshine, and abundant spring water nourishes a local oasis of mangos, bananas, lemons, oranges, and avocados.

Sights

Despite Teotitlán's significance as the capital of the sprawling governmental district of the same name, it nevertheless feels much like a small town, with a modicum of stores and services within a block or two of the central plaza. Streets run approximately east–west (uphill–downhill) and north–south. The three main east–west streets are Hidalgo, the Highway 135 ingress street that runs along the plaza's north side; José Silones, between the plaza and the church; and 5 de Mayo, a block south of the plaza along the church's south side. The main north–south streets are Josefina Ortiz de Domínguez, which runs along the west side of the plaza; Juárez, behind and east of the church; and Independencia, the Highway 182 ingress from Huautla, one block farther east (uphill).

TEOTITLÁN DEL CAMINO

DOCTOR   AU BUS   LONG-DISTANCE TELEPHONE

HIDALGO

FLETES Y PASAJES BUS   PALETERIA LA MICHOACANA

To Hwy 135, Cuicatlán, Oaxaca, Tehuacán, Puebla, and Mexico City

Plaza   COLON

TELECOM

JUÁREZ   INDEPENDENCIA

ABARROTES SANTA LUCIA ▼   CORREO (POST OFFICE) ■ ■ PRESIDENCIA MUNICIPAL

JOSÉ   SILONES

CASA DE HUÉSPEDES MARY   ■ CASA DE LA CULTURA   JOSEFINA G ORTIZ   ▼ RESTAURANT SILVIA   HOTEL DOÑA OFELIA

TEMPLO DE SAN MIGUEL ARCÁNGEL   DISNEYLANDIA ▼

INTERNET   To Hwy 182 East, Market (Wed and Sun), Huatla de Jiménez, and Tuxtepec

RESTAURANT LIBRA ▼

0   50 yds   5   DE   MAYO

0   50 m   FARMACIA MARAVILLAS   ■ FARMACIA FENIX

© AVALON TRAVEL

The town's pride is its church, the **Templo de San Miguel Arcángel,** built by Franciscan padres during the 17th century. Outside, an image of angel San Miguel decorates the pinnacle of its Roman Doric–columned facade. Inside, the ceiling is a cheery sky blue, with bright paintings of Saints John (Juan), Matthew (Mateo), Luke (Lucas), and Mark (Marcos) around the central cupola overhead. The broad church atrium out front is usually very quiet, except around September 29, when local folks honor San Miguel with processions, fireworks, and floats ridden by children dressed as angels.

Take a stroll around the adjacent town plaza, where big shady trees provide a welcome refuge from the warm afternoon sun. At night, the plaza becomes the town's central meeting ground, where couples stroll and people relax on benches attractively decorated with bright Puebla tile.

If it's Wednesday or Sunday, another focus of activity is the market on Independencia, about two blocks south of the plaza. The big Teotitlán market structure was obviously built for better times. It's presently empty as a tomb five days a week.

Accommodations

The town has three acceptable hotels, a *casa de huéspedes* (guesthouse), and a sprinkling of restaurants, one highly recommended. The best hotel is **Hotel Doña Ofelia** (Calle Ricardo Flores Magón 39, tel./fax 363/372-0220, $15 s or d in one bed, $20 d or t in two beds), three blocks west (downhill) and north from the plaza. From the plaza corner of Hidalgo and Josefina Ortiz de Domínguez, walk two blocks downhill past the secondary school to Pino Suárez, then turn right and continue one block north to Flores Magón and the hotel. Its six rooms in two stories are clean and comfortably furnished. Best of all, they open onto a shady, homey garden, with chairs and tables for relaxing. In the morning especially, birds sing, and rarely does anything disturb the tranquility. Rentals run. Rooms come with fan and hot-water shower-bath. The hotel, one of the best along Highway 135 between Oaxaca and Tehuacán, is often full; be sure to call ahead for a reservation.

The town's second-best but newer hotel has both the same name and the same kindly owner, **Ofelia Mesa Muñoz** (same phone number and prices as the Hotel Doña Ofelia). The newer hotel occupies the corner of Independencia and José Silones, a block and a half uphill east of the plaza. It's not as tightly managed, since Ofelia stays at her favorite, original hotel. The rooms, however, are just as clean and are attractively painted and highlighted with fine Puebla tile. Rooms open to an inviting shaded garden patio. And it's the only hotel in Oaxaca with an irrigation aqueduct (albeit a small one that gurgles quaintly past the edge of the patio). Unfortunately, the location suffers from noisy trucks and buses, which seem to run past the front door every few minutes during the morning. Despite the noise, this is a good second choice. Rooms come with fan and shower-bath with hot water.

Third choice goes to **Hotel Isabel** (Colonia 7, tel. 363/372-0097, $8 s, $10 d, $15 t), two blocks north of the plaza. The rooms, in an apartment-style block on the quiet edge of town, are plain and much less than immaculate, with none of the garden amenities of Ofelia's hotels. Find it from the plaza by walking two blocks down the main street, to Colonia (at the secondary school), then right (north) two blocks.

On the other hand, budget travelers may prefer the plain but homey and clean **Casa de Huéspedes Mary** (tel. 363/372-0242, $5 s, $10 d), diagonally across the street from the plaza's southwest corner.

Food

Go to Teotitlán's best, the immaculate, family-run **⚑ Restaurant Silvia** (tel. 363/372-0215, 6:30 A.M.–10 P.M. daily); from the plaza, walk a block uphill, to Juárez, and turn right, two doors around the corner. Although busily patronized by *rancheros,* businesspersons, and occasional tourists, the restaurant offers relaxing, airy patio seating in the rear. Find it open daily for *desayuno, comida,* and *cena* (breakfast, lunch, and dinner, $2–5).

A couple more good food choices are the pub-like **Disneylandia** (tel. 236/372-0164, noon–11:30 P.M., *comida* until 7 P.M. daily), also on Juárez, middle of the block; and *comedor* **Libra** (8 A.M.–8 P.M. daily, also with *comida* until around 5 P.M.), around the Juárez-5 de Mayo corner uphill.

Yet another good choice, convenient to motorists, is the highly recommended (by Doña Ofelia) **Restaurant Blanca Flor** (tel. 363/372-0326, 7 A.M.–9 P.M. daily), on Highway 135 five blocks downhill from the town plaza, just south of the big obelisk monument.

For snacks and refreshments, stop to cool off beneath the shady plaza-front portal of **Paleteria La Michoacana.** Take your pick from a host of flavors of juices, ices, and ice cream.

Information and Services

Get your groceries and yummy Jumex-brand canned juices at the small **Abarrotes Santa Lucia** (8 A.M.–9 P.M. daily), at the southeast plaza corner.

Teotitlán plaza-front establishments can supply most emergency needs. Start with the **correo** (9 A.M.–3 P.M. Mon.–Fri., no phone), in the *presidencia municipal,* southeast plaza corner; and next door, the **telégrafos** (tel. 363/372-0171, 9 A.M.–3 P.M. Mon.–Fri., 9 A.M.–12:30 P.M. Sat.), offering money orders, telex, and telegraph, but no fax. For telephone and fax, try the *larga distancia* (8 A.M.–9 P.M. daily) on Hidalgo by the bus station, half a block downhill from the plaza. Connect to the **Internet** at Travel Net (Juárez 26, at mid-block, uphill side, between Silones and Cinco de Mayo, tel. 363/372-0480, 9 A.M.–4 P.M. and 5–10:30 P.M. Mon.–Sat., 9 A.M.–4 P.M. Sun.).

For medicines, go to the **Farmacia las Maravillas** (tel. 363/372-0374, 7 A.M.–10:30 P.M. daily), of general practitioner Hector Vargas, M.D., behind the church at the corner of Juárez and 5 de Mayo. If las Maravillas doesn't have what you need,

continue uphill along 5 de Mayo half a block to **Farmacia El Fénix** (9 A.M.–9:30 P.M. daily).

For medical consultations, visit the town's favorite doctor, **Miguel Ángel Ramírez Tenorio, M.D.** (9 A.M.–2 P.M. and 5–7 P.M. Mon.–Sat.) on Hidalgo, a block downhill from the plaza, next to the bus station. Alternatively, go to the 24-hour **Seguro Social** clinic (tel. 363/372-0139) several blocks north of the town center, on Highway 182, uphill from the Highway 135–Highway 182 intersection obelisk monument.

Getting There and Away

Second-class buses operate out of terminals on Hidalgo, downhill from the plaza. First comes second-class **Autobuses Unidos** (AU) buses (tel. 363/372-0061) that connect south with Oaxaca City via Cuicatlán, northwest with Mexico City via Tehuacán and Puebla, and east with Huautla. Also, **Fletes y Pasajes** buses, three blocks farther downhill, connect south with Oaxaca City via Cuicatlán, northwest with Mexico City via Tehuacán and Puebla, and east with Huautla and Jalapa de Díaz. Additionally, the local-class white minibuses of **Transportes Regionales Sierra-Cañada-Teotitlán** (at curbside, on Hidalgo, by Autobuses Unidos) connect south with Oaxaca City via Cuicatlán, and east with Huautla and Jalapa de Díaz.

For drivers, paved Highway 182 connects Teotitlán east with Huautla in 41 miles (66 km) of scenic but winding uphill mountain road. For safety, allow 2.5 hours (or two hours in the opposite, downhill, direction). In a southerly direction, Highway 135 connects with Oaxaca City, via Cuicatlán, in a winding but easy (with caution) 100 miles (161 km). Allow about 3.5 hours of driving time, either direction. In a northerly direction, Highway 135 connects with Tehuacán (39 miles/63 km, one hour). From there, you can continue northwest to Puebla either via the toll expressway in an additional 70-mile (93-km), 1.5-hour trip (or three hours via old two-lane Highway 150).

Unleaded gasoline is available at the Pemex

gasolinera on the highway, about a mile (two km) northwest of the town plaza.

CUICATLÁN

Cuicatlán (pop. 10,000) is the commercial capital of the Cañada, the emporium for the entire high Sierra hinterland that rises immediately east of town. Cuicatlán, like Teotitlán, owes its wealth to abundant sunshine and water. In Cuicatlán, water is synonymous with the Río Grande, the river that passes just west of the highway and west of town. After nourishing a local oasis of fruit, vegetables, and grain, the Río Grande continues its good work downstream. It joins with the swarm of tributaries draining the entire Cañada basin, becoming the Río Santo Domingo, the major electrical power source at the Miguel de la Madrid dam. The river unites with the Río Papaloapan past Tuxtepec, finally feeding thirsty crops and people all the way to the Gulf of Mexico.

Sights

Cuicatlán (Place of Song) is home to a busy market, often packed with Cuicatec-speaking people, especially women, wearing their handmade *huipiles*. Head there via the turnoff road from Highway 135, which, as it becomes Avenida Hidalgo, Cuicatlán's main north–south business street, leads a mile (1.6 km) north to the plaza at the town center. There stands the church, the **Templo de San Juan Bautista**, on the plaza's east side. Juárez, the main east–west street, runs past the church half a block east to the *presidencia municipal* and continues uphill. Across the street, south, from the *presidencia* spreads the **market.** Although it's lively enough most days, the market is especially big on Sundays and overflowing around June 24, when merrymakers crowd the streets and celebrate the **Fiesta de San Juan Bautista** with costumes, parades and floats, community feasts, fireworks, and traditional dances.

Step into the cool interior of the church, and pay your respects to Saint John the Baptist reigning high, above Jesus (whom he baptized). Above all, however, see the fluttering Dove of the Holy Spirit and the glorious golden sun rays emanating from the all-seeing eye of God.

Accommodations and Food

Cuicatlán offers a trio of recommendable hotels, a good restaurant, and a number of essential services. Start with the smallest hotel, the four room *posada*-style **Hotel Casa Rivera** (5 de Mayo 6, tel. 236/374-0257, $10 s, $15 d, $15 s, $20 d with TV), on a quiet side street on the north side of the church, behind the *presidencia municipal*. Romantics will enjoy its old Mexico–style high-ceilinged rooms, rustic tiled floors and airy interior patio, with garden-view porch, and a few tables and chairs for relaxing and socializing. Rooms come with fans, private baths, and parking, but credit cards are not accepted.

In the town center, a couple of blocks uphill from the bus station, travelers might find the renovated **Casa Marina** (Calle Hidalgo, no phone, $15 s, $18 d), too convenient to pass up. It offers about 10 spare but clean rooms around a parking patio, with fans and hot-water showers and toilets; credit cards not accepted.

Alternatively, you can check out Cuicatlán's fanciest hostelry, the **Hotel Tijuana** (Juárez 9, tel. 236/374-0116, $16 s, $18 d in one bed, $21 d in two beds, $26 t), block east, uphill, from the *presidencia*. Past the inviting lobby, a stairway rises to an airy upstairs view patio, encircled by two floors of 14 immaculate, attractively decorated rooms with private hot-water shower-baths and toilets. An unusual feature of the Hotel Tijuana is the downstairs billiards room, next to a crimson-wallpapered sitting room. (The manager said the billiards room closes nightly at 10 P.M.)

As for food, you'll find the freshest fruit and vegetables in the market and the best grocery selection at the **Super El Molino** (tel. 236/374-0008, 7 A.M.–4 P.M., 5–10 P.M. daily), at the plaza's southeast corner, across the street from the church.

Cuicatlán's best place to eat by far is the clean, seafood-specialty **C Restaurant Boringuen** (tel. 236/374-0222, 8:30 A.M.–10 P.M.), on Juárez, uphill two blocks east of the plaza, on the same side as the Hotel Tijuana. Here, from her spic-and-span kitchen, the grandmotherly owner puts out a stream of tasty breakfasts (cheese omelet $2.50), Mexican specialties (leg of pork tacos $2.50, *tlayuda* $3), and shrimp and calamari ($4.50).

Information and Services

Most of Cuicatlán's service establishments are either on the town plaza or along Calle Hidalgo, the north–south Highway 135 ingress street. Although Cuicatlán still has no bank, you might be able to cash a small travelers check (or at least a $20 bill) at the grocery store **Super El Molino,** at the town plaza's southeast corner. A long-distance **telephone and Internet** access is available at the small *caseta larga distancia* (7:30 A.M.–10:30 P.M. daily), on the plaza at the east corner of Hidalgo.

Buy stamps or mail a letter at the **correo** (8 A.M.–3 P.M. Mon.–Fri.), diagonally across the street from the plaza's southwest corner, above the basketball court. Also, next door to the *correo,* send a money order or a fax at the **telecomunicaciones** (9 A.M.–3 P.M. Mon.–Fri., 9 A.M.–12:30 P.M. Sat.).

For nonprescription medicines and drugs, cross to the west, plaza-front side, of Hidalgo to **Farmacia Marilyn** (tel. 236/374-0098, 9 A.M.–9:30 P.M. daily). If, however, you need a doctor, see **Dr. Rudolfo Reyes Escalante** (tel. 236/374-0033), at Calle Centenario 30. (From the plaza, walk two blocks down Hidalgo to Centenario, then turn right half a

block.) Alternatively, go to the 24-hour public *centro de salud* on Hidalgo, three blocks downhill from the plaza.

Getting There and Away

Autobuses Unidos (tel. 236/374-0014) second-class long-distance buses operate out of their terminal on Hidalgo, about four blocks downhill from the plaza. Buses connect north with Mexico City via Teotitlán, Tehuacán, and Puebla, and south with Oaxaca City.

If, however, you have the inclination to enjoy an adventure into virtually untouristed territory, ride one of the minibuses that head from the big terminal lot, adjacent, downhill from the bus station, to indigenous Cuicateco mountain villages (go early) such as such Concepción Papalo, San Miguel Santa Flor, and Santa Maria Tlalixtac.

For **drivers,** Highway 135 connects south with Highway 190 at Telixtlahuaca, thence with Oaxaca City, a total of 63 miles (101 km). The route, paved and in good condition but winding, requires about two hours for safety.

In the northerly direction, Highway 135 connects with Teotitlán del Camino in about 37 miles (60 km). Allow about an hour and a quarter for this winding but easy (with caution) trip. Add another hour (a total of two hours) for the continuation to Tehuacá; to Puebla (a total of five hours), and Mexico City (a total of seven hours, or five hours total via the toll expressways 135 D and 150 D).

THE ISTHMUS

A trip to the Isthmus of Tehuántepec from the Oaxaca central highlands sometimes seems like a journey to another country. At the Isthmus, the North American continent narrows to a scarce 100 miles (160 km) in width; the mighty Sierras shrink to mere foothills. The climate is tropical; the land is fertile and well watered. Luxuriant groves hang heavy with almonds, avocados, coconuts, mangos, and oranges. Rivers wind downhill to the sea, springs well up at the foot of mountains, and swarms of fish swim offshore. The Isthmus is a land of abundance, and it shows in the people. Women are renowned for their beauty, independent spirit, and their incomparably lovely flowered skirts and blouses, which young and old seem to wear at any excuse.

And they have excuses aplenty, for the Isthmus is the place of the *velas,* called fiestas in other parts of Mexico. But in the Isthmus, especially in the towns of Tehuántepec and Juchitán, where *istmeño* hearts beat fastest, *velas* are something more special. Most every barrio (neighborhood) must celebrate one in honor of its patron saint. A short list names 20 major yearly *velas* in Juchitán alone. The long list, including all the towns in the Isthmus, numbers more than 100.

If you're lucky to arrive during one of these *velas,* you may even be invited to share in the fun. Local folks dress up, women in their spectacularly flowered *traje* and men with their diminutive Tehuántepec sombreros, red kerchiefs, sashes, and machetes. Sometimes entire villages or town barrios celebrate for days, eating, drinking and dancing to the beautiful

© BRUCE WHIPPERMAN

© AVALON TRAVEL

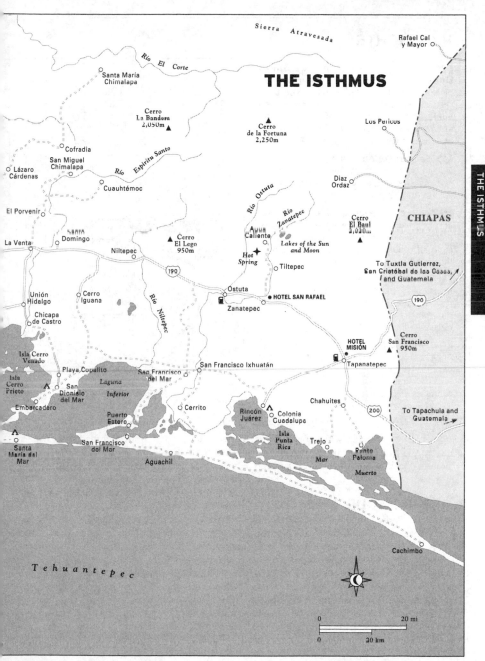

THE ISTHMUS

Sierra Atravesada

Rafael Cal
y Mayor

Río El Corte

Santa María
Chimalapa

Cerro
La Bandera
2,050m

Cerro
de la Fortuna
2,250m

Los Pericos

CHIAPAS

Cofradía

San Miguel
Chimalapa

Lázaro
Cárdenas

Río Espíritu Santo

Cuauhtémoc

Díaz
Ordaz

Cerro
El Baúl
1,030m

El Porvenir

Río Ostuta

Río Zanatepec

Agua
Caliente

Lakes of the Sun
and Moon

Santa
Domingo

Cerro
El Lego
950m

La Venta

Niltepec

Hot
Spring

Tiltepec

190

To Tuxtla Gutiérrez,
San Cristóbal de las Casas,
and Guatemala

190

Unión
Hidalgo

Cerro
Iguana

Río Niltepec

Ostuta

● HOTEL SAN RAFAEL

Zanatepec

Chicapa
de Castro

HOTEL
MISIÓN

Cerro
San Francisco
950m

Tapanatepec

Isla Cerro
Venado

Playa Copalito

San Francisco
del Mar

San Francisco Ixhuatán

Isla
Cerro
Prieto

San
Dionisio
del Mar

Laguna
Inferior

Chahuites

200

To Tapachula and
Guatemala

Embarcadero

Cerrito

Rincón
Juárez

Colonia
Guadalupe

Puerto
Entero

Isla
Punta
Rica

Trejo

Santa
María del
Mar

San Francisco
del Mar

Aguachil

Mar

Punta
Paloma

Muerto

Cachimbo

Tehuantepec

0   20 mi

0   30 km

HIGHLIGHTS

🌙 **Templo y Ex-Convento de Santo Domingo:** Around the Tehuátepec town plaza, the highlight is the church and partially restored, circa 1530 Templo y Ex-Convento de Santo Domingo. Be sure to see the recently discovered wall decorations painted by indigenous artists 450 years ago (page 327).

🌙 **Tehuántepec Market:** The native women, in their extravagant and colorful floral *huipiles*, steal the show at the Tehuántepec market (page 328).

🌙 **Around the Juchitán Plaza:** The flowers, gold filigree, and flowery embroiderered *huipiles* for sale, not to mention the all-female cadre of vendors, are the main attraction on the Juchitán plaza (page 338).

🌙 **The *Women Warriors*:** From the river bridge, enjoy the airy view and cooling breeze, then cross over to the west bank and admire the *Women Warriors*, stainless steel guardians of Juchitán (page 339).

🌙 **Balneario Tlacotepec:** Heroine Princess Donaji donated this precious crystal spring and park for Isthmus people to enjoy, something they have done with gusto for more than four centuries (page 346).

LOOK FOR 🌙 TO FIND RECOMMENDED SIGHTS, ACTIVITIES, DINING, AND LODGING.

melody of "La Sandunga," which, once you've been captured by its lovely, lilting strains, will always bring back your most cherished Isthmus memories.

PLANNING YOUR TIME

A convenient route to including the Isthmus in your Oaxaca plan would be with a circular side trip, including the vibrant market towns of Tehuántepec and Juchitán en route between Oaxaca City and the Pacific resorts. For example, you could bus, drive, or fly south to the coast, spend some days basking in the South Seas ambience of the Pacific resorts, then begin your return to Oaxaca City east along the coast by either bus, car, or tour, enjoying four days along the way exploring the colorful markets, cuisine, and sights, both manmade and natural, of the Isthmus.

For example, be sure to do plenty of strolling, and perhaps some shopping, in the fascinatingly colorful **Tehuántepec Market** hubbub, highlighted especially by the *tehuana* women in their radiantly colorful native dress. Along the way, be sure to do as the local folks do and hop aboard a *motocarro* (small motorcycle truck) for a ride around town. Later, don't miss enjoying at least one deliciously authentic Tehuántepec meal in the showplace Restaurant Scaru. With an additional day, you could enjoy a day trip to Guiengola ruined mountain fortress city, continuing on for a soak in the authentically rustic *agua caliente* (warm spring) at Jalapa del Marqués village, and/or a lake bass dinner at restful garden Restaurant Del Camino. The next day, continue east half an hour to Juchitán. Here, soak in the colorful scene with plenty of strolling around the **Juchitán plaza** and market. Along the way, be sure to see the vibrant flower and handicrafts stalls, with riots of roses and lilies and their gold filigree, exquisite flowered *huipiles*, bright hammocks, multicolored pottery, and much more. Take a break with lunch in the airy inner patio of the plaza-front Restaurant Casa Grande.

In the later afternoon, don't miss strolling a few blocks west to enjoy the breeze and view from the tranquil Río Los Perros riverbank. And especially don't miss taking a look at the monumental **Women Warriors** stainless steel sculptures overlooking the river.

Finally, enjoy another day by taking a picnic (and your bathing suit) to the historical and uniquely lovely Isthmus excursion park, at the crystalline blue springs that bubble up at **Balneario Tlacotepec,** about an hour by bus north of Juchitán.

Tehuántepec and Vicinity

Although both Juchitan and Salina Cruz are the Isthmus' big, bustling business centers, quieter, more traditional Tehuántepec remains foremost in the minds of most Istmeños as the former pre-Columbian royal capital, the seat of Cosijopí, the beloved last king of the Zapotecs. Local people are constantly reminded of their rich royal history by virtue of the Templo y Ex-Convento de Santo Domingo, the construction of which was unique in Oaxaca because it was financed by an indigenous monarch, Cosijopí. Moreover, local people can directly see their ancestors' contribution to history by glimpsing the ancient (recently discovered) floral and animal decorations that their ancestors painted on the walls of the ex-convent nearly half a millennium ago.

The town of Tehuántepec is geographically the center of the Isthmus. Roads, like spokes of a wheel, branch out in all directions, south to Salina Cruz, northeast to Juchitan, and northwest to Oaxaca City. This means that travelers from Oaxaca City most easily reach both Juchitan and Salina Cruz by passing through the fortunate town of Tehuántepec.

HISTORY

Although strictly connected only with a single location, the name Tehuántepec (Hill of the Jaguar) is, in many minds, synonymous with the entire Isthmus region: thus the label the

"Isthmus of Tehuántepec." The connection is historical, for Tehuántepec's dominance was born in events of long ago.

The earliest known settlers in the Isthmus left Olmec-style remains, which archaeologists date from as early as 4000 B.C. Much later, around 500 B.C., the Olmecs' inheritors, probably the ancestors of present-day Mixe- and Huave-speaking people, occupied the Isthmus lands. But times changed, and by A.D. 500 the Isthmus had become a strategic funnel: a trade gateway between the great civilizations, such as Teotihuacán and Monte Albán, of the Mexican central highlands, and the rich Mayan cultures of Chiapas, Yucatán, and Guatemala.

Eventually, the more populous Zapotec-speaking people displaced the Mixe and Huave in the Isthmus. By A.D. 1400, the Zapotec kings of Zaachila in Oaxaca's central valley controlled the Isthmus gateway with a mountaintop fort at Guiengola, which guarded their Isthmus capital at the present-day town of Tehuántepec.

The ambitious Aztec emperors also coveted the Isthmus gateway. In the 1440s, they sent armies to Oaxaca to pressure the Mixtec and Zapotec kingdoms, who allied themselves against the Aztecs. But forced by Aztec victories in 1486, many Zapotec people, including their king Cosijoeza, retreated from Zaachila and took refuge in Tehuántepec. There, together

TEHUÁNTEPEC

To Juchitán, Tuxtepec, and Chiapas

WEDNESDAY MARKET (*TIANGUIS*)

HEALTH CENTER — CASA DE CULTURA
TEMPLO Y EX-CONVENTO DE SANTO DOMINGO
Plaza Juárez — CATHEDRAL
TEHUÁNTEPEC MARKET — POST OFFICE — Mercado de Campesinos
PASTELERÍA DEL ISTMO — BANCO SANTANDER SERFIN — TELECOM
CASA DE DOÑA JUANA — INTERNET
SUPER ABARROTES YEMA DE ORO — Mercado Jesús Carranza
RESTAURANT ÁNGEL — FARMACIA SAN JORGE — Plaza
BANCOMER — BANORTE — LONG-DISTANCE TELEPHONE
PALACIO MUNICIPAL
TURISMO
DOCTOR
OASIS
HSBC
CAFÉ COLONIAL
RESTAURANT SCARU
HOTEL DONAJI
Plaza Laborío
TEMPLO DE LA NATIVIDAD EXCELSA

To Salina Cruz and Oaxaca

0   200 yds
0   200 m

© AVALON TRAVEL

with the Mixtecs under King Dzahuindanda, the Zapotecs, attacking from their stronghold at Guiengola, held off the Aztecs, who offered Emperor Moctezuma's daughter in marriage to King Cosijoeza as part of a peace pact.

With tranquillity established, Cosijoeza returned to reign once again over Zaachila, leaving his son, Cosijopí, as king of the Isthmus, with his court at Tehuántepec. Later, when the Spanish arrived, King Cosijopí joined with Cortés against the Aztecs. After Aztec power

was erased, Cosijopí, along with thousands of his subject-inhabitants of Tehuántepec, converted to Christianity.

Orientation

Although the Río Tehuántepec splits the Santo Domingo Tehuántepec town (pop. 52,000) along a roughly north–south line, the west-side portion, across the river via the Puente Metalico (Metal Bridge), first built for locomotives around 1900, seems like a mere suburb of the town center, east of the river. On the central plaza itself, the *presidencia municipal* occupies the south side, along Calle 5 de Mayo; the main market, **Mercado Jesús Carranza,** lies on the plaza's west, river side, along Calle Juana C. Romero; and to the northeast, past the end of main north–south street Benito Juárez, about a block and a half northeast of the plaza, stands Tehuántepec's most venerable monument, the **Templo y Ex-Convento de Santo Domingo.**

SIGHTS
Around the Plaza
First, take a stroll around the plaza, where you'll find some interesting sculptures, including noble likenesses of Miguel Hidalgo (the Father of Mexican Independence) and a pair of Tehuántepec heroes. On the north side, look for the bronze of a seated **Doña Juana Catalina Romero** (1855–1915), a Tehuántepec legend. She is famous partly for her good works,

Secondary school students practice folkloric dance in the courtyard behind the Tehuántepec *presidencia municipal.*

© BRUCE WHIPPERMAN

establishing schools for Tehuántepec children during the days when public education was a rarity in Mexico.

On the plaza's west (market) side, you'll find the bronze bust of **A. Maximino Ramón Ortiz,** the first and only governor of the Isthmus, when it was separated from Oaxaca as the territory of Tehuántepec for a few years during the 1850s. Politics, however, were not Ortiz's first love. He is best remembered as the composer of "La Sandunga," Tehuántepec's beloved theme. His ageless melody seems to perfectly capture the essence of the Isthmus in a gracefully drowsy rhythm that swings slowly, yet deliberately, like the relaxed sway of lovers in a hammock beneath the deep shade of a Tehuántepec grove.

Templo y Ex-Convento de Santo Domingo
From the plaza's northeast corner, walk north along Calle Hidalgo one block to the venerable Santo Domingo church, behind its broad fenced atrium, on the right. The aging landmark (to the left of the new church) is interesting partly because it was one of the few, if not the only, Christian churches in Mexico financed by a native ruler. Cosijopí, the last king of the Zapotecs, who was baptized as Juan Cortés de Cosijopí after his friend and ally Hernán Cortés paid for the construction with both cash and the labor of thousands of his subjects. The building was erected under the supervision of Fray Fernando de Albequerque, vicar of Tehuántepec, between 1544 and 1550.

Given the warm relations between King Cosijopí and the Spanish, it is ironic that the Inquisition authorities burned Cosijopí at the stake a generation later for continuing (and for encouraging his people) to worship the old gods.

Enter through an interior side door, off the left-aisle of the very attractive new church. Inside, old Santo Domingo's most remarkable feature is its lovely wooden *tabla* (altarpiece), with an unusual ebony Lord of Creation perched on its crest, with a dog, turtle, and deer in tow. (At last visit, the ebony statue had

THE ISTHMUS

THE ISTHMUS

been removed, but a local priest told me that it would probably be returned after the present church remodeling work is finished.)

The ex-convent section, on the old church's north side, was abandoned not long after the Reforms of the late 1850s forced the Dominicans from Mexico. It had crumbled into a virtual ruin by the mid-20th century, when local people rolled up their sleeves and began restoring it in 1953. In 1982, with the restoration complete, the townsfolk christened their ex-convent as the **Casa de la Cultura.** Now, in the evenings it resounds with the noises of young musicians and dancers at practice.

To take a look inside the restored ex-convent (tel. 971/715-0114, 9 A.M.–2 P.M. and 5–8 P.M. Mon.–Fri., 9 A.M.–2 P.M. Sat.), retrace your steps out across the atrium, turn right at Calle Hidalgo, and walk north. After two short blocks, turn right at Guerrero. Walk one long block. Just after the *centro de salud* turn right into an alley, which leads south to the Casa de la Cultura and the old convent.

Inside the Casa de la Cultura, look for the faded but still-visible flower and animal motifs that Cosijopí's long-gone artists painted on the walls three and a half centuries ago. Head upstairs where the ancient wall decorations appear as fresh as if they were painted only a generation ago. In other upstairs rooms you'll see a host of historical mementos, from ancient Olmec-style figurines to a lovely jade necklace, once scattered, but excavated piece by piece and finally reassembled here. (Sometimes the upstairs is closed. If so, it's worth seeking permission from the administrative secretary on the ground floor, in the cloister, to let you go upstairs.)

◖ Tehuántepec Market

The most colorful downtown action goes on at the **Mercado Jesús Carranza,** just across Romero from the plaza. At midday, the market overflows with life. The center of everything is the corridor street on the market's north side, which connects the plaza with the businesses along the railroad tracks behind the market.

The buzzing *motocarros* (motorcycle mini-trucks) that you see depositing and picking up passengers by the railroad track seem to be a unique Isthmus invention. They mostly follow set round-trip routes around town for a fixed price of about $0.50. When you get tired of walking, hop on for a breezy whirlwind tour of Tehuántepec's back streets.

Market vendors, especially women in *traje,* tend to be apprehensive of rubber-necking strangers with cameras in hand. A good strategy is to blend in. Get a *refresco* at one of the food stalls and find a low-profile spot in the shade where you can take in the passing scene.

Get some relief from the heat and bustle inside the roofed market building itself. If you're in the mood for shopping, plenty of handicrafts are available. On the bottom floor, stalls offer the gold filigree jewelry that the Tehuántepec women love to wear. Look farther for lots of woven goods, such as baskets, string bags of *ixtle* fiber, hand fans, and hammocks. One unusual item that you may see during the late spring are large, three-foot-long (one-meter-long) pods of decorative flowers of *coyul.*

Upstairs, via the stairway on the southwest corner by the railroad track, you'll find Tehuántepec's pride—the beautiful embroidered *tehuana* flowered blouses and skirts. Look around, decide what you want, then bargain for it. Asking prices for the prized, embroidered flower–design blouses run as much as $30, a whole outfit about $100.

Behind the market runs the **railway track,** which has the distinct appearance of being abandoned, because dozens of vendors regularly set up where trains should come roaring through. Shopkeepers, however, report that trains actually use the track occasionally—then everyone scatters with their goods (from bananas and melons to shrimp and hammocks).

Pottery, including many big, homely items—bowls, griddles, planters, pots—is for sale at the second downtown market, the lackluster Mercado 5 de Febrero, sometimes known as the **Mercado de Campesinos,** tucked at the plaza's northwest corner. Smaller for-sale items include pots painted with bright flowers as well as woven goods, such as baskets, fans, and handmade brooms and *piñatas.*

Besides the two aforementioned permanent daily markets near the plaza, country people flood into town for *tianguis* on Wednesday and Sunday. Visit the Wednesday *tianguis*, set up along north-side Calle Héroes, most easily by riding a *motocarro* from the plaza. Alternatively, from the plaza, walk north along Hidalgo past the church. Two blocks from the plaza, turn right at Guerrero and continue several blocks to the blue-trimmed San Juan Bautista church, where you turn left at Héroes. After a few blocks, you'll see the awnings stretched along side streets.

The Sunday *tianguis* is much bigger, so much so that it's held on the west side across the river, beyond the big Oaxaca highway intersection, in the open space behind the Hotel Gueixhoba.

Casa de Doña Juana Catalina Romero

The railway track so intimately close to the market is due to the speculated intimate relationship between aging President Porfirio Díaz and local beauty Doña Juana Catalina Romero (1837–1915). Doña Juana Catalina lived in the French-style mansion, now in faded white with

---

JUANA CATALINA ROMERO: HEROINE OF TEHUÁNTEPEC

Why Tehuántepec's main downtown streets, which carry such nationally renowned labels as Cinco de Mayo, Juárez, and Hidalgo, should include Juana C. Romero among them is a question nearly all adult townsfolk can immediately answer. "Doña Juana," they say, is Tehuántepec's heroine because she "built schools and helped the children of Tehuántepec." Some go on to say that she "got lots of help for Tehuántepec from her friend, Presidente Porfirio Díaz."

When pressed, most Tehuántepec folks acknowledge that she had a close (some even say intimate) relationship with Porfirio Díaz. Juana Catalina was an 18-year-old blue-blooded beauty when first introduced to Díaz in 1873. At that time, he was the celebrated general who beat the French at Puebla on May 5 (Cinco de Mayo), 1862, and heir apparent to the late President Benito Juárez. Although he must have been charmed by her beauty at their first meeting, most certainly nothing immediate came of it, since he was both middle-aged and married and she had her upper-crust reputation to preserve.

Whatever passed between them during later years has been the subject of endless gossip. In any case, she never married, and Don Porfirio, it is speculated, had the railroad tracks laid right past her house in downtown Tehuántepec so he could hop off the train and visit her with no fuss or muss.

Juana Catalina Romero is fondly remembered by Tehuántepec people for her kindness and good works.

© BRUCE WHIPPERMAN

fancy blue window awnings in need of serious renovation, that rises by the tracks. Some say that the tracks were built right out front so Díaz could visit her with ease. Until recent years Doña Juana Catalina's elderly granddaughter resided there. Lately, with her retirement, her heirs subsequently sold the house to another family.

La Cueva

If sometime you feel like an early-morning or late-afternoon walk, head for La Cueva (The Cave), as local folks call it. It's visible most of the way up the hill called Liesa, across the river about two miles (three km) west of town. La Cueva has been hallowed ground for as long as anyone remembers. Local folks tell stories about the existence of a secret passageway somewhere at the back of the cave that leads all the way to Guiengola, the "old town," now a mysterious ruin on the mountain 10 miles (16 km) to the west. (See *Excursions West of Tehuántepec* later in this chapter.)

La Cueva still draws virtually everyone in town for a pilgrimage during both Semana Santa (Holy Week) and Día de la Cruz (May 3). It's best not to try the climb during the heat of the day (allow at least an hour for the whole excursion). In order to get a head start, spend a dollar or two on a taxi or *motocarro* to take you to the base of the hill.

Plaza Laborio

A number of smaller plazas dot Tehuántepec's several barrios. If you head south along Juárez two long blocks, you'll arrive at Plaza Laborio and its adjacent blue-trimmed, storybook **Templo de la Natividad Excelsa.** Before you go inside to look around, notice that the right bell tower is tilted at a crazy angle, not unlike the Leaning Tower of Pisa. Laborio (the name of the church's barrio) residents don't seem to worry. "It's been like that for years," they say.

Plaza Laborio is mostly sleepy, except during the August 31–September 11 **Fiesta Laborio,** when residents and visitors celebrate with a long menu of feasts, dancing, fireworks, and *calendas.*

The Leaning Tower of Pisa-like angle of Templo de Natividad Excelsa concerns few, if any local residents.

© BRUCE WHIPPERMAN

Barrio de Santa María

Also worth a visit, across the river, is the Barrio de Santa María. (Get there by bearing left at the street heading diagonally left from the highway, a block or two west of the river bridge; after about two more blocks, go left again.) The main community pride and joy is the (also bright blue and white) **Templo de la Virgen de la Asunción.** The church, by the same architect who built the famous pilgrimage church in Juquila, is the focus of a busy round of barrio events. The bustle climaxes during the August 13–18 **Fiesta Patronal del Barrio de Santa María Reolotoca,** with a *calenda,* parade of flower-decorated bull-drawn carts, and ear-splitting popular dances on three successive nights. Bring your earplugs.

ACCOMMODATIONS
Under $50

Tehuántepec offers visitors at least three hotels, one of them, semi-deluxe, in the west suburb, and a humbler but acceptable pair down-town. Best choice downtown is the **(Oasis** (Melchor Ocampo 8, tel. 971/715-0008, fax 971/715-0835, julincontreras@hotmail.com, $15 s or d in one bed, $19 d in two beds, $24 t with fans; or $23 s, $40 d with a/c), a block south from the plaza hubbub, behind the *presidencia*. Although at first glance the Oasis doesn't appear very exciting, a closer examination reveals the talents of the owner, friendly English-speaking artist Julín (hoo-LEEN) Contreras, whose art decorates the hotel's restaurant wall. (She also was commissioned to do the mural in the council chamber on the second floor of the *presidencia municipal*.)

The hotel building offers four stories of 28 clean and comfortable rooms that enfold an invitingly leafy and tranquil inner patio. The rooms feature colorful, thoughtfully selected bedspreads and curtains, walls decorated with the owner's art, and private hot-water shower-baths. In most rooms, windows open to a garden, mountain, or river view. Pottery and plants selected by the owner decorate hotel niches and

© BRUCE WHIPPERMAN

quiet afternoon in Tehuántepec

corridors. In the building's inner patio, a towering *chico zapote* tree stretches skyward. Other trees around the yard supply all of the seasonal grapefruits and mangos that guests can eat. A parking lot provides security for cars. There is a good, relaxed, Restaurant Almendro (Almond Tree). VISA credit card and dogs and cats accepted. For lovers of the way Mexico "used to be," this is the place. (Besides all of the above, Julín invites guests to visit her on-site art studio and also offers Isthmus culinary tours.)

Second choice downtown goes to the **Hotel Donaji** (Juárez 10, tel. 971/715-0064, fax 971/715-0448, hoteldonaji@hotmail.com, $17 s, $23 d fan only, $27 s, $37 d with a/c), named for Oaxaca's beloved Zapoteca heroine and located two blocks south of the plaza on quiet Plaza Laborio. The hotel, recently renovated, includes a shady plant-decorated patio, filled with the melodies of tropical birds. The 48 rooms, in a big two-story block, are simply but invitingly decorated, with hot-water shower-baths, TV, and parking, but credit cards not accepted. The Donaji's major pluses are air-conditioning (desirable in warm Tehuántepec) and its location on the tree-shaded, drowsy (except during the August 31–September 11 fiesta) Plaza Laborio.

Over $50

Tehuántepec's fanciest hotel is the four-star **(Hotel Guiexhoba** (ghee-ay-SHOW-bah, Carretera Panamericana Km 250.5, Barrio Santa María, tel./fax 971/715-1710 or 971/715-0416, guiexhoba@prodigy.net.mx, $45 s, $58 d, $70 t), which deserves extra points simply for its Zapotec label, the name of a locally abundant white flower with a fragrant scent reminiscent of jasmine. The hotel has a specimen bush, which blooms during the summer rainy season, by the front entrance. Find the hotel on Highway 190, inbound from Oaxaca City on the right before the bridge.

The Guiexhoba's 36 spacious, clean, and comfortable rooms, in two stories, enclose a parking courtyard that fortunately shields rooms on its north side from highway noise. Staff are generally attentive, competent, and

THE ISTHMUS

courteous. The upstairs rooms away from the highway are quiet and have fewer people walking past the windows, whose drapes, unfortunately, must be drawn for privacy. Amenities include pool, parking, good cable TV, air-conditioning, hot-water shower-baths, credit cards accepted, and the very good Restaurant Guiexhoba.

FOOD
Groceries, Breakfasts, and Treats

Tehuántepec's freshest fruit and vegetable sources by far are the luscious mounds of avocados, bananas, carrots, lettuces, mangos, pineapples, radishes, and much more in the plaza market (be sure to peel, scrub with soap, or cook anything you buy). Likewise, find the best grocery sources, such as the **Super Abarrotes Yema** (8 A.M.–8:30 P.M. daily), by the railroads tracks just west (river side) of the market.

Breakfasts you'll probably find most conveniently at your hotel, such as the Restaurant Almendro of the Hotel Oasis and the restaurant at the Hotel Guiexhoba. Otherwise (or if you're staying at Hotel Donaji), go to the **Café Colonial,** two blocks south of the plaza, or Tehuántepec's best, the refined **Restaurant Scaru** three blocks south of the plaza.

Satisfy your sweet tooth with the baked offerings of the **Super Panadería y Pastelería del Istmo** (tel. 971/715-0808, 8 A.M.–8:30 P.M. daily). Find it on the railroad tracks, just north of the market, on the left. For evening snacks, fill up at the taco stalls lined up behind the *presidencia municipal.*

Restaurants

Tehuántepec offers a sprinkling of good sit-down restaurants. By far the most colorful is the ☾ **Restaurant Scaru** (tel. 971/715-0646, 8 A.M.–11 P.M. daily), at south-side cul-de-sac Callejon Leona Vicario 4. Here, in a graceful, airy setting, owners lovingly portray picturesque aspects of traditional Isthmus life. Walls bloom with murals of fruit, festivals, and lovely *tehuanas* in their bright, flowery costumes, while patios are sprinkled with hammocks and sheltered overhead by luxurious hand-crafted *palapas.* Saturday and Sunday afternoons 2–6 P.M., a marimba band will play "La Sandunga" to your heart's content. After such a luscious introduction, the food, from a very recognizable menu of salads, soups, and eggs ($3–5), pastas ($4–6), meats (including some game), fish, and fowl ($5–10), is no less than you would expect. Get there from the plaza by walking two long blocks south along Juárez to Plaza Laborio. Turn left and walk one block to Callejon Leona Vicario on the left; the restaurant is on the uphill side of the street. Credit cards not accepted.

Second choice goes to the good but more ordinarily picturesque restaurant at the **Hotel Guiexhoba** (tel. 971/715-1710, 7:30 A.M.–10 P.M. daily, $5–12), across the river. The food, from a typical but tasty menu of breakfasts (eggs and pancakes), lunches (hamburgers, soups, and stews), and dinners (meat, fish, fowl, and spaghetti), sometimes comes with a flaming crepe Suzette flourish. Credit cards accepted.

Back downtown, find third choice **Café Colonial** (tel. 971/715-0115, 8 A.M.–6 P.M. daily), at Juana C. Romero, two blocks south of the plaza. Owners have worked hard to recreate a corner of old Mexico, with sentimental country paintings and brightly hued stucco walls, all beneath a genuinely rustic tree limb–beamed ceiling. The food is appropriately traditional, with plenty of good breakfasts (omelet with potatoes, hotcakes, corn flakes, $2–5); Mexican *antojitos* (tacos, enchiladas, tostadas, $3–5); and a long list of entrées (pasta, meat, and seafood, $5–7).

INFORMATION AND SERVICES
Tourist Information

For travel recommendations and help in emergencies, go to the friendly **Turismo** office (on Hwy. 200 south, Salina Cruz direction, no phone, 9 A.M.–6 P.M. Mon.–Sat.), overlooking the Río Tehuántepec, two blocks west and two blocks south of the town plaza, before the river bridge.

Money

Tehuántepec has several banks, all of which have ATMs. First choice, for its Saturday hours, goes to **Banco Santander Serfin** (tel. 971/715-0916 or 971/715-0917, 9 A.M.–4 P.M. Mon.–Fri., 10 A.M.–2 P.M. Sat.) on the plaza's northwest side, corner of Romero. Otherwise, on the opposite side of the plaza, go to up and coming **Banorte** (971/715-0140, 9 A.M.–4 P.M. Mon.–Fri.) on Cinco de Mayo, south side, across from the market. Next door to Banorte, also find **Bancomer** (tel. 971/715-1253, 8:30 A.M.–4 P.M. Mon.–Fri.).

Communications

The *correo* (tel. 971/715-0106, 8 A.M.–3 P.M. Mon.–Fri.), including rapid, secure **Mexpost** service, and *telecomunicaciones* (money orders and public tel. 971/715-1197 and fax, 8 A.M.–7:30 P.M. Mon.–Fri., 9 A.M.–noon Sat.–Sun.), stand side by side at the north end of Juárez, at the plaza's northeast corner.

Long-distance telephone and photocopies are available at **Papelería La Esfera** (at the plaza's southeast corner, tel. 971/715-0042, fax 971/715-2090, 8 A.M.–8 P.M. Mon.–Sat., 9 A.M.–2 P.M. Sun.).

Internet access is at the cyber café **Alan. com** (9 A.M.–10 P.M. Mon.–Sat.) across the street from Banco Serfin, just past the plaza's northeast corner.

Health and Emergencies

A number of town pharmacies provide both over-the-counter remedies and prescription drugs. Perhaps the best stocked is the town-center branch of the **Farmacia San Jorge** (tel. 971/713-7533, 8 A.M.–8 P.M.), located in a permanent street stall, right on Romero, market side of the town plaza.

If you need to consult a doctor, you can always find one at the 24-hour *centro de salud* (Guerrero 19, tel. 971/715-0180), three blocks from the plaza. Get there by walking from the Banco Serfin at the plaza's northwest corner. After two blocks, turn right at Guerrero and continue a long block to the *centro de salud* on the right.

Alternatively, you have another good choice

with **Dr. José Manuel Vichido** (Calle Ocampo, tel. 971/715-0862, 9 A.M.–1 P.M. Mon.–Sat.). From the plaza's southeast corner, walk south one block along Juárez; turn left at the first street, Ocampo. The doctor's office is half a block farther on the left.

Police service is available from at least two sources in Tehuántepec. Call either the *policía municipal* (tel. 971/713-7000), or the emergency number (dial 066).

GETTING THERE AND AWAY

By Bus

The vintage Tehuántepec bus station was supposed to be replaced years ago by a brand-new terminal, which remains yet unused. Meanwhile, on Highway 190/200, about a mile north of the town plaza, the old bus terminal still bustles with activity. Information and reservations are accessible for all departures (tel. 971/715-0108). Get there by taxi or *motocarro* from the plaza.

Four major bus lines, first-class **Autobuses del Oriente** (ADO) and **Omnibus Cristóbal Colón** (OCC), and mixed first- and second-class **Sur** and **Autobuses Unidos** (AU), offer many connections. Departures connect north and east via Juchitán with Tuxtepec, Villahermosa, Palenque, Minatitlán, Coatzacoalcos, Mérida, Cancún and Tulum; northwest with Oaxaca City, Puebla, and Mexico City; southwest with Salina Cruz, Bahías de Huatulco, Pochutla (Puerto Ángel), and Puerto Escondido; and east via Juchitán, Tuxtla Gutiérrez, San Cristóbal las Casas, and Tapachula at the Guatemala border.

In addition, from an adjacent terminal, a pair of independent second-class cooperating lines, **Oaxaca Istmo** and **Fletes y Pasajes** offer connections northwest with Oaxaca City and west with Bahías de Huatulco, Pochutla (Puerto Ángel), and Puerto Escondido, while Fletes y Pasajes also offers connections northwest with Oaxaca City, southwest with Salina Cruz, and northeast with Juchitán.

By Car

Paved roads fan out from Tehuántepec in four

SCOOTING AROUND BY MOTOCARRO

The city of Tehuántepec's public transportation system was long ago preempted by the town's regiment of *motocarros* – small, motorcycle-driven flat-bed trucks that buzz, putt, squeal, and skid around town continuously. The center of the action is the railroad track behind the market, where all Tehuántepec *motocarros* faithfully return for passengers and cargo.

Motocarros have thus become the end-all answer to how to get around in Tehuántepec's heat. Long ago, everyone (excepting mad dogs and Englishmen) learned that too much midday walking can produce a considerable sweat at least and sunstroke at worst. If you get overheated, do as Tehuántepec people do and take a seat in the shade and cool down with an *agua* or *refresco*. Later, continue your breezy extended tour via *motocarro*. Fares run about $0.50 for an entire circuit of the town.

directions. Highway 190 connects northeast with Juchitán (17 miles/27 km), then splits north as Highway 185 at La Ventosa and continues north, via Matías Romero and Minatitlán, all the way to the Gulf of Mexico at Coatzacoalcos, a total of 166 miles (267 km). Allow about 4.5 driving hours, either way, for this relatively easy trip.

For Tuxtepec and northern Oaxaca, from cross-Isthmus Highway 185, turn onto Highway 147 at Matías Romero and continue northwest a total of 189 miles (304 km) from Tehuántepec. Allow about five hours of driving time. *Note:* In the past, some robberies have occurred on the long (two-hour), lonely Highway 147 Matías Romero–Tuxtepec leg. Although, at this writing, security appears to be little problem, authorities still advise travelers to restrict their driving to *daytime only* on this stretch.

Highway 190 connects Tehuántepec northwest with Oaxaca City along 155 miles (250 km) of well-maintained but winding highway. Allow about five hours Oaxaca City direction (uphill), 4.5 hours in the opposite direction.

Highway 200 connects Tehuántepec west with the Oaxaca Pacific coast, via Salina Cruz (9 miles/15 km), Bahías de Huatulco (100 miles/161 km, three hours), Pochutla–Puerto Ángel (124 miles/200 km, four hours), and Puerto Escondido (170 miles/274 km, five hours) of paved, moderately traveled, secure highway.

Highway 190 connects Tehuántepec east via Juchitán (17 miles/27 km) and Niltepec to Tapanatepec (78 miles/126 km) near the Chiapas border and beyond to Guatemala. Allow about 3.5 hours of driving time to Tapanatepec.

Drivers should fill up with gasoline at the Pemex *gasolinera* on the west side of the river, about a mile (two km) west of the bridge, where the road splits southwest to Salina Cruz, northwest to Oaxaca City.

EXCURSIONS WEST OF TEHUÁNTEPEC

The interesting destination trio of Guiengola, Jalapa del Marqués, and Tequisistlán can be combined into a full-day auto or taxi excursion (two days by bus) west of Tehuántepec. Along the way, enjoy a vigorous hike through pristine forest to the regal ruined fortress-city at Guiengola, a breezy boat ride on the Jalapa del Marqués reservoir, a soak in the community hot (actually just warm) spring, and a look at what is probably the world's only marble basketball court, topped off by a stop by the marble factory at Tequisistlán.

Guiengola

The mountain fortress Guiengola (ghee-ayn-GOH-lah, Big Rock in Zapotec) may have been abandoned before the Spanish arrived, but it was never forgotten. Local people refer to it as the "old town" and often hear voices when up there. If so, they rush down the mountain before dark.

Ghosts notwithstanding, an excursion to Guiengola is a chance to get some fresh air into your lungs as you enjoy the Isthmus tropical forest up close—fluttering butterflies, spiny cactus, flowery trees, and fireflies and hoot owls (if you return at dusk).

At the end of the rough jeep road that winds about four miles (six km) up Guiengola Mountain, you continue on foot via a sometimes steep two-mile (three-km), one-hour hike through summer-green (but brown in spring) tropical woodland. If you start early or leave late, you might see *venado* (deer), *javelin* (wild pigs), and, if you're very lucky, a *león* (mountain lion).

You know you're getting close to the ruins when the trail straightens out and you see a continuous series of vegetation-covered mounds and walls on both sides. You are following an ancient, regal street, lined with ruined houses of the nobility. Next, break out into the open, where a four-step unreconstructed noble pyramid, called the Pyramid of the Sun, rises at the right. On the opposite side, across a spreading, flat ceremonial plaza, another, even taller, five-step Pyramid of the Moon stands on your left. To the extreme left rises a big ball court, so well preserved that it appears as if a dozen persons could spend a weekend with machetes and a few shovels and put the place in order for a tournament on Monday.

What you see immediately around you is only the ceremonial center. Beneath the surrounding forest are dozens of mounds, remains of temples, ceremonial patios, and homes. The state of preservation is exceptional, partly because of the site's isolation. These structures of stone and mud mortar are delicate and mostly unexplored; please refrain from climbing on them.

GUIDES AND GETTING THERE

In Tehuántepec, you can pre-arrange a tour led by experienced guide Victor Velasquez Guzman (local cell tel. 044-971/111-0768, long distance in Mexico 045-971/111-0768). Victor, who furnishes a translator for his tour, is highly recommended by Julín Contreras, owner-

operator of the Oasis hotel (see Tehuántepec *Accommodations,* earlier in this chapter). Alternatively, either Julín or Tehuántepec *Turismo* (see Tehuántepec *Information*) may be able to recommend someone else.

If, on the other hand, you are lacking prior arrangements, arrive early at the Guiengola jumping-off point, by at least 9:30 A.M., to avoid the midday heat and give you time to possibly contact an on-site guide (not mandatory, but useful), most likely either José Luis Toral Sánchez or Feliciano Gonzáles Mendez, whom the government has certified as official guardians of Guiengola. You may find one or both of them either at the roadside Comedor Gema (see below), or at the uphill parking lot before the trail that leads to the ruins. The Comedor Gema and most of the highway-front *palapas* provide lunches (sometimes of armadillo, venison, iguana, coati, and other game), drinks, and bottled water (very necessary, since no water is available along the route). Once you've contacted your guide, you could either continue to Guiengola immediately or detour with your guide to Jalapa del Marqués and Tequisistlán and return to explore Guiengola in the late afternoon.

By car, **get there** by driving your own (rugged pickup truck or jeep-like, high clearance) SUV or similar rental vehicle (expensive; rental agents in Oaxaca City, Salina Cruz, and Juchitán) to the signed right turnoff that runs right past the **Comedor Gema,** about 10 miles (16 km) west, Oaxaca City direction, along Highway 190 from Tehuántepec. Otherwise, get to the Highway 190 turnoff by sharing a taxi, or, most cheaply, via the **Autotransportes Galgos de Jalapa** buses, which leave the Tehuántepec plaza in front of the market about every half hour. From the highway turnoff, get to the ruins by continuing by taxi, or thumbing a ride (offer to pay) from a truck.

Jalapa del Marqués

During Mexico's big dam boom in the 1950s, planners decided to conserve and control some of the trillions of gallons of water that flow via the Río Tehuántepec into the sea. A good idea, thought most, for flood control and irrigation during the long winter and spring drought.

The result is **Benito Juárez dam and reservoir,** which provides irrigation water, fish, and a tourist attraction for Jalapa del Marqués (pop. 3,000), the biggest town on the reservoir.

The cost for all this was that Jalapa del Marqués, originally on the bank of the Río Tehuántepec, had to be moved five miles (eight km) uphill to its present location next to Highway 190, about 18 miles (30 km) west of Tehuántepec. Now the people have everything new—wide paved streets, church, and a small museum and Casa del Pueblo cultural center.

People in Jalapa del Marqués eat a lot of fish—specifically, *mojarra* (bass). A number of restaurants cook it up and serve it for visitors; for the best, try **Del Camino** (8 A.M.–9 P.M. daily) or alternatively **Tecos** (8 A.M.–7 P.M. daily), about a kilometer past the eastern, Tehuántepec, edge of town.

The next thing to do is go fishing or take a **boat ride** on the lake. This is good anytime of year but is best in the dry winter or spring, when the silt from the summer rains has settled and the lake is invitingly clear. Arrive early enough to find one of the boatmen down at the lake before they go home for the day. They charge about $15 for a two-hour ride or fishing trip. Bring your own pole, unless you want to fish by line or net as the locals do.

A popular excursion destination is **Tres Picos,** a Zapotec ruin on the far side of the lake. There, you can explore a trio of conical stone pyramids, about 30 feet (nine meters) high, and a submerged ball court. Also, if the water is low and clear enough, perhaps your boatman will take you to see the site of the submerged old Jalapa del Marqués, where you'll be able to see the old church beneath the water or even sit on its bell tower, which at low water protrudes from the lake's surface.

Before or after your boat excursion, take a look inside the **Casa del Pueblo,** on the town plaza about 600 feet (180 meters) downhill

from the highway. Besides a number of giant fossil bones, apparently mastodon, it has a sizable collection of locally gathered pre-conquest pottery, including some very phallic-looking figurines. At this writing, the dusty collection was under lock and key. However, if you go to the *presidencia municipal* (on the opposite side of the plaza), you might find someone who will unlock the door for you.

Get to the plaza and the lakeshore boat landing by the paved main street, marked by a huge concrete Bienvenidos (welcome) portal on the highway. Continue downhill, past the central plaza (0.1 mile o/0.2 km, Casa del Pueblo on the right, uphill plaza corner). Pass a playground and traffic circle (0.4 mile/0.6 km); after another 1.4 mile (2.2 km) mostly on a dirt road, you arrive at the beach and boat landing. Go swimming (in your bathing suit) and enjoy a lakeside picnic.

Finally, you might join the folks in the community **agua caliente** (warm spring) about half a mile (one km) uphill from the highway. People begin arriving around six in the morning, when it's cool. They bring their soap and clothes to be washed and stay for hours, playing in the warm-water hot tub (about 102°F/39°C). Wear your bathing suit. If you don't have one, just go in with your clothes on like everyone else. Skinny-dipping, unless you're under three, is liable to land you in jail, besides reinforcing the local people's stereotypical view of the "loose" foreigner. Get there via the dirt street that heads uphill at the highway long-distance bus stop, a few blocks west (Oaxaca City direction) of the town entrance portal. After two blocks uphill, bear left, then turn right and pass a big electrical transformer station. Continue uphill to a low ridge, where on the right side, you'll see the women washing clothes in big tanks inside an enclosure (to keep animals out). The women are friendly and also careful to keep their waste water from the lower basins, where you'll be welcome to bathe. (The basins outside the enclosure are for animals only.)

By bus, get to Jalapa del Marqués via either the Tehuántepec central bus terminal or second-class **Autotransportes Galgos de Jalapa** bus from in front of the Tehuántepec market.

Tequisistlán

This little *municipio*, officially Santa María Magdalena Tequisistlán, was on ground too high to get gobbled up by the reservoir. Consequently, the huge-in-summer (and muddy) **Río Tequisistlán** continues to run right next to town. During the dry, hot spring this river appears very inviting for a dip into its clear, gurgling water.

Take a look inside the old church in the center of town. Here, folks enjoy the church's completely marble-floored atrium in front, especially handy for dancing during the July 20–24 festival in honor of Santa María Magdalena. On the church's side, you'll find the kicker: probably the world's only **marble basketball court.**

You can see the source of all this by going to the community **marble factory,** on Highway 190 about a mile (two km) west (Oaxaca City direction) of the town highway crossing. If you arrive during working hours (9 A.M.–1 P.M. and 5–7 P.M. Mon.–Sat.), ask someone to "please show" (*"favor de maestrar"*) you around. You'll see dozens of men and machines working beneath a shady open-air roof, cutting, grinding, and polishing dozens of beautiful pieces of marble.

In the nearby office, feast your eyes on the beautifully polished finished products. The factory will custom-make anything you want—such as the lovely marble bathroom vanity top you've always wanted, a statuesque marble cat, or some other favorite animal.

Get there by car, via Highway 190 (30 miles/50 km) Oaxaca City direction, or an hour by bus from the Tehuántepec station. Get off at the Tequisistlán crossing and hop on the local Tequisistlán bus, which shuttles folks the two miles (three km) to and from the highway about every 10 minutes.

Juchitán and Vicinity

Isthmus people associate the name Juchitán with both the town, Juchitán de Zaragoza, and the governmental district that it heads—a domain larger in extent than either the Distrito Federal or each of the four smallest Mexican states. The district of Juchitán (Place of Flowers) ranges from the Chimalapa, the roadless jungle refuge of dozens of Mexico's endangered species, south to the warm Pacific and the rich lagoons that border it.

But like any empire, Juchitán is the sum of its small parts—hidden slices of Mexico that few outsiders know, from the crystalline springs of **Tlacotepec and Laollaga** to the seemingly endless groves of the "world mango capital" at **Zanatepec** and the **vibrant market** and near-continuous **community festivals**—*velas*—of busy, prosperous Juchitán de Zaragoza.

Orientation

Juchitán (pop. 80,000) bustles with commerce all the daylight and early-evening hours. Main streets 16 de Septiembre and 5 de Septiembre steadily conduct a double stream of traffic to and from the north-side Highway 200 crossing. A few blocks to the west, the Río Los Perros (River of the Dogs, for the otters that hunt fish in the river) courses lazily southward, marking downtown Juchitán's western boundary. Traffic focuses about a mile (two km) south of the highway at the town plaza, the **Jardín Central Benito Juárez,** the town's commercial and governmental nucleus. On Calle 16 de Septiembre, on the plaza's east side, the long white classical arcade of the **palacio municipal** fills the entire block, from Calle Efrain Gómez bordering the plaza's north edge to Calle Benito Juárez on the south. Governmental offices occupy the upper floor of the *palacio,* while businesses, crafts booths, and food stalls spread across the bottom. Behind the facade, taking up the entire

THE ISTHMUS

JUCHITÁN

city block east of the plaza, is the town market, Mercado 5 de Septiembre.

SIGHTS

Around the Juchitán Plaza

A fun spot to start off (or end) your day exploring Juchitán is at a table in the graceful old-Mexico patio of Restaurant Casa Grande on Calle Benito Juárez, on the plaza's south side. Here, a hearty breakfast or a cool lunch will invigorate you for yet another few hours of relaxed plaza sightseeing.

Stroll out and admire the fine busts of Benito Juárez on the plaza's east side and Margarita Maza, his wife, on the west side,

by Calle 5 de Septiembre. On the plaza's north side, find the Monument to the Battle of September 5, 1866, where a Mexican eagle and a heroic Benito Juárez commemorate the victory of the ragtag local battalion over a superior French imperial force.

Step east, across Calle 16 de Septiembre, to the **crafts stalls** beneath the northerly (left) half of the *presidencia municipal* arcade. What you don't find downstairs you'll find in an upstairs market foyer. Stroll the aisles and choose from a host of excellent items customarily including, besides the famous Isthmus embroidered skirts and blouses, handwoven *hamacas* (hammocks); leather huaraches and *bolsas* (purses); woven

© BRUCE WHIPPERMAN

Great shade trees grace the Juchitán central plaza.

palm *tenates* and reed *canastas* (baskets), *petates* (mats), and sombreros; and gold-filigree *joyería* (jewelry). You can also find much of the same (besides a riot of flowers) at many of the stalls that line the plaza's north end.

For pottery, walk west along Calle Juárez (which borders the plaza's south side) to the block just west of the plaza. There, along the old town church's rear wall, a lineup of stalls offers an assortment of ceramics, mostly practical traditional housewares, from huge round red *ollas* (jars) and flat *comales* (griddles) to brightly painted piggy banks and flower vases.

Templo de San Vicente Ferrer and Casa de la Cultura

While you're in the vicinity, visit the town's pride, the San Vicente Ferrer church. Reach it by circling the block: Continue west on Calle Juárez, go immediately left at 5 de Mayo, then after one block turn left again at Belisario Domínguez, to the church on the left. Although the church's early history is shrouded in mystery, the present construction appears

by its style to date from the mid-19th century. Its dedication to San Vicente Ferrer, patron of survivors of the sea, appears connected to Juchitán's original founding as a refuge for survivors, perhaps of some ocean disaster, such as a terrible tsunami or hurricane, some time shortly before the conquest. Present-day Juchitecos, inheritors of their patron's zeal and ferocity, celebrate his memory with gusto to match, with no less than eight consecutive *velas,* beginning on the first Saturday of the last 15 days of May.

Across the street from the church, you might linger for a few minutes in the shady side plaza, **Parque Helidoro Charis Castro.** Here stands the bronze bust of Castro, the beloved Juchitecan *maderista* general who led the 13th Juchitecan Battalion in its bloody, but ultimately successful, revolt against dictatorial forces, from 1910 to 1914.

Afterward, look around inside the Casa de la Cultura (tel. 971/711-4589, casacult_istmo5@hotmail.com, 9 A.M.–2 P.M. and 4–8 P.M. Mon.–Fri, 9 A.M.–2 P.M. Sat.), next door, west of the church. The building, originally a Catholic school, became the Casa de la Cultura in 1972, through the efforts of celebrated Oaxaca painter Francisco Toledo. Rooms around the graceful, old-Mexico patio accommodate a café, a small archaeological museum, an art exposition gallery, and a children's library. The reception staff sells a few Spanish-language books of local history and folklore and folk music CDs.

The *Women Warriors*

As an interesting downtown side-street diversion, cross over the Río Los Perros for a look at the intriguing *Women Warriors* sculptures on the west riverbank. Head west along Juárez. Two blocks west of the plaza, from the middle of the river bridge, notice the two tall sculptures of women (in Juchiteca skirts and blouses, of course), about two stories high, in what appears to be a small neighborhood park.

Few local residents seem to know much about them, except that "they are guarding the people from the river." (Although one person did tell me that they were erected by noted sculptor and lover of Juchitán, Miguel Urban.) Get a better view of the sculptures (which, close-up, you'll see are of stainless sheet steel) by accessing the west riverbank from the pedestrian bridge a block upstream (north) from Juárez.

The riverbank is especially pleasant around sunset, when, standing on the Juárez bridge, you might catch a cooling breeze, enjoy the sky colors, and be entertained by the flocks of black grackles flying overhead and scrapping and cackling in riverbank trees as they settle down for the night.

ACCOMMODATIONS
Under $25
Very plain but right at the center of everything is plazafront **Casa de Huéspedes Echazarreta** (Benito Juárez south side, a few doors west of 16 de Septiembre, no phone or email, $10 s, $15 d). It offers about 15 barebones but clean rooms with bath, around a tranquil inner courtyard.

For more space and privacy, check out the 27-room **Hotel Victoria** (2 de Abril 29, tel. 971/711-1558, $18 s or d in one bed, $20 d in two beds with fan; add $5 for a/c), a block east and a block north of the town plaza's northeast corner. What you see is what you get: plain but clean rooms with private, hot-water shower-bath.

Back behind (adjacent east of) the market, a popular town-center choice is the once semideluxe but now rundown **Hotel Lidxi Buixa** (LEED-shee boo-EE-shah, 2 de Abril 79, tel. 971/711-1299 or 971/711-1390, $23 s, $26 d with fans, $24 s, $29 d with a/c). The 26 rooms (not too clean, take a look) all come with cable TV, pool (check to see if it's maintained) and parking. Reservations here (and at the Victoria) are generally necessary because it's very popular with out-of-town vendors, who rise around 5 A.M. to tend their market stalls across the street. Early-morning noises may consequently be a problem.

$25-50
Moving two blocks north from the plaza along 5 de Septiembre, past Miguel Hidalgo, you'll find the welcoming **Hotel Don Alex Lena Real** (16 de Septiembre 48, tel. 971/711-1064 or 971/711-0989, fax 971/711-1064, $38 s or d). The 14 very clean rooms with a choice of king-size bed or a pair of double beds come with air-conditioning, phones, cable TV, and credit cards accepted.

Continuing north, about five blocks from the plaza, find the Hotel Don Alex's sister hotel, the **Hotel López Lena Palace** (16 de Septiembre 70, tel. 971/711-1388, fax 971/711-1389, hotellopezlena@yahoo.com.mx, $34 s, $40 d, $60 t). Builders have included a modicum of extras, such as potted plants, airy staircases, and light, rose-tinted hallways, into the four-story building. The 40 spartan-chic rooms are tiled and very clean, but with barebulb reading lamps. Amenities include cable TV, phones, air-conditioning, a bar, and a reliable restaurant. Credit cards are accepted.

Over $50
Juchitán's most relaxing hotel is the resort-style ◖ **Gran Hotel Santo Domingo** (Crucero, Carretera Panamericana s/n, tel./fax 971/711-1050, 971/711-3642 or 971/711-1959, hsto@prodigy.net.mx, $44 s, $60 d, $73 t), on the highway across from both the bus station and the ingress road to town. The Gran Hotel's choice attraction is an invitingly large and luxurious pool and grassy patio, a welcome refuge for winding down from the heat and bustle. The approximately 60 rooms, in a pair of long, double-storied tiers beyond a tropical entrance foyer, are spare but clean, spacious, high ceilinged, and comfortable, with modern-standard bathrooms, air-conditioning, TV, phones, good restaurant, parking, and credit cards accepted.

FOOD
Juchitán's downtown plaza food stalls do big business all day and half the night. Especially popular with local people are the market *fondas,* bottom level at the south (right) side of the *palacio municipal.* Another, less busy *fonda* spot is on the side plaza Helidoro Charis Castro, a

block south of the main plaza, in front of the San Vicente Ferrer church.

For baked goods, go to **Panadería Nuevo Mundo** (tel. 971/711-1897, 9 A.M.–9 P.M. Mon.–Sat., 9 A.M.–3 P.M. Sun.), on 5 de Septiembre, half a block south of the plaza's southwest corner.

For pizza and spaghetti ($3–9), salads ($2–3), and more, try **Pizzería Gato Montes** (Wildcat Pizza, Colón 7, tel. 971/711-3945, 5 P.M.–midnight), with movies and entertainment starting around 7 P.M. It's a block west of the church between Belisario Domínguez and Juárez.

The class-act plaza-front restaurant, fine for a midday break, is the refined **Restaurant Casa Grande** (Juárez 12, tel. 971/711-3460, 8 A.M.–10 P.M.), in the inner patio of an ex-mansion. The mostly business and upper-class patrons choose from an international menu of soups, salads, and sandwiches ($3–5), meats and pastas ($6–9), and a number of Oaxacan regional specialties, such as *pechuga de pollo zapoteca* (breast of chicken, Zapotec style), *enchiladas de mole negro* (enchiladas with black *mole* sauce), and *chile relleno de picadillo* (chili pepper stuffed with spiced meat; all $6–12); credit cards accepted.

On the other hand, local fish lovers frequent seafood restaurant **Mariscos del Mar** (8:30 A.M.–7 P.M. daily, no phone), one block north of the plaza, at the corner of 16 de Septiembre and Hidalgo, for its long, very correctly Mexican menu of seafood and more. Have it all, including a plethora of clam, oyster, and shrimp cocktails ($3–7); seafood soups, both clear and creamed ($2–4); fish, octopus, squid, lobster, and shrimp (cooked 10 ways, $3–8); and seven styles of *cucarachas* (prawns, $3–6).

For good food in a Mexican Bohemian-style atmosphere, check out **Restaurant Los Novios** (The Sweethearts, tel. 971/712-0555, 7:30 A.M.–6 P.M.), on 5 de Septiembre, a block north of the plaza, just past the corner of Hidalgo. Amidst a colorful gallery of the owners' new-Impressionist-mode art, select from an innovative menu of breakfasts (freshly squeezed orange juice and hotcakes with bacon, $5), spaghetti (*bolognesa*, $4), and fowl (breast of chicken with chipotle sauce, $6).

Alternatively, escape temporarily from Mexico to the coffee shop–style **Restaurant Santa Fe** (tel. 971/711-1545, 7 A.M.–midnight daily except Sun.), at the Highway 200 crossing, across from the Gran Hotel Santo Domingo. In the air-conditioned 1970s-mod atmosphere, enjoy fresh coffee and fruit ($2) followed by tasty eggs, waffles, or pancakes for breakfast ($3–5), several hamburgers or salads ($4–6) for lunch, and, finally, soups, spaghetti, beef, chicken, and fish for dinner ($4–8); credit cards accepted.

ENTERTAINMENT AND EVENTS

Juchitán's substantial excess wealth goes largely to finance an impressive round of parties, locally called *velas*, in honor of a patron saint or a historically or commercially important event. The *velas* are organized and financed by entire barrios, and led by *mayordomos*, usually a well-to-do male head of household, but also including his spouse, children, and all relatives and friends, who usually add up to a major fraction of the population of an entire Juchitán barrio. The *mayordomo* family, together with male and female *capitanes* and their closest friends, make up the *mayordomía*, the core committee responsible for carrying off the celebration.

Customary activities include blossom-decorated church masses, parties in the house of the *mayordomo*, community barbecues, a parade of fruit and flower-laden floats, from which the *capitanas*, dressed like brides in their stunningly embroidered Tehuántepec outfits, throw fruit and gifts to the street-side crowds.

(*Note:* Although the *velas* are local affairs, everyone is invited, and can join the fun by paying a nominal entrance fee, customarily $5–10 per adult.)

In all, Juchitecos celebrate 20 in-town *velas*, which fill streets with merrymakers during the last half of April, virtually the entire month of May, and several days each in June, July, August, and September, a total of about 50 days

THE ISTHMUS

VELAS: FIESTAS OF THE ISTHMUS

The Isthmus *velas* amount to a near-continuous regional party. People stay up all night, sometimes for days on end of feasting, drinking, dancing, and parading with family and friends, many of whom return from afar to renew cherished old relationships. What follows is a short list that includes only the most important Isthmus *velas*. (Note: * especially recommended)

DATE	PLACE	FESTIVAL
January 18-21	Jalapa del Marqués	San Sebastián de las Flores
First Friday of Lent	San Pedro Huamelula	Carnaval
February 20-25	Matías Romero	Vela San Matías
First days of April	San Pedro Tapanatepec	Feria de Mango
April 15	Juchitán	Vela Ique Guia
April 25	Juchitán	Vela Ique Guidxi
April 27	Juchitán	Vela Paso Cru
May 3	Juchitán	Vela Guzebenda
May 3-6	Salina Cruz	Santa Cruz
May 5	Juchitán	Vela Quintu
May 8	Juchitán	Vela Guigu Dixta
May 10	Juchitán	Vela San Pedro Cantarito
May 13	Juchitán	Vela San Isidro Guete
May 15	Juchitán	Vela Guela Bene
May 16	Juchitán	Vela Iguu
Last 15 days of May	Juchitán	*Fiesta de San Vicente Ferrer
	Juchitán	Vela Biadxi
	Juchitán	Vela Calvario
	Juchitán	*Vela Angelica Pipi
	Juchitán	*Vela San Isidro Labrador
	Juchitán	*Vela San Vicente Chico
	Juchitán	*Vela San Vicente Grande
	Juchitán	*Vela de Cheguigo
Last week of May	Tehuántepec	Vela Sandunga
June 16	Juchitán	Vela San Antonio

DATE	PLACE	FESTIVAL
June 24	Juchitán	Vela San Juan Bautista
	Juchitán	Vela Taberneros
	Juchitán	Vela Coheteros
June 24-30	San Pedro Huamelula	Fiesta del Apóstol San Pedro
June 27-30	San Pedro Tapanatepec	Fiesta Patronal de San Pedro
July 21-29	Santiago Laollaga	Fiesta de Santiago Apóstol
July	Juchitán	Vela de los Niños
August 13	Juchitán	Vela Asunción
August 15	Juchitán	Vela San Jacinto
August 13-16	Jalapa del Marqués	Fiesta de la Asunción
August 13-18	Tehuántepec	*Fiesta Patronal del Barrio de Santa María Reoloteca
August 31-September 11	Tehuántepec	*Fiesta del Laborio
September 3	Juchitán	Vela de la Familia Pineda
September 4	Juchitán	Vela de la Familia López
September 5	Juchitán	Vela del Triunfo del Batallón Juchiteco de 1866
	Juchitán	Vela Superior
October 1-4	San Francisco Ixhuatan	Vela del Santa Patrón
December 26	Tehuántepec	*Vela Tehuántepec

© BRUCE WHIPPERMAN

Velas (festivals) usually start off with a *calenda* (procession) in which the women dress up in their finest flowered *huipiles*.

THE ISTHMUS

of celebrating for the entire year. This wouldn't be too excessive if it were not for the approximately 20 obligatory national holidays and the other 30 unmissable *velas* in neighboring Isthmus communities. (See the sidebar *Velas: Fiestas of the Isthmus*.)

Local folks sometimes offer droll commentaries about all this celebrating: "If you go to a *mayordomo* house, I'll tell you what you'll find . . . no bed, no stove, no shoes, just happy people and lots of friends."

Lacking a local fiesta, you might want to take in a film at the genteel art **Cinema Casa Grande** (on the plaza, south side, tel. 971-711/1074, mid- to late afternoons daily except Mon.). Enter past the patio Restaurant Casa Grande. Or, alternatively, check out the evening entertainment, beginning around 7 P.M., at the **Pizzeria Gato Montes** (see the *Food* section, preceding, for details).

INFORMATION AND SERVICES
Tourist Information
The most reliable local government *Turismo* office is in Tehuántepec. See *Information* in the *Tehuántepec and Vicinity* section.

Alternatively, in Juchitán, try travel agent **Zarymar** (5 de Septiembre 100B, tel. 971/711-2867), several blocks north of the plaza, for information, airline tickets, and car rentals.

Money
A number of downtown banks, which all have ATMs, help manage Juchitecos' money. They'll also change your money into pesos or U.S. dollars. Best choice for its long hours is **HSBC** (16 de Septiembre 52, tel. 971/712-0188, 9 A.M.–7 P.M. Mon.–Sat.), three blocks north of the plaza. Also a good bet is **Banorte** (Efrain Gómez 19, tel. 971/711-1160 or 971/711-3482, 9 A.M.–4 P.M. Mon.–Fri., 10 A.M.–2 P.M. Sat.), half a block west of the plaza's northwest corner. Third choice goes to **Banco Santander Serfin** (tel./fax 971/711-2000, 9 A.M.–5 P.M. Mon.–Fri.), at the corner of Belasario Domínguez and the extension of 16 de Septiembre, one block south of the *presidencia municipal*.

Communications
The *correo* (tel. 971/711-1272, 8 A.M.–7 P.M. Mon.–Fri., 9 A.M.–noon Sat.) is at the plaza's northeast corner, just west of the *presidencia municipal*. For a public fax or a money order, the *telecomunicaciones* (tel. 971/711-1040 or 971/712-0966, 8 A.M.–7 P.M. Mon.–Fri., 9 A.M.–noon Sat.) is on Aldama, four blocks west of 16 de Septiembre.

Internet access is available at either **La Net@.com** (tel. 971/711-0172, 9 A.M.–10 P.M. daily), on Efrain Gómez, half a block west of the plaza's northwest corner; or **Internet VIP** (16 de Sept. 22, no phone, 8:30 A.M.–8:30 P.M. daily), a block and a half north of the plaza.

Photography and Cameras
A few downtown photo shops offer both digital and film cameras and supplies and services. Try either **Foto Alta Konica** (tel. 971/711-4428, 9 A.M.–9 P.M. Mon.–Sat.), on 16 de Septiembre, east side, just north of the plaza; or **Foto Revolado Indomitable** (formerly Centro Fotográfico, 8 A.M.–8 P.M. Mon.–Sat.), on 2 de Abril, east side, a few doors before Hidalgo (a block east and a block north from the plaza's northeast corner).

Health and Emergencies
A ready source of nonprescription medicines and drugs is the 24-hour **Farmacia 24 Horas** (tel. 971/711-0312 or 971/711-0316), corner of Efrain Gómez and 2 de Abril, one block behind the north side of the *presidencia municipal*. Alternatively, go to **Farmacia Similares** (Generic Pharmacy, tel. 971/711-3126, 9 A.M.–10 P.M. daily), on 5 de Septiembre, a block south of the plaza's southwest corner.

A number of doctors maintain offices near the plaza. For example, general physician–surgeons Dr. Ruben Calvo López and Dr. Carlos Alonso Ruiz and gynecologist Doctora Anabel López Ruiz hold regular consulting hours at **Clínica San Fernando** (tel. 971/711-1569), on 16 de Septiembre between Efrain Gómez and Hidalgo, half a block north of the plaza's northeast corner.

Alternatively, go to the **Clínica Nuestra**

kid-friendly Farmacia Similares advertising

Señora de Exaltación (tel. 971/711-1378), with a very professional pharmacy, on 5 de Septiembre, east side, half a block north of the plaza. Here, general practitioner Doctor Guillermo Gonzales and gynecologist Doctora Catalina Martínez partner with several other medical specialists on call.

In a medical emergency, follow your hotel's recommendation or hire a taxi to the **General Hospital Dr. Macedonio Benítez Fuentes** (tel. 971/711-1441 or 971/711-1985), downtown on Efrain Gómez near the plaza.

In case of police or fire emergency, dial 066, the public crisis number.

Laundry

One of Juchitán's few downtown laundries is **Lavandería Puebla** (tel. 971/711-1745, 8 A.M.–7:30 P.M. daily except Sun.), at the corner of Abásolo and the Iglesia Angelica Pipi. Find it, from the plaza's northwest corner, by walking two blocks west, turning right onto Cinco de Mayo, and continuing six blocks

north to the laundry, just south of the petite neighborhood church, Iglesia Pipi.

GETTING THERE AND AWAY
By Bus

A modern long-distance *camionera central* (central bus station), at the Highway 190/200 crossing north of downtown, is the point of departure for all of the first-class and most of the second-class bus connections with both Oaxaca and national destinations. First- and second-class lines service customers from separate waiting rooms (first-class on the left, second-class on the right). The busy but clean station has snack stores and luggage-check service. Long-distance telephone and fax is available at a small office in the second-class waiting room.

Autobuses del Oriente (ADO) and affiliated lines (tel. 971/711-2565 or 971/711-1022) offer direct first-class connections north with Gulf of Mexico destinations Minatitlán, Coatzacoalcos, Villahermosa, Palenque, Merida, Cancun, and Tulum; northwest with Oaxaca City, Mexico City, Veracruz, and Tampico. Additionally, first-class carrier **Omnibus Cristóbal Colón** (OCC) (tel. 971/711-2565) and its luxury-class subsidiary, Plus, offer connections northwest with Oaxaca City, Puebla, Mexico City, and Veracruz; southwest with Salina Cruz, Bahías de Huatulco, Pochutla (Puerto Ángel), and Puerto Escondido; and east with Chiapas destinations of Tuxtla Gutiérrez, San Cristóbal las Casas, and Tapachula, at the Guatemala border.

Second-class carriers include **Autobuses del Oriente** (ADO), which offers connections north with Coatzacoalcos; southwest with Tehuántepec and Salina Cruz; and east with Tapanatepec, including all intermediate destinations. Additionally, **Autobuses Unidos** (AU) offers second-class connections northwest with Tuxtepec, Puebla, Mexico City, Orizaba, and Veracruz; and southwest with Tehuántepec and Salina Cruz, including many intermediate destinations. Moreover, **Sur** offers second-class connections north with

THE ISTHMUS

Coatzacoalcos; northwest with Oaxaca City; southwest with Bahías de Huatulco; and east with Tapanatepec and Tapachula, including intermediate destinations.

Semi-local bus connections with adjacent towns are available via the green, white, and yellow **Autotransportes Istmeños** across the side street, south, less than a block toward town from the *camionera central.*

Mostly second-class **Fletes y Pasajes** buses operate out of a separate terminal, also at the Highway 190/200 crossing but on the west side, adjacent to the Restaurant Santa Fe. Buses connect east with Chiapas destinations of Tuxtla Gutiérrez, Tapachula, and the Guatemala border; northwest, with Oaxaca City, Puebla, and Mexico City; and north with Tuxtepec and Minatitlán.

By Car

Drivers have the same highway choices and destinations as listed in *Getting There and Around* in the Tehuántepec section. Simply subtract 30 minutes driving time (and 17 miles/27 km distance) for northerly and easterly trips; add the same for northwesterly and southwesterly trips. In Juchitán, fill up with gasoline at the Pemex *gasolinera* at the Highway 190/200 town ingress crossing, next to the bus station.

North of Juchitán

A number of uniquely interesting destinations await travelers willing to venture into the foothill hinterland northwest and north of Juchitán. Foremost among them are the storied former royal Zapotec bathing **springs** that well up, blue and crystalline, at Tlacotepec and Laollaga, an hour's travel northwest of Juchitán.

Equally ripe for exploring is the stalactite-studded **limestone cave** near the town of Santo Domingo Petapa, together with the singularly successful cooperative **company town at Lagunas,** about an hour and a half north of Juchitán.

Each of these excursions can be enjoyed from Juchitán in a leisurely day by car or a long day by bus.

THE SPRINGS AT TLACOTEPEC AND LAOLLAGA

Both of these bathing resorts were part of the territory of the Zapotec royal family of King Cosijoeza. He often used the springs as a refuge during his protracted war with Aztec emperor Ahuitzotl during the 1490s. A famous traditional story recounts how love resolved the bloody conflict. Tiring of the struggle, Ahuitzotl proposed a peace pact. In exchange for allowing Aztec traders and envoys to pass through the Isthmus lands, Cosijoeza would receive Aztec princess Coyollicatzin in marriage. One day, meditating over the proposition while bathing in the Tlacotepec spring, Cosijoeza was awestruck by a stunning apparition of Coyollicatzin. Despite his apprehension, Coyollicatzin's apparition enchanted him with her beauty. Thus persuaded, Cosijoeza soon took Coyollicatzin in marriage, sealing the pact between the two nations.

Their marriage was a happy one. Children resulted, and Cosijoeza passed the springs at Tlacotepec and Laollaga to their son Cosijopí, the king of the Isthmus lands, and their daughter, Princess Donaji, both of whom continued to exercise authority after the conquest.

⟨ Balneario Tlacotepec

Storied Princess Donaji (see the sidebar *The Tragic Story of Princess Donaji* in *The Valley of Oaxaca* chapter), who after the conquest was baptized as Magdalena Donaji, donated both her Christian name and the springs and royal park at Tlacotepec to the local community, still known as Magdalena Tlacotepec.

Today, the town's springs and surrounding sanctuary are a unique asset for all Istmeño

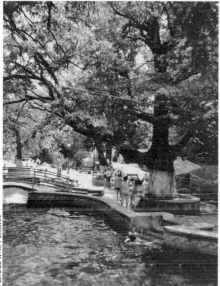
Balneario Tlacotepec, once a playground for the Tehuántepec nobility

families to enjoy, which they do en masse on sunny Sundays and holidays. The source, a clear, cool underground river, wells up from a rocky basin and fills a long, meandering, aqua-blue swimming hole. Shoals of little fish that nibble and tickle your feet hide in crannies and flit along the sandy bottom. Shady mango trees overhang the bank and spread over a rustic public strolling ground on one side. On the other, entrance side, food stalls surround a parking area.

Here you can park your (self-contained) trailer or RV or set up a tent and stay a spell, walking into the surrounding hills in the morning to enjoy wildlife and wildflowers and splashing in the cool spring in the afternoons. Custodial personnel, who keep the site clean and secure, collect nominal fees for parking and camping.

Santiago Laollaga

Laollaga (lah-oh-YAH-gah) springs mark the northern boundary of the petite *municipio* of Santiago Laollaga, which you pass through on your way to the springs. A big parking lot overlooks the main series of pools (concrete basins) built into the rocky downhill channel of the Río Laollaga. Shady trees overhang the pools, and a pair of permanent open-air *comedores* on the riverbank serve drinks and food.

Visitors equipped with a self-contained trailer or RV might enjoy a stay, parking in the lot for a day or two. Fees run only a few dollars a day. Unfortunately, the water at the main pools is sometimes a bit tainted by soap from folks washing clothes upstream. You can assure pure water by following the river a quarter mile (0.5 km) upstream to its source, a natural *ojo de agua* spring welling from the base of the hills. Here, great shady trees spread over a sandy riverbank, ripe for tent camping if you don't mind sharing the spot with a few townsfolk on weekdays, more on weekends.

Laollaga diversions might include strolls around the town and along dirt roads and trails, into the summer-lush native tropical woodlands. By local bus or car, you could explore farther afield, along the good gravel road (at the northeast corner of town, where you made your last turn left) threading the green-forested Río Los Perros valley and foothill country 15 miles (25 km) northwest to remote Santa María Guienagati.

Arrive during the last 10 days in July and join Laollaga's big **Fiesta de Santiago Apóstol** (July 20–30), which includes four separate *velas*, with fireworks, carnival rides and games, *regada* (fruit-throwing), dances, and *mojigangos* (giant dancing figures).

Small town stores can supply basic groceries. Pharmacies, a private doctor, a *centro de salud*, a post office, and a *caseta larga distancia* can provide essential services.

Getting There

Get to Tlacotepec and Laollaga from Juchitán via Ixtepec, half an hour north of Juchitán. The easiest and cheapest way to go is by one of the Ixtepec-labeled local buses that frequently head north from the Highway 190 crossing in Juchitán, across the street from the main bus station and the gas station. Half an hour

© BRUCE WHIPPERMAN

THE ISTHMUS

later, at Ixtepec, transfer to the blue-and-white Tlacotepec- or Laollaga-labeled local bus.

It's more complicated, but possible, to make your way by car. From the Highway 190/200 crossing at Juchitán, mark your odometer and head north across Highway 190/200, continuing through Ixtaltepec (five miles/eight km) to the railroad tracks at Ixtepec (9.7 miles/15.6 km). Immediately after crossing the tracks, turn left. After one block, turn right at Ixtepec's main street, Calle 16 de Septiembre. Continue five blocks (0.3 mile/0.5 km) and turn left (west) at Galeana (10 miles/16.1 km). Continue west; follow the curve right after about a mile, then after two blocks, at the police post on the right, curve left. Continue about another mile, and at a Y-intersection (11.9 miles/19.2 km) go left and continue, following the Balneario signs to the Tlacotepec springs, a total of about 18 miles (29 km).

Alternatively, for Laollaga, bear right at the abovementioned Y intersection and continue through Chihuitán (turn left at the village corner, at 16.2 miles/26.1 km) to Santiago Laollaga village center (19.2 miles/31 km). Turn right and continue a block, pass over a bridge, and, a block or two farther, at the *presidencia municipal,* turn left. Continue half a mile to the Ojo de Agua sign, turn left and continue to the *balneario* entrance after about three blocks. If you get lost, ask a shopkeeper (or point to this in your guide: *"¿Donde está El Balneario Laollaga?"* (dohn-DAY ays-TAH AYL bal-nee-AH-reeoh lah-oh-YAH-gah?), "Where is the Balneario Laollaga?).

LAGUNAS: COMPANY TOWN

If success can be measured by longevity, the industrial cooperative town of Lagunas, which began producing cement in 1942, has

© BRUCE WHIPPERMAN

The cement-manufacturing town of Lagunas seems as perfectly ordered as an industrial town could possibly be.

NORTH OF JUCHITÁN** **349**

earned its plaudits. Moreover, the unique experiment it represents seems as robust as ever. The idea began back in the 1930s, when investors were eager to exploit a mountain of local limestone that towered conveniently beside the cross-isthmus rail line. The era was, however, that of reformist President Lázaro Cárdenas, when the star of socialism was rising over Mexico from the east. The enterprise must be a cooperative, the government demanded. Investors, realizing the project's unique prospects, agreed, and Cruz Azul, a uniquely Mexican private-public cooperative, was born.

Today, the great mill beside the railroad tracks hums all day and night, producing millions of tons of cement yearly for projects from Chile to Canada. Moreover, besides supporting the livelihoods of thousands of families in the entire local hinterland, the Lagunas mill (judging from the tidy, dust-free town) appears to produce little of the cement dust that has debilitated cement-mill workers, especially in third-world countries, all over the globe.

At the town center, across the tracks from the mill, a monument erected by the workers (the Cooperadores de La Cruz Azul) honors Guillermo Alvarez, Cruz Azul's guiding light, with a pair of eternally flickering electric lamps.

Along Avenida Cooperativismo facing the plant stand the town Banamex branch, the *correo, telecomunicaciones,* and the plant superintendent's office. Badged workers, all in pressed khakis and hard hats, walk with purpose along the sidewalks. Some turn and continue along the town's main street, Avenida Cruz Azul, and continue past the hamburger shop, *centro comercial* (company store), an immaculate bakery, and the big church, dedicated to the Virgin of Guadalupe. From the commercial center, tree-lined residential streets extend past schools, a hospital, and tidy concrete houses with some of Mexico's rare, American-style unfenced yards with lawns.

SANTO DOMINGO PETAPA: LIMESTONE CAVE

Several miles past Lagunas, Santo Domingo Petapa (pop. 2,000) marks the end of the pavement. Unless you arrive during a national holiday or the August 1–4 town festival in honor of Santo Domingo, Petapa will appear as a typical sleepy Oaxaca country town. Petapa does have, however, at least one claim to fame, and that is the grand limestone cavern on the mountainside two miles (three km) beyond the town.

You will need both local permission and a local guide. The former municipal president *(president municipal)* Homero Espinoza offers to arrange both. Reach him (in Spanish, ask your hotel desk clerk to call) at tel. 972/723-4058, and arrange a date and time. If possible, Homero will arrange a guide (most likely locally experienced Ismael Juárez). Offer to pay: maybe about $40 for the guide and $20 for Espinoza.

Lacking prior arrangement, you might be able to accomplish the same directly by arriving at the *presidencia municipal* by 10 A.M. and asking for someone to guide you around the cave. You could smooth all this along by writing a letter, weeks in advance, in Spanish, addressed to the Presidente Municipal, Santo Domingo Petapa, Oaxaca, 70350, telling your date and time of arrival and that you'd be happy to pay for an experienced guide to show you the cave. Alternatively, two or three days in advance you could ask your hotel desk clerk to make the same request by telephoning the Petapa *presidencia municipal* (tel. 972/723-4068).

These preparations will give you a good chance of seeing the inside of the cave. Come equipped with sturdy shoes, hard hats (at least plastic), and, if possible, super-bright three- or four-celled flashlights. The cave, 1–2 hours' walk west of town, is large, with a towering, cathedral-like entry portal and a river flowing from its mouth. Your exploration inside will take at least two hours and extend past stalagmites and stalactites approximately half a mile (one km) into the mountainside.

THE ISTHMUS

East of Juchitán

From south to north, the grand Isthmus landscape east of Juchitán gradually changes through three distinctive panoramas. In the south, at the Pacific Ocean, the Isthmus begins as three grand, glassy lagoons, the Laguna Superior and Inferior on the west side and the Mar Muerto ("Dead Sea") on the east. This is the home ground of the Huave people, driven to the Isthmus's salty edge an age ago by the Zapotecs, to make their living mostly from the sea. North of that lies the fertile, most prized crescent of pastures, fields, and orchards of the sizable towns of Niltepec, Zanatepec, and Tapanatepec, and the Pan-American Highway, which connects them all. Farther north rise the trans-isthmus mountains, the Sierra Atravesada, heartland of the Chimalapa, a wild kingdom of sylvan forests, rushing rivers, and deep, shadowed canyons, a final refuge of rare, endangered, and yet-to-be-discovered species of plants and animals.

First access to all this is by the Pan-American Highway east of Juchitán, then by side roads north and south from junctions such as La Venta, Zanatepec, and Tapanatepec.

LA VENTA

La Venta (The Windy Place), about 18 miles (29 km) east of Juchitán, lives up to its name, so much so that the Comisión Federal de Electricidad has installed seven towering wind generators at the very spot. The ultramodern gleaming windmills, visible from the highway, whir obediently, doing their good work.

A side road leads to the windmills' base, where a display explains the project. So far, the seven 10-story generators have been able to average a continuous 500 kilowatts of power, enough for a modern Mexican village of 500 modern family homes. Currently, 500 kilowatts of electric power sells for about $1,000 per day, implying that each of the 500 families would have to fork out about $2 a day, $60 a month, for such power. Thus the experiment appears to be showing that although

not presently affordable for most Oaxacans, Mexican wind power appears promising for industry now and for home use in a future, more prosperous Mexico.

Get to La Venta by eastbound **ADO, Cristóbal Colón,** or **Sur** bus, from either of the central terminals at Tehuántepec or Juchitán. Drivers, simply head west half an hour along Highway 190/200 to La Venta.

The Chimalapa

A rough but mostly paved side road leads north from La Venta to the backcountry Chimalapa jumping-off point villages of **San Miguel Chimalapa** (14 miles/23 km) and Cuauhtémoc (17 miles/27 km). The immense million-acre Chimalapa de facto wilderness is the communal property of two Zoque-speaking indigenous communities headquartered, respectively, at San Miguel Chimalapa and the more remote **San Martín Chimalapa,** 30 rough miles (48 km) north from the Highway 185 junction at El Mezquite.

The Chimalapa Zoque people are rightly suspicious of strangers, especially now that their lands have become one of Mexico's few remaining storehouses of precious tropical hardwoods, endangered animals, and scarce minerals. Legitimate visitors to the Chimalapa wilderness, if any are allowed at all, are strictly licensed by state and local authorities and must be accompanied by community guides. If you're interested in hiking and camping in the Chimalapa, first contact the Oaxaca state tourism office in Oaxaca City (Murguia 206, tel. 951/516-0123, info@aoaxaca.com).

UNIÓN DE HIDALGO

This fair-sized *municipio* is one of the main gateways to the rich fishing grounds and tiny Huave-speaking beach villages of the **Laguna Superior.** At the end of an approximately seven-mile (11-km) mostly paved but bumpy road, you'll arrive at the big town plaza. In the vicinity you'll find groceries (**Abarrotes**

Sánchez, Altamirano 12), a neglected hotel (the **Diush'i Nga'a Naroohba'a,** at the corner of Leona Vicario Sur and Matamoros Oriente), a pharmacy (**Farmacia San Isidro,** Nicolas Bravo 13 Oriente), police (at the *palacio municipal*), a *correo,* and a *telecomunicaciones* office.

Although you'll most likely be passing through Unión de Hidalgo on the way to somewhere else, you can join the festivities (processions, mass barbecues, dancing, fruit- and gift-throwing *regadas,* carnival games and rides) if you arrive during one of the several town *velas.* The fun begins in April with the **Vela de los Pescadores** (Festival of the Fisherfolk) and continues on May 3 with the **Vela de Santa Cruz** during the *quincena* (second 15 days) of May, *velas* honor San Vicente Chico and San Vicente Ferrer Grande. Later come the *velas* in honor of San Isidro the Farmer, Santa María Santísima, and San Pedro Apóstol, June 26–30. During the first days of August, townsfolk honor Santo Domingo de Guzmán, and September 27–30 they celebrate the town's founding. Finally, they celebrate Santa Cecilia on November 22 and the Virgin of Guadalupe on December 12.

From Juchitán, get to Unión Hidalgo from the east-side Unión Hidalgo bus terminal. Best hire a taxi to take you (from the plaza, about 10 blocks along 16 de Septiembre to Calle 20 de Noviembre, thence right, east, about seven blocks, over the railroad tracks, and bear left along the gravel road a few more blocks to the terminal).

By car from Juchitán, follow Avenida 20 de Noviembre as described in the previous paragraph, past the Unión Hidalgo bus terminal. Continue straight ahead immediately onto the paved road that continues 12 miles (20 km) along the railroad track to Unión Hidalgo.

PLAYA COPALITO AND SAN DIONISIO DEL MAR

From Unión de Hidalgo, turn south and continue through Chicapa de Castro a total of about 23 miles (37 km) to Playa Copalito (Little Copal Tree Beach), a tiny (but with electricity) fishing village of thatched houses

and Huave-speaking people. A long, sandy beach built of myriad wave-washed mussel and clam shells winds along the oft mirror-smooth Laguna Superior. Motorboats and *canoas* recline lazily on the beach. A few shoreline *copal* trees provide a bit of shade, and grassy (during the summer rainy season) spaces appear fine for RV parking or tent camping.

Here, the main work for locals and diversion for visitors is fishing. *Lanchas* routinely return with a dozen one- or two-pound *lisa* (mullet), *sierra* (mackerel), or pompano. Fishermen are willing to take visitors on a half-day fishing excursion or exploration for about $15.

Since Playa Copalito is an idyllic but isolated little place, campers should arrive well equipped with tent, food, and water. Bring insect repellent; mosquitoes may be fierce certain times of the year (although they weren't a problem one wet September). Moreover, security is good here, by virtue of the local Marine detachment, right in town.

As for food, although a few village stores can probably supply some essentials, best be prepared with your own fresh fruits and vegetables. The homey *palapa* **Restaurant Playa Copalita** (8 A.M.–7 P.M. daily, $4–10) of the friendly Pinedo Castellanos family (dad Señor Martimiano, mom Señora Reynalda, and kids Celia and Leticia), *a su servicio,* will be happy to provide fresh fish dinners.

While you're in the vicinity, the pilgrimage town of San Dionisio del Mar would certainly be worth a visit. The miraculous image of San Dionisio at the town church (on the east end of town) attracts thousands of pilgrims yearly, mostly for the October 6–10 festival. Things get started right away on October 6, when a carnival sets up and food stalls begin serving traditional *atole* (a nonalcoholic corn-juice drink) and tamales for the arriving pilgrims. The next day, the *mayordomía* officials crown the queen, while everyone enjoys a community dance and barbecue at the house of the *mayordomo.* Dances continue for the next two nights, punctuated by processions with fruit and gifts thrown to the celebrants, and nightly fireworks paint the sky red, blue, and green. A basic guesthouse, **Casa**

de Huéspedes San Dionosio (at the southeast edge of the village, $5 pp, $15 pp during festival) is available for separate male and female dormitory accommodations, each with separate, shared tepid-water baths.

Getting There and Away

Get to Copalita and San Dionisio via Unión Hidalgo direct from Juchitán or La Venta. Bus travelers, catch the green bus direct to San Dionisio and Copalita at the Unión Hidalgo bus terminal in Juchitán.

Drivers heading eastbound, in Unión Hidalgo turn right (south) at the Chicapa de Castro sign. Continue another two miles (three km) to Chicapa de Castro. There, turn left in mid-village and continue southeast another 10 miles (16 km) to Copalita (turn right at the dirt road at the edge of San Dionisio) or San Dionisio (continue to the church, at the east end of town), a total of about 24 miles (39 km) from Juchitán.

You can also get to Copalita and San Dionisio by bus from La Venta. At La Venta, transfer to a local bus or *colectivo* south half an hour to Unión de Hidalgo, then transfer to the bus bound for San Dionisio–Copalita, via Chicapa de Castro. About 45 bumpy minutes later, get off at the west edge of San Dionisio at the Playa Copalito right side road (walk about one mile/two km) or continue ahead to San Dionisio.

From La Venta by car or RV, set your odometer as you head south from Highway 190/200 on the side road to Unión de Hidalgo. At 7.2 miles (11.6 km), make your way through the town, asking townsfolk "¿El camino a Chicapa?" ("The way to Chicapa?"). Arrive at Chicapa del Castro (11 miles/17.5 km), where you turn left, heading southeast toward San Dionisio. After a total of 21.6 miles (34.8 km), turn right at the edge of San Dionisio, at the dirt road to Playa Copalito (one mile/two km farther), or continue into San Dionisio del Mar, a total of about 22 miles (35 km), to the church at the east end of town.

SANTO DOMINGO ZANATEPEC

The key country town of Santo Domingo Zanatepec (pop. 10,000), on Highway 190 about 54 miles (87 km) east of Juchitán, is the point of departure for the wild and spectacularly steep Zanatepec River Canyon. There, accompanied by a guide, you can bask in a hot spring and hike to a pair of wilderness lakes.

Zanatepec, moreover, has a restaurant and hotel. For a break, stop by the mango-shaded **Restaurant Nadxielly** (tel. 994/721-0049, 6 A.M.–midnight daily), where for a few pesos you can eat all the mangos you want during April and May. The family-run establishment, well marked on the highway's north side, offers good home-style *comidas*.

Next door stands the basic **Hotel San Rafael** (Santa Domingo Zanatepec, tel. 994/721-0049, $15 s or d, $20 t with fan, $30 s, d, or t with a/c). The 20 rooms are plain but clean; parking is included.

Zanatepec can provide a number of goods and services through establishments located mostly along main street Hidalgo, which heads north from the highway. Get groceries at **Abarrotes Eli** (Hidalgo s/n, 8 A.M.–8 P.M. daily); medicines and medical consultations with **Dr. Horacio Hernández** (8 A.M.–2 P.M. and 4–6 P.M. Mon.–Sat.) at his *farmacia* on Hidalgo; *telecomunicaciones* (tel. 994/721-0142, 9 A.M.–3:30 P.M. Mon.–Fri.) and *correo* both at Hidalgo 200, next to the *presidencia municipal;* and *policía* at the *presidencia municipal* (Hidalgo 198, tel. 994/721-0260).

The Canyon of the Río Zanatepec

The hotel also serves as contact point for guide **Hermillo Toledo,** who leads parties on excursions into the Río Zanatepec Canyon during the December–May dry season. During the rainy season, the river may be too high. Access from the highway is by a gravel road to the village of Agua Caliente (nine miles/14 km); from there, visit the **warm spring,** then continue walking (about two hours) up the canyon to a pair of small lakes, the Lago del Sol (Lake of the Sun) and Lago de la Luna (Lake of the Moon). Options include expert-level rock climbing, wildlife-viewing, fishing, and wilderness camping by the river or the lakes. Expect to pay Hermillo about $30 per day, including food, for his services. Contact him through his brother, Manuel Toledo, who works at the Hotel San Rafael.

SAN PEDRO TAPANATEPEC

"Mango Capital of the World" San Pedro Tapanatepec (pop. 15,000), besides being a main access point for Rincón Juárez on the Mar Muerto, also has a number of highway-side hotels, restaurants, and services. Tapanatepec food, lodging, and services are split about evenly between the highway and the downtown, which stretches about four blocks east–west a few blocks south of the highway.

Accommodations and Food

A trio of acceptable country hotels offer lodging in Tapanatepec. Fanciest is the **Hotel Casablanca** (tel. 994/721-8039, $25 s, $35 d with fan, $30 s, $40 d with a/c), downtown on the town plaza, at Calle Melendez. The Casablanca offers about 10 comfortably furnished rooms, with private shower-baths, for about. Find it in the main business district, about four blocks south of the highway.

Back on the highway, second choice goes to **Hotel Misión** (Carretera Panamericana Km 924, tel. 994/721-8133 or 994/721-8009, $20 s or d with fan, $35 s, $40 d with a/c). The approximately 35 basic bare-bulb but clean rooms are in a motel-style layout with parking spaces in front of units. All rooms have tepid-water shower-baths and cable TV, but credit cards are not accepted. The hotel does offer relief from highway truck noise, if you get a room in the rear away from the highway. The Hotel Misión would be my first choice if the big shady pool in the rear is functioning. Check to see if it is.

Also acceptable, partly because of its good, longer-hours restaurant, is the **Posada Flor** (Carretera Panamericana Km 924, tel. 994/721-8047, $13 s, $18 d with fan, $30 s, $40 d with a/c), across the highway, on the north side, from the Hotel Misión. The approximately 15 basic but clean rooms (by the truck-noisy highway, however, so use ear plugs) have tepid-water shower-baths, cable TV, and parking, but credit cards are not accepted.

Any time other than the Fería del Mango (Mango Fair, first week of April) or the Fiesta Patronal de San Pedro (June 27–30), the hotels would not ordinarily require a reservation, provided you arrive before dark.

Groceries are conveniently available at markets on the highway, such as **Abarrotes La Flor** (tel. 994/721-8282, 8 A.M.–9 P.M. daily). First choice for a meal in Tapanatepec goes to the restaurant of the motel-style **Posada Flor** (on the north side of the highway, east end, tel. 994/721-8047, 8 A.M.–10 P.M. daily, $4–8). Second choice goes to the similarly good restaurant at the **Hotel Misión** (tel. 994/721-8133 or 994/721-8009, 8 A.M.–7 P.M. daily, $4–8).

Services

Most of Tapanatepec's service establishments are either on the highway or along the main business street, Calle Martín Melendez, parallel and about four blocks south of the highway. For money, find **Banamex** (M. Melendez 48, 9 A.M.–4 P.M. Mon.–Fri.) with ATM; for medicines, go to one of the pharmacies on the highway, or **Farmacia Espinoza** (M. Melendez 78, tel. 994/721-8192, 7 A.M.–9 P.M.). A doctor is on duty 24 hours at the **Seguro Social** clinic (16 de Septiembre 47, tel. 994/721-8119).

For a telephone, use one of the card-operated public telephones (Ladatel cards widely purchasable), on the highway and downtown. The *correo* (tel. 994/721-8215, 9 A.M. 3 P.M. Mon.–Fri.) and *telecomunicaciones* (same hours) are both on Avenida Juárez, by the *presidencia municipal* (tel. 994/721-8160). Find the **Policía Federal de Caminos** (Federal Highway Patrol, tel. 994/721-8313) on the highway.

RINCÓN JUÁREZ AND THE MAR MUERTO

Adventurers might enjoy exploring what Istmeños call the Mar Muerto, in contrast with what they call the Mar Vivo (the open ocean). Head out from Tapanatepec south about 14 miles (23 km) by a good paved road to Rincón Juárez village (pop. 1,000). Three or four seafood *palapas* line a sandy beach lapped by the gentle waves of a spreading, silvery sea. Life

THE ISTHMUS

© BRUCE WHIPPERMAN

hog heaven, at Rincón Juárez

follows the drowsy rhythms of daylight and darkness, wind and tides. Early mornings, fishermen load their nets and paddle silently out in canoes or buzz out in motorboats to try their luck. Usually, they return with about a 20-pound catch, possibly including jumbo shrimp, clams, or fish for sale to the wholesalers whose trucks arrive in early afternoon.

Visitors also can take pleasure from their own quiet routine, enjoying sunrises and sunsets, watching the flocks of pelicans, cormorants, herons, and lovely flamingo-like roseate spoonbills, and exploring the lagoon either on foot or by boat. Fishermen are willing to take parties out for wildlife-viewing or fishing excursions (expect to pay about $30 for half a day). Be prepared with your own binoculars and fishing tackle. Alternatively, launch your own boat or inflated raft right on the beach.

The prettiest spot on the Rincón Juárez shoreline is on the eastern side, at *palapa* **Restaurant Chabelita,** (9 A.M.–7 P.M. daily, $5–10) with good *lisa* (mullet) and shrimp lunches and dinners and affording a view of canoes slipping

leisurely along the glassy water. If you're planning on staying, best come supplied with fruits and vegetables and drinking water.

Unfortunately, however, despite its calm water, the Rincón Juárez immediate shoreline is useless for most beach diversions because the bottom is coated with muddy black ooze, probably related to the reason that the local body of water is called the Mar Muerto.

Fortunately, for adventurous travelers who enjoy the delights of country Mexico, there's an alternative, at **Colonia Guadalupe** village, on the shoreline about a mile east (left as you face the water). There the sandy beach and lagoon floor are clean and welcoming, and you can kick back and enjoy the charms of the beach village, with a sprinkling of fisherfolks' houses and shady *palapas* spread along a sandy spit. Offshore, seagulls and pelicans swoop and dive, and along the inland side lagoon hosts of cormorants, herons, and white ibis stalk, cackle, and preen.

The best-organized spot seems to be **Balneario Playa Sol,** with a sandy, albeit narrow, beachfront, with a clean sandy bottom that extends at least a few hundred feet off-shore. Meals are available in the Playa Sol's *palapa* restaurant, there are hammocks in the shade, and a bit of space for tenting and self-contained RV parking. Ask if someone rents horses or can supply a *canoa* or motor *lancha* for a fishing excursion. With your own rubber boat, canoe, motorboat, or kayak you could explore the Mar Muerto to your heart's content.

Other Practicalities

Back in Rincón Juárez, a restaurant-store, **Los Cocos,** provides home-cooked *comidas* and basic groceries.

Tenting and RV camping promises to be fine anywhere along the local beach for the foreseeable future. Plenty of shoreline trees provide shade and convenient branches, fine for hammocks.

Get to Rincón Juárez by bus (Tapanatepec-bound first- or second-class) from either the Juchitán or Tehuántepec central terminals. At Tapanatepec, from the highway, continue south via *colectivo* ($5) to Rincón Juárez.

By car, the Rincón Juárez trip requires about two hours, one way, from Juchitán. Set your odometer at the Juchitán Highway 190/200 crossing by the Pemex gas station. Continue east along the highway about two hours to Tapanatepec. After a total of 67 miles (108 km) (or 13 miles/21 km from Hotel San Rafael in Zanatepec), in the middle of Tapanatepec you reach the paved highway turnoff road for Rincón Juárez on the right. Continue through the town and over the only river-crossing bridge. Continue along another 14 miles (23 km) of paved road to Rincón Juárez, a total of about 74 miles (119 km) from Juchitán.

Salina Cruz and Vicinity

Salina Cruz was important long before the conquest. The *salinas* (salt-producing ponds), where many generations of native people had been harvesting salt for trade, attracted Hernán Cortés very soon after his arrival in Mexico. He also recognized Salina Cruz's strategic position on the Isthmus, where the long-sought route to China was accessible, not by a torturous trans-Sierra journey but by a short, easy passage over the narrow, low Isthmus. Cortés lost no time in acquiring the *salinas* as part of his personal domain and building ships on nearby Playa La Ventosa with which to explore the Pacific.

His efforts have been amplified by successive generations. Beginning in the 19th century and continuing to the present day, the Isthmus regularly tempts canal builders wanting to carve a sea route between the Atlantic and Pacific. President Juárez's government settled for a rail connection, begun by the American Louisiana railroad company in Salina Cruz around 1870. President Porfirio Díaz presided over the project's climax, with up-to-date Salina Cruz port

facilities built by the British company Iglesias, Pearson and Son, Ltd., around 1900.

Since the 1960s, Petróleos Mexicanos (Pemex) and other government authorities have greatly extended those early efforts with a hefty trans-isthmus pipeline funneling Gulf crude oil to a grand petrochemical complex as well as elaborate new shipping docks. From these, great loads of chemicals, crude oil, gasoline, and other fuels, minerals, fruit, and much more move out via truck, train, and ship to Mexico and the Pacific. Salina Cruz has thus become the industrial engine of the southern Mexican Pacific, employing more than 10,000 workers whose wages directly and indirectly support many tens of thousands more.

SIGHTS

Salina Cruz (pop. 80,000), Oaxaca's third-largest city, outstrips both Juchitán and Tehuántepec in hustle and bustle. In Salina Cruz, enterprise reigns and people are working. Crowds with money to spend support a host of town-center markets, stores, offices, hotels,

THE ISTHMUS

SALINA CRUZ

To Tehuantepec, Chiapas, and Oaxaca

200

200

To Bahías de Huatulco

INTERNET C-RENT

AVILA

BANCOMER

Market

5 DE MAYO

MAZATLÁN

BANORTE

CAMACHO

Plaza

CLINICA DE LAS ESPECIALIDADES

JUGUERÍA MAZATLÁN

CAFÉ

INTERNET

ITALIAN COFFEE COMPANY

BAKERY LA TOYA

MALL

ACAPULCO

★PRESIDENCIA MUNICIPAL

RESTAURANT PAPAGAYO

HEALTH FOOD

1 DE MAYO

ADO/CRISTÓBAL COLÓN/ PLUS BUSES

LABORISTA

WILFREDO CRUZ

AVILA CAMACHO

5 DE MAYO

PUERTO ÁNGEL

AV. LA PAZ

TUXPAN

ESTRELLA BLANCA BUS

AV.

21 DE NOVIEMBRE

HIDALGO

FRONTERA

TRAVEL AGENT

POST OFFICE

TELECOM

MANZANILLO

HOTEL COSTA REAL

PROGRESO

FARMACIA EL FENIX

GUAYMAS

FOTO DISCUENTO DE OAXACA

Market

MAZATLÁN

SEE DETAIL

Plaza

ACAPULCO

HOTEL CALENDAS

HOTEL RÍOS

HSBC

CENTRAL BUS TERMINAL (2ND CLASS)

To Harbor Viewpoint, Salinas del Marqués, and Hwy 200 West

COATZACOALCOS

LAUNDRY

RESTAURANT MACAO

HOTEL ALTA GRACIA

LIBERTAD

TAMPICO

LA PASADITA

PACIFICO

To Playa La Ventosa

Harbor

CAPITÁN DEL PUERTO

IMMIGRATION OFFICE

HEROES

MIRAMAR

0   200 yds

0   200 m

© AVALON TRAVEL

and restaurants. If you need to buy something, Salina Cruz is the place in the Isthmus where you're most likely to get it.

Salina Cruz's big downtown stretches in a mile-long (two-km) rectangle north and south from the town plaza. Some of the north–south streets change names at the plaza, others don't. On the plaza's east side, 5 de Mayo becomes Héroes south of the plaza, while on the plaza's west side, Avila Camacho retains the same name its entire length. West another block and north of the plaza runs Wilfredo Cruz, which becomes Tampico on the south side, while a block east of 5 de Mayo, Puerto Ángel remains the same both north and south of the plaza. Thankfully, east–west streets do not change name. From a block north of the plaza, moving successively south, are Guaymas, Mazatlán, Acapulco, and, finally, Coatzacoalcos, a block south of the plaza.

Town activity focuses at the very pungent and busy **market**, northeast of the plaza, between Guaymas and Mazatlán. Several blocks south of the plaza are the container docks along the Calle Miramar, which leads to the drowsy beach village of **Playa La Ventosa.**

Once you've gotten your fill of the sights and sounds around the plaza and market, head west to breezy harbor vista point **Faro del Marina.** Drive or ride a Salina-labeled bus or a taxi west along Acapulco, the plaza's south-side street. First you pass *dique* (DEE-kay, dry dock) no. 1 and the naval compound, then cross beneath the great rack of pipelines conducting a small river of oil and chemicals over the road. Continue, winding uphill to the summit parking lot on the right. On the harbor's near side stands the fishing fleet; on the opposite side are the smart gray naval frigates and destroyers. On the right, at the outer pier, great supertankers take on lakes of crude oil, most likely bound for Japan and the United States.

Continue west downhill to Barrio Salinas, named after Hernán Cortés's salt-producing ponds, the **Salinas del Marqués.** Although the ponds, about a mile (two km) west of the foot of the hill, still produce salt, they are as interesting for the wildlife—flocks of waterfowl,

both resident and local—that they sustain. People also live from the bounty of the *salinas*. Afternoons, next to the road that cuts north across the marshes to the highway, you can usually see men waist deep in the pond, throwing nets and hoping to haul in something for dinner.

ACCOMMODATIONS

The continuous flow of Salina Cruz visitors supports several hotels. With the exception of the beachfront hostelries in Playa La Ventosa, they are all (excepting one, Hotel Parador) near the town center.

Under $25

A good low-budget choice is the **Hotel Ríos** (Wilfredo Cruz 405, tel. 971/714-0337, $15 s or d in one bed, $20 d, t, or q in two beds), a block west, half a block south of the plaza. Here, the grandmotherly owner maintains three stories of about 20 plainly furnished but very clean rooms, arranged along corridors around an interior patio. Choose an upper room for more light and privacy. Rooms come with bath (tepid-water shower), fans, and street parking only; credit cards not accepted.

$25-50

Convenient for travelers with cars or RVs is the **Hotel El Parador** (Carretera Transistmica Km 6, Colonia Aviación, tel./fax 971/716-2951, $27 s, $30 d, $34 t). On the highway's east side, about four miles (six km) north of town, El Parador's major attraction is its big tropical pool patio, perfect for relaxing at the end of a warm, busy day. However, the rooms, although clean, generally lack light and ventilation. Consequently, some rooms may smell of *moho* (mildew), especially during the summer–fall rainy season. Inspect various rooms until you find one satisfactory. Rooms come with air-conditioning, hot-water shower-baths, and parking; credit cards not accepted.

Back in the town center, the **Hotel Altagracia** (5 de Mayo 520, tel./fax 971/714-0726 or 971/714-6225, $27 s, $33 d, $38 t), just a block and a half south of the plaza, offers another good choice. The 18 rooms, in a compact but invitingly decorated two-story block, are clean, with either one king-size or two double beds. They are tastefully decorated in modern style, with tile floors and some marble baths. Amenities include hot-water shower-baths and air-conditioning, Internet access, but street-only parking and credit cards not accepted.

Nearer to the plaza, find the **Hotel Calendas** (Puerto Ángel 408, tel./fax 971/714-4574, $35 s, $43 d, $48 t), one long block east of the plaza, just south of the corner of Acapulco and Puerto Ángel. Savvy managers have created an inviting lodging of about 20 clean, spacious, comfortably furnished rooms in two stories around a quiet interior patio, with hot-water shower-baths, TV, air-conditioning, and parking. Credit cards *are* accepted.

Fourth choice downtown goes to the pricier **Hotel Costa Real** (Progreso 22s, tel./fax 971/714-287, $38 s, $43 d, $49 t), two blocks north, half a block west of the plaza. A plus here is the good restaurant, especially handy for breakfast. Upstairs, although the approximately 30 rooms are clean and comfortable enough, they do not appear particularly well-maintained. Make sure everything works before you pay. Amenities include hot-water shower-baths, air-conditioning, TV, and parking. Credit cards are accepted.

FOOD

Food is plentiful in downtown Salina Cruz. If you're on a tight budget, the *fondas* on the market's south and west sides will satisfy with hearty country-style soups, stews, rice, tamales, and seafood, with all the tortillas you can eat. For dessert, go to one of the close-in *panaderías* (bakeries). For example, try La Toya on Acapulco near the plaza's southeast corner (8 A.M.–10 P.M. daily).

Health food fanciers will appreciate the many shelves of grains, food supplements, vitamins, ginseng, herbs, and remedies at the **Centro Naturista Aquarius** (tel. 971/714-2180, 9 A.M.–8 P.M. Mon.–Sat.) on Camacho; credit cards accepted. Find it half a block south of the the plaza's southwest corner, just past Restaurant Papagayo.

First restaurant choice goes to restful and locally popular seafood restaurant (**La Pasadita** (tel. 971/714-0356, 7 A.M.–10 P.M.) on Avila Camacho, two and a half blocks south of the plaza's southwest corner. Take a seat in their airy, tree-shaded dining room and choose from a long menu that starts out with salads (oysters Rockefeller $7, almond shrimp $9) and goes on to many styles of fish (breaded, with garlic, whole barbecued, $6–9), and in season, even jumbo prawns lobster (which they call *cucarachas*) and lobster ($10–20).

On the other hand, for Chinese food, go to refined **Restaurant Macao Cantonesa** (tel. 971/714-3834, 9 A.M.–9 P.M. daily), which carries on Salina Cruz's Asian-food tradition, also on Avila Camacho, about two blocks south of southwest the plaza-corner. Diners choose from a long, very recognizable menu, including lots of meat, fish, and chicken dishes, such as almond chicken ($7), pork chow mein ($6), and spareribs ($6). Lighter eaters can skip the meat and ask for rice and vegetables, such as broccoli, cabbage, tomatoes, and mushrooms only and get reduced prices ($3–5).

Also among the town center's recommendable sit-down eateries is **Restaurant Papagayo** (Avila Camacho 407, tel. 971/714-2084, 7 A.M.–11 P.M. daily), half a block south of the plaza's southwest corner. The Chinese-Mexican owners once offered some Asian food favorites, but now they've switched exclusively to Mexican and international specialties. These include good breakfasts (hotcakes, bacon, eggs, $3–5), lunches, or dinners (hamburgers, *tortas,* soup, salad, fish, chicken, $2–6).

For a modicum of refined tranquility and plain good food, try the dining room of the **Hotel Costa Real** (Progreso 22, 7:30 A.M.–10:30 P.M. daily, $4–12), two blocks north, half a block west of the plaza's northwest corner.

For dessert, go to the plaza-front **Italian Coffee Company;** see the *Entertainment and Events,* following.

ENTERTAINMENT AND EVENTS

True to Tehuántepec tradition, Salina Cruz folks sometimes abandon their workaday habits for fiestas. First comes the **Fiesta de la Santa Cruz**, on May 3, in a blast that includes coronation of a queen, full-costumed traditional dances, a fruit- and gift-throwing *regada* parade, carnival rides and games, and fireworks.

If you miss that fiesta, you might be lucky and get in on one later, such as the **Fiesta del Pueblo**, an all-purpose town fiesta, for several days beginning May 9; the **Fiesta de Santa Rosa de Lima** (August 26–September 2); the **Fiesta de San Francisco Asís** (October 3–5); and the **Fiesta de San Diego** (November 11–16).

If, unluckily, you miss all the fiestas, at least console yourself by going to the Starbucks lookalike **Italian Coffee Company** (9 A.M.–11 P.M. daily), right on the southeast plaza-front corner of Acapulco and Avila Camacho. Take in the refined, air-conditioned ambience, while relaxing to the soothing recorded melodies, sampling the rich espresso coffees ($1–3), snacking on sandwiches (*panini*, croissant, $2–5), or desserts (cakes and brownies, $1–2.50).

INFORMATION AND SERVICES

Money

Several banks, all with ATMs, serve downtown customers. A good first choice is **HSBC** (tel. 971/714-4476, 8 A.M.–7 P.M. Mon.–Sat.), a block south of the plaza, northeast corner of Avila Camacho and Coatzacoalcos. Alternatively, also on Avila Camacho, try **Bancomer** (tel. 971/714-0032, 8:30 A.M.–4 P.M. Mon.–Fri., 10:30 A.M.–2:30 P.M. Sat.), on the east side of the street a few steps north of the plaza; or **Banorte** (tel. 971/714-4454 or 971/714-5898, 9 A.M.–4 P.M. Mon.–Fri., 10 A.M.–2 P.M. Sat.), on the west side of the plaza, near the plaza's northwest corner.

Communications

The town *correo* (tel. 971/714-0040, 8 A.M.–7 P.M. Mon.–Fri.), with Mexpost secure mail service, and the *Telecomunicaciones*

(tel. 971/714-0891, fax 971/714-0760, 9 A.M.–7:30 P.M. Mon.–Fri., 9 A.M.–2:30 P.M. Sat. and Sun.), stand side by side four blocks north of the plaza, east side of Avila Camacho, corner of Frontera. Moreover, a *larga distancia* telephone office (7 A.M.–midnight) serves customers at the plaza's southeast corner.

A number of small storefront outlets provide Internet connection. Try **Cybernet** (7 A.M.–7 P.M. daily) near the plaza's southeast corner. Alternatively, go to **C-Rent** Internet (5 de Mayo 705, tel. 971/714-1839, 10 A.M.–4 P.M. and 6–10 P.M. Mon.–Sat.), plaza's northwest corner, across Camacho, opposite Bancomer.

Travel Agent and Car Rental

Travel agents, besides selling air tickets and reserving hotel rooms, are sometimes willing sources of information. One such agency is **Lone Star** (tel./fax 971/716-2650, lubistmo@hotmail.com, 8 A.M.–6 P.M. Mon.–Sat.), on the north outskirts, along the Tehuántepec highway, about a mile (two km) from downtown. Besides their main car rental business, they sell airline tickets, reserve hotel rooms, and provide transport.

Immigration

Being a port of entry, Salina Cruz has a **Migración** (Immigration Office, tel. 971/714-1000 or 971/714-4531, 9 A.M.–1 P.M. Mon.–Fri.), at the foot of Tampico, four blocks south of the plaza. Go there if you lose, or need an extension on, your tourist permit.

If you arrive by private boat and have inspection documentation from another Mexican port, present it for check-in at the Capitán del Puerto, located just west of Migración, across Tampico. If you arrive without Mexican inspection documentation, first go to Migración for an inspection, then to the Capitán del Puerto.

Health and Emergencies

Several pharmacies sell medicines and drugs near the plaza. For discounts, go to the big **Farmacia El Fénix** (tel. 971/714-3141, 9 A.M.–11 P.M. daily), at the northwest corner of

Avila Camacho and Guaymas, a block north of the plaza. If it can't supply you, try **Farmacia Pronto** (9 A.M.–10 P.M. daily) across the street, at the plaza northeast corner.

Of the several downtown doctors' offices, the **Clínica de Especialidades Médicas** (Medical Specialties Clinic, Avila Camacho 306, tel. 971/714-4107, 9 A.M.–8 P.M. Mon.–Sat.), west side of the plaza, offers several choices, including a gynecologist, pediatrician, ophthalmologist, urologist, and general practitioner.

Alternatively, at nearby offices, try gynecologist **Doctora Gabriela Guzman Cartas** (705 5 de Mayo, tel. 971/714-1622, 9 A.M.–1:30 P.M. Mon.–Sat.), about seven blocks north of the plaza.

In a medical emergency, either follow your hotel's recommendation or have a taxi take you to **Sanatorio del Carmen** (clinic tel. 971/714-1180, pharmacy tel. 971/714-4334), at Calle Francisco Villa 16. In a police or fire emergency, contact the *policía municipal* (tel. 971/714-0523).

Photography and Laundry

The best town source of cameras (Kodak, Konica, and Fuji), developing (both film and digital), and supplies is **Foto Discuento de Oaxaca** (tel. 971/714-4300, 9 A.M.–8 P.M. Mon.–Sat.), on Avila Camacho, half a block north of the plaza.

Get your laundry done at **Lavandería Carmel** (tel. 971/714-6105, 9 A.M.–3 P.M. and 5–10 P.M. Mon.–Sat., 9 A.M.–noon Sun.), at the southeast corner of Avila Camacho and Coatzacoalcos, a block south of the plaza's southwest corner.

GETTING THERE AND AWAY

Three terminals serve Salina Cruz bus travelers. The two first-class terminals are on the north side of town. At Calle Laborista 2, corner of Highway 200, about seven blocks north of the plaza, **Omnibus Cristóbal Colón, Plus,** and **Autobuses del Oriente** (ADO) (all contactable by local tel. 971/714-0703) offer luxury and first-class service (that can also be booked and paid for by credit card via

the **Ticket Bus** agency's toll-free Mex. tel. 800/702-8000).

Cristóbal Colón departures connect northwest with Mexico City (Norte terminal) via Tehuántepec and Oaxaca City; west with Bahías de Huatulco, Pochutla (Puerto Ángel), and Puerto Escondido; and east with Juchitán, Zanatepec, Tuxtla Gutiérrez, San Cristóbal las Casas, and Tapachula on the Guatemala border. Its subsidiary line, Plus, offers luxury-class connections northwest with Oaxaca City, Mexico City, and Veracruz, and southwest with Bahías de Huatulco.

ADO offers first-class connections north with Tehuántepec, Juchitán, Minatitlán, Coatzacoalcos, Villahermosa, Ciudad del Carmen, Tuxpan, Veracruz, and Tampico.

At the other first-class terminal, on Highway 200, four and a half blocks north of the plaza, **Estrella Blanca** and its subsidiary lines (tel. 971/714-5548) offer first- and luxury-class connections along the Highway 200 corridor with Huatulco, Pochutla–Puerto Ángel, Puerto Escondido, Acapulco (where connections may be made northwest, for Zihuatanejo, Puerto Vallarta, and the U.S. border), and Mexico City.

The second-class bus terminal (tel. 971/714-0259) is downtown, on 5 de Mayo, half a block south of the plaza. Here, **Autobuses Unidos** (AU) offers connections northwest with Oaxaca, Puebla, Mexico City, Orizaba, and Veracruz, and north with Tehuántepec, Juchitán, and Tuxtepec. **Sur** offers connections north, with Tehuántepec, Juchitán, and Coatzacoalcos; east with Zanatepec and Tapanatepec; and southwest with Astata and Bahías de Huatulco.

Drivers have the same highway choices and destinations as listed in *Getting There and Away* in the Tehuántepec section earlier in this chapter. Simply add 20 minutes to the driving time (and nine miles/15 km distance) for northerly, northwesterly, and easterly trips; subtract the same for southwesterly trips. Fill up with gasoline at the Pemex *gasolinera* on the highway, Tehuántepec direction, about four miles (six km) north of downtown.

PLAYA LA VENTOSA

Playa La Ventosa is Salina Cruz's sleepy little beach village on the historic Bahía de la Ventosa (Windy Bay), where Hernán Cortés built his first caravels to explore the Pacific. Get there by car, taxi, or white or orange Ventosa-labeled bus running west along Calle Miramar next to the container docks, four blocks south of the plaza. Drivers, bear left at the fork at the end of Miramar and continue winding over the hill toward the beach. After about two miles (three km), you get a good view of the petrochemical plant on the left, belching a swirling, hellish plume of pollution. Fortunately for Salina Cruz (but not for other towns downwind), prevailing breezes blow the smoke in a northerly direction, away from town.

About four miles (six km) from downtown, you arrive at Playa La Ventosa. One of the best places to land is **La Palapa de Chava,** the beachfront restaurant at the end of the main street through town. Friendly, knowledgeable owner Salvador Mendoza likes to tell visitors about Playa La Ventosa. He says that wood for Cortés's ships was cut inland and floated downstream via the **Río Tehuántepec,** which empties into the bay's east (left, facing the ocean) side. There, the summer rainy-season flood stains the entire Bahía Ventosa a muddy brown while depositing piles of driftwood on the east-side beach. In the dry winter and spring, the river dries to a clear trickle and the bay becomes clear and blue.

Shift your view west and notice what appears to be a tower atop the headland, a mile or two beyond the foreground bay and beach. This tower has been known for longer than anyone remembers as **El Faro de Cortés** (The Lighthouse of Cortés). The tower's builders cut a window on the seaward side, where historians believe they placed an oil lamp to guide ships to the harbor.

If the story is true, the lighthouse would be nearly five centuries old. How could this be? Without maintenance, mortar crumbles and bricks usually fall after two or three centuries. Restaurant owner Salvador Mendoza answers that experts believe that Cortés built the tower of bricks and mortar, mixed with egg whites and yolks instead of water, which made the mortar durable enough to keep the lighthouse standing straight, without any repairs, through the present day.

Activities

Wander the beach, rocky in the rainy summer and fall, sandy in the dry winter and spring. On the east side, by the river's mouth, collect shells and driftwood, watch the antics of the pelicans, seagulls, and cormorants, and, with your binoculars, look for rarer species. On the west side, explore the tide pools beneath the rocky headland, then head inland and hike the headland's forested arroyos up to the breezy hilltop for a close-up view of Cortés's lighthouse.

On another day, go on a fishing excursion and catch a load of silvery *mojarra* (bass), *lisa* (mullet), and *sierra* (mackerel) for a feast for everyone in the neighborhood. Go in your own boat or hire a boatman (figure on about $40) to take you out for half a day.

Accommodations

For accommodation, either park your RV, set up a tent, or stay in one of the Playa La Ventosa beachfront lodgings. On the far west side of the beach, beneath the headland, is a secluded, level grassy spot that appears fine for tenting. RV-equipped travelers could simply park at one of a number of likely spots down by the beach.

Otherwise, stay at La Ventosa's rustic best, sleepy **Posada Rústrian** (tel. 971/714-0450, $12 s, $24 d), so relaxing that it's worth reserving well ahead of time if you plan to arrive during high-occupancy times around Christmas, Easter, weekends, and January–April. Posada Rústrian amounts to a downscale mini-resort, perched on a breezy rise with a palm-fringed beach view. Watch for the sign on the left as you're entering town. No TV, no phones, simply about 10 basic rooms and a breezy, shaded restaurant with chairs and hammocks for resting, reading, and taking in the view. Rooms (check for maintenance and cleanliness before moving in) have fans and room-temperature private shower-baths.

Three or four alternate lodgings do exist, although none so inviting as Posada Rústrian. For example, try **Casa Limones** across the main town street from Posada Rústrian, or **Posada Miramar,** a block farther, near the end of the street on the right just before Palapa La Chava. Expect to pay about $10 per person, $20 per person during holidays.

EAST OF SALINA CRUZ: HUAVE COUNTRY

The country due east of Salina Cruz is one of the low-lying, barrier-sand spits to which many of Oaxaca's Huave-speaking people were marginalized by the more populous Zapotecs long before the Spanish arrived. The Spanish simply continued the segregation that was already in place.

The Huave appear to have grudgingly accepted their lot. They subsist mostly off of the cattle that graze whatever brush, grass, and cactus grow in the sand and the fish and shrimp that they can catch in the ocean and the lagoons.

San Mateo del Mar

San Mateo del Mar (pop. 2,000), seat of the *municipio* of the same name, has a uniquely picturesque church and a native market, making it the major destination of this eastern excursion. Get there by heading one hour east (18 miles/29 km) from the jumping-off spot on Highway 200, near Km 17.

The plaza-center of San Mateo del Mar is a block or two south (turn right) from the entrance road. The main sights are the market, which takes up much of the town plaza; the lagoon, past the plaza, a block south; and the church, just to the east of the plaza. When I was there a sullen sacristan (church keeper) didn't let me enter, claiming that the church was closed. Its colorful facade, however, is unique.

The market is where most of the town

action is. Women are the actors and Huave is the language. Dress appears to be the dividing line: The women who wear *traje*—red blouse, dark skirt, striped cloth headdress trailing a bright ribbon—seem to be the ones who speak Huave only. Besides selling a few vegetables, they mostly offer the local fish and shrimp that their husbands have caught and they've dried in the sun.

Despite their historical shyness (most likely based on a communal memory of hard experience), you might get a smile when you say *"Buenos días"* or *"Buenas tardes."* The Huave reticence shows directly in the way they build their homes. Notice the walls, the older ones of sticks or brush, now increasingly of concrete, that surround each family compound. In some country lots, concrete walls appeared to have been built even before any buildings. (This, of course, is not unlike what a significant fraction of town Mexicans do, especially the well-to-do, who have historically surrounded their houses with brawny fences and encased their windows with steel bars.)

GETTING THERE

Go by bus (ask for a "San Mateo del Mar" bus at the Salina Cruz market) or by car. The road (initially paved but potholed, finally good, all-weather gravel) takes off from near Highway 200 Kilometer 17 about three miles (five km) north of town. Turn right (or catch a San Mateo del Mar–marked bus) at the highway traffic signal and road that heads east, by the big electrical sub-station. Drivers, set your odometer. After about five blocks, follow the traffic left; continue straight about two miles (three km), passing through the traffic circle at the Pemex refinery gate. Cross the Río Tehuántepec at mile 4.7 (7.6 km). After the river bridge, follow the right road fork, and continue for about another 13 miles (21 km) through a couple of hamlets just before San Mateo del Mar, 18 miles (29 km) from Highway 200.

Santa María del Mar

If you have another two hours, continue 10 more miles (16 km) to smaller Santa María del Mar (pop. 500). Here, you'll find a sleepier town plaza and a humbler church. For a bit of beach action, turn north (left) from the plaza to the *embarcadero* (wharf), on the Laguna Inferior beach, about a mile (two km) from town. A detachment of marines guards the beach, apparently to keep order among the locals. The guards seemed unconcerned with me as I drove past their post.

A battalion of fishing *lanchas* lines a broad, breezy beach. Gentle waves wash the shallow shoreline, and dogs laze in the sun. With the added security of the marines, this appears to be an especially good spot for prepared tenters or RVers (bring water and food). The most exciting time is mid- to late afternoon, when the fishermen bring in their catches. They sell whatever they can to buyers who arrive with trucks, and load the rest on wheelbarrows, which they push home for drying. The good shrimp price that the buyers were paying—about $3.50 per pound—reflects both local and world demand.

THE ISTHMUS

BACKGROUND

The Land

On the map of North America, Mexico's state of Oaxaca (wah-HAH-kah) makes up the southern bulge of Mexico, the region where the Mexican coastline thrusts into the Pacific like the belly of a frolicking Pacific dolphin. Oaxaca is a sizable place—with about 36,800 square miles (95,400 sq. km)—and Mexico's fifth-largest state, as big as a midsize U.S. state, such as Indiana, or an entire small European country, such as Portugal.

As in Mexico as a whole, mountains rule Oaxaca's landscape. From the U.S. border, Mexico's grand pair of mother ranges, the Sierra Madre Oriental in the east and Sierra Madre Occidental in the west, sweep southward a thousand miles until they reach Oaxaca, where they bend eastward and practically merge. In Oaxaca, the ranges, respectively called the Sierra Madre de Oaxaca and the Sierra Madre del Sur, form a broad, rumpled, pine-tufted landscape, dotted with 20 peaks in excess of 10,000 feet (3,000 meters). Only the mostly narrow southern coastal plain, one large valley, and a few scattered lesser vales provide enough level cropland to support large towns. From those few valleys, a handful of streams, blocked and forced by the mountains to twist through deep canyons, make their way to the sea.

A CLOSER LOOK

Imagine navigating a high-altitude airship, borne by the tropical breezes, over Oaxaca's vivid shoreline, mountain, and valley panorama. Start your adventure in the southwest, at Oaxaca's coastal border with its neighboring state of Guerrero. Here, as you drift eastward

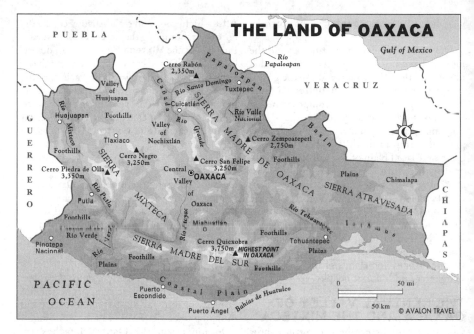

THE LAND OF OAXACA

PUEBLA
Río Papaloapan
Gulf of Mexico
VERACRUZ
Cerro Rabón 2,350m
Cañada
Río Santo Domingo
Tuxtepec
Cuicatlán
Valley of Huajuapan
SIERRA
Río Valle Nacional
Río Grande
Huajuapan
Foothills
Valley of Nochixtlán
Río Mixteco
GUERRERO
Tlaxiaco
Cerro Zempoatepetl 2,750m
MADRE
Basin
Foothills
Cerro Negro 3,250m
Cerro San Felipe 3,250m
Foothills
Cerro Piedra de Olla 3,350m
SIERRA
Central Valley
⊙ OAXACA
DE
OAXACA
Plains
Chimalapa
MIXTECA
Río Purla
Putla
of Oaxaca
SIERRA ATRAVESADA
CHIAPAS
Foothills
Río Verde
Miahuatlán
Río Atoyac
Cerro Quiexobra 3,750m HIGHEST POINT IN OAXACA
Foothills
Río Tehuantepec
Isthmus
Tehuántepec
Plains
Pinotepa Nacional
Plains
Foothills
SIERRA
MADRE
DEL
SUR
Foothills
PACIFIC OCEAN
Coastal Plain
Puerto Escondido
Puerto Ángel
Bahías de Huatulco
0   50 mi
0   50 km
© AVALON TRAVEL

above the green coastal plain directly below, the broad estuary of the **Río Verde** empties into the sea. The mightiest river system entirely within the state, the Río Verde's tributaries drain a major fraction of western Oaxaca, including the central valley, where it is known as the Río Atoyac.

As you continue easterly, the forest-swathed peaks of the Sierra Madre del Sur stretch ahead, cresting at cloud-capped 12,300-foot (3,750-meter) **Cerro Quiexobra**, Oaxaca's tallest mountain. To your right far below, Pacific waves wash a coastline indented with small bays and lined with wildlife-rich mangrove wetlands and pearly, palm-tufted strands. In succession, you pass over the small resorts of **Puerto Escondido, Puerto Ángel,** and the **Bahías de Huatulco,** where visitors flock year-round to enjoy the delights of South Seas Mexico.

TO THE ISTHMUS AND NORTH

As you continue, the coastal plain gradually broadens as the Sierra shrinks to mere foothills at the **Isthmus of Tehuántepec,** the neck

of land where Mexico (and indeed the entire North American continent) shrivels to a scant 125 miles (200 km) in width. East beyond the Isthmus, in the remote region Oaxacans call the **Chimalapa,** you spot a new range of mountains, the **Sierra Atravesada,** rising and stretching east into the neighboring state of Chiapas. The Atravesadas' isolated rugged summits, sylvan forests, and deep gorges shelter one of Mexico's last remaining troves of endangered plants, birds, mammals, and reptiles.

From the Isthmus, other Oaxaca regions beckon. Turning around to the left and heading your airship northwest, you follow the valley of the **Río Tehuántepec,** passing over the bustling, tradition-rich small cities of Juchitán and Tehuántepec and their luxuriant hinterlands of fruit, corn, and cotton. Soon, on your right toward the north, rises the grand **Sierra Madre de Oaxaca.** You see a succession of peaks stretching west a hundred miles, from the rugged homeland of the indigenous **Mixe** (MEE-shay) people in Oaxaca's northeast to the equally mountainous domain of their neighbors, the Sierra **Zapotec** at the northern center of the state.

Drawn by what you might find beyond the mountain crest, you navigate your airship due north, over the Mixe country, above the gigantic spreading massif of **Zempoaltepetl** (only 9,000 feet/2,700 meters, but composed nevertheless of a dozen separate peaks), the Mixes' holy mountain. Beyond that, the mountains gradually drop to foothills, where you see a great river-laced plain of tropical forest checkered with pasture, farms, and small towns, stretching north past Oaxaca's northern lowland border with the state of Veracruz all the way to the Gulf of Mexico. The Oaxaca portion, known as the **Papaloapan** (pah-pah-loh-AH-pahn) for the great river system that drains it, encompasses the **Chinantla** and the **Mazateca,** homelands of the indigenous Chinantec and Mazatec peoples.

THE CENTRAL VALLEY OF OAXACA AND THE MIXTECA

Continue your breeze-blown journey, now turning southwest over the Sierra Zapoteca (Zapotec Highland) country to the Valley of Oaxaca, the heartland of the Zapotec people and Oaxacan civilization for more than 3,000 years. Below you spreads Oaxaca's great highland central valley complex: farms, pastures, towns, and villages, radiating in three 50-mile fingers (east, northwest, and south) from the capital city, Oaxaca.

Drawn on by the mystery of the mist-shrouded western mountains, you continue a hundred miles northwest, following the valley of the upper **Río Atoyac,** where the Sierra de Oaxaca rises again. There, you gaze down on a broad mountain and high plateau landscape, much of it tragically eroded. Oaxacans call this the **Mixteca,** the domain of the Mixtec people, proud transmitters of a major share of Oaxaca's ancient tradition. From your high vista, you see a landscape as creased as an old chopping board, dotted with tiny settlements scattered atop rugged mesas and tucked into deep gorges.

A closer look reveals natural divisions in the land. In the center you see the **Mixteca**

Alta—high, cool, and cloud-shadowed. To the northwest, bordering the states of Guerrero and Puebla, lies the **Mixteca Baja,** a lower, desert-like plateau-land of cactus, maguey, and dwarf palm. To the south, toward the Pacific, at the place where your imaginary journey began, the mountains drop to the verdant, jungle-draped foothills, lush river canyons, and coastal farms of the **Mixteca de la Costa** (Mixtec coastal region).

CLIMATE

Despite its deep southern latitude, Oaxaca's elevation, cooling sea breezes, and summer rain showers moderate the heat of its plentiful sunshine. Most of the state, excepting the remote mountain summits, basks in the tropics, never feeling the bite of frost.

The seashore and coastal plain, including all of the Isthmus, is truly a land of endless summer. Winter days are typically warm and rainless, peaking at 82–88°F (28–31°C) and dropping to 65–75°F (18–24°C) by midnight.

Summers on the Oaxaca beaches are warmer and wetter. Mornings are usually bright and balmy, warming to around 90°F (32°C). Early afternoons, clouds often gather and bring short, sometimes heavy, cooling showers. Later, the sun reappears, drying

---

OAXACA SUMMARY

- **Land area:** 36,860 square miles/95,470 square kilometers (fifth largest among 31 Mexican states and the federal district)

- **Tallest mountain:** Cerro Quiexobra, 12,300 feet/3,750 meters

- **Population (2006):** 3,578,000 (10th largest among Mexican states)

- **Indigenous population:** 39 percent of the total

- **Population density:** 93 per square mile/36 per square kilometer the sidewalks and beaches and warming the breeze just in time to enjoy a dazzling Oaxaca *puesta del sol* (sunset).

Visitors to Oaxaca City experience similar but more temperate seasons. Midwinter days are typically mild to warm, usually peaking between 70 and 75°F (21–24°C). Expect cool but frost-free winter nights between 45 and 60°F (9–16°C). Oaxaca City summers are delightful, with afternoons typically in the mid- to upper 80s (28–32°C) and pleasant evenings in the mid-70s (24–26°C), perfect for strolling. May, before the rains, is usually the warmest, with June, July, and August highs being moderated by afternoon showers.

Visitors should take note that Oaxaca's rainfall, like all of Mexico's, is strongly seasonal.

Most years, nearly all the rainfall accumulates during the summer and early fall. Rains taper off in October and November and don't usually return until June. May, before the rains, is typically Mexico's warmest month. Relief comes with the cooling summer showers.

Many trees, especially along the coast, respond to the winter spring drought by losing their leaves by February. This might make a typical late winter–early spring Oaxaca landscape appear barren to the visitor in March even though the same area will be blooming with greenery by July or August. If you prefer lush, jungle verdure to be part of your Mexico experience, you'll enjoy plenty if you visit during the seven months from July through January.

Flora and Fauna

Luxuriant tropical foliage is one of the reasons that visitors are pleasantly surprised when they visit Oaxaca during the rainy summer–fall season. Then, excursions through Oaxaca's coastal foothill forest can often reward travelers with a bounty of exotic verdure only seen in hothouses back home: Great leafy trees are swathed with mats of vines; giant-leafed **philodendrons** climb toward the canopy, while tropical hangers-on, such as spiny, pineapple-like red **bromeliads** and big, white-flowered **orchids** perch atop available branches.

Tropical forests are not the only places that bloom. Wildflowers sprout everywhere, especially on temperate upland plateaus. There, summer rains bring carpets of roadside blossoms—petite purple daisies, blue and yellow lupine, morning glories, tiny magenta sweet peas, and dozens more.

The dry winter–spring season also brings its surprising rewards. Many trees, especially along the coast, having lost their leaves, flower in February. Hundreds of varieties of the **pea family** bloom in riotous red, pink, yellow, and white. Now and then visitors stop, attracted by something remarkable, such as a host of

white flowers blooming from the apparently dead branches of the appropriately named *palo de muerto* (tree of the dead). Other times, strikingly beautiful tree blossoms, such as the yellow, roselike *rosa amarilla*, tempt one's poetic imagination.

In dry country, cactus-like plants rule. Dotted all over the state, fields of **maguey** in ranks and files like obedient botanical battalions wait to be harvested for *mescal*. In other places, you will often see farmyards fenced with bulging nopal (prickly pear) cacti, their thick leaves studded with red **tunas** (cactus apples). And, on the road some drowsy afternoon, when you least expect it, a big **candelabra cactus** might appear around a bend, bristling with a house-size row of dozens of upright fluted green columns.

VEGETATION ZONES

Plants must adapt to the soil, sun, and rain, and Oaxaca's astonishingly diverse plant population reflects the state's varied landscape. Of Mexico's 14 major vegetation zones, ranging from high desert to tropical rainforest, at least eight occur in Oaxaca.

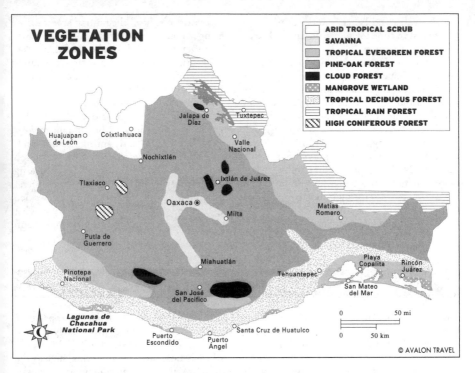

VEGETATION ZONES

ARID TROPICAL SCRUB
SAVANNA
TROPICAL EVERGREEN FOREST
PINE-OAK FOREST
CLOUD FOREST
MANGROVE WETLAND
TROPICAL DECIDUOUS FOREST
TROPICAL RAIN FOREST
HIGH CONIFEROUS FOREST

Jalapa de Díaz
Tuxtepec
Huajuapan de León
Coixtlahuaca
Valle Nacional
Nochixtlán
Tlaxiaco
Ixtlán de Juárez
Oaxaca
Milta
Matías Romero
Putla de Guerrero
Miahuatlán
Playa Copalita
Rincón Juárez
Pinotepa Nacional
Tehuantepec
San Mateo del Mar
San José del Pacífico
Lagunas de Chacahua National Park
Santa Cruz de Huatulco
Puerto Escondido
Puerto Ángel

0   50 mi
0   50 km

© AVALON TRAVEL

Directly along Oaxaca's paved national highways you can visit six of these zones: Near the seacoast lie extensive swaths of **savanna, deciduous tropical forest,** and **pine-oak forest.** Inland you can add the **tropical evergreen forest, tropical rainforest,** and **arid tropical scrub** to your botanical itinerary. Oaxaca's remaining major two vegetation zones, the **cloud forest** and **high coniferous forest,** are accessible only on high, often roadless, mountain slopes and summits.

Savanna

In their natural state, Oaxaca's savanna lands appear as flat, palm-dotted grasslands, watery during the summer and dry and brown during the winter and spring. Although much savanna has been converted to pasture or farmland, some pristine stretches lie along the coast, notably along Highway 200 near the Lagunas de Chacahua and along the Isthmus shoreline south of Highway 190, east of Juchitán.

Although grass rules the savanna, palms give it character. One of the most familiar in Oaxaca is the **Mexican fan palm,** or *palma real (Sabal Mexicana),* seasonally festooned with black fruit with leaves spread flat like a señorita's fan. The *palma real,* sometimes called the Oaxaca palm, resembles its cousin, the palmetto of the American southeast. The *palma real,* moreover, doesn't limit itself to the savanna. It appears in many other Oaxaca landscapes, notably in picturesque dwarf form in the cactus forest alongside Highway 190, just north of Huajuapan de León, in desertic northwest Oaxaca.

Visitors to Oaxaca's coastal resorts usually enjoy the sight of plenty of **coconut palms** *(Cocos nucifera),* by many measures the world's most useful tree. Local folks, who call it the *cocotero,* use nearly all of its parts: fronds for thatch, mats, and baskets; lumber for construction; and nuts for cooling drinks, fruit, candy, and oil. Nothing seems to symbolize the tropics more than a coconut palm drooping lazily over the beach or its fronds rustling gently in the tropical breeze. The coconut is completely benign with one exception: **Falling coconuts are no joke.** Watch out for them, especially during a breeze.

If you see what look like several grapefruits sprouting from a tree trunk, you are probably looking at a **gourd tree,** or *calabaza (Crescentia alata),* The mature gourds, brown and hard, were handsomely carved and fitted with gold handles for Aztec emperors to drink chocolate out of. Oaxacans, who still call them by the ancient name *jícaras,* use them as bowls (notably women, on the west Oaxaca coast, who carry them all day at market on their heads, like a hat).

Its petite, pumpkin-shaped gourds both identify and name the **sandbox tree,** or *jabillo,* because they once served as desktop boxes full of sand for drying ink. The Aztecs, however, named it the exploding tree, because its ripe fruits burst their seeds forth with a bang like a firecracker. Beware of its poisonous seeds and its irritating sap.

A **mangrove wetland** *(manglar),* a vegetation sub zone, often borders a savanna's watery seaward edge. Healthy mangrove wetlands are primary nurseries for uncounted forms of aquatic plants and animals. While a number of prime spots exist, Laguna Manialtepec, a half-hour drive west of Puerto Escondido, is one of Oaxaca's richest and most accessible mangrove wetlands.

The plant both synonymous with and essential to the mangrove wetland is the **red mangrove,** or *mangle colorado,* a tree that seems to stand in the water on stilts. Its new roots grow downward from above; a time-lapse photo would show it marching, as if on stilts, into the lagoon.

Tropical Deciduous Forest
Great swaths of this "friendly" or "short-tree" forest coat Oaxaca's coastline, especially along coastal Highway 200 around Puerto Ángel and the Bahías de Huatulco. As the label "deciduous" implies, this is the forest where the trees, in response to the dry winter weather, go dormant and lose their leaves. For visitors, the upside to all the winter barrenness is that many trees' leaves show bright fall colors; then, at the height of winter bleakness, they sprout profusions of bright red, yellow, pink, and white winter blossoms from apparently lifeless branches.

One of the most strikingly beautiful of these is the **rosa amarilla,** or yellowsilk shellseed *(Cochlospermum vitifolium).* Although not a rose, it looks every bit like a wild yellow rose when its big flowers sprout from bare branches in the early spring. After the flowers fall, leaves bud and apple-shaped green fruit grows, turning into brown pods, which pop open and release silky fluff.

The **silk cotton tree** *(Ceiba pentandra),* another of the tropical deciduous forest's major actors, yields a form of lightweight, cottony kapok fiber. Local folks, who call it the *cuajilote,* prize it for its spectacular large white (or red in cultivated varieties) blossoms with big, brushy pink stamens. In dense forest the silk cotton tree stays relatively short, but isolated it can grow to a wide-crowned giant with bulging buttresses on the lower trunk.

Lovers of Hawaii will be pleasantly surprised to find that a number of their favorite island plants are Mexican natives. The **frangipani** or **plumeria,** prized by native Mexicans for its heavenly orange blossom–like fragrance, was first classified and named as *Plumeria acutifolia* by French botanist Plumier. Pick some of its white, pink, or yellow whorl-lobed five-petaled flowers and put one behind your ear to get yourself into the mañana mood.

In Oaxaca as in Hawaii, you always know Christmas is coming because of another famous Mexico native, the **poinsettia,** or *catarina (Euphorbia pulcherrima),* first classified in 1828 by Joel R. Poinsett, an early U.S. ambassador to Mexico. Interestingly, the poinsettia's red blooms, in great abundance at Oaxaca City's Christmas fiestas, are not actually flower petals, but green leaves turned red, known technically as bracts.

Not nearly so benign is the **mala mujer** (bad woman), southern Mexico's poison ivy bush *(Cnidoscolus urens)*. Before venturing out through the Oaxaca coastal forest, ask someone to point out its drooping, oak-like, five-lobed leaves and tiny flowers. Otherwise, you might risk a stinging rash from the nettle-like hairs on the leaf surfaces and the long stalks.

If you go out on your hike but forget your makeup kit, you can improvise with the **lipstick tree,** or *achiote (Bicha orellana)*. It appears as an ordinary shrub, but marked with brownish-green soft burrs above long, heart-shaped leaves. The surprise comes when you crush the burrs and discover their bright red-orange pulp, source of annatto dye, which warriors used to make themselves look fierce and which manufacturers now use to color cheese, silk, and lipstick.

One of the showiest of roadside inhabitants is **mata ratón** (mouse killer, *Gliricidia sepium*). Despite its fragrant spring swirls of pink and white pea-like blossoms, this plant lives up to its name. Oaxacans grind its bark and leaves with cooked corn for a very effective rat and mouse poison (which, beware, is also poisonous to dogs and cats). It can be further identified by its four- to six-inch-long seedpods.

Pine-Oak Forest

About an hour's drive inland, at elevations of about 5,000 feet (1,500 meters), the tropics give way to the cooling heights of the pine-oak forest, Oaxaca's most extensive vegetation zone.

Although pine-oak forest once covered half of Oaxaca's landscape, people, beginning thousands of years ago with Oaxaca's original farmers, cleared much of it for fields, especially in the central valley and surrounding mountainsides. Nevertheless, extensive upland tracts of pine-oak forest still remain, doing their beneficent work, storing moisture, anchoring soil against erosion, and providing food and shelter for hosts of animals.

As you enter the pine-oak forest from lower elevations, you usually see the oaks first, occurring in two broad families. Mexicans identify them as either the **encino** (evergreen, small-leafed) or the **roble** (deciduous, large-leafed), both resembling oaks that dot the hills and valleys of California and the U.S. Southwest. Clustered in their branches and scattered in the shade are the *bellota* (acorns), which unmistakably mark them as oaks.

At higher elevations the oaks gradually give way to pines, which, in Oaxaca, often grow in pure stands above six or seven thousand feet (1,800–2,100 meters). Pines are easy to identify because of their long needle-like leaves, which grow in bundles, in contrast to the shorter needles of other conifers, such as spruce and fir, which commonly grow feather-shaped leaves made of rows of needles individually attached to the leaf stem.

Although pines are easily distinguished from other tree families, individual pine species are often hard to differentiate from each other. Nevertheless, examining the cones (which often conceal edible, tasty nuts) and the needles may yield identifying clues to at least a few members of this populous and very useful Mexican tree family.

Among the varieties you may encounter is the **Mexican white pine** *(Pinus ayachuite)*, similar to the white pine of the western United States. Local folks, who call it the *pinabete* or *ayacahuite*, know it by its very large (more than eight inches/20 centimeters) cones and long, four- to six-inch needles, which hang in clusters of five.

Others you might see are the **Montezuma pine,** locally called the *ocote macho* (dark three- to nine-inch dark cones, long, drooping needles, five to a bundle) or the **Aztec pine,** or *pino real* (shiny, small brown one- to two-inch cones and long, bright green needles in bundles of three—very useful for turpentine, tar, soap, and medicines).

Often associated in the same territory as pines and oaks is Mexico's renowned national tree, the **ahuehuete** (ah-way-WAY-tay), or *sabino.* Nearly every visitor to Oaxaca City sees the country's most famous specimen, at the village of Santa

María del Tule, half an hour east of the city, where droves of visitors arrive, some on bended knee, to wonder at what is known locally as El Tule. Probably the most massive tree in Latin America, it's as big around at the trunk as it is high: approximately 150 feet (46 meters).

Other more modest but still impressive *ahuehuete* specimens occur in outlying areas, often in majestic groves near water, which accounts for its name, which translates as "old one of the water." When traveling through the inland countryside, especially along stream bottoms in the Mixteca (northwest Oaxaca), you may be able to spot an old *ahuehuete* by its general appearance, unusual for Mexico: a thick, deep green crown and reddish-brown, vertically grooved bark, not unlike a California redwood. Up close you will identify it by its round, reticulated two-inch cones and its feathery green spruce-like leaves (which led botanists to classify it as a type of cypress, namely the Montezuma bald cypress, *Taxodium mucronatum*).

Tropical Evergreen Forest

In rainy foothill and low mountain areas, especially along the north Gulf slope, the lush, dense undergrowth and tall, leaf-crowned trees of the tropical evergreen forest decorate the hillsides. Here, most extensively in the north along Highway 175 around Valle Nacional, and, to a lesser extent, in the southern Sierra foothills along highways north from the Pacific coast, huge trees and vine-strewn thickets often overhang the highway. As the road curls through a dark, isolated, liana-draped canyon, momentarily you might feel as if you're traversing a forgotten corner of some prehistoric lost world, where a last remnant dinosaur might rear up at any moment.

But the bright visions of the tropical evergreen forest invariably dissipate such Jurassic Park images and jolt you back to its vivid jungle realities: A green iguana, looking every bit as primitive as a dinosaur, slithers across the road; a screeching swarm of bright green parrots swoops overhead; or a big, bird-size butterfly flutters in a roadside patch of sunlight.

Overhead, huge-leafed climbing plants, such as the **ceriman** *(Monstera deliciosa)*, hang by thick ropy vines on the trunks of accommodating trees. Local people, who know the ceriman as the *piñanona*, enjoy its sweet, juicy, corn cob–shaped fruit and find relief from aches and pains by drinking a tea brewed from its leaves.

No Oaxaca jungle trip would be complete without experiencing the **strangler fig,** known by the hideously accurate local label *matapalo* (killer tree). A strangler fig seed, once it sprouts in the crotch of a victim tree, will grow, finally entwining its host in a suffocating embrace. By then the strangler fig will have planted hairy "air roots" for ground support and will most likely go on living long after its victim has died. In a peculiarly national quirk of character, many Mexicans prize such dead victim-tree trunks. Workers scour the forests, cutting, gathering, and polishing these death embraces, to decorate living room corners or support elaborate outdoor *palapa* roofs, especially in fancy open-air restaurants.

In numerous stretches of Oaxaca's tropical evergreen forest, local folks cultivate **coffee** beneath the shady canopy. Even if coffee *(Coffea Arabica),* known to its Mexican growers as **cafeto,** weren't commercially important, people could still enjoy it as an attractive ornamental, with its shiny, ribbed green leaves and red holly-like berries. Even though coffee shrubs are quite common in Oaxaca's jungly foothills, you have to look carefully for them, because they grow best in the deep shade beneath taller trees. If you don't spot the ripe red berries, look instead for the white flowers, which are as fragrant as those of coffee's cousin, the gardenia.

Another popular import to Oaxaca's tropical forestland is the **African tulip tree** *(Spathodea campanulata).* Often seen right at roadside, a host of spectacular big red blooms caps a lush leafy crown like a host of heavenly scarlet bells.

Nearly as spectacular in its own exotic way is that cousin of the banana, the **heliconia** *(Heliconia latispatha).* Because of the resemblance, Mexicans call it the *platanillo,* or "little banana." In contrast to the fruit of the banana, the heliconia's golden-orange flower-like leaves (bracts), reminiscent of bird-of-paradise blossoms, are the main attraction. To happen upon one for the first time in a garden or in the wild—hanging amongst the greenery in descending golden-orange segments like a ladder for leprechauns—is an experience rarely forgotten.

Tropical Rainforest

This is the "forest primeval" of legend, where heavy rains nourish grand evergreen hardwoods whose great leafy crowns tower up to 200 feet (60 meters) over layers of lesser trees. Here and there, rays of sunlight shine through and nurture a luxuriant undergrowth of palms, bamboo, orchids, and bromeliads.

The rainforest gives rise to many unique, sometimes bizarre, adaptations. The big trees fortify themselves against their top-heavy bulk by developing ponderous buttresses, reaching up to a dozen feet from the ground and spreading six or eight feet from the trunk. On the other hand, shorter, lower-canopy trees commonly drop fibrous filaments, which eventually root and grow into strange, stilt-like side-trunks as far as 50 feet (15 meters) from the original trunk.

Oaxaca's rainforests, which once spread in a continuous green swath along its northern border with the state of Veracruz, are steadily being logged and replaced by farms and ranches. Nevertheless, sizable tracts still remain, much in roadless areas on both sides of Highway 175 around Valle Nacional, Isthmus Highway 185, and its offshoot, Highway 147, which runs northwest, through lowland Mixe territory, paralleling the Veracruz border.

The acknowledged king of the Mexican rainforest community is the **mahogany,** which local people, who call it the *caoba,* often point to with pride. The label refers to a number of similar trees of the genus *Swietenia,* which grow throughout the Mexican and Central American rainforests. Although the original mahogany *(Swietenia mahogany)* does not grow in Mexico, some of its cousins, such as *Swietenia macrophylla,* do. Oaxacans prize it for its handsome reddish wood, much valued

for furniture. You can identify it by its half-foot-long slender leaves and four-inch woody fruits, curved like a vulture's head, thus the tongue-twisting indigenous label *zopilo zontecomacuahuitl* (buzzard-head tree).

If, along the roadside, you spot a tall tree with diagonal slashes on its bark (for gathering sap), it's most likely either a rubber tree or the chewing-gum tree, the **chicle,** locally known as the *chicozapote.* Chewing gum, made from the chicle's sap (notice the Chiclets in every store), spread all over the world during the early 20th century and continues to gum up sidewalks and schoolroom desks from San Francisco to Samarkand. Additionally, chicle trees, known to botanists as *Acrasuzapote,* yield hard, very durable wood and, from small pinkish-white flowers, luscious round cream-colored fruits.

Of both commercial and decorative importance is the **rubber tree** *(Castilla elastica),* the source of so-called Panama rubber, once made (before synthetics) for raincoats, tennis balls, and tires. Indigenous Mexicans, who still call it the *hule* (OO-lay), have used it for millennia for making the ball for the ceremonial game of **tlatchtli.** Besides the diagonal grooves (which guide the milky sap into cups) on the trunk, you can identify the rubber tree by its foot-long elliptical leathery dark-green leaves, shiny on the top side and hairy underneath.

Among Oaxaca's most useful rainforest natives is the **chocolate tree** *(Theobromo cacao),* the "food of the gods" of the pre-conquest kings of Mexico. Before the conquest, cacao seeds served as currency. Although these days most people don't like to think of such things, historical records indicate that a healthy slave usually traded for about 100 beans; a small animal for perhaps about five. Most likely you'll identify the cacao, growing as a smallish tree beneath the forest canopy, by spotting its 10-inch (25-cm) pods, which sprout right from the trunk. Workers break open the ripe leathery yellow pods to harvest the trove of beans inside.

Arid Tropical Scrub

Although it looks a lot like a desert, Oaxaca's arid tropical scrub vegetation zone, along its

Spectacular *Organo* and *nopal* cactuses and the white flowers of the *palo muerto* ("dead" tree) are common in Oaxaca's desert-like arid tropical scrub vegetation zones.

northwest border with the states of Guerrero and Puebla, averages at least as much rainfall as San Francisco, California. In Oaxaca, however, the rain comes within a few summer months, often in cloudburst deluges that quickly drain away, leaving the people, animals, and plants to cope with six months of winter–spring drought.

The arid tropical scrub zone's most successful plants, succulents, such as the **cactuses** and their cousins the **agaves,** cope by storing moisture in fleshy leaves, trunks, and stems. None is more successful or important than the **prickly pear** *(Opuntia tuna)*, which, from its role in Aztec legend and consequent presence on the Mexican flag, is an important national symbol. Moreover, it is especially useful as a fence plant, for cattle food, and, most of all, for its delicious red *tunas*, "cactus apple" fruit, which festoon its fleshy leaves.

The prickly pear is but one member of a broad look-alike family, known in Mexico generally as the **nopal.** Another, especially benign, relative, known by botanists as *Platyopuntia,* is cultivated both for its tasty, spine-free leaves and, in Oaxaca, for red **cochineal** dye. Once commercially very important but now largely supplanted by synthetics, cochineal is still produced in a few Valley of Oaxaca communities. It turns out that a certain scale insect, *Dactylopius coccus,* loves to munch on the *Platyopuntia* cactus leaves. When the insects have eaten their fill, the people gather, dry, and crush their bodies, which yield a brilliant scarlet dye prized by weavers.

Another useful domesticated member of the arid tropical scrub community is the **maguey** (mah-GAY), or century plant, so-called because it's said to bloom once, then die, after 100 years of growth, although its lifetime is usually closer to 50 years. The maguey, moreover, has a number of well-known relatives. These include the very useful *mescal,* renowned for distilled liquor; *lechuguilla,* for *ixtle* fiber; and *sisal,* also useful for fiber. All of these, of the genus *Agave,* mature as a rose-like cluster of leathery, long pointed gray-green leaves, from which a single flower stalk eventually blooms.

Cactus-like maguey grows nearly everywhere in the state of Oaxaca.

© BRUCE WHIPPERMAN

Wondrous gardens of wild cacti proliferate in the arid tropical scrub zone of northwest Oaxaca. Hard to miss is the **bravo** (*Neobuxbaumia mexcalaensis*), which often appears right at roadside, rising as pencil-shaped fluted columns. Bravos frequently grow in spectacular grand forests stretching to far rocky horizons.

Often growing in the same habitat is the *candelabro,* or **candelabra cactus** (*Stenoceris weberi*), which, most likely, you will see in a community of stunning many-columned giants, like house-size menorahs, dotting the landscape for miles.

Cloud Forest and High Coniferous Forest

Oaxaca's two rarest plant and wildlife communities lie on the slopes and summits of high, remote mountains. Oaxaca's most accessible cloud forests coat the northern mountains north of Ixtlán de Juárez along Highway 175 and the crest of the Mazatec's holy mountain, Cerro Rabón, near Jalapa de Díaz. The easiest, safest route is to hire a local guide who can take you to these dewy mountaintops where, beginning around 6,000 feet (1,800 meters), you will first meet the plant and wildlife community of the cloud forest. Most botanists believe the cloud forest plants to be Ice Age remnants of a time when Mexico's climate was much cooler than today. The proof is in the unusual specimens, many of which appear to have been transported directly across the Gulf of Mexico from the mountain forests of Georgia or North Carolina. In Oaxacan cloud forests, you may see the brilliant reds and oranges of **liquid amber,** the lovely white flowers of **dogwood,** or the white bark and tan falling leaves of **beech.**

Besides those, you might observe some of the cloud forest's even more ancient vestiges, dating from the age of the dinosaurs. They include the giant Mexican **tree ferns** (*Cyathea mexicana*) with their long feathery fronds, dotted underside with ranks of brown spores. New fronds, which are born curling out of the treetops, account for the tree fern's local name, *rabo de mico* (monkey's tail).

Other such relics are the bromeliads and orchids, which as epiphytes merely enjoy physical support in their hosts' branches (unlike parasites, which feed on their hosts). **Bromeliads,** members of the pineapple family, love the drippy cloud-forest environment, collecting water in their cup-like leaf folds. Of the dozens of Mexican species, one of the best known is the showy *piñuela (Guzmannia lingulata),* whose roseate central leaf cluster matures from green to red, finally appearing as an exotic scarlet flower.

Among the **orchids,** you will most likely first see the very widespread *bayoneta,* or *pata de paloma* (dove's foot), which thrives in every humid Oaxaca environment from mangrove lagoons to cloud forests. You can recognize the *bayoneta* by its clusters of fleshy, drooping green leaves, topped by showy white flowers that age to a mellow golden hue.

Follow your guide even higher and you will reach the zone of **high coniferous forest,** which in Oaxaca exists only as a few scattered roadless, cloud-swathed green alpine islands, with vegetation resembling upper Rocky Mountain slopes in the United States and Canada. In Oaxaca, as you climb above about 9,000 feet (2,700 meters), you will likely pass through a zone of mixed pines, alders, and firs, reigned over by the regal **Montezuma pine** *(Pinus montezumae),* distinguished by its long, pendulous cones and rough, ruddy bark, reminiscent of the sugar pine of the western United States.

Ascending still higher, you may pass through pure stands of **sacred fir** *(Abies religiosa),* which your guide will probably know as *oyamel* or *abeto.* You can identify them by lovely violet-blue cones and typical fir-like needles, which grow in rows along the branches. Even higher, the firs will eventually thin out, giving way to bunchgrass and bushy **Mexican juniper** *(monticola),* with its edible, waxy blue berries.

For more details of Oaxaca's marvelous plants, consult M. Walter Pesman's delightfully readable *Meet Flora Mexicana* (which, unfortunately, is out of print, but major libraries often

© BRUCE WHIPPERMAN

the dewy summit cloud forest of sacred Cerro Rabón mountain, which many local Mazatec believe is inhabited by *duendes* (elfin forest spirits) have a copy). Also informative is the popular paperback *Handbook of Mexican Roadside Flora,* by Charles T. Mason Jr. and Patricia B. Mason.

MAMMALS

Although thousands of years of human hunting and habitat encroachment have generally reduced their numbers, many of Oaxaca's native animal species still thrive in the wild. While some animals sensitive to human presence, such as **jaguars, howler monkeys,** and **tapirs,** are now rarely seen in Oaxaca, others, such as **foxes, coyotes, coatimundis,** and wild pig-like **jabalís,** seem unaffected by, and sometimes even appear to benefit from, human presence.

The excitement of seeing animals in the wild is the reward of visitors who take time to visit them in their own wilderness home grounds. Sylvan stretches, such as the pine-oak woodlands coating mountainsides northeast of Oaxaca City, the thick forests of the Huatulco preserve, or the rich mangrove wetland of Manialtepec near Puerto Escondido, are ripe with wildlife-viewing opportunities for those willing to get off the beaten track and quietly watch and wait.

Armadillos, Coatimundis, Peccaries, and Bats

The benefits of quiet isolation once came to me when, lazing on a tropical beach, I spotted my first **armadillo** *(Dasypus novemcinctus).* Although it behaved much like the familiar opossum, I was struck by its reptilian-like shell. The armadillo was going about its business, nosing through the forest-edge leaf cover nearby. Not seeming to possess particularly good eyesight, the preoccupied armadillo didn't notice when I crept in for a closer look. He waddled right up and sniffed my shoe, which evidently gave him such a scare that he scuttled back into the woods in a flash.

One of the Mexicans' favorite animals is the raccoon-like **coatimundi** *(Nasua narica),* known in Mexico as *coati,* or *tejón,* the European Spanish name for badger (although

the *coati* is a completely different animal). While many urban Mexicans, charmed by the coatimundi's acrobatic antics and inquisitive nature, keep them as pets, hungry country folks enjoy them for culinary reasons. You can identify one by its long nose and straight, usually vertically held tail. Watch for them at country markets.

The pig-like **collared peccary** *(Tayassu tajacu)* is definitely *not* one of Oaxaca's endangered species. Known in Mexico as the *jabalí,* the Spanish name for the European wild boar, it is nevertheless an American native, ranging from the southwest United States through Mexico and Central and most of South America. Although it is easily distinguished by its whitish beige, collar-like marking that encircles its neck, the *jabalí* is sometimes confused with the European wild boar *(Sus scrofa),* which was introduced into the Americas as a game animal, and now thrives in the wilds of the U.S. Southeast and Pacific Coast.

The *jabalí* eats most anything and thrives in nearly all environments—often not far from towns and villages. The gray-to-brown short-haired *jabalís,* although normally shy when encountered alone, sometimes congregate in large groups and become aggressive. People have occasionally reported being chased and, in one case, forced up a tree, by collared peccaries.

Bats *(murciélagos,* moor-see-AY-lah-gohs) are widespread in Oaxaca, home to around two or three times as many bat species as the entire United States. In Oaxaca, bats were once widely worshipped, but today, as everywhere, they are both feared and misunderstood. Shortly before sundown, bats emerge from their cave and forest roosts and silently flit through the air in search of insects. Most people, sitting outside enjoying the early evening, will mistake their darting silhouettes for those of birds, who, except for owls, don't generally fly at night.

The nonvampire Oaxacan bats carry their vampire cousins' odious reputation with forbearance. They go about their good works, pollinating flowers, clearing the air of pesky gnats and mosquitoes, ridding cornfields of mice, and dropping seeds, thereby restoring forests.

Monkeys

Oaxaca's remote mountains and jungles, notably in the **Chimalapa** region in the eastern Isthmus of Tehuántepec, still shelter a number of rare and endangered species. Accompanied by a competent tracker and suitably equipped with a jeep and a week's worth of supplies, you may be lucky enough to catch glimpses of Mexico's two seldom-seen primates, the **spider** and **howler monkeys.** The black spider monkey, whom your tracker will probably know as the *chango* or *mono de araña*, congregates in groups and uses its spindly arms and legs (thus the "spider" label) and its prehensile tail to reach its favorite wild fruits. Although its entertaining antics and endearingly mischievous ways have earned the *chango* a place as a pet in many Mexican homes, its present rarity is due in large part to its contribution to the diet of many poor indigenous families.

The even rarer howler monkey, called locally *saraguato* or *aullador*, is, by contrast, extremely shy and retiring. Seldom seen even in captivity, howler monkeys *(Alouatta palliata)* withdraw far into the forest as mankind encroaches. Consider yourself lucky if somewhere in Oaxaca's eastern jungle wilderness you can draw close enough to hear a big male howler's far-off booming call. Consider yourself doubly fortunate if, on such an excursion, you also hear the chesty cry of a jaguar, the fabled *tigre.*

El Tigre

The jaguar's cunning, stealth, and strength are the stuff of Mexican legend. In ancient times, the jaguar was the supreme source from whom kings, princes, and warriors drew their power. And when Mexicans recall the old proverb etched in their memories that "Each hill has its own *tigre,*" they remember that untamable presence out there beyond the campfire, the gate, the town limits, lurking somewhere in the darkness.

The legend is well deserved; at 250 pounds and six feet (110 kilograms, two meters) in length, the jaguar *(Felis onca)* is America's largest, most powerful cat. With dark reticulated spots over a tan coat, the jaguar resembles a beefy, short-legged leopard. Although hunting and human encroachment have driven jaguars into Oaxaca's deepest forest reaches, a few still live on, mostly in the southern coast and Sierra and the northeastern isthmus, where they hunt along thickly forested stream bottoms and foothills. Unlike its more common cousin, the mountain lion, or *león,* the jaguar will eat any game. They have even been known to wait patiently for fish in rivers and stalk beaches for turtle and egg dinners. If they have a favorite food, it is probably the pig-like collared peccary.

Although government rules strictly prohibit jaguar hunting, the temptation for a poor campesino to earn a year's wages by shooting a jaguar and clandestinely selling its pelt is too great for the jaguar to survive for many more years in the wild in Oaxaca.

Despite their fearsome reputation and the demonstrated fact that they will fight back when cornered, little or no evidence indicates that jaguars are deliberate man-eaters.

Ocelots, Margays, and Jaguarundis

Although jaguars are extremely endangered, other Mexican cats are less so. Besides the bobcat and mountain lion, both familiar north of the border, three other wild cat species make their home in Oaxaca. In descending order of size, first comes the **ocelot** *(Felis pardalis).* Its appearance, like a miniature jaguar, with a spotted yellowish-tan coat and stout legs, reflects its Mexican name, *tigrillo.* Full-grown male ocelots measure about 25 pounds (10 kg) and three feet (one meter) in length. Its soft, fine fur, highly valued as a pelt, has unfortunately led to the ocelot's near-disappearance from Oaxaca's forests.

Approaching large house-cat size is the **jaguarundi,** or *leoncillo,* which, full-grown, weighs in at around 13 pounds (six kg). Although its species label *(Felis jaguarundi)* clearly puts the brownish jaguarundi in the cat family, its elongated body and long tail (totaling up to 30 inches/75 cm) gives it an otterlike overall appearance.

With its spots and diminutive size, a full-grown **margay** appears at first glance to be a baby jaguar. A closer look, however, reveals spots more aligned in rows than the jaguar's. Moreover, a domesticated margay, in contrast to the untamable jaguar, can be as endearing as your own family cat.

Like their larger cousins, the jaguarundi and margay are gradually disappearing from Oaxaca's forest wildlands. They hunt mostly along stream banks in deep remote valleys and roadless mountainsides. They feast on small game, birds, and fish, and, as a matter of self-preservation, make it their business to see you before you see them.

BIRDS

Oaxaca's coastal wetlands and upland forests straddle the southern zone of the great Pacific Flyway, the major western pathway for hosts of birds migrating south from the United States and Canada. These familiar winter visitors, such as Canada geese and ducks, including the Muscovy, black-bellied whistler, gadwall, baldpate, and shoveler, arrive and join an already-rich resident population of ibis, parrots, jacanas, egrets, herons, and anhingas, swelling the numbers into the millions.

Some of the most commonly seen residents are also the most spectacular and entertaining. The cootlike, blackish **northern jacana** *(Jacana spinosa)* amuses bird-watchers by appearing to walk on water. Actually, its clownishly large feet allow it to scoot across gardens of water-borne lily pads as if they were solid land, earning it the label "lily walker."

Always impressive is the graceful swoop of a **great blue heron** *(Ardea herodius)* gliding to rest in a Oaxacan wetland. Unmistakable because of its regal six-foot (two-meter) wing-spread and blue-gray coloring, the male great blue heron also sports a proud blue head plume. In the same marshland, you will also probably spot its smaller (about two feet, or half a meter, long), more numerous cousin, the **snowy egret** *(Egretta thula),* pure white except for its black beak. Although differing sharply in appearance, both species single-mindedly stalk

Some bird experts believe that the great grey heron and its white lookalike, the great white heron (also common in Oaxaca) belong to the same species.

© BRUCE WHIPPERMAN

through a pond ever so slowly, freezing rock-still when prey is spotted. After several seconds, pop! Down goes the bill, snaring a hapless crab, fish, or frog.

Try not to confuse the snowy egret with the smaller (18-inch) yellow-billed **cattle egret** *(Bubulcus ibis),* an African native that began appearing in Mexico around 1900. True to their name, cattle egrets usually flock around cow pastures, where they feed on the hordes of bugs that follow livestock. Local Mexican people generally identify all herons and egrets collectively as *garzas.*

Seabirds

Oaxaca's prime beach-bird actors, in addition to the swarms of gulls *(gaviotas)*, terns, sandpipers, and boobies, are **brown pelicans** and big black-and-white **frigate birds.** Their collective feeding rituals, although quite distinct, are equally entertaining. That of the brown *pelícano* (pay-LEE-cah-noh) is the most deliberate.

After spotting a school of their preferred prey, the pelicans, singly or in pairs, circle once or twice, then dive headlong into the billows, usually coming up with fish in their gullet. They rest, bobbing over the waves for a spell, seemingly waiting for their comrades to take their turns. Frigate birds (*fragatas*), by contrast, prefer either being fed or stealing food to hunting for themselves. They often reap bonuses from the efforts of villagers who haul in nets of fish right on the beach. Once the salable part of the catch is gone, kids have great fun throwing the residue overhead to a gaggle of wheeling frigate birds. In contrast to the pelicans' mannerly behavior, it's every frigate bird for itself. Frigates who miss a tossed morsel often try to snatch their fellow's prize.

Parrots

Flocks of small parrots screech, shriek, swoop, chatter, and swarm above Oaxaca's coastal mangrove lagoons and tropical foothills. The best places to spot them are in fields or pastures adjacent to thick forests, far from town. Half a dozen species—mostly green, with a patch of color on their throat or forehead—are common. If you don't get far enough into the country to see them, ask where *péricos* (PAY-ree-kohs) are for sale in big markets, such as Oaxaca City, Tlacolula, Etla, Tehuántepec, Tuxtepec, Pinotepa Nacional, and Valle Nacional.

Although you might be tempted to buy such a market parrot, don't. Like all wild animals, parrots outside of their forest homelands present manifold difficulties. For starters, they quickly chew their way out of bamboo cages. Later, your airline will probably require that you buy a special "parrot ticket" for the flight back home. Moreover, after you arrive, parrots are all but impossible to get through customs. On the other hand, if you must have a pet parrot, best buy a pair of (never a single) certified healthy birds from a pet shop back home.

Among the parrots you're most likely to encounter in Oaxaca is the foot-long **green parakeet** (*Aratinga holochlora*). A long tail and a red throat further mark the species, whose members prefer to flock in the drier woodlands above 3,000 feet (1,000 meters). Another, commonly seen in tropical lowlands, is the **Aztec parakeet** (*Aratinga astec*), at nine inches (23 cm), all green with an olive-brown throat. For superb color drawings and details, see *A Guide to the Birds of Mexico and Northern America* by Steve Howell and Sophie Webb.

REPTILES AND AMPHIBIANS
Snakes

Of Oaxaca's many dozens of snake species, the great majority couldn't harm you even if they tried. Furthermore, most snakes are shy and will clear out if you give them plenty of warning. In Oaxaca, poisonous snakes have been largely driven out of city and tourist areas. In the bush or jungle, however, carry a stick and beat the shrubbery in front of you while watching where you put your feet. When hiking or rock-climbing in the country, don't put your hands in niches you can't see into.

While such precautions minimize potential hazards, outback travelers should be prepared to encounter members of Oaxaca's most notorious snake families, the **rattlesnakes** and the **fer-de-lances.** Each occurs in a number of species, all potently venomous and generally aggressive. Mexican rattlesnakes, or **cascabeles** (kahs-kah-BAY-lays), with the same warning rattle and the diamondback markings as their north-of-the-border U.S. relatives, need little introduction. Their tropical viper-cousins, the fer-de-lances (*Bothrops atrox*), are known locally by various names, such as **nauyaca, cuatro narices, palanca,** and **barba amarilla.** Although about the same size (to six feet/two meters) and general appearance as rattlesnakes, fer-de-lances *lack warning rattles* and are consequently even more dangerous. On treks into the jungle, where the fer-de-lance commonly lives, guard against them by wearing high-topped leather boots, rustling the bushes ahead of you with a stick, and watching carefully where you put your feet.

Snakes in the tropics are not confined to land. Although very unlikely, it is possible that you may encounter a **sea snake** (*culebra* *marina)* while swimming offshore at an isolated Oaxaca beach. If small, yellow, and black, it will certainly be the *Pelamis platurus,* which, although shy, lives in groups and has been reported to inflict a serious, venomous bite. Some **eels,** which resemble snakes but have gills like fish and inhabit rocky crevices, can inflict nonpoisonous bites and should also be avoided.

The Oaxacan land counterpart of the poisonous sea snake is the **coral snake** *(coralillo),* which occurs in several species, all with bright multicolored bands that always include red. Although relatively rare, small, and shy, coral snakes occasionally bite, sometimes fatally.

Gila Monsters, Iguanas, and Geckos

The Gila monster (confined in Mexico to northern Sonora) and its southern tropical relative, the black-with-yellow-spots **escorpión,** are the world's only poisonous lizards. Despite its beaded skin and menacing, fleshy appearance, the *escorpión (Heloderma horridum)* bites only when severely provoked; even then, its venom is rarely, if ever, fatal.

The rest of Oaxaca's many lizard species are much more benign; some are even endearing. Of them, the **iguana,** locally called the *garrobo,* is most popular, mainly because of its tasty flesh. Although usually masked in the bush by its spotted green camouflage, you may glimpse an iguana scurrying, in a flash of green, across the road in front of your car or bus. Despite their fierce dinosaurian aspect, iguanas are peaceful vegetarians, often munching flowers in a favorite treetop.

One of Oaxaca's most endearing reptilian which was introduced from Europe as a game animal and now lives wild, ranging from South America to central Mexico residents is the **gecko,** known as *guerita* (blondie) in the coastal towns and villages where they are common. Visitors usually encounter them in their hotel rooms. If you hear their homey clicking sound (for which residents affectionately call them *besucona,* the "kissing one"), don't

be alarmed. Quite the contrary, for each room cannot be without its resident gecko to properly cleanse it of gnats and mosquitoes. If your room doesn't have one, ask the management to find a *guerita* for you.

Crocodiles

The crocodile *(cocodrilo* or *caiman),* once prized for its meat and hide, came close to vanishing from Oaxaca's coastal lagoons until the government stepped in to ensure its survival. Now officially protected, crocodiles are becoming increasingly common in the wild as government and private hatcheries are breeding more for the eventual repopulation of lagoons where they once were common. A coastal **crocodile hatchery** open for touring is located in Lagunas de Chacagua, west of Puerto Escondido.

Two crocodile species are native to Oaxaca. The true crocodile *(Crocodilus acutus)* has a narrower snout than its local cousin *(Caiman*

© BRUCE WHIPPERMAN

Mexican crocodiles, once hunted to near extinction, are making a comeback in Oaxaca's coastal lagoons.

crocodilus fuscus), a type of **alligator** *(lagarto)*. Although past individuals have been recorded up to 15 feet (five meters) long, wild native crocodiles are usually young and a few feet or less in length.

Sea Turtles

The story of Mexican sea turtles is similar to that of the crocodiles. They once swarmed ashore on Mexican beaches to lay their eggs. Prized for their meat, eggs, hide, and shell, the turtle populations were severely devastated. Now officially protected, growing numbers of sea turtles are hatching and returning to the sea from Oaxaca's beaches, thanks to the increasing ranks of eco-volunteers who guard against poachers. Very accessible Oaxaca turtle sanctuaries include the entire Bahías de Huatulco, a pair of home-grown sanctuaries near Puerto Escondido, and especially Playa Mazunte, near Puerto Ángel. There, a government **turtle aquarium and hatchery** occupies the site of a former turtle processing factory.

Of the four locally occurring species, the **olive ridley** *(tortuga golfina)* and the **green turtle** *(tortuga verde)* are the most common. From tour boats, sea turtles can often be seen grazing on sea grass offshore from Puerto Escondido, Puerto Ángel, and the Bahías de Huatulco.

FISH

Shoals of fish abound in Oaxacan waters. Four billfish species are found in deep-sea grounds several miles offshore: **swordfish, sailfish,** and **blue and black marlin.** All are spirited fighters, though the sailfish and marlin are generally the toughest to bring in. The blue marlin is the biggest of the four. Although 10-foot, 1,000-pound (three-meter, 450-kilogram) fish used to be brought in occasionally, four-foot, 200-pound marlin (one-meter, 90-kilogram) and 100-pound (45-kilogram) sailfish are more typical of late. Recognizing the need for conservation, forward-looking captains now encourage victorious anglers to return these magnificent "tigers of the sea" (especially the sinewy, poor-eating sailfish and blue marlin) to the deep after they've won the battle.

Billfish are not the only prizes of the sea. Serious fish lovers also seek varieties of tuna-like **jack,** such as **yellowtail, Pacific amberjack, pompano, jack crevalle,** and the tenacious **roosterfish,** named for the "comb" atop its head. These and the **yellowfin tuna, mackerel,** and **dorado,** which Hawaiians call mahimahi, are among the delicacies sought in Oaxacan waters.

Accessible from small boats offshore and by casting from shoreline rocks are varieties of **snapper** *(huachinango, pargo)* and **sea bass** *(cabrilla).* Closer to shore, **croaker, mullet,** and **Goliath fish** often can be found foraging along sandy bottoms and in rocky crevices.

Sharks and **rays** inhabit nearly all depths, with smaller fry venturing into beach shallows and lagoons. Sometimes, huge **Pacific manta rays** appear to be frolicking, their great wings flapping like birds, not far off Oaxacan shores. Just beyond the waves, local fisherfolk bring in **hammerhead, thresher,** and **leopard sharks.**

Also common is the **stingray,** which can inflict a painful wound with its barbed tail. Experienced swimmers and waders avoid injury by both shuffling (rather than stepping) and watching their feet in shallow, sandy bottoms.

Captains from marinas at Santa Cruz de Huatulco, Puerto Ángel, and Salina Cruz routinely pilot big boats equipped for four or five anglers to try for the big marlin, sailfish, and swordfish. Launches *(lanchas)* and tackle, suitable for smaller but still exciting catches, can be hired at those same marinas, in addition to Puerto Escondido and a number of other beach villages along the Oaxacan coast.

For more fish details, including a chart of species encountered in Oaxacan waters, see *Recreation* in the *Essentials* chapter.

History

An age ago—perhaps as long as 20,000 years—small bands of hardy people, ancestors of the adventurers who had crossed the Arctic land bridge from Siberia thousands of years earlier, were hunting and foraging in what is now the Valley of Oaxaca. The forests and meadows abounded with edible plants and game—from squirrels and rabbits to great Ice Age herds of camels, horses, and mammoths. Supplied with abundant food, the people multiplied.

But by around 7000 B.C. the climate had warmed several degrees, and the great game animals were extinct. Perhaps in response, the people began to sow seeds of their favorite edible wild grains, legumes, vegetables, and fruits. As their descendants still do today, those ancient Oaxacans picked out the biggest and healthiest seeds to plant for the succeeding year's crop. After many generations, their fields were blooming with domesticated beans, squash, corn, and avocados nearly as robust as those enjoyed today.

EARLY CIVILIZATION
The Village Era

Millennia later, around 2000 B.C., those early Oaxacans, supplied with the bounty of their fields, no longer had to wander in search of food and were settling into permanent villages. Although initially small—typically only a dozen houses—the villages prospered and grew. Discovered remains reveal that many aspects of Oaxacan village life have remained fundamentally unchanged. Then, as now, planting, harvesting, and preparation of food occupied most of the day. Men used flint ax-heads hafted to wooden handles to clear brush, which they would burn in preparation for seeding. Women ground corn with the familiar *mano* and *metate,* a combination roller-crusher. They patted tortillas and baked them on the flat clay *comal* (griddle) and stewed meats, beans, and chili sauces in round clay pots.

Excavated ceramic figurines reveal the villagers' dress: for women, woven cloth or frond skirts, fiber or leather sandals, and long hair, often attractively braided, plus earrings and necklaces; for men, ordinarily a simple loincloth and sandals.

Village people buried their dead family members, laid out flat, in graves near their houses. A few offerings for the afterlife accompanied the deceased: a bowl with food, drinks, favored personal objects, and jewelry, including a semiprecious stone placed in the mouth.

Gradually, population increased. By 500 B.C. some villages, such as at **San José El Mogote** about 10 miles (16 km) northwest of Oaxaca City, had grown into small towns, with as many as 500 residents. At San José El Mogote investigators have uncovered early evidence of social classes—large, regally elevated houses—and specialization, in the form of a factory where workers polished iron-rich magnetite into small mirrors, which were traded hundreds of miles away.

Gradually during the few thousand years when villages were growing into towns, abundant food and burgeoning commercial wealth lifted a small but significant fraction of Oaxacans to a privileged leisure status. They became the artists, architects, warriors, and ruler-priests—with time to think and create. Over time, they devised symbols, writing, and a calendar that tied the constant wheel of the firmament to life on earth, defining the days to plant, to harvest, to feast, to travel, and to trade. Eventually, a grand city arose.

Monte Albán

Around 500 B.C., ancestors of Oaxaca's present-day Zapotec peoples founded what many experts believe to have been the Americas' earliest metropolis. On the central valley summit known today as Monte Albán, they raised monumental platforms, pyramids, palaces, and ceremonial ball courts. These they decorated with inscriptions, in a language yet to be deciphered, recording the exploits of their god-kings. The ordinary family homes of adobe bricks, arranged around central patios, occupied the hillside just below the ceremonial summit.

For centuries, Monte Albán flourished, overflowing halfway down its hillsides. Although starting from a population of only 2,000 at its founding, Monte Albán flourished to a city of as many as 40,000 at its height a thousand years later. By A.D. 500 Monte Albán encompassed three square miles (seven sq. km), interlaced with vegetable and flower gardens and spreading to several monumental neighborhood sub-centers downhill.

Although Monte Albán ruled, upwards of two dozen subsidiary cities administered local areas throughout Oaxaca. Their ruins litter the present-day state: sites such as Yucuita and Monte Negro near Nochixtlán, in the Mixteca Alta, Cerro de las Minas in the Mixteca Baja, and Dainzu and Lambityeco in the central valley. War appears to have been a scourge of Oaxaca's early cities. Like Monte Albán, and in contrast to most village-era sites, most cities lay atop defensible hilltops.

Monte Albán's days were nevertheless numbered. After dominating Oaxaca and beyond for more than a thousand years, its power was fading fast by around A.D. 750. Although experts argue over what combination of drought, disease, war, or overpopulation ended Monte Albán's glory days, they agree that it was virtually abandoned by A.D. 1000 and eclipsed by a crowd of tussling city-states. A similar mysterious fate befell other southern and central Mexican cities, most notably Teotihuacán, Monte Albán's great rival metropolis in the north.

Teotihuacán

Although founded half a millennium later than Monte Albán, Teotihuacán grew rapidly, attaining population and wealth on a par with the ancient world's great cities by A.D. 300. Its epic pyramids still stand, not far north of Mexico City, along a grand avenue of fearsome, ruby-eyed stone effigies of Quetzalcoatl, the feathered serpent king of gods.

After Teotihuacán was abandoned around A.D. 700, a host of its former vassal cities rose to power, among them Xochicalco, in the highlands in the present state of Morelos, an hour's drive south of Mexico City.

The Living Quetzalcoatl

Xochicalco became renowned as a center of learning, where noble families sent their sons to study the healing arts, astronomy, architecture, and agriculture. A prominent student among them was **Topiltzín** (literally, Our Prince), who left Xochicalco in A.D. 968 to found his own city-state, Tula, north of old Teotihuacán.

After an enlightened 20-year rule, Topiltzín became so revered that his people began to know him as the living incarnation of Quetzalcoatl, the plumed-serpent god of gods. He was not universally loved, however. Jealous priests, who hated Quetzalcoatl-Topiltzín's persuasive opposition to their bloody rites of human sacrifice, drugged him with alcohol. He awoke, bleary-eyed, in bed with his sister. Devastated by shame, Quetzalcoatl-Topiltzín banished himself from Tula with a band of retainers. In A.D. 987, they headed east, toward Yucatán. Although he sent word he would reclaim his kingdom during the 52 year cyclical calendar year of his birth, Ce Acatl, Quetzalcoatl-Topiltzín never returned. Legends say that he sailed east and rose to heaven as the morning star.

The Rise of Oaxacan City-States

By A.D. 1000, the power vacuum left by the demise of Monte Albán had been filled by its dozens of former tributary cities, whose rulers carved out their own little kingdoms, mostly in the central valley and the Mixteca. Each had a dominant town, typically with a population of 5,000–10,000, which ruled a dispersed walking-distance village hinterland of about 100 square miles (250 sq. km) and 10,000 or 20,000 people. Some of these, notably **Zaachila** and **Mitla**, near present-day Oaxaca City, remain thriving towns, still dominating their districts, while others, such as **Yagul**, near Mitla; **Huijazoo**, in the Etla Valley northwest of Oaxaca City; and **Guiengola**, in the Isthmus west of Tehuántepec, are uninhabited ruins.

8-Deer and the Mixtec Invasion

In A.D. 1011, not long after the great Quetzalcoatl-Topiltzín had trekked east, another renowned noble, known to historians as 8-Deer, the calendar name-date of his birth, was born in Oaxaca. Scholars have learned details of his life through pre-conquest hieroglyphic documents, collectively called **codices** (or singularly, codex). Although most were destroyed by Spanish priests all over Mexico early in the conquest, eight Oaxaca codices, folded deerskin hieroglyphic books whitened with lime, survived, all from the Mixtec region of Oaxaca, respectively called Becker I, Becker II, Bodley, Colombino, Nuttall, Sánchez Solis, Selden, and Vienna. Six of these eight Mixtec codices commemorate 8-Deer's adventures. Among the most enlightening, Codex Nuttall records 8-Deer's given name as **Tiger Claw**, portending his ruthless exploits.

As Monte Albán's power faded, the Mixtec city-states, west and northwest of the central valley, thrived. But overpopulation, and perhaps pressure from Xochicalco and the Toltecs (People of Tula), forced ambitious Mixtec nobles to look southward at the fertile lands of the Oaxaca central valley.

The stage for Mixtec expansion was set when 8-Deer Tiger Claw came of age. He moved quickly, forming alliances and setting his rivals against one another. Codex Nuttall depicts one of 8-Deer Tiger Claw's expeditions. It shows him, along with two allies, 4-Tiger and 9-Water, spears and shields in hand, crossing a lake by canoe toward an island, the Hill of Mixtlatl. The document records the expedition's three consecutive dates: 10-Serpent, 11-Death, and 12-Deer, of A.D. 1046, when 8-Deer was in his 35-year-old fighting prime.

After bringing the entire Mixteca, from the Tehuacán Valley in the north to the coastal stronghold at Tututepec, under his control, 8-Deer led Mixtec armies southeast from his capital at **Tilantongo** and defeated a number of Zapotec central valley city-states. Although 8-Deer met his end as a sacrifice victim in Cuilapan, not far south of present-day Oaxaca City, in 1061, Mixtec nobles ruled on as an elite minority in Zaachila, Mitla, and other valley city-states. They preserved their dominance by the tactic of political marriage, taking daughters of the Zapotec nobility as near-hostage wives who raised Mixtec-speaking heirs.

Although only a relatively few of the original Mixtec speakers remain living today in the central valley, the old Mixtec influence lives on in the Zapotec-Mixtec stylistic fusion of the architecture, pottery, jewelry, and other remains found at Zaachila, Mitla, Monte Albán, and other sites. Admire the elaborately fine **greca** mosaic frets decorating the Mitla ruins and you're enjoying the Mixtec influence; likewise, at the Museo de las Culturas de Oaxaca, in the Centro Cultural de Santo Domingo in Oaxaca City, Mixtec craftsmanship and sophistication gleam from the **golden mask of death** and the trove of gold and turquoise jewelry taken from **Tomb 7** at Monte Albán.

The Aztecs Invade Oaxaca

At the time the Mixtecs were consolidating their rule of the Valley of Oaxaca, the Aztecs (People of Aztlán), a collection of seven aggressive immigrant subtribes, had eclipsed the Toltec civilization that Quetzalcoatl-Topiltzín had founded north of present-day Mexico City. After migrating from a mysterious **western land of Aztlán** (Land of the Herons) into the lake-filled valley that Mexico City now occupies, around 1250, the Aztecs' fiercest tribe, whose members called themselves the **México** (MAY-shee-kah), clawed its way to dominion over the Valley of Mexico. In 1325, the México founded their capital, Tenochtitlán, on an island in the middle of the valley-lake. During the next century, Tenochtitlán grew into a magnificent city, from which Aztec armies, like Roman legions, marched out and subdued kingdoms for hundreds of miles in all directions.

In 1434, the Aztecs, under Emperor Itzcóatl, conquered the northern Mixtec domains in the Tehuacán Valley; several years later his successor, Moctezuma Ilhuicamina, attacked southward, defeating Atonaltzin, the Mixtec lord of Coixtlahuaca. Besides yielding booty and a small army of captives, the victory opened the path to the entire Mixteca and the Valley of Oaxaca.

By 1488, the Aztecs were firmly fixed in the valley, having established a garrison at **Huaxyacac,** the site of present-day Oaxaca City. From that point, however, the Aztecs found their access to the remainder of the central valley and the coveted southern lands of Tehuántepec blocked by the strong Zapotec city-state of Zaachila. After several years of frustrating bargaining, the Aztecs, then under Emperor Ahuizotl, hammered out a treaty with **Cosijoeza** (koh-see-hoh-EY-zah), the king of Zaachila, for peaceful access toward Tehuántepec in the southeast. Cosijocza soon regretted the concession. In 1494, the Aztecs broke the agreement and seized and subjugated Mitla, at the eastern end of the Valley of Oaxaca. Enraged, Cosijoeza rushed his forces southeast and fortified their Isthmus hilltop bastion at Guiengola, which blocked the Aztecs' progress to their southern capital at Tehuántepec and Chiapas beyond.

After a seven-month siege of Guiengola, the frustrated Aztecs again resorted to diplomacy. They proposed a new alliance, in the form of a marriage between King Cosijoeza and **Coyollicatzin** (koh-yoh-yee-KAH-tseen), the daughter of the new Aztec Emperor Moctezuma I. The Aztecs' hidden agenda: They expected Coyollicatzin to spy upon Cosijoeza; true love, however, won out as Coyollicatzin refused to play the pawn and remained loyal to her husband Cosijoeza. The Aztecs eventually made peace in return for tribute. Cosijoeza turned his Tehuántepec domain to his son **Cosijopí** and returned home to reign over his Zapotec people at Zaachila in the central valley.

Despite a king's ransom in yearly tribute—mounds of quetzal feathers, dozens of sacks of cochineal, hundreds of pounds of gold, thousands of bolts of cloth—the Aztecs' millions of Oaxacan subjects always seemed to be rebelling someplace until the Spanish conquistadores arrived and toppled the Aztecs from power in 1521.

THE CONQUEST

Although Christopher Columbus and the generation of explorers who followed him had discovered a new world in America, their dreams of riches had eluded them. In Spain's new Caribbean island colonies both gold and native workers, who had mostly died from European diseases, were scarce. A new wave of adventurers, among them **Hernán Cortés,** a minor nobleman from the poor Spanish province of Extremadura, turned their vision toward new fabled empires—perhaps even the elusive Cathay—beyond the setting sun. In Cuba, Cortés patched together a motley force of 550 men, an assortment of small ships, a few horses and cannons and sailed west in early 1519. By the time they landed on Mexico's Gulf Coast on April 22, 1519, Cortés's men, torn by dissension and realizing the impossible odds against them, were near mutiny.

Cortés, however, cut his losses and exploited his opportunities with extraordinary aplomb. He won over the doubters, isolated the dissenters, and ended any thoughts of retreat to Cuba by burning his ships. Next he capitalized on the lucky coincidence that he had landed on the Mexican coastline in the Aztec year of Ce Acatl, exactly the same 52-year cyclical anniversary year in which Quetzalcoatl-Topiltzín had vowed to return from the east to reclaim his kingdom.

As he led his band of adventurers westward over the mountains toward the Aztec capital of Tenochtitlán, Cortés played Quetzalcoatl to the hilt, awing local leaders. Coaxed by **Doña Marina,** his wily native translator-mistress-confidante, local chiefs began to add their armies to Cortés's march against their Aztec oppressors.

Tenochtitlán, Capital of the Empire

A few months later, inside the gates of Tenochtitlán, the Venice-like island metropolis, it was the Spaniards' turn to be awed: by gardens full of animals, gold, and palaces, and a great pyramid-enclosed square where tens of thousands of people bartered goods gathered from all over the empire. Tenochtitlán, with perhaps a quarter of a million people, was the great capital of an empire as large and rich as any in Europe.

Moctezuma II, the lord of that empire, fearing that Cortés was in fact the god Quetzalcoatl incarnate, had followed Cortés's progress toward Tenochtitlán with trepidation. Wishing not to offend, Moctezuma II had sent Cortés sumptuous gifts of gold, coupled with warnings to stay away. Encouraged by the gold, Cortés demanded an early audience with the emperor, who pathetically surrendered himself to Cortés's custody and "donated" his entire empire to the Spanish crown.

Spaniards Enter Oaxaca

With his position temporarily secure, Cortés dispatched emissaries west, east, and south. To Oaxaca he sent Hernando Pizarro and Diego de Ordaz, each with small detachments, to reconnoiter for riches. Pizarro searched for gold in the Papaloapaon basin around Tuxtepec and later the Chinantla, while Ordaz passed through the Mixtec kingdoms of Yanhuitlán and Sosola on his way to the Gulf Coast.

The Aztecs Force a Spanish Retreat

Meanwhile, however, the people of Tenochtitlán were rioting against Spanish brutality. On July 1, 1520, with Moctezuma II mortally wounded by his own countrymen, Cortés and his men, forced by the sheer numbers of rebellious Mexicans, retreated, hacking a bloody path through thousands of screaming Aztec warriors to safety on the lakeshore.

Hearing the news of Cortés's defeat, Mexican garrisons in Oaxaca dealt a similar blow against the local Spanish expeditions, attacking and killing dozens of Spaniards and their indigenous allies.

Although Cortés was down, he wasn't out. In succeeding months, as his forces regathered strength in the Valley of Mexico, he pushed the conquest of the south. Alonso de Avila arrived in Oaxaca in late 1520 and accepted the ambassadors of Zapotec kings Cosijoeza

and Cosijopí, who were more than willing to ally themselves against their Aztec overlords. Concurrently, other Spanish expeditions thrust into Oaxaca: Gonzalo de Sandoval successfully counterattacked against the Aztec garrisons, while Juan Cedeño obtained the submission of the Chinantecs and the northern Zapotecs.

Tenochtitlán Falls and Oaxaca Is Conquered

In late 1521, reinforced by fresh soldiers, horses, a small fleet of armed sailboats, and 100,000 indigenous allies, Cortés retook Tenochtitlán. The stubborn defenders, led by Cuauhtémoc, Moctezuma's nephew, fell by the tens of thousands beneath a smoking hail of Spanish grapeshot. The Aztecs, although weakened by smallpox, refused to surrender. Cortés found, to his dismay, that he had to destroy the city in order to take it.

Soon after Cortés's triumph, the Zapotec kings Cosijoeza and Cosijopí sent ambassadors declaring their submission to him and his king, Charles V. This alarmed the Mixtecs, who, with the backing of the Chinantec king of Tuxtepec, declared war on the Zapotecs. At the request of his new Zapotec allies, Cortés dispatched Francisco de Orozco in December 1521 and Pedro de Alvarado a month later with a few hundred infantry and a handful of cavalry to pacify Oaxaca. After a few skirmishes, Orozco took possession of Huaxyacac, the site of present-day Oaxaca City, which the Aztec garrisons had occupied since 1456. A few hours later, on the same day, December 25, 1521, padre Juan Díaz celebrated the first Catholic mass in Oaxaca territory. A month later at the same spot, Alvarado, with the help of padre Bartolomé de Olmedo, helped negotiate a peace agreement between the Mixtecs and Zapotecs.

With the valley and northern Oaxaca pacified, Cortés sent Alvarado to conquer the Oaxacan Pacific coast. On March 4, 1522, Alvarado defeated Casandoo, the Mixtec king of Tututepec, and with colonists displaced from the Valley of Oaxaca by Cortés's orders, he founded the Villa Segura de la Frontera

(Secure Village of the Frontier). He went on to pacify the whole coast, including Tonameca, Pochutla, Huatulco, and Astata, all the way east to Tehuántepec.

NEW SPAIN

With much of the former Aztec empire firmly in his grip and his lieutenants continuing to lead their forces in triumph in all directions, Cortés anticipated the grand domain that would eventually expand to more than a dozenfold the size of old Spain. He wrote his king, Charles V, "The most suitable name for it would be New Spain of the Ocean Sea, and thus in the name of your Majesty I have christened it."

Even as he was building the new Mexico City atop the ruins of old Tenochtitlán, Cortés dreamed of a kingdom of his own. His first information of the fertile, spring-like Valley of Oaxaca came from his own scouts and from the ambassadors the Oaxacan kings had sent Cortés moved quickly to carve out his Oaxaca domain, sending orders with Pedro de Alvarado to remove all Spanish settlers from the valley.

When Cortés personally arrived in Oaxaca in 1523 he found to his chagrin that the settlers that he had previously ordered out of the valley had returned and were squatting on the land he wanted for himself. He sent the instigators to Mexico City in chains and dispersed the settlers again. He granted his friends and relatives, including his son Martín and his two illegitimate daughters, *encomiendas* (rights to land and native labor) at strategic points all over Oaxaca, then, in October 1524, marched off on an exhausting two-year expedition to Honduras.

By the time Cortés returned in 1526, the settlers had again returned and reestablished their village at Huaxyacac. Moreover, they had petitioned the king of Spain, Carlos I, for a charter for their settlement, which they had christened **Antequera,** in honor of the ancient Granada town of the same name. To Cortés's great displeasure, the petition was granted, by royal decree, on September 14, 1526.

Undeterred, Cortés took charge and began building his Valley of Oaxaca domain. He staked out the best bottomland, built haciendas, and set his native laborers to planting wheat and sugarcane. Cortés then traveled to Huatulco and Tehuántepec, where he built a port and ships to explore the Pacific. Concurrently, Cortés strengthened his alliance with King Cosijopí, who reciprocated by converting (along with thousands of his Tehuántepec subjects) to Christianity, taking the name Juan Cortés Cosijopí.

Hernán Cortés, Marquis of the Valley of Oaxaca

Cortés realized that his de facto kingdom needed both a queen and royal recognition, so he traveled to Spain in 1528 to get both. A year later he returned with his young noble bride, Juana de Zúñiga, and the grand title of Marqués del Valle de Oaxaca, which included a singularly generous grant of land, subjects, and privileges. For many years thereafter, he and his heirs received upward of 80,000 gold pesos a year from tens of thousands of indigenous subjects on three million acres of domain scattered from the Valley of Mexico through the present states of Morelos, Mexico, Guerrero, and Veracruz to Oaxaca.

Cortés's Valley of Oaxaca holdings, the crown jewel of his domain, encompassed most of the best valley land. In a wide, 350,000-acre swath, it stretched 25 miles, including 34 villages and towns, from Etla in the north to Coyotepec in the south. Excluded, however, was the one-league square (two square miles) of the town of Antequera, which grew into the present-day Oaxaca City.

The Missionaries

While the conquistadores scoured the countryside for gold and subjugated the local people, missionaries began arriving to heal, teach, and baptize them. The Dominicans were the first and most numerous in Oaxaca. Padre Minaya built the first Oaxaca convent, dedicated to Saint Paul, in Antequera around 1530. Other Dominicans settled in Tlaxiaco, Etla, and Tehuántepec, where King Cosijopí financed a church for them in 1538. Other orders—Franciscans, Augustinians, Bethlehemites, and more—soon joined them. Missionary authorities customarily enjoyed a sympathetic ear from Charles V and his successors, who earnestly pursued Spain's Christian mission, especially when it coincided with their political and economic goals.

Besides saving souls, the missionaries introduced new plants, flowers, and vegetables, and useful European crafts, such as ironwork, glassmaking, wool processing, and pottery glazing. They learned native tongues and wrote catechisms in Zapotec, Mixtec, and other local dialects. Within a few dozen years, the fields, orchards, and vineyards dotted with dozens of churches around the Valley of Oaxaca and beyond testified to the dedication of both the missionaries and their native converts.

Unfortunately, in order to speed the process of conversion, which the missionaries viewed as a sort of divine manifest destiny, native temples, idols, and paintings were destroyed. Historical records were irretrievably lost. The Spaniards also banned native song and dance, fearing that they kept alive old beliefs.

Although the missionaries on the whole provided a kinder, gentler counterbalance to the often brutal and exploitative conquistadores and colonists, they were not entirely blameless. In their zeal to build churches, convents, and monasteries, they also demanded the backbreaking labor of the newly converted. Moreover, those resistant to conversion were dealt with harshly, sometimes beaten, tortured, or killed.

In Oaxaca, however, which was primarily a Dominican stronghold, *indígenas* were spared the worst excesses of the more zealous Franciscans. **Bartolomé de las Casas,** a Dominican friar, devoted his life to fighting for the rights of the native people. This champion of social justice earned the sobriquet "Apostle of the Indians."

The King Takes Control

By 1530, the crown, through the Council of the Indies, had begun to wrest power away from Cortés and his conquistador lieutenants. Cortés had granted many of them rights of **encomienda:** taxes and labor of an indigenous district. In exchange, the **encomendero,** who often enjoyed the status of feudal lord, pledged to look after the welfare and souls of his native charges.

From the king's point of view, though, tribute pesos collected by *encomenderos* translated into losses to the crown. Moreover, many *encomenderos* callously exploited their indigenous wards for quick profit, sometimes selling them as slave labor in mines and on plantations. Such abuses, coupled with European-introduced diseases, began to reduce the native population at an alarming rate.

By 1540, strongly influenced by Dominican padre Bartolomé de las Casas, the outspoken "Apostle of the Indians," the king and his councilors realized that the native Mexicans were in peril, and without their labor New Spain would vanish.

They acted decisively. New laws would shift power toward the crown and limit abuses to the king's native subjects. Decreed in 1542 and enforced by a powerful *visitador* (inspector general), the **New Laws of the Indies** abolished perpetual rights of *encomienda,* outlawed slavery of native Mexicans, and limited their labor and tribute payments.

Although Oaxacan colonists protested vehemently, some native groups benefited. With the support of the new bishop of Antequera, Juan López de Zárate, and the missionary padres, Zapotecs around the Valley of Oaxaca mounted a legal fight against excessive *encomienda* payments.

COLONIAL OAXACA
Congregación

Despite the Valley of Oaxaca Marquesate, Spanish garrisons, a score of Spanish-run haciendas, a few mines, and the capital town Antequera, Oaxaca had a sparse population of no more than a thousand Spaniards around 1550. On the other hand, the native population, while reduced, still numbered several hundred thousand, widely dispersed over the entire territory, and largely controlled by the hereditary native nobility. The Spanish authorities, in order to break the hold of the old chiefs on the natives, began moving indigenous populations into *congregaciones:* new townships in potentially productive areas—valleys, mines, and along royal roads. Each township had its *cabecera* (head town) and *sujeto* (subject) villages. Indigenous governing councils, supervised by Spanish agents, were responsible for local order and collection of tribute.

The missionary clergy initially went along with *congregación* because it led to more converts, but after a generation of seeing the cruel reality of people displaced from their land and traditions, opposed it. In 1604, although the policy was officially abandoned and some of the people returned to their original way of life, many did not. Their descendants remain living in the original *cabeceras,* which comprise a significant portion of present-day Oaxaca's 570 *municipios,* or governmental townships.

The natives, in being shifted toward traditional Spanish occupations, in which they worked mines, harvested sugarcane and wheat, and tended sheep and cattle, were forced to abandon the way of life that had sustained them for millennia. In a few generations, even the memory of their extensive irrigation works—diversion dams and canals that fed terraced fields—was lost.

The severe consequences of this forgotten water-conservation tradition have become acute in modern Oaxaca. An increasing population has led to lack of bottomland, forcing families to poor uplands that without irrigation cannot sustain them. Slash-and-burn dry farming, noncontour plowing, overgrazing, and overcutting of forest have turned large tracts of Oaxaca into eroded wasteland.

Population Collapse

In a real sense, European disease, rather than the conquistadores, subdued Mexico. Despite the missionary fathers' most benign efforts and the most beneficial effects of the king's New Laws, typhus, measles, smallpox, and other European plagues wiped out about 90 percent of the Mexican indigenous population within a few generations after the conquest. Although estimates vary, most experts agree that pre-conquest Mexico's 15–25 million native population had shrunk to a mere 1.3 million by 1650.

Oaxaca's figures reflect a similar tragedy. Of a population that archaeologists estimate at around two million in 1500, only 150,000 remained in 1650. In some cases, such as the mines of Santa Catalina Martir, in 1580, a combination of overwork and disease killed thousands; those remaining simply fled into the hills. In the southern Valley of Oaxaca towns, plagues reduced thriving towns such as Teitipac, Ocotlán, and Miahuatlán from populations of thousands to a few dozen inhabitants nearly overnight.

POPULATION CHANGES IN NEW SPAIN

	EARLY COLONIAL (1570)	LATE COLONIAL (1810)
peninsulares	6,600	15,000
criollos	11,000	1,100,000
mestizos	2,400	704,000
indígenas	3,340,000	3,700,000
negros	22,000	630,000

Today's Mexicans can look forward to the year 2019, the 500th anniversary of Cortés's landing, when Mexico's native-speaking population will have largely recovered to its pre-conquest level of approximately 25 million.

The Changing Role of the Church

During the colonial era, civil and church authorities increasingly came into conflict with missionary orders, whose independent status derived directly from papal authority, in contrast to locally administered ("secular") clergy, who answered to local bishops. Disputes often revolved around treatment of the natives, whose welfare missionaries often outspokenly championed. The kettle, always bubbling, sometimes boiled over. In 1647, Bishop Cerda Benevente of Antequera tried to kick all Dominican fathers out of their churches; in 1749 Bishop Maldonado tried to replace 27 Dominicans with clergy under his control. The issue of power was finally settled in 1767 when the King of Spain expelled all Jesuit missionaries from his New World colonies. This chilled the liberal activist tendencies of clergy everywhere in Mexico and led to an increasingly conservative church establishment.

During Spain's Mexican colonial twilight, the church, increasingly profiting from the status quo, became fat and largely complacent. The biblical tithe—one-tenth of everything, from crops and livestock to rents and mining profits—filled church coffers. By 1800, the church owned half of Mexico. Moreover, all clergy (including the lay church officers) and the military were doubly privileged. They enjoyed right of *fuero* (exemption from civil law) and could be prosecuted by ecclesiastical or military courts only.

The Colonial Economy

In trade and commerce, New Spain existed for the benefit of the mother country. Spaniards enjoyed absolute monopolies by virtue of the complete prohibition of foreign traders and goods. Colonists, as a result, paid dearly for often shoddy Spanish manufactures. The Casa de Contratación, the royal trade regulators, always ensured the colony's yearly balance of payments would result in deficit, which would be made up by bullion shipments from New Spain mines (from which the crown raked 10 percent off the top).

If New Spain was a tradition-bound feudal domain, Oaxaca was even more so. The crown regulated nearly everything. Any kind of enterprise required a royal license, issued through a bureaucracy that required bribes as part of the cost of doing business. Wealth flowed directly from the labor of the native people. Although Oaxaca people produced lots of corn, wheat, cattle, sheep, wool, and some silk, **cochineal** was by far Oaxaca's most valuable export.

Whatever native people produced, they all had to pay taxes, whether directly to the local collector or as tribute to the *encomendero* owner of the estate where they lived. For many poor native families, the problem of getting enough to eat year-round was doubly acute because of the seasonal nature of their produce. They began to rely upon *alcaldes mayores,* local royal officials, for cash advances on crops, especially cochineal. Through their official posts, *alcaldes mayores* enjoyed a monopoly, which forced local folks to sell to them for a pittance. This hated monopoly payment system, known as *repartmiento,* although officially forbidden, was rampant during the mid-1600s, when a swarm of Oaxaca uprisings led to the killing of Tehuántepec's greedy *alcalde mayor* and a number of his henchmen by an angry crowd of native cochineal producers.

Reform didn't come until the 18th century, when Spanish authorities saw the light and banned the *repartmiento* system, replacing the *alcaldes mayores* with less corruptible salaried agents known as *intendentes.*

The bustling cochineal trade led to boom times in colonial Oaxaca. The region, previously a backwater, neglected by Mexico City authorities, benefited from a monopoly on cochineal production after 1745. The population tripled during the 1700s, reaching 20,000 and making the city of Oaxaca (whose name was officially changed from Antequera in 1786) New Spain's third-largest city by 1800.

The benefits of the new prosperity did not extend equally to all Oaxacans, however. As the administrative center for the entire region, most wealth flowed to Oaxaca City, where a rich elite, of mostly Spanish-born government and church officials and owners of large estates, raked in the lion's share of the profits. Below them, a modicum of treasure and respectability trickled down to the small locally born white and mixed-blood professional and merchant class. Finally, the great majority of mixed and pure native descent who did the hard work—the spinners, weavers, masons, shoemakers, bakers, farmers, and laborers—plugged along as best they could at the city's least desirable margins.

Despite its faults, New Spain lasted three times longer than the Aztec empire. By most contemporary measures, both Oaxaca in particular and New Spain as a whole were prospering in 1800. The native and mixed-blood labor force was completely subjugated and increasing, and the galleon fleets were carrying home increasing tonnages of silver, gold, and cochineal worth many millions of gold pesos. Spanish authorities, however, failed to recognize that Mexico had changed in 300 years.

COCHINEAL – NATURE'S RICHEST RED DYE

Cochineal (cochinilla) is a prized rich scarlet dye, long cultivated in Mexico before the conquest. The Spanish, immediately seeing its export value, expanded production, especially in Oaxaca, where it became a major source of cash for native Oaxacans faced with increasing tribute demands. The rise of the textile industry in England, the Low Countries, France, and Spain further propelled demand for Oaxacan cochineal, renowned as the most brilliant, richest red dye in the world. The word spread, and, by its peak during the 17th and 18th centuries, Spain's cochineal trade extended as far as China. Although largely replaced by cheaper synthetic dyes by 1900, cochineal is still locally cultivated in the Valley of Oaxaca.

The actual source of the dye is the female of a type of scale insect, Dactyloplus coccus, which feeds off a variety of nopal (prickly pear) cactus. Typically, families or village cooperatives own patches of nopal, from which they brush the female beetles during the fall harvest. The beetles are then dried, ground, and boiled in water. The resulting dye suspension is filtered and evaporated leaving pure crimson cochineal crystals, still preferred by many Valley of Oaxaca weavers.

A demonstration farm dedicated to the revival of cochineal welcomes visitors to see its experimental cactus garden and small museum at Santa María Coyotepec, on the highway about four miles (six km) south of the Oaxaca airport. (For contact and visitation details, see The Valley of Oaxaca chapter or visit www.aztecacolor.com.)

The cochineal beetle thrives on the leaves of nopal cactus, very common in Oaxaca.

Criollos, the New Mexicans

Nearly three centuries of colonial rule gave rise to a burgeoning population of more than a million criollos—Mexican-born descendants of Spanish colonists, many rich and educated—to whom top status was denied.

High government, church, and military office had always been the preserve of a tiny but powerful minority of *peninsulares*—European-born Spaniards. Criollos (kree-OH-yohs) could only watch in disgust as unlettered, unskilled *peninsulares* (derisively called *gachupines*—wearers of spurs) were boosted to authority over them.

Although the criollos stood high above the mestizo (mixed native-Spanish), *indígena*, and black (African Mexican) underclasses, that seemed little compensation for the false smiles, the deep bows, and the costly bribes that *gachupines* demanded.

Mestizos, *Indígenas*, and African Mexicans

Upper-class luxury existed by virtue of the sweat of Mexico's mestizo, *indígena*, and black laborers and servants. African slaves were imported in large numbers during the 17th century after typhus, smallpox, and measles epidemics had tragically wiped out as much as 90 percent of the indigenous population. In Oaxaca, a small African-born black population of around 2,000 in 1650 rose gradually to approximately 10,000, both pure and mixed, by 1800. Although the African Mexicans contributed significantly (crafts, healing arts, dance, music, drums, and marimba), they had arrived last and experienced discrimination from everyone.

INDEPENDENCE

The chance for change came during the aftermath of the French invasion of Spain in 1808, when Napoléon Bonaparte replaced King Ferdinand VII with his brother Joseph on the Spanish throne. Most *peninsulares* backed the king; most criollos, however, inspired by the example of the recent American and French revolutions, talked and dreamed of independence. One such group, urged on by a firebrand parish priest, acted.

El Grito de Dolores

"¡Viva México! Death to the Gachupines!" Father **Miguel Hidalgo**'s impassioned *grito* from the church balcony in the Guanajuato town of Dolores on September 16, 1810, ignited passions. A mostly *indígena*, machete-wielding army of 20,000 coalesced around Hidalgo and his compatriots, **Ignacio Allende** and **Juan Aldama.** Their ragtag mob raged out of control through the Bajío, killing hated *gachupines* and pillaging their homes.

Hidalgo advanced on Mexico City but, unnerved by stiff royalist resistance, retreated and regrouped around Guadalajara. His rebels, whose numbers had swollen to 80,000, were no match for a disciplined, 6,000-strong royalist force. Hidalgo (now "Generalisimo") fled north but was soon apprehended, defrocked, and executed. His head and those of his comrades—Aldama, Allende, and Mariano Jiménez—were hung from the walls of the Guanajuato granary (site of the slaughter of 138 *gachupines* by Hidalgo's army) for 10 years as grim reminders of the consequences of rebellion.

The 10-Year Struggle

Others carried on, however. A former student of Hidalgo, mestizo **José María Morelos,** carried the Independence struggle to Oaxaca in earnest by defeating the Oaxaca capital's royalist defenders on November 25, 1812. He set up a revolutionary government and fanned the flames with his liberationist newspaper *El Correo Americano del Sur (The American Post of the South)* until seriously defeated in Michoacán a year later. The victorious royalists retook Oaxaca City on January 29, 1814, sending defending *insurgente* commander Ramón Rayón fleeing north to Tehuacán, Puebla.

Although the royalists seriously damaged the rebel cause by capturing and executing Morelos in December 1815, Morelos's compatriot **Vicente Guerrero** continued the fight, joining forces with criollo royalist Brigadier **Agustín de Iturbide.** Their **Plan de Iguala** promised **"Three Guarantees"**—the renowned Trigarantes: Independence, Catholicism, and Equality—which their army (commanded by Iturbide, of course) would enforce. On September 21, 1821, Iturbide rode triumphantly into Mexico City at the head of his army of Trigarantes. Mexico was independent at last.

But the cost of the struggle had been great, especially in Oaxaca. Ten years of war had decimated the cochineal industry and sent Oaxaca's rich Spaniards and their capital fleeing to Mexico City and Europe. The criollo professional and business class now found themselves at the top of the social ladder, but with little money for rebuilding. Everyone tightened their belts as Oaxaca industry reverted to traditional products: soap, *aguardiente* (white lightning, a kind of alcohol) distillation, *pulque* (native beer), wool, leather, and pottery.

Moreover, in Mexico as a whole, independence had resolved few grievances except to expel the *peninsulares*. With an illiterate populace and no experience in self-government, Mexicans began a tragic 40-year love affair with a fantasy: the general on the white horse, the gold-braided hero who could save them from themselves.

The Rise and Fall of Agustín I

Iturbide—crowned Emperor Agustín I by the bishop of Guadalajara on July 21, 1822—soon lost his charisma. Attempting to assert his authority, Iturbide dissolved the national Congress on October 31, igniting a roar of protests. Among the loudest protesters was Iturbide's military governor of Oaxaca, Colonel Antonio de León. In a pattern that became sadly predictable for succeeding generations of topsy-turvy Mexican politics, ambitious commanders issued *pronunciamientos,* declarations against the government. Supporting *pronunciamientos* followed, and old revolutionary heroes Guerrero, Guadalupe Victoria, and Nicolás Bravo endorsed a "plan"—the Plan of Casa Mata (not unlike Iturbide's previous Plan de Iguala)—to dethrone Iturbide in favor of a republic. Iturbide, his braid tattered and brass tarnished, abdicated in mid-February 1823.

On June 1, 1823, carried away by liberationist zeal, León set up a local provisional government that declared Oaxaca to be a "free and independent" state and wrote a state constitution. Simultaneously, delegates in Mexico City were doing the same, creating the republic of the Estados Unidos Mexicanos (United Mexican States), which Oaxaca soon joined.

The country overflowed with republican zeal. Oaxacans rewrote their state constitution to conform with the federal document, creating a governor, bicameral legislature, local governments, and state departments, including public instruction and the **Institute of Sciences and Arts** (now the Benito Juárez Autonomous University). Graduates of the Institute, notably Mexico's famous pair of presidents, Benito Juárez and Porfirio Díaz, both of indigenous descent, gradually began to fill the leadership vacuum left by the departed Spanish elite.

The Disastrous Era of Santa Anna

Antonio López de Santa Anna, the eager 28-year-old military commander of Veracruz, whose *pronunciamiento* had pushed Iturbide from his white horse, maneuvered to gradually replace him. Throughout the latter 1820s the government teetered between liberal and conservative hands six times in three years. Finally, unhappy with the 1828 presidential election result, Santa Anna "pronounced" in favor of the losing candidate, old independence *insurgente* Vicente Guerrero. This put Santa Anna at odds with government commanders all over the country—especially in Oaxaca City, which he attacked—but he soon found himself seriously besieged in the fortress-like convent of Santo Domingo.

But Lady Luck, as usual, intervened in favor of Santa Anna. At the height of the siege, on November 20, 1829, government agents discovered that a Spanish force was being assembled in Cuba to re-invade Mexico. Faced with the external threat, former bitter enemies soon joined hands. On January 5, 1829, Santa Anna rushed from Oaxaca City with a combined force that, a few months later, defeated an abortive Spanish invasion attempt on the

Gulf at Tampico. People called Santa Anna "The Victor of Tampico."

In 1831, a rebellious, still-powerful Vicente Guerrero was kidnapped in Acapulco and handed over to agents of conservative President Anastasio Bustamante in Huatulco. He was taken to Oaxaca City and executed at the old convent in Cuilapan on February 14, 1831. Later, upon the initiative of young Oaxaca legislative deputy **Benito Juárez,** Guerrero's remains were placed in an elaborate silver urn and reinterred during six days of solemn ceremonies at Santo Domingo convent in the city.

In late 1832, the national government was bankrupt; mobs demanded the ouster of President Bustamante in retaliation for Guerrero's execution. Santa Anna issued a *pronunciamiento* against Bustamante, which Congress soon obliged, elevating Santa Anna to "Liberator of the Republic" and "Conqueror of the Spaniards" and naming him president in March 1833. More interested in the hunt than the prize, Santa Anna quickly resigned his office to Vice President Gómez Farías.

Santa Anna would pop in and out of the presidency like a jack-in-the-box 10 more times before 1855. First, he foolishly lost Texas to rebellious Anglo settlers in 1836. He later lost his leg (which was buried with full military honors) fighting the emperor of France.

Santa Anna's greatest debacle, however, was to declare war on the United States with just 1,839 pesos in the treasury. With his forces poised to defend Mexico City against a relatively small 10,000-man American invasion force, Santa Anna inexplicably withdrew. U.S. Marines surged into the "Halls of Montezuma," Chapultepec Castle, where Mexico's six beloved Niños Héroes cadets fell in the losing cause on September 13, 1847.

In the subsequent Treaty of Guadalupe Hidalgo, Mexico lost two-fifths of its territory—the present states of New Mexico, Arizona, California, Nevada, Utah, and Colorado—to the United States. Mexicans have never forgotten; they have looked upon gringos with a combination of admiration and disgust ever since.

Despite the national debacle, Oaxaca prospered under the 1848–1852 governorship of Benito Juárez. Among his first acts was to deny Santa Anna, who was fleeing from U.S. invaders, transit across Oaxaca territory. Besides keeping the peace, Juárez opened hundreds of elementary schools, a swarm of teacher's academies, and nearly wiped out the state debt. Improved roads and new bridges attracted Italian investment in mines; new coffee production began to replace Oaxaca's lost cochineal output. English entrepreneurs built a textile and hat factory, and artisans in Atzompa, near Oaxaca City, resumed producing their renowned pottery again in earnest. Oaxaca City's population swelled by more than 25 percent, to 24,000, between 1844 and 1854.

But for Santa Anna, however, enough was not enough. Called back as president for the last and 11th time in 1853, Santa Anna, now "His Most Serene Highness," financed his final war against the liberals by selling off a part of southern New Mexico and Arizona, known as the Gadsden Purchase, for $10 million.

REFORM, CIVIL WAR, AND INVASION
The Reforms

Mexican leaders finally saw the light and exiled Santa Anna forever. While conservatives fumbled, searching for a king to replace Santa Anna, liberal leaders (whom Santa Anna had exiled or kept in jail) stirred up their own successful revolution. Benito Juárez, having triumphantly returned to the Oaxaca governorship, and others plunged ahead with three controversial reform laws: the Ley Juárez, Ley Lerdo, and Ley Iglesias. These *reformas,* integrated into a new liberal Constitution of 1857, directly attacked the privilege and power of Mexico's corporate landlords, clergy, and generals: Ley Juárez abolished *fueros,* the separate military and church courts; Ley Lerdo forbade excess corporate (read: church) landholdings; and Ley Iglesias reduced or transferred most church power to the state.

Despite their liberal authors' good intentions,

some of the reform provisions resulted in negative consequences. Although Ley Lerdo (the "Law of the Divestiture of the Property of the Dead Hand") succeeded in wiping out bloated church landholdings, it also forced thousands of native communities to sell their traditional land. Such sales invariably benefited the few rich individuals who could afford to buy, at the expense of the great mass of native Mexicans who became landless as a result. The consequence was equally negative. It created a new class of superlandowners: *latifundistas,* who soon ruled small kingdoms with impunity all over Mexico.

Oaxaca, fortunately, ran counter to the national trend. Lack of local capital and isolation from Mexico City led to little investment in Oaxaca land, so most communal holdings remained in indigenous hands. Moreover, of the several hundred church parcels sold in Oaxaca, one-third were, surprisingly, bought by native Mexicans.

Alarmed by the reforms, conservative generals, priests, and businessmen and their mestizo and *indígena* followers revolted. The resulting **War of the Reforms** (not unlike the U.S. Civil War) ravaged the countryside for three long years until the victorious liberal army paraded triumphantly in Mexico City on New Year's Day 1861. In a thumping congratulations from the electors, Juárez outdistanced all rival candidates and became president in March 1861.

Juárez and Maximilian

Benito Juárez, the leading *reformista,* had won the day. His similarity to his contemporary, Abraham Lincoln, is legend: Juárez had risen from humble Zapotec native origins to become a lawyer, a champion of justice, and the president who held his country together during a terrible civil war. Like Lincoln, Juárez's triumph didn't last long.

Imperial France (taking advantage of U.S. preoccupation with its civil war) invaded Mexico in January 1862. Despite a formidable French force, which eventually ballooned to 60,000, Mexican regulars and guerrillas achieved a number of victories, several under the leadership of Oaxacan colonel (later general) **Porfirio Díaz.** Díaz rocketed to fame as the "Victor of Puebla" whose troops routed the French on May 5 (Cinco de Mayo), 1862. The French nevertheless managed to occupy Mexico City and several state capitals, including Oaxaca City, by summer 1864.

After two costly years pushing Juárez's liberal army into the hills, the French installed the king Mexican conservatives thought the country needed. Austrian Archduke Maximilian and his wife Carlota, the very models of modern Catholic monarchs, were crowned emperor and empress of Mexico in June 1864.

The naive **Emperor Maximilian I** was surprised that some of his subjects resented his presence. Meanwhile, Juárez refused to yield, stubbornly performing his constitutional duties in a somber black carriage one jump ahead of the French occupying army. After Díaz's signal victories at Carbonera and Miahuatlán in Oaxaca in late 1866, the climax came in May 1867, when liberal forces besieged and defeated Maximilian at Querétaro. Juárez, giving no quarter, sternly ordered Maximilian's execution by firing squad on June 19.

Juárez Reelected; Díaz Rebels

Benito Juárez's tumultuous popular approval and reelection to the presidency in October 1867 was not without its costs. His critics, notably Sebastián Lerdo de Tejada and Porfirio Díaz (who retired from active military duty to seek the presidency himself) accused Juárez of heavy-handed constitutional violations. Under Díaz's influence, a number of military commanders stirred up local uprisings. Undeterred, Juárez worked day and night at the double task of reconstruction and reform. Single-mindedly, he pushed to amend the Constitution of 1857, a course that triggered a major armed revolt, the Rebellion of La Noria, by Díaz in 1871 to "restore the purity" of the constitution against Juárez's alleged transgressions. Although his political momentum was weakened, Juárez was reelected president over both Tejada and Díaz in October 1871, but, exhausted, he succumbed to a heart attack on July 18, 1872. In

PORFIRIO DÍAZ: HERO OR VILLAIN?

Porfirio Díaz, Mexico's most controversial and longest-serving president, was born in the city of Oaxaca on September 15, 1830. His parents, José de la Cruz Díaz and Petrona Mori, were of poor Mixtec-mestizo origin. Porfirio's father died when he was three, and he spent his childhood working at odd jobs to support his mother while attending public and parochial schools. He entered seminary in Oaxaca in 1843, dropped out after three years, and resumed studies in law at the Institute of Arts and Sciences, where he briefly taught in 1854.

A seminal event occurred for young Porfirio in 1854, when it was publicly announced that the entire faculty of the institute unanimously supported the notorious conservative dictator Antonio López de Santa Anna. Díaz asked that his abstention be recorded, and when publicly accused of siding with the liberal cause, he declared his support for General Juan Álvarez, leader of the liberal rebellion in Guerrero. The die was thus cast: For the next 50 years, Díaz never wavered from the image of a resolute, determined liberal, who possessed the courage of his convictions.

Forced to flee, Porfirio joined a rebel guerrilla band in the northern Sierra and later, in 1856, the Oaxaca National Guard, where he found purpose fighting for Benito Juárez's lib-eral side during the civil War of the Reforms. His valor and ability elevated him to the rank of brigadier general at the time of the liberal triumph in 1861.

During the imperialist French intervention, his military reputation skyrocketed when his forces defeated the French army at Puebla on May 5, 1862, the still celebrated Cinco de Mayo national holiday. After 25 battles and the liberation of Oaxaca, Puebla, and Mexico City, Díaz retired from the military in 1867 at the age of 37.

It turned out that Díaz's insatiable ambition was driving him toward the presidency. He opposed Juárez and Lerdo de Tejada in the 1871 election, which, with no clear winner, was thrown into Congress, where Juárez was re-elected. Díaz revolted unsuccessfully; Juárez died and Lerdo de Tejada became president. Díaz rebelled again, in 1876, promulgating the doctrine of *No Reelección* in his Plan of Tuxtepec. Lerdo de Tejada fled, and Porfirio Díaz finally assumed the presidency legally on May 5, 1877.

Mexico, however, remained a hotbed of revolt. Díaz found that he had to put some of his democratic principles aside to remain in office and keep the country together. He reasoned in essence that, after all, if you don't have a government, you can't have democracy. His treatment

his honor, Oaxaca City fathers renamed their city, officially, **Oaxaca de Juárez.**

The passing of Benito Juárez, the stoic partisan of reform, signaled hope to Mexico's conservatives. They soon got their wish: General Don Porfirio Díaz, the "Coming Man," was elected president in 1876.

ORDER AND PROGRESS
Pax Porfiriana

Don Porfirio is often remembered wistfully, as old Italians remember Mussolini: "He was a bit rough, but, dammit, at least he made the trains run on time."

Although Porfirio Díaz's humble Oaxaca mestizo origins were not unlike Juárez's, Díaz was not a democrat: When he was a general, his officers often took no captives; when he was president, his country police, the *rurales,* shot prisoners in the act of "trying to escape."

Order and progress, in that sequence, ruled Mexico for 34 years. Foreign investment flowed into the country; new railroads brought the products of shiny factories, mines, and farms to modernized Gulf and Pacific ports. Mexico balanced its budget, repaid foreign debt, and became a respected member of the family of nations.

Oaxaca also gained material benefits from the Porfiriato, the label Mexican historians attach to Díaz's long rule. The Mexico City rail link, which arrived in 1892, was the high of captured local rebels – *Matalos en caliente* (Kill them on the spot) – was typically brutal.

Díaz retained enough of his liberal idealism to follow his own *No Reeleccíon* prescription and stepped down from the presidency in 1880 to become governor of Oaxaca, but after that he was re-elected consecutively and held office for 28 more years, until 1911.

The 34-year period (1876-1910) known as the Porfiriato was marked by stability and modernization. A stable Mexico attracted foreign investment. Mostly American and British entrepreneurs and engineers expanded railroads from a mere 400 miles in 1876 to 15,000 miles by 1910. New factories, mills, and mines blossomed along the railroads, which brought raw materials and took away manufactured goods to cities and modernized ports.

In 1908, Díaz hinted in an interview that he would retire in 1910 at the age of 80. This encouraged his growing political opposition, and when Díaz changed his mind and stood for another term in 1910, he was opposed by northern factory owner Francisco I. Madero, who campaigned on Díaz's original *No Reeleccíon* slogan. Díaz had Madero jailed and won election to his eighth presidential term.

But this time, Díaz was too tired to keep the lid on; his long rule collapsed partly because of its own success. Díaz had transformed the country. In many ways it reflected his original liberal vision of a stronger, richer, and better-educated Mexico, with a democratic balance of power and a procedure for orderly succession. But Díaz's failures, driven by cynicism, complacency, and a thirst for dominance, produced a regime that, like a dinosaur, fell under its own weight on May 31, 1911.

Porfirio Díaz, in exile in Paris, complaining of French food and yearning for some home-cooked Oaxacan fare, died on July 2, 1915.

young General Porfirio Díaz

point of three decades of public works improvement: bridges, roads, ports, electricity, sewage, an elegant theater, an Isthmus rail line, a state museum, and an enlarged Institute of Arts and Sciences. Rich foreign and Mexican investors dug dozens of new mines and built scores of factories, producing shoes, soap, hats, matches, glassware, cigarettes, and beer. In the southern mountains, coffee farms proliferated after the government offered a rebate for planting 2,000 coffee trees or more. Oaxaca City's population doubled, to nearly 40,000, during Díaz's rule.

The human price, nevertheless, was high. The rich, who included hundreds of resident foreigners, soaked up most of the profits while Oaxaca's poor, who lacked the money to benefit directly from the new civic improvements, struggled along as best they could. And although in Oaxaca most natives were able to hold on to their land, nationally Díaz's government did not intervene to prevent more than a hundred million acres—one-fifth of Mexico's land area (including most of the arable land)—being turned over to rich Mexicans and foreigners. Poor Mexicans suffered the most. By 1910, 90 percent of Mexico's *indígenas* had lost their traditional communal land. In the spring of 1910, a smug, now-cultured, and elderly Don Porfirio anticipated with relish the centennial of Hidalgo's Grito de Dolores.

REVOLUTION AND STABILIZATION
"¡No Reelección!"

Porfirio Díaz himself had first campaigned on the slogan *¡"No Reelección!"* It expressed the idea that the president should step down after one term. Although Díaz had stepped down once in 1880, for an interregnum as Oaxaca's governor, in 1884 he got himself elected president again and remained in office for 26 consecutive years. In 1910, **Francisco I. Madero,** a short, squeaky-voiced son of rich landowners, opposed Díaz under the same banner.

Although Díaz had jailed him before the election, Madero refused to quit campaigning. From a safe platform in the United States, he called for a revolution to begin on November 20. The response in Oaxaca was typical: In the countryside, a few leaders rallied around Madero's banner, but Díaz had them rounded up and then got his nephew, Félix, installed as governor.

After all, *"¡No Reelección!"* is not much of a platform. But millions of poor Mexicans were going to bed hungry, and Díaz hadn't listened to them for years.

Villa and Zapata

In May 1910, those millions of poor Mexicans began to stir. In Oaxaca, a swarm of small rebellions broke out, then coalesced into a general revolution, which toppled Félix Díaz from the governorship. Simultaneously, up north in Chihuahua, followers of **Francisco (Pancho) Villa,** an erstwhile ranch hand, miner, peddler, and cattle rustler, began attacking the *rurales,* dynamiting railroads, and raiding towns. Meanwhile, in Morelos state, just north of Oaxaca, horse trader, farmer, and minor official **Emiliano Zapata** and his *indígena* guerrillas were terrorizing rich *hacendados* and forcibly recovering stolen ancestral village lands. Zapata's movement gained steam and by mid-May had taken the Morelos state capital, Cuernavaca. Meanwhile, Madero crossed the Río Grande and joined with Villa's forces, who took Ciudad Juárez. Soon the *federales,* government army troops, began deserting in

droves, and on May 25, 1911, Díaz submitted his resignation.

As Madero's deputy, General Victoriano Huerta, put Díaz on his ship of exile in Veracruz, Díaz confided: "Madero has unleashed a tiger. Now let's see if he can control it."

Madero's star, nevertheless, was still rising. As he paraded triumphantly into Mexico City, revolutionary state governments were blossoming all over the country. Benito Juárez's son, Benito Juárez Maza, served briefly as Oaxaca's *maderista* governor in 1911–1912 until he was killed in a local skirmish.

The Fighting Continues

Emiliano Zapata turned out to be that very tiger whom Madero had unleashed. Meeting with Madero in Mexico City, Zapata fumed over Madero's go-slow approach to the "agrarian problem," as Madero termed it. By November 1912, Zapata had denounced Madero. *"¡Tierra y Libertad!"* ("Land and Liberty!") the Zapatistas cried, as Madero's support faded. The army in Mexico City rebelled; Huerta forced Madero to resign on February 18, 1913, then ordered him executed four days later.

The rum-swilling Huerta ruled like a Chicago mobster; general rebellion, led by the **"Big Four"**—Villa, Alvaro Obregón, and Venustiano Carranza in the north, and Zapata in the south—soon broke out. Pressed by the rebels and refused U.S. recognition, Huerta fled into exile in July 1914.

Meanwhile in Oaxaca, fighting between liberals and conservatives, much like the wars for Independence and the Reforms, laid waste to the countryside, killing commerce and sending foreign investors fleeing. But unlike the rest of the country, Oaxaca had no majority class of landless campesinos and consequently no great radical cause or leader to champion it.

Disgusted with the barbaric war of attrition ravaging the rest of the country, many Oaxaca leaders publicly repudiated the "Big Four" and declared Oaxaca a "sovereign" republic and tried to deny access to revolutionary outsiders.

Moreover, Oaxacan conservatives made a serious error in betraying and murdering Jésus

Carranza, brother of El Primer Jefe (First Chief) Venustiano Carranza. Soon Carranzista battalions invaded Oaxaca and quickly defeated local forces, sending Oaxacan leaders scurrying to Mexico City or to the mountains, where they fought on for years as guerrillas.

The national struggle ground on for three more years as authority see-sawed between revolutionary factions. Finally Carranza, who controlled most of the country by 1917, got a convention together in Querétaro to formulate political and social goals. The resulting Constitution of 1917, while restating most ideas of the Reformistas' 1857 constitution, additionally prescribed a single four-year presidential term, labor reform, and subordinated private ownership to public interest. Every village had a right to communal *ejido* land, and subsoil wealth could never be sold away to the highest bidder.

The Constitution of 1917 was a revolutionary expression of national aspirations and, in retrospect, represented a social and political agenda for the entire 20th century. In modified form, it has lasted to the present day.

Obregón Stabilizes Mexico

On December 1, 1920, General Alvaro Obregón legally assumed the presidency of a Mexico still bleeding from 10 years of civil war. Although a seasoned revolutionary, Obregón was also a negotiator who recognized that peace was necessary to implement the goals of the revolution. In four years, his government pacified local uprisings, disarmed a swarm of warlords, executed hundreds of *bandidos,* obtained U.S. diplomatic recognition, assuaged the worst fears of the clergy and landowners, and began land reform.

With Obregón as an example, Oaxaca's new governor **García Vigil** went to work. Despite the irritant of remnant revolutionary guerrilla bands in the countryside, Vigil pushed a successful land reform and wrote a new constitution, which is essentially in effect today. His tax reform plans, however, ran into trouble with Oaxaca's rich landowners and came to nothing when he was assassinated in 1924.

At the national level, Obregón's success set the stage for Plutarco Elías Calles, Obregón's Secretaría de Gobernación and handpicked successor, who won the 1924 national election. Aided by peace, Mexico returned to a semblance of prosperity. Calles brought the army under civilian control, balanced the budget, and shifted Mexico's revolution into high gear. New clinics vaccinated millions against smallpox, new dams irrigated thousands of previously dry acres, and campesinos received millions of acres of redistributed land.

Simultaneously, Calles threatened foreign oil companies, demanding they exchange their titles for 50-year leases. A moderate Mexican supreme court decision over the oil issue and the skillful arbitration of U.S. Ambassador Dwight Morrow smoothed over both the oil and church troubles by the end of Calles's term.

Calles, who started out brimming with revolutionary fervor and populist zeal, became increasingly conservative and dictatorial. Although he bowed out peaceably in favor of Obregón (the constitution had been amended to allow one six-year nonsuccessive term), Obregón was assassinated two weeks after his election in 1928. Calles continued to rule for six more years through three puppet-presidents: Emilio Portes Gil (1928–1930), Pascual Ortiz Rubio (1930–1932), and Abelardo Rodríguez (1932–1934).

Calles Forms the PRI

In 1929, President Calles united three of Mexico's major constituencies: the country poor (represented by the Confederación Nacional de Campesinos, CNC), the workers (Confederación de Trabajadore Méjicanos, CTM), and the middle classes (Confederación Nacional de Organizaciones Populares, CNOP). Calles christened his new super political party the **Partido Revolucionario Institucional** (Institutional Revolutionary Party), or **PRI,** or, pronounced simply, the "pree."

The PRI dominated Mexican, and especially Oaxacan, politics during the 60 years after its founding. PRI presidents handpicked their PRI successors, who always got elected. Federal government contracts and salary money flowed from PRI headquarters in Mexico City to state and municipal officials, who were nearly always loyal local members of the PRI.

Oaxaca, isolated from the national economy and with no influential revolutionary ex-general to demand its fair share of national patronage, was consistently underfunded and mostly ignored by the central government. Nevertheless, despite a severe earthquake in 1931 and general economic depression, Oaxacans managed some modest public works improvements during the 1930s and early 1940s. A paved road to Monte Albán led to important archaeological discoveries; other new highways branched out from the valley to the Mixteca, the Isthmus, and to Puerto Ángel. Oaxaca City residents benefited from a few improvements, such as a new water works and restoration of the opera house. But revolution and hard times had taken their toll: In 1940, Oaxaca City's population, about 40,000, was still the same as in 1910.

Lázaro Cárdenas, President of the People

Although he had received Calles's blessing for the 1934 presidential election, ex-general Lázaro Cárdenas, the 40-year-old former governor of Michoacán, immediately set his own agenda. Cárdenas worked tirelessly to fulfill the social prescriptions of the revolution. As morning-coated diplomats and cabinet ministers fretted in his outer office, Cárdenas ushered in delegations of campesinos and factory workers and sympathetically listened to their problems.

In his six years of rule, Cárdenas moved public education and health forward on a broad front, supported strong labor unions, and redistributed 49 million acres of farmland, more than any president before or since.

Cárdenas's resolute enforcement of the constitution's Artículo 123 brought him the most renown. Under this pro-labor law, the government turned over a host of private companies to employee ownership and, on March 18, 1938, expropriated all foreign oil corporations.

In retrospect the oil corporations, most of which were British, were not blameless. They had sorely neglected the wages, health, and welfare of their workers while ruthlessly taking the law into their own hands with private police forces. Although Standard Oil cried foul, the U.S. government did not intervene. Through negotiation and due process, U.S. companies eventually were compensated with $24 million plus 3 percent interest. In the wake of the expropriation, President Cárdenas created Petróleos Mexicanos (Pemex), the national oil corporation that continues to run all Mexican oil and gas operations to the present day.

Manuel Avila Camacho

Manuel Avila Camacho, elected in 1940, was the last general to be president of Mexico. His administration ushered in a gradual shift of Mexican politics, government, and foreign policy as Mexico allied itself with the U.S. cause during World War II. Foreign tourism, initially promoted by the Cárdenas administration, ballooned. Good feelings surged as Franklin Roosevelt became the first U.S. president to officially cross the Río Grande, when he met with Camacho in Monterrey in April 1943.

As World War II moved toward its 1945 conclusion, both the United States and Mexico were enjoying the benefits of four years of governmental and military cooperation and mutual trade in the form of a mountain of strategic minerals, which had moved north in exchange for a similar mountain of U.S. manufactures that moved south.

CONTEMPORARY MEXICO AND OAXACA
The Mature Revolution

During the decades after World War II, beginning with moderate President **Miguel Alemán** (1946–1952), Mexican politicians gradually honed their skills of consensus and compromise as their middle-aged revolution bubbled along under liberal presidents and sputtered haltingly under conservatives. Doctrine required of all politicians, regardless of stripe, that they be "revolutionary" enough to be included beneath the banner of the PRI, Mexico's dominant political party.

Mexico's revolution hasn't been very revolutionary about **women's rights,** however. The PRI didn't get around to giving Mexican women, millions of whom fought and died alongside men during the revolution, the right to vote until 1953.

Alemán's government in 1947 began construction of a huge power and irrigation dam in the Río Papaloapan watershed of northern Oaxaca. The resulting **Miguel Alemán Dam,** completed a few years later, created a mammoth 2.3-million-acre reservoir. Although providing a large chunk of the region's growing electricity demand and an assured irrigation supply for thousands of new fruit, dairy, and vegetable farms, the project required the painful relocation of many thousands of poor Mazatec, Chinantec, and Mixe *indígena* families.

Political Trouble in Oaxaca

Meanwhile, in Oaxaca City, trouble was breaking out, triggered by the unpopular actions of Governor Edmund Sánchez Cano. Merchants, who objected to his new taxes, and students, who resented the governor's interference in university affairs, got together and occupied the state government palace. Before the dust settled, federal troops were occupying the city and Mexico's second-in-command, the Secretaría de Gobernación, had forced Governor Sánchez's resignation and taken over the state government.

Trouble erupted again in 1951. This time, the dispute had roots among coffee farmers in Oaxaca's southern Sierra. Growers, far removed from Oaxaca City, had been shipping their coffee directly from Pacific ports or by remote roads directly to Mexico City, where they had developed strong commercial and political connections. Although responsible for Oaxaca's major export, coffee growers enjoyed little influence among state officials in Oaxaca City. One of these growers, Mayoral Heredia, had become a close family friend of President Miguel Alemán, who endorsed Heredia's successful PRI candidacy for governor of Oaxaca in 1950.

Upon taking office in December 1950, Heredia replaced the local politicos with his own Mexico City cadre, then proceeded with plans to modernize Oaxaca's agriculture, with subsidies paid by new state taxes. The ensuing dispute revolved fundamentally around the question of power: Who should control Oaxaca—the city leaders as usual, or Mexico City–oriented appointees?

Soon, most townspeople—notably among them, local businesspeople and university professors and students—lined up angrily against the governor. The governor's sole supporters were the state police, who, in the heat of action, shot two protesting university students. After a one-day national student strike and weeks of daily protests, the merchant-student-professor coalition mounted a **citywide general strike.** Finally, President Alemán had to send in a federal regiment to restore order. Discredited, Governor Heredia was forced to replace his cabinet with city leaders. They reversed his modernization plans: They judged the present dirt roads adequate and found no need for tractors or irrigation. Oaxaca agriculture would sputter along as it had for the past hundred years. Rebuffed, Governor Heredia soon resigned in July 1952.

Political Activism of the 1960s and 1970s

Women, voting for the first time in a national election, kept the PRI in power by electing liberal **Adolfo López Mateos** in 1958. Resembling Lázaro Cárdenas in social policy, López Mateos redistributed 40 million acres of farmland, forced automakers to use 60 percent domestic components, built thousands of new schools, and distributed hundreds of millions of new textbooks. *"La electricidad es nuestra"* ("Electricity is ours"), Mateos declared as he nationalized foreign power companies in 1962.

Despite his left-leaning social agenda, unions were restive under López Mateos. Protesting inflation, workers struck; the government retaliated, arresting Demetrios Vallejo, the railway union head, and renowned muralist David Siqueiros, former Communist party secretary.

Despite the troubles, López Mateos climaxed his presidency gracefully in 1964 as he opened the celebrated National Museum of Anthropology, appropriately located in Chapultepec Park, where the Aztecs had first settled 20 generations earlier.

In 1964, as several times before, the outgoing president's Secretaría de Gobernación succeeded his former chief. Dour, conservative **Gustavo Díaz Ordaz** immediately clashed with liberals, labor, and students. The pot boiled over just before the 1968 Mexico City Olympics. Reacting to a student rebellion, the army occupied the National University; shortly afterward, on October 2, government forces opened fire with machine guns on a peaceful downtown rally crowd, killing hundreds and wounding thousands.

The Mexico City troubles reignited political activism in Oaxaca. Local university students, organized as the **Federación Estudiantil de Oaxaca (FEO),** mounted a successful campaign in support of bus drivers in 1970. In 1972, the students joined with workers and poor farmers, forming the **Coalición de Obreros, Campesinos, y Estudiantes de Oaxaca (COCEO).** They led off with a fight on behalf of sidewalk vendors to prevent the Saturday market being moved to the city's southern outskirts. After that, a disgruntled student splinter faction set off three small bombs: in the PRI-dominated union office, at an English-language library, and in the (empty) folk-dance amphitheater on the hill above the city. Fortunately, no one was injured. Later, in the mid-1970s, the COCEO supported and helped organize rural land invasions by villagers, organized and supported city workers' unions, and backed hillside squatters on the city's northern edge.

The actions in the capital inspired activists in other parts of Oaxaca. In Juchitán, on the Isthmus, students united with workers and poor farmers to form the **Coalición Obero, Campesino, y Estudiantil del Istmo (COCEI).** Unlike its Oaxaca City counterpart, the COCEI had a strong indigenous Zapotec cultural orientation, with women exerting important, although behind-the-scenes, leadership roles. Moreover, their cultural unity produced unusual militancy and political skill. Through a series of actions—strikes, boycotts, marches, and demonstrations—they opposed city-hall cliques and local *caciques* (bosses) at the painful cost of 20 of their number killed or kidnapped by police, soldiers, and hired thugs. Their payment in blood, however, led to significant improvements in working and living conditions for poor people in Juchitán and other Isthmus communities. Moreover, they forced the local establishment politicos to recognize their legitimacy by winning the 1980 local elections and making Juchitán one of the few towns in Mexico without a PRI-dominated city government.

Meanwhile, back in Oaxaca City, student influence peaked, then faded in 1977 over a dispute that started with election of the university (Universidad Autonoma de Benito Juárez de Oaxaca, UABJO) rector, equivalent to a university president in the United States. Actions escalated until snipers were killing people in university buildings. As police stepped in to restore order, students protested and organized strikes. Fed up with the turmoil, merchants, property owners, and the local PRI organized their own anti-student shutdown, triggering a student-worker march upon the central plaza. State police opened fire, killing one and wounding dozens. That night, the federal government clamped down. Troops took control, and Zárate Aquino, the third Oaxaca governor to be forced from office within a generation, left permanently. Soldiers patrolled the city for nine months, demonstrations were banned, and the anti-establishment COCEO coalition collapsed.

Having had to deal with a generation of Oaxacan political turmoil, the federal government began to direct more resources to Oaxaca. Federal expenditures and employment in Oaxaca City doubled during the 1970s. Improved roads linked villages to the city; electric lines extended into formerly isolated mountain villages; a host of schools and health centers proliferated; and many villages and towns got clean water systems for the first time. With the money and power flowing from

Mexico City, Oaxaca's local merchant and professional old guard gradually lost their influence over state government.

New Mexican Industrialization

Despite its serious internal troubles, Mexico's relations with the United States were cordial. President Lyndon Johnson visited and unveiled a statue of Abraham Lincoln in Mexico City. Later, President Díaz Ordaz met with President Richard Nixon in Puerto Vallarta.

Meanwhile, bilateral negotiations produced the **Border Industrialization Program.** Within a 12-mile strip south of the U.S.–Mexico border, foreign companies could assemble duty-free parts into finished goods and export them without any duties on either side. Within a dozen years, a swarm of such plants, called *maquiladoras,* were humming as hundreds of thousands of Mexican workers assembled and exported billions of dollars worth of shiny consumer goods—electronics, clothes, furniture, pharmaceuticals, and toys—worldwide.

Concurrently, in Mexico's interior, Díaz Ordaz pushed Mexico's industrialization ahead full steam. Foreign money financed hundreds of new plants and factories. Primary among these was the giant Las Truchas steel plant at the new industrial port and town of Lázaro Cárdenas at the Pacific mouth of the Río Balsas.

Very little of Mexico's new industrial development reached Oaxaca, however. Oaxaca's sparse industry, with few exceptions, remained simple, producing raw materials or goods for local consumption only.

Oil Boom, Economic Bust

Discovery in 1974 of gigantic new oil and gas reserves along Mexico's Gulf Coast added fuel to Mexico's already rapid industrial expansion. During the late 1970s and early 1980s, billions in foreign investment, lured by Mexico's oil earnings, financed other major developments—factories, hotels, power plants, roads, airports—all over the country.

A modest share of Mexico's new oil wealth trickled to Oaxaca, in increased government jobs, infrastructure construction, and the new cross-Isthmus pipelines and Salina Cruz oil refinery, completed in 1977. Soon 3,000 Oaxacan workers were processing 800,000 barrels of Gulf crude a year into gasoline, diesel and jet fuel, and liquid propane and butane, which tank trucks, railway cars, and ocean tankers distributed all over Mexico and the Pacific Rim.

The negative side to these expensive projects was the huge dollar debt required to finance them. President **Luis Echeverría Alvarez** (1970–1976), diverted by his interest in international affairs, passed Mexico's burgeoning balance of payments deficit to his successor, **José López Portillo.** As feared by some experts, a world petroleum glut during the early 1980s burst Mexico's ballooning oil bubble and plunged the country into financial crisis. When the 1982 interest came due on its foreign debt, Mexico's largest holding company couldn't pay the $2.3 billion owed. The peso plummeted more than fivefold, to 150 per U.S. dollar. At the same time, prices doubled every year.

In the mid-1980s President **Miguel de la Madrid** (1982–1988) was straining to get Mexico's economic house in order. He sliced government and raised taxes, asking rich and poor alike to tighten their belts. Despite getting foreign bankers to reschedule Mexico's debt, de la Madrid couldn't stop inflation. Prices skyrocketed as the peso deflated to 2,500 per U.S. dollar, becoming one of the world's most devalued currencies by 1988.

Such economic belt-tightening invariably hits the poor hardest, and Oaxacans are among Mexico's poorest. Oaxaca's families average only about $2,000 income per year—about one-third of the Mexican average, and less than a tenth of the U.S. average. The problem is much worse for Oaxaca's dirt-poor, who, in Oaxaca City, make up about one-third of the population. Their yearly average family income hovers somewhere around $1,000, less than $100 per month. With basic food prices not much different from those in the United States, hunger, if not outright starvation, has been an everyday fact for many Oaxacans for as long as they can remember.

Salinas de Gortari, Solidaridad, and NAFTA

Public disgust led to significant opposition during the 1988 presidential election. The conservative National Action Party candidate Michael Clothier and liberal National Democratic Front candidate Cuauhtémoc Cárdenas ran against the PRI's Harvard-educated technocrat Carlos Salinas de Gortari. Although Salinas de Gortari eventually won the election, his showing, barely half of the vote, was the worst ever for an Institutional Revolutionary Party president.

Salinas de Gortari, nevertheless, lost no time getting started. His biggest domestic success was the popular "Solidarity" (Programa Nacional de Solidaridad, PRONASOL) program, which aided poor communities in locally run self-help, cultural, sanitation, health, agricultural, and other projects. Especially targeted were small, mostly indigenous Oaxaca coffee producers who, through local Solidaridad committees, received hundreds of interest-free loans.

Salinas de Gortari's major international achievement, despite significant national opposition, was the North American Free Trade Agreement (NAFTA), which the Canadian, U.S., and Mexican legislatures ratified in 1993.

The Zapatista Revolt

However, on the very day in January 1994 that NAFTA took effect, rebellion broke out in Oaxaca's neighboring state of Chiapas. A small but well-disciplined campesino force, calling itself **Ejército Zapatista Liberación Nacional** (Zapatista National Liberation Army, EZLN), or "Zapatistas," captured a number of provincial towns and held the former governor of Chiapas hostage.

The Zapatista revolt rattled Oaxaca. In a social trend that had been growing at least since the Isthmus Zapotec community became politicized and formed the COCEI during the 1970s, indigenous communities all over the state began pushing for their rights under the Mexican constitution. Prime actors in this movement have been liberationist Catholic priests and nuns, especially in remote country parishes.

Although successful clergy-led projects have sprung up all around Oaxaca, the Isthmus provides the most successful examples. Under the leadership of clergy, in dozens of communities around Tehuántepec, thousands of indigenous people—Mixe, Chontal, Huave, Zapotec, and others—have organized self-help, cultural, political, and communal work programs. Their moneymaking activities range from raising coffee, sheep, and chickens to milling corn and producing pottery, which they sell in the Tehuántepec, Salina Cruz, and Juchitán markets.

One of the most successful organizations in all this ferment has been the **Unión de Comunidades de la Region del Istmo** (UCIRI, www.uciri.org), headquartered in Lachaviza, north of Tehuántepec. Fed up with corrupt middlemen and discouraged by the lack of governmental help, small coffee growers banded together and now represent 3,000 growers in 50 communities. Besides working together in production, transportation, and sales, they organize cooperative self-education (especially in organic farming) and run a savings bank, a clinic, and cooperative grocery, hardware, and drug stores.

The Zapatista revolt has struck the common chord—of autonomy—among virtually all of Oaxaca's indigenous social-political groups. Echoing the Zapatistas in Chiapas, their political goals usually include the right of self-rule by their own traditional means.

A National Tragedy

In mid-1994, Mexico's already tense political drama veered toward tragedy. While Salinas de Gortari was trying to settle the Zapatista revolt, Luis Donaldo Colosio, Salinas's handpicked presidential candidate, was gunned down just months before the August balloting. However, instead of disintegrating, the nation united in grief; opposition candidates eulogized their fallen former opponent and later earnestly engaged his replacement, stolid technocrat **Ernesto Zedillo,** in Mexico's first presidential election debate.

In a closely watched election relatively unmarred by irregularities, Zedillo piled up a solid plurality against his PAN (National Action Party) and PRD (Revolutionary Democratic Party) opponents. By perpetuating the PRI's 65-year hold on the presidency, the electorate had again opted for the PRI's familiar, although imperfect, middle-aged revolution.

A New Economic Crisis

Zedillo, however, had little time to savor his victory. The peso, long propped up by his predecessor's fiscal policies, lost one-third of its value in the few days before Christmas 1994. The peso kept falling, and to stave off a worldwide financial panic, in February 1995 U.S. President Bill Clinton secured an unprecedented multibillion-dollar international loan package for Mexico.

Although economic disaster was temporarily averted, the cure for the country's ills required another painful round of belt-tightening for poor Mexicans. During 1995, national inflation soared. More and more families became unable to purchase staple foods and basic medicines. Malnutrition increased sixfold, and diseases such as cholera and dengue fever resurged in the countryside.

The Political Cauldron Bubbles On

At the same time, Mexico's equally serious political ills seemed to defy cure. Raul Salinas de Gortari, an important PRI party official and the former president's brother, was arrested for money laundering and political assassination. As popular sentiment began to implicate Carlos Salinas de Gortari himself, the former president fled Mexico to an undisclosed location.

Meanwhile, as negotiations with the rebel Zapatistas sputtered on and off in Chiapas, popular discontent erupted in Oaxaca's western neighbor-state, Guerrero, leading to the massacre of 17 unarmed campesinos at Aguas Blancas, in the hills west of Acapulco, by state police in June 1995. One year later, at a demonstration protesting the massacre, a new, well-armed revolutionary group, **Ejército Popular Revolucionario** (People's Revolutionary Army, EPR), made its appearance. Scarcely two months later, on August 28, EPR guerrillas killed more than two dozen police and soldiers at several southwest Mexico locations, including four sailors at the naval garrison in Huatulco, Oaxaca. Soon, platoons of soldiers and police were scouring rural Guerrero, Oaxaca, Michoacán, and other states, searching homes and arresting suspected dissidents.

At the same time, although the official negotiations with the Zapatista rebels were stalled over the issue of indigenous rights, the Zedillo government gained momentum in addressing other local grievances in Chiapas by building new rural electrification networks and refurbishing health clinics. Similar federal action seemed to be forthcoming in Oaxaca also when, in early 1996, President Zedillo recognized that "success or failure of [his] social policy" depended on Oaxaca and announced an unprecedented $1 billion in federal expenditures in Oaxaca for the upcoming fiscal year.

The rough federal army and police searches, arrests, and jailings have energized a flurry of political action. Oaxacan human rights groups, already protesting against unpunished violence, have upped the pressure for reforms at the state and national level. The official **Comisión Estatal de Derechos Humanos** (Oaxaca State Human Rights Commission, CNDH) hears complaints and issues "nonbinding and autonomous recommendations" to relevant authorities.

Fortunately, foreign visitors in Oaxaca have been unaffected by such disputes. In Oaxaca City especially, and along well-traveled highways, in resorts, towns, and sites of touristic interest, foreign visitors are generally much safer than in their home cities in the United States, Canada, or Europe.

Economic Recovery and Political Reforms

The best news for which the Zedillo

government could justly claim credit was the dramatically improving national economy. By mid-1998, annual inflation had dropped below 15 percent, investment dollars were flowing back into Mexico, the peso had stabilized at about eight to the U.S. dollar, and Mexico had paid back every penny of its borrowed U.S. bailout money.

Moreover, in the political arena, although the justice system in Oaxaca and other states left much to be desired, a pair of unprecedented events signaled an increasingly open political system. In the 1997 congressional elections, voters elected a host of opposition candidates, depriving the PRI of an absolute congressional majority for the first time since 1929. A year later, in early 1998, Mexicans were participating in their country's first **primary elections**—in which voters, instead of political bosses, chose party candidates.

Although Ernesto Zedillo's presidential ride had been rough, he entered the twilight of his 1994–2000 term able to take credit for an improved economy, some genuine political reforms, and relative peace in the countryside. The election of 2000 revealed, however, that the Mexican people were not satisfied.

End of an Era:
Vicente Fox Unseats the PRI

During 1998 and 1999 the focal point of opposition to the PRI's three-generation rule had been shifting to relative newcomer Vicente Fox, former President of Coca-Cola Mexico and clean former PAN governor of Guanajuato.

Fox, who had announced his candidacy for president two years before the election, seemed an unlikely challenger. After all, the minority PAN had always been the party of wealthy businessmen and the conservative Catholic right. But blunt-talking, six-foot-five Fox, who sometimes campaigned in *vaquero* boots and a 10-gallon cowboy hat, preached populist themes of coalition building and "inclusion." He backed up his talk by carrying his campaign to hardscrabble city barrios, dirt-poor country villages, and traditional outsider groups, such as Jews.

In a relatively orderly and fair July 2, 2000, election, Fox decisively defeated his PRI opponent Labastida, 42 percent to 38 percent, while PRD candidate Cárdenas polled a feeble 17 percent. Fox's win also swept a PAN plurality (223/209/57) into the 500-seat Chamber of Deputies lower house (although the Senate remained PRI-dominated).

Nevertheless, in pushing the PRI from the all-powerful presidency after 71 consecutive years of domination, Fox had ushered Mexico into a new, more democratic era.

Despite stinging criticism from his own ranks, **President Zedillo,** whom historians were already praising as the real hero behind Mexico's new democracy, made an unprecedented early appeal for all Mexicans to unite behind Fox.

On the eve of Fox's December 1, 2000, inauguration, Mexicans awaited his speech with hopeful anticipation. He did not disappoint them. Although acknowledging that he couldn't completely reverse 71 years of PRI entrenchment in his one six-year term, he vowed to ride the crest of reform, by revamping the tax system and reducing poverty by 30 percent, by creating a million new jobs a year through new private investment in electricity and oil production, and by forming a new common market with Latin America, the United States, and Canada.

He promised, moreover, to secure justice for all by a much-needed reform of police, the federal attorney general, and the army. Potentially most difficult of all, Fox called for the formation of an unprecedented congressional "Transparency Commission" to investigate a generation of past grievances, including the 1968 massacre of student demonstrators and assassinations of, among others, a Roman Catholic cardinal in 1993 and a popular presidential candidate in 1994.

Vicente Fox, President of Mexico

Wasting little time getting started, President Fox first headed to Chiapas to confer with indigenous community leaders. Along the way, he shut down Chiapas military bases and removed dozens of military roadblocks. Back in Mexico City, he sent the long-delayed **peace plan,** including the **indigenous bill of rights,** to Congress. Zapatista rebels responded by journeying en masse from Chiapas to Mexico City, where, in their black masks, they addressed Congress, arguing for indigenous rights. Although by mid-2001 Congress had passed a modified version of the negotiated settlement, and the majority of states had ratified the required constitutional amendment, indigenous leaders condemned the legislation plan as watered down and unacceptable, while proponents claimed it was the best possible compromise between the Zapatistas' demands and the existing Mexican constitution.

On the positive side, by mid-2002 Vicente Fox could claim credit for cracking down on corruption and putting drug lords in jail, negotiating a key immigration agreement with the United States, keeping the peso stable, clamping down on inflation, and attracting a record pile of foreign investment dollars.

Furthermore, Fox continued to pry open the door to democracy in Mexico. In May 2002, he signed Mexico's first **freedom of information act,** entitling citizens to timely copies of all public documents from federal agencies. Moreover, Fox's long-promised **"Transparency Commission"** was taking shape. In July 2002, federal attorneys were taking extraordinary action. They were questioning a list of 74 former government officials, including ex-President Luis Echeverrí, about their roles in government transgressions, notably political murders and the University of Mexico massacres during the 1960s and 1970s.

But, Mexico's economy, reflecting the U.S. economic slowdown, began to sour in 2001, losing half a million jobs and cutting annual growth to 2.5 percent, down from the 4.5 percent that the government had predicted. Furthermore, a so-called "Towelgate" furor (in which aides had purchased dozens of $400 towels for the presidential mansion) weakened Fox's squeaky-clean image.

During 2002 and 2003, the Mexican economy continued its lackluster performance,

increasing public dissatisfaction. In the July 7, 2003, congressional elections, voters took their frustrations out on the PAN and gave its plurality in the Chamber of Deputies to the PRI. When the dust settled, the PRI total had risen to 225 seats, while the PAN had slipped to 153. The biggest winner, however, was the PRD, which gained more than 40 seats, to a total of about 100.

The best news of 2004 was not political, but economic. The Mexican economy, reflecting that of the United States, began to recover, expanding at a moderate (if not robust) rate of about 4 percent, while exports to the United States also increased.

By mid-2005, despite only modest political gains and with his term mostly spent, critics were increasingly claiming that Vicente Fox was a lame-duck president who had run out of time to accomplish what he promised. But Fox, despite a hostile congress that almost continuously blocked his legislative proposals, could claim some solid accomplishments. During his first five years, he had pushed through significant gains in indigenous rights, national reconciliation and government transparency, drug enforcement, U.S.–Mexico immigration policy, social security reform, housing, and education. Moreover, in addition to nurturing a recovering economy, no one could deny that Fox had kept exports robust, the peso strong against the dollar and had clamped the lid on inflation.

Unfortunately, despite President Fox's efforts at the national level, serious political trouble surfaced in Oaxaca in mid-2006. It started mildly enough. In May 2006, Oaxaca's statewide teachers union went on their perennial strike for much-needed higher wages. They accused PRI governor Ulises Ruiz of diverting millions of dollars in education funds to his controversial pet public works projects. Soon, hundreds of teachers were camping out in the *zócalo* and staging daily political rallies. Their rhetoric increasingly focused on the credibility of Governor Ruiz, who consistently refused to negotiate with them.

By mid-June, when teachers began

barricading streets around the *zócalo,* Ruiz sent in his police, who brutally manhandled the nonviolent middle-class demonstrators. The protest escalated quickly. The teachers allied themselves with their left-leaning supporters, forming an umbrella protest organization, the APPO (Popular Assembly of the People of Oaxaca), and added the demand that Governor Ruiz must step down.

During the summer months of July, August, and September, the protests turned violent. Highways were blocked, buses were burned, a radio station was occupied, and several people were shot to death. By October, downtown Oaxaca City resembled a ghost town. Tourism had evaporated, and consequently, all businesses, including hotels and restaurants, had shut their doors.

The focus then shifted to Mexico City, where teachers, negotiating with federal authorities, got their requested wage increase. Furthermore, the federal Chamber of Deputies voted overwhelmingly that Governor Ruiz must vacate his office.

In late October, President Vicente Fox, spurred by the killing of an American news reporter, acted. He sent a brigade of federal troops and police to Oaxaca, who removed the street barricades and dispersed the protestors while inflicting only minimal injuries. The local townspeople, breathing a sigh of relief, turned out, and in two days they swept up the mess, painted over the accumulated graffiti, opened their businesses, and filled the streets, buying flowers to celebrate the November 1–2 Day of the Dead holiday.

At this writing, in February 2008, the teachers have gotten their raise and returned to work, and peace has continued for an entire year in Oaxaca. Although it's still usually quiet around the *zócalo,* visitors are beginning to return. Merchants and restaurateurs are serving an increasing flow of customers, and hotels are placing lodging discounts on their websites and accepting reservations.

And lastly, what's very important for visitors to realize is that, through all of the recent political trouble, the people of Oaxaca have overwhelmingly remained appreciative of visiting travelers and are now increasingly looking forward to again sharing their celebrated handicrafts, delicious cuisine, and beloved fiestas with all visitors who come to their lovely city and surrounding valley.

The Election of 2006

During the first half of 2006, as Vicente Fox was winding down his presidency, Mexicans were occupied by the campaign to elect his successor. Most headlines went to the PRD candidate, the mercurial leftist-populist Andres Manuel López Obrador, former mayor of Mexico City. Trying hard not to be upstaged was the steady, no-nonsense PAN candidate, Harvard-educated centrist-conservative Felipe Calerón, a leading light of President Fox's cabinet.

On Sunday, July 2, 2006, 42,000,000 Mexicans cast their ballots. In an intensely monitored election marred by very few irregularities, unofficial returns indicated that voters had awarded Calderón a paper-thin plurality. Four days later, after all returns were certified, the Federal Electoral Institute announced the official vote tally: only about 22 percent for the PRI candidate, Roberto Madrazo, with the remaining lion's share divided nearly evenly, with 38.7 percent going to Obrador and 39.3 percent for Calderón. This result, the Federal Electoral Institute ruled, was too close to declare a winner without a recount.

Besides the close Obrador-Calderón vote, the election results revealed much more. Not only were the 32 electoral entities (31 states and the Federal District) divided equally, with 16 going for Obrador, and 16 for Calderón, the vote reflected a nearly complete north-south political schism, with virtually all of the 16 PAN-majority states forming a solid northern bloc, while the 16 PRD-voting states did the same in the south. Furthermore, the election appeared to signal a collapse of PRI power; with no state (nor the Federal District) giving either a majority or a plurality to Robverto Madrazo.

A howl of protest came from Obrador and his PRD followers after the election results were announced. They claimed the PAN had stolen the election. They jammed the Federal Electoral Institute with lawsuits, alleging a host of irregularities and ballot stuffing incidents, and demanding a complete recount of all 42,000,000 ballots. They yelled, marched, blocked Mexico City's Paseo de la Reforma and camped in the *zócalo* central plaza.

Election Aftermath

For a month, the questionable ballots were gathered and examined exhaustively by the Supreme Election Tribunal, an impeccable panel of federal judges. They found that the recount shifted the margin by only by a few thousand votes away from Calderón to Obrador. On September 6, the Federal Electoral Institute declared Calderón the president-elect by a margin of about 240,000 votes, or a bit more than one-half of a percent of the total vote.

Obrador and his supporters screamed foul even louder and threatened to ignore Calderón and/or block his presidency. On September 16, Mexican Independence Day, Obrador convened hundreds of thousands of his supporters in the Mexico City *zócalo* that declared him the legitimate president. In the succeeding days, the PRD's obstructionist tactics reached an outrageous climax when a handful of PRD senators and deputies made such a ruckus during a joint session of the federal legislature that they prevented the President of Mexico, for the first time in history, from delivering his annual state of the union address. Mexican voters, watching the PRD's melodramatic tactics on television, began, in increasing numbers, to say enough was enough. National polls showed that more than two-thirds of Mexicans disapproved of the PRD's protest behavior. By October, many of the PRD's leaders agreed, further isolating Obrador and his rump government to a footnote in Mexican history. Mexico's new democracy, given a gentle shove forward ten years earlier by President Ernesto Zedillo and nurtured for six more years by Vicente Fox, seemed to have again surmounted a difficult crisis and emerged stronger.

An important result of the 2006 election, initially overshadowed by the intense struggle over the presidential vote, but potentially crucial, was the federal legislative vote, in which PAN emerged as the biggest winner by far. The final results showed that voters had given PAN candidates strong pluralities of 206/127/106 over the PRD and PRI, respectively, in the 500-seat federal Chamber of Deputies, and 52/29/33 in the 128-seat Senate, with the remainder of seats scattered among minor parties. This result may bode well for Mexican democracy. With some cooperation (most likely from the PRI) Felipe Calderón may be able to use his party's pluralities to further the national political and economic reform agenda Vicente Fox promised six years earlier, but could only partially deliver.

Calderón Takes Charge

As he prepared for his December 1, 2006 inauguration, Felipe Calderón not only appeared to be moving ahead with many of his predecessor's original proposals, but he also seemed to be reaching out to the PRI and the PRD with some new ideas. These, although containing many of PAN's pro-business pro-NAFTA ideas, also appeared to borrow considerably from the liberal-populist agenda of Obrador and the PRD. Only much-needed cooperation will allow their country to make progress toward the bright but elusive vision of a just and prosperous motherland for all Mexicans.

Calderón wasted no time getting started. He immediately attacked Mexico's most immediate problem by declaring war on Mexico's drug lords. Right away he replaced most of the federal police chiefs, many suspected of corruption. He then put the Mexican army in charge of his war on drugs, eventually assigning 30,000 Mexican soldiers to seek and destroy criminal drug networks, especially in the most drug-infested states of Michoacán, Guerrero, and Sinaloa and the border towns of Tijuana, Ciudad Juárez, and Nuevo Laredo, where criminal drug gangs had been assassinating incorruptible judges and local police officials and officers.

Peace Reigns in Oaxaca

Concurrently, Felipe Calderón dealt head-on with the violent elements of the Oaxaca political protests. Within a month of his inauguration, Oaxaca police, using a minimum of force, rounded up dozens of the protest ringleaders and sequestered them far away in a Michoacán prison to await trial. To the relief of Oaxaca people, the remainder of the APPO demonstrators were never again allowed to push their protest to the city center, thus bringing peace to the lovely downtown heart of Oaxaca. Peace, at this writing, still reigns in downtown Oaxaca.

Calderón Visits the United States

Despite Mexico's immediate security problems, Felipe Calderón found time to tend to the Mexican economy and politics, both national and international. Under his steady hand, during 2007, the Mexican economy continued to bubble along at a moderate annual growth rate of about 2.5 percent, inflation was kept at a low 4 percent, and the peso retained its value below 11 pesos to the U.S. dollar.

On the world stage, President Calderón made his first international trip, initially to California for three days, then east to the Midwest and New York. On February 13, 2008, he addressed a joint session of the California legislature, emphasizing cooperation. "Collaboration and shared responsibility," he said, were the keys to joint California–Mexico progress. In the same address, he thrust himself into the U.S. immigration debate by declaring that "Mexican and Mexican-American workers are a large reason for the dynamic economy of California," and that Mexican "immigration should be legal, safe, and organized."

Government and Economy

GOVERNMENT AND POLITICS
The Constitution of 1917

Mexico's governmental system is rooted in the Constitution of 1917, which incorporated many of the features of its reformist predecessor of 1857. State constitutions, including Oaxaca's, must conform to the federal Constitution, which, with some amendments, remains identical to the 1917 document. Although drafted at the behest of conservative revolutionary Venustiano Carranza by his handpicked Querétaro "Constitucionalista" congress, the 1917 Constitution was greatly influenced by Alvaro Obregón and generally ignored by Carranza during his subsequent three-year presidential term.

Whereas many articles resemble those of its U.S. model, the Constitution of 1917 contains provisions developed directly from Mexican experience. **Article 27** addresses the question of land. Private property rights are qualified by societal need, subsoil rights are public property, and foreigners and corporations are severely restricted in land ownership. Although the 1917 constitution declared *ejido* (jointly held) land inviolate, recent 1994 amendments allow, under certain circumstances, the sale or use of communal land as loan security.

Article 23 severely restricts church powers. In declaring that "places of worship are the property of the nation," it stripped churches of all title to real estate, without compensation. **Article 5** and **Article 130** banned religious orders, expelled foreign clergy, and denied priests and ministers all political rights, including voting, holding office, and even criticizing the government.

Article 123 establishes the rights of labor: to organize, bargain collectively, strike, work a maximum eight-hour day, and receive a minimum wage. Women are to receive equal pay for equal work and be given a month's paid leave for childbearing. Article 123 also establishes social security plans for sickness, unemployment, pensions, and death.

On paper, Mexico's constitutional

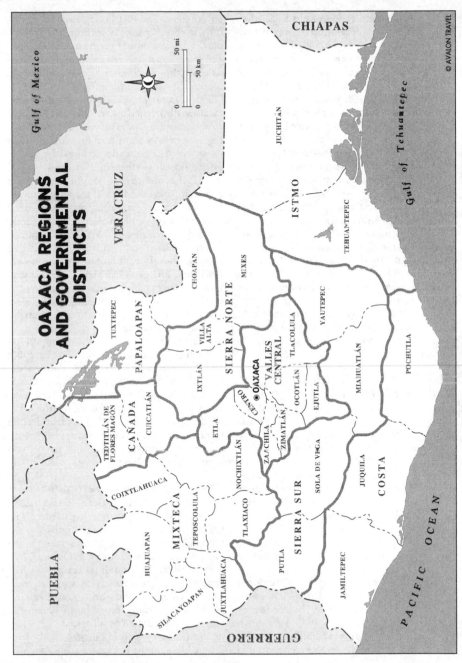

**OAXACA REGIONS
AND GOVERNMENTAL
DISTRICTS**

government structures appear much like their U.S. prototypes: a federal presidency, a two-house (Senate and Chamber of Deputies) congress, and a supreme court, with their counterparts in each of the 31 states and the Mexico City Distrito Federal. Political parties field candidates, and all citizens vote by secret ballot.

In Oaxaca, local federal elections determine Oaxaca's national legislative delegation: **11 deputies** *(diputados)* of the approximately 500-seat lower house and **four senators** *(senadores)* of the 120-odd upper house seats. **PRI dominance** of Oaxaca elections, although not as complete as in the past, still continues, with a plurality of Oaxaca's deputies and senators usually being PRI members.

Although ideally providing for **separation of powers,** the Constitution of 1917 subordinates both the legislative and judicial branches, with the courts being the weakest of all. The supreme court, for example, can only, through repeated deliberations, decide upon the constitutionality of legislation. Five separate individuals must file successful petitions for writs *amparo* (protection) on a single point of law in order to effect constitutional precedent.

The President, the PRI, and the PAN

Despite Mexico's increasingly active legislative bodies, Mexican presidents still enjoy greater powers than their U.S. counterparts. They can suspend constitutional rights under a state of siege, can officially initiate legislation, veto all or parts of bills, refuse to execute laws, and replace state officers. The federal government, moreover, retains nearly all taxing authority, relegating the states to a role of merely administering federal programs.

Mexican presidents successively built upon their potent constitutional mandate during the last three generations of the 20th century. The **Partido Revolucionario Institucional** (Institutional Revolutionary Party, PRI), whose handpicked candidates held the presidency continuously from 1929 to 2000, became an extralegal parallel government, as powerful as or more so than the formal constitutional government. The PRI is organized hierarchically, in three separate labor, farmer, and "popular" (this last mostly government, business, and professional workers) columns, which send delegates from local committees to state and, ultimately, national conventions.

Past Mexican presidents, as heads of the PRI, traditionally reigned at the top of the party apparatus, sending orders through the national PRI delegates, who in turn looked after their respective state delegations. The delegates reported on the performance of the state and local PRI committees to get out the vote and carry out party mandates. If the local committee's performance was satisfactory, then federal subsidies, public works projects, election funds, and federal jobs flowed from government coffers to the state and local level through PRI organizations. In your hometown, if you were not in the PRI or didn't know someone who was, you might have found it difficult to get a small business loan, crop subsidy, government apartment, teaching job, road-repair contract, or government scholarship.

The successful election of PAN opposition presidential candidate Vicente Fox in 2000, although erasing PRI executive dominance, still left the Senate (and later, in 2003, also the Chamber of Deputies) under PRI control. Consequently, President Fox found himself in much the position of a U.S. president, having to negotiate, sometimes unsuccessfully, with legislators from the opposition party (and sometimes even his own party).

State and Local Government

Oaxaca, like all 31 Mexican states, has an elected governor and state legislature. The Oaxaca voters elect 42 representatives to the state legislature, which holds its sessions in the Palacio de Gobierno, adjacent to Oaxaca City's central plaza. With minimal tax powers, the state government is mostly relegated to oversight of federal public works, social welfare, health, and education programs in 30 regional administrative **distritos** (districts).

Distritos vary widely in extent, from the largest, Juchitán, in the Isthmus, to tiny Zaachila, the smallest, in the central valley, not far south of Oaxaca City. Although second smallest in area, Oaxaca's most populous and economically most important district is the Centro district, which contains the capital, Oaxaca City.

Oaxaca's 30 *distritos* are in turn divided, often along ethnic lines, into a host of 570 **municipios** (townships), each with its *cabecera* (head town) and subsidiary *agencias,* usually country villages, each of which oversees a scattering of surrounding *rancherias* (hamlets). Oaxaca's crazy quilt of 570 *municipios,* by far the most of any Mexican state, reflects Oaxaca's ethnic richness. Many of the *municipios* encompass a single ethnic group whose members are united by common kinship, language, and costume.

Its *municipios* are where much of Oaxaca's civic action is. If you get a traffic ticket, you'll probably be told to go to the *municipio's presidencia municipal* (like a city hall) to pay your fine and recover your driver's license. From the *presidencia municipal* reigns the *municipio's*

publicly elected *presidente* (like a mayor), *alcaldes* (judges), and *regidores* (administrators) of various ranks, who oversee the *municipio's policía municipal* and organize public works.

Parallel to and interlocking with this formal Spanish-derived hierarchy is the less formal indigenous **consejo de ancianos** (council of elders), members of which attain their status by a cumulative lifetime of civic service. Operating mostly by discussion and consensus, the council of elders (which sometimes includes the *presidente* and other elected officials) gets its way through discussion, persuasion, and final approval or veto of civic proposals.

Oaxaca's former progressive governor and legislature, in 1995, recognized indigenous demands for local election by traditional **Usos y Costumbres** (Use and Custom) procedures. Now, a majority of (but by no means all; notably not Oaxaca City) *municipios* elect their mayor and city council members in town hall meetings.

Although *municipios* collect minimal

The *presidencia municipal,* as shown here at Tamazulapan in the Mixteca, is the seat of the local *municipio* (city-county or township) governmental unit.

monetary taxes, they often require community members to perform *tequio* (public service) in lieu of taxes. For men, such work might be repairing a local bridge or police or fire duty; women, on the other hand, might perform childcare or sweep the city streets or the municipal market.

Since colonial times, authorities have recognized eight traditional Oaxacan ethno-geographic regions: Valles Centrales, Sierra Norte, Papaloapan, Istmo, Costa, Sierra Sur, Mixteca, and the Cañada. Later, during the republican era, these traditional regions were subdivided into governmental-economic districts, now aggregating 30 in number, each presided over by a district capital through which state tax monies are distributed and elections for both state and federal legislative and executive offices are organized. After the capital Oaxaca City, the district capitals, notably Tlacolula, Ocotlán, and Zaachila in the Valles Centrales; Tuxtepec in the Papaloapan; Juchtán in the Istmo; Juquila in the Sierra Sur; and Juxtlahuaca and Tlaxiaco, in the Mixteca; rank among the state of Oaxaca's most fascinating destinations, and are described in detail in this book.

Political Reform

Reforms in Mexico's stable but top-heavy "Institutional Revolution" has come only gradually. Characteristically, street protests were brutally put down at first, with officials only later working to address grievances. Dominance by the PRI led to widespread cynicism and citizen apathy. Regardless of who got elected, the typical person on the street used to tell you that office-holders were bound to retire with their pockets full.

Nevertheless, during the last dozen years of the 20th century, Mexico took significant strides toward pluralism. Minority parties increasingly were electing candidates to state and federal office. Although none captured a majority of any state legislature, the strongest non-PRI parties, such as the conservative pro-Catholic **Partido Acción Nacional (PAN)** (National Action Party) and the liberal-left **Partido Revolucionario Democratico (PRD)** (Revolutionary Democratic Party), elected governors. As early as 1986, minority parties were given federal legislative seats, up to a maximum of 20, for winning a minimum of 2.5 percent of the national presidential vote. In the 1994 election, minority parties received public campaign financing, depending upon their fraction of the vote.

Following his 1994 inaugural address, in which he called loudly and clearly for more reforms, President **Ernesto Zedillo** quickly began to produce results. He immediately appointed a respected member of the PAN opposition party as attorney general—the first non-PRI cabinet appointment in Mexican history. Other Zedillo firsts were federal Senate confirmation of supreme court nominees and the attorney general, multiparty participation in the Chiapas peace negotiations, and congressional approval of the 1995 financial assistance package received from the United States. Zedillo, moreover, organized a series of precedent-setting meetings with opposition leaders, which led to a written pact for political reform and the establishment of permanent working groups to discuss political and economic questions.

Of major symbolic importance was Zedillo's campaign and inaugural vow to separate both his government and himself from PRI decision-making. He kept his promise, becoming the first Mexican president in as long as anyone could remember who did not choose his successor.

A New Mexican Revolution

Finally, in 2000, like a Mexican Gorbachev, Ernesto Zedillo, the man responsible for many of Mexico's earlier democratic reforms, watched as PAN opposition reformer Vicente Fox swept Zedillo's PRI from the presidency after a 71-year rule. Moreover, despite severe criticism from his own party, Zedillo quickly called for the country to close ranks behind Fox. Millions of Mexicans, still dazed but buoyed by Zedillo's statesmanship and Fox's epoch-making victory, eagerly awaited Fox's inauguration address on December 1, 2000.

He promised nothing less than a new revolution for Mexico and backed it up with concrete proposals: reduce poverty by 30 percent with a million new jobs a year from revitalized new electricity and oil production, a Mexican Silicon Valley, and free trade between Mexico, all of Latin America, and the United States and Canada. He promised justice for all, through a reformed police, army, and the judiciary. He promised conciliation and an agreement with the Zapatista rebel movement in the south, including a bill of rights for Mexico's native peoples.

But six years later, with his grand vision only fractionally fulfilled, no one can fairly say that Vicente Fox didn't set a good example. Like few Mexican presidents before him, he remained true to his belief in a democratic presidency: negotiating, haranguing, cajoling, and compromising with a cadre of legislators who stubbornly blocked nearly all of his reform proposals.

Time and again Vicente Fox admitted the messiness and difficulty of the democratic process. But he also remained convinced and committed that there could be no turning from the democratic path for Mexico. In a 2004 interview, he pointed out that, at least, he had ended "Presidencialismo," the decades-old Mexican habit of bowing to a strong, sometimes even ruthless, president. And perhaps that is how historians will remember Vicente Fox: as the president who, with courage and honesty, truly did begin a New Mexican Revolution, by earnestly leading his country along the difficult but true path to a more just and prosperous future for all Mexicans.

It was truly a bold vision, and five years

SOCIOECONOMIC STATISTICS: OAXACA VS. MEXICO VS. THE UNITED STATES

	OAXACA	MEXICO	U.S.
Approximate average daily income per active worker	$10	$25	$110
Corn productivity	.5 ton/acre	.5 ton/acre	1.6 ton/acre
Tractor use by farmers	25%	40%	100%
Infant mortality	2%	2%	.7%
Inhabitants per doctor	1,200	670	400
Average grade attained in school	6.0	8.5	13
Illiteracy	20%	9%	3%
Population (year 2000)	3,578,000	101,400,000	298,000,000
Yearly population growth	1.1%	1.2%	1.4%

Sources: Mexican government census, U.S. Census Statistical Abstract, World Bank, and the *U.S. Government Book of Facts*

ECONOMIC ACTIVITY – REGIONAL VS. NATIONAL

The following figures represent categories by percent of population engaged in the activity and percent of value of total output.

	AGRICULTURE	INDUSTRY	CONSTRUCTION	COMMERCE
MEXICO				
Population	23%	21%	7%	13%
Value of Output (% of total)	7%	23%	5%	22%
OAXACA				
Population	53%	12%	5%	8%
Value of Output (% of total)	18%	13%	5%	20%

later, nearing the twilight of his six-year term, Fox could only claim partial success. He admitted that the path to democracy, which he believes cannot be reversed, would continue to be messy and difficult. His unfinished agenda therefore will be a challenge to his successor Felipe Calderón, who in his brief but emphatic inauguration speech on December 1, 2006, vowed to continue Mexico's difficult but non-reversible march toward a truly just, democratic, and prosperous homeland for all of Mexico's people.

THE ECONOMY
Postrevolutionary National Gains

By many measures, Mexico's 20th-century revolution appears to have succeeded. Since 1910, illiteracy has plunged from 80 percent to 10 percent; life expectancy has risen from 30 years to nearly 70; infant mortality has dropped from a whopping 40 percent to about 2 percent; and, in terms of caloric intake, most Mexicans are eating about twice as much as their turn-of-the-century forebears.

Decades of near-continuous economic growth account for rising Mexican living standards. The Mexican economy rebounded from its 1982 and 1995 recessions and has recovered, although only modestly, from its 2001–2002 recession, because of its plentiful natural resources; diversified manufacturing, such as cars, steel, and petrochemicals; steadily increasing tourism; exports of fruits, vegetables, and cattle; and its large, willing, low-wage workforce.

Mexican governments during the 1970s and 1980s skillfully exploited Mexico's economic strengths. The **Border Industrialization Program** has led to millions of jobs in thousands of border *maquiladora* factories, from Tijuana to the mouth of the Río Grande. Foreign trade, a strong source for new Mexican jobs, has burgeoned since the 1980s, due to liberalized tariffs as Mexico joined the General Agreement on Tariffs and Trade (GATT) in 1986 and NAFTA in 1994. As a result, Mexico has become a net exporter of goods and services to the United States, its largest trading partner. Although Mexico suffered a peso collapse of about 50 percent (in relation to the U.S. dollar) in 1995, the Zedillo administration acted

	TRANSPORTATION	PRIVATE SERVICES	GOVERNMENT SERVICES
MEXICO			
Population	4%	16%	13%
Value of Output (% of total)	9%	14%	20%
OAXACA			
Population	3%	8%	10%
Value of Output (% of total)	9%	15%	20%

Note: Population percentages, from year 2000 census figures, do not add to 100 percent because some respondents declined to categorize their occupations.

quickly. Belt-tightening measures brought foreign investment flowing back to Mexico by 1997 and annual inflation, which had initially surged, cooled down to around 6 or 7 percent during 2003.

But, during 2004 and 2005, despite high prices for its oil, rock-bottom inflation, large payments of money from Mexicans working in the United States, and a balanced budget, the Mexican economy still didn't produce the million jobs a year it needed to keep up with population increase. Although some of the sluggishness could be blamed on the hurricane that devastated Cancún in fall 2005, most experts agree that Mexico's largest economic problem is lack of ability to compete, especially with respect to Asian countries, especially China, which floods Mexico with low-cost goods, while Mexico sells very little to China in return. A serious marker of all this appeared in 2004, when China replaced Mexico as the United States' second-largest import source, jumping to about 14 percent of U.S. imports, compared to Mexico, at around 10 percent.

Many economists suggest that Mexico, in order to breathe permanent new life into its economy, needs fundamental structural reforms, such as more flexible labor rules, more effective tax collection (hardly anyone pays any income tax), and the possibility of private investment to modernize the energy and oil industries.

The Oaxacan Economy

Despite huge gains, Mexico's Revolution of 1910 is incomplete. In Oaxaca, it remains especially so. Oaxaca lags behind the rest of Mexico by many measures of economic success. Median income, for example, hovers at about half the national average. The year 2000 national census figures indicate that median daily earnings per active worker stood at about $3 for Oaxacans and about $6 for Mexicans in general. Such numbers demonstrate the difficult reality confronting the poorest Oaxacan families. When asked by 2000 census takers to categorize their incomes, a whopping 28 percent of Oaxacan active wage earners said they received no income. The next two higher categories, totaling about 20 percent (one in five)

INCOME DISTRIBUTION – REGIONAL VS. NATIONAL

Approximate percent of workforce that earns the equivalent US$ per day:

	$0	$0-2	$2-4	$4-8	$8-12	$12-20	$20-40	MORE THAN $40
MEXICO	8%	4%	9%	32%	18%	15%	8%	4%
OAXACA	27%	6%	11%	23%	8%	9%	3%	12%

Note: Estimated from the 2000 Mexican national census. Percentages do not add to 100 percent because some respondents declined to categorize their earnings.

reported incomes of between zero and $2 and between $2 and $4 per day, respectively.

A look at more government figures provides clues as to who most of Oaxaca's poor are. According to recent figures, **agriculture**—overwhelmingly corn farming, but also cattle, fruit, and fish—occupies about half of Oaxaca's active workers, but accounts for only one-fifth of the value of Oaxaca's yearly economic output. The remaining four-fifths is generated by the other half of Oaxaca's workers who are, consequently, responsible for approximately four times as much production value as the farmers.

At the human level, the typical Oaxacan lives on a farm and is poor, even by Mexican standards. The typically six-member family, dad José, 36; mom María, 31; three kids, 2, 6, and 11; and grandma, 56; earn next to no cash income and must subsist on what they can produce and gather. This generally is limited to corn, squash, beans, eggs, garden vegetables, an occasional chicken or turkey, and maybe a little wild game. Staples that they don't produce must be bought or bartered for at the village market. So once a week María bundles up some tomatoes, carrots, and potatoes from her garden and maybe one of her half dozen young roosters. With her middle child in tow, she walks the six miles uphill to the village. With luck, María will return by early evening,

having sold or traded everything for perhaps a liter of cooking oil, a kilo of sugar, a spool of thread, and a yard or two of bright ribbon.

While María is at the market, José pulls weeds for a few hours in his *milpa* (cornfield). Although his acreage is small, perhaps no more than two or three acres, he usually manages two harvests of corn a year. In a good season, this might amount to two tons, as long as he keeps the mice and rats away from it. Every year he stores about a ton of corn for home consumption and sells the other ton for about $100 to Conasupo, the government commodity agency. If all goes well, he reckons, in three years he'll save enough to replace his family's present stick-and-adobe, dirt-floor house with a new, sturdy two-room concrete house with an interior water tap and a toilet.

Solving the Problems

Like José, many thousands of Oaxacan farmers must struggle to better their lot. The government is generally sympathetic to their efforts and recognizes that Oaxaca, with its plentiful sun and adequate (but sharply seasonal) rainfall, is a potential trove of grain, fruit, fiber, meat, and fish for the rest of the country and maybe even for export. But the problems are manifold. Although Oaxaca has expanses of rich land, especially in the Isthmus, the Papaloapan, and the central valley, about a fifth of Oaxaca's land, especially in the Mixteca, is useless because of severe erosion. Another third is partly so. Before the conquest, much of Oaxaca's farmland was terraced and irrigated, not unlike the millet terraces of Nepal and the rice terraces of Bali. Although Oaxacans largely lost that precious knowledge, it could be relearned, and the old water channels and hillside terraces (which are still visible at many locations) could be restored.

Meanwhile, on the present land, productivity could be greatly increased. To raise corn production from the current half ton per acre to the U.S. level of two tons per acre would require mechanization, fertilizer, an irrigation water supply, and the know-how to make everything come together. At present, however, only about one-fifth of Oaxaca's farmers have access to a tractor (compared to 38 percent nationwide); very few have the money for fertilizer; only about 15 percent have access to irrigation water; and most have completed five years or less of schooling. Nevertheless, a focused, long-term government-to-people partnership, not unlike the Tennessee Valley Authority in the United States, could restore prosperity in the Oaxacan countryside.

One route to a better life for many Oaxacans has been to get out. Census figures indicate that about 40 percent of people born in Oaxaca are living and working in other parts of Mexico, the United States, or Canada. While Oaxacan people don't want to leave home, lack of local jobs forces them to. Unlike northern Mexican states close to U.S. cities filled with people who want to buy Mexican-made shoes, telephones, mops, lamp fixtures, and bicycles, Oaxaca, in the far south, is surrounded by other equally disadvantaged Mexican states. Oaxaca, with few nearby markets, attracts only a dribble of new factories and consequently generates scant new jobs. If Oaxaca had oil or gold, the story would be much different.

Although emigration has slowed Oaxaca's population growth in general, Oaxaca City is an exception. Country people seeking a better life started arriving in Oaxaca City in the 1940s when the population was about 40,000, and they're still coming. Most estimates put Oaxaca City's rising population at around 375,000. All the new neighbors make life more crowded for the average Oaxaca City family—parents with two or three children—who typically must manage on about $10 per day. The survival mode for many such city families has been enterprise: Mom takes in laundry or starts a neighborhood store on the front porch; Dad works one or two jobs; and both Mom and Dad sell *taquitos* out front on Saturday and Sunday nights. Oaxacans, like everyone, do what they must to get by.

Tourism

Partly because of their isolation and difficult economic circumstances, Oaxaca folks are in many ways like people of yesteryear. Unlike richer people in some parts of Mexico and much of the United States, Canada, and Europe, most Oaxacans have yet to join the headlong race into the future. And therein lies Oaxaca's charm. The native women's bright traditional costumes, the venerable, monumental buildings, the stick-and-adobe thatched houses, the *vaqueros* on horseback, the oxcarts, all of which symbolize backwardness and poverty in some eyes, are a sentimentally picturesque sight to increasing numbers of visitors, both domestic and foreign.

But as a visitor, *please remember the reality behind Oaxaca's charm.* Please be tolerant, generous in your gratuities, and bargain gently. If you do, Oaxacans will welcome your presence and try even harder to make your visit worthwhile.

State and federal government planners years ago recognized Oaxaca tourism's potential benefits. Their strategy, formulated in the late 1980s, is yielding results. While tourist visitations have burgeoned, Oaxaca City's proud old monuments have been restored, the central plaza blooms with old Mexico charm, village-run tourist accommodations have sprouted in the countryside, and the coastal Bahías de Huatulco resort continues to grow gradually while retaining its precious tropical forest hinterland.

This is all good news if Oaxaca's increasing tide of visitors doesn't ruin the charm that they came to enjoy in the first place. Instead, let's hope that Oaxaca's culture and natural assets will be enriched *because* of their tourist value. If so, campesinos will preserve, rather than wipe out, the local wildlife because they realize that visitors come *because* of the wildlife. For the same reason, artisans will fashion more enticing handicrafts, people will continue to dress up and dance in their bright costumes, towns will build museums and conserve their old monuments, and archaeologists will restore crumbled cities to their original glory.

ECOTOURISM AND SOCIALLY RESPONSIBLE TRAVEL

Latter-day jet travel has brought droves of vacationing tourists to developing countries largely unprepared for the consequences. As the visitors' numbers swell, power grids black out, sewers overflow, and roads crack under the strain of accommodating more and larger hotels, restaurants, cars, buses, and airports.

Worse yet, armies of vacationers drive up local prices and begin to change native customs. While visions of tourists as sources of fast money replace traditions of hospitality, television wipes out folk entertainment, Coke and Pepsi substitute for fruit drinks, and prostitution and drugs flourish.

Some travelers have said enough is enough and are forming organizations to encourage visitors to travel with increased sensitivity to native people and customs. They have developed travelers' codes of ethics and guidelines that encourage visitors to stay at local-style accommodations, use local transportation, and seek alternative vacations and tours, such as language-study and cultural programs and people-to-people work projects.

A number of especially active socially responsible travel groups sponsor tours all over the world, including Oaxaca. These include organizations such as **Global Exchange, Green Tortoise, Green Globe,** and **Third Eye Travel.** They all have websites that can be accessed via Internet search engines, such as Google and Yahoo, or the umbrella website www.sociallyresponsible.com.

The related ecotourism movement promotes socially responsible tourism through the strategy of simultaneous enjoyment and enhancement of the natural environment. Oaxaca has become an ecotourism center partly because of the dedication of Oaxaca-based Ron Mader, founder and moving force behind the superb website www.planeta.com. Log on and you'll find virtually everything you need to know about Oaxaca-based ecotourism, from nature tour companies and village recycling projects to indigenous handicrafts cooperatives and international conferences.

Guests at the *cabaña ecoturística* at Santa María Yavesia village enjoy an airy view balcony.

© BRUCE WHIPPERMAN

People and Culture

Let a broad wooden chopping block represent the high plain, the *altiplano* of Mexico; imagine hacking at one half of it with a sharp cleaver until it is grooved and pocked. That fractured surface resembles Mexico's central highlands, where most Mexicans have lived for millennia. The most severely shattered southern end of the Mexican landscape encompasses Oaxaca, whose rugged topography has isolated its original inhabitants behind high ridges and yawning barrancas for untold generations. In their seclusion, they developed separate tongues and hierarchical societies that viewed outsiders with suspicion and hostility, as odd-speaking, barely human barbarians from across the canyon or behind the mountains. When the Spanish conquerors arrived in Oaxaca, they found a region divided among hundreds of separate subtribes, speaking 16 main languages broken down into scores of mutually unintelligible dialects. The Oaxacans' own divisions, as much as Spanish horses and steel, led to their quick downfall.

The Spanish merely added their own layers atop the existing divisions—of territory, language, caste, class, and wealth—that continue to shape both Mexico and Oaxaca to the present day.

Mesoamerica

Although Oaxacan native peoples are divided by their diverse languages and rugged topography, they nevertheless share many folk customs, not only with each other but with tens of millions of other native peoples in a broad belt, beginning around Mexico's Tropic of Cancer and stretching south and east to Honduras and El Salvador. Anthropologists call the entire region Mesoamerica, a single label reflecting its broad cultural unity. Anthropologists believe that this universal symphony of belief and practice flows from tenaciously held traditions handed down from Mexico's great pre-conquest civilizations. And nowhere are these folk practices more persistent than in Oaxaca, Mesoamerica's heartland. If you're curious about how most

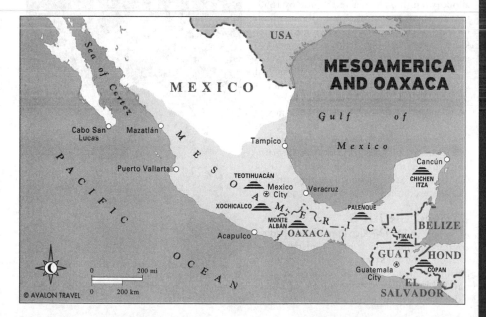

Americans lived before Columbus and Cortés, you needn't look any farther than the Oaxaca countryside.

POPULATION

The Spanish colonial government and the Roman Catholic religion provided the glue that over 400 years has welded Mexico's fragmented population into a nation. In recent years, increased emigration, mostly to the United States, has slowed the growth of the population of both Mexico at large and Oaxaca. At about 98 million in 2000, Mexico's population is growing at less than one percent per year, less than half the pace of previous decades. The same is true for Oaxaca's population, which stood at about 3.4 million in the year 2000.

A growing population was not always the case in Mexico. Historians estimate that European diseases, largely measles and smallpox, probably wiped out as many as 20 million—perhaps 95 percent—of Mexico's *indígena* population within a few generations after Cortés stepped ashore in 1519. Oaxaca's population dropped correspondingly from a pre-conquest level of about two million to a mere 150,000 by 1650. Oaxaca's native peoples, ironically, can look forward to the year 2019, five centuries after Cortés, when their population will have recovered approximately to its pre-conquest level.

By 1600, Mexico's indigenous population had dropped so low that the Spanish began to import sizable numbers of **African slaves,** whose numbers swelled to several tens of thousands by 1650. Although much of the African lineage has been absorbed into Mexico's general population, several thousand African Mexicans still maintain separate small communities in the Costa Chica, the coastal region spreading both east and west from the Oaxaca–Guerrero border.

ETHNIC GROUPS

Although by 1950 Mexico's population had recovered to 25 million, it was completely transformed. The **mestizo,** a Spanish-speaking person of mixed blood, had replaced the pure native Mexican, the *indígena* (een-DEE-hay-nah), as the typical Mexican.

This trend is not as strong in Oaxaca. Although perhaps three of four Mexicans would identify themselves as mestizo, only about half of Oaxacans probably would. Among many native Oaxacans, the label "mestizo" borders on the derogatory, despite the long colonial tradition that, by virtue of their part-European blood, mestizos were elevated to the level of *gente de razón*—people of "reason" or "right."

The typical mestizo family enjoys many of the benefits of the modern world. They typically own a modest concrete house in town. Their furnishings, simple by developed-world standards, will often include an electric refrigerator, washing machine, propane stove, television, and a car or truck. The children go to school every day, and the eldest son sometimes even looks forward to college.

Above the mestizos, a tiny **criollo** (Mexican-born, European blood) minority, a few percent of the total population, inherits the privileges—wealth, education, and political power—of their colonial Spanish ancestors.

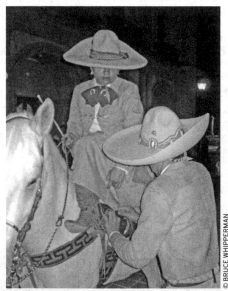

© BRUCE WHIPPERMAN

A *charra* (gentlewoman cowgirl), in traditional Spanish-origin costume, prepares to exhibit her riding skills.

TAKING PEOPLE PICTURES

Like most folks everywhere, typical Oaxacan people on the street rarely appreciate strangers taking their pictures. The easiest route to overcoming this is a local friend, guide, or even a willing interpreter-bystander who can provide an introduction. Lacking that, you'll need to be at least semi-fluent in Spanish in order to introduce yourself or say something funny to break the ice.

A sometimes useful way to go is to offer to send them a copy of their picture. If they accept, make sure that you follow through. If somehow the picture doesn't come out, at least send them a picture of you, explaining why.

Although it's becoming less common, some people still believe that they might lose their souls if they let you take their picture. In such a case, humor again might help (or perhaps offering to let them take a picture of you first).

Markets are wonderful picture-taking places but pose challenges. Vendors are often resistant, to the point of hostility, if you try to take their picture behind their sumptuous pile of tomatoes or stack of baskets. The reasons aren't hard to understand. They're grumpy partly because sales are probably disappointing, and, since they have to stay put, they probably feel used. Buying something from them might go a long way toward soothing their feelings.

As for church picture-taking, remember churches are places of worship and not museums. Don't be rude by trying to take pictures of people at the altar. Moreover, churches are usually dark inside, and, unless you have a flash-suppress option or unusually high-speed film, your flash will disturb worshippers.

The typical **indígena** family lives in a small adobe house in a remote valley, subsisting on corn, beans, and vegetables from their small, unirrigated *milpa* (cornfield). They usually raise chickens, a few pigs, and sometimes a cow, and have electricity, but no sewage connection. Their few hundred dollars a year cash income isn't enough to buy even a small tractor or refrigerator, much less a truck. The *indígenas* (or, mistakenly but commonly, Indians), by the usual measurements of income, health, or education, squat at the bottom of the social ladder. (See also *Indigenous Groups* later in this chapter.)

Sizable **African Mexican** communities, or *negros,* descendants of 17th- and 18th-century African slaves, live in the Gulf states and along the Guerrero–Oaxaca coastline. Last to arrive, they experience discrimination at the hands of everyone else and are integrating very slowly into the mestizo mainstream.

SHARED OAXACAN CUSTOMS
Settlement Patterns
Oaxaca's present 570 *municipios* (townships),

each with its main town and market, reflect community boundaries often dating back more than a thousand years. Although the Spanish imposed their civic pattern of church, *presidencia* (city hall), and major stores and prominent residences all clustered around a central plaza, the native people still hold to their tradition of concentrating their homes in a number of barrios (neighborhoods) on the outskirts. Native peoples have sometimes stretched the Spanish pattern, reverting to their ancient **"empty town"** custom. Here, only the mestizo and criollo elite permanently live in town, while natives maintain empty in-town houses, which they occupy only during market and ceremonial occasions. Most of their days they spend by their country *milpas.*

Birth, Life, and Death
Christian baptism is everyone's first major life event; it's so important that a number of communities believe that a baby is not fully human until baptized. If an unbaptized baby dies, the parents must make haste to bury the body immediately, with little ceremony.

MESOAMERICAN CALENDAR

The Mixtec and Zapotec ancestors of present-day Oaxacans ordered their lives with the same calendric system as many Mesoamerican linguistic groups, including the Maya, the Aztecs (Nahuatl), the Tarascans (Purépecha), and many others. Their system combined two major calendric cycles. First, they used the agricultural calendar, tied to the seasons and derived from the approximately 365-day (more accurately 365.2422) cycle of the sun through the background of stars and constellations.

The Mesoamerican counting system was basic to the calendar's operation. The Mesoamericans didn't count by decimals, but rather used a vigesimal (20-count) system. They logically divided their agricultural year into 18 "months" of 20 days each, with a five-day short month at the year-end. A given day, for example, might be called, instead of June 11 or June 12, 5-Deer or 6-Deer and so forth.

They tracked ceremonial dates, such as birthdays, with a separate ritual or divinatory calendar of 260 days that combined 20 separate named days with numbers one through 13. Succeeding days were identified as, for example, 2-Water, 3-Monkey, 4-Dog, and so on.

A given date was a unique coincidence of both calendars, which you can imagine as a pair of meshed cogwheels, turning in lockstep. As you picture the calendric cogwheels turning, at a given moment a certain cog (marked as 5-Deer, for example) in the solar calendar will always be meshing with some slot (marked as 3-Monkey, for example) in the ritual calendar, producing a unique combination of two numbers and two names (since the solar and the ritual calendars have different − 365 vs. 260 − respective totals of cogs and slots). For example, June 11, 1999, might be represented by the unique coincidence of cog 5-Deer and slot 3-Monkey; June 12, 1999, by 6-Deer and 4-Dog; June 13 by 7-Deer, 5-Water; and so on. (Note that the solar calendar progresses through named "months," such as "Deer" in the example, while the ritual calendar does not.)

In this system dates are unique, but only for a determined time period, because the entire calendric cycle repeats itself after all dual-number-dual-name combinations have occurred. This happens every 52 solar years (or, in days, 52 times 365, 18,980 days). During this time the intermeshed ritual calendar

---

If not, the spirit of the unbaptized baby might escape and become a *nagual* (nah-WAHL), a malevolent animal that will harm people who cross its path.

Baptism is also the time when the web of *compadrazgo* relationships starts to influence a person's life. This begins when parents designate their *compadres* (best friends) as *padrinos* (godparents) to their newly born. As children mature, with parental consent they designate their own *compadres*. Formal ceremonies often solemnize *padrino* and *compadrazgo* bonds, which might continue through generations of loyal *padrino* and *compadre* relationships.

With babies, nursing often lasts two or three years, or at least until the next child comes along. Preschool children experience little imposed discipline except the responsibility of watching after younger siblings. Loud or disruptive children might get spanked or shunned, however. Formal schooling is usually considered so important that families often sacrifice so that children, especially boys, may attend at least six grades of school. Although children of poorer parents experience few, if any, puberty rites, richer parents often honor their children, especially girls, with a number of Catholic ceremonies, such as first communion, confirmation, blessing of their pet animals, and *quinceana* (coming out) at age 15. Among poorer populations, a girl becomes an adult with marriage, often by age 14 or 15. A boy enters manhood through either marriage or entering *servicio* (community service). He's expected to pay community assessments and perform *tequio* (communal must pass through exactly the same number of days. Dividing 18,980 by its number of 260 cogs, you come up with the exactly 73 revolutions that the ritual calendar must undergo in the same 52 solar years.

Besides the Mixtecs and Zapotecs, all other Mesoamerican groups probably feared that cataclysmic events might occur at the end of each 52-year period, measured from some mythical beginning. High priests and presumably the populations at large observed solemn ceremonies, performed sacrifices, and watched the sky for auspicious portents, such as a bright overhead star, a conjunction of planets, or a comet, on the eve of their 52 year cyclical "millennium."

Knowledge of the Zapotec and Mixtec calendars is gradually being accumulated. Scholars believe that they have been used since at least the early urban stage, around 500 B.C., approximately the founding of Monte Albán. Alfonso Caso, the discoverer of Monte Albán's earliest stages, associated a common but undeciphered Monte Albán glyph, of a headdress in profile, with the solar year. For Caso, this indicated that certain personages wearing such headdresses either interpreted, read, or manipulated the calendar. The ritual calendar, called *piye* in Zapotec, was also certainly used at Monte Albán.

As in other parts of Mesoamerica, persons were named by their birth date, such as 8-Deer, 3-Dog, or 7-Monkey, in the ritual calendar. Such name-dates occur as glyphs associated with personages recorded in stone or on the surviving hieroglyphic paper books, called *codices*, such as the Codex Nuttall.

The Mesoamericans, as the Europeans, had to apply corrections to keep the solar calendar in correspondence with the seasons. This will happen only if the year averages, over the millennia, 365.2422 days. The presently used Gregorian calendar (which was instituted by Pope Gregory VIII in 1582) corrects the solar year approximately to 365.2425 days (compared to the actual 365.2422) by omitting the leap year every three out of four centuries. Therefore, although the years 1700, 1800, and 1900 were not leap years (that is, they were permitted only 365 days, instead of 366), the year 2000 was permitted 366 days. The Mayans, scholars believe, did a little better than this; they corrected the solar calendar to 365.2420 days.

work) service. As a young man matures, he is expected to fulfill the duties of a series of increasingly important *cargos* (offices). If successful, at middle age he is rewarded with the rank of *principal* (elder) and admitted to the village council of elders.

Death is usually marked by 24 hours of mourning while the body lies in state at home, usually with candles, incense, and flowers. Wrapped in a *petate* (reed mat) or a coffin, the body is buried, along with the deceased's favored trinkets, and perhaps favorite food. Rituals continue periodically thereafter, especially at nine days as well as one year after burial.

Marriage, Family, and Inheritance

Traditional marriage is an alliance between families, initiated by the groom's parents, often through a go-between. Girls marry as early as 14, boys at 16 or 17. The more well-to-do marry later. Often prospective grooms and brides perform services for the other's family, sometimes even taking up temporary residence (but not sleeping with their intended) while everyone gets acquainted. The contents of the couple's dreams often carry weight in the decision to marry. Polyandry, marriage of a woman to two brothers, although sanctioned in some communities, is not common. On the other hand, well-to-do husbands, while remaining married, sometimes support additional women in separate households.

Although extended families generally encompass two, three, or four generations, couples often establish their own households after the birth of their first child. Even though both the wife's and the husband's relatives enjoy equal kinship status, couples are more likely to live near the husband's relatives. Other practices are male-weighted. Boys usually inherit more land than their sisters, and family names, nearly always Spanish, are inherited from the father. Among some Mixtecs and Mazatecs, the father's first name, interestingly, becomes his children's surname. (This is not unlike the practice among some northern Europeans—"Johnson," "Svensen," and "Mendelsohn," for example.)

Household Life

The basic house has a single room, a dirt floor, stick-and-adobe walls, and a thatched roof. Better houses have more rooms, adobe or concrete walls, a concrete floor, and perhaps a flush toilet. Household goods hang on pegs and nails all around the walls. Overhead, rafters support grain and other heavy storage. Beds are either on floor mats or hammocks. A small altar with saint and candle occupies one corner, with the kitchen in the other. Cooking is either over open fire or on an adobe stove. Tortillas are heated on a flat adobe *comal* (griddle); beans, chilies, and stews are cooked in pottery jars *(ollas)* or metal pots over the open fire. Women grind corn by rolling with their stone *mano* on the *metate* basin. They grind chilies in their *molcajete* (mortar).

Men do the heavier outside work: clearing, burning, farming, building, repairing, plus fishing, hunting, and tending cattle and horses. If fields are far from the homestead, men sometimes take up temporary residence there during planting and harvest. Women cook, sew, wash clothes, gather fruit, flowers, and wild herbs, and tend household animals, such as pigs, goats, chickens, and turkeys. Women do most, if not all, of the marketing. Both men and women carry heavy loads.

Dress

Verbal descriptions pale in comparison to the color and excitement of a Oaxaca town fiesta or big market day. Country people, especially in remote areas, still wear the traditional cottons that blend the Spanish and native styles. Men usually wear the Spanish-origin fiber **sombrero** (literally, shade-maker) on their heads, loose white cotton shirt and pants, and leather **huaraches** on their feet. Women's dress is often more colorful. It can include a **huipil** (long, sleeveless dress), often embroidered in bright floral and animal motifs, or a handwoven **enredo** (wraparound skirt that identifies the wearer with a particular locality). A very common addition is the Spanish-tradition all-purpose woven shawl **(rebozo),** which can carry a baby, a bag of corn, or maybe even a chicken or two, as well as protect from the rain or sun. A *faja* (waist sash) and, in the winter, a *quech-quémitl* (shoulder cape) complete the costume.

Making a Living

The great majority of Oaxacan indigenous people cultivate native corn, along with a number of other secondary crops, such as beans, squash, pumpkins, potatoes, chili peppers, and tomatoes. Depending upon soil and climate, they may also harvest potatoes, maguey (for alcoholic drinks), and fruits, such as mangos, papaya, chirimoya, *zapote,* and avocado. Other native crops might be cotton or maguey for *ixtle* fiber, and perhaps cocoa beans, *hule* (rubber), and chicle (chewing gum) for cash. Locally cultivated introduced cash crops include wheat, bananas, coffee, sugarcane, sesame seeds, and peanuts.

Many families or sometimes entire villages specialize in crafts, such as pottery, cloth weaving, or basketry. Although the appearance of cheap, machine-made cloth has weakened the tradition, many Oaxacan women still weave family garments with the ancestral backstrap loom. Treadle looms, introduced by the Spanish and operated by either men or women, are common around Oaxaca City. Potters, both women and men, practice their craft all over Oaxaca. Methods vary; they might confine themselves to the native hand-coiling or the Spanish-introduced potter's wheel, or use a combination of both. (See *Arts and Crafts* later in this chapter.)

Governmental and Religious Institutions

Although women exercise considerable behind-the-scenes influence, men customarily occupy the formal community leadership positions. Minor *presidencia* (city hall) positions are usually appointive; senior positions, such as *regidor* (administrator), *alcalde* (judge), and *presidente* (mayor) are often elective. In-town native homes cluster in one or more barrios on the outskirts. A town *regidor* acts as a representative agent for one or more barrios.

Paralleling such formal civil institutions are the religious, which center on the *mayordomía*, the office responsible for the oft-elaborate ceremonial trappings and yearly fiesta of the barrio's patron saint. The barrio's *regidor* or one of its *cofradías* (religious fraternities) designates the *mayordomo* for a one-year *mayordomía* responsibility. If donations for the patronal fiesta are inadequate, the *mayordomo*, often a wealthy individual, is expected to add a generous contribution of his or her own. Although this may spell temporary poverty for the *mayordomo*, the reward is great community prestige. A lifetime of such service will often assure election to the status of elder (*principal* or *anciano*) and exalted (so exalted that elders are rarely prosecuted for wrongdoing) membership in the council of elders, upon whose resources and sage advice the community relies.

RELIGION

Although the vast majority of Oaxacan *indígenas* consider themselves Catholics, their religion blends the catechism of the missionary fathers with ancient native beliefs. Deities in their age-old Mesoamerican pantheon assume thinly disguised identities among the host of Catholic saints. Besides paying obeisance at the village church altar, Oaxacan country folks also appease mountain, water, and underworld spirits with offerings and sacrifices at sacred summits, springs, and caves. Before killing a deer, for example, a hunter often asks permission of the *señor del monte* (lord, or spirit, of the mountain). Sometimes *hechiceros* (wizards) or *ancianos* lead entire communities in cornfield

Catholicism is practiced by the vast majority of Oaxacans. Here, Puerto Escondido people fete their beloved Virgen de la Soledad.

ceremonies for a successful harvest, with flower offerings, candles, food, and sacrificial turkeys and chickens.

Other old beliefs persist. Many folks, especially in remote areas, believe that *animas* (spirits) of the dead, besides the Catholic God and the saints, influence the living. Appeasement of *animas* peaks on November 1 and 2, respectively, the Day of All Saints and Day of the Dead, when many families gather all night at graves of their departed, with candles, flowers, incense, and the deceased's favorite foods. People also appease saints for favors; however, if prayers are not answered, a person may also punish a saint by abusing its figurine. Sometimes evil dwarfs, the devil, or malevolent female spirits lure men to ruin. At birth, people acquire *tonos*, powerful guardian spirits, often in the guise of mountain lions, jaguars, and eagles, who, if treated with respect, might protect them throughout life. Sickness, commonly thought to be afflicted by an evil spell, loss of soul by fright, or "bad air" *(mal aire)*, is

© BRUCE WHIPPERMAN

THE VIRGIN OF GUADALUPE

Conversion of the *indígenas* was sparked by the vision of Juan Diego, a humble farmer. On the hill of Tepayac north of Mexico City in 1531, Juan Diego saw a brown-skinned version of the Virgin Mary enclosed in a dazzling aura of light. She told him to build a shrine in her memory on that spot, where the Aztecs had long worshipped their "earth mother," Tonantzín. Juan Diego's brown virgin told him to go to the cathedral and relay her instruction to Archbishop Zumárraga.

The archbishop, as expected, turned his nose up at Juan Diego's story. The vision returned, however, and this time Juan Diego's brown virgin realized that a miracle was necessary. She ordered him to pick some roses at the spot where she had first appeared to him (a true miracle, since roses had been previously unknown in the vicinity) and take them to the archbishop. Juan Diego wrapped the roses in his rude fiber cape, returned to the cathedral, and placed the wrapped roses at the archbishop's feet. When he opened the offering, Zumárraga gasped: imprinted on the cape was an image of the brown virgin herself – proof positive of a genuine miracle.

In the centuries since Juan Diego, the brown virgin – La Virgen Morena, or Nuestra Señora La Virgen de Guadalupe – has blended native and Catholic elements into something uniquely Mexican. In doing so, she has become the virtual patroness of Mexico, the beloved symbol of Mexico for *indígenas*, mestizos, *negros*, and criollos alike.

In the summer of 2002, Pope John Paul journeyed to Mexico to perform a historic gesture. Before millions of joyous faithful, on July 31, 2002, the frail aging pontiff elevated Juan Diego to sainthood, thus making him Latin America's first indigenous person to be so honored.

treated by the incantations of a traditional village healer *curandero* or *curandera*.

Healers employ other remedies, such as consumption or avoidance of certain foods, sucking (to remove the mysterious object causing the illness), herbs and poultices, and also modern medicine. Especially common is a steam bath in the traditional *temascal*, a permanent wood or stone structure or temporary mat-covered brush hut, which many Oaxacan households maintain individually (rather than communally).

Catholicism, spreading its doctrine of equality of all persons before God and incorporating native gods into the church rituals, eventually brought the native Mexicans into the fold. Within a hundred years of the Conquest, nearly all natives had accepted the new religion, which raised the universal God of all humankind over local tribal deities.

Every Mexican city, town, and village celebrates the cherished memory of their Virgin of Guadalupe on December 12. This celebration, however joyful, is but one of the many fiestas that Mexicans, especially the *indígenas,* rejoice in. Each village holds its local fiesta in honor of its patron saint, who is often a thinly veiled sit-in for some local pre-Cortesian deity. Themes appear Spanish—Christians vs. Moors, devils vs. priests—but the native element is strong, sometimes dominant. During Semana Santa (Holy Week) at Pinotepa Nacional in coastal Oaxaca, for example, Mixtec people, costumed as Jews, shoot arrows skyward, simultaneously reciting traditional Mixtec prayers.

LANGUAGE
Oaxacan Indigenous Languages

Linguists recognize 16 separate languages spoken in Oaxaca today. Experts identify each of them with one of five language families. North American language family names are conventionally derived by combining the names of the northernmost and southernmost languages of the group. Thus, Otomanguean, Oaxaca's most widespread language family, derives its label from Otomi, spoken northwest of Mexico City, and Mangue, spoken

Nearly everyone at Valley of Oaxaca markets is a native speaker of the Zapotec dialect, a tonal language.

© BRUCE WHIPPERMAN

The same is true for Oaxaca's other major languages—Zapotec, Mazatec, Chinantec, and Mixe—and to a lesser degree, for the minor languages.

Few nonindigenous people, whether foreigners or Mexican, have made the intense effort required to speak and understand a Oaxacan native language. All of the Otomanguean languages, like the Chinese dialects, are **tonal.** This means that a given word takes on different meanings depending upon the pitch—low, high, rising, or falling—with which it is enunciated. Consequently, in big market towns, Spanish is often the lingua franca of buying and selling. Nevertheless, at many country markets, aware visitors notice many people, usually older folks, who speak no Spanish at all.

Please take note that the Spanish names for the Zapotec, Mixtec, Mazatec, and Chinantec languages are *Zapoteco, Mixteco, Mazateco,* and *Chinanteco,* while the respective home territories of each group are the Zapoteca, Mixteca, Mazateca, and Chinantla.

INDIGENOUS GROUPS

Although anthropologists and census takers classify them according to language groups (such as Mixtec, Zapotec, or Nahua), *indígenas* typically identify themselves as residents of a particular locality rather than by language or ethnic grouping. And although as a group they are referred to as *indígenas* (native, or aboriginal), individuals are generally made uncomfortable (or may even feel insulted) by being labeled as such.

While the mestizos are the emergent self-conscious majority class, the *indígenas* remain mostly invisible, keeping to their country hamlets, except during town market days and fiestas. Typically, they are politically conservative, socially traditional, and tied to the land. On market day, the typical *indígena* family might make the trip into town. They bag up some tomatoes, squash, or peppers, and tie up a few chickens or a pig. The rickety country bus will often be full, and the mestizo driver may wave them away, giving preference to his friends,

in southeast Mexico. All of Oaxaca's native language speakers occupy pretty much the same territories that they did at the time of the conquest. The Otomanguean, by location, moving generally west to east, are: **Amusgo, Chatino, Trique, Mixtec, Chocho, Ixcatec, Popoluca, Cuicatec, Mazatec, Chinantec,** and **Zapotec.** A language pair of eastern Oaxaca, **Mixe** (MEE-shay) and **Zoque** (SOH-kay), probably distantly related to Mayan dialects, are often lumped into a second family, the Mixe-Zoque family. Three other languages are the only representatives of their respective families. **Nahuatl** (the language of the Aztecs) of the Uto-Aztecan family; **Chontal,** of the Hokan-Coahuiltecan family; and **Huave,** of its own family, Huave.

Understanding in Oaxaca is further complicated by a proliferation of **dialects.** Mixtec speakers from Jamiltepec, on the Pacific coast, for example, do not generally comprehend the Mixtec dialect of a town, such as Tlaxiaco, across half a dozen ridges 100 miles away.

INDIGENOUS LANGUAGES

The 2000 national census figures list populations of those over five years old who speak an indigenous Oaxacan language:

PERCENTAGE OF TOTAL

Language	Population	Oaxacans	Important Centers in Oaxaca
Zapotec	377,000	13.5%	Tlacolula, Juchitán, Pochutla
Mixtec	245,000	8.8%	Tlaxiaco, Huajuapan de León, Jamiltepec
Mazatec	174,000	6.5%	Huatla de Jiménez, Jalapa de Díaz
Chinantec	108,000	3.9%	Valle Nacional, Ojatitlán
Mixe	105,000	3.8%	Ayutla, Zacatepec
Chatino	40,000	1.4%	Nopala, Juquila
Trique	15,200	.55%	Tilapa
Huave	13,700	.49%	San Mateo del Mar, San Dionisio del Mar
Cuicatec	12,000	.43%	Cuicatlán
Nahua	11,000	.39%	Salina Cruz, Tuxtepec
Zoque	5,300	.19%	San Miguel Chimalapa, Santa María Chimalapa
Amusgo	4,800	.17%	San Pedro Amusgos
Chontal	4,600	.16%	Santiago Astata
Chocho	500	.018%	Coixtlahuaca
Popoluca	500	.018%	Santiago Chazumba
Ixcatec	200	.0072%	Ixcatlán
Totals	**1,076,000**	**38.7%**	

leaving the *indígenas* to trudge stoically along the road.

Their lot, nevertheless, has been slowly improving. *Indígena* families now often have access to a local school and a clinic. Improved health has led to a large increase in their population. Official census counts, however, probably run low. *Indígenas* are traditionally suspicious of government people, and census takers, however conscientious, seldom speak the local dialect.

Recent figures nevertheless indicate that about 40 percent of Oaxacans are *indígenas*— that is, they speak one of Oaxaca's 16 native languages. Of these, about a fifth speak no Spanish at all. These fractions, moreover, are changing only gradually. Many *indígenas* prefer the old ways.

Once a year, in mid-July, thousands of indigenous people, from hundreds of ethnically distinct Oaxaca communities, converge on Oaxaca City for the **Guelaguetza** (gay-lah-GHET-sah) folk dance festival. Dazzled by the whirling color and spectacle, visitors begin to grasp the richness and sheer magnitude of Oaxacan folk tradition. Although their diversity is staggering, the simple fact is that the majority—about three of every five—of indigenous Oaxacans speak some dialect of one of two languages, Zapotec or Mixtec. Of these, the most numerous and visible are the Zapotecs, the people whom visitors encounter first in excursions from Oaxaca City.

Zapotecs

The Spanish label "Zapoteco" comes from Aztec, rather than Zapotec, tradition. The Zapotecs call themselves **Ben Zaa**, or "People of the Clouds." The Aztecs heard this as Tsapotécatl, or "Zapote People," a less-than-flattering "fruit eater" label.

Zapotec speakers, who number upward of 400,000, make up about one-third of Oaxaca's native people. The Zapotecs, moreover, are the most visible for more reasons than their numbers. In contrast to the Mixtecs, the Zapotecs, led by their kings Cosijoeza and Cosijopí, allied themselves with the Spanish right from the beginning. Nearly unique among Mexican indigenous groups, Zapotecs have figured prominently in national politics. Mexico's most beloved president, Benito Juárez, was of pure Zapotec origin. Lately, Zapotecs, including many women, have strongly influenced politics and government in the Isthmus through the **Coalición Obero, Campesino, y Estudiantil de Istmo** (Confederation of Workers, Farmers, and Students of the Isthmus, COCEI).

Zapotec influence goes much further. Although frequented by nearly all of Oaxaca's indigenous groups, a number of Oaxaca's largest native markets, such as Oaxaca City, Tlacolula, Tehuántepec, and Juchitán, are run by Zapotecs. Backcountry centers, where Zapotecs own and manage most stalls and stores, are hostile to penetration by mestizo merchants.

Individual Zapotec-speaking persons usually identify themselves more strongly with region or locale than language. (You might expect this, since the several Zapotec regional dialects are virtually separate languages, differing as much as French, Spanish, Italian, and Portuguese.) Living and work patterns, likewise, depend much more on locale—tropical coast, cool mountain, or highland valley—than ethnicity. Oaxaca's four Zapotec regions (and their important market centers), moving clockwise from Oaxaca's center, are the central valley (Oaxaca City, Tlacolula, Ocotlán), northern Sierra (Ixtlán, Yalalag, Villa Alta), Isthmus (Tehuántepec, Juchitán), and southern Sierra (Miahuatlán, Pochutla).

Zapotec communities, moreover, are generally skillful at resolving disputes. If informal means—neighborly discussion, arbitration, or the council of elders—fail, then the argument will nearly always be resolved in the local court. Blood feuds, common in some Oaxacan indigenous communities, are rare among the Zapotecs.

Although Zapotec speakers are gradually adopting new ways, many still remember the old gods, especially the god of rain, fertility, and lightning, known as Cocijo, in the central valley. On masks you may see him as a lizard. He controls the clouds and may even release *granizo* (hail) onto a wrongdoer's crops. Some southern Zapotecs visualize the world as an island in a vast sea, watched down upon by Cocijo and his retinue-hierarchy of heavenly hosts.

Other old beliefs persist. Influential animals, such as the *correcamino* (roadrunner), who brings good luck; the *tecolote* (small owl), who brings bad; and the *mariposa* (butterfly), who signifies death; are important actors in Zapotec fables. Besides mysterious incantations, Zapotec traditional healers, both men and women, use a wealth of herbal cures: wild garlic for high blood pressure, cloves for toothaches, *rosa de fandango* (a type of mint) for conception, *epazote morada* (a type of basil) for worms.

Although midwives traditionally preside over birthing, fathers are expected to be present to ensure a healthy baby. Pregnant women are often exhorted not to eat honey or mamey fruit. If possible, mothers are treated royally after giving birth. They traditionally remain in bed for three weeks, get plenty of massages, take *temascal* steam baths, and eat lots of chicken, chilies, and salt.

Mixtecs

It's probably not an accident that the Mixtecs' self-label, Nyu-u Sabi, "People of the Rain" (or "Clouds") has the same meaning as the Zapotecs' name for themselves. Linguists estimate that around 3,000 years ago, they were, in fact, the same people. They're not the same today, however. Their languages, although related, are mutually unintelligible, and their homelands are on opposite sides of Oaxaca.

The Mixtecs, who number around 350,000, comprise about a quarter of all Oaxacan native speakers. Nearly all live in three geographic zones in western Oaxaca: the Mixteca Baja, Mixteca Alta, and Mixteca de la Costa. The Mixteca Baja is the dry plateau-land basin of the Río Mixteco, which runs adjacent to the Puebla–Guerrero border, about 100 miles (160 km) west by northwest of Oaxaca City. Major centers are Santiago Juxtlahuaca in the southwest and Huajuapan de León in the north. Bordering the Mixteca Baja to the southwest is the Mixteca Alta, a highland of pine-tufted peaks cut by lush deep canyons. Its major market centers, moving from north to south, are Tamazulapan, Teposcolula, and Tlaxiaco. Bordering the Mixteca Alta on the south is the Mixteca de la Costa, a roughly 50-by-50-mile (160-sq.-km) region of hills and valleys abutting the Guerrero border on the west and spreading southward from the foothills to the mangrove-fringed coastline. Its major centers are Pinotepa Nacional in the center and Santiago Jamiltepec to the east.

A few thousand Mixtec speakers also occupy a pair of intriguingly isolated enclaves: Cuyamecalco (near the market town of San Juan Chiquihuitlán) in the northern Sierra, and around Mixtequilla, the "Little Mixteca" just north of Tehuántepec, in the Isthmus.

Although Mixtec-speaking people have passed down a rich heritage, as a group they are now among Oaxaca's poorest. Of the Mixteca's three regional groupings, the people in the Costa are generally the best off. Santiago Jamiltepec, for example, where Mixtec-speakers compose 70 percent of the population, has many Mixtec shop owners, in contrast to upland Mixtec centers where mestizos often dominate commerce.

Exceptions notwithstanding, most Mixtecs are subsistence farmers. Agriculture is typically based on age-old slash-and-burn methods. Fields lie fallow for five years, then brush is burned, cleared, and the ground planted with corn, usually employing a *coa* (digging stick). Oxen, when they are used for plowing or hauling, are often rented. Irrigation, except near valley-bottom creeks, is not common. On the coast, the warmer climate allows more options for cash crops, such as bananas, mangos, *panela* (brown sugar from cane), cotton, and peanuts, although distribution is limited and local.

Another cash possibility that Mixtecs have not generally developed is coffee, which mestizo, Trique, and European immigrant growers harvest successfully on the Mixteca Alta's semitropical forested mountainsides, using Mixtec day labor.

Moreover, despite their proximity to rich ocean resources, very few coastal Mixtecs fish. Instead, they buy dried fish from the many African Mexicans, descendants of African slaves, whose modest houses and fields dot the coastline.

Nevertheless, the Mixtecs seem to have cornered the palm-frond weaving market. In the dry Mixteca Baja, homeland to wild forests of short palms, people gather and dry the fronds, and whenever two hands are free, everyone—father, mother, children, grandmother, grandfather—weaves them into everything, from mats and hats to toys and baskets.

Lack of good roads hinders market access all over the Mixteca. A large proportion of Mixtec homesteads lie at the end of foot trails, along which produce must be hauled by hand or burro. Even if a farmer could harvest a ton of mangos (potentially worth maybe $500) from his four trees, how could he, his wife, a baby, and two children, and three neighbors

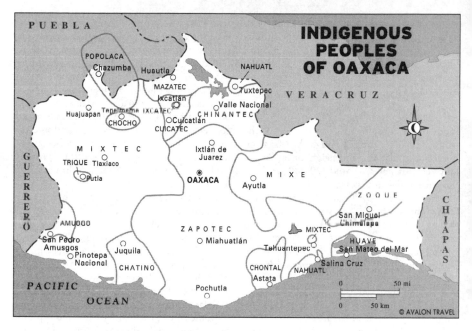

haul them five miles by trail, then 20 miles by dirt road, to some market where people have the money to buy his mangos? He tells himself that maybe he and his neighbors will get together, widen the trail and buy a used truck. Yes . . . someday.

Faced with such odds, instead of saving for that someday truck, many Mixtec farmers opt to accumulate prestige by fulfilling *compadrazgo* (contributing to friends) or *mayordomía* (religious festival) obligations. Although such charitable action often leads to poverty, generosity, in the Mixtec (and Mexican) mind is, after all, much preferable to parsimony.

Coastal Mixtec women enjoy an unusual degree of autonomy. Besides often handling family purse strings and doing all the marketing, they typically keep their own family names and own property independently of their husbands. For some Mixteca Alta and Mixteca Baja men, traveling to the coast is believed to be dangerous, partly for fear that some Costa Mixteca woman, through witchcraft, might steal (or disable) their penis. So, men, watch out for the women, especially around the Pinotepa Nacional market, where they often wear their best finery, which customarily includes an heirloom *pozahuanco* (wraparound skirt) of brilliant natural-dyed red cochineal and deep purple horizontal stripes. From afar, you'll easily recognize them, carrying themselves proudly, with their hat-like *jícara* (gourd bowl) tipped whimsically on their heads. Some women sell hand-loomed *pozahuancos* in the market. The authentic ones, by which coastal Mixtec women judge each other, sell for $150 or more.

Mazatecs

In contrast to the Zapotecs and Mixtecs, the Mazatec territory, the Mazateca, is relatively concentrated into a roughly 35-by-50-mile (56-by-80-km) corner at Oaxaca's very northern tip. Mazatec villages and farms spread across two very fertile climatic zones: lush semitropical forested uplands and tropical rainforest river bottomland of the Río Papaloapan basin. Major market centers are

Jalapa de Díaz and Huautla de Jiménez, both in the western highlands. Important subsidiary centers, many in the highlands around Huautla, are Cosolapa, Santa María Chilchotla, Huehuetlán, Eloxotitlán, San José Tenango, Mazatlán, Chiquihuitlán, and Ayautla. The eastern lowland has no dominant Mazatec center, partly because of the displacement of thousands of families during construction of the Miguel Alemán Dam. Although the Mazatecs' homeland spills over into neighboring Puebla and Veracruz states, around 170,000, or about 90 percent, live in Oaxaca.

The Mazatecs' own name for their homeland, Ampaad, which translates as the "Place Where the People Are Born," reflects their own creation myth. Legends say that the great tropical trees of Ampaad gave birth to three types of people: giants; ordinary-size humans, who became the present Mazatecs; and smaller people, who became the monkeys. The label "Mazatec" derives from the Aztec Nahuatl language and translates as "People of the Deer."

Left largely to themselves, the Mazatecs have retained many of their own traditions. Many of these they hold in common with their Chocho-, Popoloca-, and Ixcatec-speaking neighbors, whose tongues linguists sometimes lump into a Mazatec-language subfamily. Their isolation has left Mazatec speakers among the least hispanicized of Oaxacans; as a group, as many as 40 percent speak little or no Spanish.

In 1944, government planners initiated the **Papaloapan Project,** which called for a huge hydroelectric works in the Mazatec heartland. The project's centerpiece, christened as the Miguel Alemán Dam and Reservoir in 1955, created a mammoth lake in the Mazatec lowland, drowning hundreds of thousands of acres of fertile Papaloapan basin forest and farmland. Although water and electric power were the projected benefits, the human cost turned out to be enormous. Mazatec society was torn by the forced removal of 22,000 poor Mazatec people to unfamiliar, often undesirable territory. Fortunately, the rest of the Mazatec population, largely in the western highlands around Huautla de Jiménez, remained undisrupted. Mexican authorities have since generally avoided such socially disruptive mega-projects.

Although most Mazatec families are subsistence corn, bean, and squash farmers, many cultivate fruits (mango, mamey, *zapote,* papaya, banana, and avocado) and coffee as cash crops on their fertile acreage. Although some farmer cooperatives have found national and international markets for their fruit and coffee, many individuals seem content to sell their produce for low local prices at Huatla de Jiménez and other Mazateca markets.

Mazatec women are renowned for their costumes and adornments. At markets and festivals especially, watch for them in their famously bright *huipiles,* horizontally striped in the middle, vertically on the sides. Beneath the *huipil* they often wear a loom-woven blue and white horizontally striped skirt. Their hair is also part of their decoration. They keep it soft and dark with a preparation called *pistle,* made from the core of the mamey fruit, and typically braid it with bright ribbons. Many women take pride in their home embroidery and hand-woven cotton, silk, and wool, which they sometimes sell at markets.

As in the past, scarcity of priests weakens Catholic influence in the Mazateca. Priestly visits are so rare that many Mazatec campesino couples have two or three children by the time they enjoy a Catholic church wedding ceremony. When a priest does arrive, rustic churches are customarily thronged with husbands and wives bringing children for baptism. For the ceremony, they buy a small lead cross, which they hang with a bright ribbon around their child's neck. In addition to Catholic baptism, Mazatec parents sometimes ask a diviner to read the ancient *tonalpohualli* 260-day ritual calendar to discover their newborn's *tona* or *tono* (guardian spirit).

Mazatec people often gather for non-Catholic religious rites in fields and at sacred springs, caves, or mountains. Mazatec people especially venerate El Rabón peak, which towers over Jalapa de Díaz, and whose 0.6-mile-high (one-km) vertical rock wall is said never to have been scaled. There on that lofty summit live the *dueñes* (earth spirits), who must be appeased with prayers and *copal* incense for the return of lost souls. In the Mazateca lowland, *brujos* (witch doctors) carry out similar ceremonies at Cabeza de Tilpan cave near San José Tenango.

Traditional *curandero* or *curandera* healers are very busy in the Mazateca. Among their weapons against illness, many include natural forest-gathered hallucinogens. Common are *hongos alucinantes* (hallucinogenic mushrooms), *semillas de la Virgen* (seeds of the Virgin) or *ololiuhqui*, and *hojas de la pastora* (leaves of the shepherdess). These, used by either the patient or the healer, will induce enlightening visions that may lead to a cure.

Chinantecs

Although Oaxaca's approximately 100,000 Chinantec-speaking people live on some of Mexico's best-watered land, the majority are poor. Inaccessibility, tropical forests that were not easily tillable, and lack of gold or silver relegated the Chinantecs to the margin during colonial times. The Chinantecs' homeland, the Chinantla, is a 70-by-40-mile (112-by-64-km) region around the important market town of Valle Nacional, in northeast Oaxaca. The Chinantla's natural division into eastern lowland (Chinantla Grande) and western upland (Chinantla Pichinche) was apparent to the first Spanish arrivals in the 1520s. For the Spanish conquistadores, the Chinantecs weren't pushovers. After years of seesaw skirmishes, the Spanish mounted their final push at Yetzelalag. Chinantec legend recounts that at the battle's height the Chinantec warriors invoked their gods, who opened the mountain, allowing them to escape. Nevertheless, the Chinantecs submitted to three centuries of labor on Spanish tobacco and sugarcane plantations and cattle ranches.

Although the Spanish colonial policy of *congregación* led to the abandonment of many original town sites, the upland Chinantla retained a number of important market centers. Among the most important and colorful are Sochiapan, Tlacozintepec, Usila, Quiotepec,

and San Pedro Yolox in the western uplands; Valle Nacional and San Lucas Ojitlán in the center; and Petlalpa, Lalana, and Jocotepec in the southwest lowlands.

During the 19th century, new colonists introduced coffee, pineapple, and rice agriculture, which, with the Papaloapan Project, continues in modern form today. Although the project forced painful relocations on thousands of lowland Mazatec and Chinantec peoples, it ended their isolation. Government jobs, schools, clinics, electricity, and sanitary and water systems changed life forever in the Chinantec lowlands. At the height of the disorder, swarms of protests erupted. Oaxacan bishops denounced government relocation efforts: "The *indígenas* continue to be the ones always exploited, those who must pay the price of any progress."

For good or bad, the Papaloapan Project lifted the native residents' health, literacy, and general standard of living at the expense of erasing many of their age-old ways of life. In contrast to the Chinantla highlands, few traditional markets function in the lower Chinantla. On the other hand, the government-planned communal and corporate plantations have greatly increased productivity. The Chinantla regularly produces the lion's share of Oaxaca's tobacco, rice, sugarcane, chilies, and pineapples. The workers, however, receive only a minimum of the benefits. Most profits flow to the government agencies, which control everything—seeds, planting, credit, harvesting, and marketing.

Nevertheless, tradition still rules in much of the upper Chinantla. In the minds of many Chinantec-speakers, the old fertility gods "Father and Mother Maize" still command the rain even though their prayers are Catholic. The cosmos is still a battleground between day, ruled by the young and vigorous sun, and night, ruled by the twinkling old stars. Some still believe that Creation's original people, who refused to bow down before the god-sun, were changed to monkeys and banished to the forest forever for their error. In some villages, *rayos,* powerful members of lightning cults, can still hurl lightning bolts against neighboring villages and know how to defend the home village against reverse attacks.

Mixes and Zoques

Their cultural and common Mayan linguistic linkages have led most experts to believe that the original Mixe and Zoque (MEE-shay and SOH-kay) people, together with the Popoluca of present Veracruz state, occupied a single territory. Invasions, first by the Zapotecs and Aztecs and then the Spanish, forced the present territorial divisions. The Mixes (pop. 100,000) occupy the mountainous belt that stretches about 100 miles (160 km) from the central valley's eastern edge to the most easterly Mixe center, San Juan Guichicovi, several miles short of the cross-isthmus highway-rail line. Thirty-five miles (55 km) farther east, Zoque territory (pop. 5,000), divided between two sprawling *ejido* grants, begins. From the Santa María Chimalapa–San Miguel Chimalapa line it spreads east, across the wild Chimalapa mountainous jungle to the Chiapas border. The few remaining Popoluca-speakers are limited to a few isolated villages in eastern Veracruz state.

Despite several costly campaigns, the Spanish force of arms never really conquered the Mixes. If they were conquered at all, it was by 16th-century Dominican missionaries who accomplished with kindness what Spanish guns and steel could not. By the end of the colonial era, they had established nine vicarages, among them Juquila Mixes, San Miguel Quetzaltepec, Asunción Puxmecatan, Ayutla, and San Juan Guichicovi, which all remain important Mixe market towns. Ayutla, closest to the central valley, is dominant.

Anthropologists generally describe Mixe traditions as "less developed" than other Oaxacan groups. They describe a "culture unsuited to the environment," as if the Mixe ways of life first flowered in fairer, more fertile lands and never completely adjusted to the cold, marginal mountainous regions where the Mixes fled in the face of foreign invasions. Such a speculation also explains the Mixes' well-known wariness and avoidance of outside contact. The Zoque,

by contrast, adapted relatively easily to Spanish ways and share little of the Mixes' shyness.

Spanish attempts to congregate the Mixes into towns were only minimally successful. Mixe people largely moved back into the countryside, leaving little-used empty houses in town. Today most live in country hamlets clinging to mountainsides, with individual houses built on level stilt platforms.

Turbulence has marred the Mixes' recent history. In 1938, President Lázaro Cárdenas wanted to reward the Mixe people for their support of the Republic against the infamous 1865 French Intervention. He persuaded the Oaxaca legislature to award them semi-autonomous status in an all-Mixe district. However, a dispute broke out over the location of the district capital. The towns of Ayutla, Cacalotepec, and Zacatepec had their leading supporters, but Luis Rodríguez of Zacatepec was the most ruthless. While the others protested weakly, he led a four-year reign of terror—kidnapping, cattle rustling, torture, murder, and pillage—with the implicit support of Governor Vicente González. In 1943, Rodríguez cut off the feet and tongue of one prominent opponent and had another assassinated on the steps of the Government Palace in Oaxaca City. Enough was enough for Governor Sánchez Canom, who left Oaxaca City to intervene. But while he was gone, Rodríguez got him replaced. After that, Rodríguez was in complete control, murdering opponents with impunity, collecting tribute from towns and even 10 percent from religious fiestas and holding 500 prisoners in forced labor. Even after his death in 1952, his heirs tried to extend their reign until the 1970s. Despite Luis Rodríguez's notorious legacy, Zacatepec remains the Mixe district capital to the present day.

In 1972, partly in response to the trouble, Mixe people organized themselves into the grass-roots social-political Federación Mixe. They soon coalesced with the already-existing local Worker's Federation of Chinantecs, Zapotecs, and Mixes and the national General Union of Workers and Farmers of Mexico (UGOCM).

Mixe and Zoque social traditions closely follow Mesoamerican patterns. Mixe religion has striking parallels to those described in the Maya sacred book, the *Popol Vuh*. Their legends say that the Mixe god Kondoy was hatched from an egg, grew rapidly, and traveled, battling Aztec armies. He returned and arranged the world in the Mixe image, then retired to the Mixe sacred mountain, Zempoaltepetl, where he still lives.

Belief in the *nagual* persists among the Mixes. If an unbaptized baby dies, the parents must make haste to bury the body immediately, with little ceremony. If not, the spirit of the unbaptized baby might escape and become a *nagual,* a malevolent animal that will harm people who cross its path. Sometimes the *nagual* takes human form as a witch that can transform itself into an animal or other scary form and cause general mischief and illness by infusing some type of object into the victim's body. Traditional healers combine a number of remedies, such as *temascal* steam bathing, rubbing with herbs, prayers, sucking, and vision-inducing plants, to remove such infusions.

Chatinos

The southern Sierra country of the nearly 40,000 strong Chatinos is a 1,200-square-mile (3,072-sq.-km) enclave surrounded by Mixtecs on the west, Zapotecs on the north and east, and mestizos and African Mexicans on the south coast. Their language, part of the Zapotec subfamily, resembles Sierra Zapotec. Chatino market centers, besides the central and dominant Santa Catarina Juquila, are Panixtlahuaca, San Juan Quiahije, San Pedro Juchatengo, Nopala, and Zacatepec. Besides its commercial and political influence, Santa Catarina Juquila is a major pilgrimage center, especially for the hundreds of thousands of faithful who arrive on December 8 to honor their beloved Virgin of Juquila.

Most Chatino families are subsistence farmers; Zapotec and mestizo traders dominate commerce in the market centers. In addition to the customary corn, beans, and squash, farmers also cultivate coffee, either as day laborers or on their own land, in which case they sell the surplus for cash at the market.

Amusgos

The approximately 30-by-30-mile (48-by-48-km) Amusgo territory straddles the Oaxaca–Guerrero border. Only about 5,000 of 40,000 Amusgo speakers live in Oaxaca, around the small centers of Cacahuatepec and San Pedro Amusgos, while the remainder live on the Guerrero side, near the centers of Ometepec, Xochistlahuaca, and Tlacoachistlahuaca.

Linguists reckon that the Amusgo language, a member of the Mixtec language subfamily, separated from Mixtec between 2000 and 1000 B.C. Around A.D. 1000 the Amusgos came under the domination of the strong coastal Mixtec kingdom of Tututepec. In 1457 they were conquered by the Aztecs and not long after, by the Spanish in the 1520s. Decimation of the Amusgo population by disease during the 16th century led to the importation of African slave labor, whose descendants, known locally as *negros* or *costeños,* live along the Guerrero–Oaxaca coastline.

Although the Amusgo population eventually recovered, many of the old colonial-era haciendas remained intact until modern times. The Amusgos, isolated from the mainstream of modern Mexican life, retain their age-old corn-bean-squash farming tradition. Moreover, they have received little attention from anthropologists or archaeologists, although several likely archaeological mounds exist near Amusgo villages.

Amusgo women are nevertheless famous for their hand-embroidered *huipiles,* whose colorful floral and animal designs fetch willing customers in Oaxaca tourist centers. Even better, Amusgo women often wear their *huipiles,* appearing as heavenly visions of spring on dusty small-town side streets.

Triques

About 50 miles (80 km) farther north from the Amusgo territory, about 15,000 Trique (TREE-kay) people live in their 20-by-15-mile (32-by-24-km) highland pocket of the Mixteca Alta. You'll see plenty of them in the Juxtlahuaca town market—especially Trique women—selling their brilliant red-striped wool *huipiles* in the middle of the town square. Long ago, the

Trique fled into the mountain vastness, from first Mixtec, then Aztec, and finally Spanish, invaders. Some of their main centers are San Isidro Chicahuaxtla, San Juan Copala, and Tilapa, all south of Juxtlahuaca and north of Putla de Guerrero.

The Trique have only grudgingly accepted outside authority. Rebellions broke out often during the colonial era and later. In 1843 Trique forces rebelled against state and federal authorities, who needed five years to jail and execute the responsible leaders. Subsequently, during the later 19th and 20th centuries, coffee became a major Trique product and coffee beans became their money, which traders turned into alcohol and guns. Rebellion, which again required federal forces to suppress, broke out in Copala in 1956. The federal garrison remains in Copala to the present day.

Only at Chicahuaxtla, in the high Mixteca country (just off of Hwy. 125, about 25 miles/40 km west of Tlaxiaco), did Christianity have much effect. This was due to the compassionate persuasion of Father Gonzales Lucero hundreds of years ago. Consequently, much of the Trique's folklore survives to the present day. An oft-told creation myth describes the sun and the moon, gods who once lived in a *calabaza* (calabash), but who broke out and rode a rabbit and a cat into the heavens to light the world. Around March 25, traditional *curanderos* lead services to appease the old gods at a sacred cave near Copala, about 13 miles (20 km) down the highway south of Juxtlahuaca. They sacrifice a lamb and a goat while the gathered crowd offers incense and flowers.

Chochos, Ixcatecs, and Popolucas

Emigration and Spanish literacy are fast reducing the number of speakers of Chocho, Ixcatec, and Popoluca, three related tongues of the dry canyonlands of northwest Oaxaca. Of the three, the Chocho people are dominant in their extensive homeland around Coixtlahuaca and subsidiary centers of Tequixtepec and Tepelmeme. If you're going to hear any of the Chocho language, it will probably be in the market at Tepelmeme de Morelos, just off the Oaxaca–Puebla expressway about 15 miles (24 km) north of Coixtlahuaca.

Defeated by the Mixtecs in the 1300s and the Aztecs a hundred years later, the Chochos were again subdued by Spanish conquistadores Orozco and Alvarado in 1522 and later converted by Dominican Father Fermín Abrego. Coixtlahuaca was a thriving Chocho and Ixcatec market until around 1900, but loss of topsoil to erosion has forced many families to emigrate.

If you're going to hear any Ixcatec at all, it will be in Ixcatlán, the sole Ixcatec *municipio*, accessible by dirt road about 20 miles (32 km) northeast from Coixtlahuaca. The same is approximately true of Popoluca, whose few remaining speakers in Oaxaca live in the sliver of territory by the Puebla border, around Santiago Chazumba on Highway 125.

Cuicatecs

The Cuicatec language, by contrast, is holding its own, due to the isolation and richness of the homeland of the Cuicatecos ("People of Song"). About 15,000 Cuicatec people inhabit their present territory, mainly the *municipios* of Concepción Pápalo, San Juan Tepeuxila, San Pedro Teutila, and Santiago Nacaltepec in the mountains east of district capital Cuicatlán and south of the Río Santo Domingo canyon.

Archaeological digs around Pápalo and other sites reveal Toltec influences, hinting that the Cuicatec lands may have been a haven for some of the refugees from the fall of Tula, the Toltec capital in the north, around A.D. 1060.

Historians believe that Cuicatec speakers numbered about 60,000 before the conquest. They were defeated by both the Aztecs, around 1456, and Spanish soldiers, commanded by conquistador Martín Mezquita, in 1526. Nevertheless, during the colonial era the Cuicatecs resisted both Catholic conversion and forced plantation labor by fleeing into the mountains, where they remain today. Although the Dominicans established a church in Pápalo in 1630 and tried to convert them, Catholic influence remains weak. The old gods, notably *jáiko,* the lord of their sacred mountain, Cerro

Cheve, still live on in the hearts and minds of many Cuicatec people.

Today you might hear some Cuicatec spoken at the busy market at Cuicatlán, where Cuicatec women come down from the mountains to sell their highland handicrafts: wool serapes and jackets, flower- and animal-motif embroidered *huipiles,* and palm-leaf sombreros, *petates,* and *cestas* (hats, mats, and baskets, respectively).

Cuicatec people also earn cash collectively from the concession in which they allow the paper mill in Tuxtepec to harvest some of their forest trees. The money goes to finance community projects.

Huaves

The Isthmus territory of the Huave people encompasses the shoreline of the big tidal Lagunas Superior, Inferior, and the Mar Muerto. About 15,000 Huave-speaking people live there, notably around the villages of San Mateo del Mar, Santa María del Mar, San Dionisio del Mar, and San Francisco del Mar.

The Huave language, not clearly identified with any other language family, is generally classified in a family of its own. This is supported by studies by colonial historians, indicating that the Huave may have migrated from the Nicaraguan Pacific coast and settled around present-day Jalapa del Marqués on the Isthmus. The more-numerous Zapotecs, invading around 1375, forced them to the edges of the lagoons, where they now live.

Generally ignored and neglected by everyone, the Huaves hold on to many pre-conquest beliefs. In the absence of Catholic priests, native *curanderos* practice thinly veiled pagan rites in some village churches.

Although they subsist mainly on corn, beans, chilies, vegetables, and occasional meat, Huave-speaking people earn cash from their fish catches. Men sell fresh fish to wholesalers who arrive afternoons at the shoreline villages, while women sell the surplus as dried fish at Salina Cruz, Tehuántepec, and Juchitán markets.

Nahuas

Along the coast, in a 20-mile (32-km) strip west of Salina Cruz and with the small town of Morro de Mazatán at its center, lies an enclave of Nahua (Nahuatl- or Aztec-speaking people). Besides this small region, several thousand more Nahuatl speakers live in two other small Oaxaca enclaves in the north, one around Tuxtepec and the other next to the Puebla border, wedged between Mazatec, Ixcatec, Chocho, and Popoluca territories. Such Nahuatl enclaves are probably remnants of early colonies established by the Aztec emperors after their armed expansion into Oaxaca in the 1400s.

Chontals

Finally, a few miles farther west lies the Chontal (sometimes known as "Tequistlatec") territory. The Chontals are most visible on the coast, at Santiago Astata and San Pedro Huamelula. Today, about 25,000 speakers of Chontal, a language of the Hokan language family (widespread, from the north Gulf Coast to Central America), live in their approximately 1,000-square-mile (2,560-sq.-km) domain.

The Chontals are among the least modernized of Oaxaca indigenous groups. They have always tenaciously resisted invasion (though many in the zone due west of Tequisistlán have adopted the Zapotec language). Although many live near the coast, they do little fishing. They live mostly by corn-based subsistence farming, emigrating to the Isthmus or elsewhere for cash employment.

Relatively unaffected by Catholicism, their traditions remain strong. A popular fable is of their folk-hero King Fane Kansini, whom, legend says, an elderly couple hatched as an infant from an egg that they had found. The old couple soon discovered that the infant had supernatural powers. As he matured, Fane Kansini acquired the burning desire to save his people from the Zapotecs. He invented body armor and a wondrous new kind of arrow, which he used to defeat the Zapotec king in battle and thus save the Chontal people from annihilation. The Chontal-Zapotec mutual enmity continues to the present time.

Festivals and Events

Mexicans love a party. Urban families watch the calendar for midweek national holidays that create a *puente* (bridge) to the weekend and allow them to squeeze in a three- to five-day mini-vacation. Visitors should likewise watch the calendar. Such holidays (especially Christmas and Semana Santa, pre-Easter week) mean packed buses, roads, and hotels, especially around Oaxaca's beach resorts.

Country people, on the other hand, await their local saint's day or holy day. The name of the locality often provides the clue. For example, in Santa Cruz Papalutla, just east of Oaxaca City, expect a celebration on May 3, El Día de la Santa Cruz (Day of the Holy Cross). People dress up in their traditional best, sell their wares and produce in a street fair, join a procession, get tipsy, and dance in the plaza.

Bullfighting

Oaxaca, unique among Mexican states, has no bullfights. Benito Juárez, as governor during the 1850s, was instrumental in outlawing bullfights in Oaxaca. In his honor, they remain banned.

FIESTAS

The following calendar lists national and notable Oaxacan holidays and festivals. For many more details, see the destinations cited. Call ahead to confirm dates. If you happen to be where one of these is going on, get out of your car or bus and join in!

January

- January 1: **¡Feliz Año Nuevo!** (New Year's Day; national holiday), especially in Santiago Jamiltepec and Teotitlán del Valle.

- January 6: **Día de los Reyes** (Day of the Kings), especially in Santos Reyes Nopala—traditional gift exchange; townsfolk perform favorite traditional dances.

- January 13–17: **Fiesta del Dulce Nombre de Jesús** (Festival of the Sweet Name of Jesus), in Santa Ana del Valle, Tlacolula, and Zimatlán—troupes perform many traditional dances, including the Dance of the Feathers.

- January 17: **Día de San Antonio Abad**—decorating and blessing animals.

- January 20–21: **Fiesta de San Sebastián,** especially in San Pedro and San Pablo Tequixtepec, Pinotepa Don Luis, and Jalapa de Díaz.

- January 25: **Fiesta del Apóstol de San Pablo** (Festival of Apostle St. Paul), in Mitla—masses, processions, feast, fireworks, *jaripeo* (bull roping and riding), and dancing.

February

- February 2: **Día de Candelaria,** especially in Tututepec—plants, seeds, and candles blessed; procession and bullfights.

- February 5: **Constitution Day** (national holiday)—commemorates the constitutions of 1857 and 1917.

- February 24: **Flag Day** (national holiday).

- February: During the four days before Ash Wednesday (46 days before Easter Sunday), usually in late February, many towns, especially San Juan Colorado, Putla, Pinotepa Don Luis, and Juxtlahuaca, celebrate **Carnaval**—Mardi Gras–style extravaganzas.

- February–March: Celebrations continue during Cuaresma (Lent), especially in Santiago Jamiltepec and Pinotepa Nacional, for several weeks.

March

- Second Friday of Lent (nine days after Ash

Wednesday): **Fiesta del Señor del Perdón** (Festival of the Lord of Forgiveness), in San Pedro and San Pablo Tequixtepec—big pilgrimage festival.

- Second Friday of Lent: **Fiesta del Señor de Piedad,** in Santiago Astata.

- Fourth Friday of Lent (23 days after Ash Wednesday): **Fiesta del Señor de Misericordias,** in Santa María Huatulco.

- Fourth Friday before Easter Sunday: **Fiesta of Jesus the Nazarene,** in Huaxpaltepec.

- Week before Palm Sunday: **Week of Ramos,** especially in Jamiltepec.

- Friday before Good Friday (11 days before Easter Sunday): **Feria Comercial** (Commercial Fair), in Huautla de Jiménez—many traditional folk dances.

- March 18–19: **Fiesta de San José,** in Valle Nacional; on the weekend closest to March 10 in San José El Mogote.

- March 21: **Birthday of Benito Juárez,** the "Hero of the Americas" (national holiday), especially in Benito Juárez's birthplace, Guelatao—a whirl of traditional dances.

- March 21–31: **Juegos Florales** (Flower Games), in Oaxaca City.

April

- April. **Semana Santa** (pre-Easter Holy Week, culminating in Domingo Santa—Easter—national holiday), in many locales, especially San Juan Colorado, Pinotepa Don Luis, and Pinotepa Nacional.

- Good Friday, two days before Easter Sunday: **Fiesta de la Santa Cruz de Huatulco** (Festival of the Holy Cross of Huatulco).

- Saturday before Easter Sunday: **Sábado de Gloria** in San Miguel Tequixtepec—people, called *mecos,* don masks and do a kind of adult trick or treat for the occasion.

- First week in April: **Feria del Mango** (Mango Fair), in Tapanatepec.

- April 26–29: **Fiesta de San Pedro Mártir de Verona,** in San Pedro Yucunama.

May

- May 1: **Labor Day** (national holiday).

- May 3: **Fiesta de la Santa Cruz** (Festival of the Holy Cross), in many places, especially Salina Cruz, Tehuántepec, and Unión Hidalgo.

- May 5: **Cinco de Mayo** (national holiday)—celebration of the defeat of the French at Puebla in 1862.

- May 10: **Mothers' Day** (national holiday).

- May 10–12: **Fiesta of the Coronation of the Virgin of the Rosary.**

- May 11–16: **Fiesta de San Isidro Labrador** (Festival of Saint Isador the Farmer), in Ixcatlán.

- May 15–30: **Velas de San Vicente Ferrer,** in Juchitán (also many more—see the

It's hard to predict what you'll see on the street during a Oaxaca City festival.

sidebar *Velas: Fiestas of the Isthmus* in *The Isthmus* chapter).

- Late May–early June: **Feria Tuxtepec,** in Tuxtepec—big expo and folkloric dance festival.

June

- June 2–3: **Fiesta de San Antonio de Padua,** in Jalapa de Díaz.

- June 23–24: **Fiesta de San Juan Bautista** (Festival of St. John the Baptist), especially in Tuxtepec, Valle Nacional, Cuicatlán, and Coixtlahuaca.

- June 25: **Fiesta de San Pedro,** in Santa María Huamelula; June 27–30 in San Pedro Tapanatepec; June 29 in San Pedro Amusgos; June 26–30 in Unión Hidalgo.

- June 26–30: **Fiesta de Santa María Santísima** in Unión Hidalgo.

- June 26–30: **San Isidro el Labrador** (Saint Isador the Farmer) in Unión Hidalgo.

- June 29: **Fiesta de San Pablo y San Pedro** (Festival of St. Paul and St. Peter); June 21–28 in San Pedro Pochutla.

July

- July 1–15: **Fiesta of the Precious Blood of Christ,** in Teotitlán del Valle—featuring the Danza de la Pluma (Dance of the Feather).

- Usually (see *Oaxaca City* chapter for details) on the two Mondays following July 16: **Lunes de Cerro** or **Guelaguetza** in Oaxaca City—all-Oaxaca dance extravaganza.

- July 20–24: **Fiesta de Santa María Magdalena** (Festival of St. Mary Magdalene), in Tequisistlán.

- July 20–30: **Fiesta de Santiago Apóstol** (Festival of St. James the Apostle), in Santiago Laollaga; July 22–27 in Suchilquitongo; July 23–26 in Jamiltepec and in Pinotepa Nacional; and July 25 in Juxtlahuaca.

August

- August 1–5: **Fiesta de Santo Domingo de Guzmán,** in Unión Hidalgo.

- August 13–18: **Fiesta del Barrio de Santa María Relatoca,** in Tehuántepec.

- August 14: **Fiesta de la Virgen de la Asunción** (Festival of the Virgin of the Assumption), in Tlaxiaco; August 15 in Nochixtlán; August 13–16 in Huazolotitlán.

- August 25–29: **Fiesta de San Bartolomé,** in San Bartolomé de Quiliana; August 23–24 in San Bartolo Tuxtepec; August 24–27 in San Bartolo Coyotepec.

- August 26–September 2: **Fiesta de Santa Rosa de Lima,** in Salina Cruz; August 28 in Ojitlán.

- August 31–September 11: **Fiesta Laborio,** in Tehuántepec.

September

- September 7–8: **Fiesta de la Vírgen de La Navidad,** in Huautla de Jiménez.

- September 7–9: **Fiesta del Señor de La Natividad** (Festival of the Lord of the Nativity), in Teotitlán del Valle.

- September 11: **Fiesta de la Virgen de los Remedios,** in Jamiltepec.

- September 14: **Charro Day** (Cowboy Day), all over Mexico—rodeos.

- September 16: **Independence Day** (national holiday)—mayors everywhere reenact Father Hidalgo's 1810 Grito de Dolores from city hall balconies on the night of September 15.

- September 21: **Fiesta of San Mateo,** in Calpulalpan.

- September 23–30: **Fiesta de la Preciosa Sangre de Cristo** (Festival of the Precious Blood of Christ), in Tlacochahuaya—eight days of processions, dances, fireworks, and food.

- September 27–29: **Fiesta de San Miguel,** in San Miguel Tequixtepec and Teotitlán del Camino—highlights include traditional dances, such as the Cristianos y Moros (Christians and Moors).

October

- October 1–2: **Fiesta de San Miguel Arcangel,** in Puerto Ángel.

- First Sunday in October: **Fiesta de la Virgen del Rosario** (Festival of the Virgin of the Rosary), in San Pedro Amusgos.

- October 3–5: **Fiesta de San Francisco Asis,** in Salina Cruz.

- October 6–8: **Fiesta de San Dionisio,** in San Dionisio del Mar—pilgrimage.

- Second Sunday in October: **Fiesta del Santo Cristo de Tlacolula** (Festival of the Holy Christ of Tlacolula), in Tlacolula.

- Second Monday in October: **Fiesta de los Lunes del Tule,** in Santa María del Tule—locals in costume celebrate with rites, folk dances, and feats of horsemanship beneath the boughs of their beloved great cypress tree.

- Third Sunday in October: **Fiesta de Octubre,** in Tlaxiaco—includes fireworks, basketball and *pelota mixteca* (traditional ball game) tournaments, and popular dances.

- October 12: **Día de la Raza** (Columbus Day)—national holiday that commemorates the union of the races.

November

- November: **Fiestas de Noviembre,** in Puerto Escondido—features the big folk dance festival **Fiesta Costeño.**

- November 1: **Día de Todos Santos** (All Saints Day)—in honor of the souls of children; the departed descend from heaven to eat sugar skeletons, skulls, and treats on family altars.

masks for the Day of the Dead

- November 2: **Día de los Muertos** (Day of the Dead), especially in Tuxtepec and Cacahuatepec—in honor of ancestors; families visit cemeteries and decorate graves with flowers and favorite foods of the deceased.

- November 11–16: **Fiesta de San Diego,** in Salina Cruz.

- November 13: **Fiesta de San Marcos,** in San Marcos Tlapazola (tourist Yu'u town in the Valley of Oaxaca).

- November 20: **Revolution Day** (national holiday)—anniversary of the revolution of 1910–1917.

- November 22: **Fiesta de Santa Cecilia,** in Unión Hidalgo.

- November 25: **Fiesta de Santa Catarina,** in Santa Catarina Ixtepeji.

- November 29: **Fiesta de San Andrés,** in San Juan Colorado.

December

- December 1: **Inauguration Day**—national government changes hands every six years: 2006, 2012, 2018 . . .

- December 8: **Día de la Purísima Concepción** (Day of the Immaculate Conception).

- December 8: **Fiesta de la Vírgen de la Soledad,** in Oaxaca and Juxtlahuaca.

- Late November–December 8: **Fiesta de la Virgen de Juquila,** in Santa Catarina Juquila—Oaxaca's biggest fiesta.

- December 8–11: **Fiesta de Nuestra Señora de la Concepción,** in Santa María Huatulco.

- December 12: **Día de Nuestra Señora de Guadalupe** (Festival of the Virgin of Guadalupe), nationwide—processions, music, and dancing honoring the patroness of Mexico.

- December 16–18: **Fiesta de la Virgen de la Soledad,** in Oaxaca City.

- December 16–24: **Christmas Week**—week of *posadas* and piñatas, with midnight mass on Christmas Eve.

- December 19–22: **Fiesta de Santo Tomás Apóstol,** in Ixtlán de Juárez.

- December 23: **Fiesta de los Rábanos** (Festival of the Radishes), in Oaxaca City.

- December 24: **Nochebuena** (Christmas Eve), in Oaxaca City and Yucunama.

- December 25: **¡Feliz Navidad!** (Christmas Day; national holiday)—Christmas trees and gift exchange.

- December 26: **Vela Tehuántepec,** in Tehuántepec—everyone in town dances to the lovely melody of the *Sandunga.*

- December 31: **New Year's Eve.**

Arts and Crafts

Oaxaca abounds with attractive, reasonably priced handicrafts. A sizable fraction of Oaxacan families still depend upon homespun items—clothing, utensils, furniture, native herbal remedies, religious offerings, adornments, toys, musical instruments. Many such traditions reach back thousands of years, to the beginnings of Mesoamerican civilization. The accumulated knowledge of manifold generations of artisans has in many instances resulted in finery so prized that whole villages devote themselves to the manufacture of a certain class of goods.

Shops and markets in Oaxaca City and the Valley of Oaxaca towns of Teotitlán del Valle, Santa Ana del Valle, Tlacolula, Mitla, San Bartolo Coyotepec, San Martín Tilcajete, Santo Tomás Jalieza, Ocotlán, Arrazola, and Atzompa are Oaxaca's most renowned sources of handicrafts. And, although most crafts are not made in the coastal resorts of Huatulco and Puerto Escondido, each has several good private handicrafts stores and a number of crafts markets where local folks maintain stalls stuffed with their homemade goods. Moreover, the rich cornucopia of crafts from other Mexican centers, such as the neighboring state of Guerrero, the Lake Pátzcuaro region of Michoacán, and around Guadalajara, spills over to Oaxaca.

Handicrafts (*artesanías,* ar-tay-sah-NEE-ahs) shoppers who venture away from the Oaxaca City center and the coastal tourist enclaves to the source villages and towns will most likely benefit from lower prices, wider choices, and, most importantly, the privilege of meeting the artisans themselves. There, perhaps in a patio shop on a dusty Teotitlán del Valle side street or an Arrazola family patio, you might encounter the people and perhaps view the painstaking processes by which they fashion humble materials—clay, wool, cotton, wood, metal, straw, leaves, bark, paper, leather—into irresistible works of art.

Bargaining

Bargaining comes with the territory in Mexico and needn't be a hassle. On the contrary, if done with humor and moderation, bargaining can be an enjoyable path to encountering Mexican people and gaining their respect, and even friendship. The local crafts market is where bargaining is most intense. For starters, try offering half the asking price. From there on, it's all psychology: You have to content yourself with not having to have the item. Otherwise, you're sunk; the vendor will probably sense your need and stand fast. After a few minutes of good-humored bantering, ask for *el último precio* (the final price), in which, if it's close, you may have a bargain.

BASKETRY AND WOVEN CRAFTS

Weaving straw, leaves, and reeds is among the oldest of Oaxacan crafts traditions. Mat- and basket-weaving methods and designs go back as far as 5,000 years and are still used today.

The drier regions of Oaxaca are sources of fronds from the dwarf palms that populate the hillsides. In the Mixteca, in places such as Huajuapan de León and Coixtlahuaca and the east side of the Valley of Oaxaca around Tlacolula, you might see people sitting on a doorstep or at a bus stop or even walking down the street while weaving a **petate** (mat) or **tenate** (tumpline basket) of creamy white palm leaf, prized for its soft, pliable texture. All over Oaxaca, nearly everyone uses *petates,* from vacationers, for stretching out on the beach, to local folks, for keeping tortillas warm and shielding babies from the sun. *Tenates* have been raised to nearly a fine art in a number of Oaxaca localities, such as San Luis Amatlán, near Ejutla in the southern Valley of Oaxaca. There, craftspeople interweave dyed fibers with the natural palm, creating attractive, sensitively executed geometric designs.

Carrizo, a bamboo-like reed that grows on stream banks all over Oaxaca state, is the

Handmade reed *canastas* (baskets with handle) rank among Oaxaca's most prized handicrafts.

source of stronger, more rigid baskets, usually called *canastas* when they have handles, *tenates* when they don't. Well-known Valley of Oaxaca sources are San Juan Guelavía and Magdalena Teitipac, on the east side, and Santa Ana Zegache near Ocotlán in the south. Familiar variations include the prized *tenate para tortillas,* round at the top and tapering to square at the base, and *cajas para pájaros* (birdcages), sometimes fashioned in two, three, or four levels.

A third important weaving fiber in Oaxaca is **ixtle,** the dried strands from the leaves of maguey and related agave-family plants. Artisans all over Oaxaca craft *ixtle* into useful items, such as ropes for pulling, string bags for carrying, and hammocks for relaxing.

CLOTHING AND EMBROIDERY

Although *traje* (ancestral tribal dress) has become uncommon in Oaxaca City, significant numbers of Oaxacan native women make and wear *traje,* especially in the Mazateca,

Chinantla, and Zapotec Sierra in the north, the Isthmus in the southeast, the coastal Mixteca in the southwest, and the Trique in the Mixteca Alta in the west.

The most common *traje* garment is the **huipil,** a full, square-shouldered, short- to mid-sleeved dress, often hand-embroidered with animal and floral designs and embellished with ribbons. Probably the most popular Oaxaca *huipiles* are the captivating designs from San Pedro de Amusgos (Amusgo tribe; white cotton embroidered with abstract colored animal and floral motifs). Others nearly as prized include the Trique styles from around San Andrés Chicahuaxtla (white cotton, richly embroidered red stripes, interwoven with green, blue, and yellow, and hung with colored ribbons); Mazatec, from Huautla de Jiménez (white cotton with bright flowers embroidered in multiple panels, crossed by horizontal and vertical purple and magenta silk ribbons); and Isthmus Zapotec, from Tehuántepec (brightly colored cotton densely embroidered with either geometric designs or a field of flamboyant, multicolored flowers).

Oaxaca shops and stalls also sell other, less common types of *traje.* These include the **quechquémitl** (shoulder cape), often made of wool and worn as an overgarment in winter, and the **enredo,** a full-length skirt that wraps around the waist and legs like a Hawaiian sarong.

Mixtec women in Oaxaca's warm southwest coastal region around Pinotepa Nacional commonly wear the *enredo,* known locally as the **pozahuanco** (poh-sah-WAHN-koh), below the waist and, when at home, go bare-breasted. When wearing their *pozahuancos* in public, they usually tie a **mandil,** a wide apron, around their front side.

Women weave the most prized *pozahuancos* using cotton thread dyed a light purple with secretions of tidepool-harvested snails *(Purpura patula pansa)* and silk dyed deep red with cochineal, an extract from the dried bodies of a locally cultivated scale insect, *Dactylopius coccus.* On a typical day, two or three women will be selling handmade *pozahuancos* at the Pinotepa Nacional market.

Ropa Típica

Colonial-era Spanish styles have blended with native *traje,* producing a wider class of dress, known generally as *ropa típica.* Lovely embroidered *blusas* (blouses), *rebozos* (shawls), and *vestidos* (dresses) fill shop racks and market stalls all over Oaxaca. Among the most popular is the so-called **Oaxaca wedding dress,** made of cotton with a crochet-trimmed riot of diminutive flowers hand-stitched about the neck and yoke. Some of the finest examples are made in San Antonino Castillo Velasco, just north of Ocotlán on the Valley of Oaxaca's south side.

In contrast to women, only a small fraction of Oaxacan men—members of remote groups, such as mountain Mazatec and Chinantecs in the north, the Mixes in the east, and rural Chatinos and Amusgos in the southwest—wear *traje.* Nevertheless, shops offer some fine men's *ropa típica,* such as wool jackets and serapes for highland or winter wear and *guayaberas,* hip-length pleated tropical dress shirts.

Fine *bordado* (embroidery) embellishes much traditional Oaxacan clothing, *manteles*

Oaxaca wedding dress

© BRUCE WHIPPERMAN

(tablecloths), and *servilletas* (napkins). As everywhere, women define the art of embroidery. Although some work is still handmade at home, cheaper machine-made factory lace and needlework is more commonly available in shops.

Among the most renowned handmade example is the embroidery of Santo Tomás Jalieza, the "town of belts" *(cinturones)*, in the Oaxaca central valley south of Coyotepec. Although best known for their attractive embroidered cloth and leather belts, the townsfolk have adapted their colorful designs to clothing, purses, bags, and much more.

LEATHER

Some Oaxaca shops offer selections of locally produced *huaraches* from around Miahuatlán in the south valley and Yalalag, north in the Sierra Juárez. Shops import most other leather goods from other Mexican centers, such as Guadalajara and León. For unique and custom-designed articles you'll probably have to confine your shopping to the expensive tourist resort shops. For the more usual though still attractive leather items, such as purses, wallets, belts, coats, and boots, veteran shoppers go to Mercado Juárez or Mercado de Artesanías in Oaxaca City.

GLASS AND STONEWORK

Glass manufacture, unknown in pre-Columbian times, was introduced by the Spanish. Today factories scattered all over Mexico turn out mountains of **burbuja** (boor-BOO-hah) bubbled-glass tumblers, goblets, plates, and pitchers, usually in blue, yellow, green, or red.

Artisans work stone, mostly near sources of supply. Puebla and Tequisistlán (in the Oaxaca isthmus) are Mexico's main sources of decorative **onyx** *(onix,* OH-neeks). Factory shops turn out the galaxy of mostly roughhewn, cream-colored items, from animal charms and chess pieces to beads and desk sets, which you'll see on some Oaxaca City curio shop shelves.

Cantera, a volcanic tufa stone, occurs in pastel shades from pink to green and is quarried in several locations in the Valley of Oaxaca. Most preferred is the light jade-green *cantera* from Magdalena Etla, northwest of Oaxaca City. It has replaced the original but exhausted green *cantera* source that supplied stone for most of Oaxaca City's original buildings. An open-air *cantera* workshop, with many examples of expertly sculptured *cantera* (by Hwy. 190 in Suchilquitongo, at the Valley of Oaxaca's northeast corner), welcomes visitors.

For a keepsake from a truly ancient Oaxacan tradition, don't forget the hollowed-out stone **metate** (may-TAH-tay), or corn-grinding basin, and the three-legged **molcajete** (mohl-kah-HAY-tay), a mortar for grinding chilies. Most examples you'll see in Oaxaca are from Teitipac, in the west valley near Tlacolula (where you'll most likely see for-sale examples during the big Sunday market).

JEWELRY

Gold and silver were once the basis for Mexico's wealth. Her Spanish conquerors plundered a mountain of gold—ritual offerings, necklaces, pendants, rings, plates—masterfully crafted by a legion of indigenous jewelers. Unfortunately, much of that native tradition was lost as the colonial Spanish denied Mexicans access to precious metals and introduced Spanish methods. Nevertheless, a small native gold-working tradition survived the dislocations of the 1810–1821 War of Independence and the 1910–1917 Revolution. Meanwhile, silver crafting, moribund during the 1800s, was revived in Taxco, Guerrero, during the 1920s, principally through the joint efforts of architect-artist William Spratling and the local community.

Today, spurred by the tourist boom, jewelry-making is thriving in Mexico. Taxco, where guilds, families, and cooperatives produce sparkling silver and gold adornments, is the acknowledged center. Several Oaxaca shops offer Taxco-made jewelry—shimmering ornamental butterflies, birds, jaguars, serpents, turtles, and fish from the pre-conquest tradition. Pieces, mostly in silver, vary from humble but attractive trinkets to glittering necklaces, silver candelabras, and place settings for a dozen, sometimes embellished with precious stones.

Oaxaca also has a healthy local jewelry-making tradition. Acknowledged leader in Oaxaca City is the family firm of **Oro de Monte Albán.** Their several city and coastal resort shops offer replicas of the ancient Mixtec designs, notably of many pieces found at Monte Albán's Tomb 7.

Tehuántepec women *(tehuanas)* have created a demand for elaborate **gold filigree jewelry,** made from fine wires and often decorated with pearls and precious stones. The finest, ranging from 10 to 18 karat (42–75 percent pure) gold, is more often kept in safe deposit boxes and used only on ceremonial occasions. Much more common is *chapa de oro,* gold look-alike filigree that contains no gold at all. Women sell this jewelry in Oaxaca City, at the north-central entrance of the 20 de Noviembre market and in the Isthmus, at the Juchitán and Tehuántepec markets.

Buying Silver and Gold

Silver and gold jewelry, the finest of which is crafted in Taxco, Mexico City, Guanajuato, and Oaxaca, is sold in a number of shops in Oaxaca City, Huatulco, and Puerto Escondido.

One hundred percent pure silver is rarely sold because it's too soft. Silver (most of which is sent from processing mills in the north of Mexico to be worked in Taxco shops) is nearly always alloyed with 7.5 percent copper to increase its durability. Such pieces, identical in composition to sterling silver, should have ".925," together with the initials of the manufacturing jeweler, stamped on their back sides. Other, less common grades, such as "800 fine" (80 percent silver), should also be stamped.

If silver is not stamped with the degree of purity, it probably contains no silver at all and is an alloy of copper, zinc, and nickel, known by the generic label "alpaca," or "German" silver. Once, after haggling over the purity and prices of his offerings, a street vendor handed me a shiny handful and said, "Go to a jeweler and have them tested. If they're not real, keep them." Calling his bluff, I took them to a jeweler, who applied a dab of hydrochloric acid to each piece. Tiny, tell-tale bubbles of hydrogen revealed the cheapness of the merchandise, which I returned the next day to the vendor.

Some shops price sterling silver jewelry simply by weighing, which typically translates to about $1 per gram. If you want to find out if the price is fair, ask the shopkeeper to weigh it for you.

Oaxaca City itself is a gold jewelry center, mainly due to the skill and enterprise of the family-owned Oro de Monte Albán business. They maintain three shops, two in Oaxaca City and one in Puerto Escondido.

People universally prize pure gold, partly because, unlike silver, it does not tarnish. Gold, nevertheless, is rarely sold pure (24 karat); for durability, it is alloyed with copper. Typical purity levels, such as 18 karat (75 percent) or 14 karat (58 percent), should be stamped on the pieces. If not, chances are they contain no gold at all.

WOOD CARVING AND MUSICAL INSTRUMENTS
Masks

Spanish and Native Oaxacan traditions have blended to produce a multitude of masks—some strange, some lovely, some scary, some endearing, all interesting. The tradition flourishes in Oaxaca and the strongly indigenous neighboring states of Michoacán, Guerrero, and Chiapas. Here campesinos gear up all year for the village festivals—especially Semana Santa (Easter week), early December (Virgin of Guadalupe), and that of the local patron, whether it be San José, San Pablo, San Pedro, Santa Barbara, Santa María, or one of a host of others. Every local fair has its favored dances, such as the **Dance of the Conquest, the Christians and Moors, the Old Men,** or the **Tiger,** in which masked villagers act out age-old allegories of fidelity, sacrifice, faith, struggle, sin, and redemption.

Although artisans craft Oaxaca masks of many materials—from stone and ebony to coconut husks and paper—wood, where available, is the medium of choice. For the entire year, workers carve, sand, and paint to ensure that each participant will be properly disguised for the festival. Although Oaxaca's larger municipalities usually have their cadres of mask makers, towns in the coastal Mixteca region, notably Santa María Huazolotitlán and Pinotepa Don Luis, are among Oaxaca's busiest authentic mask sources.

The popularity of masks has resulted in an entire made-for-tourist mask industry, which has led to mass-produced duplicates, many cleverly antiqued. Examine the goods carefully; if the price is high, don't buy unless you're convinced it's a real antique.

Alebrijes

Tourist demand has made zany wooden animals called *alebrijes* (ah-lay-BREE-hays) a Oaxaca growth industry. Virtually every family in certain Valley of Oaxaca villages—notably Arrazola and San Martín Tilcajete—runs a factory studio. There, piles of *copal* wood, which men carve and women finish and

alebrijes, zany wooden animals carved from *copal* wood

intricately paint, become whimsical giraffes, dogs, cats, iguanas, gargoyles, and dragons, including most of the possible permutations in between. The farther from the source you get, the higher the *alebrije* price becomes; what costs $5 in Arrazola will probably run about $10 in Oaxaca City and $30 in the United States, Canada, or Europe.

Musical Instruments

Virtually all of Mexico's guitars are made in Paracho, Michoacán (southeast of Lake Chapala), north of Uruapan. There, scores of cottage factories turn out guitars, violins, mandolins, ukuleles, and a dozen more variations every day. Products vary widely in quality, so look carefully before you buy. Make sure that the wood is well cured and dry; damp, unripe wood instruments are more susceptible to warping and cracking.

METALWORK

Several Oaxaca City family factories turn out fine cutlery, forged ironwork, and a swarm of bright tinware mirror frames, masks, and glittering Christmas decorations.

Cutlery tradition—knives, machetes, scissors, swords, and more—arrived in Oaxaca with the Spanish. Today, several family shops offer their wares in town shops and market stalls, notably at the Benito Juárez market in Oaxaca City.

Traditional **ironwork,** admittedly heavy to carry home in your luggage, is made to order, boxed, and shipped at a number of specialty shops in Oaxaca City. Some of the more commonly requested items, such as medieval-style lanterns and garden benches, are available on display.

Tinware (*hojalata,* oh-hah-LAH-tah), especially the colorfully lacquered Christmas decorations—winsome angels, saints, Santas, butterflies, and fruits—constitute Oaxaca City's most sought-after metal craft. Running closely behind are the hosts of old-fashioned lead figures—soldiers, ballerinas, antique automobiles, angels—and fancy silvery mirror frames, metal boxes, birds, flowers, and much

Tinware ornaments are the Oaxaca City specialty of a few artisan families.

© BRUCE WHIPPERMAN

more. Many downtown handicrafts shops, in addition to stalls at the 20 de Noviembre market and the Mercado de Artesanías (Handicrafts Market), sell metal work.

Moreover, be sure to ask at the same shops and stalls for **milagros,** one of Mexico's most charming forms of metal work. Usually of brass, they are of homely shapes—a horse, dog, or baby, or an arm, head, heart, or foot. The faithful pin them, along with a prayer, to the garments of their favorite saint, whom they hope will intercede to cure the ailment or fulfill the wish designated by the *milagro.*

PAPER AND PAPIER-MÂCHÉ

Papier-mâché has risen to nearly a fine art in Tonalá, Jalisco. Many Oaxaca handicrafts stores stock small flocks of Tonalá-made birds, cats, frogs, giraffes, and other animal figurines, meticulously crafted by building up repeated layers of glued paper. The results—sanded, brilliantly varnished, and polished—resemble fine sculptures rather than the humble newspaper from which they were fashioned.

Other paper goods you shouldn't overlook include **piñatas** (durable, inexpensive, and as Mexican as you can get), available in every town market; colorful, decorative **cutout banners** (string overhead at your home fiesta) from San Salvador Huixcolotla, Puebla; and **amate,** wild fig tree bark paintings in animal and flower motifs, from Xalitla and Ameyaltepec, Guerrero.

POTTERY AND CERAMICS

The Valley of Oaxaca is the focus of a vibrant pottery tradition. Many of the most celebrated examples come from the village of Atzompa, a few miles northwest of the city. Traditionally popular for their green-glazed clay pots, dishes, casseroles, and bowls, Atzompa potters have evolved a host of fresh styles, from graceful vases and plates blooming with painted lilies to red clay pots and bowls inscribed with artfully flowing blossoms.

sun-moon traditional motif ceramics

San Bartolo Coyotepec village, south of the city, has acquired equal renown for its **black pottery** *(barro negro)*, sold all over the world. Doña Rosa, now deceased, pioneered the crafting of big round pots without using a potter's wheel. Now made in many more shapes by Doña Rosa's descendants, the pottery's celebrated black hue is produced by the reduction (reduced air) method of firing, which removes oxygen from the clay's red (ferric) iron oxide, converting it to black (ferrous) iron oxide. Workers burnish the result to produce an exquisite, pearly sheen.

Although most latter-day Oaxacan potters are aware of the health dangers of **lead pigments,** some for-sale pottery may still contain lead. The hazard comes from low-fired pottery in which the lead has not been firmly melted into the glaze. Acids in foods such as lemons, vinegar, and tomatoes dissolve the lead pigments, which, when ingested over a period of time, can result in lead poisoning. In general, the hardest, glossiest, high-fired stoneware, that has been twice fired, is the safest for dinnerware.

Although Mexican pottery tradition is as diverse as the country itself, some varieties stand out. Among the most prized is the so-called **Talavera** (or Majolica), the best of which is made by a few family-run workshops in Puebla. The names Talavera and Majolica derive from Talavera, the Spanish town from which the tradition migrated to Mexico in the 1500s. Prior to that, it was extensively crafted on the Spanish Mediterranean island of Majorca (thus the *majolica* label), from a blending of ancient Arabic, Middle-Eastern, and North African ceramic styles. Shapes include plates, bowls, jugs, and pitchers, hand-painted and hard-fired in intricate bright yellow, orange, blue, and green floral designs. So few shops make true Talavera these days that other, cheaper look-alike grades, made around Guanajuato, are more common, selling for a small fraction of the price of the genuine article.

WOOLEN WOVEN GOODS

Mexico's finest wool weavings come from Teotitlán del Valle and the neighboring town of Santa Ana del Valle, less than an hour's drive east of Oaxaca City. Although they learned to work wool from the Spanish, the weaving tradition, continued by Zapotec-speaking families, dates back at least a thousand years before the conquest. Most families still carry on the arduous process, making everything from scratch. They gather the dyes from wild plants and the bodies of insects and sea snails. They hand-wash, card, spin, and dye the wool and even travel to remote mountain springs to gather water. The result, they say, is *vale la pena* (worth the pain): intensely colored, tightly woven carpets, rugs, and wall hangings that retain their brilliance for generations.

Although many handicrafts shops and a host of stalls in all the Oaxaca City markets sell the Teotitlán and Santa Ana weavings, a trip to Teotitlán (where Santa Ana weavers send most of their products for sale) is a must for Valley of Oaxaca first-time visitors.

ESSENTIALS

Getting There

BY AIR
From the United States and Canada

The majority of foreign visitors reach Oaxaca by air, and a large fraction of those through Mexico City. There, travelers transfer to flights bound for Oaxaca City, Puerto Escondido, or Bahías de Huatulco–Puerto Ángel. Two possible exceptions are Mexicana Airlines and American Airlines flights, which in the past have connected (but at this writing do not) directly with Huatulco from Los Angeles and Dallas, respectively.

Most air travelers launch their Oaxaca vacations through the Mexico City gateways of **Atlanta, Chicago, Dallas, Denver, Houston, Los Angeles, Miami, New York, Orlando, Phoenix, San Antonio, San Francisco,** or **Tijuana.** Nearly all flights involve an airplane change at the large, super-busy Mexico City Airport. (At this writing, **three flights go from the United States Oaxaca-direct:** Two are the quick 2.5-hour Oaxaca-direct Huatulco-direct Continental Airlines flights from Houston; the other is the new Avolar Airlines Tijuana–Oaxaca flight).

Although only a few scheduled flights go directly to Mexico City from the northern

© BRUCE WHIPPERMAN

United States and Canada, **charters** do, especially during the winter. In locales near Boston, Buffalo, Calgary-Edmonton, Cleveland, Detroit, Minneapolis, Montreal, Ottawa, Seattle, Toronto, Vancouver, and Winnipeg, consult a travel agent or website for charter flight options. Be aware that charter reservations, which often require fixed departure and return dates and provide minimal cancellation refunds, decrease your flexibility.

Air travelers can save money by shopping around, through independent ticket agents and the airlines, both by telephone and the Internet. Don't be bashful about trying for the best price. Make it clear to the airline or agent that you're interested in a bargain. Ask the right questions. Are there special incentive, advance-payment, night, midweek, tour-package, or charter fares? Peruse the ads in your Sunday newspaper travel section for bargain-oriented travel agencies. An agent usually costs you no money, although some don't like discounted tickets because their fee often depends on a percentage of ticket price. Nevertheless, many agents will work to get you a bargain.

You also may be able to save money by booking an air/hotel package. Mexicana (tel. 800/531-9321, www.mexicana.com) and Aeromexico (tel. 800/237-6639, www.aero mexico.com) and most others routinely offer Oaxaca air/hotel packages.

From Europe, Latin America, and Australasia

A few airlines fly across the Atlantic directly to Mexico City. These include **Lufthansa,** which connects directly from Frankfurt, and **Aeroméxico,** which connects directly from Paris and Madrid. In Mexico City, several connections, including Oaxaca City, Puerto Escondido, and Huatulco, are available, mostly via Mexicana, Aeroméxico, Magnicharter, Aviacsa and affiliated airlines. See Oaxaca City, Puerto Escondido, and Huatulco *Getting There and Away* sections for details.

From Latin America, **Aeroméxico** connects directly with Mexico City, from Sao Paulo, Brazil; Santiago, Chile; and Lima,

Peru. A number of other Latin American flag carriers also fly directly to Mexico City. From there, easy Oaxaca connections are available via Mexicana Airlines and Aeroméxico Airlines and their respective affiliate airlines, Aerocaribe and Aeromar.

Very few flights cross the Pacific directly to Mexico, except for **Japan Airlines,** which connects Osaka-Tokyo to Mexico City, via Vancouver. More commonly, travelers from Australasia routinely transfer at Los Angeles, Phoenix, or San Francisco for connections to Mexico City, thence Oaxaca.

Baggage, Insurance, "Bumping," and In-Flight Meals

Tropical and temperate Oaxaca makes it easy to pack light. (See the *Packing Checklist* sidebar.) Veteran tropical travelers often condense their luggage to carry-ons only. Airlines routinely allow a carry-on (not exceeding 45 inches in combined length, width, and girth) and a small book bag or purse. Thus relieved of heavy burdens, your trip will become much simpler. You'll avoid possible luggage loss and long baggage check-in lines by being able to check in directly at the boarding gate.

Even if you can't avoid having to check luggage, loss of it needn't ruin your vacation. **Always carry your irreplaceable items in the cabin with you.** These should include all cameras, checks, credit cards, eyeglasses, money, passport, prescription drugs, tickets, and traveler's keys.

At the X-ray security check, insist that your film and cameras be hand-inspected. Regardless of what attendants claim, repeated X-ray scanning will fog any film, especially the sensitive ASA 400 and 1,000 high-speed varieties. (You can assure both protection and hand inspection for your film by packing it in the special lead-lined film bags available in any good camera store.)

Travelers packing lots of expensive baggage, or who (because of illness, for example) may have to cancel a nonrefundable flight or tour, might consider buying **travel insurance.** Travel agents routinely sell packages that

AIRLINES SERVING OAXACA

At this writing, only one of the following scheduled airlines (Continental) connects directly (with no plane change) with Oaxaca City (OAX) and Huatulco (HUA). The remainder connect directly with Mexico City (MX), where connecting flights continue on to the Oaxaca destinations of Oaxaca City, Huatulco-Puerto Ángel, and Puerto Escondido. The following departures are listed alphabetically by airline and geographically from west to east and south to north.

AIRLINE	ORIGIN	DESTINATIONS
Aerocalifornia tel. 800/237-6225 www.aerocalifornia.com.	Tijuana .... MX	
Aeroméxico tel. 800/237-6639 www.aeromexico.com	Los Angeles .... MX Ontario (California) .... MX San Diego .... MX Seattle .... MX Tijuana .... MX Phoenix .... MX Tucson .... MX San Antonio .... MX Houston .... MX New York .... MX Atlanta .... MX Orlando .... MX Miami .... MX	
Air Canada tel. 888/247-2262 www.aircanada.com	Toronto .... MX	
American tel. 800/433-7300 www.aa.com	Dallas .... MX Miami .... MX	

include baggage, trip cancellation, and default insurance. Baggage insurance covers you beyond the customary $1,250 domestic, $400 international baggage liability limits, but check with your carrier. **Trip cancellation insurance** pays if you must cancel your prepaid trip, while default insurance protects you if your carrier or tour agent does not perform as agreed. Travel insurance, however, can be expensive. Traveler's Insurance Company, for example, offers about $1,000 of baggage insurance per person for two weeks for about $50. Carefully weigh both your options and the cost against benefits before putting your money down.

AIRLINE	ORIGIN	DESTINATIONS
Aviacsa tel. 800/967-5263 www.aviacsa.com	Tijuana .... MX Las Vegas .... MX Houston .... MX	
Avolar www.avolar.com.mx	Tijuana .... OAX	
Continental tel. 800/231-0856 www.continental.com	Houston .... MX OAX HUA Newark .... MX	
Delta tel. 800/221-1212 www.delta.com	Los Angeles .... MX Dallas .... MX Atlanta .... MX New York .... MX	
Mexicana tel. 800/531-7921 www.mexicana.com	Los Angeles .... MX San Jose .... MX Tijuana .... MX San Francisco .... MX Oakland .... MX Portland .... MX Las Vegas .... MX Denver .... MX San Antonio .... MX Chicago .... MX Toronto .... MX New York .... MX Montreal .... MX Miami .... MX	
U.S. Airways **(formerly America West)** tel. 800/363-2597 www.usairways.com	Phoenix .... MX	

It's wise to reconfirm both departure and return flight reservations, especially during the busy Christmas and Easter seasons. This is a useful strategy—as is prompt arrival at check-in—against getting "bumped" (losing your seat) because of the tendency of airlines to overbook the rush of high-season vacationers.

For further protection, if possible get your seat assignment and boarding pass included with your ticket.

Airlines generally try hard to accommodate travelers with dietary or other special needs. When booking your flight, inform your travel agent or carrier of the necessity of a low-sodium, low-cholesterol, vegetarian, or lactose-reduced meal or other requirements.

BY BUS

As air travel rules in the United States, bus travel rules in Mexico. Hundreds of sleek luxury- and first-class bus lines with romantic names such as Elite, Estrella de Oro (Star of Gold), and Estrella Blanca (White Star) roar out daily from the border, headed south.

Since U.S. bus lines ordinarily terminate just north of the Mexican border, you must usually disembark, collect your things, and, after having filled out the necessary but very simple paperwork at the immigration booth, proceed on foot across the border to Mexico, where you can bargain with a local taxi driver to drive you the few miles ($2–4) to the *camionera central* (central bus station). (*Note:* Do not cross the border into Mexico without a **valid passport;** U.S. border authorities may not allow you to return without one.)

Finally, at the bus station, handy words to have in mind are *taquilla* (ticket booth), *guardaequipajes* (baggage checkroom), *llegada* (arrival), *salida* (departure), and *sanitario* or *baño* (toilet or bathroom).

First- and luxury-class bus service in Mexico is generally cheaper and at least as good as in the United States. Tickets for comparable trips in Mexico cost less than half (as little as $60 for a 1,000-mile/1,600-km trip), compared to perhaps $150 in the United States.

In Mexico, as on U.S. buses, you often have to take it as you find it. *Asientos reservados* (reserved seats), *boletos* (tickets), and information must generally be obtained in person at the bus station, and credit cards and travelers checks are sometimes not accepted. Reserved bus tickets are typically nonrefundable, so don't miss the bus. On the other hand, plenty of buses roll south almost continuously. Two basic routes are available, either through Mexico City or down the Pacific coast all the way.

Pacific Coast Route

The route to Oaxaca along the Pacific shore, although the longest, requiring one or two transfers and at least three full 24-hour days, is the most scenic. Try to go luxury class all the way; the small additional cost is well worth it. Cross the border at **Tijuana, Mexicali,** or **Nogales,** where you can choose from at least three bus lines along the Pacific coast route, via combined National Highways 15 and 200, via Mazatlán, Puerto Vallarta, Zihuatanejo, Acapulco, and, finally, Puerto Escondido, in Oaxaca. At the border, get a bus as far south as you can, maybe even **Elite** all the way to Acapulco; or if not, at least to Tepic or Puerto Vallarta, where you change to a bus headed south for, most likely, Lázaro Cárdenas, Zihuatanejo, or Acapulco, at the end of your second day. There, you catch a third bus, which will take you at least to Acapulco, and at most to Puerto Escondido by the end of your third day. On the other hand, make it easy on yourself and stretch the trip to five days by resting overnight in Puerto Vallarta and Zihuatanejo along the way. In Puerto Vallarta, stay at Hotel Rosita (tel. 322/223-2185, tel./fax 322/223-2000, sales@hotelrosita.com, www.hotelrosita.com, $50) or Casa Corazon (tel./fax 322/222-6364, U.S.-Canada toll-free tel. 866/648-6893, www.casacorazonvallarta.com, corazon@yahoo.com, on the beach, $40–50 d). In Zihuatanejo, stay at Hotel Irma (tel./fax 755/554-8003, 755/554-8472 info@mcrx.com, www.mcrx.com, on the beach, $60–80 d) or Posada Citlali (tel./fax 755/554-2043, citlali@zihuatanejo.com.mx, a block from the beach, $35 d).

Mexico City Route

This is the quickest bus route to Oaxaca, typically about 36 hours from the south Texas border, a day longer from California or Nogales, Arizona, via Guadalajara. From the western United States, cross the border at Tijuana, Mexicali, or Nogales. From the United States Midwest, Southeast, and East, cross the border at Laredo to Nuevo Laredo or McAllen to Reynosa. For the most speed and comfort, at only a small extra cost, go by luxury-class bus to Mexico City.

Mexico City has four bus terminals—north, east, south, and west (respectively, Terminal Norte, Terminal Tapo, Terminal Sur, and

Terminal Poniente). You will most likely arrive in the Terminal Norte, although a few buses from the west via Guadalajara might arrive at Terminal Poniente. For an overnight rest break, Guadalajara is especially handy, at basic but clean and moderately priced Hotel La Serena (tel.33/3600-0910, fax 33/3600-1974, reservas@aranzazu.com.mx, with pool and restaurant, conveniently adjacent to the bus station, $38 d).

In any case, at Mexico City, if you're heading to Oaxaca City, from Terminal Norte, board an **Autobuses del Oriente (ADO)** or **Cristóbal Colón** bus, via the Puebla expressway (*autopista* or *corta*) to Oaxaca City. If you're heading for the Oaxaca Pacific coast, best board an **Estrella Blanca** affiliate (such as **Turistar** or **Futura**) or an **Estrella de Oro** bus bound for Acapulco, where you can transfer to a Puerto Escondido–bound bus.

If somehow the above connections are not available at Terminal Norte (or Terminal Poniente), share a taxi (don't try it by public transit) to Terminal Sur (or Terminal Tapo for Oaxaca City via ADO) and catch an Estrella Blanca subsidiary (such as Elite, Turistar, Futura, Flecha Roja, or Transportes Cuauhtémoc) all the way to Puerto Escondido via Acapulco. If you miss the direct Puerto Escondido connection, settle for an express connection to Acapulco, where plenty of local departures head out southeast for Puerto Escondido.

Get across town to your continuing bus terminal via *taxi especial* (private taxi) or *colectivo* (collective taxi). Although such a trip is possible by public transportation, don't try it. If you do, you're either a Mexico City veteran traveling light and know what you're getting into or are willing to bear a load of frustration, pain, and the dirty looks from fellow passengers as you unwittingly poke them with your bulging backpacks and luggage in a crowded subway or local bus.

BY CAR OR RV

If you're adventurous and like going to out-of-the-way places, but still want to have all the comforts of home, you may enjoy driving your car or RV to Oaxaca. On the other hand, consideration of cost, risk, wear on both you and your vehicle, and the congestion hassles in towns may change your mind.

Mexican Car Insurance

Mexico does not recognize foreign insurance. When you drive into Mexico, Mexican auto insurance is at least as important as your passport. At the busier crossings, you can get it at insurance "drive-ins" just north of the border. The many Mexican auto insurance companies are government-regulated; their numbers keep prices and services competitive.

Sanborn's Mexico Insurance (Sanborn's Mexico, P.O. Box 310, McAllen, TX 78502, toll-free 800/222-0158, tel. 956/686-3601, www.sanbornsinsurance.com), one of the best-known agencies, certainly seems to be trying hardest. It offers a number of books and services, including the *Recreational Guide to Mexico*, a good road map, "smile-by-mile" *Travelog* guide to "every highway in Mexico," hotel discounts, and more. Much of the above is available to members of Sanborn's Sombrero Club.

Alternatively, look into **Vagabundos del Mar** (tel. 800/474-2252, www.vagabundos.com), an RV-oriented Mexico travel club offering memberships that include a newsletter, caravaning opportunites, discounts, insurance, and much more.

MEXICO CITY DRIVING RESTRICTIONS

To reduce smog and traffic gridlock, authorities have limited which cars can drive on which days in Mexico City, depending upon the last digit of their license plates. If you violate these rules, you risk getting an expensive ticket. On Monday, no vehicle may be driven with final digits 5 or 6; Tuesday, 7 or 8; Wednesday, 3 or 4; Thursday, 1 or 2; Friday, 9 or 0. Weekends, all vehicles may be driven.

DRIVING DISTANCES

NOTE: DISTANCES ARE SHOWN AS MILES/KILOMETERS.
APPROXIMATE DRIVING TIMES ARE SHOWN AS HOURS:MINUTES.

━━━ MAIN ROAD   ━━━ EXPRESSWAY

© AVALON TRAVEL

Mexican car insurance runs from a bare-bones rate of about $6 a day for minimal $10,000/$50,000 (property damage/medical payments) coverage to a more typical $12 a day for more complete $20,000/$100,000 coverage. On the same scale, insurance for a $50,000 RV and equipment runs about $30 a day. These daily rates decrease sharply for six-month or one-year policies, which run from about $200 for the minimum to $400–1,600 for complete, high-end coverage.

If you get broken glass, personal effects, and legal expenses coverage with these rates, you're lucky. Mexican policies don't usually cover them.

You should get something for your money, however. The deductibles should be no more than $300–500, the public liability per occurrence/medical payments per person/per occurrence should be about double the ($25,000/$25,000/$50,000) legal minimum, and you should be able to get your car fixed in the United States and receive payment in U.S. dollars for losses. If not, shop around.

A Sinaloa Note of Caution

Although *bandidos* no longer menace Mexican roads (but loose burros, horses, and cattle still do), be cautious in the infamous marijuana- and opium-growing region of Sinaloa state north of Mazatlán. It's best not to stray from Highway 15 between Culiacán and Mazatlán or from Highway 40 between Mazatlán and Durango. Curious tourists have been assaulted in the hinterlands adjacent to these roads.

The Green Angels

The Green Angels have answered many motoring tourists' prayers in Mexico. Bilingual teams of two, trained in auto repair and first aid, help distressed tourists along main highways. They patrol fixed stretches of road at least twice daily by truck. To make sure they stop to help, pull completely off the highway and raise your hood. You may want to hail a passing motorist or trucker with a Mexican cell phone to call the Mexico Tourism–Green Angels hotline

(tel. 800/903-9200, or all-purpose emergency direct tel. 078) for you.

If, for some reason, you have to leave your vehicle on the roadside, don't leave it unattended. Hire a local teenager or adult to watch it for you. Unattended vehicles on Mexican highways are quickly stricken by a mysterious disease, the symptoms of which are rapid loss of vital parts.

ROAD SAFETY

Hundreds of thousands of visitors enjoy safe Mexican auto vacations every year. Their success is due in large part to their frame of mind: Drive defensively, anticipate and adjust to danger before it happens, and watch everything – side roads, shoulders, the car in front, and cars far down the road. The following tips will help ensure a safe and enjoyable trip.

- **Don't drive at night.** Range animals, unmarked sand piles, pedestrians, one-lane bridges, cars without lights, and drunk drivers are doubly hazardous at night.

- Although **speed limits** are rarely enforced, *don't break them.* Mexican roads are often narrow and shoulderless. Poor markings and macho drivers who pass on curves are best faced at a speed of 40 mph (64 kph) rather than 75 mph (120 kph).

- **Drive on sand only sparingly.** Even with four-wheel drive, you'll eventually get stuck if you drive either often or casually on beaches. When the tide comes in, who'll pull your car out?

- **Slow down** at the *topes* (speed bumps) at the edges of towns and for *vados* (dips), which can be dangerously bumpy and full of water.

- Extending the **courtesy of the road** goes hand-in-hand with safe driving. Both courtesy and machismo are more infectious in Mexico; on the highway, it's much safer to spread the former than the latter.

Mexican Gasoline

Pemex, short for Petróleos Mexicanos, the government oil monopoly, markets diesel fuel and two grades of unleaded gasoline: 92-octane *premio* (PRAY-mee-oh) and 87-octane Magna (MAHG-nah). Magna is good gas, yielding performance similar to that of U.S.-style regular unleaded gasoline. (My original car, whose manufacturer recommended 91-octane, ran well on Magna.) It runs about $0.65 per liter (or about $2.50 per gallon at this writing). On main highways, Pemex makes sure that major stations (typically spaced about 30 miles apart in the countryside) stock Magna.

Gas Station Thievery

Although the problem has abated considerably in recent years (by the hiring of young female attendants), boys who hang around gas stations to wash windows are notoriously light-fingered. When stopping at the *gasolinera,* make sure that your cameras, purses, and other moveable items are out of reach. Also, make sure that your car has a lockable gas cap. If not, insist on pumping the gas yourself, or be super-watchful as you pull up to the gas pump to make certain that the pump reads zero before the attendant pumps the gas.

A Healthy Car

Preventive measures spell good health for both you and your car. Get that tune-up (or that long-delayed overhaul) *before,* rather than after, you leave.

Carry a stock of spare parts, which will be more difficult to get and more expensive in Mexico than at home. Carry an extra tire or two, a few quart bottles of motor oil, oil and gas filters, fan belts, spark plugs, tune-up kit, ignition points, and fuses. Be prepared with basic tools and supplies, such as screwdrivers, pliers including Vice-Grip, lug wrench, jack, adjustable wrenches, tire pump, tire pressure gauge, steel wire, and electrical tape. For breakdowns and emergencies, carry a folding shovel, a husky rope or chain, a gasoline can, and flares or red highway markers.

DETOUR INTO A CORNFIELD

Driving hazards – poorly marked roads, potholes, pedestrians, roadside horses, cattle, burros, and rattletrap cars and trucks with no lights – make rural nighttime driving in Oaxaca an iffy proposition. Add speed to the mix and you have a recipe for close calls at least and disaster at worst.

I was only doing about 30 or 35 miles per hour (about 50 or 55 kph), and although the road was paved (something that probably lulled me into complacency), it was dark, wet, gravelly, and completely lacking either a white center line or edge markings.

I blundered into a sharp left curve and in a split second found that I had to either roll my car or leave the road. I chose the latter and hurtled into someone's tall-corn *milpa.* As green stalks slapped the windshield and I bounced up and down like a Ping-Pong ball, I wondered if I was going to go over a cliff (this was hilly country), something that probably would have postponed publication of this book indefinitely.

This time I was lucky. After a very long second or two, my little truck lurched to a stop, tilted at a crazy sideways angle against a big round boulder. Somehow something managed to seriously crack the front windshield and cave in both passenger-side doors, but the car didn't roll, and miraculously the motor would still run.

What does a writer on a short deadline do on such an occasion? Go get help and get rolling again if possible. The only problem: I was way out in the country, 100 miles (160 km) from the crane (Tow truck? No way!) that seemed necessary to pull my truck from where it was lodged over the boulders and up the long embankment.

It turned out that I couldn't have been in a better place to get help. I climbed out of the cornfield to a nearby village, where, at 9 P.M.

Car Repairs in Mexico

The American big three—General Motors, Ford, and Chrysler—as well as Nissan and Volkswagen are represented by extensive dealer networks in Mexico. Latecomers Toyota and Honda are also represented, although to a lesser extent. Getting your car or truck serviced at such agencies is straightforward. While parts will probably be higher in price, shop rates run about one-third to one-half U.S. prices, so repairs will generally come out cheaper than back home.

The same may not be true for repairing other makes, however. Mexico has few, if any, other car or truck dealers; consequently, officially certified mechanics for other Japanese, British, and European makes are hard to find.

Nevertheless, many ingenious Mexican independent mechanics can fix any car that comes their way. Their humble *talleres mecánicos* (tah-YER-ays may-KAH-nee-kohs) dot town and village roadsides everywhere.

Although the great majority of Mexican mechanics are honest, beware of unscrupulous operators who try to collect double or triple their original estimate. If you don't speak Spanish, find someone who can assist you in negotiations. *Always* get a cost estimate, including needed parts and labor, in writing, even if you have to write it yourself. Make sure the mechanic understands, then ask him to sign it before he starts work. Although this may be a hassle, it might save you a much nastier hassle later. Shop labor at small, independent repair shops should run $10–20 per hour. For much more information, and for entertaining anecdotes of car and RV travel in Mexico, consult Carl Franz's *The People's Guide to Mexico*.

Bribes (Mordidas)

The usual meeting ground of the visitor and Mexican police is in the visitor's car on a highway or downtown street. To the tourists, such an encounter may seem mild harassment by the police, accompanied by vague threats of going to the police station or impounding the car for such-and-such a violation. The tourist often

---

on Saturday night, everybody was out and about. I asked a man, named German ("Herman"), who, it seems, knew Agustín, who had a tractor. Agustín, German said, was at his girlfriend's house, where we went next.

Agustín came outside for a conference. Given his tractor, it was not a question of if the job could be done, but when.

"Can't we wait until tomorrow?" Agustín asked. "It's dark now. Best to try in the morning."

My deadline pushed me on.

"You may be right, but if possible I'd like to try now. I've got 1,500 pesos ($150) cash. It's yours if you pull my *camioneta* out of the *milpa*."

By this time a small crowd had gathered around. Several of us piled into German's truck and headed to Agustín's place, where Agustín maneuvered a huge green John Deere tractor with seven-foot (two-meter) wheels out of his barn. Agustín's brother went to get a long cable and met us at the site.

With about five guys helping me, we wrapped the cable around the axle. I got behind the steering wheel and, miracle of miracles, Agustín and his tractor, like the strong right hand of God, pulled my *camioneta* straight up the rocky incline and onto the road.

Overjoyed, I immediately wanted to fulfill my promise to Agustín. I started counting out the $10 bills, one by one. When I got to eight or nine, Agustín protested.

"Stop. That's enough."

I distributed the rest of the bills to the other men and was about to leave when someone spied that the crash had flattened the right front tire. Quickly, one of the men replaced it with my spare, and I was ready to go. I thanked everyone all round again and headed out through the Oaxaca night, shaken but unhurt and grateful to my kind rescuers.

goes on to say, "It was all right, though . . . we paid him $20 and he went away . . . Mexican cops sure are crooked, aren't they?"

And, I suppose, if people want to go bribing their way through Mexico, that's their business. But calling Mexican cops crooked isn't exactly fair. Police, like most everyone else in Mexico, have to scratch for a living, and they have found that many tourists are willing to slip them a $20 bill for nothing. Rather than crooked, I would call them hungry and opportunistic.

Instead of paying a bribe, do what I've done a dozen times: Remain cool, and if you're really guilty of an infraction, calmly say, "Ticket, please." *("Boleto, por favor")*. After a minute or two of stalling, and no cash appearing, the officer most likely will not bother with a ticket, but will wave you on with only a warning. If, on the other hand, the officer does write you a ticket, he will probably keep your driver's license, which you will be able to retrieve at the *presidencia municipal* (city hall) the next day in exchange for paying your fine.

Crossing the Border

Squeezing through the border traffic bottlenecks during peak holidays and rush hours can easily take two or three hours. Avoid crossing 7–9 A.M. and 4:30–6:30 P.M. Moreover, with latter-day increased U.S. homeland security precautions, the return, northbound border crossing, under the best of conditions, generally takes at least an hour waiting in your car, along with a hundred or more other frustrated drivers. (*Note:* Do not cross the border into Mexico without a **valid passport** for everyone in your party. U.S. border authorities will probably not let you return without one.)

Highway Routes from the United States

If you've decided to drive to Oaxaca, you have your choice of four general routes. At safe highway speeds, from the Mexican border these routes require as many as five days or as few as two days, depending on your route.

The longest but most scenic route is the **Pacific route,** which starts out as Mexican National Highway 15 from the border at Nogales, Sonora, an hour's drive south of Tucson, Arizona. Soon you join Highway 15D *cuota autopista* (toll expressway)—or continue along old *libre* (free) Highway 15—proceeding southward smoothly, over cactus-studded plains mountains that give way to irrigated farms and groves and palmy tropical coastal plain by the time you arrive in Mazatlán. Follow the *periféricos* (peripheral bypasses) that conduct traffic past the congested downtowns of Hermosillo, Guaymas, Culiacán, and Mazatlán. Between these centers, you can speed along via the *cuota* Highway 15D expressway virtually the entire way. If you prefer not to pay the high tolls (around $60 total for a passenger car, much more for multiple-wheeled RVs) you should stick to the old *libre* Highway 15. Hazards, bumps, and slow going might force you to reconsider, however.

At **Tepic,** the Pacific route leaves Highway 15–15D and continues south via Highway 200, winding past tobacco farms and mango orchards, through lush forest, climbing vine–hung canyons, crossing a score of rivers, past a host of palm-tufted beaches, and passing the renowned vacation lands of **Puerto Vallarta, Manzanillo, Ixtapa-Zihuatanejo,** and **Acapulco.** Finally, several days after you crossed the border, you arrive at the heart of the tropical Oaxaca coast at Puerto Escondido or Puerto Ángel.

A speedier variation on the Pacific route is the **Pacific-Mexico City route,** which starts out as the Pacific route but departs from the Pacific coast, eastward, at Tepic, continuing along Highway 15 or 15D past Guadalajara, via Toluca to Mexico City.

Across town, at the Los Reyes southeast-side suburb, pick up the Puebla–Veracruz expressway Highway 150D, where you continue about an hour past Puebla to a fork. Follow the south fork expressway, via Tehuacán and Nochixtlán, to Oaxaca City. This nearly all-expressway route minimizes the road time from the western U.S. border to three very long, or, to be safe, four days to Oaxaca. *Note:* Be sure to arrive in Mexico City on a day of the week when driving restrictions (determined by the last digit of your license plate; see the sidebar *Mexico City Driving Restrictions*) do not apply to your car.

If, however, you're driving to Oaxaca from the central United States, go via the **central route,** crossing the border at El Paso to Ciudad Juárez, Chihuahua. There, National Highway 45, preferably via the *cuota* multilane expressway (or, if not, the old *libre* two-lane highway), leads you southward past high, dry plains and the cities of Chihuahua and Jiménez (use *periféricos* to bypass downtowns). Continue via Highway 49 southwest, through Gómez Palacio and the silver colonial cities of Zacatecas to San Luis Potosí, where you connect with Highway 57 expressway, via Querétaro, to the northern outskirts of Mexico City.

At that point, best use the east-bound *periférico* expressway via Carpio and Tezcoco instead of trying to fight your way through downtown Mexico City. At Los Reyes on the southeast side of town, pick up Highway 150D, the expressway east to Puebla, where you continue southeast via the toll expressway to Oaxaca (as described two paragraphs above). To be safe, allow three daytime-only driving days for this route.

Folks heading to Oaxaca from the eastern and southeastern United States probably save the most time by crossing the border from McAllen, Texas, to Reynosa and taking the **eastern route** to Oaxaca. Continue south, via Highway 97 then Highway 101, to Ciudad Victoria, bypassing the downtown by the *perférico*. Then connect with Highway 80 to Tampico. There, again bypass the downtown and pick up Highway 105 south headed for Tempoal de Sánchez. After a long, winding, mountain climb via Huejutla de Reyes, you reach Pachuca and continue southward via expressway Highway 85 to Mexico City. At Carpio in the northern suburb, take the east

HIGHWAY ROUTES FROM THE U.S. BORDER TO OAXACA

ROUTE	VIA	MILES/KM	HOURS AT THE WHEEL	TRAVEL DAYS
Pacific	Nogales-Mazatlán Puerto Vallarta Acapulco-Puerto Ángel	1,911/3,075	46	5
Pacific-Mexico City	Nogales-Mazatlán Guadalajara-Mexico City Puebla-Oaxaca City	1,749/2,814	34	3
Central	Ciudad Juárez-Chihuahua Torreón-Zacatecas Querétaro-Mexico City Puebla-Oaxaca City	1,370/2,204	29	3
Eastern	Reynosa-Ciudad Victoria Tampico-Pachuca-Mexico City Puebla-Oaxaca City	967/1,556	22	2

bypass expressway, via Tepexpan and Tezcoco, continuing to east-bound expressway 150D for Puebla. There, you continue southeast to Oaxaca City (as described three paragraphs above). If you start off at dawn each morning, you could probably get to Oaxaca safely in two driving days, under optimal conditions. Best do it in three leisurely days, including two overnights.

BY TOUR

For travelers on a tight time budget, a prearranged tour package can provide a hassle-free route for sampling Oaxaca's attractions. For tour information, read on, call a travel agent, or visit a travel website (see *Internet Resources*).

If, however, you prefer a self-paced vacation, or desire thrift over convenience, you should probably defer tour arrangements to Oaxaca guides and agencies whom you can contact upon arrival (or before departure by telephone, fax, or email, see the *Travel and Tour Agencies and Guides* section in the *Oaxaca City* chapter and *Getting Around* in *The Valley of Oaxaca* chapter). Many Oaxaca tour agencies as close as your hotel telephone or lobby-front tour desk can customize a tour for you.

Special Tours and Study Options

Oaxaca's rich archaeological and cultural heritage provides a focus for some noteworthy tour-study programs. Some of the agencies that offer such options include Adventures into Art, Elderhostel, Field Guides, Journey Mexico, Manos de Oaxaca, Mexi-Maya Tours, Siemer and Hand, and Zapotec Tours.

A pair of **Elderhostel** (11 Lafayette Ave., Boston, MA 02111, 877/454-5768, www.elderhostel.org) tours lead participants on Oaxaca explorations: "Oaxaca: Spanish Language and Hispanic Culture" emphasizes local traditions, food, and fiestas, plus lots of practice in conversational Spanish; "Dia de Los Muertos (Day of the Dead) in Oaxaca" centers on the happy Mexican tradition of celebrating their beloved departed in joyous gravesite, food, flower- and candle-festooned family fiestas. Both programs include visits to the archaeological sites

of Monte Albán and Mitla and appreciation of indigenous tradition through visits to pottery, weaving, and woodcraft villages and evening excursions to enjoy Oaxacan food and folkloric music and dance. Accommodations can include both hotel rooms and homestays with Mexican families.

Florida-based **Zapotec Tours** (407/332-0707, toll-free 800/446-2922, fax 407/264-0709) arranges two exciting and enlightening Oaxaca tours: a "Taste of Oaxaca" gastronomical tour (beginning of October), a "Day of the Dead" cultural tour, focused on the celebrated November 1–2 Day of the Dead festival. For many details, visit www.zapotel.com.

Journey Mexico (toll-free U.S. tel. 800/513-1587, Mexico tel. 322/225-9821, info@journeymexico.com, www.journeymexico.com) organizes custom or group outdoor, people-to-people-oriented tours that include off-the-beaten-track villages in the Oaxaca northern mountains and southern tropical coast. The group tour starts in Oaxaca City and the Valley of Oaxaca archaeological sites and crafts villages. The itinerary continues with hiking around the Sierra Norte villages of Benito Juárez and Cuajimoloyas. Tours usually climax with explorations, including sea turtle conservation and wildlife-viewing, in the tropical coastal villages around Puerto Ángel.

The Illinois-based **Mexi-Mayan** (12S675 Knoebel Dr., Lemont, IL 60439, 630/972-9090, toll-free 800/337-6394, fax 630/972-9393, www.meximayan.com) tours feature broad museum-quality cultural experiences, customarily including visits to museums, historical and archaeological sites, crafts villages, and markets. In past years, they have regularly led groups on a popular Oaxaca Day of the Dead tour. Sometimes itineraries include extensions to Oaxaca's palmy coastal resorts.

Birding tour outfitter **Field Guides** (800/728-4953, fax 512/263-0117, fieldguides@fieldguides.com, www.fieldguides.com) leads Oaxaca tours centering on the wildlife-rich foothill forests and lagoons of the tropical coast. Along the way, trips often include archaeological and historical sites and colorful native markets.

Siemer and Hand Travel (50 Osgood Place, Suite 230, San Francisco, CA 94111, 415/788-4000 or 800/451-4321, fax 415/788-4133, www.siemerhand.com), a broad-based high-end tour agency, specializes in both individual and group educational tours. Their Oaxaca group tours have recently included "Birding in Oaxaca," in cooperation with the Massachusetts Audubon Society, and "Textiles of Mexico City and the Valley of Oaxaca" that also includes historical and cultural highlights, in cooperation with the California Academy of Sciences.

Oaxaca arts and crafts tours, often in cooperation with art institutes and museums, are the specialty of **Travel Adventures into Art** (3030 Bridgeway, Sausalito, CA 94965, tel./fax 415/492-8166, taia1@mindspring.com, www.home.mindspring.com/~taia1), run by President Joan LeVine Mellion. Tours frequently occur during the springtime (for cooking) and July (for the Guelaguetza dance festival), and Day of the Dead (November 1 and 2) and Christmas–New Year's. Other tours have focused on a special interest, such as contemporary art, textiles, or women artists. Hands-on tours emphasize actually doing art, such as painting, pottery, or photography, in a Oaxaca setting.

Adventuresome travelers hankering for something unusual might check out **Manos de Oaxaca** (Oaxaca tel. 951/571-3695, traditions mexico@yahoo.com or mindling@comcast.net, www.manos-de-oaxaca.com), of artisan-guide and Oaxaca lover Eric Mindling. His bliss is leading like-minded folks in explorations of traditional clay and fiber arts by country artisans in communities in Valley of Oaxaca, the Mixteca, and the Coast. The approach is people to people, the accommodations sometimes rustic, the prices very reasonable, but the rewards potentially great. Eric customarily leads about four or five 7- to 10-day tours per year.

Getting Around

BY AIR

Travelers on tight time budgets find it useful to save a day by flying, instead of driving or busing, over the Sierra between Oaxaca City and the Pacific resorts of Puerto Ángel, Bahías de Huatulco, and Puerto Escondido.

Mexicana Airlines affiliate **Click** (reservations in Mexico tel. 800/125-5425) flights connect Oaxaca City with Mexico City, Huatulco, and Puerto Escondido.

Alternatively, light charter airlines (in the general aviation terminal, the building to the right as you face the main terminal) connect Oaxaca City with various points within Oaxaca. **Aerotucan** (in Oaxaca City, Alcalá 201, upper floor, suite 204, tel. 951/501-0530, toll-free outside Oaxaca Mex. tel. 800/640-4148, infor@aerotucan.com.mx, www.aerotucan.com.mx) regularly connects Oaxaca City with Puerto Escondido, Huatulco, Tuxtla Gutiérrez, and Puebla.

From the same general aviation terminal, **Aerovega** (tel. 951/516-2777), the dependable local air-taxi service, routinely connects Oaxaca City with Puerto Escondido and Huatulco.

Local Flying Tips

Mexican airlines have operating peculiarities that result from their tight budgets. For example, don't miss a flight—you might lose half the ticket price. Adjusting your flight date may cost 25 percent of the ticket price. Get to the airport at least an hour ahead of time. Last-minute passengers are often "bumped" in favor of early-bird standbys. Conversely, go to the airport and get in line if you must catch a flight that the airlines have claimed to be full—you might get on anyway. Keep your luggage small so you can carry it on. Lost luggage victims receive scant compensation in Mexico.

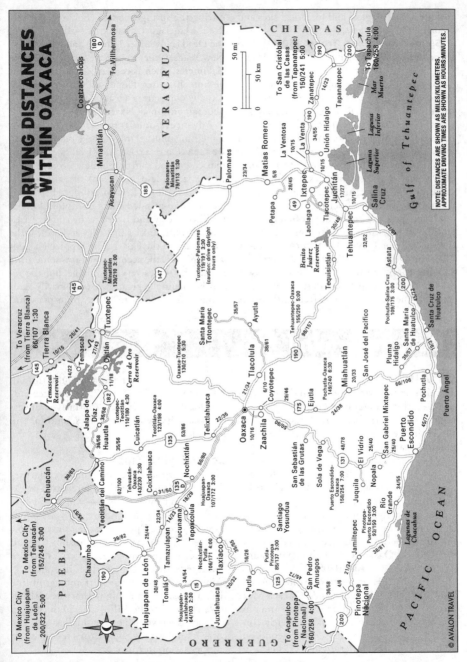

BY BUS

The bus is the king of the Oaxaca road. A host of lines connect virtually every town and most villages in Oaxaca. Three distinct levels of service—luxury or super-first class, first class, and second class—are generally available. **Luxury-class** (usually called something like Primera Plus or Ejecutivo, depending upon the line), super-deluxe express coaches speed between major towns, seldom stopping en route. In exchange for somewhat higher fares (about $50 Oaxaca City–Puerto Escondido, for example, compared with $40 for first class), luxury-class passengers enjoy rapid passage and airline-style amenities: plush reclining seats, air-conditioning, on-board toilet, video, and aisle attendant.

Although much less luxurious, **first-class** service costs less, is frequent, and always includes reserved seating. Additionally, passengers usually enjoy soft reclining seats and air-conditioning (if it is working). Besides making regular stops at or near most towns and villages en route, first-class bus drivers, if requested, will usually stop and let you off anywhere along the road.

Second-class bus seating is unreserved. In outlying parts of Oaxaca, there is a class of buses even beneath second class, but given the condition of many second-class buses, it usually seems as if third-class buses wouldn't run at all. Such buses are the stuff of travelers' legends: the recycled old GMC, Ford, and Dodge school buses that stop everywhere and carry everyone and everything to the smallest villages tucked away in the far mountains. As long as there is any kind of a road to it, such a bus will most likely go there.

Now and then, you'll read a newspaper story of a country bus that went over a cliff somewhere in Mexico, killing the driver and a dozen unfortunate souls. The same newspapers never bother to mention the half-million safe passenger trips the same bus provided during its 15 years of service prior to the accident.

Second-class buses are not for travelers

© BRUCE WHIPPERMAN

In Oaxaca, if there's a road to it, a second-class bus probably goes there.

with weak knees or stomachs. You will often initially have to stand, cramped in the aisle, among a crowd of campesinos. They are warm-hearted people, but poor, so don't tempt them with open, dangling purses or wallets bulging in back pockets. Stow your money safely away. After a while, you will probably be able to sit down. Such privilege, however, comes with obligation, such as holding an old lady's bulging bag of carrots or a toddler on your lap. But if you accept your burden with humor and equanimity, who knows what favors and blessings may flow to you in return.

Tickets, Seating, and Baggage

Oaxaca bus lines do not ordinarily publish schedules or fares. You have to ask someone (such as your hotel desk clerk) who knows, or call (or have someone call) the bus station. Only a few travel agents handle bus tickets. If you don't want to spend the time to get a reserved ticket yourself, hire someone trustworthy to do it for you. Another way of doing it all is to get to the bus station early enough on your traveling day to ensure you'll get a bus to your destination.

Although some first-class bus lines accept credit cards and issue computer-printed tickets at their major stations, many reserved bus tickets are sold for cash and handwritten, with a specific *número de asiento* (seat number) on the back. If you miss the bus, you lose your money. Furthermore, airlines-style automated reservations systems have not yet arrived at the smaller Oaxacan bus stations. Consequently, you can generally buy reserved tickets only at the *salida local* (local departure) station. (An agent in Tehuántepec, for example, cannot ordinarily reserve you a ticket on a bus that originates in Oaxaca City, a day's travel down the road.)

Request a reserved seat number, if possible, from numbers 1–25 in the *delante* (front) to *medio* (middle) of the bus. The rear seats are often occupied by smokers, drunks, and general rowdies. At night, you will sleep better on the *lado derecho* (right side) away from the glare of oncoming traffic lights.

© BRUCE WHIPPERMAN

On second-class buses, seats are unreserved – first-come, first-served.

Baggage is generally secure on Oaxaca buses. Label it, however. Overhead racks are often too cramped to accommodate airline-size carry-ons. Carry a small bag of your crucial items on your person; pack clothes and less essential items in your checked luggage. For peace of mind, watch the handler put your checked baggage on the bus and watch to make sure it is not mistakenly taken off the bus at intermediate stops.

If, somehow, your baggage gets misplaced, remain calm. Bus employees are generally competent and conscientious; if you are patient, recovering your luggage will become a matter of honor for many of them. Baggage handlers are at the bottom of the pay scale; a tip for their mostly thankless job would be very much appreciated.

On long trips, carry food, drinks, and toilet paper. Station food may be dubious and the sanitary facilities ill-maintained.

If you are waiting for a first-class bus at an intermediate *salida de paso* (passing station), you often have to trust to luck that there will be an empty seat. If not, your best option may be to ride a usually much more frequent second-class bus.

BY CAR, TAXI, TOUR, OR HITCHHIKING

Getting around by car in Oaxaca has its pluses and minuses. On the minus side, cars are expensive to rent and roads are often narrow and usually shared with pedestrians, horses, cows, and burros. On the plus side, driving allows you to go where you want on your own schedule. For details on road conditions, mileage, and driving times, see the destination chapters. For tips on driving to Mexico from the United States, as well as within Mexico, see *Getting There* earlier in this chapter.

Rental Car

Car and jeep rentals are an increasingly popular transportation option for Oaxaca travelers. They offer mobility and independence for local sightseeing and beach excursions. In Oaxaca City, Huatulco, and Puerto Escondido, the gang's at least partially there. If you make a reservation, they will meet your flight. Agents stationed regularly at the Oaxaca airport are Hertz (tel. 951/516-8268, hertz_oax@hotmail.com, www.hertz.com), Alamo (tel./fax 951/514-8534, fax 951/514-8686, oaxalamo@hotmail.com), and Europcar (tel. 951/516-8258, www.europcar.com.mx). In Puerto Escondido, contact Budget (tel. 954/582-0312, budget33@hotmail.com, www.budget.com). In Huatulco, Thrifty (at airport tel. 958/581-9000, in Crucecita tel. 958/587-0010, or Mex. toll-free tel. 800/021-2277, www.thrifty.com), or Hertz (at airport tel. 958/581-9092, in Tangolunda tel. 958/581-0588), or Europecar (at airport tel. 958/581 9094, in Crucecita, tel. 958/581-0552).

During the winter high season, especially, make reservations in the United States and Canada prior to departure.

Rental agencies generally require drivers to have a valid driver's license, passport, a major credit card, and may require a minimum age of 25. Some local companies do not accept credit cards, but offer lower rates in return.

Oaxaca car rentals are not cheap. With a 15 percent or more "value added" tax tacked on and mandatory Mexican car insurance, they run more than in the United States. The cheapest possible rental car, usually a vintage, well-used, stick-shift VW Beetle, runs $30–60 per day or $200–450 per week, depending on location and season. Prices are steepest during high Christmas–New Year's and pre-Easter weeks. Before departure, use the international agencies' (Thrifty, Hertz, Alamo, Budget, and Europecar) toll-free numbers to shop around for availability, prices, and reservations. During non-peak seasons, you may save lots of pesos by waiting till arrival and renting a car through a local agency. Shop around, starting with the agent in your hotel lobby or the local yellow pages (under "Automóviles, renta de").

Car insurance that covers property damage, public liability, and medical payments is an *absolute must* and is required by Mexican law. Although it is customarily included in the price of your rental car, make certain that you're covered before signing the deal. **Collision insurance** is not usually included and costs extra. However, major credit cards, such as American Express, often do furnish coverage that supplements your personal car insurance. Double-check your coverage with both your auto insurance agent and your credit card company before leaving for Mexico.

If you get into an accident in Mexico without insurance, you will be in deep trouble, probably jail. Safe driving in Oaxaca requires more caution and less speed than back home. (For important car safety and insurance information, see *Getting There* earlier in this chapter.)

Taxis

The high prices of rental cars make taxis a viable option for local excursions. Cars are luxuries, not necessities, for most Oaxacan families. Travelers might profit from the local money-saving practice of piling everyone in a taxi for Sunday park, beach, and fishing outings. You may find that an all-day taxi and driver (who, besides relieving you of driving, will become your impromptu guide) will cost less than a rental car.

The magic word for saving money by taxi is **colectivo:** a taxi that you share jointly with other travelers. Your first place to practice getting a taxi will be at the airport, where *colectivo* tickets are routinely sold from booths at the terminal door.

If, however, you want your own private taxi, ask for a *taxi especial,* which will probably run about three or four times the individual tariff for a *colectivo.*

Your airport experience will prepare you for in-town taxis, which in Oaxaca do not have meters. **You must establish the taxi price before getting in.** Bargaining comes with the territory in Mexico, so don't shrink from it, even though it may seem a hassle. If you get into a taxi without an agreed-upon price, you are letting yourself in for a more serious, potentially nasty hassle later. If your driver's price is too high, he'll probably come to his senses as soon as you hail another taxi.

After a few days, getting taxis around town will be a cinch. You'll find you don't have to take the high-ticket taxis lined up in your hotel driveway. If the price isn't right, walk toward the street and hail a regular taxi.

In town, if you can't seem to find a taxi, it may be because they are all hanging around waiting for riders at the local stand, called a taxi *sitio.* Ask someone to direct you to it: Say *"Excúseme. ¿Donde está el sitio taxi, por favor?"* ("Excuse me. Where is the taxi stand, please?").

Tours and Guides

For many Oaxaca visitors, locally arranged tours offer a hassle-free alternative to rental car or taxi sightseeing. Hotels and travel agencies, many of whom maintain front-lobby travel and tour desks, offer a bounty of sightseeing, water sports, bay cruise, fishing, and wildlife-viewing tour opportunities. (For details, see the destination chapters.)

Hitchhiking

Most everyone agrees hitchhiking is not the safest mode of transport. If you're unsure, don't do it. Hitchhiking doesn't make a healthy steady travel diet, nor should you hitchhike at night.

The recipe for trouble-free hitchhiking requires equal measures of luck, savvy, and technique. The best places to catch rides are where people are already arriving and leaving, such as bus stops, highway intersections, gas stations, RV parks, and on the highway out of town.

Male-female hitchhiking partnerships seem to net the most rides (although it is technically illegal for women to ride in commercial trucks). The more gear you and your partner have, the fewer rides you will get. Pickup and flatbed truck owners often pick up passengers for pay. Before hopping onto the truck bed, ask how much *(¿cuánto cuesta?)* the ride will cost.

Visas and Officialdom

PASSPORTS, TOURIST CARDS, AND VISAS
Your Passport

Your passport (or birth or naturalization certificate) is your positive proof of national identity; without it, your status in any foreign country is in doubt. Don't leave home without one. In fact, U.S. Immigration rules require that all **U.S. Citizens must have a valid passport in order to re-enter the U.S.** United States citizens may obtain passports (allow four to six weeks) at local post offices. For-fee private passport agencies can speed this process and get you a passport within a week, maybe less.

Entry into Mexico

For U.S. and Canadian citizens, entry by air into Mexico for a few weeks could hardly be easier. Airline attendants hand out tourist cards *(tarjetas turísticas)* en route and officers make them official by glancing at passports and stamping the cards at the immigration gate. Business travel permits for 30 days or fewer are handled by the same simple procedures.

In addition to the entry fee, Mexican immigration officials require that all entering U.S. citizens 15 years old or over must present proper identification—either a valid U.S. passport, original (or notarized copy) of your birth certificate, military ID, or state driver's license, while naturalized citizens must show naturalization papers (or a laminated naturalization card) or valid U.S. passport.

Canadian citizens must show a valid passport or original birth certificate. Nationals of other countries (especially those such as Hong Kong, which issue more than one type of passport) may be subject to different or additional regulations. For advice, consult your regional Mexico Tourism Board Office (see the sidebar *Mexico Tourism Board Offices*) or local Mexican consulate. Very complete and up-to-date Mexico visa and entry information for nationals of virtually all of the world's countries is available at the Toronto, Canada, Consulate website (www.consulmex.com).

More Options

For more complicated cases, get your tourist card early enough to allow you to consider the options. Tourist cards can be issued for multiple entries and a maximum validity of 180 days; photos are often required. If you don't request multiple entry or the maximum time, your card will probably be stamped single entry, valid for some shorter period, such as 90 days. If you are not sure how long you'll stay in Mexico, request the maximum (180 days is the absolute maximum for a tourist card; long term foreign residents routinely make semiannual "border runs" for new tourist cards).

Student and Business Visas

A visa is a notation stamped and signed on your passport showing the number of days and entries allowable for your trip. Apply for a student visa at the consulate nearest your home well in advance of your departure; the same is true if you require a business visa of longer than 30 days. One-year renewable student visas are available (sometimes with considerable red tape). An ordinary 180-day tourist card may be the easiest option, if you can manage it.

Entry for Children

Children under 15 can be included on their parents' tourist cards, but complications occur if the children (by reason of illness, for example) cannot leave Mexico with both parents. Parents can avoid such red tape by getting a passport and a Mexican tourist card for each of their children.

Oaxaca travelers should hurdle all such possible delays far ahead of time in the cool calm of their local Mexican consulate rather than

MEXICO TOURISM BOARD OFFICES

More than a dozen Mexico Tourism Board (Consejo de Promoción Turístico de Mexico, CPTM) offices and scores of Mexican government consulates operate in the United States, Canada, Europe, South America, and Asia. Consulates generally handle questions of Mexican nationals abroad, while Mexico Tourism Boards serve travelers heading for Mexico.

For straightforward questions and Mexico regional information brochures, contact the Tourism Board (U.S./Can. tel. 800/44-MEXICO or 800/446-3942, Europe tel. 00-800/111-2266, www.visitmexico.com). If you need more details and read a bit of Spanish, you might find visiting www.cptm.com.mx helpful also. Otherwise, contact one of the North American, European, South American, or Asian Mexico Tourism Boards directly for guidance.

IN NORTH AMERICA

From Alaska, Arizona, California, Colorado, Hawaii, Idaho, Montana, Nevada, Utah, Washington and Wyoming, contact the **Los Angeles** office (1880 Century Park East, Suite 511, Los Angeles, CA 90067, tel. 310/282-9112, fax 310/282-9116, losangeles@visitmexico.com). From Alberta, British Columbia, Alberta, Saskatchewan, and the Yukon and Northwest Territories, contact the **Vancouver** office (999 W. Hastings St., Suite 1110, Vancouver, BC, V6C

2W2, tel. 604/669-2845, fax 604/669-3498, mgto@telus.net).

From Arkansas, Colorado, Louisiana, New Mexico, Oklahoma, and Texas, contact the **Houston** office (4507 San Jacinto, Suite 308, Houston TX 77004, tel. 713/772-2581, fax 713/772-6058, houston@visitmexico.com). From Alabama, Florida, Georgia, Mississippi, Tennessee, North Carolina, Puerto Rico, and South Carolina, contact the **Miami** office (5975 Sunset Drive #305, Miami, FL 33143, tel. 786/621-2909, fax 786/621-2907, miami@visitmexico.com).

From Illinois, Indiana, Iowa, Kansas, Kentucky, Michigan, Minnesota, Missouri, Nebraska, North Dakota, Ohio, South Dakota, and Wisconsin, contact the **Chicago** office (225 North Michigan Ave., 18th Floor, Suite 1850, Chicago, IL 60601, tel. 312/228-0517, fax 312/228-0515, chicago@visitmexico.com).

From Connecticut, Delaware, Kentucky, Maine, Maryland, Massachusetts, New Hampshire, New Jersey, New York, Pennsylvania, Rhode Island, Vermont, Virginia, Washington D.C., and West Virginia, contact the **New York** office (400 Madison Avenue, Suite 11C, New York, NY 10017, tel. 212/308-2110, fax 212/308-9060, newyork@visitmexico.com).

From Ontario, Manitoba, and the Nunavut Territory, contact the **Toronto** office (2 Bloor St. West, Suite 1502, Toronto, Ontario M4W

---

the hot, hurried atmosphere of a border or airport immigration station.

Entry for Pets

A pile of red tape may delay the entry of dogs, cats, and other pets into Mexico. Be prepared with veterinary-stamped health and rabies certificates for each animal. For more information, contact your regional Mexico Tourism Board (see the sidebar *Mexico Tourism Board Offices*), or your local Mexican Consulate.

Don't Lose Your Tourist Card

If you do, be prepared with a copy of the original, which you should present to the nearest federal Migración (Immigration) office (on duty at Oaxaca City, Puerto Escondido, and Huatulco airports) and ask for a duplicate tourist permit. Lacking this, you might present some alternate proof of your date of arrival in Mexico, such as a stamped passport or airline ticket. Savvy travelers carry copies of their tourist cards while leaving the original safe in their hotel rooms.

Car Permits

If you drive to Mexico, you will need a permit for your car. Upon entry into Mexico, be ready

3E2, tel. 416/925-0704, fax 416/925-6061, toronto@visitmexico.com).

From New Brunswick, Newfoundland, Nova Scotia, Prince Edward Island, and Quebec, contact the **Montreal** office (1 Place Ville Marie, Suite 1931, Montreal, Quebec H3B2C3, tel. 514/871-1052 or 514/871-1103, fax 514/871-3825, montreal@visitmexico.com).

IN EUROPE

In Europe, travelers may either contact the all-Europe Mexico tourism information (tel. 00-800/111-2266, www.visitmexico.com) or contact the local offices directly.

London: Wakefield House, 41 Trinity Square, London EC3N 4DJ, England, UK, tel. 207/488-9392, fax 207/265-0704, uk@visitmexico.com.

Frankfurt: Taunusanlage 21, D-60325 Frankfurt-am-Main, Deutschland, tel. 697/103-3383, fax 697/103-3755, germany@visitmexico.com.

Paris: 4 Rue Notre-Dame des Victoires, 75002 Paris, France, tel. 1/428-69612, 1/428-69613, fax 1/428-60580, france@visitmexico.com.

Madrid: Calle Velázquez 126, 28006 Madrid, España, tel. 91/561-3520, 91/561-1827, fax 91/411-0759, spain@visitmexico.com.

Rome: Via Barbarini 3-piso 7, 00187 Roma, Italia, tel. 06/487-4698, fax 06/487-3630, fax 06/420-4293, italy@visitmexico.com.

IN SOUTH AMERICA

Contact the Mexico Tourism Board in Brazil, Argentina, or Chile.

Sao Paulo: Alameda Administrativo, Rocha Azevedo 882, Conjunto 31, Tercer Andador, Sao Paulo, Brazil, 01410-002, tel. 3088-2129, fax 3083-5005, brasil@visitmexico.com.

Buenos Aires: Avenida Santa Fe 920, 1054 Buenos Aires, Argentina, tel. 1/4393-7070, 1/4393-8235, fax 1/4393-6607, argentina@visitmexico.com.

Santiago: Felix de Amesti #128, primer piso, Los Condes, Santiago de Chile, tel. 562/583-8426, fax 562/583-8425, chile@visitmexico.com.

IN ASIA

Contact the Mexico Tourism Board in either Japan or China.

Tokyo: 2-15-1-3F, Nagata-Cho, 2-chome, Chiyoda-ku, Tokyo, Japan 100-0014, tel. 335/030-290, fax 335/030-643, japan@visitmexico.com.

Beijing: San Li Dongwajie 5, Chaoyang 100600, Beijing, Peoples Republic of China, tel./fax 106/532-1717, 106/532-1744, jamezcua@visitmexico.com.

with originals and copies of your proof-of-ownership or registration papers (state title certificate, registration, or notarized bill of sale), current license plates, and current driver's license. The auto permit fee runs about $30, payable only by non-Mexican bank MasterCard, Visa, or American Express credit cards. (The credit-card-only requirement discourages those who sell or abandon U.S.-registered cars in Mexico without paying customs duties.) Credit cards must bear the same name as the vehicle proof-of-ownership papers.

The resulting car permit becomes part of the owner's tourist card and receives the same length of validity. Vehicles registered in the name of an organization or person other than the driver must be accompanied by a notarized affidavit authorizing the driver to use the car in Mexico for a specific time.

Border officials generally allow you to carry or tow additional motorized vehicles (motorcycle, another car, large boat) into Mexico but will probably require separate documentation and fee for each vehicle. If a Mexican official desires to inspect your trailer or RV, go through it with him.

Accessories, such as a small trailer, boat shorter than six feet, CB radio, or outboard motor, may be noted on the car permit and must leave Mexico with the car.

For more details on motor vehicle entry and what you may bring in your baggage to Mexico, you might also consult the AAA (American Automobile Association) *Mexico TravelBook.* See the *Unique Guide and Tip Books* section in *Suggested Reading* at the end of this book.

Since Mexico does not recognize foreign automobile insurance, you must buy Mexican automobile insurance. (For more information on this and other details of driving in Mexico, see *Getting There* earlier in this chapter.)

Crossing the Border and Returning Home

Squeezing through border bottlenecks during peak holidays and rush hours can be time-consuming. Avoid crossing 7–9 A.M. and 4:30–6:30 P.M.

Just before returning across the border with your car, park and have a customs *(aduana)* official **remove and cancel the holographic identity sticker that you received on entry.** If possible, get a receipt *(recibo)* or some kind of verification that it's been canceled *(cancelado).* Tourists have been fined hundreds of dollars for inadvertently carrying uncanceled car entry stickers on their windshields.

At the same time, return all other Mexican permits, such as tourist cards and hunting and fishing licenses. Also, be prepared for Mexico exit inspection, especially for cultural artifacts and works of art, which may require exit permits. Certain religious and pre-Columbian artifacts, legally the property of the Mexican government, cannot be taken from the country.

If you entered Mexico with your car, you cannot legally leave without it except by permission from local customs authorities, usually the Aduana (Customs House) or the Oficina Federal de Hacienda (Federal Treasury Office).

All returnees are subject to U.S. immigration and customs inspection. These inspections have become generally more time-consuming since September 11, 2001. The worst bottlenecks are at busy border crossings, especially Tijuana and, to a lesser extent, Mexicali, Nogales, Juárez, Nuevo Laredo, and Matamoros, all of which should be avoided during peak hours.

United States law allows a fixed value ($400 at present) of duty-free goods per returnee. This may include no more than one liter of alcoholic spirits, 200 cigarettes, and 100 cigars. A flat 10 percent duty will be applied to the first $1,000 (fair retail value, save your receipts) in excess of your $400 exemption. You may, however, mail packages (up to $100 value each) of gifts duty-free to friends and relatives in the United States. Make sure to clearly write "unsolicited gift" and a list of the value and contents on the outside of the package. Perfumes (over $5), alcoholic beverages, and tobacco may not be included in such packages.

Improve the security of such mailed packages by sending them by Mexpost class, similar to U.S. Express Mail service. Even better (but much more expensive), send them by Federal Express or DHL international couriers, which maintain offices in Oaxaca City, Puerto Escondido, Huatulco, Tuxtepec, Salina Cruz, Juchitan, and other larger Oaxaca towns.

U.S. Government Customs and Wildlife Information

For more information on U.S. customs regulations important to travelers abroad, read or download the useful pamphlet *Know Before You Go,* by visiting the U.S. Customs and Border Patrol website (www.cpb.gov). Click on "Travel" at the top of the home page, then scroll down to *Know Before You Go.*

For more information on the importation of endangered wildlife products, contact the Fish and Wildlife Service (1849 C. St. NW, Washington, DC 20240, toll-free tel. 800/344-WILD, www.fws.gov).

Recreation

ON THE BEACH

It's easy to understand why many Oaxaca vacationers stay right at the beach. And not just at the popular crystalline stretches around the Bahías de Huatulco, Puerto Ángel, and Puerto Escondido. Some adventurers flee the resorts to find even more pristine strands hidden in far corners along the entire Oaxaca coast. There they discover solitude and wildlife-rich shorelines varying from mangrove-edged lagoons and algae-decorated tidepools to shoals of pebbles and sand of a dozen colors and consistencies.

Sand makes the beach, and Oaxaca has plenty, from warm, black mica dust to cool, velvety white coral. Some beaches drop steeply to turbulent, close-in surf fine for fishing. Others are level, with gentle, rolling breakers made for surfing and swimming.

Oaxaca's beaches yield fascinating troves of shells and treasures of flotsam and jetsam. **Beachcombing** is more rewarding during the summer storm season when big waves deposit acres of fresh shells—among them clams, combs of Venus, conch, cowries, limpets, olives, sand dollars, scallops, starfish, and whelks.

During the summer–fall rainy season, beaches near river mouths are often fantastic outdoor galleries of wind- and water-sculpted snags and giant logs deposited by the downstream flood.

Viewing Wildlife

Wildlife watchers should keep quiet and always be on the alert. Animal survival depends on them seeing you first. Occasional spectacular offshore sights, such as whales, dolphins, and manta rays, or an onshore giant constrictor, beached squid or octopus, crocodile, or even a

© BRUCE WHIPPERMAN

Playa Mazunte's broad curve seems made for long beach strolls.

jaguar looking for turtle eggs may reward those prepared to wait and watch for them. Don't forget your binoculars and Steve Howell and Sophie Webb's *A Guide to the Birds of Mexico and Northern America.*

WATER SPORTS

Swimming, surfing, windsurfing, snorkeling, scuba diving, and kayaking are Oaxaca's water sports of choice. For details on local conditions, favorite spots, equipment, and rental shops, see the destination chapters of this book.

Safety First

As viewed from Oaxaca beaches, the Pacific Ocean usually lives up to its name. Many protected inlets, safe for child's play, dot the coastline. Unsheltered shorelines, on the other hand, can be deceiving. Smooth water in the calm forenoon often changes to choppy in the afternoon; calm ripples lapping the shore in March can grow to hurricane-driven walls of water in November. Such storms can wash away sand, changing a wide gently sloping beach into a steep rocky one plagued by turbulent waves and treacherous currents.

Undertow, whirlpools, crosscurrents, and occasional oversized waves can make ocean swimming a fast-lane adventure. Getting unexpectedly swept out to sea or hammered onto the beach bottom by a surprise breaker are potential hazards.

Never attempt serious swimming when tipsy or full of food; *never* swim alone where someone can't see you. *Always* swim beyond the breakers (which come in sets of several, climaxed by a big one, which breaks highest and farthest from the beach). If you happen to get caught in the path of such a breaker, avoid it by diving under and letting it roll harmlessly over you. If you do get caught by a serious breaker, try to roll and tumble with it (as football players tumble) to avoid injury.

Poisonous sea snakes, although rare and shy, do inhabit Oaxaca waters. Much more common, especially around submerged rocks, is the **moray eel.** Don't stick your fingers or toes in any concealed cracks.

Now and then, swimmers get a nettle-like **jellyfish sting.** Be careful around coral reefs and beds of sea urchins; corals can sting (like jellyfish), and you can get infections from coral cuts and sea-urchin spines. Shuffle along sandy bottoms to scare away stingrays before stepping on one. If you're unlucky, its venomous tail-spines may inflict a painful wound.

For advice on what to do if you suffer a coral scratch or jellyfish sting or become injured from sea-urchin spines and sting-rays, see *Sea Creatures* in the *Health and Safety* section later in this chapter.

Snorkeling and Scuba Diving

Many exciting clear-water sites, such as the **Bahías de Huatulco** and **Playa Estacahuite** near Puerto Ángel and **Playa Angelito** near Puerto Escondido, await both beginner and expert snorkelers and divers. Veteran divers usually arrive during the dry winter and early spring when river outflows are mere trickles, leaving offshore waters clear. In Huatulco and Puerto Escondido, professional dive shops rent equipment, provide lessons and guides, and transport divers to choice sites.

While convenient, rented equipment is often less than satisfactory. To be sure, serious divers bring their own gear. This might include wetsuits in the winter, when some swimmers begin to feel cold after an unprotected half hour in the water.

Surfing, Sailing, Windsurfing, and Kayaking

Oaxaca has the Mexican Pacific's acknowledged best (but most challenging) surfing beach, the renowned **Playa Zicatela** "pipeline" at Puerto Escondido. The surf everywhere is highest and most exciting during the July–November hurricane season, when big swells from storms far out at sea attract platoons of surfers to favored beaches.

Other lesser but still popular intermediate-level surfing spots are **Playa Zipolite** near Puerto Ángel, **La Boca** at Huatulco, and Playa Chacahua, an hour's drive west of Puerto Escondido.

SPRINGS, CAVES, AND WATERFALLS

A trove of crystalline springs *(aguas termales)*, limestone caves *(grutas)*, and gushing waterfalls *(cascadas)* fills the state of Oaxaca. Refer to the specific destination chapters for details (* means especially recommended).

- **The Valley of Oaxaca:** *Hierve El Agua, *San Sebastián de las Grutas

- **Pacific Resorts and Southern Sierra:** Chacalapa, Balneario El Paraíso, Aguas Termales Atotonilco, Charquito Atotonilco Warm Springs

- **The Mixteca:** *Apoala, *Tamazulapan, Juxtlahuaca (*Laguna Encantada, *San Miguel de la Cueva), Yosundua (Cascada Esmeralda)

- **Northern Oaxaca:** Ixtlán de Juárez (Arco de Yagela), Valle Nacional (*Balnearios Monte Flor and El Zuzul), San José Chiltepec, Jalapa de Díaz (*Río Uluapa), Huautla de Jiménez (Las Regaderas, *Nindo-Da-Gé, and Sotano de San Agustín)

- **The Isthmus:** Jalapa del Marqués, *Magdalena Tlacotepec, *Santiago Laollaga

---

Sailboarders and sailboaters can often find the moderately breezy conditions that they love during the Oaxaca winter or spring. Then they gather to enjoy the near-ideal conditions at many coves and inlets near the resorts.

Kayakers who, by contrast, are happiest in tranquil waters, also do well in the winter and spring in sheltered coastal bays and coves, notably the **Bahías de Huatulco.** Mangrove lagoons, furthermore, especially **Laguna Manialtepec** near Puerto Escondido, and Laguna Chacahua farther west, or Laguna Corrallero, near Pinotepa Nacional, near Oaxaca's western border, offer abundant kayaking opportunities.

While beginners can have fun with the equipment available from rental shops, serious surfers, sailboarders, sailboaters, and kayakers should pack their own gear.

POWER SPORTS

Power sports, such as waterskiing, parasailing, and personal watercraft riding, are not widespread on Oaxaca beaches. In parasailing, a motorboat pulls while a parachute lifts you, like a soaring gull, high over the ocean. After 10 minutes, they deposit you (usually gently) back on the sand. Personal watercraft are like snowmobiles except they operate on water, where, with a little practice, even beginners can quickly learn to whiz over the waves.

Although the luxury hotels at Huatulco provide experienced crews and equipment for such activities, practice while sober and with caution. Moreover, you, as the paying patron, have a right to expect that your providers and crew are themselves both cautious and sober besides being well equipped.

Beach Buggies and ATVs

Some visitors enjoy racing along the beach and rolling over dunes with beach buggies and ATVs (all-terrain vehicles—*motos* in Mexico); balloon-tired, three- or four-wheeled motor scooters; and mini-jeeps. While certain resort rental agencies cater to the growing use of such vehicles, limits are in order. Of all the proliferating high horsepower beach pastimes, these are the most intrusive. Noise, exhaust and gasoline pollution, injuries to operators and bystanders, and scattering of wildlife and destruction of their habitats have led (and I hope will continue to lead) to the restriction of beach buggies and ATVs on beaches and in forest habitats.

TENNIS AND GOLF

Most Oaxacans are working too hard to be playing much tennis and golf. Consequently, tennis and golf courses are nearly completely restricted to Oaxaca City and the Bahías de Huatulco. If you are planning on a lot of golf and tennis, check into one of the several

FISH

A bounty of fish dart, swarm, jump, and wriggle in Oaxaca's surf, reefs, lagoons, and offshore depths. While many make delicious dinners (albacore, red snapper, pompano), others are tough (sailfish), bony (bonefish), and even poisonous (puffers). Some grow to half-ton giants (marlin, Goliath fish), while others are diminutive reef-grazers (parrot fish, damselfish, angelfish) whose bright colors delight snorkelers and divers. Here's a sampling of what you might find underwater or on your dinner plate.

- **albacore** *(albacora, atún):* 2–4 feet in size; blue; found in deep waters; excellent taste
- **angelfish** *(angel):* one foot; yellow, orange, blue; reef fish*
- **barracuda** *(barracuda, picuda):* two feet; brown; deep waters; good taste
- **black marlin** *(marlin negro):* six feet; blue-black; deep waters; good taste
- **blue marlin** *(marlin azul):* eight feet; blue; deep waters; poor taste
- **bobo** *(barbudo):* one foot; blue, yellow; found in surf; fair taste
- **bonefish** *(macabi):* one foot; blue or silver; found inshore; poor taste
- **bonito** *(bonito):* two feet; black; deep waters; good taste
- **butterfly fish** *(muñeca):* six inches; black, yellow; reef fish*

- **chub** *(chopa):* one foot; gray; reef fish; good taste
- **croaker** *(corvina):* two feet; brownish; found along inshore bottoms; rare and protected
- **damselfish** *(castañeta):* four inches; brown, blue, orange; reef fish*
- **dolphinfish, mahimahi** *(dorado):* three feet; green, gold; deep waters; excellent taste
- **grouper** *(garropa):* three feet; brown, rust; found offshore and in reefs; good taste
- **grunt** *(burro):* eight inches; black, gray; found in rocks, reefs*
- **jack** *(toro):* 1–2 feet; bluish-gray; offshore; good taste
- **mackerel** *(sierra):* two feet; gray with gold spots; offshore; good taste
- **mullet** *(lisa):* two feet; gray; found in sandy bays; good taste
- **needlefish** *(agujón):* three feet; blue-black; deep waters; good taste
- **Pacific porgy** *(pez de pluma):* 1–2 feet; tan; found along sandy shores; good taste
- **parrot fish** *(perico, pez loro):* one foot; green, pink, blue, orange; reef fish
- **pompano** *(pómpano):* one foot; gray; inshore bottoms; excellent taste
- **puffer** *(botete):* eight inches; brown; inshore; poisonous

Oaxaca City or Huatulco hotels with easy access to these facilities. Use of hotel tennis courts is sometimes included in your hotel tariff. If not, fees will run about $10 per hour. Golf greens fees, which begin at about $50 for 18 holes, are usually extra.

FISHING

Experts agree that the Oaxaca coast is a world-class deep-sea and surf fishing ground. Sportfishing enthusiasts routinely bring in dozens of species from among the several hundred that have been identified in Oaxaca waters.

Surf Fishing

Most good fishing beaches away from the immediate resort areas will typically have only a few locals (mostly with nets) and fewer visitors. Oaxacans do little sportfishing. Most either make their living from fishing or do none at all. Some local folks catch fish for supper with nets. Consequently, few Oaxaca shops sell fishing equipment. Plan to bring your own, including hooks, lures, line, and weights.

In any case, the cleaner the water, the more interesting your catch. On a good day, your

- **red snapper** *(huachinango, pargo):* 1-2 feet; reddish pink; deep waters; excellent taste
- **roosterfish** *(pez gallo):* three feet; black, blue; deep waters; excellent taste
- **sailfish** *(pez vela):* five feet; blue-black; deep waters; tough, poor taste
- **sardine** *(sardina):* eight inches; blue-black; offshore; good taste
- **sea bass** *(cabrilla):* 1-2 feet; brown, ruddy; reef and rock crevices; good taste
- **shark** *(tiburón):* 2-10 feet; black to blue; in- and offshore; good taste
- **snook** *(robalo):* 2-3 feet; black-brown; found in brackish lagoons; excellent taste
- **spadefish** *(chambo):* one foot; black-silver; found along sandy bottoms, reef fish*
- **swordfish** *(pez espada):* five feet; black to blue; deep waters; good taste
- **triggerfish** *(pez puerco):* 1-2 feet; blue, rust, brown, black; reef fish; excellent taste
- **wahoo** *(peto, guahu):* 2-5 feet; green to blue; deep waters; excellent taste
- **yellowfin tuna** *(atún amarilla):* 2-5 feet; blue, yellow; deep waters; excellent taste
- **yellowtail** *(jurel):* 2-4 feet; blue, yellow; offshore; excellent taste

*Fish that are generally too small to be considered edible.

A netful of fish caught inshore will generally contain both edible and non-edible, even poisonous, examples, such as the two speckled black puffers, at the top.

© BRUCE WHIPPERMAN

reward might be *sierras, cabrillas,* porgies, or pompanos pulled from the Oaxaca surf.

You can't have everything, however. Foreigners cannot legally take Mexican abalone, clams, coral, lobster, rock bass, sea fans, seashells, shrimp, or turtles. Nor are they supposed to buy them directly from fishermen.

Deep-Sea Fishing

Santa Cruz de Huatulco and, to a lesser extent, Puerto Escondido and Puerto Ángel, are well-known jumping-off-spots for the big prize marlin and sailfish.

A deep-sea boat charter generally includes the boat and crew for a full or half day, plus equipment and bait for 2–6 persons, not including food or drinks. The full-day price depends upon the season. Around Christmas and New Year's and before Easter (when reservations will be mandatory), a boat can run $400 at Huatulco, less during low season and at the other spots.

Renting an entire big boat is not the only choice. *Pangas,* outboard launches seating up to six passengers, are available for as little as $40, depending on the season. Once, six of my friends hired a *panga* for $50, had a great time, and came back with a boatload of big tuna, jack, and mackerel. A restaurant cooked them up as a banquet for a dozen of us in exchange for the extra fish, and I discovered for the first time how heavenly fresh *sierra veracruzana* can taste.

Bringing Your Own Boat

If you're going to be doing lots of fishing, your own boat may be your most flexible and economical option. One big advantage is you can go to the many excellent fishing grounds the charter boats do not frequent. Keep your equipment simple, scout around, and keep your eyes peeled and ears open for local regulations and customs, plus tide, wind, and fish-edibility information.

Fishing Licenses and Boat Permits

Anyone, regardless of age, who is either fishing or riding in a fishing boat in Mexico is required to have a fishing license. Although Mexican fishing licenses are obtainable from certain bait and tackle stores and car insurance agents or at government fishing offices everywhere along the coast, save yourself time and trouble by getting both your fishing licenses and boat permits by mail ahead of time from the Mexican Department of Fisheries. Call at least a month before departure (U.S. tel. 619/233-4324, fax 619/233-0344) and ask for (preferably faxed) applications and the fees (which are reasonably priced, but depend upon the period of validity and the fluctuating exchange rate). On the application, fill in the names (exactly as they appear on passports) of the people requesting licenses. Include a cashier's check or a money order for the exact amount, along with a stamped, self-addressed envelope. Address the application to the Mexican Department of Fisheries (Oficina de Pesca), 2550 5th Ave., Suite 15, San Diego, CA 92103-6622.

Freshwater Fishing

Oaxaca has four large reservoirs: Yosocuta, in the Mixteca near Huajuapan de León; Cerro de Oro and Miguel Alemán, in the north near Tuxtepec; and Benito Juárez Reservoir, in the Isthmus not far from Tehuántepec. Their shorelines are scenic and easily accessible, and their waters are home to several varieties, mostly *mojarra* (bass), plentiful enough for local folks to a make living cooking fish dinners.

Accommodations

Oaxaca has lodgings to suit every style and pocketbook: world-class resorts, small beachside hotels, bed-and-breakfasts, homey *casas de huéspedes* (guesthouses), friendly trailer parks, community-maintained tourist lodgings (see Tourist Yu'u and *Community Cabañas Ecoturísticas Accommodations* in the *Northern Oaxaca* chapter), and many miles of breezy beaches, ripe for camping.

In Oaxaca city, the busy **high seasons,** when hotel reservations are generally necessary, are July, Day of the Dead (late October through early November), and mid-December until Janurary 6, the Day of the Kings. On the coast, high seasons are also mid-December through January 6, plus mid-February through Easter, and the months of July and August. Excellent, quiet **low-season** times to visit anywhere in Oaxaca are November after the Day of the Dead and the month of January after January 6, when prices are low and the weather is consistently temperate and dry.

The dozens of accommodations described in this book are positive recommendations— checked out in detail—good choices from which you can pick according to your taste and purse.

Hotel Rates

The rates listed in this book are U.S. dollar

equivalents of peso prices, taxes included, as quoted by the hotel management at the time of writing. They are intended as a general guide only, and probably will only approximate the asking rate when you arrive. Some readers unfortunately try to bargain by telling desk clerks that, for example, the rate should be $30 because they read it in this book. This is unwise, because it makes hotel managers and clerks reluctant to quote rates for fear readers might hold their hotel responsible for such quotes. As private businesses, hotels are free to raise their rates; conversely, if the price is too high, customers are entitled to take their business elsewhere.

In Oaxaca, hotel rates depend strongly upon inflation and season. To cancel the effect of the fluctuating Mexican peso, rates are reported in U.S. dollars. However, when settling your hotel bill, you should always insist on paying in pesos cash or by credit card, which by law must be marked in pesos.

Websites listed in the *Internet Resources* section might be a useful supplement to the accommodations described in the destination chapters.

Saving Money

The hotel prices quoted here are **rack rates:** the maximum tariff, exclusive of packages and promotions, that you would pay if you walked in off the street and rented an unreserved room for one day. Savvy travelers seldom pay the maximum. Since most hotel clerks will tell you that their hotel doesn't give **discounts** *(discuentos)*, it's best not to use that forbidden word. Instead, always inquire if there are any **promotions or packages** *(promociones o paquetes,* proh-moh-see-OH-nays oh pah-KAY-tays)*. At any time other than the high seasons, you can generally bargain for a lowered price. Don't be shy; if the hotel asking price is $60, offer $40. At best, you'll get what you want; at worst, you can always take your business elsewhere. Often discounts (Shh!) come as one or two free days for a one-week stay. Promotional packages available during slack seasons sometimes include free extras, such as breakfast, a car rental, a boat tour, or a sports rental. A

travel agent and/or Internet travel site can be of great help in shopping around for such bargains.

You will virtually always save money if you deal in pesos only. Insist on booking your lodging for an agreed price in pesos and paying the resulting hotel bill in pesos, rather than dollars. The reason is that dollar rates quoted by hotels are often based on the hotel desk exchange rate, which is sometimes as much as 10 percent less favorable than the bank exchange rate. For example, if the desk clerk tells you your hotel bill is $1,000, instead of handing over the dollars, ask him or her how much it is in pesos. Using the desk conversion rate, the clerk might say something like 10,000 pesos (considerably less than the 11,000 pesos that the bank might give for your $1,000). Pay the 10,000 pesos or have the clerk mark 10,000 pesos on your credit card slip, and save yourself $90.

GUESTHOUSES, BED-AND-BREAKFASTS, AND HOMESTAYS

A growing fraction of Oaxaca City lodgings fall into these categories. On city residential side streets, often several blocks removed from the tourist zone, are many of the *casas de huéspedes* (guesthouses), bed-and-breakfasts, and homes where increasing numbers of families are renting rooms to visitors.

Such lodgings vary from scruffy to spic-and-span, humble to luxurious. At minimum, you can expect a plain room, a shared toilet and hot-water shower, and plenty of atmosphere for your money. Rates are highest in Oaxaca City and the Bahías de Huatulco, ranging between $20 and about $100 for two. Discounts are often available for long-term stays.

Note: Oaxaca bed-and-breakfasts are generally (but not always) rather expensive, since they are a lodging style sought out by mostly North American travelers accustomed to paying high prices. If you want to save money, check out the Mexican version of the same thing, the homier *casa de huéspedes.*

In addition to the guesthouse, bed-and-breakfast, and homestay-style lodgings listed in the destination chapters of this book, you should also consult the many classified advertisements of the local tourist newspapers, especially in Oaxaca City and Puerto Escondido, and travel websites in the destination chapters and the *Internet Resources* section of this book. Moreover, Spanish Language School, common in Oaxaca City, usually recommends a list of homestays (family accommodations) to their participants.

APARTMENTS AND HOUSE RENTALS

For longer stays in Oaxaca City, many visitors prefer the convenience and economy of an apartment or house rental. Choices vary, from spartan studios to deluxe homes big enough for entire extended families. Prices depend strongly upon season and amenities, from $350 per month for the cheapest to around $1,000 for the most luxurious.

At the low end, you can expect a clean, furnished apartment with kitchen and bathroom and once- or twice-a-week housecleaning service. Higher up the scale, houses vary from moderately luxurious homes to sky's-the-limit mansions, blooming with built-in designer luxuries, such as a swimming pool or tennis court, and including at least a gardener, cook, and maid.

Shopping Around

The *Oaxaca City* chapter of this book recommends several solid guesthouse, bed-and-breakfast, and apartment rentals. You can find many more through on-the-spot local contacts, such as the tourist newspapers' want ad sections, websites, neighborhood For Rent or *Renta* signs, and local listing agents. If you prefer making rental arrangements prior to arrival, you can usually email, fax, telephone, or write managers—many of whom speak English—directly, using the contact information given in the destination chapters of this book. Furthermore, the *Internet Resources* section of this book also recommends a number of apartment and house rental listing sources in Oaxaca City and Puerto Escondido.

COMMUNITY *CABAÑAS ECOTURÍSTICAS*

More than a dozen rural communities, mostly on the east side of the central Valley of Oaxaca, the Northern Sierra, and the Mixteca, encourage visitors to come and stay in their tourist lodges, called *cabañas ecoturísticas* (ecotouristic cabins). These are government-built, rustic but comfortable, modern-standard cabins, managed and maintained by a community-appointed *gerente* (manager). *Cabañas* typically have two separate one-room units that sleep up to six persons each and share a single flush toilet and shower-bath between them. Units rent for about $10–20 per night per person, or $30–50 per group, with towels, blankets, flush toilets, and hot-water showers.

For additional details on *cabañas,* see the specific destinations with *cabañas* in *The Valley of Oaxaca* chapter (Santa Ana del Valle, San Miguel del Valle, Hierve El Agua, San Sebastian de las Grutas), the *Northern Oaxaca* chapter (Benito Juárez, Cuajimoloyas, Los Llanos, Ixtepeji, Ixtlán de Juárez), and the *Mixteca* chapter (Apoala, San Miguel Tequixtepec, Tepelmeme de Morelos, Huamelulpan, and Yosocuta).

LOCAL HOTELS

Locally owned and operated hotels make up most of the recommendations of this book. Many veteran travelers find it hard to understand why people come to Oaxaca and spend $200 a day for a super-plush hotel room when simpler but comfortable alternatives run as little as $30.

In Oaxaca City, many such hotels are within easy walking distance of the town center, with its lovely plaza, restored old monuments, restaurants, and shops. In the Puerto Escondido and Puerto Ángel resorts, most of them are either right on the beach or very near it. Local hotels, which depend at least as much on Mexican tourists as foreigners, generally have clean, large rooms, often with private view balconies, ceiling fans, and toilet and hot-water bath or shower. What they often lack are the plush extras—air-conditioning, cable TV, phones, tennis courts, exercise gyms, spas, and saunas—of the luxury resorts.

Booking local hotels is straightforward. Many of them can be emailed and all of them can be dialed or faxed directly (from the United States, dial 011-52, followed by the telephone or fax number given in this book) for information and reservations. If your Spanish is rusty, ask for someone who speaks English (ask, in Spanish: *"¿Por favor, hay alguien que habla Inglés?"*—por fah-VOR, AY ahhl-ghee-AYN KAY AB-lah een-GLAYS?). Always ask about money-saving packages and promotions when reserving.

INTERNATIONAL-CLASS RESORTS

Oaxaca visitors enjoy several beautiful, well-managed international-class resort hotels in Oaxaca City and the Bahías de Huatulco. Their super-deluxe amenities, moreover, need not be overly expensive. While high-season room tariffs ordinarily run $100–300, low-season packages and promotions sometimes cut these prices by half or even more. Shop around for savings through travel agents, and by calling the hotels directly through the toll-free 800 numbers cited for each hotel in the Oaxaca City and Bahías de Huatulco accommodations sections.

CAMPING, *PALAPAS*, AND TRAILER PARKS

Although Oaxaca has only a sprinkling of formally maintained places for camping, many inviting beach and inland country spots are customarily used informally. For camping locations, see the maps at the beginning of each destination chapter. For descriptions and details, see specific destinations.

Beach Camping

Camping at beaches is popular among middle-class Mexican families, especially during the Christmas–New Year's week and during Semana Santa, the week before Easter. Other times, tent and RV campers usually find prospective camping spots uncrowded. The best beach spots typically have a shady palm grove for camping and a *palapa* (palm-thatched) restaurant that serves drinks and fresh seafood. (Heads up for falling coconuts, especially in the wind.) Cost for parking and tenting is often minimal, typically only the price of food at the restaurant.

Beach days are often perfect for swimming, strolling, and fishing; nights are usually balmy—too warm for a sleeping bag, but fine for a hammock (which allows more air circulation than a tent). Good tents, however, keep out mosquitoes and other pests, which may be further discouraged with good bug repellent. Tents are generally warm inside, requiring only a sheet or light blanket for cover.

As for **camping on isolated beaches,** opinions vary, from dire warnings of *bandidos* to bland assurances that all is peaceful along the coast. The truth is probably somewhere in between. Trouble is most likely to occur in the vicinity of resort towns, notoriously, on the outskirt beaches of Puerto Escondido, where a few local thugs have harassed isolated campers.

When scouting out a place to camp, a good general rule is to arrive early enough in the day to get a feel for the place. Buy a soda at the *palapa* or nearby store and take a stroll around. Say *"Buenos días"* to the people along the way; ask if the fishing is good: *"¿Pesca buena?"* Use your common sense. If the people seem friendly, ask if it's *seguro* (safe). If so, ask permission: *"¿Es bueno acampar acá?"* ("Is it OK to camp around here?"). You'll rarely be refused.

Beach *Palapas*

Visitors can still rent beachfront *palapas* (thatched houses) in Puerto Escondido and Zipolite, near Puerto Ángel, adjoining Mazunte and Ventanilla, and east of Puerto Escondido, at Roca Blanca and Playa Chacahua. Amenities typically include beds or hammocks, a shady thatched porch, cold running water, a kerosene stove, and shared toilets and showers, for $10 per day per person.

The bad news is that security has been a problem in some *palapas,* notably at Puerto

Escondido. The good news is that the Puerto Ángel area has some of the better *palapas,* such as Lo Cósmico and Shambhala. The best news of all is that *palapas* are usually right on the beach, so you can walk right out your front door onto the sand, where surf, shells, and sea-birds will be there to entertain you.

Mountain and Backcountry Camping

Oaxaca's mountain and rural backcountry offer additional camping opportunities. Private owners and communities maintain picnic areas and informal campgrounds at choice sites, such as springs, waterfalls, caves, *sabineras* (cypress groves), and on rivers and reservoir shorelines.

Invariably, such inland sites are on private (*particular*—par-tee-koo-LAHR) or communal land. As a courtesy, you should obtain permission to set up camp either from the site manager, the closest neighboring restaurant or house, or at the nearest *presidencia municipal* or *agencia.* Such permission, sometimes for a small fee, is usually granted almost automatically. Please reciprocate by keeping your campfire, if permitted, modest and under control, respecting local etiquette (don't swim or sunbathe in the nude), cleaning up thoroughly, and carrying away all your trash.

For an informative and entertaining discussion of camping in Mexico, check out *The People's Guide to Mexico* by Carl Franz.

RV Trailer Parks

Campers who prefer company to isolation usually stay in trailer parks. Oaxaca has five modest but recommendable RV trailer parks: two in Oaxaca City, two in Zipolite by the beach, near Puerto Ángel, and one in Puerto Escondido, on the beach. For more details, see the destinations chapters.

Food and Drink

Some travel to Mexico for the food. True Mexican food is old-fashioned, homestyle fare requiring many hours of loving preparation. Such food is short on meat and long on corn, beans, rice, tomatoes, chilies, spices, onions, eggs, and cheese.

Mexican food is the unique end-product of thousands of years of native tradition. It is based on corn—*teocentli,* the Aztec "food of the gods"—called *maíz* (mah-EES) by present-day Mexicans. In the past, the typical Mexican woman spent much of her time grinding and preparing corn: soaking the grain in limewater (which swells the kernels and removes the tough seed-coat) and grinding the bloated seeds into meal on a stone *metate.* Finally, she would pat the meal into tortillas and cook them on a hot, baked mud griddle.

Sages (men, no doubt) have wistfully imagined the gentle pat-pat-pat of women all over Mexico to be the heartbeat of Mexico, which they feared would someday cease. Fewer women these days make tortillas by hand. The gentle pat-pat-pat has been replaced by the whir and rattle of automatic tortilla-making machines in myriad *tortillerías,* where women and girls line up for their family's daily kilo-stack of tortillas.

Tortillas are to the Mexicans as rice is to the Chinese and bread to the French. A Mexican family meal, more often than not, is some mixture of sauce, meat, beans, cheese, and vegetables wrapped in a tortilla, which becomes the culinary be-all: the food, the dish, and the utensil all wrapped into one.

This most Mexican style of meal usually includes one or two of a number of specialties known by Mexicans as **antojitos** and known to everyone else as "Mexican food." These are the familiar burritos, chiles rellenos, enchiladas, guacamole, nachos, quesadillas, refried beans, tacos, tamales, and other combinations of beans, cheese, corn, eggs, meat, sauces, and spices that make up the menus of Mexican deep-fried pork-skin rinds *(chicharrones)*

restaurants in the United States and Canada. (For more about Oaxacan food in particular, see the sidebar *A Oaxacan Menu* in the *Oaxaca City* chapter.)

Hot or Not?

Much food served in Mexico is not "Mexican." Eating habits, as most other Mexican customs, depend upon social class. Upwardly mobile Mexicans typically shun the corn-based native food in favor of the European-style food of the Spanish colonial elite: chops, clams, cutlets, fish, omelets, pasta, potatoes, rice, soups, and steaks.

Such fare is often as bland as Des Moines on a summer Sunday afternoon. *"No picante"*—not spicy—is how the Mexicans describe bland food. *"Caliente"* or *"Calor,"* the Spanish words that describe "hot" water or weather, do not, in contrast to English usage, also imply spicy, or *picante.*

Vegetarian Food

Strictly vegetarian cooking is the exception in Mexico, although a few macrobiotic-vegetarian restaurants and health-food stores have opened in Oaxaca City, Puerto Escondido, Puerto Ángel, and Huatulco. Meat is such a delicacy for most Oaxacans that they can't understand why people would give it up voluntarily. If vegetable-lovers can manage with beans, cheese, corn, eggs, fruit, and *legumbres* (vegetables) and not be bothered by a bit of *manteca de cerdo* (pork fat), Mexican (and Oaxacan) cooking will suit them fine.

If you require strictly vegetable fare, all is not lost. Even a humble Mexican *comedor* or *fonda* will almost always be able to fill some hot corn tortillas with fresh diced tomatoes, avocados, and onions, add some piquant fresh *salsa,* and serve it all up as several tasty and nutritious hot tacos.

Seafood

Early chroniclers wrote that Aztec Emperor Moctezuma employed a platoon of runners to bring fresh fish 300 miles (480 km) from the sea to his court every day. On the Oaxaca

Pacific coast, fresh seafood is fortunately much more available from scores of shoreline establishments, ranging from thatched beach *palapas* to five-star hotel restaurants.

Oaxaca seafood is literally there for the taking. When strolling on the beach, I have seen well-fed, middle-class local vacationers breaking and eating oysters and mussels right off the rocks. Villagers up and down the coast use small nets (or bare hands) to retrieve a few fish for supper, while communal teams haul in big nets full of silvery, wriggling fish for sale right on the beach.

Despite the plenty, Oaxaca seafood prices reflect high worldwide demand, even at the humblest seaside *palapa*. The freshness and variety, however, make even the typical dishes seem bargains at any price.

Fruits and Juices

Squeezed vegetable and fruit juices (*jugos,* HOO-gohs) are among the widely available delights of Oaxaca. Among the many establishments—restaurants, cafés, and *loncherías*—willing to supply you with your favorite *jugo,* the *jugerías* (juice bars) are often the most fun. Colorful fruit piles usually mark *jugerías.* If you don't immediately spot your favorite fruit, ask anyway; it might be hidden in the refrigerator.

Besides your choice of pure juice, a *jugería* will often serve **licuados.** Into the juice, they whip powdered milk, your favorite fruit, ice, and sugar to taste for a creamy afternoon pick-me-up or evening dessert. One big favorite is a cool banana-chocolate *licuado,* which comes out tasting like a milk shake, minus the calories.

Alcoholic Drinks

The Aztecs usually sacrificed anyone caught drinking alcohol without permission. The later, more lenient, Spanish attitude toward getting *borracho* (soused) has led to a thriving Mexican renaissance of alcoholic beverages: *aguardiente,* Kahlua, *mescal, pulque,* and tequila. **Mescal,** distilled from the fermented juice of the maguey (century) plant, was introduced by the Spanish colonists in Oaxaca, where the best *mescales* are still made. Quality **tequila** (mostly made near Guadalajara) and *mescal* both come 76 proof (38 percent alcohol) and up. A small white worm, endemic to the maguey plant, is often added to each bottle of factory *mescal* for authenticity.

Pulque, although also made from the sap of the maguey, is locally brewed (but not distilled), to a small alcohol content, between beer and wine. The brewing houses are sacrosanct preserves, circumscribed by traditions that

---

CATCH OF THE DAY

- **Ceviche** (say-VEE-chay): a chopped raw fish appetizer as popular on Oaxaca beaches as sushi is on Tokyo side streets. Although it can contain anything from conch to octopus, the best ceviche consists of diced young *tiburón* (shark) or *sierra* (mackerel) fillet and plenty of fresh tomatoes, onions, garlic, and chilies, all doused with lime juice.

- **Filete de pescado:** fish fillet breaded (*empanizada*), sautéed *al mojo* (ahl-MOH-hoh) with butter and garlic, or smothered in *mole.*

- **Pescado frito** (pays-KAH-doh FREE-toh): fish, pan-fried whole; if you don't specify that it be cooked *a medio* (lightly), the fish may arrive well done, like a big, crunchy french fry.

- **Pescado veracruzana:** a favorite everywhere. Best with *huachinango* (red snapper) smothered in a savory tomato, onion, chili, and garlic sauce. *Pargo* (snapper), *mero* (grouper), and *cabrilla* (sea bass) are also popularly used in this and other specialties.

- **Shellfish:** *ostiones* (oysters) and *almejas* (clams) by the dozen, *langosta* (lobster) and *langostina* (crayfish) *asado* (broiled), *al vapor* (steamed), or *frito* (fried). Pots of fresh-boiled *camarones* (shrimp) are sometimes sold on the street by the kilo; restaurants will make them into *cóctel* (cocktail) or prepare them *en gabardinas* (breaded) at your request.

A TROVE OF FRUITS AND NUTS

Besides carrying the usual temperate fruits, *jugerías* and especially markets are seasonal sources of a number of exotic (followed by an *) varieties.

- **avocado** *(aguacate* – ah-wah-KAH-tay): Aztec aphrodisiac

- **banana** *(platano):* many kinds – big and small, red and yellow

- *chirimoya**: green scales, white pulp, sometimes called an *anona*

- *ciruela**: looks like (but tastes better than) a small yellow-to-red plum

- **coconut** *(coco):* coconut "milk," called *agua coco*, is a wonderful and healthy thirst quencher

- **grapes** *(uvas):* August–November season

- *guanabana**: looks, but doesn't taste, like a green mango

- **guava** *(guava):* delicious juice, widely available canned

- **lemon** *(lima real* – LEE-mah ray-AHL): uncommon and expensive; use lime instead

- **lime** *(limón* – lee-MOHN): abundant and cheap; douse salads with it

- *mamey** (mah-MAY): yellow, juicy fruit, excellent for jellies and preserves

- **mango:** king of fruit, in 100 varieties June–November

- **orange** *(naranja* – nah-RAHN-ha): often greenish-yellow skin but sweet and juicy

- **papaya:** said to aid digestion and healing

- **peach** *(durazno* – doo-RAHS-noh): delicious and widely available as canned juice and fruit

- **peanut** *(cacahuate* – kah-kah-WAH-tay): home roasted and cheap

- **pear** *(pera):* fall season

- **pecan** *(nuez):* for a treat, try freshly ground pecan butter

- *piña anona**: looks like a thin ear of corn without the husk; tastes like pineapple

- **pineapple** *(piña):* huge, luscious, and cheap

- **strawberry** *(fresa* – FRAY-sah): local favorite

- **tangerine** *(mandarina):* sweet, juicy, and common around Christmas

- **watermelon** *(sandía* – sahn-DEE-ah): perfect on a hot day

- **yaca** (YAH-kah): relative of the Asian jackfruit, with pebbly green skin, round, and as large as a football; yummy mild taste

- **zapote** (sah-POH-tay): yellow, fleshy fruit, said to induce sleep

- *zapote colorado**: brown skin, red, puckery fruit, like persimmon; commonly, but incorrectly, called *mamey*

Sandía (watermelon) is best during Mexico's rainy summer season.

© BRUCE WHIPPERMAN

Tepache (fermented sugar cane juice) and *pulque* (fermented juice of maguey) sell in native markets by the glass.

While *pulque* comes from an age-old indigenous tradition, **cerveza** (beer) is the beverage of modern mestizo Mexico. Full-bodied and tastier than "light" U.S. counterparts, Mexican beer enjoys an enviable reputation.

Those visitors who indulge usually know their favorite among the many brands, from light to dark: Superior, Corona, Pacífico, Tecate (served with lime), Carta Blanca, Modelo, Dos Equis, Bohemia, Tres Equis, and Negra Modelo. Nochebuena, a flavorful dark brew, becomes available only around Christmas.

Mexicans have yet to develop much of a taste for *vino* (wine), although some domestic wines, such as the Baja California labels Monte Xanic, Domecq, and Cetto, are often quite good and sometimes excellent.

Bread and Pastries

Excellent locally baked bread is a delightful surprise to many first-time visitors to Oaxaca. Small bakeries everywhere put out trays of hot, crispy-crusted **bolillos** (rolls) and sweet **panes dulces** (pastries). They range from simple cakes, muffins, cookies, and doughnuts to fancy fruit-filled turnovers and puffs. Half the fun occurs before the eating: Grab a tray and tongs, peruse the goodies, and pick out the most scrumptious. With your favorite dozen finally selected, you take your tray to the cashier, who deftly bags everything up and collects a few pesos (two or three dollars) for your whole mouthwatering selection.

exclude both women and outsiders. The brew, said to be full of nutrients, is sold to local *pulquerías* and drunk immediately. If you are ever invited into a *pulquería,* it will be an honor you cannot refuse.

Aguardiente, by contrast, is the notorious fiery Mexican "white lightning," a locally cane-fermented and distilled, dirt-cheap ticket to oblivion for poor Mexican men.

Tips for Travelers

Access for Travelers with Disabilities

Mexican airlines and hotels (especially the large ones) have become sensitive to the needs of travelers with disabilities. Open, street-level lobbies and large, wheelchair-accessible elevators and rooms are available in nearly all Pacific Mexico resort (and some smaller, especially boutique) hotels. Furthermore, most street-corner curbs accommodate wheelchairs.

Both Mexico and United States law forbids travel discrimination against otherwise qualified people with disabilities. As long as your disability is stable and not liable to deteriorate during passage, you can expect to be treated like any passenger with special needs.

Make reservations far ahead of departure and ask your agent to inform your airline of your needs, such as boarding wheelchair or in-

© BRUCE WHIPPERMAN

Monte Albán now has a wheelchair-accessible lift to the archaeological site's North Platform, near the main entrance.

flight oxygen. Be early at the gate to take advantage of the preboarding call.

For many helpful details to smooth your trip, get a copy of *Survival Strategies for Going Abroad* by Laura Hershey, published in 2005 by **Mobility International USA** (132 E. Broadway, Suite 343, Eugene, Oregon 9/401, tel. 541/343-1284 voice/TDD, fax 541/343-6812, www.miusa.org). Mobility International is a valuable resource for many disabled lovers of Mexico, for it encourages disabled travelers with a goldmine of information and literature and can provide them with valuable Mexico connections. They publish a regular newsletter and provide information and referrals for international exchanges and homestays.

Similarly, **Partners of the Americas** (1424 K St. NW, Suite 700, Washington, D.C. 20005, tel. 202/628-3300 or 800/322-7844, fax 202/628-3306, info@partners.net, www.partners.net), with chapters in 45 U.S. states, works to improve understanding of disabilities and facilities in Mexico and Latin America. It maintains communications with local organizations and individuals whom disabled travelers may contact at their destinations.

TRAVELING WITH CHILDREN

Children are treasured like gifts from heaven in Mexico. Traveling with kids will ensure your welcome most everywhere. On the beach, take extra precautions to make sure they are protected from the sun.

A sick child is no fun for anyone. Fortunately, clinics and good doctors are available even in most small towns. When in need, ask a storekeeper or a pharmacist, *"¿Dónde hay un doctor, por favor?"* ("¿DOHN-day eye oon doc-TOHR por fah-VOHR?"). In most cases, within five minutes you will be in the waiting room of the local physician or hospital.

Children who do not favor typical Mexican fare can easily be fed with always available eggs, cheese, *hamburguesas,* milk, oatmeal, corn flakes, bananas, cakes, and cookies.

Your children will generally have more fun if they have a little previous knowledge of Mexico

© BRUCE WHIPPERMAN

Kids love beaches, but protect them with sunscreen.

and a stake in the trip. For example, help them select some library picture books and magazines so they'll know where they're going and what to expect, or give them responsibility for packing and carrying their own small travel bag.

Be sure to mention your children's ages when making air reservations; child discounts of 50 percent or more are often available. Also, if you can arrange to go on an uncrowded flight, you can stretch out and rest on the empty seats.

For more details on traveling with children, check out *Adventuring with Children* by Nan Jeffries.

Senior Travelers

Age, according to Mark Twain, is a question of mind over matter: If you don't mind, it doesn't matter. Mexico is a country where whole extended families, from babies to great-grandparents, live together. Elderly travelers will benefit from the respect and understanding Mexicans accord to older people. Besides these encouragements, consider the number of retirees already in havens in Puerto Vallarta,

Guadalajara, Manzanillo, Oaxaca, and other regional centers.

Certain organizations support and sponsor senior travel. Leading the field is **Elderhostel** (11 Ave. de Lafayette, Boston, MA 02111-1746, toll-free tel. 800/454-5768, www.elderhostel .org). Request one of their Elderhostel U.S. and international catalogs of special tours, study, homestays, and people-to-people travel programs.

Some books also feature senior travel opportunities. One of the pithiest is *Unbelievably Good Deals and Great Adventures You Can't Have Unless You're Over 50,* by Joan Rattner Heilman, published by McGraw Hill (2003). Its 200 pages are packed with details of how to get bargains on cruises, tours, car rentals, lodgings, and much, much more.

For seniors with online access (as close as your neighborhood library these days) the **Internet** is a gold mine of senior-oriented travel information. For example, on the Google search engine (www.google.com) home page, I typed in "Senior Travel" and netted more than 90 million responses. Near the top of the list was the **Transitions Abroad** site (www.transitions abroad.com), which offers a gold mine of a sub-site (www.transitionsabroad.com/listings/travel/ senior) with a load of useful resources, centering around senior traveling and living abroad.

Gay and Lesbian Travelers

The great majority of visitors find Oaxaca people both gracious and tolerant. This extends from racial color-blindness to being broad-minded about sexual preference. As long as gay and lesbian visitors don't flaunt their own preference, they will find acceptance most anywhere in the state of Oaxaca.

As a result, both Oaxaca City and, to a smaller extent, the coastal resorts have acquired a growing company of gay- and lesbian-friendly hotels, bars, and entertainments. For example, for Oaxaca City hotel, restaurant, and nightlife details, visit the gay-oriented travel website www.go-oaxaca.com.

Some gay- and lesbian-oriented Internet and print publishers also offer excellent travel guidebooks. One of the most experienced is **Damron Company** (415/255-0404 or 800/462-6654, www.damron.com), which publishes, both in print and by Internet subscription, the *Damron Women's Travel* and *Damron Men's Travel* guidebooks, containing a wealth of gay and lesbian travel information, including some listings in Oaxaca.

If you're interested in more gay and lesbian travel information, advice, and services, check out the San Francisco **Purple Roofs** Internet agency (wheretostay@purpleroofs.com, www .purpleroofs.com). They offer Oaxaca hotel, nightlife, and travel agent listings, plus a multitude of services, from tours and air tickets, to travel insurance and hotel reservations.

Health and Safety

STAYING HEALTHY

In Oaxaca as everywhere, prevention is the best remedy for illness. For those visitors who confine their travel to the beaten path, a few basic common-sense precautions will ensure vacation enjoyment.

Resist the temptation to dive headlong into Mexico. It's no wonder that people get sick—broiling in the sun, gobbling peppery food, guzzling beer and margaritas, then discoing half the night—all in their first 24 hours. An alternative is to give your body time to adjust. Travelers often arrive tired and dehydrated from travel and heat. During the first few days, drink plenty of bottled water and juice, and take siestas.

Immunizations and Precautions

A good physician can recommend the proper preventatives for your Oaxaca trip. If you are going to stay pretty much in town, your doctor will probably suggest little more than updating your basic typhoid, diphtheria-tetanus, hepatitis, and polio shots.

For camping or trekking in remote tropical areas—below 4,000 feet/1,200 meters—doctors often recommend a gamma-globulin shot against hepatitis A and a schedule of chloroquine pills against malaria. While in backcountry areas, use other measures to discourage mosquitoes—and fleas, flies, ticks, no-see-ums, "kissing bugs" (see *Chagas' Disease and Dengue Fever* later in this chapter), and other tropical pesties—from biting you. Common precautions include sleeping under

mosquito netting, burning *espirales mosquito* (mosquito coils), and rubbing on plenty of pure DEET (n,n dimethyl-meta-toluamide) "jungle juice," mixed in equal parts with rubbing (70 percent isopropyl) alcohol. Although super-effective, 100 percent DEET dries and irritates the skin.

Sunburn

For sunburn protection, use a good sunscreen with a sun protection factor (SPF) rated 15 or more, which will reduce burning rays to one-fifteenth or less of direct sunlight. Better still, take a shady siesta-break from the sun during the most hazardous midday hours. If you do get burned, applying your sunburn lotion (or one of the "caine" creams) after the fact usually decreases the pain and speeds healing.

Safe Water and Food

Although municipalities have made great strides in sanitation, food and water are still potential sources of germs in some parts of Oaxaca. Although it's probably safe most everywhere, except in a few upcountry localities, it's still probably best to drink bottled water only. Hotels, whose success depends vitally on their customers' health, generally provide *agua purificada* (purified bottled water). If, for any reason, the available water is of doubtful quality, add a water purifier, such as "Potable Aqua" brand (get it at a camping goods stores before departure) or a few drops per quart of water of *blanqueador* (household chlorine bleach) or *yodo* (tincture of iodine) from the pharmacy.

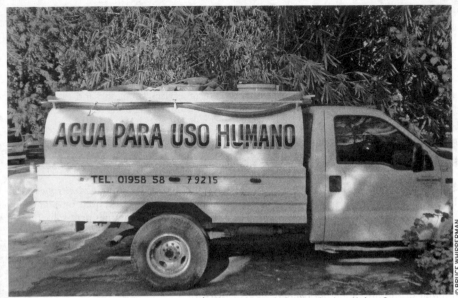

© BRUCE WHIPPERMAN

Drinking water is sometimes scarce and/or available only by truck at outlying Oaxaca villages and countryside.

Pure bottled water, soft drinks, beer, and fresh fruit juices are so widely available it is easy to avoid tap water, especially in restaurants. Ice and *paletas* (iced juice-on-a-stick) may be risky, especially in small towns.

Washing hands before eating in a restaurant is a time-honored Mexican ritual that visitors should religiously follow. The humblest Mexican eatery will generally provide a basin to *lavar las manos* (wash the hands). If it doesn't, don't eat there.

Hot, cooked food is generally safe, as are peeled fruits and vegetables. These days milk and cheese in Mexico are generally processed under sanitary conditions and sold pasteurized (ask, *"¿Pasteurizado?"*) and are typically safe. Mexican ice cream used to be both bad-tasting and of dubious safety, but national brands available in supermarkets are so much improved that it's no longer necessary to resist ice cream while in town.

In recent years, much cleaner public water and increased hygiene awareness have made salads—once shunned by Mexico travelers—generally safe to eat in tourist-frequented Oaxaca cafés and restaurants. Nevertheless, lettuce and cabbage, particularly in country villages, are more likely to be contaminated than tomatoes, carrots, cucumbers, onions, and green peppers. In any case, you can try dousing your salad in *vinagre* (vinegar) or plenty of sliced *limón* (lime) juice, the acidity of which kills some but not all bacteria.

First-Aid Kit

In the tropics, ordinary cuts and insect bites are more prone to infection and should receive immediate first aid. A first-aid kit with aspirin, rubbing alcohol, hydrogen peroxide, water-purifying tablets, household chlorine bleach or iodine for water purifying, swabs, bandages, gauze, adhesive tape, Ace bandage, chamomile *(manzanilla)* tea bags for upset stomachs, Pepto-Bismol, acidophilus tablets, antibiotic ointment, hydrocortisone cream, mosquito repellent, knife, and good tweezers is a good precaution for any traveler and mandatory for campers.

HEALTH PROBLEMS
Traveler's Diarrhea

Traveler's diarrhea (known in Southeast Asia as "Bali Belly" and in Mexico as *turista* or "Montezuma's Revenge") sometimes persists, even among prudent vacationers. You can suffer *turista* for a week after simply traveling from California to Philadelphia or New York. Doctors say the familiar symptoms of runny bowels, nausea, and sour stomach result from normal local bacterial strains to which newcomers' systems need time to adjust. Unfortunately, the dehydration and fatigue from heat and travel reduce your body's natural defenses and sometimes lead to a persistent cycle of sickness at a time when you least want it.

Time-tested protective measures can help your body either prevent or break this cycle. Many doctors and veteran travelers swear by Pepto-Bismol for soothing sore stomachs and stopping diarrhea. Acidophilus, the bacteria found in yogurt, is widely available in the United States in tablets and aids digestion. Warm *manzanilla* (chamomile) tea, used widely in Mexico (and by Peter Rabbit's mother), provides liquid and calms upset stomachs. Temporarily avoid coffee and alcohol, drink plenty of *manzanilla* tea, and eat bananas and rice for a few meals until your tummy can take regular food.

Although powerful antibiotics and antidiarrhea medications such as Lomotil and Imodium are readily available over *farmacia* counters, they may involve serious side effects and should not be taken in the absence of medical advice. If in doubt, consult a doctor.

Chagas' Disease and Dengue Fever

Chagas' disease, spread by the "kissing" (or, more appropriately, "assassin") bug, is a potential hazard in the Mexican tropics. Known locally as a *vinchuca,* the triangular-headed, three-quarter-inch (two-cm) brown insect, identifiable by its yellow-striped abdomen, often drops upon its sleeping victims from the thatched ceiling of a rural house at night. Its bite is followed by swelling, fever, and weakness and can lead to heart failure if left untreated. Application of drugs at an early stage can, however, clear the patient of the trypanosome parasites that infect victims' bloodstreams and vital organs. See a doctor immediately if you believe you're infected.

Most of the precautions against malaria-bearing mosquitoes also apply to dengue fever, which does occur (although uncommonly) in outlying tropical areas of Mexico. The culprit here is a virus carried by the mosquito species *Aedes aegypti.* Symptoms are acute fever, with chills, sweating, and muscle aches. A red, diffuse rash frequently results, which may later peel. Symptoms abate after about five days, but fatigue may persist. A particularly serious, but fortunately rare, form, called dengue hemorrhagic fever, afflicts children and can be fatal. See a doctor immediately. Although no vaccines or preventatives exist, other than deterring mosquitoes, you should nevertheless see a doctor immediately.

For more good tropical preventative information, get a copy of the excellent pamphlet distributed by the International Association of Medical Advice to Travelers (IAMAT, see *Medical Care* later in this section).

Scorpions and Snakes

While camping or staying in a *palapa* or other rustic accommodation, watch for scorpions, especially in your shoes, which you should shake out every morning. Scorpion stings and snakebites are rarely fatal to an adult but are potentially very serious for a child. Get the victim to a doctor calmly but quickly. (For more snakebite details, see *Reptiles and Amphibians* in the *Flora and Fauna* section of the *Background* chapter.)

Sea Creatures

While snorkeling or surfing, you may suffer a coral scratch or jellyfish sting. Experts advise you to wash the afflicted area with ocean water and pour alcohol (rubbing alcohol or tequila) over the wound, then apply hydrocortisone cream available from the *farmacia.*

Injuries from sea-urchin spines and sting-ray barbs are painful and can be serious. Physicians recommend similar first aid for both: remove the spines or barbs by hand or with tweezers, then soak the injury in as-hot-as-possible fresh water to weaken the toxins and provide relief. Another method is to rinse the area with an antibacterial solution—rubbing alcohol, vinegar, wine, or ammonia diluted with water. If none are available, the same effect may be achieved with urine, either your own or someone else's in your party. Get medical help immediately.

Tattoos

All health hazards don't come from the wild. A number of Mexico travelers have complained of complications from black henna tattoos. When enhanced by the chemical dye PPD, an itchy rash results that can lead to scarring. It's best to play it safe: If you must have a vacation tattoo, get it at an established, professional shop.

MEDICAL CARE

For medical advice and treatment, let your hotel (or if you're camping, the closest *farmacia*) refer you to a good doctor, clinic, or hospital. Mexican doctors, especially in medium-sized and small towns, practice like private doctors in the United States and Canada once did before health insurance, liability, and group practice. They will come to you if you request it; they often keep their doors open even after regular hours and charge reasonable fees.

You will receive generally good treatment at the many local hospitals in Oaxaca's tourist centers and larger towns. If you must have an English-speaking, American-trained doctor, the **International Association for Medical Assistance to Travelers (IAMAT)** publishes an updated booklet of qualified member physicians, some of whom practice in Oaxaca City, Puerto Escondido, and Huatulco. IAMAT (1623 Military Road, #279, Niagra Falls, NY 14304, tel. 716/754-4883; or in Canada at 40 Regal Rd., Guelph, Ontario N1K 1B5, tel. 519/836-0102, or 1287 St. Clair Ave. W, Toronto, Ontario M6E 1B8, tel. 416/652-0137, info@iamat.org or www.iamat.org) also

---

MEDICAL TAGS AND AIR EVACUATION

Travelers with special medical problems should consider wearing a medical identification tag. For a reasonable fee, **Medic Alert** (2323 Colorado Ave., Turlock, CA 953812, California 95382, tel. 209/668-3333, toll-free tel. 888/633-4398, www.medicalert.org) provides such tags, as well as an information hotline that will inform doctors of your vital medical background.

In life-threatening emergencies, highly recommended **Aeromedevac** (Gillespie Field Airport, 681 Kenney St., El Cajon, CA 92020, toll-free tel. 800/462-0911, from Mexico 24-hr.toll-free tel. 001-800/832-5087, www.aeromedevac.com) provides high-tech jet ambulance service from any Mexican locale to a U.S. hospital for roughly $20,000.

Alternatively, you might consider the similar services of **Med-Jet Assistance** (Birmingham, Alabama, Intl. Airport, 4900 69th St., Birmingham AL, 35206, toll-free U.S. tel. 800/963-3538, www.medjet.com; in emergencies, world-wide, call U.S. tel. 205/595-6626 collect).

---

distributes a very detailed *How to Protect Yourself Against Malaria* guide, together with worldwide malaria risk and communicable disease charts.

For more useful information on health and safety in Mexico, consult Drs. Robert H. Paige and Curtis P. Page's *Mexico: Health and Safety Travel Guide* (Tempe AZ, Med to Go Books, 2004) and Dirk Schroeder's *Staying Healthy in Asia, Africa, and Latin America* (Berkeley, CA: Avalon Travel Publishing, 2000).

SAFETY

Occasional knifepoint robberies and muggings have marred the once-peaceful Puerto Escondido nighttime beach scene. Walk alone and you invite trouble, especially along Playa Bachoco and the unlit stretch of Playa

Principal between the east end of the *adoquín* and the Hotel Santa Fe. If you have dinner alone at the Hotel Santa Fe, avoid the beach and return by taxi or walk along the highway to Pérez Gasga back to your hotel.

Fortunately, such problems seem to be confined to the beach. Visitors are quite safe on the Puerto Escondido streets themselves, often more so than on their own city streets back home.

Safe Conduct

Mexico is an old-fashioned country where people value traditional ideals of honesty, fidelity, and piety. Crime rates are low; visitors are often safer in Mexico than in their home cities.

This applies even more strongly in Oaxaca. Don't be scared away by headlines about kidnappings and drug-related murders in border cities such as Tijuana and Ciudad Juárez, or car hijackings in bad Mexico City neighborhoods. Violent crime is nearly unknown in Oaxaca City. Around the *zócalo,* women are often seen walking home alone at night. Nevertheless, some Oaxaca neighborhoods are friendlier than others. If you find yourself walking in a locality at night that doesn't feel too welcoming, do not hesitate to hail a taxi.

Although Oaxaca is very safe with respect to violent crime, you should still take normal precautions against petty theft. Stow your valuables in your hotel safe, don't wear showy jewelry or display wads of money, and especially at a crowded market, keep your camera and valuables protected in a waist belt, secure purse, or zipped pockets. If you're parking your car for the night, do it in a secure garage or a guarded hotel parking lot.

Even though four generations have elapsed since Pancho Villa raided the U.S. border, the image of a Mexico bristling with *bandidos* persists. And similarly for Mexicans: despite the century and a half since the *yanquis* invaded Mexico City and took half their country, the communal Mexican psyche still views gringos (and, by association, all white foreigners) with revulsion, jealousy, and wonder.

Fortunately, the Mexican love-hate affair with foreigners does not usually apply to individual visitors. Your friendly *"buenos días"* ("good morning") or *"por favor"* ("please"), when appropriate, is always appreciated, whether in the market, the gas station, or the hotel. The shy smile you will most likely receive in return will be your small, but not insignificant, reward.

Women

Your own behavior, despite low crime statistics, largely determines your safety in Mexico. For women traveling solo, it is important to realize that the double standard is alive and well in Mexico. Dress and behave modestly and you will most likely avoid embarrassment. Whenever possible, stay in the company of friends or acquaintances; find companions for beach, sightseeing, and shopping excursions. Ignore strange men's solicitations and overtures. A Mexican man on the prowl will invent the sappiest romantic overtures to snare a gringa. He will often interpret anything but a firm "no" as a "maybe," and a "maybe" as a "yes."

Men

For male visitors, alcohol often leads to trouble. Avoid bars and cantinas; and if, given Mexico's excellent beers, you can't abstain completely, at least maintain soft-spoken self-control in the face of challenges from macho drunks.

The Law and Police

While Mexican authorities are tolerant of alcohol, they are decidedly intolerant of other substances such as marijuana, psychedelics, cocaine, and heroin. Getting caught with such drugs in Mexico usually leads to swift and severe results.

Equally swift is the punishment for nude sunbathing, which is both illegal in public and offensive to Mexicans. Confine your nudist colony to very private locations.

Although with decreasing frequency lately, traffic police in Oaxaca sometimes seem to watch foreign cars with eagle eyes. Officers seem to inhabit busy intersections and one-way streets, waiting for confused tourists to

MACHISMO

I once met an Acapulco man who wore five gold wristwatches and became angry when I quietly refused his repeated invitations to get drunk with him. Another time, on the beach near San Blas, two drunken campesinos nearly attacked me because I was helping my girlfriend cook a picnic dinner. Outside Taxco I once spent an endless hour in the seat behind a bus driver who insisted on speeding down the middle of the two-lane highway, honking aside oncoming automobiles.

Despite their wide differences (the first was a rich criollo, the campesinos were *indígenas,* and the bus driver mestizo), the common affliction shared by all four men was machismo, a disease that seems to possess many Mexican men.

Machismo is a sometimes reckless obsession to prove one's masculinity, to show how *macho* one is. Men of many nationalities share the instinct to prove themselves. Japan's *bushido* samurai code is one example. Mexican men, however, often seem to try the hardest.

When confronted by a Mexican braggart, male visitors should remain careful and controlled. If your opponent is yelling, stay cool, speak softly, and withdraw as soon as possible. On the highway, be courteous and unprovocative; don't use your car to spar with a macho driver. Drinking often leads to problems. It's best to stay out of bars or cantinas unless you're prepared to deal with the macho consequences. Polite refusal of a drink may be taken as a challenge. If you visit a bar with Mexican friends or acquaintances, you may be heading for a no-win choice of a drunken all-night *borrachera* (binge) or an insult to the honor of your friends by refusing.

For women, machismo also requires cautious behavior. In Mexico, women's liberation is long in coming. Few women hold positions of power in business or politics. Machismo requires that female visitors obey the rules or suffer the consequences. Keep a low profile; wear bathing suits and brief shorts only at the beach. Follow the example of your Mexican sisters: Make a habit of going out in the company of friends or acquaintances, especially at night. Mexican men believe an unaccompanied woman wants to be picked up. Ignore such offers; any response, even refusal, might be taken as a "maybe." If, on the other hand, there is a Mexican man whom you'd genuinely like to meet, the traditional way is an arranged introduction through family or friends.

Mexican families, as a source of protection and friendship, should not be overlooked – especially on the beach or in the park, where, among the gaggle of kids, grandparents, aunts, and cousins, there's room for one more.

make a wrong move. If they whistle you over, stop immediately or you will really get into hot water. If guilty, say *"Lo siento"* ("I'm sorry") and be cooperative. Although the officer probably won't mention it, he or she is usually hoping that you'll cough up a $20 *mordida* (bribe) for the privilege of driving away. Don't do it. Although he may hint at confiscating your car, calmly ask for an official *boleto* (written traffic ticket), if you're guilty, in exchange for your driver's license (have a copy), which the officer will probably keep if he writes a ticket. If after a few minutes no money appears, the officer will most likely give you back your driver's license rather than go to the trouble of writing the ticket. If not, the worst that usually will happen is you will have to go to the *presidencia municipal* (city hall) the next morning and pay the $20 to a clerk in exchange for your driver's license.

The customarily tranquil state of Oaxaca has occasionally experienced episodes of public unrest. Recent conflicts have been the result of the longstanding backlog of unsettled grievances that run from local land disputes and protest strikes by underpaid teachers, such as the teacher strike that paralyzed Oaxaca City for several months during 2006, all the way up to unsolved political kidnappings and assassinations.

In recent years, the aggrieved, often local community delegations have petitioned local authorities for redress and set up camp in plain view for visitors to see in the Oaxaca *zócalo*. There is no reason for visitors to be alarmed about such lawful demonstrations as long as they remain peaceful. During 1996–2006, such protests were generally tolerated by local Oaxaca authorities and could be considered a positive sign of a maturing Oaxacan democracy.

Pedestrian and Driving Hazards

Although Oaxaca's potholed pavements and "holey" sidewalks won't land you in jail, one of them might send you to the hospital if you don't watch your step, especially at night. "Pedestrian beware" is especially good advice on Mexican streets, where it is rumored that some drivers speed up rather than slow down when they spot a tourist stepping off the curb. Falling coconuts, especially frequent on windy days, constitute an additional hazard to unwary campers and beachgoers.

Driving Mexican country roads, where slow trucks and carts block lanes, campesinos stroll the shoulders, and horses, burros, and cattle wander at will, is hazardous—doubly so at night.

Information and Services

MONEY
The Peso: Down and Up

Overnight in early 1993, the Mexican government shifted its monetary decimal point three places and created the "new" peso (now known simply as the "peso"), which, at this writing, trades at about 11 per U.S. dollar. Since the peso value sometimes changes rapidly, U.S. dollars have become a much more stable indicator of Mexican prices; for this reason they are used in this book to report prices. You should, nevertheless, always use pesos to pay for everything in Mexico.

Since the introduction of the new peso, the centavo (one-hundredth of a new peso) has reappeared, in coins of 10, 20, and 50 centavos. Incidentally, the dollar sign, "$," also marks Mexican pesos. Peso coins *(monedas)* in denominations of 1, 2, 5, 10, and 20 pesos, and bills, in denominations of 20, 50, 100, 200, and 500 pesos, are common. Since banks like to exchange your travelers checks for a few crisp large bills rather than the often-tattered smaller denominations, ask for some of your change in 50- and 100-peso notes. A 500-peso note, while common at the bank, may look awfully big to a small shopkeeper, who might be hard-pressed to change it.

Banks, ATMs, and Money-Exchange Offices

Mexican banks, like their North American counterparts, have lengthened their business hours. Hong Kong Shanghai Banking Corporation (HSBC) maintains the longest hours: as long as Mon.–Sat. 8 A.M.–7 P.M. Banamex (Banco Nacional de Mexico), generally the most popular with local people, usually posts the best in-town dollar exchange rate in its lobbies; for example: *Tipo de cambio: venta 10.799, compra 10.933*, which means it will sell pesos to you at the rate of 10.799 per dollar and buy them back for 10.933 per dollar.

ATMs (automated teller machines), or *cajeros automáticos* (kah-HAY-rohs ahoo-toh-MAH-tee-kohs), have become the money sources of choice in Mexico. Virtually every bank has a 24-hour ATM, accessible (with proper PIN identification code) by a swarm of U.S. and Canadian credit and ATM cards. *Note:* Some Mexican bank ATMs will "eat" your ATM card if you don't retrieve it within about 15 seconds of completing your transaction. Retrieve your card *immediately* after getting your cash.

Although one-time bank charges, typically about $2 per transaction, for ATM cash remain small, the money you can usually get from a single card is limited to about $300 or less per day.

Even without an ATM card, you don't have to go to the trouble of waiting in long bank service lines. Opt for a less-crowded bank, such as Bancomer, Banco Serfín, HSBC, or a private money-exchange office *(casa de cambio)*. Often most convenient, such offices often offer long hours and faster service than the banks, for a fee (as little as $0.50 or as much as $3 per $100).

Keeping Your Money Safe

Travelers checks, the traditional prescription for safe money abroad, are widely accepted in Oaxaca. Even if you plan to use your ATM card, buy some U.S. dollar travelers checks (a well-known brand such as American Express or Visa) as an emergency reserve. Canadian travelers checks and currency are not as widely accepted as U.S. travelers checks, and European and Asian travelers checks are even less so. Unless you like signing your name or paying lots of per-check commissions, buy denominations of $50 or more.

In Oaxaca as everywhere, thieves circulate among the tourists. Keep valuables in your hotel *caja de seguridad* (security box). If you don't particularly trust the desk clerk, carry what you cannot afford to lose in a money belt. Pickpockets love crowded markets, buses, and airport terminals where they can slip a wallet out of a back pocket or dangling purse or a camera from its belt case in a blink. Guard against this by carrying your wallet in your front pocket, your camera in your purse or daypack, and your purse, waist pouch, and daypack (which clever crooks can sometimes slit open) on your front side.

Don't attract thieves by displaying wads of money or flashy jewelry. Don't get sloppy drunk; if so, you may become a pushover for a determined thief.

Don't leave valuables unattended on the beach; share security duties with trustworthy-looking neighbors, or leave a bag with a shopkeeper nearby.

Tipping

Without their droves of visitors, Mexican people would be even poorer. Deflation of the peso, while it makes prices low for outsiders, makes it rough for Mexican families to get by. The help at your hotel typically get paid only a few dollars a day. They depend on tips to make the difference between dire and bearable poverty. Give the *camarista* (chambermaid) and floor attendant 20 pesos every day or two. And whenever uncertain of what to tip, it will probably mean a lot to someone—maybe a whole family—if you err on the generous side.

In restaurants and bars, Mexican tipping customs are similar to those in the United States: tip waiters, waitresses, and bartenders about 15 percent for satisfactory service.

Credit Cards

Credit cards, such as Visa, MasterCard, and, to a lesser extent, American Express and Discover, are widely honored in the hotels, restaurants, crafts shops, and boutiques that cater to foreign tourists. You will generally get better bargains, however, in shops that depend on local trade and do not so readily accept credit cards. Such shops sometimes offer discounts for cash sales.

Whatever the circumstance, your travel money will usually go much further in Oaxaca than back home. Despite the national 17 percent ("value added" IVA) sales tax, local lodging, food, and transportation prices will often seem like bargains compared to the developed world. Outside of the pricey high-rise beach-front strips, pleasant, palmy hotel room rates often run $50 or less.

COMMUNICATIONS
Using Mexican Telephones

Although Mexican phone service has improved in the last decade, it's still sometimes hit-or-miss. If a number doesn't get through, you may have to redial it more than once. When someone answers (usually *"Bueno"*) be especially courteous. If your Spanish is rusty, say, *"¿Por favor, habla inglés?"* (¿POR fah-VOR,

PACKING CHECKLIST

Use this list as a last-minute check to make sure that you've packed all of the items essential to your Mexico trip:

NECESSARY ITEMS
___ camera, film (expensive in Mexico)
___ comb
___ guidebook, reading books
___ inexpensive watch, clock
___ keys, tickets
___ lightweight clothes, hat for sun
___ money, ATM card, and/or travelers checks
___ mosquito repellent
___ prescription eyeglasses
___ prescription medicines and drugs
___ purse, waist-belt carrying pouch
___ sunglasses, sunscreen
___ swimsuit
___ toothbrush, toothpaste
___ passport
___ windbreaker

USEFUL ITEMS
___ address book
___ birth control
___ checkbook, credit cards
___ contact lenses
___ dental floss
___ earplugs
___ first-aid kit
___ flashlight, batteries
___ immersion heater
___ lightweight binoculars
___ portable radio/cassette player
___ razor

___ travel booklight
___ vaccination certificate

NECESSARY ITEMS FOR CAMPERS
___ collapsible gallon plastic bottle
___ dish soap
___ first-aid kit
___ hammock (buy in Mexico)
___ insect repellent
___ lightweight hiking shoes
___ lightweight tent
___ matches in waterproof case
___ nylon cord
___ plastic bottle, quart
___ pot scrubber/sponge
___ sheet or light blanket
___ Sierra Club–style metal cup, fork, and spoon
___ single-burner stove with fuel
___ Swiss army knife
___ tarp
___ toilet paper
___ towel, soap
___ two nesting cooking pots
___ water-purifying tablets or iodine

USEFUL ITEMS FOR CAMPERS
___ compass
___ dishcloths
___ hot pad
___ instant coffee, tea, sugar, powdered milk
___ moleskin (Dr. Scholl's)
___ plastic plate
___ poncho
___ short (votive) candles
___ whistle

AH-blah een-GLAYS?)—"Please, do you speak English?"). If you want to speak to a particular person (such as María), ask, *"¿María se encuentra?"* (¿mah-REE-ah SAY ayn-koo-AYN-trah?).

Since November 2001, when telephone numbers were standardized, Mexican phones operate pretty much the same as in the United States and Canada. In Oaxaca City, for example, a complete telephone number is generally written like this: 951/514-4709. As in the United States, the "951" denotes the telephone area code, or *lada* (LAH-dah), and the 514-4709 is the number (except in the case of a calling a cell phone, see below) that you dial locally. If you want to dial this number long distance *(larga distancia),* **first dial "01" (like "1" in the United States),** then 951/514-4709. All

Mexican telephone numbers, with only three exceptions, begin with a three-digit *lada,* followed by a seven-digit local number. (The exceptions are Monterrey, Guadalajara, and Mexico City, which have two-digit *ladas* and eight-digit local numbers. The Mexico City *lada* is 55; Guadalajara's is 33; Monterrey's is 81. (For example, a complete Guadalajara phone number would read 33/6897-2253.)

Although **Mexican cellular telephones** are as universally used as those in the United States and Canada, at this writing they operate a bit differently. Generally, in order to call a local cellular number, for example, the Oaxaca local number 951/514-4709, you must prefix it with "044." Thus, in Oaxaca City and Valley, dial 044-951/514-4709. However, outside of Oaxaca City and the Valley of Oaxaca, for example, in Puerto Escondido, you call a cellular number by first dialing "045." Thus, from Puerto Escondido calling Oaxaca, simply dial 045-951/514-4709.

In Oaxaca towns and cities, direct long-distance dialing is the rule—from hotels, public phone booths, and efficient private computerized telephone offices. The cheapest, often most convenient, way to call is by buying and using a public telephone **Ladatel telephone card** *(tarjeta telefónica).* Buy them in 30-, 50-, and 100-peso denominations at the many outlets—minimarkets, pharmacies, liquor stores—that display the blue and yellow Ladatel sign.

Calling Mexico and Calling Home

To call Mexico direct from the United States, first dial 011 (for international access), then 52 (Mexico country code), followed by the Mexican area code and local number. For example, from the United States, call a Oaxaca local number such as 514-4709 by dialing 01152-951/514-4709. Again, you must **dial cellular phone numbers a bit differently,** by entering a "1" before the area code. Thus, if Oaxaca City local number 514-4709 were a cellular number, from the United States you must dial 01152-1-951/514-4709.

For station-to-station **calls to the United States from Mexico,** dial 001 plus the U.S. area code and the local number. For example, to call San Diego (area code 619) local number 388-5390, from Mexico, simply dial 001-619/388-5390. For calls to other countries, ask your hotel desk clerk or see the easy-to-follow directions in the local Mexican telephone directory.

By far the cheapest way to call home (about $0.50 per minute) is via one of the many public telephones with your Ladatel phone card.

Beware of certain private "To Call Long Distance to the U.S.A. Collect" (or "by Credit Card") telephones installed prominently in airports, tourist hotels, and shops. Tariffs on these phones often run as high as $10 per minute (with a three-minute minimum), for a total of $30, whether you talk three minutes or not. Always ask the operator for the rate, and if it's too high, buy a 30-peso ($3) Ladatel phone card for a (six-minute) call home.

In smaller towns, with no public street telephones, you must often do your long-distance phoning in the *larga distancia* (local phone office). Typically staffed by a young woman and often connected to a café, the *larga distancia* becomes an informal community social center as people pass the time waiting for their phone connections.

Post, Telegraph, and Internet Access

Mexican *correos* (post offices) operate similarly, but more slowly and less securely, than most of their counterparts all over the world. Mail services usually include *lista de correo* (general delivery, address letters *"a/c lista de correo"*), *servicios filatelicas* (philatelic services), *por avión* (airmail), *giros* (postal money orders), and Mexpost secure and fast delivery service, sometimes from separate Mexpost offices.

Mexican ordinary (non-Mexpost) mail is sadly unreliable and pathetically slow. If, for mailings within Mexico, you must have security, use the efficient, reformed government Mexpost (like U.S. Express Mail) service. For international mailings, check the local Yellow

Pages for widely available DHL, Federal Express, or UPS courier service.

Telégrafos (telegraph offices), usually near the post office, send and receive *telegramas* (telegrams) and *giros* (money orders). *Telecomunicaciones* (Telecom), the new high-tech telegraph offices, add computerized telephone and public fax to the available services.

Internet service, including personal email access, has arrived in Oaxaca cities and larger (and even smaller) towns. Internet "cafés" are becoming increasingly common, especially in the Oaxaca City, Huatulco, Puerto Escondido, and Puerto Ángel resort centers. Online rates run $1–2 per hour.

Electricity and Time

Mexican electric power is supplied at U.S.-standard 110 volts, 60 cycles. Plugs and sockets are generally two-pronged, nonpolar (like the pre-1970s U.S. ones). Bring adapters if you're going to use appliances with polar two-pronged or three-pronged plugs. A two-pronged polar plug has different-sized prongs, one of which is too large to plug into an old-fashioned nonpolar socket.

The entire state of Oaxaca and all surrounding states operate on U.S. Central Time, the same as Mexico City and central U.S. states such as Nebraska, Illinois, Tennessee, and Louisiana.

RESOURCES

Glossary

Many of the following words have a social-historical meaning; others you will not find in the usual English–Spanish dictionary.

abarrotesía grocery store

aguardiente Mexican "white lightning": cheap distilled liquor made from sugarcane

alcalde mayor or municipal judge

alebrije fanciful wooden animal, mostly made in Arrazola and Tilcajete villages

alfarería pottery

andador walkway, or strolling path

antojitos native Mexican snacks, such as tamales, chiles rellenos, tacos, and enchiladas

artesanías handicrafts

artesano, artesana craftsman, craftswoman

asunción the assumption of the Virgin Mary into heaven (as distinguished from the *ascención* of Jesus into heaven)

atole a popular nonalcoholic drink made from corn juice

audiencia one of the royal executive-judicial panels sent to rule Mexico during the 16th century

autopista expressway

ayuntamiento either the town council or the building where it meets

barrio a town or village district or neighborhood, usually centered around its own local plaza and church

bienes raíces literally "good roots," but popularly, real estate

boleto ticket, boarding pass

brujo, bruja male or female witch doctor or shaman

caballero literally "horseman," but popularly, gentleman

cabaña ecoturísticas bungalow lodging for tourists

cabercera head town of a municipal district, or headquarters in general

cabrón literally, a cuckold, but more commonly, bastard, rat, or S.O.B.; sometimes used affectionately

cacique local chief or boss

calenda procession, usually religious, as during a festival

camionera bus station

campesino country person; farm worker

canasta basket, usually of woven reeds, with handle

cantera local volcanic stone, widely used for colonial-era Oaxaca monuments

Carnaval celebration preceding Ash Wednesday, the beginning of the fasting period called Lent. Carnaval is called Mardi Gras in the United States

casa de huéspedes guesthouse, often operated in a family home

cascada waterfall

caudillo dictator or political chief

centro de salud health center/clinic

charro gentleman cowboy

chingar literally, to "rape," but also the universal Spanish "f" word, the equivalent of "screw" in English

Churrigueresque Spanish Baroque architectural style incorporated into many Mexican colonial churches, named after José Churriguera (1665-1725)

científicos literally, scientists, but applied to President Porfirio Díaz's technocratic advisers

coa (estaca) digging stick, used for planting corn

Cocijo Zapotec god of rain, lightning, and thunder

cofradía Catholic fraternal service association, either male or female, mainly in charge of financing and organizing religious festivals

colectivo a shared public taxi or minibus that picks up and deposits passengers along a designated route

colegio preparatory school or junior college

colonia suburban subdivision/satellite of a larger city

comal a flat pottery griddle, for cooking/heating tortillas

comida casera home-cooked food

comida corrida economical afternoon set meal, usually with four courses – soup, rice, entrée, and dessert

compadrazgo the semi-formal web of village and barrio **compadre** and **padrino** relationships that determine a person's lifetime obligations and loyalties

compadre a semi-formalized "best friend" relationship that usually lasts for life

comunal refers to the traditional indigenous system of joint decision-making and land ownership and use

Conasupo government store that sells basic foods at subsidized prices

correo mail, post, or post office

criollo person of all-European, usually Spanish, descent born in the New World

Cuaresma Lent (the 46 days of pre-Easter fasting, beginning on Ash Wednesday)

cuota toll, as in **cuota autopista,** toll expressway

curandero, curandera indigenous medicine man or woman

damas ladies, as in "ladies room"

Domingo de Ramos Palm Sunday

ejido a constitutional, government-sponsored form of community, with shared land ownership and cooperative decision-making

encomienda colonial award of tribute from a designated indigenous district

farmacia pharmacy, or drugstore

finca farm

finca cafetelera coffee farm

fonda foodstall or small restaurant, often in a traditional market complex

fraccionamiento city sector or subdivision, abbreviated "Fracc."

fuero the former right of Mexican clergy and military to be tried in separate ecclesiastical and military courts

gachupín "one who wears spurs"; a derogatory term for a Spanish-born colonial

gasolinera gasoline station

gente de razón "people of reason"; whites and mestizos in colonial Mexico

gringo once-derogatory but now commonly used term for North American whites

grito impassioned cry, as in Hidalgo's Grito de Dolores

hacienda large landed estate; also the government treasury

hamaca hammock

hechicero a "wizard" who often leads native propitiatory ceremonies

hidalgo nobleman or noblewoman; called honorifically by "Don" or "Doña"

hojalata tinware

indígena indigenous or aboriginal inhabitant of all-native descent who speaks his or her native tongue; commonly, but incorrectly, an **indio** (Indian)

jacal native label for thatched, straw, and/or stick country house

jaripeo bull roping and riding

jejenes "no-see-um" biting gnats, most common around coastal wetlands

judiciales the federal "judicial," or investigative police, best known to motorists for their highway checkpoint inspections

jugería stall or small restaurant providing a large array of squeezed vegetable and fruit **jugos** (juices)

juzgado the "hoosegow," or jail

lancha launch (small boat)

larga distancia long-distance telephone service, or the **caseta** (booth or office) where it's provided

licencado academic degree (abbrev. Lic.) approximately equivalent to a bachelor's degree in the United States

lonchería small lunch counter, usually serving juices, sandwiches, and **antojitos**

machismo; macho exaggerated sense of maleness; person who holds such a sense of himself

mañanita early-morning mass

mano a hand, or the stone roller used to grind corn on the flat stone **metate**

mayordomo community leader responsible for staging a local Catholic religious festival

mescal alcoholic beverage distilled from the fermented hearts of maguey (century plant)

mestizo person of mixed native and European descent

metate a slightly concave, horizontal stone basin for grinding corn for tortillas

milagro literally a miracle, but also a small religious wish medal, often pinned to an altar saint by someone requesting divine intervention

milpa a small, family-owned field, traditionally planted in corn, beans, and squash

mirador viewpoint, overlook

molcajete a stone mortar and pestle, used for hand-grinding, especially chilies and seeds

mordida slang for bribe; "little bite"

olla a pottery jug or pot, used for stewing – vegetables, meats, beans, coffee

padrino, padrina godfather or godmother, often the respective **compadres** of the given child's parents

palapa an open, thatched-roof structure, usually shading a restaurant

panela rough brown cane sugar, sold in lumps in the market

panga outboard motor-launch (**lancha**)

papier-mâché the craft of glued, multilayered paper sculpture, centered in Tonalá, Jalisco, where creations can resemble fine pottery or lacquerware

Pemex acronym for Petróleos Mexicanos, the national oil corporation

peninsulares the Spanish-born ruling colonial elite

peón a poor wage-earner, usually a country native

periférico peripheral boulevard

petate all-purpose woven mat, from palm fronds

piciete wild tobacco

piñata papier-mâché decoration, usually in animal or human form, filled with treats and broken open during a fiesta

plan political manifesto, usually by a leader or group consolidating or seeking power

Porfiriato the 34-year (1876–1910) ruling period of president-dictator Porfirio Díaz

posada Christmas Eve procession in which participants, led by costumed Holy Mary and Joseph, knock on neighborhood doors and implore, unsuccessfully, for a room for the night

pozahuanco horizontally striped hand-woven wraparound skirt, commonly worn in the Oaxaca's coastal Mixtec district

pozole stew of hominy in broth, usually topped by shredded meat, cabbage, and diced onion

presidencia municipal the headquarters, like a U.S. city or county hall, of a Mexican **municipio**, county-like local governmental unit

preventiva state-funded local police

principal, anciano a respected elder, often a member of a council of elders, whom the community consults for advice and support

pronunciamiento declaration of rebellion by an insurgent leader

pueblo town or people

puente literally a "bridge," but commonly a holiday weekend, when hotel reservations are highly recommended

pulque the fermented juice of the maguey plant, approximately equivalent in alcoholic content to wine or strong beer

puta whore, bitch, or slut

quinta a villa or upscale country house

quinto the colonial royal "fifth" tax on treasure and precious metals

ramada a temporary shade roof, usually of palm fronds

regidor a community official, often a town council member, responsible for specific government functions, such as public works

retablo altarpiece, often of ornately carved and gilded wood

retorno cul-de-sac

ropa típica traditional dress, derived from the Spanish colonial tradition (in contrast to *traje*, traditional indigenous dress)

rurales former federal country police force created to fight *bandidos* (bandits) and suppress political dissent

Sabi Mixtec god of rain

sabino Mexican cypress tree

Semana Santa Holy Week, the week preceding Easter Sunday

servicios the ladder of increasingly responsible public tasks that, if successfully performed, leads to community approval, prestige, and leadership for a given individual by middle age

tapete wool rug, made in certain east-side Valley of Oaxaca villages

taxi especial private taxi, as distinguished from *taxi colectivo,* or collective taxi

telégrafo telegraph office, lately converting to high-tech *telecomunicaciones (telecom),* that also offers computerized telephone and public fax services

temazcal traditional indigenous sweat room, rock-enclosed and heated by a wood fire, usually used for healing, especially by women after childbirth

tenate basket of woven palm leaf, with tumpline instead of a rigid handle

tepache a wine, fermented from *panela* (sugarcane juice)

tequio an obligatory communal task, such as local road work, street sweeping, or child care, expected of all adult villagers from time to time

tianguis literally "awning," but now has come to mean the awning-decorated native town market

tono a usually benign animal guardian spirit

topil lowest municipal job, of messenger, filled by youngest teenage boys

vaquero cowboy

vecindad neighborhood

yanqui Yankee

zócalo the popular label originally for the Mexico City central plaza; now the name for central plazas all over Mexico, including Oaxaca

Spanish Phrasebook

Your Mexico adventure will be more fun if you use a little Spanish. Mexican folks, although they may smile at your funny accent, will appreciate your halting efforts to break the ice and transform yourself from a foreigner to a potential friend.

Spanish commonly uses 30 letters – the familiar English 26, plus four straightforward additions: ch, ll, ñ, and rr, which are explained in "Consonants," below.

PRONUNCIATION

Once you learn them, Spanish pronunciation rules – in contrast to English – don't change. Spanish vowels generally sound softer than in English. (*Note:* The capitalized syllables below receive stronger accents.)

Vowels

a like ah, as in "hah": *agua* AH-gooah (water), *pan* PAHN (bread), and *casa* CAH-sah (house)

e like ay, as in "may:" *mesa* MAY-sah (table), *tela* TAY-lah (cloth), and *de* DAY (of, from)

i like ee, as in "need": *diez* dee-AYZ (ten), *comida* ko-MEE-dah (meal), and *fin* FEEN (end)

o like oh, as in "go": *peso* PAY-soh (weight), *ocho* OH-choh (eight), and *poco* POH-koh (a bit)

u like oo, as in "cool": *uno* OO-noh (one), *cuarto* KOOAHR-toh (room), and *usted* oos-TAYD (you); when it follows a "q" the **u** is silent; when it follows an "h" or has an umlaut, it's pronounced like "w"

Consonants

b, d, f, k, l, m, n, p, q, s,
t, v, w, x, y, z, and ch
   pronounced almost as in English; **h** occurs,
   but is silent – not pronounced at all.

c like k as in "keep": *cuarto* KOOAR-toh
   (room), Tepic tay-PEEK (capital of Nayarit
   state); when it precedes "e" or "i," pronounce **c** like s, as in "sit": *cerveza* sayr-VAY-
   sah (beer), *encima* ayn-SEE-mah (atop).

g like g as in "gift" when it precedes "a," "o,"
   "u," or a consonant: *gato* GAH-toh (cat),
   hago AH-goh (I do, make); otherwise, pronounce **g** like h as in "hat": *giro* HEE-roh
   (money order), *gente* HAYN-tay (people)

j like h, as in "has": *Jueves* HOOAY-vays
   (Thursday), *mejor* may-HOR (better)

ll like y, as in "yes": *toalla* toh-AH-yah (towel),
   ellos AY-yohs (they, them)

ñ like ny, as in "canyon": *año* AH-nyo (year),
   señor SAY-nyor (Mr., sir)

r is lightly trilled, with tongue at the roof of
   your mouth like a very light English d, as in
   "ready": *pero* PAY-doh (but), *tres* TDAYS
   (three), *cuatro* KOOAH-tdoh (four).

rr like a Spanish r, but with much more emphasis and trill. Let your tongue flap. Practice
   with *burro* (donkey), *carretera* (highway),
   and Carrillo (proper name), then really let go
   with *ferrocarril* (railroad).

Note: The single small but common exception
to all of the above is the pronunciation of Spanish **y** when it's being used as the Spanish word
for "and," as in "Ron y Kathy." In such case, pronounce it like the English ee, as in "keep": Ron
"ee" Kathy (Ron and Kathy).

Accent

The rule for accent, the relative stress given to
syllables within a given word, is straightforward.
If a word ends in a vowel, an n, or an s, accent
the next-to-last syllable; if not, accent the last
syllable.

   Pronounce *gracias* GRAH-seeahs (thank you),
orden OHR-dayn (order), and *carretera* kah-ray-
TAY-rah (highway) with stress on the next-to-last
syllable.

   Otherwise, accent the last syllable: *venir* vay-
NEER (to come), *ferrocarril* fay-roh-cah-REEL
(railroad), and *edad* ay-DAHD (age).

   Exceptions to the accent rule are always
marked with an accent sign: (á, é, í, ó, or ú),
such as *teléfono* tay-LAY-foh-noh (telephone),
jabón hah-BON (soap), and *rápido* RAH-pee-doh
(rapid).

BASIC AND COURTEOUS EXPRESSIONS

Most Spanish-speaking people consider formali-
ties important. Whenever approaching anyone
for information or some other reason, do not forget the appropriate salutation – good morning,
good evening, etc. Standing alone, the greeting
hola (hello) can sound brusque.

Hello. *Hola.*
Good morning. *Buenos días.*
Good afternoon. *Buenas tardes.*
Good evening. *Buenas noches.*
How are you? *¿Cómo está usted?*
Very well, thank you. *Muy bien, gracias.*
Okay; good. *Bien.*
Not okay; bad. *Mal* or *feo.*
So-so. *Más o menos.*
And you? *¿Y usted?*
Thank you. *Gracias.*
Thank you very much. *Muchas gracias.*
You're very kind. *Muy amable.*
You're welcome. *De nada.*
Goodbye. *Adios.*
See you later. *Hasta luego.*
please *por favor*
yes *sí*
no *no*
I don't know. *No sé.*
Just a moment, please. *Momentito, por
favor.*
**Excuse me, please (when you're trying to
get attention).** *Disculpe* or *Con permiso.*
**Excuse me (when you've made a boo-
boo).** *Lo siento.*
Pleased to meet you. *Mucho gusto.*
How do you say...in Spanish? *¿Cómo se
dice...en español?*
What is your name? *¿Cómo se llama usted?*

Do you speak English? *¿Habla usted inglés?*

Is English spoken here? (Does anyone here speak English?) *¿Se habla inglés?*

I don't speak Spanish well. *No hablo bien el español.*

I don't understand. *No entiendo.*

How do you say...in Spanish? *¿Cómo se dice...en español?*

My name is . . . *Me llamo...*

Would you like . . . *¿Quisiera usted...*

Let's go to . . . *Vamos a...*

TERMS OF ADDRESS

When in doubt, use the formal *usted* (you) as a form of address.

I *yo*

you (formal) *usted*

you (familiar) *tu*

he/him *él*

she/her *ella*

we/us *nosotros*

you (plural) *ustedes*

they/them *ellos* (all males or mixed gender); *ellas* (all females)

Mr., sir *señor*

Mrs., madam *señora*

miss, young lady *señorita*

wife *esposa*

husband *esposo*

friend *amigo* (male); *amiga* (female)

sweetheart *novio* (male); *novia* (female)

son; daughter *hijo; hija*

brother; sister *hermano; hermana*

father; mother *padre; madre*

grandfather; grandmother *abuelo; abuela*

TRANSPORTATION

Where is . . . ? *¿Dónde está . . . ?*

How far is it to . . . ? *¿A cuánto está . . . ?*

from...to . . . *de...a . . .*

How many blocks? *¿Cuántas cuadras?*

Where (Which) is the way to . . . ? *¿Dónde está el camino a . . . ?*

the bus station *la terminal de autobuses*

the bus stop *la parada de autobuses*

Where is this bus going? *¿Adónde va este autobús?*

the taxi stand *la parada de taxis*

the train station *la estación de ferrocarril*

the boat *el barco*

the launch *lancha; tiburonera*

the dock *el muelle*

the airport *el aeropuerto*

I'd like a ticket to . . . *Quisiera un boleto a . . .*

first (second) class *primera (segunda) clase*

roundtrip *ida y vuelta*

reservation *reservación*

baggage *equipaje*

Stop here, please. *Pare aquí, por favor.*

the entrance *la entrada*

the exit *la salida*

the ticket office *la oficina de boletos*

(very) near; far *(muy) cerca; lejos*

to; toward *a*

by; through *por*

from *de*

the right *la derecha*

the left *la izquierda*

straight ahead *derecho; directo*

in front *en frente*

beside *al lado*

behind *atrás*

the corner *la esquina*

the stoplight *la semáforo*

a turn *una vuelta*

right here *aquí*

somewhere around here *por acá*

right there *allí*

somewhere around there *por allá*

road *el camino*

street; boulevard *calle; bulevar*

block *la cuadra*

highway *carretera*

kilometer *kilómetro*

bridge; toll *puente; cuota*

address *dirección*

north; south *norte; sur*

east; west *oriente (este); poniente (oeste)*

ACCOMMODATIONS

hotel *hotel*

Is there a room? *¿Hay cuarto?*

May I (may we) see it? *¿Puedo (podemos) verlo?*

What is the rate? *¿Cuál es el precio?*

Is that your best rate? *¿Es su mejor precio?*

Is there something cheaper? *¿Hay algo
más económico?*
a single room *un cuarto sencillo*
a double room *un cuarto doble*
double bed *cama matrimonial*
twin beds *camas gemelas*
with private bath *con baño*
hot water *agua caliente*
shower *ducha*
towels *toallas*
soap *jabón*
toilet paper *papel higiénico*
blanket *frazada; manta*
sheets *sábanas*
air-conditioned *aire acondicionado*
fan *abanico; ventilador*
key *llave*
manager *gerente*

FOOD
I'm hungry *Tengo hambre.*
I'm thirsty. *Tengo sed.*
menu *carta; menú*
order *orden*
glass *vaso*
fork *tenedor*
knife *cuchillo*
spoon *cuchara*
napkin *servilleta*
soft drink *refresco*
coffee *café*
tea *té*
drinking water *agua pura; agua potable*
bottled carbonated water *agua mineral*
bottled uncarbonated water *agua sin gas*
beer *cerveza*
wine *vino*
milk *leche*
juice *jugo*
cream *crema*
sugar *azúcar*
cheese *queso*
snack *antojo; botana*
breakfast *desayuno*
lunch *almuerzo*
daily lunch special *comida corrida (or el
menú del día depending on region)*

dinner *comida (often eaten in late afternoon);
cena (a late-night snack)*
the check *la cuenta*
eggs *huevos*
bread *pan*
salad *ensalada*
fruit *fruta*
mango *mango*
watermelon *sandía*
papaya *papaya*
banana *plátano*
apple *manzana*
orange *naranja*
lime *limón*
fish *pescado*
shellfish *mariscos*
shrimp *camarones*
meat (without) *(sin) carne*
chicken *pollo*
pork *puerco*
beef; steak *res; bistec*
bacon; ham *tocino; jamón*
fried *frito*
roasted *asada*
barbecue; barbecued *barbacoa; al carbón*

SHOPPING
money *dinero*
money-exchange bureau *casa de cambio*
**I would like to exchange traveler's
checks.** *Quisiera cambiar cheques de
viajero.*
What is the exchange rate? *¿Cuál es el tipo
de cambio?*
How much is the commission? *¿Cuánto
cuesta la comisión?*
Do you accept credit cards? *¿Aceptan
tarjetas de crédito?*
money order *giro*
How much does it cost? *¿Cuánto cuesta?*
What is your final price? *¿Cuál es su último
precio?*
expensive *caro*
cheap *barato; económico*
more *más*
less *menos*
a little *un poco*
too much *demasiado*

HEALTH

Help me please. *Ayúdeme por favor.*
I am ill. *Estoy enfermo.*
Call a doctor. *Llame un doctor.*
Take me to . . . *Lléveme a . . .*
hospital *hospital; sanatorio*
drugstore *farmacia*
pain *dolor*
fever *fiebre*
headache *dolor de cabeza*
stomach ache *dolor de estómago*
burn *quemadura*
cramp *calambre*
nausea *náusea*
vomiting *vomitar*
medicine *medicina*
antibiotic *antibiótico*
pill; tablet *pastilla*
aspirin *aspirina*
ointment; cream *pomada; crema*
bandage *venda*
cotton *algodón*
sanitary napkins use brand name, e.g.,
   Kotex
birth control pills *pastillas anticonceptivas*
contraceptive foam *espuma anticonceptiva*
condoms *preservativos; condones*
toothbrush *cepilla dental*
dental floss *hilo dental*
toothpaste *crema dental*
dentist *dentista*
toothache *dolor de muelas*

POST OFFICE AND COMMUNICATIONS

long-distance telephone *teléfono larga
   distancia*
I would like to call . . . *Quisiera llamar a . . .*
collect *por cobrar*
station to station *a quien contesta*
person to person *persona a persona*
credit card *tarjeta de crédito*
post office *correo*
general delivery *lista de correo*
letter *carta*
stamp *estampilla, timbre*
postcard *tarjeta*
aerogram *aerograma*

air mail *correo aereo*
registered *registrado*
money order *giro*
package; box *paquete; caja*
string; tape *cuerda; cinta*

AT THE BORDER

border *frontera*
customs *aduana*
immigration *migración*
tourist card *tarjeta de turista*
inspection *inspección; revisión*
passport *pasaporte*
profession *profesión*
marital status *estado civil*
single *soltero*
married; divorced *casado; divorciado*
widowed *viudado*
insurance *seguros*
title *título*
driver's license *licencia de manejar*

AT THE GAS STATION

gas station *gasolinera*
gasoline *gasolina*
unleaded *sin plomo*
full, please *lleno, por favor*
tire *llanta*
tire repair shop *vulcanizadora*
air *aire*
water *agua*
oil (change) *aceite (cambio)*
grease *grasa*
My...doesn't work. *Mi...no sirve.*
battery *batería*
radiator *radiador*
alternator *alternador*
generator *generador*
tow truck *grúa*
repair shop *taller mecánico*
tune-up *afinación*
auto parts store *refaccionería*

VERBS

Verbs are the key to getting along in Spanish.
They employ mostly predictable forms and
come in three classes, which end in *ar*, *er*, and
ir, respectively:

to buy *comprar*
I buy, you (he, she, it) buys *compro, compra*
we buy, you (they) buy *compramos, compran*

to eat *comer*
I eat, you (he, she, it) eats *como, come*
we eat, you (they) eat *comemos, comen*

to climb *subir*
I climb, you (he, she, it) climbs *subo, sube*
we climb, you (they) climb *subimos, suben*

Here are more (with irregularities indicated):

to do or make *hacer* (regular except for *hago*, I do or make)
to go *ir* (very irregular: *voy, va, vamos, van*)
to go (walk) *andar*
to love *amar*
to work *trabajar*
to want *desear, querer*
to need *necesitar*
to read *leer*
to write *escribir*
to repair *reparar*
to stop *parar*
to get off (the bus) *bajar*
to arrive *llegar*
to stay (remain) *quedar*
to stay (lodge) *hospedar*
to leave *salir* (regular except for *salgo*, I leave)
to look at *mirar*
to look for *buscar*
to give *dar* (regular except for *doy*, I give)
to carry *llevar*
to have *tener* (irregular but important: *tengo, tiene, tenemos, tienen*)
to come *venir* (similarly irregular: *vengo, viene, venimos, vienen*)

Spanish has two forms of "to be":

to be *estar* (regular except for *estoy*, I am)
to be *ser* (very irregular: *soy, es, somos, son*)

Use *estar* when speaking of location or a temporary state of being: "I am at home." *"Estoy en casa."* "I'm sick." *"Estoy enfermo."* Use *ser* for a permanent state of being: "I am a doctor." *"Soy doctora."*

NUMBERS
zero *cero*
one *uno*
two *dos*
three *tres*
four *cuatro*
five *cinco*
six *seis*
seven *siete*
eight *ocho*
nine *nueve*
10 *diez*
11 *once*
12 *doce*
13 *trece*
14 *catorce*
15 *quince*
16 *dieciseis*
17 *diecisiete*
18 *dieciocho*
19 *diecinueve*
20 *veinte*
21 *veinte y uno* or *veintiuno*
30 *treinta*
40 *cuarenta*
50 *cincuenta*
60 *sesenta*
70 *setenta*
80 *ochenta*
90 *noventa*
100 *ciento*
101 *ciento y uno* or *cientiuno*
200 *doscientos*
500 *quinientos*
1,000 *mil*
10,000 *diez mil*
100,000 *cien mil*
1,000,000 *millón*
one half *medio*
one third *un tercio*
one fourth *un cuarto*

TIME

What time is it? *¿Qué hora es?*
It's one o'clock. *Es la una.*
It's three in the afternoon. *Son las tres de la tarde.*
It's 4 A.M. *Son las cuatro de la mañana.*
six-thirty *seis y media*
a quarter till eleven *un cuarto para las once*
a quarter past five *las cinco y cuarto*
an hour *una hora*

DAYS AND MONTHS

Monday *lunes*
Tuesday *martes*
Wednesday *miércoles*
Thursday *jueves*
Friday *viernes*
Saturday *sábado*
Sunday *domingo*

today *hoy*
tomorrow *mañana*
yesterday *ayer*
January *enero*
February *febrero*
March *marzo*
April *abril*
May *mayo*
June *junio*
July *julio*
August *agosto*
September *septiembre*
October *octubre*
November *noviembre*
December *diciembre*
a week *una semana*
a month *un mes*
after *después*
before *antes*

Suggested Reading

Some of these books are informative, others are entertaining, and all of them will increase your understanding of both Mexico and Oaxaca. Some are easier to find in Oaxaca than at home, and vice versa. Many of them are out of print, but www.amazon.com, www.barnesandnoble.com, or libraries may have used copies. Take some along on your trip. If you find others that are especially noteworthy, let us know.

HISTORY

Blanton, E. Richard, Gary M. Feinman, Stephen A. Kowaleski, and Linda M. Nicholas. *Ancient Oaxaca.* Cambridge, New York, and Melbourne: Cambridge University Press, 1999. A scholarly account of pre-Columbian Oaxaca history, for the serious reader.

Brunk, Samuel. *Emiliano Zapata: Revolution and Betrayal in Mexico.* Albuquerque: University of New Mexico Press, 1995. A detailed narrative of the renowned revolutionary's turbulent life, from his humble birth in Anenecuilco village in Morelos through his de facto control of Mexico City in 1914–1915 to his final betrayal and assassination in 1919. The author authoritatively demonstrates that Zapata, neither complete hero nor complete villain, was simply an incredibly determined native leader who paid the ultimate price in his selfless struggle for land and liberty for the campesinos of southern Mexico.

Calderón de la Barca, Fanny. *Life in Mexico, with New Material from the Author's Journals.* New York: Doubleday, 1966. Edited by H. T. and M. H. Fisher. An update of the brilliant, humorous, and celebrated original 1913 book by the Scottish wife of the Spanish ambassador to Mexico.

Casasola, Gustavo. *Seis Siglos de Historia Gráfica de Mexico (Six Centuries of Mexican Graphic History).* Mexico City: Editorial Gustavo Casasola, 1978. Six fascinating encyclopedic volumes, in Spanish, of Mexican history in pictures, from 1325 to the present.

Chance, John K. *Conquest of the Sierra*. Norman: University of Oklahoma Press, 1990. Professor Chance uses archival sources to trace the evolution of colonial society, principally the northern Sierra Zapotec communities and how they adapted their religion, customs, and settlement patterns in response to the pressures of Spanish rule.

Collis, Maurice. *Cortés and Montezuma*. New York: New Directions Publishing Corp., 1999. A reprint of a 1954 classic piece of well-researched storytelling, Collis traces Cortés's conquest of Mexico through the defeat of his chief opponent, Aztec Emperor Montezuma. He uses contemporary eyewitnesses—notably Bernal Díaz del Castillo—to revivify one of history's greatest dramas.

Cortés, Hernán. *Letters from Mexico*. Translated by Anthony Pagden. New Haven: Yale University Press, 1986. Cortés's five long letters to his king, in which he describes contemporary Mexico in fascinating detail, including, notably, the remarkably sophisticated life of the Aztecs at the time of the conquest.

De las Casas, Bartolome. *A Short Account of the Destruction of the Indies*. New York: Penguin Books, 1992. The gritty but beloved Dominican Bishop, renowned as Mexico's "Apostle of the Indians" writes passionately of his own failed attempt to moderate and humanize the Spanish conquest of Mexico. Undoubtedly, de las Casas' sad tale made a great impression on Spain's King Charles V, who, in 1542, the same year the book was written, promulgated the liberal New Laws of the Indies, which outlawed slavery 320 years before Abraham Lincoln's Emancipation Proclamation.

Díaz del Castillo, Bernal. *The Discovery and Conquest of Mexico*. Translated by Albert Idell. London: Routledge (of Taylor and Francis Group), 2005. A soldier's still-fresh tale of the Conquest from the Spanish viewpoint.

Garfias, Luis. *The Mexican Revolution*. Mexico City: Panorama Editorial, 1985. A concise Mexican version of the 1910–1917 Mexican revolution, the crucible of present-day Mexico.

Gugliotta, Bobette. *Women of Mexico*. Encino, CA: Floricanto Press, 1989. Lively legends, tales, and biographies of remarkable Mexican women, including several from Oaxaca.

León-Portilla, Miguel. *The Broken Spears: The Aztec Account of the Conquest of Mexico*. New York: Beacon Press, 1962. Provides an intriguing contrast to Díaz del Castillo's account.

Meyer, Michael, and William Sherman. *The Course of Mexican History*. New York: Oxford University Press, 2003. An insightful, 700-plus-page college textbook in paperback. A bargain, especially if you can get it used.

Novas, Himlice. *Everything You Need to Know About Latino History*. New York: Plume Books (Penguin Group), 1994. Chicanos, Latin rhythm, La Raza, the Treaty of Guadalupe Hidalgo, and much more, interpreted from an authoritative Latino point of view.

Ridley, Jasper. *Maximilian and Juárez*. New York: Ticknor and Fields, 1999. This authoritative historical biography breathes new life into one of Mexico's great ironic tragedies, a drama that pitted the native Zapotec "Lincoln of Mexico" against the dreamy, idealistic Archduke Maximilian of Austria-Hungary. Despite their common liberal ideas, they were drawn into a bloody no-quarter struggle that set the Old World against the New, ended in Maximilian's execution, the insanity of his wife, and the emergence of the United States as a power to be reckoned with in world affairs. The defeat of France and Maximilian in Mexico was aided by U.S. support of the Juárez government. The Monroe Doctrine became a reality; and never again would a European power invade Mexico or any other country in the Americas.

Ruíz, Ramon Eduardo. *Triumphs and Tragedy: A History of the Mexican People*. New York: W.W. Norton, Inc., 1992. A pithy, anecdote-filled history of Mexico from an authoritative Mexican American perspective.

Simpson, Lesley Bird. *Many Mexicos.* Berkeley: University of California Press, 1962. A much-reprinted, fascinating broad-brush version of Mexican history.

ARCHAEOLOGY

Flannery, Kent, and Joyce Marcus. *The Cloud People.* New York: Academic Press, 1983. Eminently authoritative authors trace the divergent evolution of the Zapotec and Mixtec peoples as revealed by the archaeological record.

Marcus, Joyce, and Kent Flannery, contributor. *Zapotec Civilization.* London and New York: Thames and Hudson, 1996. The distinguished authors trace the evolution of Valley of Oaxaca civilization, from 10,000 B.C. to the conquest, using the results from recent finds to shed light on the roots of Oaxaca's dominant linguistic group. The expertly documented text is elegantly illustrated with hundreds of maps, drawings, and photos, including many aerial views of Oaxaca archaeological sites.

Paddock, John, ed. *Ancient Oaxaca.* Palo Alto, CA: Stanford University Press, 1966. An eminent Oaxaca archaeologist edits this richly illustrated compendium of articles by major discoverers of Zapotec, Mixtec, and other antiquities.

Winter, Marcus. *Oaxaca, the Archaeological Record.* Mexico, D.F.: Minutiae Mexicana, 1992. A distinguished Oaxaca resident investigator skillfully traces a concise history of Oaxaca's pre-conquest inhabitants, based on finds at Monte Albán, Mitla, and dozens of other Valley of Oaxaca and mountain sites.

UNIQUE GUIDE AND TIP BOOKS

American Automobile Association. *Mexico TravelBook.* Heathrow, FL: 2003. Published by the American Automobile Association (1000 AAA Drive, Heathrow, FL 32746-5063). Short but sweet summaries of major Mexican tourist destinations and sights. Also includes information on fiestas, accommodations, restaurants, and a wealth of information relevant to car travel in Mexico. Available in bookstores, or free to AAA members at affiliate offices.

Church, Mike and Terry. *Traveler's Guide to Mexican Camping.* Kirkland, WA: Rolling Homes Press (order by tel. 425/825-7846, P.O. Box 2099, Kirkland, WA 98083-2099, www.rollinghomes.com). This is an unusually thorough guide to trailer parks all over Mexico, with much coverage of the Pacific Coast in general and the Guadalajara region in particular. Detailed maps guide you accurately to each trailer park cited and clear descriptions tell you what to expect. The book also provides very helpful information on car travel in Mexico, including details of insurance, border crossing, highway safety, car repairs, and much more.

Forgey, Dr. William. *Traveler's Medical Alert Series: Mexico, A Guide to Health and Safety.* Merrillville, IN: ICS Books, 1991. Useful information on health and safety in Mexico.

Franz, Carl. *The People's Guide to Mexico.* Emeryville, CA: Avalon Travel Publishing, 13th edition, 2006. An entertaining and insightful A-to-Z general guide to the joys and pitfalls of independent economy travel in Mexico.

Gilford, Judith. *The Packing Book.* Berkeley, CA: Ten Speed Press, fourth edition, 2006. The secrets of the carry-on traveler, or how to make everything you carry do double and triple duty. All for the sake of convenience, mobility, economy, and comfort.

Graham, Scott. *Handle With Care: Guide to Socially Responsible Travel in Developing Countries.* Chicago: The Noble Press, 1991. Should you accept a meal from a family who lives in a grass house? This insightful guide answers this and hundreds of other tough questions for people who want to travel responsibly in the third world.

Jeffrey, Nan. *Adventuring with Children*. Ashland, MA: Avalon House Publishing, 1995. This unusually detailed book starts where most travel-with-children books end. It contains, besides a wealth of information and practical strategies for general travel with children, specific chapters on how you can adventure—trek, kayak, river-raft, camp, bicycle, and much more—successfully with the kids in tow.

Mader, Ron. *Adventures in Nature Mexico*. Emeryville, CA: Avalon Travel Publishing, 1998. An internationally acknowledged expert on ecotravel in Latin America details dozens of environmentally sensitive adventure tours in Mexico and Oaxaca. Destinations range widely, from scuba diving off Cozumel and exploring lost Mayan cities to jeeping through the Copper Canyon to rescuing turtle eggs on Oaxaca beaches. (Although used copies are available from amazon.com and at libraries, this book, a classic, is out of print. Nevertheless, Oaxaca resident Ron Mader has updated much of the book in his superb website www.planeta.com.)

Werner, David. *Where There Is No Doctor*. Berkeley, CA: Hesperian Foundation (1919 Addison St., Berkeley, CA 94704, tel. 888/729-1796, www.hesperian.org), 1992. How to keep well in the tropical backcountry.

Whipperman, Bruce. *Moon Acapulco, Ixtapa & Zihuatanejo*. Berkeley, CA: Avalon Travel, fourth edition, 2008. The most comprehensive guidebook, with an abundance of detail of not only the famous resorts, but the little-known untouristed treasures, from the mountains to the sea, of Oaxaca's neighboring state of Guerrero.

Whipperman, Bruce. *Moon Pacific Mexico*. Emeryville, CA: Avalon Travel Publishing, eighth edition, 2007. A wealth of information for traveling the Pacific coast route, through Mazatlán, Guadalajara, Puerto Vallarta, Manzanillo, Colima, Michoacán, Ixtapa-Zihuatanejo, Acapulco, and Oaxaca.

FICTION

Bowen, David, ed. *Pyramids of Glass*. San Antonio, TX: Corona Publishing Co., 1994. Two dozen-odd stories that lead the reader along a month-long journey through the bedrooms, the barracks, the cafés, and streets of present-day Mexico.

Boyle, T. C. *The Tortilla Curtain*. New York: Penguin-Putnam 1996; paperback edition, Raincoast Books, 1996. A chance intersection of the lives of two couples, one affluent and liberal Southern Californians, the other poor homeless illegal immigrants, forces all to come to grips with the real price of the American Dream.

Cisneros, Sandra. *Caramelo*. New York: Alfred A. Knopf, 2002. A celebrated author weaves a passionate, yet funny, multigenerational tale of a Mexican-American family and of their migrations, which, beginning in Mexico City, propelled them north, all the way to Chicago and back.

De la Cruz, Sor Juana Inez. *Poems, Protest, and a Dream*. New York: Penguin, 1997. Masterful translation of a collection of love and religious poems by the celebrated pioneer (1651–1695) Mexican feminist-nun.

De Zapata, Celia C., ed. *Short Stories by Latin American Women: The Magic and the Real*. New York: Random House Modern Library 2003. An eclectic mix of more than 30 stories by noted Latin American women. The stories, which a number of critics classify as "magical realism," were researched by editor Celia de Zapata, who got them freshly translated into English by a cadre of renowned translators; includes a foreword by celebrated author Isabel Allende.

Doerr, Harriet. *Consider This, Señor*. New York: Harcourt Brace, 1993. Four expatriates tough it out in a Mexican small town, adapting to the excesses—blazing sun, driving rain, vast untrammeled landscapes—meanwhile interacting with the local folks while the local folks observe them, with a mixture of fascination and tolerance.

Finn, María, ed. *Mexico in Mind*. New York: Vintage Books, 2006. The wisdom and impressions of two centuries of renowned writers, from D. H. Lawrence and John Steinbeck to John Reed and Richard Rodríguez, who were drawn to the timelessness and romance of Mexico.

Fuentes, Carlos. *Where the Air Is Clear*. New York: Farrar, Straus, and Giroux, 1971. The seminal work of Mexico's celebrated novelist.

Fuentes, Carlos. *The Years with Laura Díaz*. Translated by Alfred MacAdam. New York: Farrar, Straus, and Giroux, 2000. A panorama of Mexico from Independence to the 21st century through the eyes of one woman, Laura Díaz, and her great-grandson, the author. One reviewer said that she, "as a Mexican woman, would like to celebrate Carlos Fuentes; it is worthy of applause that a man who has seen, observed, analyzed and criticized the great occurrences of the century now has a woman, Laura Díaz, speak for him."

Jennings, Gary. *Aztec*. New York: Atheneum, 1980. Beautifully researched and written monumental tale of lust, compassion, love, and death in pre conquest Mexico.

Nickles, Sara, ed. *Escape to Mexico*. San Francisco: Chronicle Books, 2002. A carefully selected anthology of 20 odd stories of Mexico by renowned authors, from Steven Crane and W. Somerset Maugham to Anaïs Nin and David Lida, who all found inspiration, refuge, adventure, and much more in Mexico.

Peters, Daniel. *The Luck of Huemac*. New York: Random House, 1981. An Aztec noble family's tale of war, famine, sorcery, heroism, treachery, love, and, finally, disaster and death in the Valley of Mexico.

Rulfo, Juan. *The Burning Plain*. Austin: University of Texas Press, 1967. Stories of people torn between the old and new in Mexico.

Rulfo, Juan. *Pedro Paramo*. Evanston, IL: Northwestern University Press, 1994. Rulfo's acknowledged masterpiece, first published in 1955, established his renown. The author, thinly disguised as the protagonist, Juan Preciado, fulfills his mother's dying request by returning to his shadowy Jalisco hometown, Comala, in search of his father. Although Preciado discovers that his father, Pedro Páramo (whose surname implies "wasteland"), is long dead, Preciado's search resurrects his father's restless spirit, which recounts its horrific life tale of massacre, rape, and incest.

Traven, B. *The Treasure of the Sierra Madre*. New York: Hill and Wang, 1967. Campesinos, *federales*, gringos, and *indígenas* all figure in this modern morality tale set in Mexico's rugged outback. The most famous of the mysterious author's many novels of oppression and justice in Mexico's jungles.

Villaseñor, Victor. *Rain of Gold*. New York: Delta Books (Bantam, Doubleday, and Dell), 1991. The moving, best-selling epic of the gritty travails of the author's family. From humble rural beginnings in the Copper Canyon, they flee revolution and certain death, struggling through parched northern deserts to sprawling border refugee camps. From there they migrate to relative safety and an eventual modicum of happiness in Southern California.

ARTS, CRAFTS, AND ARCHITECTURE

Baird, Joseph. *The Churches of Mexico, 1530–1810*. Berkeley: University of California Press, 1962. Mexican colonial architecture and art, illustrated and interpreted, with many monumental examples from Oaxaca.

Barbash, Shepard, and Vicki Ragan. *Oaxaca Wood Carving*. San Francisco: Chronicle Books, 1993. Ragan's luscious color images and Barbash's interesting, authoritative text highlight the best of Oaxacan wooden *alebrijes*, masks, dolls, toys, and much more.

Chibnik, Michael. *Crafting Tradition: The Making and Marketing of Oaxaca Wood Carvings.* Austin, Texas: Univ. of Texas Press, 2003. Authoritative study of the phenomenally popular growth of *alebrijes,* Oaxaca's fanciful wooden animals. This carefully researched work covers all you need to know about the history, crafting, artistry, and the social and economic ramifications of Oaxacan woodcrafts in particular and handicrafts in general.

Fishgrund, Andrea Stanton. *Zapotec Weavers of Teotitlán.* Santa Fe: University of New Mexico Press, 1999. Authoritative, richly color-illustrated description of the history, economics, and techniques, both traditional and contemporary, of the textile weavers of Teotitlán del Valle, in the Valley of Oaxaca.

Martínez Penaloza, Porfirio. *Popular Arts of Mexico.* Mexico City: Editorial Panorama, 1981. An excellent pocket-sized exposition of Mexican art and handicrafts.

Morrill, Penny C., and Carol A. Berk. *Mexican Silver.* Atglen, PA: Shiffer Publishing Co. (4880 Lower Valley Road, Atglen, PA 19310), 2001. Lovingly written and photographed exposition of the Mexican silvercraft of Taxco, Guerrero, that was revitalized through the initiative of Frederick Davis and William Spratling in the 1920s and 1930s. Color photos of many beautiful museum-quality pieces supplement the text, which describes the history and work of a score of silversmithing families who developed the Taxco craft under Spratling's leadership. Greatly adds to the traveler's appreciation of the beautiful Taxco silvercrafts.

Muller, Robert J. *The Architecture and Sculpture of Oaxaca, 1530s to 1980s.* Tempe: Arizona State University, 1995. An informative stone-by-stone guide to Oaxaca's monumental buildings, mostly churches. The author's solid commentary vivifies visits to every church of note in Oaxaca and transforms what might be humdrum sightseeing for the reader-traveler into recognition, understanding, and appreciation.

Sandoval, Judith Hancock. *Shopping in Oaxaca.* Oaxaca: Government of Oaxaca, 1998. The serious shopper's and wholesaler's guide to Oaxacan crafts, even including some food. The author illustrates a plethora of examples in black and white and authoritatively lists nearly every source of Oaxacan folk craft, from individual artisans to nearly every established crafts shop in the entire state. Has been available at crafts stores and the federal-state tourist information office on the plaza in Oaxaca City.

Sayer, Chloë. *Arts and Crafts of Mexico.* San Francisco: Chronicle Books, 1990. All you ever wanted to know about your favorite Mexican crafts, from papier-mâché to pottery and toys and Taxco silver. Beautifully illustrated by traditional etchings and David Lavender's crisp black-and-white and color photographs.

PEOPLE AND CULTURE

Augur, Helen. *Zapotec.* New York: Doubleday and Co., 1954. One woman's view of Oaxaca's history and culture: a tapestry of Oaxacan tradition from the Mixteca to the Isthmus and ancient Monte Albán to present-day Oaxaca City.

Castillo, Ana, ed. *Goddess of the Americas.* New York: Riverhead Books, 1996. Here a noted author has selected from the works of seven interpreters of Mesoamerican female deities to provide readers with visions of goddesses that range as far and wide as Sex Goddess, the Broken-Hearted, the Subversive, and the Warrior Queen.

Chinas, Beverly Newbold. *Isthmus Zapotecs: A Matrifocal Culture of Mexico.* New York: Harcourt-Brace-Jovanovich, 1997. How a female-dominant culture functions in Oaxaca.

Cohen, Jeffrey. *Cooperation and Community: Economy and Society in Oaxaca.* Austin: University of Texas Press, 1999. A pithy, authoritative account of the history, economy, politics, and folkways of the Santañeros—the people of the weaving village of Santa Ana del

Valle, in the Valley of Oaxaca. Here, time-honored customs—*compadrazgo, guelaguetza, promesas*—fuse with latter-day realities to produce a culture simultaneously modern and traditional.

Cordrey, Donald, and Dorothy Cordrey. *Mexican Indian Costumes.* Austin: University of Texas Press, 1968. A lovingly photographed, written, and illustrated classic on Mexican native peoples, including many Oaxacan groups.

Covarrubias, Miguel. *Indian Art of Mexico and Central America.* New York: Knopf, 1957. A classic work by the renowned interpreter of *indígena* art and design.

Edinger, Steven T. *The Road from Mixtepec.* Fresno, CA: Asociación Cívica Benito Juárez (P.O. Box 12320, Fresno, CA 93706), 1996. A compassionately researched and photographed account of the people of San Juan Mixtepec, in the Mixteca Alta region of Oaxaca. The author, through his solid anecdotal narrative, relates the story of how a people whose means of existence have been gradually degraded for the past four hundred years maintain their lives, spirit, and traditions only by repeated emigration to work as marginal farm laborers in northern Mexico and the United States.

Greenberg, James. *Blood Ties: Life and Violence in Rural Mexico.* Tucson: University of Arizona Press, 1993. The author reveals, with a wealth of personal anecdotes, the cultural underpinnings beneath decades of deadly feuding between two leading Chatino towns in Oaxaca's southern Sierra.

Haden, Judith Cooper, and Matthew Jaffe. *Oaxaca, the Spirit of Mexico.* New York: Artisan, division of Workman Publishing, Inc., 2002. Simply the loveliest, most sensitively photographed and crafted coffee-table book of Mexico photography yet produced. Photos by Haden, text by Jaffe.

Leslie, Charles M. *Now We Are Civilized.* Detroit: Wayne State University Press, 1960. A now-classic anecdotal study of the worldview and ways of the Zapotec people of Mitla, Oaxaca.

Martinez, Zarela. *The Food and Life of Oaxaca.* New York: Macmillan, 1997. Martinez, a New York restaurateur, leads her readers on an intriguing tour of Oaxacan folkways by way of the palate. Features chapters on Oaxaca's seven *moles,* 150 recipes, and two dozen photos of finished gastronomical creations.

Medina, Sylvia López. *Cantora.* New York: Ballantine Books, 1992. Fascinated by the stories of her grandmother, aunt, and mother, the author seeks her own center by discovering a past that she thought she wanted to forget.

Nader, Laura. *Harmony, Ideology, Justice, and Control in a Zapotec Mountain Village.* Palo Alto, CA: Stanford University Press, 1990. How some northern Sierra Zapotecs solve disputes, using religion-based ideas of harmony to achieve social control.

Palmer, Colin A. *Slaves of the White God: Blacks in Mexico.* Cambridge, MA: Harvard University Press, 1976. A scholarly study of why and how Spanish authorities imported African slaves into the Americas and how they were used afterward. Replete with poignant details taken from Spanish and Mexican archives describing how the Africans struggled from bondage to eventual freedom.

Romney, Kimball, and Romaine Romney. *The Mixtecs of Juxtlahuaca.* Huntington, NY: Robert E. Krieger Publishing Co., 1966. Authors study the contemporary Mixtec culture of the western Mixteca. Pithy examples, especially of the organization of fiestas, still ring true despite the generation elapsed since the research was done.

Stephen, Lynn. *Zapotec Women.* Austin: University of Texas Press, 1992. Study of how women run much of the local economy and a significant fraction of the politics in the Oaxaca Isthmus districts of Tehuántepec and Juchitán.

Toor, Frances. *A Treasury of Mexican Folkways.* New York: Bonanza Books, 1947, reprinted 1985. An illustrated encyclopedia of vanishing Mexicana—costumes, religion, fiestas, burial practices, customs, legends—compiled during the celebrated author's 35 years' residence in Mexico in the early 20th century.

Trilling, Susana. *Seasons of My Heart.* New York: Ballantine Publishing Group, 1999. The celebrated Oaxaca author, chef, and cooking teacher leads her readers on a culinary journey of the seven regions of Oaxaca. Along the way, they stop by market towns, mountain hamlets, shoreline villages, and lush highland valleys, visiting the friends with whom she refined the dozens of recipes that introduce the best of Oaxacan cooking. *Seasons of My Heart* is the companion volume to Trilling's National Public Television series on Oaxacan cooking.

Wauchope, Robert, ed. *Handbook of Middle American Indians.* Vols. 7 and 8. Austin: University of Texas Press, 1969. Authoritative but aging surveys of important native-speaking groups in northern, central (vol. 8), and southern (vol. 7) Mexico.

GOVERNMENT, POLITICS, AND ECONOMY

Campbell, Howard. *Zapotec Renaissance: Ethnic Politics and Cultural Revival in Southern Mexico.* Albuquerque: University of New Mexico Press, 1994. A history of how the Zapotecs around Juchitán, Oaxaca, fought city hall and won.

Dillon, Samuel, and Preston, Julia. *Opening Mexico: The Making of a Democracy.* New York: Farrar, Strauss and Geroux, 2005. Former Mexico City *New York Times* bureau chiefs use their rich personal insights and investigative journalistic skill to tell the story of the latter-day evolution of Mexico's uniquely imperfect democracy. Their story begins during the 1980s, tracing the decay of the 71-year-rule of the PRI, to its collapse, with the election of opposition candidate Vicente Fox in 2000. The actors are vivid and manifold, from rebellious anti-government campesinos in Chiapas and Oaxaca and high federal officials conspiring with druglords to teachers striking for fair pay and an end to political assassination of their colleagues.

Murphy, Arthur D., and Alex Stepick. *Social Inequality in Oaxaca.* Philadelphia: Temple University Press, 1993. A sociopolitical history of grassroots underclass activism in Oaxaca City during the 1960s, 1970s, and 1980s.

Poleman, Thomas T. *Agricultural Development in the Mexican Tropics.* Palo Alto, CA: Stanford University Press, 1964. The successes, failures, and consequences of Mexico's great dam project in Oaxaca's Papaloapan basin.

Rubin, Jeffry W. *Decentering the Regime.* Winston-Salem, NC: Duke University Press, 1997. Ethnicity, radicalism, and democracy in Juchitán, Oaxaca.

FLORA AND FAUNA

Goodson, Gar. *Fishes of the Pacific Coast.* Stanford, CA: Stanford University Press, 1988. More than 500 beautifully detailed color drawings highlight this pocket version of all you ever wanted to know about the ocean's fishes (including common Spanish names) from Alaska to Peru.

Howell, Steve N. G., and Sophie Webb. *A Guide to the Birds of Mexico and Northern America.* Oxford: Oxford University Press, 1995. All the serious bird-watcher needs to know about Mexico's rich species treasury. Includes authoritative habitat maps and 70 excellent color plates that detail the males and females of around 1,500 species. (For a more portable version, check out Steve Howell's *Bird-Finding Guide to Mexico,* 1999.)

Mason Jr., Charles T., and Patricia B. Mason. *Handbook of Mexican Roadside Flora.* Tucson: University of Arizona Press, 1987. Authoritative identification guide, with line illustrations, of all the plants you're likely to see in the Oaxaca region.

Morris, Percy A. *A Field Guide to Pacific Coast*

Shells. Boston: Houghton Mifflin, 1974. The complete beachcomber's Pacific shell guide.

Pesman, M. Walter. *Meet Flora Mexicana.* Globe, AZ: D. S. King, 1962. Delightful anecdotes and illustrations of hundreds of common Mexican plants. Out of print.

Wright, N. Pelham. *A Guide to Mexican Mammals and Reptiles.* Mexico City: Minutiae Mexicana, 1989. Pocket-edition lore, history, descriptions, and pictures of commonly seen Mexican animals.

Internet Resources

A number of websites may be helpful in preparing for your Oaxaca trip.

GENERAL TRAVEL

Internet Travel Sites
**www.travelocity.com,
www.expedia.com**
Major sites for airline and hotel bookings

Travel Insurance
**www.travelinsure.com,
www.worldtravelcenter.com**
Both good for general travel insurance and other services

Mexico Car Insurance

Sanborn's Insurance
www.sanbornsinsurance.com
Site of Sanborn's Insurance, the long-time, very reliable Mexico auto insurance agency, with the only north-of-the-border adjustment procedure. Get your quote online, order their many useful publications, and find out about other insurance you many have forgotten.

SPECIALTY TRAVEL

Elderhostel
www.elderhostel.org
Site of Boston-based Elderhostel, Inc., with a huge catalog of ongoing study tours, including, at this writing, two in Oaxaca.

Mobility International
www.miusa.org
Site of Mobility International, wonderfully organized and complete, with a flock of services for travelers with disabilities, including many people-to-people connections in Mexico.

Purple Roofs
www.purpleroofs.com
One of the best general gay travel websites is maintained by San Francisco–based travel agency Purple Roofs. It offers, for example, details about several gay-friendly Oaxaca hotels, in addition to a wealth of gay-friendly travel-oriented links worldwide.

Go Oaxaca
www.go-oaxaca.com/overview/gay.html
A small page that lists a number of gay-friendly bars, restaurants, nightclubs, and a few gay-friendly hotels in Oaxaca City.

U.S. GOVERNMENT

U.S. State Department
www.state.gov/travelandbusiness
The U.S. State Department's very good travel information site. Lots of headings and links to a swarm of topics, including Mexican consular offices in the United States, U.S. consular offices in Mexico, travel advisories, and links to other government information, such as importation of food, plants, and animals, U.S. customs, health abroad, airlines, and exchange rates.

MEXICO IN GENERAL

Mexico Tourism Board
www.visitmexico.com
The official website of the public-private Mexico Tourism Board; a good general site for official information, such as entry

requirements. It has lots of summarily informative sub-headings, not unlike an abbreviated guidebook. If you can't find what you want here, call the toll-free information number 800/44-MEXICO (800/446-3942), or email contact@visitmexico.com.

Mexico Online
www.mexonline.com

Very extensive, well-organized commercial site with many subheadings and links to Mexico's large and medium destinations, and even some in small destinations. For the state of Oaxaca, they cover Oaxaca City, Huatulco, Puerto Ángel, and Puerto Escondido. For example, for Oaxaca, their linked sub-page www.mexonline.com/cityguide-oaxaca.htm is typical, with manifold links, including about many dozens of accommodations, from luxury hotels to modest bed-and-breakfasts. Excellent.

MexConnect
www.mexconnect.com

An extensive Mexico site, with dozens upon dozens of subheadings and links, especially helpful for folks thinking of traveling, working, living, or retiring in Mexico.

Mexico Desconocido
www.mexicodesconocido.com.mx

The site of the excellent magazine *Mexico Desconocido* (Undiscovered Mexico) that often features unusual, untouristed destinations, many in the state of Oaxaca. It links to a large library of past articles, which are not unlike a Mexican version of National Geographic Traveler. Solid, hard-to-find information, in good English translation, if you can get it. (The site is so voluminous that the automatic translator tends to bog down at the effort.)

On the initial home page, find the small magnifying glass and dialog box, labeled "buscar" ("find") at the upper right. I typed in "Oaxaca" and got 206 informative hits about places and things in Oaxaca, each linked to an article in the magazine.

On the Road in Mexico
www.ontheroadin.com

Very helpful, regularly updated information and photos of Mexico trailer parks and campgrounds. Includes accurate and very usable maps to loads of out-of-the-way, hard-to-find locations, many along the Pacific coast, including Oaxaca.

OAXACA CITY AND OAXACA IN GENERAL

Planeta.com
www.planeta.com

Superb life project of Latin America's dean of ecotourism, Oaxaca resident Ron Mader, who furnishes a comprehensive English-language clearinghouse of everything ecologically correct, from rescuing turtle eggs on the Oaxaca Coast to preserving the cloud forests in the Oaxaca's northern Sierra Juarez. Contains dozens of subheadings competently linked for maximum speed. Check out www.planeta.com/oaxaca.html for a block-long list of information-packed links of everything you need to know about Oaxaca.

Oaxaca Secretary of Tourism
www.oaxaca.travel

Very detailed website of the Oaxaca Secretary of Tourism. Good Tourist Guide section with archaeological sites, recipes, churches, museums, festivals, myths and legends, murals, handicrafts, and more. The site goes the extra step farther and provides extensive information (accessible by clicking on the home-page Oaxaca map) about off-the-tourist-track country villages. Much of the detailed information remains untranslated into English, however.

Oaxaca Mio
www.oaxaca-mio.com

Good commercial site, with lots on history, culture, sights, hotels, and services in Oaxaca City and Valley. Oaxaca coast coverage, including Puerto Escondido and Huatulco, is still informative, but not nearly so extensive.

Oaxaca Info
www.oaxacainfo.com

Joint website of the Oaxaca Hotel Association and U.S.-based Zapotec Tours and Oaxaca-based Oaxaca Tours. Includes much good travel information, with (mostly up-market) hotels and restaurants in Oaxaca City and lots of background information on festivals, museums, maps, and much more. It has separate, but much smaller, Huatulco and Puerto Escondido sections.

Go Oaxaca
www.go-oaxaca.com

Good website of editor Oscar Garcia Carrizosa, of the *Go Oaxaca* newspaper. He includes plenty, from real estate and a chat room to tours and classifieds listing bed-and-breakfasts and for-rent apartments and rooms, with links to grassroots pages, such as the English-language library, the hospitality club, and a child welfare organization.

Oaxaca Times
www.oaxacatimes.com

The website of the *Oaxaca Times* newspaper. It has links to restaurants, galleries, handicrafts shops, services, plus a handy classified section usually including a long list of Oaxaca City apartment, house, homestay, and bed-and-breakfast rentals.

Vacation Rentals
www.vrbo.com, www.choice1.com

A pair of very useful sites for picking a vacation rental house, condo, or villa, with information and reservations links to individual owners. Prices vary from moderate to luxurious. Coverage extends over much of the Mexican Pacific, and, especially in www.vrbo.com, many listings in Oaxaca City, Puerto Escondido, and Huatulco.

OAXACA COAST

Tomzap
www.tomzap.com/oaxaca.html

This project of Mexico lover Tom Penick is a very informative site, especially for down-scale corners of Oaxaca. It's unusually detailed about Puerto Escondido, Puerto Ángel, Zipolite, Mazunte, and the Bays of Huatulco. Information includes hotels, travel, history, surfing, scuba and snorkeling, and much more, with much helpful advice on what to enjoy and what to avoid. Very Good. (*Note:* Be aware, however, that some information is out of date.)

Huatulco Hotel Association
www.hoteleshuatulco.com.mx

Useful site of the Huatulco Hotel Association, with links to about four dozen hotels, ranging modest to plush (two to five stars), including prices for some of the hotels. The remaining information (restaurants, events, tour operators, water sports, and land sports) would be more useful if it were in English.

Huatulco Magazzine
www.huatulco.magazzine.net

Site of the reliable local free tourist magazine, with useful links to all of its advertisers, from real estate and rental cars to handicrafts shops and 3-, 4-, and 5-star hotels.

El Sol de la Costa
www.elsoldelacosta.com

Extensive and authoritative commercial site of the excellent Puerto Escondido bilingual tourist newspaper *El Sol de la Costa,* Warren Sharpe, editor and publisher. It's especially useful for hotels, restaurants, sights, and services and also includes much cultural background, especially on local indigenous culture and traditions. A handy classified section usually lists a number of vacation rentals by owner.

Puerto Real Estate
www.puertorealestate.com

Very good website of Puerto Real Estate; besides home sales, it lists and photo-illustrates many vacation rental villas, condos, and apartments ($3000–4000/week) and offers trip-planning services.

Zicatela Properties
www.zicatelaproperties.com

Excellent site of Puerto Escondido's Zicatela Properties real estate company. It's especially good for moderately priced apartment, condo, and vacation home rentals (as low as $250/week). It also lists a number of services to help newcomers settle into Puerto Escondido.

Index

Map Index

Photo Credits

All photos © Bruce Whipperman

page 4: Masks for the Day of the Dead, Oaxaca City

page 5: Crafts store display, Mazunte; Puerto Escondido people fete their beloved Virgen de la Soledad with a grand Dec. 8 processional regatta around the bay; pink angel woodcraft, San Bartolo Coyotepec museum

page 6: The celebrated Capilla Abierta (Open Chapel) graces the grand, grassy atrium of Teposcolula's Ex-convento de San Pedro y San Pablo; woodcrafts bowls and alebrijes, Tlacolula market

page 7: Luscious red Oaxaca watermelons seem common enough to be a native fruit, although they were originally cultured in Central Asia; Volunteers do an important job, rescuing, incubating, and finally being rewarded by watching hundreds of sea-turtle hatchlings return to the ocean

page 8: Cloister, Museo de las Culturas de Oaxaca, Oaxaca City, © Bruce Whipperman

page 9: Bright pink bugambilia and plumy coconut palms are so common that most folks are convinced that they are native to Mexico, but they're not; San Agustinillo's "double beach" has an eastern half and a mirror-image twin beach on its west side

page 10: Poking fun of death, especially around the Nov. 1 and 2 Day of the Dead, is part of Oaxaca tradition

page 11: Sleepy time at Tlacolula Market

www.moon.com

For helpful advice on planning a trip, visit www.moon.com for the **TRAVEL PLANNER** and get access to useful travel strategies and valuable information about great places to visit. When you travel with Moon, expect an experience that is uncommon and truly unique.

HANDBOOKS | METRO | OUTDOORS | LIVING ABROAD

MAP SYMBOLS

▦ Expressway	**C**	Highlight	✗	Airfield	⚲	Golf Course
▦ Primary Road	○	City/Town	✗	Airport	**P**	Parking Area
⎯ Secondary Road	◉	State Capital	▲	Mountain	◭	Archaeological Site
░ Unpaved Road	◉	National Capital	✦	Unique Natural Feature	⬥	Church
▬ Trail	★	Point of Interest			⬛	Gas Station
⋯ Ferry	●	Accommodation	↘	Waterfall	⬭	Glacier
▬ Railroad	▼	Restaurant/Bar	▲	Park	▦	Mangrove
▦ Pedestrian Walkway	■	Other Location	⬛	Trailhead	▦	Reef
▦ Stairs	Λ	Campground	⛷	Skiing Area	▦	Swamp

CONVERSION TABLES

°C = (°F - 32) / 1.8
°F = (°C x 1.8) + 32
1 inch = 2.54 centimeters (cm)
1 foot = 0.304 meters (m)
1 yard = 0.914 meters
1 mile = 1.6093 kilometers (km)
1 km = 0.6214 miles
1 fathom = 1.8288 m
1 chain = 20.1168 m
1 furlong = 201.168 m
1 acre = 0.4047 hectares
1 sq km = 100 hectares
1 sq mile = 2.59 square km
1 ounce = 28.35 grams
1 pound = 0.4536 kilograms
1 short ton = 0.90718 metric ton
1 short ton = 2,000 pounds
1 long ton = 1.016 metric tons
1 long ton = 2,240 pounds
1 metric ton = 1,000 kilograms
1 quart = 0.94635 liters
1 US gallon = 3.7854 liters
1 Imperial gallon = 4.5459 liters
1 nautical mile = 1.852 km

MOON OAXACA

Avalon Travel
a member of the Perseus Books Group
1700 Fourth Street
Berkeley, CA 94710, USA
www.moon.com

Editor: Kevin McLain
Series Manager: Kathryn Ettinger
Copy Editor: Kay Elliott
Graphics and Production Coordinator:
    Elizabeth Jang
Cover Designer: Elizabeth Jang
Map Editor: Kevin Anglin
Cartographers: Brice Ticen, Kat Bennett
Proofreader: Leah M. Gordon
Indexer: Rachel Kuhn

ISBN-10: 1-59880-088-4
ISBN-13: 978-1-59880-088-3
ISSN: 1533-3949

Printing History
1st Edition – 2000
5th Edition – October 2008
5 4 3 2 1

KEEPING CURRENT

If you have a favorite gem you'd like to see included in the next edition, or see anything
that needs updating, clarification, or correction, please drop us a line. Send your
comments via email to feedback@moon.com, or use the address above.